Cases on Digital Technologies in Higher Education: Issues and Challenges

Rocci Luppicini
University of Ottawa, Canada

A.K. Haghi
University of Guilan, Iran

Information Science REFERENCE

INFORMATION SCIENCE REFERENCE
Hershey · New York

Director of Editorial Content:	Kristin Klinger
Director of Book Publications:	Julia Mosemann
Acquisitions Editor:	Lindsay Johnston
Development Editor:	Elizabeth Ardner
Typesetter:	Gregory Snader
Production Editor:	Jamie Snavely
Cover Design:	Lisa Tosheff
Printed at:	Yurchak Printing Inc.

Published in the United States of America by
Information Science Reference (an imprint of IGI Global)
701 E. Chocolate Avenue
Hershey PA 17033
Tel: 717-533-8845
Fax: 717-533-8661
E-mail: cust@igi-global.com
Web site: http://www.igi-global.com/reference

Library of Congress Cataloging-in-Publication Data

Cases on digital technologies in higher education : issues and challenges / Rocci Luppicini and A.K. Haghi, editors.
p. cm.
Includes bibliographical references and index.
Summary: "This book focuses on the institutionalization of technology into education, specifically, discussing the integration of technology (and new techniques) into various areas of higher education"--Provided by publisher.
ISBN 978-1-61520-869-2 (hardcover) -- ISBN 978-1-61520-870-8 (ebook) 1. Education, Higher--Effect of technological innovations on--Case studies. 2. Education, Higher--Computer-assisted instruction--Case studies. 3. Educational technology--Case studies. I. Luppicini, Rocci. II. Haghi, A. K.
LB2395.7.C414 2010
378.00285--dc22
2009040712

British Cataloguing in Publication Data
A Cataloguing in Publication record for this book is available from the British Library.

List of Reviewers

M. Ciocoiu, *Technical University of Asachi, Romania*
A. Hamrang, *Education Consulting, UK*
R. Janardhanam, *University of North Carolina, USA*
L. K. Maquire, *University of Wollongong, Australia*
V. Mottaghitalab, *University of Guilan, Iran*
F. Nagiyev, *Azerbaijan State Oil Academy, Azerbaijan*
P. Poulin, *CNRS, France*
G. M. Spinks, *University of Wollongong, Australia*
S. Thomas, *Mahatma Gandhi University, India*
G.G. Wallace, *University of Wollongong, Australia*
J. Cibert, *CNRS, France*
H. Courtois, *University of Joseph Fourier, France*
J. Kamm, *University of Toledo, USA*
N. Kulov, *Russian Academy of Sciences, Russia*
D. Lukas, *Technical University of Liberec, Czech Republic*
S. Maamir, *University of Boumerdes, Algeria*
D. Peyrade, *CNRS, France*
L. A. Pothan, *Bishop Moore College, India*
D. Rondot, *IUT, France*
V. Tura, *Al. I. Cuza University, Romania*
J. Venugopal, *National University of Singapore, Singapore*
G. E. Zaikov, *Russian Academy of Sciences, Russia*
B. Zeghmati, *University of Perpignan, France*

Table of Contents

Selected Readings

Detailed Table of Contents

Preface

TECHNOLOGY: THE LONG ROAD

If technology is the question, what is the answer? And conversely, if technology is the answer, what is the question? Since the onset of the industrial revolution, the societal conceptualization of technology has changed from a view of technology as a tool or technique to a view of technology as a system. Pre-industrial revolution technology was represented by new tools and techniques (E.g., agricultural tools, spears, gunpowder, steam engine, etc) which could be used to manipulate the environment in specific ways. This conceptualization gave way to the view of technology as a system during the industrialization of society when new techniques were developed for restructuring organizations around systematic operations and mechanisms of production within which humans operated. This shift marked the birth of modern technological systems and the rise of new types of social complexities that emerged as traditional ways of life and society began to be threatened. Technology was no longer a set of visible tools and objects to manipulate; it was now a complex system that separated human work and activity from human values and ways of life that defined individuals and society. This view of modern technological systems was equated with concerns about human freedom and fear of a new form of slavery. Ellul (1966) described technological systems as powerful innovations that came with a heavy price that created a dilemma for its users:

"The individual is in a dilemma: either he decides to safeguard his freedom of choice, chooses to use traditional, personal, moral, or empirical means, thereby entering into competition with a power against which there is no efficacious defence and before which he must suffer defeat; or he decides to accept technical necessity, in which case he will be the victor, but only by submitting irreparably to technical slavery" (p.84)

The second major shift in the conceptualization of technology was a shift inside, which arose with the onset of the information age. Over the last forty years, the conceptualization of technological systems has gradually changed from a technological system outside of human culture and values to one that is now part of everyday life and meaning. This is partly due to the proliferation of technological innovation and scientific advances. It is also due to the ongoing institutionalization of technology into education and the public sphere. Under this view, technological systems are interwoven within our lives and social institutions as intermediating forces that help shape experience, interaction, communications, and knowledge innovation. It is this conceptualization of technology that comes closest to capturing the complexity and breadth of issues that challenge us today. This is particularly salient in higher education where the preoccupation with technology to advance knowledge innovation is a priority. To this end, Cases on Digital Technologies in Higher Education: Issues and Challenges focuses on the institutionalization of technology into education. More specifically, it focuses on the integration of technology (and new techniques) into various areas of higher education.

HIGHER EDUCATION: FROM THEN TO NOW

Perhaps better than any academic in the 20th century, Whitehead was deeply interested in the area of the connection between educational development and the rhythm of growth. Whitehead (1929) viewed education as an organic growth process where the student and subject matter evolved together. He believed the aim of education could be divided into three fundamental stages: (1) the stage of romance, (2) the stage of precision, and (3) the stage of generalization. In the first stage, educational experiences arise through emotional engagement of young learners as they engage with diverse subject matter in a way that inspires and fulfills a need for stimulation and enjoyment. In the second stage, learning takes on a new direction by focusing more on specific areas of mastery as found in the sciences and technical subjects, including logic and spoken languages. The final phase, generalization, attempts to integrate elements of romance and precision into a general framework of useful knowledge that can be deployed in real contexts. Unfortunately, the lack of romance within the educational system has turned many students off of learning and reduced the potency of Higher Education. As argued by Whitehead (1929), "The justification for a university is that it preserves the connection between knowledge and the zest of life, by uniting the young and the old in the imaginative consideration of learning" (Whitehead 1929, p. 93). Whitehead has contributed a formidable challenge for universities that academics are still striving for today.

What new technologies bring into education (on a good day) is a means to rekindle some of the lost romance with learning that Whitehead was so concerned about. New technologies offer greater flexibility in teaching and learning by providing more opportunities for instructors to adapt teaching to student interests and different learning styles. The question is, how these new learning opportunities can be realized. If, as Whitehead (1938) believes, "The task of a University is the creation of the future" (p. 233), then there is an onus on developers and instructors to make sure that the future is a bright one and that technology is complimentary to university teaching rather than being contradictory.

DIGITAL TECHNOLOGY IN CONTEMPOARY HIGHER EDUCATION

As a key centre of adult education, social meaning creation, and socio-political debate, institutions of higher education are at the forefront of our technological interface with life and society. Technological innovation within university research centres, university library resource developments, and new tools available for teaching and learning are nurturing in new educational approaches and debates concerning the appropriate use of new technologies. As is demonstrated in this volume, absolute support for or opposition against technology in society has given way to more nuanced relationships. This follows a view of technology as a complex systems intertwined in a web of human interests and needs that require study in order to draw out challenges encountered and lessons learned about new technologies applied to various contexts of higher education.

In terms of objective, this co-edited volume attempts to provide a collection of practical case studies (and essays) exploring the application of digital technologies in higher education along with strategies to address new challenges facing educational institutions in the 21st century. It does so by juxtaposing a selected set of perspectives from educators, researchers, designers, and developers working in key areas of higher education. Taken together, the set of chapters within this edited volume help to illustrate through practical case studies and essays how digital technology is playing an important role in higher education. This book will be of interest to those affected by digital teaching and learning within institutions of higher education along with university administrators and researchers working in this area.

ORGANIZATION

In terms of organization, Cases on Digital Technologies in Higher Education: Issues and Challenges is divided into 17 chapters focusing on particular themes of interest revolving around digital technologies in higher education. They are as follows:

Chapter 1, entitled, "ELATE: Evolving an E-Learning Faculty Wiki", is a case study focusing on the creation of an e-learning wiki to support faculty in their work at Kansas State University. This chapter reviews key research literature and pedagogical theories on wikis. It also addresses practical challenges connected to the planning and building of a wiki site by dealing with important considerations such as, intellectual property policies, accessibility issues, content development issues, and publicity issues linked to the launch of the ELATE wiki to the Wikisphere.

Chapter 2, entitled, "Open Source and Bridging the Digital Divide" is a case study focusing on contemporary conceptualizations of open source and the digital divide with a focus on key considerations including operating systems, software, inexpensive hardware, and technological access issues. The chapter ends with a discussion of practical implications of open source in higher education and future directions. It provides a timely discussion of key concerns faced by institutions of higher education around the world.

Chapter 3, entitled, "A Conversation Approach to Electronic Collections Development Within University Libraries", explores student perspectives on electronic collections development within university libraries. This case uses a conversational modeling framework derived from student focus group discussion data to uncover student perspectives and factors affecting students' stances towards current and future electronic collections development trends. It also identifies a number of conversation modeling strategies used by students in fostering perspective sharing to inform consensual decision-making in contexts where communication gaps surrounding technology and its use in society exist.

Chapter 4, entitled, "Education Technology in Teacher Education: Overcoming Challenges, Realising Opportunities", explores the use of educational technologies within a pre-service teacher education program in New Zealand. This case discusses challenges and opportunities faced within teacher training for pre- and in-service teachers. To this end, it investigates the integration of educational technology to leverage a trans-disciplinary learning activity. This case highlights key teacher training challenges revolving around task complexity and possible resistance to change in higher education.

Chapter 5, entitled, "Wikis as open educational resources in higher education: Overcoming challenges, realizing potential", provides a case study on open wiki use within a single online postgraduate course at Massey University in New Zealand. Specifically, the case focuses on the use of open wiki technology at WikiEducator as a teaching presentation tool and as a production tool used by learners within the context of an instructional design project. This chapter discusses practical challenges and opportunities associated with wiki use in contemporary higher education.

Chapter 6, entitled, "Doctoral Faculty 2020: Preparing For the Future in Educational and Organizational Leadership", offers an insightful case study on faculty competencies within an organizational leadership doctoral program. The case identifies key skills necessary for doctoral faculty in leadership programs based on a review of relevant literature and interviews with faculty. This case study takes a serious look at the new competencies needed by doctoral faculty to meet the instructional needs within current and future context of doctoral level instruction.

Chapter 7, entitled, "Technoethical Study of Electronic Technology Ab/Use at University", explores how university students view non-work related use of electronic technology within universities (I.e., electronic monitoring technology and personal use of electronic technologies). This chapter highlights student experiences and ethical stances concerning non-work related use of electronic technologies within universities as well as the variables that affect their decision to engage in or not engage in personal electronic technology use during class. Drawing on research literature and conversational data derived from online group work, this study sheds light on attitudes and factors affecting students' ethical stances towards non-work related technology use at university.

Chapter 8, entitled, "Faculty Training and Mentoring at a Distance: Learning Together in the Virtual Community", provides an insightful review of selected work on instructor practices and faculty training in the context of online course design and delivery. This chapter reviews two selected cases (Delgado Community College and Excelsior Community) to identify key online faculty training challenges in different contexts. This chapter illustrates the importance of understanding organizational changes associated with current efforts to improve faculty development for online teaching in higher education.

Chapter 9, entitled, "The Potential for Student Engagement Using Clickers in a Large Introductory Class", reports on findings from an innovative pilot project focused on the integration of a personal response system (clicker technology) into an undergraduate classroom. Personal response systems were integrated into a large introductory class in Communications with the aim of leveraging student engagement and learning opportunities during lectures. This chapter discusses key challenges associated with student engagement along with suggested exercises to take advantage of this technology in the classroom.

Chapter 10, entitled, "'The Knee Bone Connected to the Thigh Bone': A Case Study of Teaching Anatomy Engineering Students Using State-of-The-Art Anatomical Software", presents a study on teaching Bioengineering at Newcastle University using a variety of selected tools (I.e., Primal Pictures, anatomical software, teaching material, peer to peer learning). The case explores how Bioengineering students used technology to construct an understanding of anatomical principles. Based on written feedback from students , this chapter provides evidence that the integration of new technologies promotes positive learning experiences and a deep knowledge of anatomical descriptions among students.

Chapter 11, entitled, "Improvement of Engineering Students Education by E-learning", provides an insightful look at the growth of e-Learning in engineering education. The chapter explores various ways to develop e-Learning in engineering education with an emphasis on the international design of e-Learning, within selected developing countries. The authors show how new advances in technology allow the realization of a more distributed structure of knowledge transfer that can benefit developing countries that lack core resources and infrastructure.

Chapter 12, entitled, "Purpose-Oriented Small Software: A Case Study for Some Engineering Subjects" provides a novel approach to engineering education. It presents an alternative approach that places instructional focus on sophisticated uses of general purpose software rather than focusing on specific computer applications. To this end, it discusses educational advantages of purpose-oriented small software which can be designed as a cost-effective way to leverage undergraduate student learning in engineering.

Chapter 13, entitled, "Managing Learning Activities in E-Learning Systems", delves into learning activity management systems as new tools to facilitate the design and management of online collaborative learning. The chapter highlights how new learning design tools allow instructors to better organize and monitor learning activities within e-learning systems. The chapter also addresses challenges and possible solutions to improve the management of e-learning systems.

Chapter 14, entitled, "Architectural Web Portal and Interactive CAD Learning in Hungary", presents the teaching web portal of the Faculty of Architecture at Szechenyi Istvan University and demonstrates how it can be used to leverage learning. This chapter explores how this teaching web portal can accommodate a diversity and complexity of architecture, while being attentive to professional standards. This chapter proposes that this system can help students to become more self-directed learners.

Chapter 15, entitled, "WIRE: A Highly Interactive Blended Learning for Engineering Education", takes a sobering look at blended learning and the challenge of integrating it into a coherent learning model that effectively sustains interaction between teacher and students. This study offers innovative strategies for combining online and face-to-face learning environments into a semester course. Findings are presented and key points are discussed.

Chapter 16, entitled, "Competitive Design of Web-Based Courses in Engineering Education", addresses the ongoing challenge of trying to design web-based courses to augment university learning. This chapter contributes an innovative approach applied to the design of web-based engineering courses. To this end, the chapter identifies key areas of focus needed to optimize the design of web-based engineering courses subject to a variety of constraints. It also highlights the need for customized approaches to web-based course design.

Chapter 17, entitled, "Web-Based Approaches in Engineering Education", takes a step back from the web-based course design in engineering education in order to conceptualize its most important elements to address within the context of e-learning. This provides practical insight into the requirements of engineering education for the 21st century by focusing on factors including, facility constraints, inadequacies of e-learning, and training techniques within engineering instruction.

Additional material has been added to further augment the breadth and depth of coverage within this case book. These selected readings help further the coverage on digital technologies in higher education. They are as follows:

Chapter 18, entitled, "A Needs Analysis Framework for the Design of Digital Repositories in Higher Education", addresses the various motivations and needs connected to virtual repository development in college and university settings. It posits a needs analysis framework to guide the design of digital repositories in Higher Education. To this end, it describes a needs analysis framework applied to the Australian higher education sector, the Carrick Exchange.

Chapter 19, entitled, "ICT Integration Efforts in Higher Education in Developing Economies: The Case of Addis Ababa University, Ethiopia", applies a modified version of Tearle's model (2004) to examine the integration of ICTs within the educational setting of developing economies with limited resources. To this end, the chapter assesses the challenges faced by teachers and management at Addis Ababa University in Ethiopia.

Chapter 20, entitled, "Game Informed Virtual Patients Catalysts for Online Learning Communities and Professional Development of Medical Teachers", focuses on the complexities of medical education and issues relating to practice, professional development, and learning. This chapter describes how virtual patient resources are used to create new learning tools and resources has contributed to aid professional development of those engaged in teaching medical students at the University of Edinburgh.

Because the issues related to digital technology in higher education are so broad, this edited volume is necessarily selective. It attempts to advance in its own modest way a selective synthesis of key contemporary work on technology to help guide individuals within institutions of higher education faced with technological change. This edited volume makes a concerted effort to place a strong emphasis in the area of engineering education. Because engineers are the key proponents and creators of technology, there is a special need in engineering education to address technological concerns and find solutions that will help maximize the utility of new digital technologies and minimize their adverse effects. By juxtaposing case work from engineering education with other academic areas in Higher Education, new opportunities for scholarly exchange may be realized. Despite the modest aims of this project, this co-editor realizes that it is not possible to please everyone. It is hoped that this volume of practical case studies and essays will be helpful to individuals in all areas within institutions of Higher Education. Critical comments and suggestions are welcome.

Sincerely,

Rocci Luppicini, University of Ottawa, Canada

REFERENCES

Whitehead, A. (1929). The Aims of Education and Other Essays. New York: Macmillan.

Whitehead, A. (1938). Modes of Thought. New York: Macmillan.

Chapter 1
ELATEwiki:
Evolving an E-Learning Faculty Wiki

Shalin Hai-Jew
Kansas State University, USA

Roger W. McHaney
Kansas State University, USA

ABSTRACT

A small team at Kansas State University worked to plan, create and launch an e-learning wiki to support faculty in their work. The advantages of the wiki technology—with its technological affordances of wide access and dissemination, digital content archival, multimedia expressiveness, remote collaboration, subscribability, and the reversibility of postings –appealed to this team. Even initially, there seemed to be opportunities for building novice and professional capacities in e-learning through the co-creation and sharing of information, problem-solving, and virtual community building. This chapter describes the research literature and pedagogical theories on wikis. It addresses the team's efforts in exploring and then building the wiki site. Additionally, this explains the team's rationales in terms of the intellectual property policies, the work to create accessibility, the wiki's fortuitous naming, the seeding of the wiki with contents, its low-key branding strategy, and the publicity plan for a "hard launch" of the ELATEwiki to the Wikisphere. This also describes the datamining techniques used to track use of the site and how those affect the site's continuing evolution. Finally, this chapter will provide perspectives on the work of a wiki-master in a peer-to-peer, collaborative, and open wiki.

ELATE: EVOLVING AN E-LEARNING FACULTY WIKI

A wiki used to develop particular subject matter works as a socio-technical space. The open hypertext affordances of wiki technologies enhance intercommunications and collaborative editing, but to succeed, the participants must bring their good will and expertise; the people are the ones who create and maintain the community. The users sustain wikis with continuous addition and refinement of digital information and contents. This case study discusses the creation and deployment of wiki technology in higher education to support e-learning

DOI: 10.4018/978-1-61520-869-2.ch001

Figure 1. A screenshot of the ELATEwiki

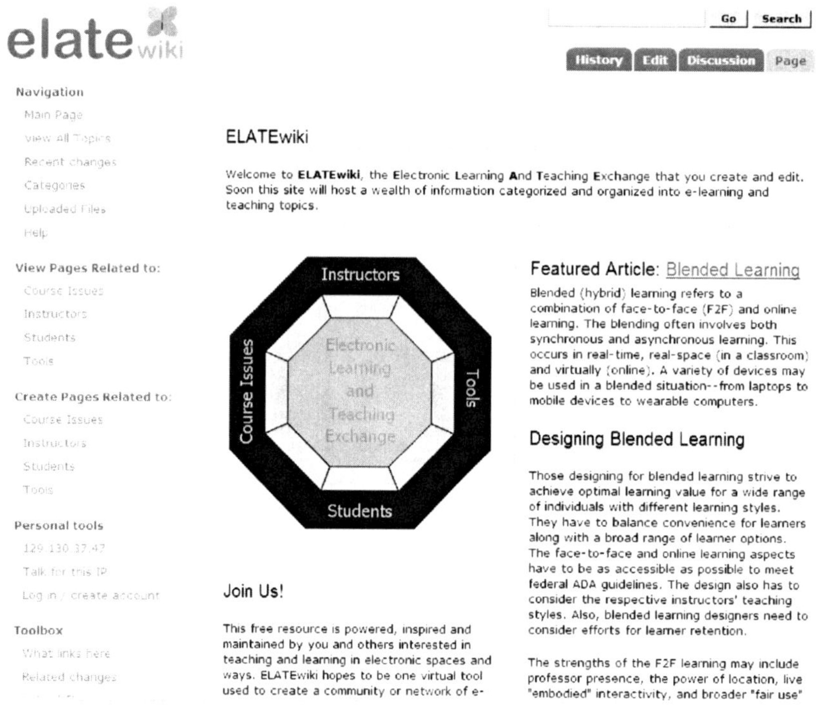

faculty, administrators, staff, and learners. The name of ELATEwiki stands for “E-Learning and Teaching Exchange”.

INTRODUCTION

The conversation began at the Division of Continuing Education (DCE) at Kansas State University (K-State) among members of the Distance Education Leadership group to support e-learning faculty members. This group had worked to launch a digital newsletter and to create a social site for both e-learning faculty and learners. Although ample on-campus teaching exchanges already existed, it became apparent that more was needed, particularly for those in geographically dispersed locations. The group decided to explore the use of a wiki to support those engaged in e-learning both on and off the K-State campuses. The exploration was conducted over several months, and then the project went dormant for half a year. Interest in this “thought experiment” was renewed at the end of Dec. 2008, and the project received modest funding and high-level political support on the campus shortly thereafter. ELATEwiki launched in early Mar. 2009.

AN ENVIRONMENTAL SCAN

Initially, the team conducted an environmental scan to see if there was an existing wiki that would fulfill the needs at the campus. They found some that dealt with e-learning technologies; they explored others that were designed for particular universities, subject areas, and courses. They found some that dealt with education in general but not any that dealt with the breadth of issues in e-learning. They also probed some electronic publications and blogs. If such a shared space existed stably in the Wikisphere, the Web 2.0 approach would be to join up and participate—to the benefit of all, through democratized knowledge access and sharing.

Next, the team reviewed the research literature to find out the latest word on wiki uses in teaching and learning. By the time of ELATEwiki's launch, wikis had long become part of an "emerging trend" of use for knowledge management and sharing. Since W. Cunningham's creation of the first wiki in 1994, wikis have sparked various innovations in the intervening 15 years; this technology has diffused widely with uses in both password-protected spaces as well as semi-public and wholly public spaces.

The reading that occurs on a wiki has been described as a "hypertextual" and non-linear sort of reading and connecting to a variety of contents through unpredictable paths:

The biggest advantage, and probably also the biggest disadvantage, of traditional reading is that the reader feels he cannot lose his orientation. On the other hand, a reader of hypertext tends to find himself astray in randomness and flexibility. When the reader cruises through a hypertext, his decision on which link to follow next is mostly decided by the stimulation provided by the Web page rather than a pre-set reading plan; in this sense, he loses his orientation as soon as the reading starts (Zhang, Aug. 2006, p. 25).

Researchers observe: "Wiki technology utilization is growing at a dramatic rate. Empirical evidence indicates this technology is sustainable" (Majchrzak, et al. 2006, as cited in Hester & Scott, 2008, pg. 6).

SOME OF THE RESEARCH LITERATURE

The research literature shows a wide use of wikis for innovative educational purposes. The innovations involve applications in teaching and learning, digital content management, as well as technological advancements into geographical awareness, mobile collaborations, and the activation of social spaces.

Wikis for Learning

Wikis have been employed for numerous student collaborations for learning (Raitman, Augar, & Zhou, 2005). They offer online concept formation as part of pre-class priming (Bower, 2007). A wiki may strengthen student value-added note-taking for collaborative notes based on instructor slides (O'Neill, 2005). Collaborations around wikis are interdisciplinary (Reinhold, Aug. 2006). E-learning environments have been enhanced through the use of supplementary wikis (Giannoukos, Lykourentzou, Mpardis, Nikolopoulos, Loumos, & Kayafas, July 2008). Others contain domain content materials such as an online science resource (Forte & Bruckman, Oct. 2007). Another wiki serves as a repository of code snippets (Mwai, 2006). Wikis may build learner capacities (Bruns & Humphreys, Oct. 2007) in primary, secondary and tertiary education.

Digital Content Management

In terms of information management, wikis may be treated with suspicion "for management, social and legal reasons" but are used to the management of tacit knowledge in various industries (Hasan, Meloche, Pfaff & Willis, 2007, p. 35). Wikis are used to capture, store and distribute organizational knowledge (Hester, Apr. 2008) or to support helpdesk staff (Klein & Smith, Oct. 2008). They enhance organizational decision-making and collaboration (Hill, Gaudiot, Hall, Marks, Prinetto, & Baglio, Sept. 2006).

Geographical Awareness

Various wiki projects offer location-awareness to connect to the physical context of users; these "geowikis" are being used on a campus (Schuler, Grandhi, Laws, Jones, & Bajaj, 2007, pp. 2639 – 2644); by bicyclists for navigation, decision-making, and live social interactivity to serve users who have "significant individual differences in purpose, attitude, and abilities" but focus on action / riding / exploring and sharing their experiences (Priedhorsky, Jordan, & Terveen, Oct. 2007, p. 93).

Mobile Collaborations

People collaborate through mobile devices with interactions mediated through an audio wiki (Wang, Roe, Pham, & Tjondronegoro, Mar. 2008). Physical books may be digitally annotated through a wiki to bridge the information sharing between the physical and digital (Wu, Robinson, & Mazalek, Feb. 2008). Political collaboration has occurred around wikis (Makice, Aug. 2006).

Activated Social Spaces

Social spaces where users may create contents may be activated via technological affordances in order to activate what C. Shirky calls a "latent group." Such groups may be nurtured to contribute contents but in studies of such groups, the power law distribution applies, which finds a minority group contributing a majority of the contents, which benefit the larger whole. It's been suggested that such a predictable imbalance of disproportionate contributions is to be expected (Shirky, 2008). Researchers have identified some 14 motivational categories for contributing to open virtual communities like those enabled by wikis: altruism, belonging, collaboration, egoism, egotism, emotional support, empathy, knowledge, power, reciprocity, reputation, self-esteem, self-expression, and wisdom" (Moore & Serva, 2007, p. 154). The technological affordances of a wiki may give contributors "a sense of accomplishment, collectivism, and benevolence, while working with exceptional freedom and ease. "The values of reputation, community, reciprocity, altruism and autonomy are fostered both by the people and the technology, effectively creating a near-utopian society in which individuals voluntarily collaborate and learn together" (Kuznetsov, 2006, p. 6). Human-facilitated wiki management will require some skills in activating the various motivations to encourage participation.

METHODS

Given the dispersed aspects of information on the Web, much less the Wikisphere, it would seem critical for the e-learning wiki to form a persona and a reputation as an end destination early on to merely survive. This would mean the contents would have to be fresh and valid; the social networks created would have to be people who are leaders and change agents in their fields; the audience would have to be defined and served clearly early on and continually. With the speed of changes on the Web and Wikisphere, the clock had already started running on this project before it had even been conceptualized. The domain field of higher education would require an even greater sense of importance for maintaining high informational quality standards. The expectations of quality from faculty nationally and internationally would require responsiveness regarding feedback to the site. The interface would have to be intuitive and supportable on a very modest budget (in the upper three digits).

University-Based Considerations

The team considered cost-benefit scenarios. What could K-State gain from this peer-to-peer wiki endeavor? What were potential risks? Who was the competition? How would the quality of the postings be established? How could the site be an end-destination for those on the Web and not just a way-station, in terms of the majority of users? What sorts of legal considerations were needed?

In line with the Web 2.0 sharing of intellectual resources—made available through Creative Commons™ copyright releases, M.I.T.'s Open Courseware, and other sharing endeavors—K-State wanted to share more of its intellectual property and expertise. It also has an interest in creating a wider digital footprint in the social sphere of the Web, in part to showcase its various online degree and certificate programs. Another perceived benefit was that of creating a stronger community of practice, both from the K-State community and the larger network of e-learning instructors (potentially K-20), technological staff, and administrators. Based on these and other considerations, the group determined a need for an interactive wiki to build communities and networks of practice across distance and institutional boundaries. They also brainstormed potential contents for the wiki to meet a range of needs, in the hopes of attracting and maintaining continuing interest from a range of potential participants.

Brainstormed Contents

The brainstormed contents include curricular design; the challenges of going global with e-learning courses and trainings; general e-learning technologies; automated learning; virtual and F2F events to build instructor community; online learner supports; reusability and open sharing; online teaching strategies; regulatory concerns; accessibility; educational resources; professional development opportunities, and other "branches." The idea though was to let the wiki evolve without building branches that would not be populated right away with some contents. Clearly, however, the wiki contents must go beyond showcasing what already exists on the Internet and Web. (See the Appendix for a visual of these ideas.)

Potential Risks

Wikis apparently have met with varying success. "There are currently plenty of other active open-access wikis, with varying success: some recruit many users and achieve sustainability, while others strive to attract sufficient active contributors, irrespective of the topic of the wiki" (Roth, 2007, p. 119). Research has found failures to contribute to wikis based on many reasons. In one case, they cited "economic reasons, issues of identity, and a lack of group norms. "A critical factor in its failure, however, was the lack of its integration into existing work practices and project governance" (Giordano, 2007, p. 269). This phenomenon suggests that there is a large challenge to turning casual visitors into actual contributors and community editors.

The potential risks would also not be minimal. There could be the risk of silence, of non-participation, or of a failure to launch. This endeavor would be one of many thousands of existing wikis with various purposes (McFedries, 2006). Promoting cross-institutional knowledge management across a variety of educational institutions in both higher education and K-12 would mean a different set of logistical challenges than building for one institution with (theoretically) one workplace culture.

The lack of an incubation period for the wiki would mean that it would be live (accessible and public) from the moment of its creation, ready or not. This feature of the wiki might discourage participation by some who would prefer some space to consider options. "While this removes impediments to collaboration, it often deters participants who would rather incubate ideas before bringing them to the group" (Burrow, 2004, p. 77).

There could be legal liabilities created if the team did not work closely with the university's legal counsel to put in solid policies and practices into place. There could be academic battles that get transferred onto the wiki. There could be plenty of digital graffiti, which would need human time investment to clean off and address. There would need to be protection also of the university's academic standing and image, depending on the posting of certain content types.

Technological Considerations

The wiki team debated whether to use a wiki farm or to host the wiki on the university's own servers using an open-source technology. They considered server load in terms of multimedia in podcasts, audiocasts, animated slideshows, and other digital artifacts. The group considered whether to launch a wiki as a private enterprise, a wholly public enterprise, or a mix. They also considered whether to build privately first and then launch to public when the time seemed right. (They decided that writing privately to a limited audience would result in a different voice and feel, so they decided that the spirit of a public wiki should involve public work from the beginning.) They debated issues of avatar and individual telepresence creation. They considered the power of social regulation to maintain site quality, and debated whether or not to use a wikimaster, albeit backed up by the best controls that a wiki technology could offer.

They sampled various types of wiki technologies to determine what functionalities they wanted based on their perceived needs. Interestingly, wiki technologies now already seem to include the four paradigms of "global editability" mentioned by Di Iorio & Vitali (2005, pp. 36 – 37). These include the writable web (the phenomena of users being producers), external layered contributions (hyperlinking out), anthologies (the ability to combine information) and collaborative editing (user co-revision and co-editing). Ultimately, they decided on MediaWiki, an open-source wiki technology that underlies Wikipedia™. This technology was popular and included various plug-ins for the integration of various digital objects like video embeds. Learning synchronously about the technology with the live launch would mean that technological snafus could occur.

WIKI MASTER METHOD AND ONTOLOGY

Wiki masters are jokingly referred to as benevolent dictators in the Wikisphere. One writer asserts with tongue-in-cheek that open content communities often spawn merit-based "dictatorships" by necessity: "The need for 'dictatorship' arises from the difficulty inherent to decision making in large, voluntary, and consensus oriented communities" (Reagle, 2007, p. 149). He balances that with an additional comment in his observations of leaders in Web-based communal spaces: "Leaders whose autocratic actions exceed their accumulated merit/charisma risk being hounded to death within their community, or the community forking" (Reagle, 2007, p. 152). He notes that leaders need to make continuing important contributions to keep their positions, no matter if they are founding leaders.

A range of considerations emerges with supporting a wiki. There are questions not only of soliciting participants and participation but of virtual community evolution over the long term, the management of information over time [with one group suggesting letting unused aspects of a wiki fade away (Stickel, Holzinger, & Ebner, 2008)].

Extreme messages and behaviors may be encouraged with the openness of wikis (Bryant, Forte, & Bruckman, 2005, p. 1). "Some people are ignorant, some are malicious, and some are just bad writers. Yet, Wikipedia seems to work" (Priedhorsky, Chen, Lam, Panciera, Terveen, & Riedl, 2007, p. 259). Damage is serious, involving misinformation, mass deletions of contents, partial deletions, offensive writing, spam, nonsense, and other types (p. 266).

That aspect of open communications may conflict with the academic rigor required in most fields (Costa, Nhampossa, & Aparicio, 2008, p. 169). As more virtual participation grows and magnifies, conflicts follow, with a need for coordination (Kittur, Suh, Pendleton, & Chi, 2007, p.

453). Theoretically, participants to a wiki should be maintaining order and "safeguarding the equality, innovation and accuracy of Wiki" (Jing & Fan, 2008, p. 204). Participants may employ the power of self-correction (Farkas, 2008) to the various entries.

The team felt the need for human oversight of the wiki because of the importance of academic contents. Also, there are ambitions to potentially develop special interest groups within the wiki, who specialize in particular branches of wiki information. In a sense, while the branding for Kansas State University would be very light, the contents could rebound indirectly to the university. Having a very credible and high profile professor would allay some of the inherent distrust of wikis as conveyers of reliable information, with their high mutability (Kittur, Suh, & Chi, 2008). Human leadership of the wiki could also enhance the sense of transparency about wiki provenance and institutional support. The contents would go through a de facto peer review. Wiki contents are being developed in the same way the *Oxford English Dictionary* was, with volunteer readers composing more than 400,000 definitions of word usage: "Lacking wiki software meant organizing over five million slips to form this collective intelligence project, a process that lasted from 1857 until 1928" (Harris, 2007, p. 26).

A number of factors make judgment quality difficult on wikis—particularly the number of articles; the diverse contents; unknown contributors, and purposeful abuse by site visitors (Lim, Vuong, Lauw, & Sun, 2006, n.p.). Managing "edit-war"(s) will be challenging (Viégas, 2007, p. 1), particularly with high contributors or article curators, with stakes in the definitions and understandings.

The management work surrounding a wiki is no light feat. The research indicates a range of categories of work: "Editing Work, Social and Community Support Actions, Border Patrol, Administrative, Collaborative Actions and Disposition, Meta-Content Work, (and) Undifferentiated Work" (Kriplean, Beschastnikh, & McDonald, 2008, p. 50).

Dr. Roger W. McHaney (ProfRogerMc) was invited to serve as the wiki master for this endeavor early on. He created two "sysop" (systems operator) accounts, one with his catchy name and then one as "WikiKeeper" to handle more of the administrative, non-academic related aspects of wiki management. He re-named the wiki master role to "wiki keeper" to reflect his sense of caretaking of the wiki rather than the centralized "master." He developed an ontology early on as a kind of macro-structure to the wiki's contents. "Ontologies are unambiguous representations of concepts, relationships between concepts (such as a hierarchy), ontologically significant individuals, and axioms" (Hepp, Siorpaes, & Bachlechner, 2007, p. 55). Given the diversity of points-of-views, values, and fields, it was understood that a more natural ontology would be defined by participants as the site evolved. The terms would need to have "conceptual consistency" over time (p. 55) and may need to be grouped and fine-tuned by the wiki master to ensure small spelling and meaning differences would not result in particular portions of content becoming orphaned with regard to the larger classification scheme.

In essence, the initial ontology was viewed more as a starting point than as an enforced, permanent structure for the site. A primary motivation for creating this structure was the belief that potential users might not develop an initial contribution without a clear and relatively simple way to add value to the site. And further they might wonder how to connect their entries in meaningful ways. And further, many may not understand or desire to learn wikitext or wiki conventions. For those reasons, four general categories were created. The ontology areas---course issues, instructors, students, and tools---are meant to provide a high level organization for e-learning and are viewed by the team to fill a role similar to the tags used by most social bookmark services. The conceptualization is represented in the visualization that has been built into the site.

Over time, the team envisions users attaching more "tags" to their entries by creating and using Wikimedia category names which automatically provide hyperlinks to groups of articles. This enables one article to belong to several categories and makes it easier for readers to find and view articles or interest.

In the same way social bookmarking services (such as Digg, Yahoo!Buzz, Del.icio.us, Technorati.com, stumbleupon.com, and kaboodle.com) allow users to organize their bookmarks with informal tags instead of traditional, rigid hierarchies, the team envisions ELATEwiki users will determine and add tags as the field of e-learning evolves and changes. In a sense, the well-defined practice of collaboratively creating and maintaining tags, also known as folksonomy, is being applied to ensure keywords are generated using a bottom-up approach.

RESULTS

Wikimedia software was installed to comply with the team's implementation recommendations for ELATEwiki. As stated earlier, MediaWiki is popular open source software used in a wide range of wiki applications including Wikipedia. As such, it is regularly updated, is continually scrutinized for security, and has an active community of users. A K-State server with a clustered environment having two nodes (so if one server goes down, the site should still be available, served from the second node) was preloaded with PHP 5.2.8 and MySQL database software and was used as a hosting platform for the installation which was initiated in late January of 2009 in K-State's Office of Mediated Education (OME). Version 1.13.3 of the software (1.13.3) was obtained, unzipped, and loaded onto the server. Properties on the uploaded configuration folder were set to make it writable so the install script would run. An SQL database was created and the MediaWiki installer was run. Once the software was in place, several customizations were done to give ELATEwiki the desired appearance. First, the cavendish wiki skin setting was used. Next, a logo, created by a K-State graphic artist, was uploaded to the server and a setting in the localsettings.php file ($wgLogo) was used to point to it. See Figure 2.

Development of Templates

MediaWiki content comprises articles which represent specific topics. The informal term, wiki page, generally refers to a single article that has, at a minimum, a title and a body. Occasionally, a wiki page only will have a title, in which case it is called a stub. Stubs are created by a user who may not possess the required knowledge to develop an article but hopes someone else will notice the incomplete entry and add to it.

In general, articles are written and maintained by a community of users. While this openness can foster incredible creativity and result in amazing emergent outcomes, problems can also develop. For instance, the contents of pages created by different users can be organized in vastly different ways making the site seem disorganized and lacking cohesion. Conventions for citing sources and providing credit for original material can

Figure 2. A visualization of the ELATEwiki ontology

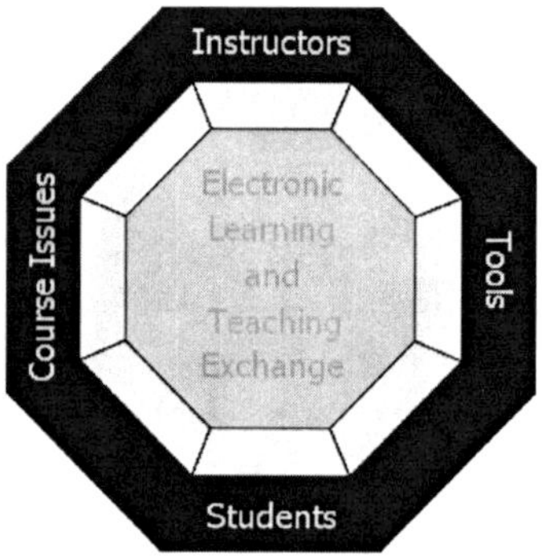

Figure 3. ELATEwiki logo (Mendoza, 2009)

elate wiki

become confusing and take a variety of forms. Mechanisms for tagging and linking pages can be set up in various fashions making navigation difficult. Taken separately, none of these issues would result in much more than maintenance headaches but taken together, particularly on a site with constant dynamic use, a wiki could quickly be rendered unusable.

To provide a sense of direction to ELATEwiki, a series of templates were devised to coincide with the general ontology developed for the site. The templates were envisioned as a series of page structures pre-loaded with category tags to make a new user's assimilation into the community easier and to increase user productivity while lowering the learning curve.

Initially, four templates were developed, one for each of the categories suggested by the team--- course issues, instructors, students, and tools. The templates were constructed of wikitext and loaded on the site. Figures 4 and 5 provide views of the template used for a new article related to instructor issues.

Although simple, a potential site contributor without knowledge of wikitext might find it difficult to take the first step and create a new page whereas the template helps automate this process. In addition to the subtitles which can be changed in the template, a category tag has been added to cluster this page with all others related to instructors. Two additional sections---'See Also' and 'References'---have also been added to the initial templates.

Creating a New Page

With the templates in place and a general structure defined as a starting point, the process for creating new pages was automated. First a set of

Figure 4. ELATEwiki instructor template

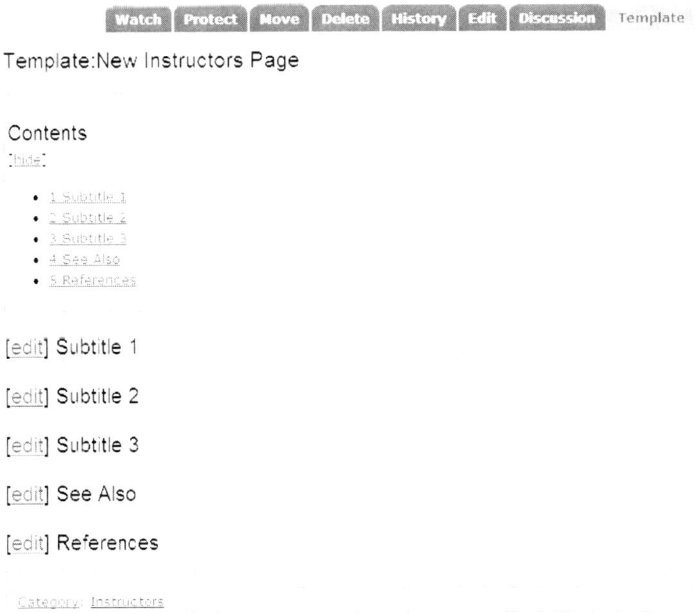

Figure 5. Wikitext for new instructors page template

links were added to the 'Main Page' sidebar so a user can easily access the new page templates. Figure 5 shows a portion of the sidebar. The 'Create Pages Related to:' grouping provides a set of easy links for a potential contributor to bring up her desired page template in the edit mode. Figure 6 provides a look at the sidebar code. It can be accessed by typing: MediaWiki:sidebar into the search box and then pressing the 'edit' button to reveal the wikitext.

The 'Create_Instructors_Page' directive is located in the wikitext for the sidebar. This directive is linked to the display text 'Instructors'. 'Create_Instructors_Page and the three other 'Create' directives all bring up pages that prompt the user for a new article title and then proceed to load that into the appropriately tagged template. Figure 7 provides a view of 'Create_Instructor_Page' and Figure 8 shows the associated wikitext.

The following image shows the Wikitext on the back end that creates this functionality for site visitors.

In order to use the inputbox on the page, the following code had to be added to the configuration file, LocalSettings.php, found on the Wiki server: 'require_once("extensions/inputbox.php"); // added' (Moore & Barber, 2008). Additionally, the wikitext shown in Figure 8 loads the page template using the: 'preload=Template:New_Instructors_Page' command.

Tagging Entries

Additional tags can be formulated and added to the template should the author desire. For instance, if the topic being written involved an instructor's use of a course management system, a category tag such as: [[Category:Course Management System]] could be added and this would provide further indexing capacity. The category tags will ensure searches will bring up the list of pages related to a particular category. Once an article is created and tagged, it will be listed in the appropriate categories. The full range of categories can be accessed by pressing the 'Categories' link under 'Navigation' on the MediaWiki sidebar. The user can then select a category of interest and view all the related articles. Figure 10 provides an example

Figure 6. Wikitext for ELATEwiki sidebar

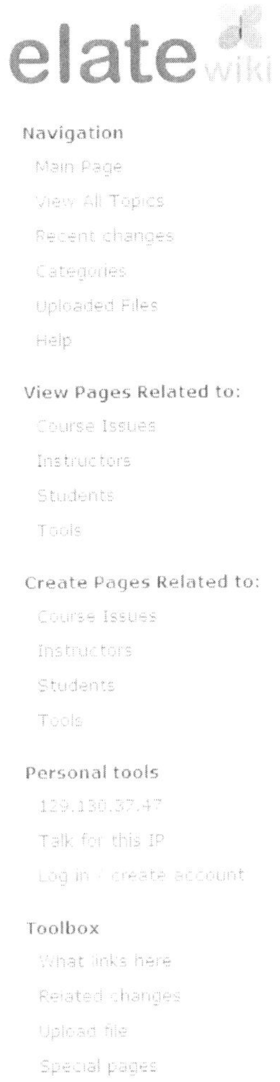

of the pages under the category 'Course Issues' early in ELATEwiki's development.

Launching ELATEwiki

Once the initial capabilities were developed to make ELATEwiki easier to use, a multiphase launch was conducted. The first phase in the process was to seed a number of articles to help set the tone for the wiki and to add a measure of value immediately apparent to potential users. Several articles in each of the major categories were developed and posted. The articles were written with varying length, quality and completeness. Several brief stubs were also included. Various combinations of images, new tags, existing tags, links (both internal and external), references (following American Psychological Association citation guidelines), new categories, and videos were included in the initial pages to provide examples for future users of the site. This first phase was conducted by the wikimaster and another user with high privilege level. This step was viewed as both a seeding operation and an experiment to help uncover potential problems and issues that might arise when a larger group enters the site.

The second phase of the launch was to invite a group of local e-learning experts to enter the site as browsers, contributors, and editors. These individuals had limited knowledge of the wiki's mechanics and were invited, in part, to help "stress test" the wiki. The actions of these users were monitored and helped fine tune various settings and help understand the level of editing work required by the wikimaster and others in the community. Several lessons were learned during this phase. For instance, page titles can be changed by 'moving' an article to a new name. The move tab is not available to all users but just those with administrative privileges. Another item coming to light at this time was the need to include embedded video in the contributed pages. An extension for MediaWiki called VideoFlash had to be installed to accomplish this. The following steps were taken to provide users with the desired capability: 1) A file called videoflash.php in the extensions directory of the MediaWiki installation was created; 2) The system administrator copied and pasted the code provided on MediaWiki's website into the videoflash file. The code can be found at http://www.mediawiki.org/wiki/Extension:VideoFlash; and finally, 3) This line of code was added to the LocalSettings.php file: require_once("extensions/videoflash.php").

With those items loaded. The wiki was capable of displaying embedded video from YouTube and other sites. Figure 11 provides an example.

The third phase of the launch involved inviting

Figure 7. Sidebar code

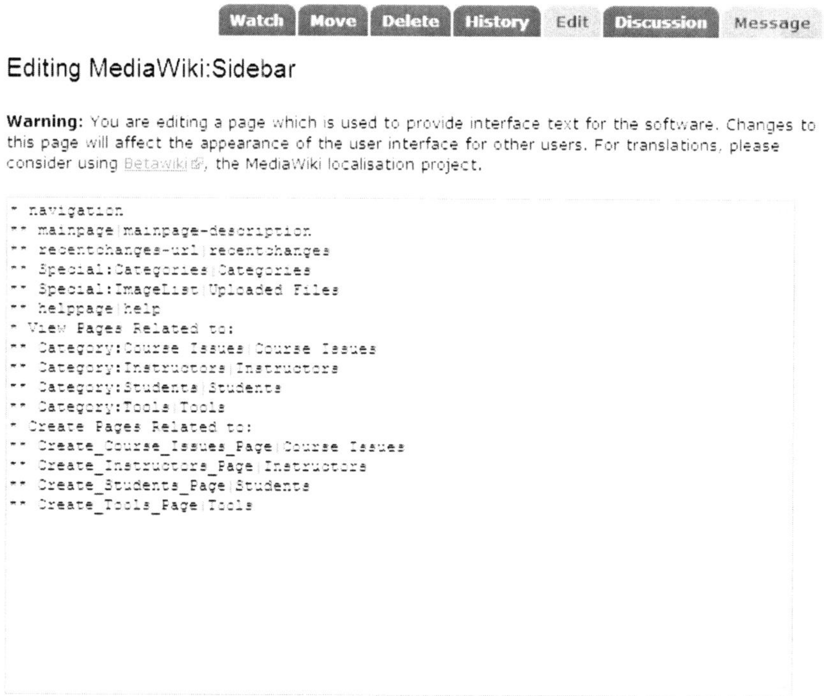

Figure 8. Create instructors page

a larger group into ELATEwiki. By this time, the team was confident the site was robust enough to support additional traffic and to provide a useful set of material to the larger e-learning and teaching community. A number of invitations were sent out to potential users via electronic mailing lists, through conference presentations, email lists, and contacts at various campuses and other organizations. This phase of expansion was not conducted until a robust legal disclaimer was placed on the site by one of Kansas State University's attorneys.

As a larger group began using ELATEwiki, additional features were requested. These requests resulted in the installation of further extensions to the MediaWiki software. Among these were ImageMagick which allows the automatic generation of thumbnail images and enables image scaling on the wiki. The WikiArticleFeeds Extension was

Figure 9. Wikitext for create instructors page

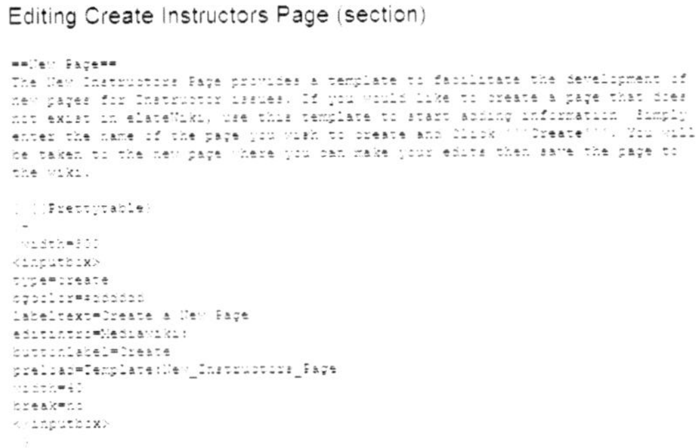

Figure 10. Pages by category for 'course issues'

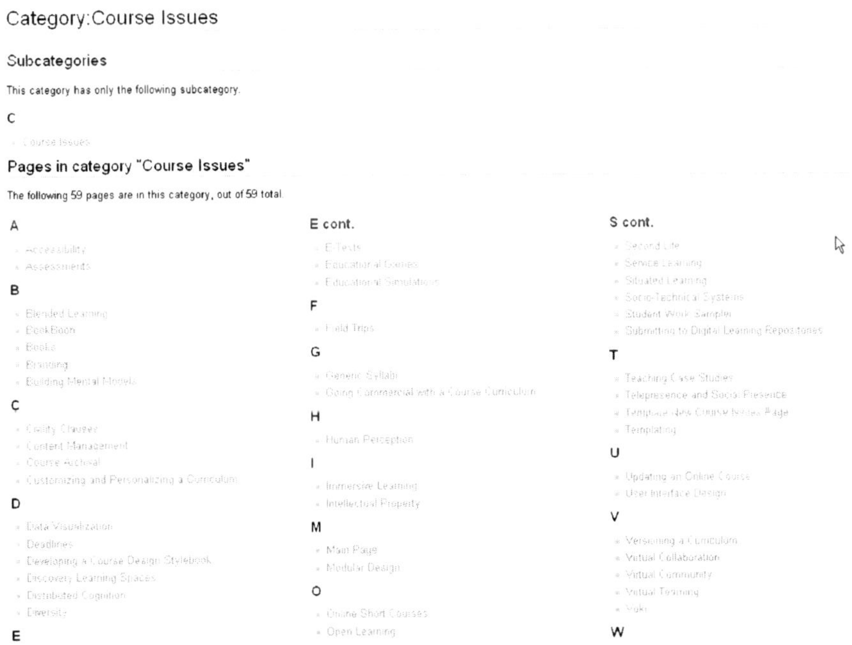

installed to allow users to create RSS feeds within ELATEwiki for export to other sites. As the site became more popular, spam and vandalism became a problem so the RECAPTCHA plug-in for MediaWiki was added to the site to prevent anonymous editors from adding hyperlinks without first verifying they were not 'bots.' Another extension added was ANYSITE which allows embedding a live Website within a wiki page. This extension was added so BookBoon.com was able to offer free student textbooks to users directly through ELATEwiki. Others have begun using ANYSITE to illustrate various Websites with dynamic rather than static screen captures.

Figure 11. Embedded video in an example article

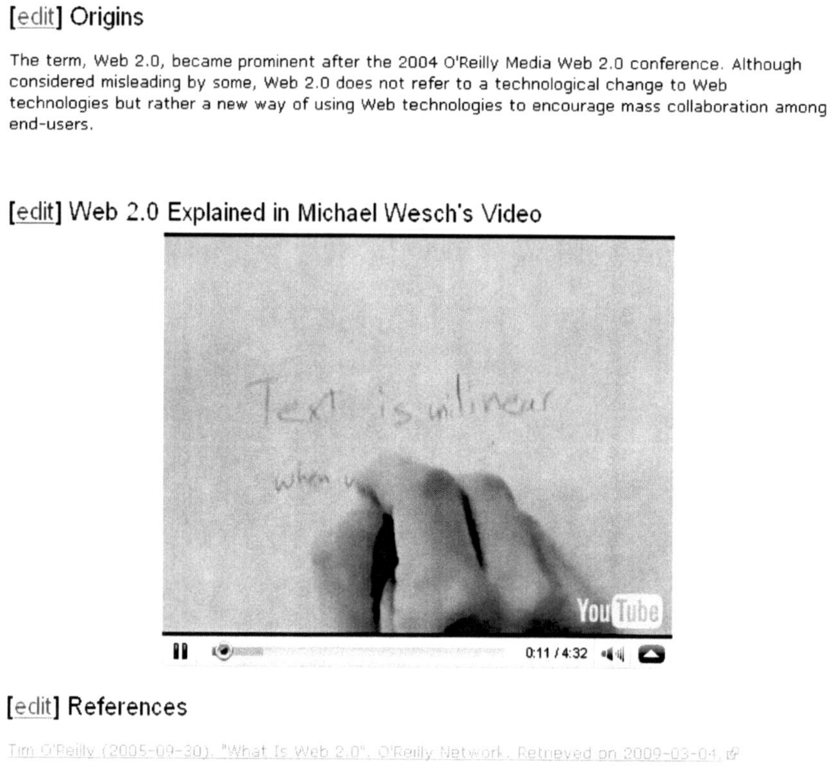

DISCUSSION

Wikis appear to have a bright future in e-learning and teaching. Since a primary advantage of e-learning is to free both instructor and student from the twin tyrannies of geography and time, it makes sense that a related teaching exchange should function in the same way. Although wikis have been used in a variety of applications and for different purposes ranging from public websites (Mader, 2008) to knowledge bases (p. 32) and many areas between (such as blogs, directories, project management, and communication sites), the strengths of wiki technology reside within its collaborative nature. The MediaWiki™ technology has been malleable, particularly regarding the integration of other technologies. ELATEwiki is poised to enable a teaching exchange by leveraging the power of the Web and taking advantage of MediaWiki's collaborative features.

While the technical aspects of implementing a wiki involve a steep learning curve and formal help material can be difficult to acquire and assimilate, the most daunting development challenge is attracting a critical mass of users from which a community of practice will emerge. While a number of traditional methods (such as publicity, conference presentations, and word of mouth) exist for accomplishing this and some authors have suggested steps for success in the process (Mader, 2008), in the emerging, networked world of Web 2.0, it might be better to view the process through a fresh set of eyes.

C. Shirky, in *Here Comes Everybody: The Power of Organizing without Organizations*, provides a perspective that may help in accomplishing the site's ultimate goal of reaching a critical mass (Shirky, 2008). Shirky suggests in order for a social tool to succeed, three components must be in place: *Promise, Tools, and Bargain* (p. 260).

He cautions these items are not to be viewed as a recipe for success but instead as components in a complex set of interactions needing close attention. It is then that success might be achieved. Shirky suggests among these three components, "[t]he promise creates the basic desire to participate." (p. 261). The promise is the key and essential piece that convinces potential users to take the plunge and use a portion of their already constrained time in order to contribute in meaningful ways. The promise has to offer more than the explicit outward trappings such as 'to be a dynamic and useful e-learning and teaching exchange where meaningful information can be stored and accessed.' Instead it has to appeal at the implicit, personal level. For instance, motivating promises might be: 'using this site will provide a potential audience for your hard work and it will be appreciated by others who work in your field' or 'you will be providing a valuable academic service for your peers' or 'this is the chance to get in on the ground floor of something with the potential to become very big and be very important'. If potential users understand the promise and find it coincides with their needs and desires, then the possibility of success is improved.

The tools are a more obvious component for the ELATEwiki project. Most are derived from MediaWiki and its community-developed capabilities. Additional tools, such as the ontology, templates, categories, seeded entries, input boxes, and menus have also been added to ensure users can easily understand how to use and join the community. A watchlist may be created to monitor updates to particular parts of the site. A good social tool must be designed to accomplish the task intended and it must fit the skill levels of those intending to use it (p. 269). While the promise can draw in users, a poorly designed or selected tool set can have just the opposite effect and drive away potential users. And with the world of choices out there, often a social site may only get one chance from a potential user.

The bargain is the most complex aspect of a social group because it involves the behaviors of various users as well as the response of the supplier of the promise and tools. In the case of ELATEwiki, the bargain is that contributions will be maintained, improved, and used by others. The site will maintain a 'neutral tone' regarding controversial issues and will allow people to post entries which will be edited by others. Part of the bargain then becomes posting and editing content to ensure peers will also post and edit content.

The ultimate success of the ELATEwiki project will hinge on achieving the correct balance between these three aspects of social group formation: promise, tools, and bargain. In essence this creates an intersection between governance and group dynamics/use and if this intersection appeals to a critical mass of users, the project will succeed and enjoy a long useful existence.

FUTURE ELATION

The potential for ELATEwiki will depend in part on the building of the socio-technical environment that is co-created between the wiki originators and those who participate in this site. This bargain will result in a cooperative environment with many long-term benefits for academic and larger communities. For instance, there is hope that if the contents are of sufficient quality and applicability, wikibooks may be created for uses in e-learning courses. The Creative Commons™ licensing agreement provides for that possibility. It is possible that virtual cross-functional work teams may emerge, collaborate and develop solutions to particularly thorny academic issues. Professional alliances may form around shared virtual, blended, and face-to-face events. Organizations with a focus on e-learning or teaching may find the infrastructure useful and incorporate this resource into their knowledge dissemination processes.

CONCLUSION

Starting with a small team at Kansas State University and a set of physical resources such as a server and technical support, an e-learning and teaching exchange wiki called ELATEwiki has been launched to support faculty and administrators in their work. The project aims to leverage the advantages of wiki technology such as wide access and dissemination, digital content archival, collaboration, subscribability, and reversibility of postings to interest a community of virtual (and local) collaborators for a long-term and successful development of a free educational resource. C. Shirky's suggested components in the successful deployment of a social tool---promise, tools and bargain---are being formulated in a way the team hopes will appeal to a wide audience leading to an active and growing repository of cutting edge knowledge.

To share the experiences of ELATEwiki's development, this chapter has been developed to chronicle the project starting with a literature review and ending with physical implementation details before concluding with the social challenges facing the development of any viable online community. It is hoped the readers of this chapter will visit http://www.ELATEwiki.org and add their knowledge to the material on the site and help make this a useful knowledgebase for current and future e-learning educators, administrators, staff, and learners. ELATEwiki's affordances may contribute to this fast-growing field, in a shared endeavor of mutual discovery and sharing.

ACKNOWLEDGMENT

The team members working on ELATEwiki deserve the kudos for their planning and hard work: Dr. Bettie Minshall, Ellen Stauffer, Ron Jackson, Lynda Spire, Dr. Roger McHaney and Dr. Shalin Hai-Jew (team lead). Dr. Sue Maes provided budgetary support for this project. Peter Paukstelis, legal counsel at K-State, provided superb support in the development of the site's policies and Terms of Service. Dr. Vicki Clegg provided helpful advice. Andrea Mendoza designed the logo, and Josh Works provided some initial setup work and continuing support. Dave Bollman and Josh McCune offered helpful advisement regarding using wiki software. Thanks to all for their contributions. Most of all, thanks to the many engaged in e-learning who have contributed to ELATE, and also to those who will in the future.

REFERENCES

Bower, M. (2007). Independent, synchronous and asynchronous—An analysis of approaches to online concept formation. Presented at ITiCSE '07. Dundee, Scotland

Bruns, A., & Humphreys, S. (2007). Building collaborative capacities in learners: The M/cyclopedia project revisited. Presented at WikiSym '07. Montréal, Québec.

Bryant, S. L., Forte, A., & Bruckman, A. (2005). *Becoming Wikipedian: Transformation of participation in a collaborative online encyclopedia. Presented at GROUP '05*. FL: Sanibel Island.

Burrow, A. L. (2004). Negotiating access within Wiki: A system to construct and maintain a taxonomy of access rules. Presented at HT '04. Santa Cruz, CA.

Costa, C. J., Nhampossa, J. L., & Aparicio, M. (2008) Wiki content evaluation framework. Presented at SIGDOC '08. Lisbon, Portugal.

Di Iorio, A., & Vitali, F. (2005). From the writable Web to global editability. Presented at HT '05. Salzburg, Austria. ACM. 36.

Farkas, M. (2008). CMS the wiki way: Maintaining library web content with a wiki. In Practice: Technology. *American Libraries*, *39*(11), 35.

Forte, A., & Bruckman, A. (2007). Constructing text: Wiki as a toolkit for (collaborative?) learning. Presented at WikiSym'07. Montréal, Québec.

Giannoukos, I., Lykourentzou, I., Mpardis, G., Nikolopoulos, V., Loumos, V., & Kayafas, E. (2008). *Collaborative e-learning environments enhanced by wiki technologies. Presented at PETRA '08* (pp. 1–5). Athens, Greece: ACM.

Giordano, R. (2007). An investigation of the use of a wiki to support knowledge exchange in public health. Presented atGROUP '07. Sanibel Island, FL, ACM. 269.

Harris, C. (2007). Can we make peace with Wikipedia? *School Library Journal.* Retrieved from www.alj.com

Hasan, H., Meloche, J. A., Pfaff, C. C., & Willis, D. (2007). *Beyond ubiquity: Co-creating corporate knowledge with a wiki.* Presented at the International Conference on Mobile Ubiquitous Computing, Systems, Services and Technologies. UBICOMM 2007, IEEE. 35.

Hepp, M., Siorpaes, K., & Bachlechner, D. (2007). *Harvesting wiki consensus: Using Wikipedia entries for knowledge management.* Semantic Knowledge Management.

IEEE Internet Computing. 55. Hester, A. (2008). Innovating with organizational wikis: Factors facilitating adoption and diffusion of an effective collaborative knowledge management system. Presented at SIGMIS-CPR '08. Charlottesville, Virginia. ACM. 161-163. Hester, A. J. & Scott, J. E. (2008). A conceptual model of wiki technology diffusion.

In *Proceedings of the 41st Hawaii International Conference on System Sciences.* 1-8. Hill, M. D., Gaudiot, J.-L., Hall, M., Marks, J., Prinetto, P., & Baglio, D. (2006). A wiki for discussing and promoting best practices in research. *Communications of the ACM, 49*(9), 63-64.

Jing, H., & Fan, Y. (2008). Usability of wiki for knowledge management of knowledge-based enterprises. Presented at 2008 International Symposium on Knowledge Acquisition and Modeling. IEEE, 204.

Kittur, A., Suh, B., & Chi, E. H. (2008). Can you ever trust a wiki? Impacting perceived trustworthiness in Wikipedia. Presented at CSCW '08. San Diego, CA.ACM, 477.

Kittur, A., Suh, B., Pendleton, B. A., & Chi, E. H. (2007). He says, she says: Conflict and coordination in Wikipedia. In Proceedings of the Online Representation of Self. San Jose, CA. ACM, 453.

Klein, R., & Smith, M. (2008). *Pursuing the peak of excellence: Wiki as a knowledge base. Presented at SIGUCCS '08* (pp. 167–171). Portland, OR: ACM.

Kriplean, T., Beschastnikh, I., & McDonald, D. W. (2008). Articulations in WikiWork: Uncovering valued work in Wikipedia through Barnstars. Presented at CSCW '08. San Diego, CA. ACM, 50.

Kuznetsov, S. (2006). Motivations of contributors to Wikipedia. *ACM SIGCAS Computers and Society, 36*(2).

Lim, E.-P., Vuong, B.-Q., Lauw, H. W., & Sun, A. (2006). Measuring qualities of articles contributed by online communities. In *Proceedings of the 2006 IEEE / WIC / ACM International Conference on Web Intelligence*. IEEE.

Mader, S. (2008). *Wikipatterns*. Indianapolis, IN: Wiley Publishing.

Makice, K. (2006). *PoliticWiki: Exploring communal politics. WikiSym 2006* (pp. 105–118). Odense, Denmark: ACM.

McFedries, P. (2006) It's a wiki, wiki world. Technically Speaking. IEEE Spectrum. Retrieved Jan. 22, 2009, from < www.spectrum.ieee.org >. 88.

Mendoza, A. (2009). ELATEwiki logo.

Moore, A., & Barber, L. R., Jr. (2008). Wiki-based extension fact sheets. Journal of Extension: 46(3). *Extension Journal, Inc. retrieved from:*http://www.joe.org/joe/2008june/tt1.php on March 4, *2009).*

Moore, T. D., & Serva, M. A. (2007). Understanding member motivation for contributing to different types of virtual communities: A proposed framework. Presented at SIGMIS-CPR '07. St. Louis, MS.

Mwai, N. (2006). Creation of a wiki-based code snippet repository. Student poster abstract. In *Proceedings of the Consortium for Computing Sciences in Colleges*. 293.

O'Neill, M. E. (2005, Feb.). Automated use of a wiki for collaborative lecture notes. *SIGCSE '05*. St. Louis, MS.

Priedhorsky, R., Chen, J., Lam, S. T. K., Panciera, K., Terveen, L., & Reidl, J. (2007). Creating, destroying, and restoring value in Wikipedia. GROUP'07. Sanibel Island, FL. ACM, 259 &266.

Priedhorsky, R., Jordan, B., & Terveen, L. (2007). *How a personalized geowiki can help Bicyclists share information more effectively*. Presented at WikiSym '07. Montréal, Québec.Raitman, R., Augar, N., & Zhou, W. (2005). Employing wikis for online collaboration in the e-learning environment: Case study. In *Proceedings of the Third International Conference on Information Technology and Applications* (ICITA '05). IEEE.

Reagle, J. M., Jr. (2007). Do as I do: Authorial leadership in Wikipedia. Presented at WikiSym '07. Montréal, Québec.

Reinhold, S. (2006). WikiTrails: Augmenting wiki structure for collaborative, interdisciplinary learning. Presented at WikiSym '06. Odense, Denmark.

Roth, C. (2008). Viable wikis: Struggle for life in the Wikisphere. Presented at WikiSym '07. Montréal, Québec.

Schuler, R. P., Grandhi, S. A., Laws, N., Jones, Q., & Bajaj, S. (2007). *Finding your way with CampusWiki: A location-aware wiki. CHI 2007: Work-in-Progress. San Jose, CA.Shirky, C. (2008). Here Comes Everybody: The Power of Organizing without Organizations*. New York: Penguin Group.

Stickel, C., Holzinger, A., & Ebner, M. (2008). Useful oblivion versus information overload in e-learning examples in the context of wiki systems. In *Proceedings of the ITI 2008 30th International Conference on Information Technology Interfaces*. Cavtat, Croatia. 171 – 176.

Viégas, F. B. (2007). The visual side of Wikipedia. In *Proceedings of the 40th Hawaii International Conference on System Sciences*. IEEE.

Wang, L., Roe, P., Pham, B., & Tjondronegoro, D. (2008). An audio wiki supporting mobile collaboration. Presented at SAC '08. Fortaleza, Ceará, Brazil.

Wu, C.-S. A., Robinson, S. J., & Mazalek, A. (2008). Turning a page on the digital annotation of physical books. In *Proceedings of the Second International Conference on Tangible and Embedded Interaction* (TEI'08). Bonn, Germany.

Zhang, Y. (2006). Wiki means more: Hyperreading in Wikipedia. Presented at HT'06. Odense, Denmark.

FURTHER READING

Anderson, C. (2006). *The Long Tail: Why the Future of Business is Selling Less of More*. New York: Hyperion Books.

Benkler, Y. (2007). *The Wealth of Networks: How Social Production Transforms Markets and Freedom*. New Haven, CT: Yale University Press. (Original work published 2006)

MediaWiki.org. (2009). See http://www.mediawiki.org/wiki/MediaWiki.

Richardson, W. (2006). *Blogs, Wikis, Podcasts, and Other Powerful Web Tools for Classrooms*. Thousand Oaks, CA: Corwin Press.

Shirky, C. (2008). *Here Comes Everybody: The Power of Organizing without Organizations*. New York: Penguin Group.

Surowiecki, J. (2005). *The Wisdom of Crowds*. New York: Random House. (Original work published 2004)

Tapscott, D., & Williams, A. D. (2008). *Wikinomics*. New York: Penguin Group.

"Wiki." (2009, June 23). Retrieved June 30, 2009, from http://en.wikipedia.org/wiki/Wiki

APPENDIX: SUPPORTING MATERIAL

Figure 12. DE faculty wiki content ideas (initial draft)

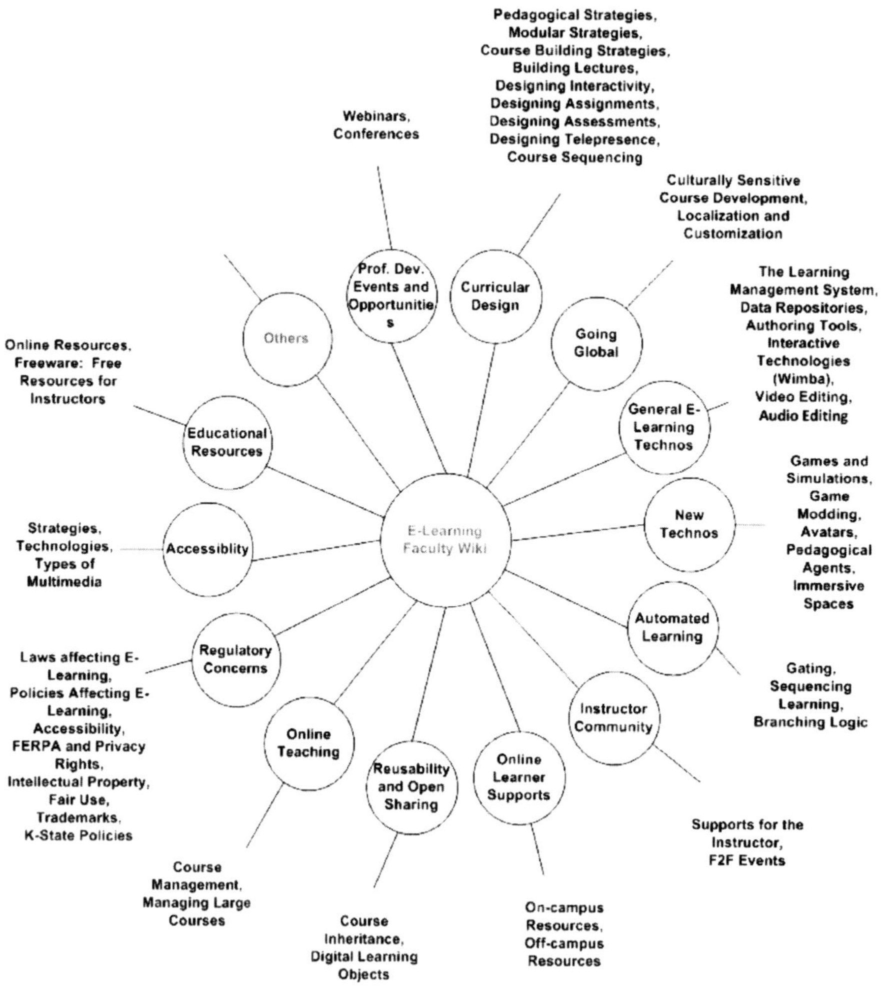

DE Faculty Wiki Content Ideas (Draft)

Abstract

A small team at Kansas State University worked to plan, create and launch an e-learning wiki to support faculty in their work. The advantages of the wiki technology—with its technological affordances of wide access and dissemination, digital content archival, multimedia expressiveness, remote collaboration, subscribability, and the reversibility of postings –appealed to this team. Even initially, there seemed to be opportunities for building novice and professional capacities in e-learning through the co-creation and sharing of information, problem-solving, and virtual community building. This chapter describes the research literature and pedagogical theories on wikis. It addresses the team's efforts in exploring and then building the wiki site. Additionally, this explains the team's rationales in terms of the intellectual property policies, the work to create accessibility, the wiki's fortuitous naming, the seeding of the wiki with contents, its low-key branding strategy, and the publicity plan for a "hard launch" of the ELATEwiki to the Wikisphere. This also describes the datamining techniques used to track use of the site and how those affect the site's continuing evolution. Finally, this chapter will provide perspectives on the work of a wiki-master in a peer-to-peer, collaborative, and open wiki.

Questions and Answers

1. What are some challenges with ELATEwiki going live right from the beginning? How were soft and hard launches used to gradually push this wiki into the public consciousness?

ELATEwiki had challenges with its original identity or branding. It had some light competitors in the Wikisphere. It had a core group of educators who may not have had much experience going live to a worldwide audience with their initial writing drafts. There were concerns that "shy" individuals may not wish to contribute to the wiki given those terms—of being live right away. The soft launches brought in some early contributors to work on their wiki entries without the perceptual pressure of the world's eyes on their work. Then, as the writing became stronger and the contents more diverse, hard launches occurred to gain a wider readership and quality of editing.

2. What features of technology are needed in a collaborative software that is the center of a virtual community? Why? Why is it important for this technology to be flexible, adaptable, and integrative?

Wikis do need to be stable and robust to handle the traffic of site visitors. They also need to be able to integrate various functionalities and other technologies to work in a digital space. The expectation for collaborative software is that it be compatible with multimedia and be more dynamic than simple text.

3. What are some challenges for the wikikeeper and the larger ELATEwiki community in maintaining relevance in terms of information? How may the interdisciplinary aspects of the wiki be encouraged?

The wikikeeper needs to maintain an awareness of the cutting-edge e-learning issues and technologies, as well as the deeper issues within particular domain fields. He or she also has to maintain standards. This means constant vigilance with regard to reviewing new entries and ensuring overlap is kept to a minimum.

4. How may the wikikeeper and the ELATEwiki community attract "new blood" and maintain a fresh community of supportive participants?

He or she has to maintain wide contacts and maintain a welcoming stance to all. It will be important to maintain numerous channels of outreach to the academic, business, military, and other communities with insights on e-learning. The wikikeeper can use the power of the Web to publicize the wiki and enhance visibility with search engines, social tagging, and through forming partnerships with relevant third-parties.

5. Review the ELATEwiki's legal policies. What legal challenges did the team anticipate, and how did they work to head off legal challenges?

The policies show concerns about intellectual property protections (including trademark protections), privacy and confidentiality rights, the use of the contents for advisement (instead of informational purposes), online identity management, and civility. The wiki also has a minimum age requirement to ensure that the legal strictures apply and are legally enforceable. The policies show clarity about their non-endorsement of linked sites. The university also reserved the right to access private account information if necessary to address policy enforcement issues. The policies also allow modification of the service without notification.

6. Some wikis were found to have geographical awareness and mobile uses in augmented reality spaces. Other wikis focus on audio; some focus on video. What are some fresh applications of wiki technologies in terms of cutting-edge applications?

Geographical, mobile, location-aware, audio-and video-based wikis just offer richer ways for people to interact and to share knowledge beyond text. Real-time synchronous interactions may also occur more readily on real-time location-sensitive wikis. These will enrich the types of interchanges and learning by individuals and co-located virtual and real "local" communities.

7. Examine some of the multimedia (audio and video) embedded in this site. Brainstorm some additional ways that multimedia may be used to enhance communications. Also, how may multimedia enhance virtual community building?

Multimedia may humanize the contributors to a site by showing their real selves and enable nonverbal communication cues. Avatars may be used to show more idealized selves. Various types of social presence and telepresence may be conveyed using various technologies. Such technologies may be used to transport users of the site into others' circumstances with a greater sense of veracity and reality.

8. What new branches of e-learning should the current ELATEwiki integrate for greater relevance?

This will depend on how the site has evolved.

9. Online events have a way of drawing visitors to a site. What sorts of guest appearances, events, or other "draws" may be created to bring people to the site?

Renowned personages from e-learning and the Wikisphere may conduct live events. They may host various solicitations for types of contents to develop particular "branches" or pieces of the Wikisphere. There may be fresh roll-out or other information that may be debuted on the site.

10. Conversion of "lurkers" and "site visitors" to contributors can be a very tough endeavor. What strategies can you think of to "convert" site visitors into long-term contributors?

The research talks about strategies to help individuals acclimate to a site and to feel some ownership over the contents. Running a site in an ethical and professional way also may enhance the trust that others feel about sharing information and experiences.

Epilogue and Lessons Learned

1. A lot may be achieved with a small budget, human good will, and hard work. In a time of budget crunches, it is important to still push forward and enhance the workplace and professional relationships to provide more mutual support to each other. A well designed wiki may stand in for some more expensive information-sharing solutions.
2. Technologies that lie at the heart of virtual communities of practice need to be highly flexible and adaptable to meet the continuing needs of users. This has to be combined with a leadership willing to add innovative technologies and approaches.
3. It takes a lot of hard work to bring contributing users to a site and to maintain high quality information. This is a hands-on endeavor and not as simple as just setting up a space. The work is continuous and critical, for the success of the wiki endeavor.

Chapter 2
Open Source and Bridging the Digital Divide:
A Case Study

Heidi L. Schnackenberg
SUNY Plattsburgh, USA

Edwin S. Vega
SUNY Plattsburgh, USA

ABSTRACT

This case study involves the adoption of new technologies by a developing nation. The leader of the country, in consultation with an advisory non-profit agency must weigh the benefits and drawbacks of commercial products versus open source/low-cost options. He must also consider ways of remaining sensitive to cultural traditions and norms when introducing these new innovations.

INTRODUCTION

For 10 years, the African nation of Zado was in constant turmoil and suffered extreme civil unrest. Essentially destroyed, the country had to rebuild itself almost entirely. From amongst the turmoil emerged an unexpected leader, Nazir Bunta. After working tirelessly on humanitarian efforts for several years, Bunta was selected as Prime Minister when Zado finally held its first election in a decade. Over the last six years, Prime Minister Bunta has worked hard to rebuild Zado's infrastructure. Hospitals, schools, factories, farms, and many other vitally necessary institutions have been erected and repaired. Humanitarian organizations are working hard to reunite families and re-integrate refugees who fled to neighboring countries during the civil war. Children are once again attending school and the elderly and infirmed are receiving consistent medical care. Programs for job training and retraining are enabling employees to re- enter the work force and help Zado's economy to right itself and thrive. Clean water is available and electricity is rapidly being restored to most regions in the nation. Overall, the quality of life for most Zadorians has improved dramatically.

Now that his nations most basic needs have been taken care of and citizens are beginning to thrive, Prime Minister Bunta can begin to look ahead at his country's future. While Zado has gained economic and political status with the rest of Africa and much of the western world, they are sorely lacking in

DOI: 10.4018/978-1-61520-869-2.ch002

technological ability, equipment and connectivity in general. Being a progressive leader, the Prime Minister realizes the criticality of entering the age of technology, but doesn't quite know how to get there. An intelligent man, Bunta wants to consider his options and enlist the help of informed individuals. Hearing of a non-profit organization, PacemMundus (PacemM.), that has been completing successful work in other parts of Africa, the Prime Minister contacts the main office.

CASE DESRIPTION

PacemMundus is located in central Europe and is co-run by the European Union and the United States. Volunteers and staff come mostly from these two regions and have various levels of education, but a university degree and intensive training with the organization are required by all. While there are many divisions of PacemM., the technology division is one of the fastest growing areas. It's also well-funded through private donations and non-profit divisions of many microchip and computer corporations. Consequently, the tech division has a full complement of qualified staffers and an even larger number of volunteers. One of the full-time staff members who often works with some of the higher-profile clients is Theo Walters. Theo has a Masters Degree in Educational Technology from an accredited university in the United States and has spent several years working for large computer and software corporations. He also taught computer courses part time at his local community college. Approximately five years ago, Theo started a management position at PacemMundus. Since that time, he has worked on technology initiatives with the governments of several countries in Asia and Africa. He recently learned that he was advise Prime Minister Nazir Bunta of Zado and assist in bringing the country's technology infrastructure into the 21st century. The first meeting with Bunta is to be held at the Prime Minister's palace in Muta, Zado's capital city.

Prior to his departure, Theo gathers a team of his best staff to travel to Zado and conduct a needs assessment. In general, the team found that essentially no technology infrastructure exists in Zado. Although cell phones are becoming quite prevalent (exponentially more so than landlines), computer technology is sorely lacking. What did exist before the civil war is now demolished and what is left is out of date. Due to this situation, most of the citizens do not have many tech skills and those who do have them have mostly left the country. While the Prime Minister sees technology and a technology-saavy citizenship as crucial to the continuing growth of Zado, the Zadorians are not as keen. For over a decade, they have been scrambling to simply remain alive and keep their families safe. Now that stability has come to their country, they are finally getting a chance to prosper and enjoy the simple things in life again. While this is difficult and constant work, they relish in the idea of simply getting back to where they were before the war. Becoming technology literate does not figure into that equation. Although progressive, Prime Minister Bunta is not out of touch with his people and has sympathy with their resistance to his new passion. To complicate matters more, Zado is not wealthy. In fact, it is outright poor. Even though the economy is flourishing more each day, there really is no excess to invest in technology and technology training. Zado will need to depend on the generosity of non-profit organizations and charities.

Once he heard his teams report and perceptions, Theo struggled with his recommendations to Prime Minister Bunta. Given that Zado has no money to spare for the technology initiative, Theo knows that the best solution for hardware and software is to use low/no cost and open source products. There is a wealth of open source operating systems and applications which won't cost Zado anything except funding for tech support and training. In addition, $99 laptops are being created and proliferated by a research group in Vermont who received a large grant from the National Science Foundation (NSF). The laptops are robust and low-cost, distributed and used in developing countries and by those in need. The laptop, called the EIN, contains parts that are hardy, so that they can survive in rugged terrain, utilizing an external drive rather than a hard drive, mobile networking, and most intriguing, a low power system tolerating even a hand crank to charge it. While $99 for a quality machine doesn't seem like much money, Theo knows that it may be a formidable price tag for Prime Minister Bunta and Zado. However, it is one of the best options available.

Issues of training and tech support for the open source or low cost hardware and software options are more complicated and Theo isn't entirely certain what to propose. While it's true that open source products are easy to acquire and freely available, those characteristics also usually indicate that they come without guaranteed technological support or training. This is a particular drawback for a population that will likely need these services in abundance. One solution would be for PacemMundus to set up its own tech support system and training workshops for Zadorians. However, given the fact that it is a non-profit organization, it is unlikely that management will support such a proposal. Another option would be to encourage Prime Minister Bunta to purchase the "extra package" that can come with the EIN. The option for the extra package was included two years ago when the Vermont group found itself running short of funds and turned to an extremely successful software company, OptiComp, to help underwrite some of the costs. In exchange, OptiComp requested that the group offer their operating system with the EIN for only $5.00 per computer. While the extra $5.00 per machine is a small price to pay for the Vermont group to gain continuing support, it does add many complications to offering the EIN and its extra package as an option to countries like Zado.

The primary issue that arises from the inclusion of the extra package is that it adds an additional fee onto a machine that may already have too high of a price tag. If Zado purchases 10,000 machines at $99 each, it will cost them $990,000. If they purchase 10,000 of the EINs with the extra $5 package, it will cost a total of $1040, 000. That is an extra $50,000 that Zado could certainly use for other things and that OptiComp surely doesn't need as profit.

A further complication of the extra package may be that it could give the perception that while OptiComp is being charitable, it is at the same time trying to create a captive market. By offering the operating system at a hugely reduced cost (it is $500 per system in the United States and $750 in the EU) and providing free technical support and user training, OptiComp has then ingratiated itself into a society that may or may not be able to evaluate or have the resources to learn any other product in the future. That could be viewed as yet another way in which the western world is trying to impose it's values, systems, and lifestyles on other parts of the globe which may, or may not, welcome it. While proliferating technology may seem sensible from a western perspective, for developing countries it simply may not be a priority. Proponents of technological diffusion argue that it can help developing countries to solve challenges, such as crop production, pollution, and water contamination. While that may be true to a certain extent, leaders in countries like Zado argue that a resource, however powerful, is not useful if no one has the time or skill to utilize it. Training and skill development are important, but when considered in the context of an individual's daily life, it often doesn't appear feasible. How does a Zadorian woman with seven children, who washes, cooks, cleans, and cares for her family all without modern conveniences spare any time to learn the necessary skills to operate a computer? Even if she acquires the skills, how does she make the time to utilize the computer to research more hygienic processes or cures for childhood maladies? And if she acquires the skills and makes the time, how can she afford the equipment? While Theo knows all of these perspectives well, it still doesn't make his decision about what to recommend to Prime Minister Bunta any clearer.

FUTURE TRENDS

Open-source operating systems and software have a bright future. With the advent of Web 2.0, user-centered design and collaborative knowledge and product creation are standard fare. Whereas previously, users only trusted technologies that were corporately produced and sold, consumers are now realizing that they can obtain software, operating systems and even hardware that are better quality, and either cheaper or free. To a certain extent, software manufacturers facilitated this new consumer attitude by continually marketing faulty products at a fairly high cost. Once a new generation of computer users realized that they could make and share the same if not better products at no cost, the open-source movement really began intensify. Open-source is so important in current technology culture that it has been embedded into the very tenets of the newest generation of the World Wide Web.

Despite the ever-increasing prevalence and quality of open-source operating systems and software, the ability of the global population to access technology has dichotomized. In most general terms, citizens in wealthier countries own or can access computers, and therefore possess more advanced technological abilities, while citizens of developing countries do not have access to technology nor possess the corresponding skill set. Of course, this overly broad characterization differs between and within countries based on gender, ethnicity, socio-economic status, and a host of other factors. Although excellent operating systems and software now exist and are free, and a limited amount of hardware resources are also available at low or no cost, there are still individuals and populations that do not and cannot utilize technology. This gap in availability, accessibility and use of technology is considered the "Digital Divide." It has been formally recognized since the mid-1990's, but was certainly in existence prior to that time, likely since desktop computers became affordable for use in the home. Unfortunately, rather than global access to technology slowly growing over time, the disparity between the have and have-nots has steadily expanded as innovations have developed.

Given that software, hardware, and operating systems have evolved and demystified to the point where the average computer users can have some facility with them, and yet many countries, cultures, and peoples do not have access to these resources, where does that leave the intersection of the two in the future? It seems a natural match to pair excellent, free resources with communities that would like technology but cannot afford to purchase the products. At the heart of the matter, it appears that a host of other factors exist that are more powerful than simply the availability of open-source in working to bridge the gap in the Digital Divide. Cultural considerations, political strategies, and powerful economic forces are all at play when technology is introduced to developing countries. It is not a simple case of fulfilling a need (or perceived need), but rather a complex labyrinth of considerations that must be navigated slowly, and with care. In the long term however, persisting in closing the gap in the Digital Divide is a necessary and critical endeavor which both the open-source community and commercial interests must constantly continue to pursue.

REFERENCES

Al-Fahad, M. (2008). *Bridging the Global Digital Divide*. Saarbrucken, Germany: VDM Verlag.

Bell, R., Jung, J., & Zacharilla, L. (2009). *Broadband Economies: Creating the Community of the 21st Century*. New York: Intelligent Community Forum.

Chinn, M. D., & Fairlie, R. W. (2006). The Determinants of the Global Digital Divide: A Cross-Country Analysis of Computer and Internet Penetration. *Oxford Economic Papers*, *59*(1), 16–44. doi:10.1093/oep/gpl024

Close the Gap International. (2009). *Close the Gap: Bridging the Digital Divide*. Retrieved February 3, 2009, from http://www.close-the-gap.org/pages/frontend/Home.aspx?menuitem=17

Colford, S. (2009, December/January). Explaining Free and Open Source Software. *Bulletin of the American Society for Information Science and Technology*, *35*(2), 10–15. doi:10.1002/bult.2008.1720350205

Creative Commons. (2009). Creative Commons. Retrieved February 3, 2009, from http://creativecommons.org

Digital Divide Network. (2009). *Digital Divide Network*. Retrieved.

Dovey, J. (2009). *New Media: A Critical Introduction* (2nd ed.). New YorkRoutledge.

February 3, 2009, from http://www.digitaldivide.net

Hargittai, E. (April 2002). Second Level Digital Divide: Differences in People's Online Skills. *First Monday*, *7*(4-1). Retrieved February 3, 2009, from http://firstmonday.org/issues/issue7_4/hargittai/index.html

James, J. (2003). *Bridging the Global Digital Divide*. Northampton, MA: Edward Elgar Publishing.

Kagami, M., Masatsugu, T., & Giovannetti, E. (Eds.). (2004). *Information Technology Policy and the Digital Divide: Lessons for Developing Countries*. Northampton, MA: Edward Elgar Publishing.

Lakhani, K. R., & von Hippel, E. (2003, June). How Open Source Software Works: "Free" User to User Assistance. *Research Policy*, *32*(6), 923–943. doi:10.1016/S0048-7333(02)00095-1

Lee, S. T., Kim, H., & Gupta, S. (2009). Measuring Open Source Software Success. *Omega*, *32*(2), 426. doi:10.1016/j.omega.2007.05.005

Lerner, J., & Tirole, J. (2003). Some Simple Economics of Open Source. *The Journal of Industrial Economics*, *51*(2), 197–234.

Odamtten, T., & Millard, J. (2009, January). Learning from Others Within the Landscape of "Transitional Economies" and the Challenge in ICT Development for African Countries. *Society*, *23*(1), 51–61.

Open Content Alliance. (2009). *Open Content Alliance: Building a Digital Archive of Global Content for Universal Access*. Retrieved February 3, 2009, from http://www.opencontentalliance.org

Patterson, S. J., & Radtke, J. M. (2009). *Strategic Communications for Nonprofit Organization: Seven Steps to Creating a Successful Plan* (2nd ed.). Hoboken, NJ: John Wiley & Sons, Inc.

Raymond, E. S. (1999). *The Cathedral & the Bazaar: Musings on Linux and Open Source by an Accidental Revolutionary*. Sabastopol, CA: O'Reilly & Associates, Inc.

Tapscott, D., & Williams, A. D. (2006). *Wikinomics: How Mass Collaboration Changes Everything*. New York: Penguin Group.

Tiemann, M. (2009). *History of the OSI*. Retrieved February 3, 2009, from http://www.opensource.org/history

Von Hippel, E., & von Krogh, G. (2003, March-April). Open Source Software and the "Private-Collective" Innovation Model: Issues for Organization Science. *Organization Science*, *14*(2), 209–223. doi:10.1287/orsc.14.2.209.14992

Warshauer, M. (2003). Demystifying the Digital Divide. *Scientific American*, *289*(2), 6, &42.

Warshauer, M. (2004). *Technology and Social Inclusion: Rethinking the Digital Divide*. Cambridge, MA: The MIT Press.

Weber, S. (2005). *The Success of Open Source*. Cambridge, MA: Harvard University Press.

Whitehurst, J. (2009, January/February). Open Source: Narrowing the Divides Between Education, Business, and Community. *Educause*, *44*(1), 70.

FURTHER READING

Al-Fahad, M. (2008). *Bridging the Global Digital Divide*. Saarbrucken, Germany: VDM Verlag.

Bell, R., Jung, J., & Zacharilla, L. (2009). *Broadband Economies: Creating the Community of the 21st Century*. New York: Intelligent Community Forum.

Chinn, M. D., & Fairlie, R. W. (2006). The Determinants of the Global Digital Divide: A Cross-Country Analysis of Computer and Internet Penetration. *Oxford Economic Papers*, *59*(1), 16–44. doi:10.1093/oep/gpl024

Close the Gap International. (2009). *Close the Gap: Bridging the Digital Divide.* Retrieved February 3, 2009, from http://www.close-the-gap.org/pages/frontend/Home.aspx?menuitem=17

Colford, S. (2009, December/January). Explaining Free and Open Source Software. *Bulletin of the American Society for Information Science and Technology*, *35*(2), 10–15. doi:10.1002/bult.2008.1720350205

Creative Commons. (2009). *Creative Commons*. Retrieved February 3, 2009, from http://creativecommons.org

Digital Divide Network. (2009). *Digital Divide Network*. Retrieved February 3, 2009, from http://www.digitaldivide.net

Dovey, J. (2009). *New Media: A Critical Introduction* (2nd ed.). New York: Routledge.

Hargittai, E. (April 2002). Second Level Digital Divide: Differences in People's Online Skills. *First Monday, 7*(4-1). Retrieved February 3, 2009, from http://firstmonday.org/issues/issue7_4/hargittai/index.html

James, J. (2003). *Bridging the Global Digital Divide*. Northampton, MA: Edward Elgar Publishing.

Kagami, M., Masatsugu, T., & Giovannetti, E. (Eds.). (2004). *Information Technology Policy and the Digital Divide: Lessons for Developing Countries*. Northampton, MA: Edward Elgar Publishing.

Lakhani, K. R., & von Hippel, E. (2003, June). How Open Source Software Works: "Free" User to User Assistance. *Research Policy*, *32*(6), 923–943. doi:10.1016/S0048-7333(02)00095-1

Lee, S. T., Kim, H., & Gupta, S. (2009). Measuring Open Source Software Success. *Omega*, *32*(2), 426. doi:10.1016/j.omega.2007.05.005

Lerner, J., & Tirole, J. (2003). Some Simple Economics of Open Source. *The Journal of Industrial Economics*, *51*(2), 197–234.

Odamtten, T., & Millard, J. (2009, January). Learning from Others Within the Landscape of "Transitional Economies" and the Challenge in ICT Development for African Countries. *Society*, *23*(1), 51–61.

Open Content Alliance. (2009). *Open Content Alliance: Building a Digital Archive of Global Content for Universal Access*. Retrieved February 3, 2009, from http://www.opencontentalliance.org

Patterson, S. J., & Radtke, J. M. (2009). *Strategic Communications for Nonprofit Organization: Seven Steps to Creating a Successful Plan* (2nd ed.). Hoboken, NJ: John Wiley & Sons, Inc.

Raymond, E. S. (1999). *The Cathedral & the Bazaar: Musings on Linux and Open Source by an Accidental Revolutionary*. Sabastopol, CA: O'Reilly & Associates, Inc.

Tapscott, D., & Williams, A. D. (2006). *Wikinomics: How Mass Collaboration Changes Everything*. New York: Penguin Group.

Tiemann, M. (2009). *History of the OSI*. Retrieved February 3, 2009, from http://www.opensource.org/history

Von Hippel, E., & von Krogh, G. (2003, March-April). Open Source Software and the "Private-Collective" Innovation Model: Issues for Organization Science. *Organization Science*, *14*(2), 209–223. doi:10.1287/orsc.14.2.209.14992

Warshauer, M. (2003). Demystifying the Digital Divide. *Scientific American, 289*(2), 6, &42.

Warshauer, M. (2004). *Technology and Social Inclusion: Rethinking the Digital Divide*. Cambridge, MA: The MIT Press.

Weber, S. (2005). *The Success of Open Source*. Cambridge, MA: Harvard University Press.

Whitehurst, J. (2009, January/February). Open Source: Narrowing the Divides Between Education, Business, and Community. *Educause*, *44*(1), 70.

APPENDIX: SUPPORTING MATERIALS

Abstract

This case study involves the adoption of new technologies by a developing nation. The leader of the country, in consultation with an advisory non-profit agency must weigh the benefits and drawbacks of commercial products versus open source/low-cost options. He must also consider ways of remaining sensitive to cultural traditions and norms when introducing these new innovations.

Questions

1. If you were Theo, what would you recommend to Prime Minister Bunta?

Answers here may vary. However, perhaps the best solution for Prime Minister Bunta and Zado is to purchase a quantity of the EIN, without the optional operating system from OptiComp, and load the machines with open source software. The Prime Minster could then build a number of tech centers around the country and equip them with the EIN and some infrastructure for Internet connectivity. This would be a good way to allow citizens to become acquainted with computer technologies at no cost and in their own way. It would be a non-threatening way to introduce the innovations in which the Prime Minister so strongly believes.

2. Are there technology alternatives for Zado other than the ones described above?

Other alternatives that the Prime Minister could consider would be to acquire refurbished or second-hand machines from charities. Charities may even be able to provide some new machines. There may also be individuals in these organizations who could act as tech support in various parts of the country. Another option would be for the Prime Minister to negotiate a deal with a prosperous computer company and promise purchase of a certain amount of machines in a stipulated timeframe if the company could provide them at a reasonable price. This of course, would create a market base for a western company, but it is an option.

3. If Theo decides to recommend open source and low cost hardware, how can tech support be arranged? (Assume that PacemMundus will not fund and organize on-going technical support.)

One way, and perhaps the best way, to arrange tech support for Zado would be for PacemMundus to train a corps of key Zadorians who could become the first wave of tech support. This first wave could then train others. This would allow all the stakeholders to essentially get what they want. PacemMundus could run a short term program and help Zado, but yet not be responsible for on-going support. Zadorians themselves could provide the skills and training necessary to do something which the Prime Minister originally envisioned outsourcing. Perhaps most importantly, since Zadorians would be supplying tech support to their countryfolk, then the risk of western values and customs creeping in via a technology initiative would be severely minimized.

4. If you were Prime Minister Bunta, how would you negotiate a middle ground between your citizens lack of enthusiasm for technology and your vision for moving Zado into the 21st century?

Perhaps the best way for the Prime Minister to negotiate a compromise between proliferation of his vision and any resistant factions is to show his citizens what technology can do for them and how it can possibly improve the quality of their lives. As illustrated in answer 3, if the Prime Minister set up well-staffed tech centers and allowed people to come to them on their own, free of charge, it could go a long way in convincing those who are resistant to change and computer technologies.

5. What are the advantages to purchasing OptiComp's operating system with the EIN? What are the drawbacks?

One advantage of purchasing and using OptiComp's operating system is the consistent availability of tech support to the citizens of Zado (as well as any other system users). Another advantage of learning and using this operating system is that it is one of the most well-known in the world and if Zadorians became familiar with it, those skills could potentially enable them to compete better on a global scale for various types of employment. The drawbacks to using this operating system are the initial unnecessary added cost, the potential that Zado will be become a captive market for OptiComp, and the fact that a significant cost might be incurred for each upgrade that the company produces.

6. Once Prime Minister Bunta and Theo Walters finish working together, what can the Prime Minister do to be more self-reliant when it comes to technological decisions?

Once Theo and Prime Minster Bunta part company, a wise move for the Prime Minister would be to send a group of his best and brightest citizens to universities around the world so that they can become knowledgeable about technology and technological advances. These individuals could have their education fully funded, with the condition that once they finish school they would need to return to Zado and help advise the current administration on technological issues. Another thing that the Prime Minister could do directly is to introduce himself to some of the leading technology developers and hardware/software company leaders. In that way, he could call on these colleagues for advice and information when the need arose.

Epilogue

Over the long term, Theo's recommendations and Prime Minister Bunta's approaches to his technology initiative could have varied and far-reaching outcomes. They essentially frame how Zado will evolve with respect to technology, technological skills, and advances in technology. If the Prime Minister acquires technology and eases his citizens into its uses and benefits, all while being sensitive to their cultural and daily needs, it's likely that Zadorians could not only adopt, but even embrace technology. Educating his society in technology skills and having a select force who can advise and drive technology issues will also help the Prime Minister to make sound choices for Zado in the future.

Some of the lessons that can be learned from this case are:

1. The benefits and drawbacks of commercial technology products versus open-source/low cost options.
2. The importance of always providing some sort of training and support when implementing a technology initiative.
3. The criticality of remaining sensitive to cultural traditions and norms when introducing new innovations.

Chapter 3
A Conversation Approach to Electronic Collections Development Within University Libraries

Rocci Luppicini
University of Ottawa, Canada

Laura Bratanek
University of Ottawa, Canada

ABSTRACT

Electronic collections development within university libraries is transforming university research and academic life. This case explores the topic of electronic collections development within university libraries from a student perspective. By mobilizing Conversation Theory (CT) and a conversational modeling framework, a case on electronic collections development is presented that utilizes research literature and focus group discussion data derived from undergraduate students within a large urban university. Findings reveal student perspectives and factors affecting students' stances towards current and future electronic collections development trends. In addition, the findings indicate a variety of conversation modeling strategies are used by students in fostering perspective sharing and mutual understanding about electronic collections development. This case sheds light on electronic collections development from a student perspective and offers recommendations on how to use conversation modeling to leverage mutual understanding and consensual decision-making in contexts where communication gaps surrounding technology and its use in society exist.

DOI: 10.4018/978-1-61520-869-2.ch003

BACKGROUND: ELECTRONIC COLLECTIONS DEVELOPMENT WITHIN UNIVERSITY LIBARIES

Evaluating the success of large scale developments within organizations like universities is both necessary and difficult. It is necessary because of the limited time and limited amount of public resources available to invest in organizational change. It is difficult because of the complexity of the development itself (i.e., technical considerations, costs) and by the complexity of the social context (i.e., presence of different stakeholder groups, competing interests, knowledge, and communication gaps).

One particularly important large scale development within higher education revolves around library collections development trends. University libraries are core parts of most, if not all, universities and central to upholding university mandates to pursue excellence in academic research and university education. But what happens when shifts in publishing technology begin to transform university libraries and how they serve their users? Electronic collections are publications (e.g., monographs, edited books, journals) offered in electronic format (such as e-books and e-journals). More specifically, an e-book or e-journal within an electronic collection is a "text, in digital form, or a book converted into digital form, or digital reading material, or a book in a computer file format, or an electronic file of words and images displayed on a desktop, note-book computer, or portable device, or formatted for display on dedicated e-book readers" (Rao, 2003, p.86-7).

In 1971, Michael Hart pioneered the first major electronic book library (Project Gutenberg) as a small digital repository project. Now, less than forty years later, libraries around the world have large electronic collections as part of their regular library holdings. This represents a major technological and organizational shift within the publishing industry, as well as a shift in education and society. As stated by Rao (2003), "The e-book is the most important development in the world of literature since the Gutenberg press and is destined to change the reading habits of many over the next several years" (p.85). This technology-driven change is having a particularly strong influence on university library services, challenging the traditional roles of university libraries (and librarians) in keys areas including cataloguing, circulation, digital preservation, and user services. This is partly due to the complex relationship between stakeholder groups and new technologies (Nelson, 2008; Poftak, 2001). Connaway (2001) notes, "Perhaps the greatest challenge of the digital library is its dependency on strong alliances between publishers, authors, librarians and e-book providers. Together they will need to provide electronic content through new technologies and delivery systems to meet the increasing demands of technology-savvy users" (p.349). In examining the implications of e-books in academic libraries and how libraries must adapt to new technologies, Jantz (2001) indicates, "In this advancing digital library era, we are tantalizing our users by offering rapid access to digital sources and simultaneously frustrating them by not providing effective end-to-end processes that enable ease of use" (p.104).

Perhaps the biggest problem in reorienting university libraries for the technological society of the 21st century lies in providing information concerning user needs and making a business case for such an expenditure. This will be beneficial to the largest user group—the students. As stated by Hernon, Hopper, Leach, Saunders, and Zhang (2007), "Given the financial commitment that many libraries make to acquiring e-books and the need for evidence of use to justify the expenditures, it is important to study student preferences and changing information-gathering behaviours" (p.3). Furthermore, if students are unaware of the fact that these resources are offered, or do not know how to use them, perhaps it would be useful for the library to invest in campaigns to further educate students about information gathering techniques

(Rowlands & Nicholas, 2008). Based on this information, there is warrant for studies from a student perspective. By examining the perception of students, it may be possible to better understand user interests and key challenges associated with electronic collections development efforts.

In terms of chapter organization, the next section describes electronic collections development situated within a theoretical framework of conversation theory (CT). Next, the chapter reports on an electronic collections case within a university context based on a conversation approach adapted to this case. Finally, the chapter concludes with a discussion of key challenges and opportunities of researching complex development initiatives within university contexts where multiple stakeholder groups and interests must be reconciled.

SETTING THE STAGE: CONVERSATION AT THE ROOT OF ORGANIZATIONAL LIFE AND LEARNING

This chapter focuses on the topic of electronic collections development within university libraries from a student perspective. It addresses the question of whether students believe their university should focus collections development on print, electronic, or both types of publications. The scope of this case is mainly concerned with e-book and e-journal development trends within university libraries (rather than all electronic resource development trends within universities). This allows for a more in-depth focus on one area of electronic resource development that is receiving a particularly high level of attention within universities and creating broader public debate. In terms of theoretical grounding for this case, a grounded conversation framework is used to assess student perspective sharing on electronic collections development within a university library. This framework is chosen because it is well suited to the study of conversational processes and perspective sharing situated within specific social contexts.

This chapter is oriented towards the study of electronic collections development from a student perspective and draws on Conversation Theory (CT) established by Gordon Pask in the 1960s and 1970s. CT is a constructivist-based theory of teaching and learning that specifies the necessary conditions needed for human and artificial systems to learn. The theory explains how mutual understanding and knowledge emerges through modeling human and machine learning conversations (Pask, 1975). As stated by Boyd (2004), "Conversation Theory portrays and explains the emergence of knowledge by means of multilevel agreement-oriented conversations among participants, supported by modeling facilities and suitable communication and action interfaces" (p.179). CT describes learning conversations as exchanges between conversational agents (humans and/or machine) where learning emerges through the creation of symbolic representations acquired through conversational interaction and attention directing strategies (Scott, 2001).

In terms of application, CT provides the theoretical framework and can be used as a research tool to study complex conversational processes within face-to-face and online contexts. CT offers a means to study how individuals generate multiple perspectives and shared meaning underlying knowledge creation and decision-making processes (Harri-Augstein & Thomas, 1991). CT has been applied in a variety of organizational contexts to explain second-language learning, self-organized learning, software design, and organizational learning for person–job matching (see Boyd, 2004 for a review).

How does CT work when applied to a university learning context? In the current case exploring student perspectives on e-book development within their university library, a learning conversation typically involves two steps: (1) a student (receiver) shares a concept with another student (sender) when the receiver is able to make sense

Figure 1. Learning conversation about e-collections development

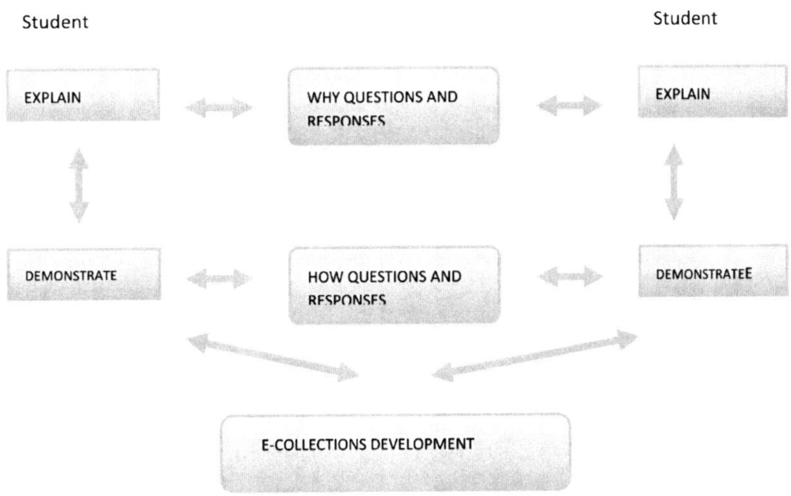

of the sender's explanation (demonstrate) and (2) the receiver and the sender understand one another when the receiver is able to make sense of the sender's explanations of the receiver's explanations (explain). In the most basic learning conversation model there is a minimum of two levels of interaction to leverage mutual understanding/knowledge of the how and why of a topic (learning conversation). To illustrate:

In the above conversation model only two students are represented for simplicity, however, conversations can involve many more students. In the actual case presented in this chapter, focus groups consisting of 4 students per group share group member perspectives about e-book development within focus group conversations. Students are directed to actively engage in focus group discussion in an effort to reach mutual understanding and agreement about the core discussion question. To this end, the case presented uses CT as a framework for analyzing multiple perspectives and shared meaning grounded within focus group discussions designed to allow students to exchange views on e-book development within their university libraries.

CASE DESCRIPTION

Case Context

The main library is situated in the heart of a large urban North American university (henceforth the University). The library has a growing collection of e-journals and over 320 000 e-books. Electronic resources can be accessed by students and faculty both on and off campus. The electronic journals and e-books are accessed through e-journal and e-book databases which provide varying levels of options for searching content, downloading content, and exporting references to citation databases (i,e., RefWorks). The library is intended to serve the academic and research needs of over 30 000 faculty, students, and staff across multiple faculties, schools, university institutes, and research centres. As the largest group of library users are the undergraduate students, data collection and analysis is focused on uncovering undergraduate student perspectives.

Electronic Collections Development Concerns

University libraries are faced with difficult challenges in deciding how to invest limited funding for collections development. On the one hand, e-books, e-journals, and other electronic resources are providing new opportunities for library collections development with the potential of lowering purchasing costs, increasing library resource access, and preserving valuable library storage space. On the other hand, it is unclear as to whether or not the largest group of university library users (the students) is in favour of focusing limited university library funding on electronic resource developments. This raises several questions: Do students prefer print or electronic resources at their university library? What are the perceived advantages and disadvantages of electronic library resources according to students? What are the perceived advantages and disadvantages of traditional print based library resources according to students? What is the student position(s) on electronic resource development trends within university libraries?

Given that students are a major stakeholder group in universities, as they pay tuition used in library resource development, it is important to understand the student perspective on current and future library developments that impact all students. Unfortunately, there is a paucity of research focusing on student beliefs and attitudes concerning electronic resource development within their own university. Without contextually specific information on student views of library resource development, it is difficult to make informed decisions that meet the needs and interests of the university library's largest user base.

Data Collection and Analysis Tools for Exploring Electronic Collections Development

Regarding data collection, two main data sources were employed. First, focus group conversation data was examined from MSN transcripts derived from 24 focus group conversations of 4 members per group. Using a focus group conversation question assigned by the researcher, student participants carried out online focus groups discussions using MSN instant messaging software. The main focus group question was as follows: Current trends in electronic publishing (i.e., e-books, e-journals) create new challenges and opportunities for university libraries with limited budgets. Should your university focus collections development on print, electronic, or both types of publications?" Results were compiled and stripped of any information that would identify individual students. Second, using the ERIC database, a keyword search (e-books AND e-journal AND electronic resource) was carried out to find peer reviewed articles published in the last ten years. A document analysis was used in advanced data analysis to help situate focus group findings within the larger research context.

Data analysis entailed a line-by-line coding of each focus group conversation transcript separately to identify themes within the data. The findings were then compared across the 24 focus group conversation transcripts to highlight common themes, uncover student perspectives, and identify key challenges and possible solutions. More specifically, the complete analysis presented below demonstrates: a) how students perceive current and future e-book developments within their university library; and b) how conversational strategies participate in multiple perspective sharing and collaborative learning processes within university teaching and learning contexts.

FINDINGS: KEY THEMES, ISSUES, AND CHALLENGES

E-Book Use at University

What are the main themes highlighted within student perspectives on university library collections development? When asked whether the

University should focus collections development on print, electronic, or both types of publications, the majority of focus group members indicated a preference for focusing on both print and electronic resources. A number of reasons were offered by students, including personal preference, educational need, information amount, conservation of library space, reliability issues, information retention, access flexibility, and risk reduction. These themes are illustrated in the following selection of student conversation excerpts:

- "But universities need to find a balance between these two publications because people will most likely prefer to use one over the other and one type should not be favoured in terms of funding over the other" (personal preference).
- "I am a firm believer in print media as well as print publications when it comes to education" (educational need).
- "Living in our so called "information age" I feel we should use both electronic and hard copy forms of publication. Why reduce the amount of scholarly information we can place in project while only using hard copy information" (information amount).
- "I wouldn't want to see the library reduced in size any I think balance is a more important aspect than to have millions and millions of resources all in one medium" (conservation of library space).
- "This is because it would be unreliable to just have electronic publications, because if the network was to fail or have some technological problem, there would be no back up resource to look for" (reliability issues).
- "I agree that it is personal preference, however there are many current print references that may still be informative and important in years to come and I don't think that they should be eliminated" (information retention).
- "I think that having the information available in both mediums would be most effective. This would allow access to the entirety of the university library from home as well as having the ability to spread books across a table in order to compare and contrast different articles with ease" (access flexibility).
- "Technology is amazing up until it doesn't work. If you put all your eggs in one basket you can end up with nothing. I think there has to be a balance between both print and electronic resources" (risk reduction).

A second major area of focus group conversation revolved around the discussion of advantages and disadvantages of electronic and print library collection items. The breakdown of advantages and disadvantages of electronic and print library collections appears in Figure 2.

The above graph illustrates students' perceptions concerning the advantages and disadvantages of electronic and print library collections. Students perceived the advantages of electronic library collections to far outweigh their disadvantages. One student stated, "I think that focusing on electronic publications would be most beneficial for our changing times. It is far more accessible to students at home who may not be able to travel to libraries often, and it is easy to locate a particular item" (excerpt). A second student indicated the environmental benefits of electronic collections should be considered, "Think of all the books published a year, all of the paper that is needed, and all of the trees that are cut down. By using e-books and e journals we are doing our part to contribute positively to the environment. This is an excellent way to start living green" (excerpt). A third student pointed out the benefit of electronic text duplicability, "You don't have to worry about someone else returning a copy of a journal on time, it won't get lost, you can copy an electronic file and have it indefinitely" (excerpt). Despite the many advantages of electronic collections,

Figure 2. Breakdown of advantages and disadvantages of electronic and print library collections

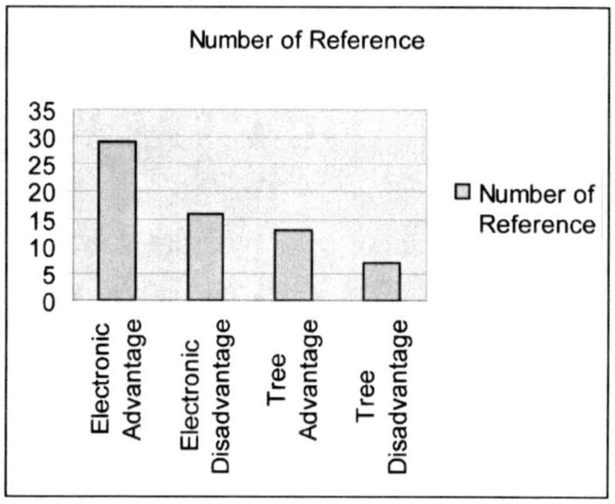

a number of disadvantages were highlighted as well. One student discussed the fear of technology failure, "There will always be a technological breakdown in a system and you may not be able to access your e-books" (excerpt). Another student mentioned the risk of violating intellectual property policies, "If the universities didn't do the exchange through a university mediator we risk purchasing fraudulent or falsified texts from falsified publishers" (excerpt). A third student noted the increased risk of plagiarism associated with the copy/paste opportunities with electronic text, "It also make plagiarism all too easy and tempting for those ignorant enough to believe that they won't get caught by professors who also have computers" (excerpt).

Although less advantages and disadvantages were attributed to print collections, a moderate level of discussion revolved around advantages and disadvantages of print. One major advantage identified is connected to the tangibility of a printed text. As stated by one student, "Print publications are also useful because some people simply prefer reading from a text where they can flip the pages and have it right there in their hands, as opposed to viewing something from a computer screen" (excerpt). Another student mentioned, "with a book I can read anywhere. Do a lot of studying in bed!" (excerpt). A second major theme concerned library research experience. One student mentioned, "I personally would much rather read a book for info than read if off a computer screen, and I think navigating a library (whether in bookshelves, newspapers etc) is much more rewarding than typing words into a search database' (excerpt). At the same time, students noted a number of disadvantages with a printed library collection. One student stated, "There is nothing more frustrating than needing a book that someone else has already taken out and it will not be back in time for you to use it for your project" (excerpt). Another student noted that "printed sources can be out dated and not updated on a regular basis with that information" (excerpt).

What do students believe about the future of university library collections development? This topic was moderately discussed within focus group conversations, the majority of which tended to predict the eventual demise of printed library collections in favour of electronic. One student stated that, "online resources are certainly the wave of the future and need to be focused on for any university to remain relevant in society" (excerpt). A second student stated, "Knowledge is always evolving, so university should evolve with it. Everything is becoming electronic, so students should be equipped with the skills to utilize it after they graduate" (excerpt). Another student linked a similar prediction to generational differences, "I think that as years go on and the younger generations get used to working on a computer, they will not be interested in opening a book and doing research, they will do all of their work online or through e-journals, it is happening already" (excerpt). Other students commenting on the near future (as opposed to the distant future) indicated a small niche for print-based collections in some circumstances, "So basically while it is important to keep certain hard copies, favoring digital files (while not abandoning print) in the near future seems to be the best, realistic option" (excerpt). A second student conveyed skepticism concerning the pace at which a complete shift to electronic library collections is possible, "I somehow feel we are a long way away from transference of hard copy to Internet as it is probably a quite lengthy process, and much more decision making must be made until this happens in reality" (excerpt).

What intervening valuables are perceived to influence collections development trends? During the focus group conversations, a number of students articulated fairly nuanced perspectives of library collections development linked to underlying factors such as budgetary considerations and security issues. In discussing budgetary considerations, one student noted "If the University is bigger and has the resources it should have both prints and e-books" (excerpt). A second student added to this, "Financially if it is necessary to choose one I think they should choose electronic" (excerpt). However, the allocation of limited funding to library collections development was seen as a high priority. As noted by another student, "I am sure that as it [electronic library collections] becomes more and more common, the budgets will have to be altered and make allowances for the necessary changes to be made" (excerpt).

Conversational Strategies Used in Online Discussion

Data analysis carried out on the focus group data revealed four types of conversational strategies used by students: (1) clarification, (2) expansion, (3) justification, and (4) counter argument. These strategies were discerned from focus group discussions and defined below. Table 1 provides a breakdown of each strategy, along with descriptions and their evaluative dimension used to guide conversational analysis.

Table 1. Breakdown of each strategy

Conversation Type	Description	Evaluative Dimension
Conversation for Clarification	Participants attempt to make the meaning of something clearer by reworking presented questions or explanations. The aim is to ensure adequate clarity and detail for something to be mutually understood.	Do participants provide enough clarity and detail for something to be mutually understood?
Conversation for Expansion	Participants attempt to expand the scope of understanding of something by asking additional questions and exploring new possibilities. The aim is to build on incomplete information by seeking information and exchanging conjectured explanations.	Do participants build on incomplete information by seeking new information and exchanging conjectured explanations?
Conversation for Justification	Participants attempt to validate or rationalize something to others by offering (logical) arguments. The aim is to use (logical) arguments to reach a mutually acceptable position about something.	Do participants posit logical arguments in an effort to reach a mutually acceptable position about something?
Conversation for Counter Argument	Participants attempt to challenge a perspective posited using logical counter arguments. The aim is to refute something or provide an alternative explanation.	Do participants posit objections to a participant perspective using logical counterarguments to prove that some posited position or explanation is inadequate?

The above-mentioned conversation types manifested themselves within MSN focus group conversations in a variety of ways.

First, conversations for clarification were observed as students attempted to inform each other of details that were not clear within initial explanations:

Excerpt 1: Conversation for clarification

Student 1: Should your university focus collections development on print, electronic or both types of publications?

Student 3: I'm unsure what collections development is, can someone explain?

Student 2: Like in the future should they work to improve their collection of hard copies or focus more on acquiring more electronic sources

Student 1: Yes. That's the question.

Student 3: I understand. Thanks.

In this excerpt, a basic learning conversation for clarification is illustrated as student 1 provides a question which is not understood completely by student 2. The question is understood by student 2 who provide an example with added details on print collection items ('hard copies') or electronic collection items ('electronic sources'). This demonstrates a mutual understanding of the student 1 question by student 2, which is shared with student 3. The ongoing conversation involving student 3 confirmed this. This clarification process was moderately present in focus group conversation data.

Second, a conversation for expansion is observed as students attempted to supplement incomplete information by asking additional questions to help orient and sustain conversation by exploring avenues of inquiry not previously considered.

Excerpt 2: Conversation for Expansion

Student 5: And we also need to consider the economic consequences of dramatically reducing the use of print industries.

Student 6: While not forgetting about the advantages to the environmental economy of doing just that.

In this excerpt, student 5 applies mutual understanding gained from previous focus group conversation to speculate on a potential new area to explore (economic consequences) that has not been considered. Student 6 (receiver) demonstrates understanding of the content expressed by student 5 (sender) by applying the same conversational modeling strategies to introduce another new potential area to explore (environmental consequences) that has not been considered. This "opening up" of the learning conversation to new possibilities was moderately present in focus group conversation data.

Third, a conversation for justification is observed as students attempt to rationalize something to other members of the focus group conversation by offering arguments for choosing, print, electronic, or both collections development varieties.

Excerpt 3: Conversation for justification

Student 8: Should your university focus collections development on print, electronic or both types of publications?

Student 7: I believe both types of publications are useful to students as well as professors. It is not always possible to have internet access, so it could be easier to simply take out a book and read it whenever you can. Also, electronically publish-

ing can possess problems that books, DVDs and such will not have. For instance, there could be a corruption in the file or there could be a problem with the computer systems or internet, which make it hard for a person to have access immediately.

In this excerpt, a basic learning conversation for justification is illustrated as student 7 provides a demonstration of understanding the questions by answering it ('I believe both types of publications are useful'). Student 7 effectively justifies his or her understanding of the question asked through references made how electronic texts are accessed (internet access) and how print texts are accessed (take out a book from library). This "how to" understanding is augmented through justifications of "why" there are problems with relying only on electronic publications (because of corrupted file limitations, because of access problems). Under a conversation framework, the receiver (student 7) is able to demonstrate a mutual understanding of the sender's question (student 8) by providing justifications which explain how and why a position was taken. The justification processes within learning conversation was moderately present in focus group conversation data.

Fourth, a conversation for counter-argumentation is observed as students attempt to challenge a perspective posited using logical counter arguments.

Conversation for counter-argumentation

Student 12: Perhaps most importantly, electronic resources cost less to acquire, and even less to maintain

Student 11: Until your computer crashes that is

Student 12: Unless every computer crashes at the same time, I don't think that is a major concern. You should always make backups

Student 13: Yeah you just never know with electronic sources...they seem to be so convenient but then comes the day when you need a book or article desperately and your computer won't turn on.

Student 14: And not everyone has access to more than one computer, and when your pressed for time you don't really want to be searching for another computer

In this excerpt, student 12 posits an explanation ('electronic resources cost less to acquire') which other focus group members challenge. Mutual understanding of the explanation is demonstrated through a counter-argument ('until your computer crashes') made by student 11 (receiver). Student 12 (sender) then offers a counter-argument to this new point ('unless every computer crashes') in an attempt to address the first-counter argument with an alternative explanation (computer crashes are not a major concern because they are widely available). This, in turn, is mutually understood by student 13 and student 14 as demonstrated through additional counter-arguments against the original position of student 11 ('electronic resources cost less to acquire'). The counter-argument processes within learning conversation was less present in focus group conversation data compared to other conversation types uncovered.

SOLUTIONS AND RECOMMENDATIONS

What is particularly interesting about these findings lies in the connection between student perspectives of current and future library collections development. While most students emphasized the importance of electronic and print based library collection options, they tended to align themselves with the 'new generation' of 'technologically advanced citizen of the rapidly expanding 'information society'. The outlook of the future and perceptions of current intervening variables suggest that the future is future is electronic and there may be little students can do to resist or avoid this. It is noteworthy that a few students argue for student input in the decision-making process concerning library collections development planning. One student stated, "If the school is having problems funding both types of publishing's, than it should ask the students, through a vote, whether they would agree to an increase in fees, in order for them to have both electronic and print publications. That way there are not any complaints about not having enough resources for projects, and everyone knows and agrees to where their money is going" (excerpt). A second student added that their contribution to the university warranted their input in such large scale decisions affecting them, "It is the students that pay there way through University, 15 grand a year. If students want to read from e-journals or from print, they should have this option" (excerpt). This reinforces the possible utility of conversation theory (or a similar approach) as highly relevant in providing a theoretical framework for integrating student perspectives into university decision-making processes. Moreover, conversation analysis findings revealed that most, if not all, students were able to engage in learning conversations on a focused topic using a variety of conversation strategies (types) to help leverage mutual understanding and perspective sharing.

Despite the fact that conversation modeling strategies were found to be a useful tool for navigating complex and controversial areas of shared human interest (university library collections development debate), there are limitations to note. The primary limitation of this approach is that it is time consuming and requires invested interest of all stakeholders to continue learning conversations to completion (the point at which mutual understanding and consensual agreements are reached).

Assuming that adequate time and interest are available, one recommendation in this chapter is to apply conversation modeling strategies to all stakeholder groups (administration, faculty, library staff, and students), independently and combined, until mutual understanding is achieved and a set of acceptable solutions are identified, which all stakeholders can agree to. Given that this is time consuming, it has limited application in complex areas of shared human interest where competing values and multiple perspectives need to be understood to inform democratic decision-making which takes all perspectives and views into consideration. This type of approach is particularly important in this case, where controversies are deeply rooted in ethical tensions arising from competing assumptions underlying new technologies and their application.

REFERENCES

Boyd, G. (2004). Conversation theory. In Jonassen, D. (Ed.), *Handbook of educational communications and technology* (pp. 125–145). Mahwah, NJ: Laurence Erlbaum and Associates.

Connaway, L. S. (2001). A web-based electronic book (e-book) library: The netLibrary model. *Library Hi Tech*, *19*(4), 340–349. doi:10.1108/07378830110411961

Harri-Augstein, S., & Thomas, L. (1991). *Learning conversations*. London: Routledge.

Hernon, P., Hopper, R., Leach, M. R., Saunders, L. L., & Zhang, J. (2007). E-book use by students: Undergraduates in economics, literature, and nursing. *Journal of Academic Librarianship*, *33*(1), 3–13. doi:10.1016/j.acalib.2006.08.005

Jantz, R. (2001). E-books and new library service models: An analysis of the impact of E-book technology on academic libraries. *Information Technology and Libraries*, *20*(2), 104–115.

Nelson, M. R. (2008). E-books in higher education: Nearing the end of the era of hype? *EDUCAUSE Review*, *43*(2), 40–56.

Pask, G. (1975). *The cybernetics of human learning and performance: A guide to theory and research*. London: Hutchinson.

Perez, R. C., & Alaman, X. (2002). Creating E-books in a distributed and collaborative way. *The Electronic Library*, *20*(4), 288–295. doi:10.1108/02640470210438883

Poftak, A. (2001). Getting a read on E-books. *Technology & Learning*, *21*(9), 22–36.

Rao, S. S. (2003). Electronic books: A review and evaluation. *Library Hi Tech*, *21*(1), 85–93. doi:10.1108/07378830310467427

Rowlands, I., & Nicholas, D. (2008). Understanding information behaviour: How do students and faculty find books? *Journal of Academic Librarianship*, *34*(1), 3–15. doi:10.1016/j.acalib.2007.11.005

Scott, B. (2001). Conversation theory. A constructivist dialogical approach to educational technology. *Cybernetics & Human Knowing*, *8*(4), 25–46.

FURTHER READING

Appleton, L. (2004). The use of electronic books in midwifery education: The student perspective. *Health Information and Libraries Journal*, *21*(4), 245–252. doi:10.1111/j.1471-1842.2004.00509.x

Appleton, L. (2005). Using electronic textbooks: Promoting, placing and embedding. *The Electronic Library*, *23*(1), 54–63. doi:10.1108/02640470510582736

Armstrong, C., Edwards, L., & Lonsdale, R. (2002). Virtually there? E-books in UK academic libraries. *Program*, *36*(4), 216–227.

Armstrong, C., & Lonsdale, R. (2005). Challenges in managing e-books collections in UK academic libraries. *Library Collections, Acquisitions & Technical Services*, *29*(1), 33–50. doi:10.1016/j.lcats.2004.12.001

Bailey, T. P. (2006). Electronic book usage at a master's level I university: A longitudinal study. *Journal of Academic Librarianship*, *32*(1), 52–59. doi:10.1016/j.acalib.2005.10.004

Ball, D. (2005). A new model for procuring E-books. *New Review of Academic Librarianship*, *11*(1), 1–11. doi:10.1080/13614530500417479

Ball, D. (2006). Innovative models for procuring e-books. *Serials*, *19*(1), 28–31. doi:10.1629/1928

Bell, R. (2009). E-books in practice: The librarian's perspective. *Learned Publishing*, *22*(1), 18–22. doi:10.1087/095315108X378730

Buczynski, J. A. (2006). Faculty begin to replace textbooks with "freely" accessible online resources. *Internet Reference Services Quarterly*, *11*(4), 169–179. doi:10.1300/J136v11n04_11

Clyde, L. A. (2005). Electronic books. *Teacher Librarian*, *32*(5), 45.

Corbeil, J. R., & Valdes-Corbeil, M. E. (2007). Are you ready for mobile learning? *EDUCAUSE Quarterly*, *30*(2), 51–58.

Dodero, J. M., Aedo, I., & Diaz, P. (2002). Participative knowledge production of learning objects for E-books. *The Electronic Library*, *20*(4), 296–305. doi:10.1108/02640470210438892

Gibbons, S. (2001). Growing competition for libraries. *Library Hi Tech*, *19*(4), 363–367. doi:10.1108/07378830110411989

Goodwin-Jones, B. (2003). E-books and the tablet PC. *Language Learning & Technology*, *7*(1), 4–8.

Hellwig, S. J., Monroe, E. E., & Jacobs, J. S. (2000). Making informed choices: Selecting children's trade books for mathematics instruction. *Teaching Children Mathematics*, *7*(3), 138–143.

Jantz, R., & Bell, R. (2002). English advice manuals online at Rutgers: A partnership in a new course using digital books and web technology. *Library Hi Tech Journal*, *20*(3), 318–324. doi:10.1108/07378830210444513

Landoni, M., & Hanlon, G. (2007). E-book reading groups: Interacting with e-books in public libraries. *The Electronic Library*, *25*(5), 599–612. doi:10.1108/02640470710829578

Latal, K. L. (2007). The eBooks puzzle: An entertaining examination of love-hate issues surrounding eBooks. *Against the Grain*, *19*(4), 64-64.

McClelland, R. J., & Hawkins, N. (2006). Perspectives on the use and development of a broad range of e-books in higher education and their use in supporting virtual learning environments. *The Electronic Library*, *24*(1), 68–82. doi:10.1108/02640470610649254

Rowhani, S., & Sedig, K. (2005). E-books plus: Role of interactive visuals in exploration of mathematical information and E-learning. *Journal of Computers in Mathematics and Science Teaching*, *24*(3), 273–298.

Rowlands, I., Nicholas, D., Jamali, H. R., & Huntington, P. (2007). What do faculty and students really think about e-books? *Aslib Proceedings*, *59*(6), 489–511. doi:10.1108/00012530710839588

Shamir, A., & Korat, O. (2006). How to select CD-ROM storybooks for young children: The teacher's role. *The Reading Teacher*, *59*(6), 532–543. doi:10.1598/RT.59.6.3

Shamir, A., & Korat, O. (2007). Developing an educational e-book for fostering kindergarten children's emergent literacy. *Computers in the Schools*, *24*(1), 125–143. doi:10.1300/J025v24n01_09

Song, Y., & Fox, R. (2008). Using PDA for undergraduate student incidental vocabulary testing. *ReCALL*, *20*(3), 290–314. doi:10.1017/S0958344008000438

Wilkins, V. (2007). Managing e-books at the University of Derby: A case study. *Program: Electronic Library and Information Systems*, *41*(3), 238–251. doi:10.1108/00330330710774129

Wilson, R., Landoni, M., & Gibb, F. (2002). A user-centred approach to e-book design. *The Electronic Library*, *20*(4), 322–330. doi:10.1108/02640470210438865

Woodward, H. (2007). Acquiring E-books for academic libraries. *Liber Quarterly: The Journal of European Research Libraries*, *17*(1-4), 174–179.

APPENDIX: SUPPORTING MATERIAL

Abstract

This case explores the topic of electronic collections development within university libraries from a student perspective. By mobilizing Conversation Theory (CT) and a conversational modeling framework, a case on electronic collections development is presented which utilizes research literature and focus group conversational data derived from undergraduate students within a large urban university.

Questions and Answers

1. What is the overall problem(s) in this case?

The overall problem in this case is that the student perspective on electronic collections development should be understood to determine if students prefer a focus on print, electronic, or both types of publications. The case presents conversation modeling as a method of obtaining mutual understanding in situations where communication gaps exist.

2. What are the factors affecting the problem(s) related to this case?

Academic libraries must make the most of their limited resources and the largest user group (students) must feel they have input on collections development at the institution they attend and support. The issues are complex and there are many stakeholders; as a result of this, there is a communication gap. The concerns of these stakeholders must be understood in their unique contexts, rather than generalizing to all universities.

3. Discuss managerial, organizational, and technological issues and resources related to this case.

Managerial – Evaluating the success of large developments in organization is necessary and difficult. User needs must be understood and met and the best use of scarce resources must be determined.

Organizational – The individual organization must be taken in context for stakeholders' needs to be met and users must be made aware of what is offered to them. The organization must change within the evolving technological environment.

Technological – Technology has changed over time and as a result, potential services that can be offered by libraries have changed. These changes must be adapted to (by purchasing computers, electronic documents, etc.).

4. What role do decision-makers play in the overall planning, implementation, and management of print and electronic collections development within universities?

The decision-makers in universities (administration, faculty, and library staff) must decide on how to invest funding for collections development while also meeting the needs of students. Additionally, they must decide on issues of broader concern such as long-term information retention, environmental concerns, and providing the technological support students need to make use of the library resources.

5. What are the possible alternatives and pros and cons of each alternative, as indicated by students, facing the organization in dealing with the problem(s) related to the case?

Focus on electronic – Advantages included increased accessibility, environmental benefits, and electronic text duplicability. Disadvantages highlighted by students included fear of technology failure, violations of intellectual property policies, and increased risk of plagiarism.

Focus on print – Key advantages given by students included a preference for tangibility of printed text and preferences for the traditional library research experience. Disadvantages of print included the limited physical holdings and outdated information.

Shared focus on print and electronic – It was indicated by students that personal preference, educational need, information amount, conservation of library space, reliability issues, information retention, access flexibility, and risk reduction were key to focusing on both print and electronic resources.

6. What are some of the tools and techniques that should be considered in solving the problem(s) related to the case?

Conversation Theory (CT) can be used to help understand the complex conversational processes within face-to-face and online contexts and create shared meaning. Conversation modeling strategies can be a useful tool for understanding complicated issues. Additionally, this technique can be applied to help understand the perspectives of other stakeholder groups (administration, faculty, and library staff).

7. What is the final solution that can be recommended to the management of the organization described in the case? Provide your arguments in support of the recommended solution.

Perspective sharing and collaborative learning processes within the individual context should be discovered and acceptable solutions should be indentified and agreed upon. This can be done through conversation modeling strategies applied to all stakeholder groups (administration, faculty, library staff, and students). By applying conversation modeling to each of these groups, best-practices for collections development could be created for the individual library to meet the needs of each of these groups.

Epilogue

One of the most interesting findings in this chapter addresses the role of CT in addressing the challenge of multiple perspective sharing and consensual decision making within organizations. It would be interesting to test the conversational modeling strategies used by students in a follow-up case using mixed focus groups involving all key stakeholders (students, administration, faculty). This could provide a useful indicator of mutual understanding (or lack of understanding) between university stakeholder groups that could help identify gaps in communication and understanding that could be used to inform interventions designed to improve student-faculty-administration relations and leverage collaboration within universities.

Lessons Learned

1. There are no quick and easy solutions to electronic collections development within a university. This is because of the many stakeholder groups and competing interests that are challenging to overcome.
2. Each university is a complex system which requires context specific analyses. The study of library collections development initiatives cannot be generalized across universities and must be tailored to each context.
3. Conversational approaches to study perspective sharing and collaborative learning has its limits. The major limit in this study was the time required to analyze data. It provides a rich level of detail, at the expense of efficiency.

Chapter 4
Education Technology in Teacher Education:
Overcoming Challenges, Realizing Opportunities

Peter Rawlins
Massey University, New Zealand

Benjamin Kehrwald
Massey University, New Zealand

ABSTRACT

This chapter examines the use of educational technologies in teacher education programs through the exploration of a single professional practice course in a pre-service teacher education program in New Zealand. This case highlights the opportunities associated with teacher educators' unique role in promoting and supporting the use of educational technologies amongst pre-service teachers. It examines the use of a single complex learning activity to integrate education technology into other subject studies and realize some of the transformative potentials associated with the use of technologies in education. It also identifies the challenges of leveraging these opportunities in the face of (a) a complex and demanding role for teacher educators and (b) the forces of change in higher education.

INTRODUCTION

The uptake of digital educational technologies in education has been a focal point of wider initiatives to promote educational development and emerging ideals of twenty-first century education. These initiatives position digital technologies not only as tools for education providers to improve the outcomes of educational programs, but also as tools for learners who are participating in contemporary societies which increasingly rely on digital technologies for a range of personal and professional pursuits.

Teacher educators have particular roles to play in promoting the use of educational technologies in two contexts: First, as higher education practitioners, they are concerned with the appropriate use of technology in the service of higher learning. In this context, the use of digital technologies serves the needs of increasingly diverse groups of learners by creating powerful, flexible, personalized and connected learning experiences. Second, as

DOI: 10.4018/978-1-61520-869-2.ch004

practitioners in dedicated professional education programs for teachers, they are concerned with the modeling of exemplary technology-enhanced education and creating learning experiences which help teacher trainees link their experiences as learners to excellent technology-enhanced teaching. In this context, the use of digital technologies in higher education produces flow-on effects for technology-enhanced education in schools and other educational settings.

Despite these roles, there are distinct disconnects between the operation of teacher education programs and the needs of pre-service teachers which create tensions between the intended applications of educational technologies and the realities of educational technology use in teacher education. These include: (a) teacher educators' disconnect from contemporary practice in schools due to their place outside the schooling sector; (b) the difference between teacher educators' limited experiences of educational technologies, as either learners or teachers, and their roles in modeling effective practice for pre-service teachers; and (c) the disconnect between the intent of teacher education programs to produce teachers capable of responding to change throughout their careers in a dynamic schooling sector and the unwillingness of teacher educators who deliver those programs to embrace change, especially with regard to educational technologies. These tensions background the main focus of the case outlined in this chapter.

This chapter examines the use of educational technologies in teacher education programs through the exploration of a single professional practice course in a pre-service teacher education course in New Zealand. This case outlines the integrated use of educational technologies within a teacher education program to demonstrate the potential application of educational technologies to the teacher education staff and model effective use of educational technologies to the pre-service teachers. The following discussion highlights the lessons learned in the first generation of this new learning activity and some recommendations for future versions of the course.

ORGANIZATION BACKGROUND

The College of Education at Massey University (New Zealand) provides teacher education to pre-service and in-service teachers in a range of educational contexts, including a significant number of early childhood, primary and secondary school teachers. The College offers undergraduate Bachelor of Education programs for pre-service teachers without degrees, Graduate Diplomas in Teaching for those with degrees but not teaching qualifications, and Master of Education and Doctor of Education programs for in-service educators in a range of contexts.

As New Zealand's leading provider of higher education at a distance, Massey University has been at the forefront of distance education for teachers in New Zealand. This focus has included the integration of digital technologies into educational programs as part of efforts to improve the flexibility and quality of programs delivered at a distance. More recently, this use of educational technologies has also featured in on campus delivery as part of 'hybrid' or 'blended' learning in which individual courses or programs are offered using a blend of not only modes of delivery but also approaches to teaching and learning.

The case study discussed in this chapter is part of the professional practice course for the Graduate Diploma of Teaching (Secondary), a one year pre-service teacher education program for secondary teachers offered by the College of Education at Massey University. The 120 credit program consists of two Integrated Teaching Studies courses (45 credits), three subject studies courses (45 credits), and two professional practice courses (30 credits). The program enrolls an average of 160 students each year

The program is offered via a blended delivery mode with approximately half of the students based at one of the two campuses in either Palmerston North or Napier; the rest of the students studying at a distance. Although the Palmerston North and Napier based students are often referred to as 'internal' students in reality the distinction is that these students engage in the Integrated Teaching Studies (ITS) courses through a face to face mode of delivery while the 'distance' students study the ITS courses through a online 'virtual school' environment, with a compulsory three and half day block course in Palmerston North. While it is recognized that the activities that these two groups of students undertake cannot, in all circumstances, be the same, they are designed to offer the students equivalent learning opportunities. In all other respects there is little distinction between the two groups of students. The three subject studies courses (math, English, science etc.) are all extramural courses, with all students studying through a blended delivery of on-line learning and compulsory contact courses in Palmerston North. The professional practice courses involve a total of 15 weeks of practicum in a variety of secondary schools.

The philosophy that underpins the Graduate Diploma program is strongly influenced by the belief that teaching and learning are dynamic processes. Learning to teach is viewed as a journey towards a synthesis of the theory and the practice through knowledge, understanding, reflection, and integration. Teaching is viewed as a 'craft' activity involving nuanced understanding of teaching and learning processes as well as combination of skills and expertise in linking such understanding to practical activity in context. Emphasis is placed on cognitive and sociocultural theoretical perspectives that value socially constructed knowledge and authentic learning experiences, both for prospective teachers and their future students. In order for such abstract ideas to be meaningful, prospective teachers must have a context for learning where they are surrounded with real educational problems that can be identified, analyzed and solved by applying their growing understandings of the craft of teaching. This philosophy is consistent with the Graduating Teaching Standards developed by the New Zealand Teachers' Council which acts as the professional standard for judging new teachers' preparedness for entering the teaching profession.

The teachers graduating from this program are entering an educational sector that is changing at an ever increasing rate. As such, teaching, as a craft, needs to continually adapt to better suit the needs of contemporary learners. In recognition of this fact one of the desired outcomes of our program is that students become critical assessors of the school settings they go into. They are asked to examine and reflect on what they see and do, with an eye towards building on the positive components and adapting the things that need change. In this context, approaches to teacher education which provide students with a set of discrete skills that quickly become outdated are not likely to be as successful as approaches which provide new/aspiring teachers with a set of dispositions towards adapting their pedagogy to make use of future educational opportunities. Key amongst these opportunities will be the use of educational technologies as powerful pedagogical resources that will allow teachers to help students learn in fundamentally different ways, and for classrooms to look very different than they do today. To appreciate these opportunities, our students must be exposed to authentic uses of educational technologies during their pre-service teacher education program.

SETTING THE STAGE: OPPORTUNITIES AND CHALLENGES

Opportunities

The use of educational technologies is motivated by a set of perceived opportunities to improve the outcomes of educational programs and re-focus those programs on learners and learning. First, universities, polytechnics, colleges and other education providers are using educational technologies to improve access to educational opportunities and to widen participation in higher and further education. Motivated by changed revenue streams (Ryan, 2001), the emergence of global markets for education (Gouthro, 2002), the imperatives of lifelong learning associated with globalization and local (national) imperatives related to societal needs (Birzea, 2000; Starkey, 2002), universities are employing educational technologies to open and cater to new markets for their programs. Educational technologies are seen as a means to overcome the limits of time and space in order to allow more learners, including those who are not able to participate in traditional place-based education, to participate in rich, engaging, interactive learning activities as part of formal distance and blended education.

Following the drive to open new markets for higher and further education, providers are using educational technologies to increase the flexibility of teaching and learning within formal education (Jona, 2000). This increased flexibility includes modes of delivery (e.g. technology enhanced distance education, wholly online delivery and blended face-to-face or distance education) and modes of interaction (e.g., synchronous or asynchronous). Flexibly delivered education includes flexibilities in place of study, pace of study, topics of study, qualification structures and progression, roles and responsibilities of stakeholders and costs associated with study for both the learner and the education provider. This flexibility has affected approaches to teaching and learning (e.g. situated and social vs. self-contained and self paced) and the design of programs, courses, units of work and types of assessment.

One of the benefits of this flexibility is the ability to add an experiential dimension to learning through the use of active learning approaches which are situated in authentic contexts. For example, educational technologies can be used to create sites for activity as in the case of online learning environments and immersive virtual worlds. Alternately, technology can be used to link learners to authentic activity in context as in the use of mobile digital technologies to allow learners to record and discuss practical activity wherever they are. When coupled with highly flexible, convenient communication provided by email, instant messaging, asynchronous discussion or synchronous conferencing, educational technologies create a powerful combination of context, communication and purposeful activity which enhances the learning experience. Learners are able to use technology not only to *learn about* particular content, but *learn to do* particular content-specific tasks and *learn to be* practitioners by assuming certain specialist roles in context (Brown & Duguid, 2000). Moreover, teaching staff are able to assume roles which seem them participate in the community as role models and lead by example.

Another result of the flexibility afforded by educational technologies has been the ability to better cater to the needs of adult learners, particularly through a focus on authentic learning contexts, learner agency and a learner-centered view of learning programs. The focus on the learner is not unique to adult learning, but it has a particular significance in that context due to the likelihood of variation between learners who have accumulated a wealth of life experience and related learning. There may be very significant differences in existing ability, knowledge and motivation between individuals within cohorts of adult learners (Mayes, 2004). Educational technologies offer an opportunity to address particular needs of individual learners through increasingly individualized pedagogies made possible via the flexibility of technology-mediated learning.

Challenges

Accompanying these opportunities is a set of practical challenges which create barriers to the effective use of educational technologies. One of the key challenges is the willingness and ability of teaching staff to engage in new (or changed) ways of doing things. Individual teaching staff members have abilities, knowledge and motivation to engage in practice in particular ways. These issues affect their willingness to engage in innovative practices which are often associated with the use of educational technology. Further, their abilities to engage in innovative practice should not be assumed. While most experienced teacher-practitioners can be regarded as skilled with certain aspects of teaching, several factors work against their abilities to stay up-to-date with technology enhanced teaching practices. These include (a) the breakneck speed of technological evolution compared with the relatively slow pace of change in educational systems; (b) the limited investment in teacher professional development relative to technology hardware and infrastructure; and (c) availability of various technologies in different educational contexts. The result is a widening gap between the technology 'cans' and 'cannots'. As with the learners themselves, innovative applications of educational technologies involving groups of teaching staff must accommodate a range of skills, attitudes and abilities as part of a developmental approach to the use of those technologies.

Another of the key challenges is the expectations learners bring to formal education. Returning to the issue of individual difference mentioned above, each learner brings a particular set of expectations to the educational situation. Particularly with adult learners, these expectations and based on experience, attitudes, motivation and values. These expectations include levels of flexibility; roles and responsibilities for themselves as learners, teaching staff and for the institution as a provider of education; views on assessment; notions of authenticity and relevance; preferences with regard to learning activity; and ideas about their own likelihood of success. While these expectations influence learning activity in general, they also have a particular affect on learners' willingness to engage in new, novel or unfamiliar learning situations (Jona, 2000). Experience shows that this can be a significant challenge to innovative approaches to teaching and learning with technology.

CASE DESCRIPTION

Technology Applications: Opportunities for Improvement

The Graduate Diploma program has recently undergone a review process through which a number of key recommendations emerged. Notably, the review specifically highlighted the needs to (a) increase the use of information and communications technology (ICT, as it is commonly known in New Zealand, referred to as educational technologies in this chapter) in its widest application, (b) increase emphasis on critique and debate within the program, and (c) make better use of learning approaches intended for adult learners. The teaching team identified that effective use of educational technologies informed by sociocultural learning principles was consistent with these three key recommendations. Although a number of the teaching staff in the program were increasingly modeling effective teaching practice *through* technology, rather than *with* or *about* technology, this tended to be rather sporadic and unplanned. A more formal and systematic approach was required. As such, educational technologies were identified as one of the key threads that would be embedded through all of the courses in the program.

Despite this general agreement, there was extensive debate on the level of integration, how this might be achieved, and anxiety about whether the teaching team had the expertise to undertake this task. E-portfolios and better use of on-line Learning Management Systems (LMS) were identified as two important facets of this innovation but there remained uncertainty as to how existing activities could be adapted to more fully integrate educational technologies to improve learning. Redesigning and rewriting a whole program is a lengthy process, complicated by internal and external accreditation procedures. This lead-in time did, however, provided the time to undertake professional development and to trial a number of activities within the existing course structures. To this end, two of the teaching team undertook to redesign the new educational technologies unit within the existing ITS course structure. Due to the timing of the decision to redesign this unit, and for pragmatic reasons associated with the lead-in time for study guide material it was decided that this new unit would be trialed with the internal students only.

The redesign of the unit was, in part, intended to demonstrate the practicalities and the potential of incorporating technology through all our courses. It has subsequently been used during professional development opportunities with teaching staff as an example that they can deconstruct and examine in depth for its key features.

Historically, the potential of new educational technologies as a pedagogical tool had been addressed primarily through a single unit of work late in the one year program. This unit attempted to make links between conceptual theories of learning through technology, but tended to be a series of short, de-contextualized activities introducing students to discrete applications such as PowerPoint and the World Wide Web, combined with a series of printed readings highlighting some of the theoretical possibilities of technology to enhance learning. Material was often presented to students in a transmissive mode with no apparent recognition of prior knowledge or learning, and little opportunity for the students to link the new knowledge and skills to existing knowledge or prior learning in a meaningful way. The reality was that the material was presented in a manner where examples of what *could* be achieved were presented to the students without them being asked to do anything as part of their learning, e.g., *create* or *evaluate* the merit of any significant examples of their own. Learners were *learning about* educational technologies without *learning how* to use them (Brown & Duguid, 2000).In essence the students were exposed to a series of potentially powerful tools without proper attention being paid to how they might integrate these tools into their own teaching in order to enhance their own students' learning.

The timing and indeed the very existence of the new educational technology unit was also questioned. Within any program, discussions of when students should be exposed to key ideas are often hotly debated amongst the program's teaching team. While some subscribed to the view that students must be exposed to key ideas before they go out on their teaching practicum, others argued that some ideas are so important that if students are to fully appreciate the subtleties that will help to embed these ideas as a fully integrated part of learning, they must first have a level of practical experience of what actually happens in schools. Moreover some of the teaching team pointed out the irony of trying to help students understand about how educational technologies can be integrated into the everyday classroom, through a standalone activity which was conducted after much of their practicum had been completed. In essence, teaching staff were trying to convince students that educational technologies were not just an 'add-on' by doing exactly that, adding it on.

Furthermore, the predominantly transmissive method of delivery of this unit appeared to be inconsistent with its philosophical goal. This unit sought to open the student teachers' eyes to how learning in their classroom can be fundamentally different through alignment to sociocultural principles, and the affordances that technology offers in creating this new learning environment. Contemporary sociocultural theories of learning increasingly recognize the situated nature and interpersonal dimension of knowledge, and the impact of the social environment in promoting and directing learning (Sfard, 2003). Central to these theories is the notion of a 'community of practice'.

A community of practice is an intrinsic condition for the existence of knowledge not least because it provides the interpretive support necessary for making sense of its heritage. Thus, participation in the cultural practice in which any knowledge exists is an epistemological principle of learning. The social structure of this practice, its power relations, and its conditions for legitimacy define possibilities for learning. (Lave & Wenger, 1991, p. 98)

Accordingly, learning is conceived as social and collaborative activity in which people develop their thinking together through the practices of the community. The learner is both shaping and being shaped by the 'community of practice'. Rather than asking what kinds of cognitive processes and conceptual structures are involved in learning, sociocultural perspectives ask "what kinds of social engagements provide the proper context for learning to take place" (Even & Tirosh, 2002, p. 232).

If educational technologies have the potential to enhance students' ability to investigate and construct their own learning in a sociocultural setting then surely presenting a set of discrete de-contextualized tools is inconsistent with this philosophical position. Accordingly, it was decided that students should be provided with an authentic context by giving them the opportunity to learn something new using a technology enhanced environment.

Technology Application: The Redeveloped Learning Tasks

The new unit of work for learners combined two units that had previously been taught in the program—the 'new educational technologies' unit and an 'educational issues' unit—where students explored an educational issue such as plagiarism or text bullying. It was intended that the new unit would embed a greater understanding of the pedagogical potential that educational technologies offer, both for the students and, particularly, for the teaching team. The design of the new unit also considered the conceptual framework of the program that encouraged the use of authentic learning experiences to help prospective teachers appreciate the pedagogical advantages of using such experiences in their own teaching. By exposing students to activities where technology was an integral part of the learning, thus providing them with an opportunity to learn in a fundamentally different way, it was hoped that the unit would be a both a transformative approach to the use of technology, and a transformative learning experience for the students. Although it was recognized that the new unit did not address a number of the concerns raised about the full integration of technology throughout the program, it provided a useful example of what was possible and helped to stimulate more discussion on the topic of the integrated use of educational technologies within the teaching team.

Within the new unit, students were asked to work in small groups to investigate a contemporary educational issue and produce a 10 minute docudrama that was to be presented to the wider cohort of students as a DVD. The activity was specifically designed to promote learner agency by providing them with a broad assignment brief and then the freedom and time to meet that brief in a way that they felt was appropriate. Students had two weeks of dedicated class time plus an additional two weeks to explore their educational issue and compile their docudrama. They were encouraged to be creative and innovative in their presentations and in their use of a wide range of technologies. They had access to digital video cameras and a computer room where they could do digital editing. Some students had previous experience with digital editing, so they were asked to step back and teach the other members of their group how to use the software. Similarly, other students brought a range of media or drama related skills which proved useful in the overall design of the project. Two program staff were also available to help with the content, design or any technical aspects of the project; students accessing these services according to their groups' needs. Although the two teaching staff had a degree of expertise they were open about the limitations to their knowledge and skill set. Indeed, in many instances it was noted that students from one group were often asking the 'experts' from other groups to help them, rather than the teaching staff. In this regard the students and staff constituted a community of learners, recognizing the wide range of expertise within the group and helping to break down the hierarchical distinctions of teacher/student often associated with many learning situation.

The DVDs produced by the students were shown on the last day of the course and, consistent with sociocultural perspectives of learning and assessment, were peer-assessed by the rest of the students. A second component of the assignment asked the group to discuss the merits of using educational technologies as a pedagogical tool and to provide some contextual examples of where their use might enhance the learning experience for students. This was assessed by the two teaching team members.

Although students had worked in small groups before this had tended to be on projects where the task could be divided up amongst the members of the group who worked individually, only coming together immediately prior to the submission date to compile the assignment. This project differed in that the members of the group had to fulfill a large number of roles. They had to be writers, actors, cameramen, editors and producers. This resulted in them working closely together, often causing some tension amongst the members. This was seen as a positive outcome of the activity as it reflected the diverse nature of teachers in schools. It was seen as an opportunity for the students to develop their professional working relationship skills.

As identified earlier, it was anticipated that there may be some student resistance to engaging with both the activity and the educational technology. The diverse nature of ages, backgrounds and expectations of the student body may have potentially created a number of challenges to the success of this trial. In particular, students' expectation of their roles and the roles of the teacher in the learning process, notions of authenticity and relevance, and preferences with regard to learning activity were all identified as challenges that would need to be overcome. Despite these concerns, the students embraced the activity with vigor and indeed formal feedback at the end of the year identified this activity as a highlight for the year for many students. They commented that not only was it an enjoyable activity, but they could identify the potential of re-conceptualizing the learning environment through the use of educational technologies and authentic activities.

CURRENT CHALLENGES FACING THE ORGANISATION

Despite the motives for re-conceptualizing the use of educational technologies within the program, there were a number of significant challenges to the effective use of technology to achieve the ends identified within the case above.

Firstly, there is still some significant resistance amongst some staff to the practical changes required to integrate technology in to the program. This resistance can be linked to issues of both willingness and ability of staff to engage with technology-enhanced teaching, including (a) the familiarity of staff with various educational technologies and their application within the program (b) changed staff roles in technology-enhanced learning activities and the willingness of staff to reconsider their roles in reconfigured teacher-student relationships (c) concerns that students may not have the necessary technical skills to effectively engage with a technology enhanced program and question about whether it is our job to up-skill them (d) issues of equitable access to broadband, computers, and other educational technologies, especially for our distance students.

Secondly, while openly promoting a philosophical position of preparing students to be critical examiners of the school sector they are entering, teacher educators are often guilty of failing to critically examine their own practice. Students graduating from our program will often be faced with resistance to change and the new ideas they bring into the schools. Teacher educators pride themselves that they equip their students with a set of critical analysis skills that will allow the trainee teachers to examine the education practices in schools and adapt them to meet the changing needs of students. However, while espousing this philosophy on the one hand teacher educators are reticent to apply such analytical skills to their own programs and practices. There have been some pockets of significant resistance to embracing new ways of doing things that more accurately reflect the changes needs of a contemporary school sector.

Thirdly, this activity was undertaken with the internal students in the program. As stated, this was for a number of pragmatic reasons associated with lead-in time for study guides. However, it is recognized that the students being on-campus does afford them greater access to each other, to equipment, and to staff and other expertise. Teaching staff are currently investigating how this activity might be adapted, or what comparable activities might be designed, that are consistent with the philosophical underpinnings of the activity.

SOLUTIONS AND RECOMMENDATIONS

The challenges identified in this case foreshadow a number of tensions and related questions that teacher educators must face as they modernize pre-service teacher education programs to better prepare students for an increasingly technological school sector. The tensions include potential conflicts around the currency of teacher educators' accumulated knowledge and their roles in preparing teachers for current and future classrooms; the tensions between good face-to-face teaching and similarly good technology-enhanced teaching; friction between the intent of technology enhanced teaching and the realities of blended learning.

More particularly, this case highlighted three main challenges to the integration of educational technologies within the program in quesiton: teacher resistence to change, the need to be appropriately critical about the application and use of educational technologies and the need to create an equitable use of educaitonal technologies for all students.

Regarding teacher resistance, a number of potential solutions emerged to address the concerns highlighted above. Although much of the resistance is vocalised as 'it can't be done', in reality this often means 'I don't know how to do it'. As such, on-going professional development for the teaching team, and sharing of 'what works? and why?', will need to occur. This includes: instructional design to help staff identify aspects of their course that are better suited to the interactions afforded by on-line learning environments, greater familiarity with the tools available within the universities LMS and other Web 2.0 tools, greater awareness of the range of educational technologies available (e.g. mobile phones, graphics and CAS calculators, still and video photography, data loggers etc.) and their uses, on-going sharing and deconstructing of activities that utilise educational technologies to enhance the learning environment; continuing use of staff discussion forums to both debate issues relating to the use educational technologies and illustrate how this debate can occur outside a face-to-face environment.

Regarding the critical application of educational technologies, the case highlights the key point that educational technologies cannot be assumed to be 'good' or 'beneficial', and that changing our existing activites and learning environments may not necessarily improve the learning experiences and outcomes for our pre-service teachers. Decisons about the 'when' and 'how' to use a technologically enhanced learning environment must be pedagogically driven. We must ensure that educational technologies are applied to a particular purpose in a carefully thought out way in order to achieve the intended aims, particular where those aims involve the modelling of technology use. This will require continuing discussion about the conceptual framework that underpins our programme and the nature of the learning environment that will operationalise this framework. In essence the teaching team must continue to examine the purpose of the programme and how that purpose might be best met.

Regarding the quesiton of equity between internal and extramural students, the recommended course of action is careful attention to equity issues which arise for on- and off-camputs students. Breifly, the two key issues which emerged from this case were (a) the time required for asynchronous approaches to collaborative work and (b) the relative qualities of the interactive process for students who are physically distant from one another. In general, off campus students were seen to be disadvantaged by the process as described above. The advantages of timely face-to-face interaction experienced by on-campus students translated to much more time consuming negotiation via asynchronous commuication for the off-campus students. The response to these issues is still forthcoming, but the suggested approach involves developing modified version of the docudrama activity which can be supported at a distance; provides a high-quality learning expeirence and balances out the resource demands of the task with the resrouces available to off-campus students.

REFERENCES

Birzea, C. (2000). *Education for democratic citizenship: a lifelong learning perspective*. Strasbourg, Germany: Council for Cultural Co-operation.

Brown, J. S., & Duguid, P. (2000). *The social life of information*. Boston: Harvard Business School Press.

Even, R., & Tirosh, D. (2002). Teacher knowledge and understanding of students' mathematical learning. In English, L. D. (Ed.), *Handbook of international research in mathematics education* (pp. 219–240). Mahwah, NJ: Lawrence Erlbaum.

Gouthro, P. A. (2002). Education for sale: at what cost? Lifelong Learning and the marketplace. *International Journal of Lifelong Education, 21*(4), 334–346. doi:10.1080/02601370210140995

Gunn, C. (2000). *Identity, Control and Changing Reality*. Paper presented at the ASCILITE 2000. Retrieved May 1, 2009, from http://www.ascilite.org.au/conferences/coffs00/papers/cathy_gunn_keynote.pdf

Jona, K. (2000). Rethinking the design of online courses. Paper presented at the ASCILITE. Retrieved from http://www.ascilite.org.au/conferences/coffs00/

Lave, J., & Wenger, E. (1991). *Situated learning: Legitimate peripheral participation*. New York: Cambridge University Press.

Mayes, J. T. (2004). *Learner centred pedagogy: Individual differences between learners*. JISC e-Learning Models Desk Study. Retrieved October 20, 2006, from http://www.jisc.ac.uk/uploaded_documents/Stage%202%20Learning%20Styles%20(Version%201).pdf

Ryan, Y. (2001). The provision of learner support services online. In *The changing faces of virtual education* (pp. 71–94). Vancouver, BC: The Commonwealth of Learning.

Sfard, A. (2003). Balancing the unbalanceable: The NCTM standards in light of theories of learning mathematics. In Kilpatrick, J., Martin, W. G., & Schifter, D. (Eds.), *A research companion to Principles and Standards for School Mathematics* (pp. 353–392). Reston, VA: National Council of Teachers of Mathematics.

Starkey, H. (2002). *Active citizenship and the lifelong learning agenda.* Paper presented at the Danish EU Presidency Conference: Lifelong learning - learning for adults in the 21st century, Snekkersten, Denmark.

FURTHER READING

Bauer, J., & Kenton, J. (2005). Toward *Technology* Integration in the Schools: Why It Isn't Happening. *Journal of Technology and Teacher Education, 13*(4), 519–546.

Bebell, D., Russell, M., & O'Dwyer, L. (2004). Measuring Teachers' Technology Uses: Why Multiple-Measures Are More Revealing. *Journal of Research on Technology in Education, 37*(1), 45–63.

Carneiro, R. (2006). Motivating School Teachers to Learn: can ICT add value? *European Journal of Education, 41*(3/4), 415–435. doi:10.1111/j.1465-3435.2006.00274.x

Dexter, S., & Riedel, E. (2003). Why Improving Preservice Teacher Educational Technology Preparation Must go beyond the College's Walls. *Journal of Teacher Education, 54*(4), 334–346. doi:10.1177/0022487103255319

Gracanin, D. (2003, Aug 11-13). *Combining traditional and web-based distance learning in information technology education.* Paper presented at the International Conference on Information Technology, Newark, NJ.

Kynigos, C., & Argyris, M. (2004). Teacher beliefs and practices formed during an innovation with computer-based exploratory mathematics in the classroom. *Teachers and Teaching, 10*(3), 247–273. doi:10.1080/1354060042000204414

McCormick, R. (2004). Collaboration: The Challenge of ICT. *International Journal of Technology and Design Education, 14*(2), 159–176. doi:10.1023/B:ITDE.0000026495.10503.95

O'Hanlon, C. (2009). Resistance is Futile. *T.H.E. Journal, 36*(3), 32–36.

Otero, V., Peressini, D., Meymaris, K. A., Ford, P., Garvin, T., & Harlow, D. (2005). Integrating Technology into Teacher Education. *Journal of Teacher Education, 56*(1), 8–23. doi:10.1177/0022487104272055

Perraton, H., Creed, C., & Robinson, B. (2002). *Teacher education guidelines: Using open and distance learning.* Paris: UNESCO, Higher Education Division.

Rye, S. A. (2007). Flexibility, technology, and the daily life practices of distance students living beyond the digital mainstream. *Geoforum, 38*(5), 1028–1039. doi:10.1016/j.geoforum.2007.02.003

Sahin, I., & Shelley, M. (2008). Considering students' perceptions: The distance education student satisfaction model. *Educational Technology & Society, 11*(3), 216–223.

Sigren, P. (2003, Jul 31-Aug 02). *Open distance learning in higher educational systems: A technological approach within a social constructivistic perspective.* Paper presented at the International Conference on Education and Information Systems - Technologies and Applications (EISTA 03), Orlando, FL.

Sun, P. C., Tsai, R. J., Finger, G., Chen, Y. Y., & Yeh, D. (2008). What drives a successful e-Learning? An empirical investigation of the critical factors influencing learner satisfaction. *Computers & Education, 50*(4), 1183–1202. doi:10.1016/j.compedu.2006.11.007

Vannatta, R. A., & Beyerbach, B. (2000). Facilitating a Constructivist Vision of Technology Integration among Education Faculty and Preservice Teachers. *Journal of Research on Computing in Education*, *33*(2), 132.

KEY TERMS AND DEFINITIONS

Blended Learning: Learning situations in which the 'blend' includes combinations of modes of delivery and approaches to teaching and learning. Blended learning can be viewed as a means to producing a good fit between learning designs and the needs of learners in particular contexts.

Educational Technologies: Networked digital computing and communications technologies which are employed in the service of teaching and learning as part of education.

Extramural Delivery: Refers to off campus delivery of educational programs, also called 'distance education' in many contexts.

In-Service Teacher Education: Refers to programs targeted at practicing teachers. In-service teacher education is a form of continuing education and professional development.

Pre-Service Teacher Education: Also called 'initial teacher education', this refers to education programs for individuals who lack any formal teaching qualifications and may lack any teaching experience.

APPENDIX: SUPPORTING MATERIAL

Abstract

This chapter examines the use of educational technologies in teacher education programs through the exploration of a single professional practice course in a pre-service teacher education program in New Zealand. This case highlights the opportunities associated with teacher educators' unique role in promoting and supporting the use of educational technologies amongst pre- and in-service teachers. It examines the use of a single complex learning activity to integrate education technology into other subject studies and realise some of the transformative potentials associated with the use of technologies in education. It also identifies the challenges of leveraging these opportunities in the face of (a) a complex and demanding role for teacher educators and (b) the forces of change in higher education.

Questions and Answers

1. What is the overall problem presented in this case?

The case highlights both opportunities and challenges associated with the integration of educational technologies into teacher education. In particular, the case highlights some of the systemic challenges which prevent the effective use of educational technologies in this program.

2. What factors contribute to the limited quality of the application of educational technologies in teacher education programs?

Three main disconnects are identified in this chapter: (a) teacher educators' disconnect from contemporary practice in schools due to their place outside the schooling sector; (b) the difference between teacher educators' limited experiences of educational technologies, as either learners or teachers, and their roles to model effective practice for pre-service teachers; and (c) the disconnect between the intent of teacher education programs to produce teachers capable of responding to change throughout their careers in a dynamic schooling sector and the unwillingness of teacher educators who deliver those programmes to embrace change, especially with regard to educational technologies.

3. Generally, what advantages are associated with the use of educational technologies as discussed in this case?

Briefly, the advantages discussed in the case include: improved access to educational opportunities, the ability of education providers to open and cater to new markets and increased flexibility in formal educational programs. The benefits of flexibility include changed approaches to how, when and where programs are delivered, including particular attention to the needs of adult learners.

4. What common barriers or challenges do universities and other education providers face in the innovative use of educational technologies?

The challenges noted include learner expectations, the ability and willingness of staff to change and conflicts between existing institutional infrastructure (policy, procedure) and new or innovative ways of doing things. Notably, these challenges are seen as systemic, not technical.

5. What organizational challenges were encountered in this case?

In this particular case, four key challenges emerged:

1. The disconnect between teacher educators experiences of education technology and their need to use it effectively
2. The resistance of teacher staff to change their teaching activities
3. The need to model effective practices
4. Equity issues between modes of delivery.

Epilogue and Lessons Learned

The challenges identified in this case foreshadow a number of tensions and related questions and that teacher educators must face as they modernize pre-service teacher education programs to better prepare students for an increasingly technological school sector. The tensions include potential conflicts around the currency of teacher educators accumulated knowledge and their roles in preparing teachers for current and future classrooms; the tensions between good face-to-face teaching and similarly good technology-enhanced teaching; friction between the intent of technology enhanced teaching and the realities of blended learning.

The questions include: To what extent can we expect our teaching staff to change deeply held beliefs about what they think good teaching and learning is, and how this is achieved? What rate of change can we reasonably expect? What is the uptake rate amongst our teacher educators? What institutional changes need to occur to support these initiatives? What role do our student teachers have in this transformational process? What challenges will they face? How do we as teacher educators continue to support these change processes?

Therefore, the effective use of technology as part of teacher education is not a foregone conclusion of institutional imperatives to integrate technology into teaching. it must be carefully supported with a combination of technological development and professional development for teachers.

Chapter 5
Wikis as Open Educational Resources in Higher Education:
Overcoming Challenges, Realizing Potential

Benjamin Kehrwald
Massey University, New Zealand

P. A. Danaher
The University of Southern Queensland, Australia

ABSTRACT

*Open wikis such as WikiEducator (WE) (*http://www.wikieducator.org/Main_Page*) lie at the intersection of two significant applications of learning technology: open educational resources (OERs), which are freely available materials that can be shared, modified, adapted, and reused in diverse learning contexts; and collaborative authoring environments. This chapter presents a case study of the use of open wikis in a single online postgraduate course in the College of Education at Massey University (New Zealand). The case discussion includes an illustration of the use of open wiki technology at WikiEducator within the course from two different points of view: the use of wikis as a presentation tool by the course teaching staff; and as a production tool by learners seeking to create OERs as part of an instructional design project. The chapter also links the challenges and opportunities associated with these points of view to wider possibilities and pressures attending the terrain in which contemporary higher education is situated.*

INTRODUCTION

The merit of wikis in education is a point of debate. Proponents hail them as potentially glamorous and exciting learning tools (Pan & Bonk, 2007), as providing a flexible, cost effective, and user friendly interface for student interaction and collaboration (Schwartz, Clark, Cossarin, & Rudolph, 2004), as allowing productive brainstorming among learners (Challborn & Reimann, 2005), as enhancing students' collective cognition while enabling (and requiring) new pedagogical approaches by teachers (Lund & Smørdal, 2006), as drawing on the best features of print and orality (Ferris & Wilder,

DOI: 10.4018/978-1-61520-869-2.ch005

2006), as exhibiting affordances that promote community-focused enquiry (Wheeler, Yeomans, & Wheeler, 2008), and for their versatile applicability across disciplines as varied as financial security (O'Neill, Schuchardt, Pankow, Porter, Seiling, Branch, & Miller, 2007) and teachers' professional development (Foley & Chang, 2006). Detractors cite technical difficulties associated with installing and using some wikis (Challborn & Reimann, 2005), course design not necessarily maximizing the possible utility of wikis (Choy & Ng, 2007), an ambivalence about the lack of attribution of individual authorship of wiki content potentially reducing its quality (Kamel Boulos, Maramba, & Wheeler, 2006), and a recognition that good wiki design cannot compensate for poor pedagogical approaches to group-based assignments (Robertson, 2008).

This debate positions open wikis as potentially powerful tools for a variety of educational applications. However, as with all innovative uses of technology, there are a number of challenges associated with their use in context. This chapter examines the opportunities offered by the use of open wikis in higher education and the possible challenges faced in their use. The chapter is structured around the following sections:

- The organization's background, including the basis for openness and the link between openness and OERs
- Setting the scene, including wikis as OERs and a focus on WE
- The case description, highlighting course delivery and use of technology, the use of WE, and the rationale for using the technology in that way
- Two crucial current challenges facing the organization in maximizing WE's potential utility
- Solutions and recommendations, linking those two challenges to broader issues confronting contemporary higher education.

ORGANIZATION BACKGROUND

The chapter is based on a case study of the use of open wikis in a single online postgraduate course in the College of Education at Massey University (New Zealand). The case discussion includes an illustration of the use of open wiki technology at WE within the course from two different points of view. The first point of view is the use of wikis as a presentation tool by the course teaching staff. The discussion highlights the perceived advantages of this approach and anticipated challenges faced by faculty in the use of open wikis. This discussion also articulates issues for faculty in terms of their role in both teaching (for example, subject matter experts, learning facilitators, and learner support) and administration (for example, responding to institutional imperatives around the production of teaching materials and the management and administration of formal educational programs) The second point of view is the use of wikis as a production tool by learners seeking to create OERs as part of an instructional design project. The analysis identifies opportunities for the enrichment of learning experience provided by the use of open wikis as well as the challenges faced by teaching staff in supporting learning in this environment. Particular issues canvassed include the addition of authenticity to learning and explicit support for collaborative activity provided by features of the technology, to some extent contradicted by current limitations of that technology.

A Basis for Openness

The concept of 'openness' denotes a flexible approach which emphasizes freedom from barriers to the creation and use of particular resources. The openness referred to in the context of OERs is informed by old and new academic traditions in the sharing and application of knowledge for the common good; the provision of open education; the development of free open source software; and the connected, collaborative culture of networks that has emerged with the evolution of the Internet. The influences of these traditions frame the background in considering the effectiveness of OERs in this chapter.

More specifically, the Cape Town Open Education Declaration highlights the ethos of openness which underpins these open initiatives:

This emerging open education movement combines the established tradition of sharing good ideas with fellow educators and the collaborative, interactive culture of the Internet. It is built on the belief that everyone should have the freedom to use, customize, improve and redistribute educational resources without constraint. Educators, learners and others who share this belief are gathering together as part of a worldwide effort to make education both more accessible and more effective. (Cape Town Open Education Declaration, para 2, http://www.capetowndeclaration.org/read-the-declaration)

Thus open learning involves the flexible provision of education and emphasizes learner choice in what is studied, how it is studied, and where study takes place. The ethos of open learning is one of sharing and use of knowledge. Historically, open learning has embraced flexible modes of delivery to remove barriers and improve learners' access to educational opportunities. For this reason, open learning is often associated with distance education and educational technologies which create opportunities for flexible delivery and offer learners increased control over their learning process. While open learning is not limited to activities in distance education or with educational technologies, these activities, in combination with the ethos of open learning, underpin the OER movement.

However, the Cape Town Open Education website also emphasizes that openness in education and related activities is an ever-changing notion:

Open education is a living idea. As the movement grows, this idea will continue to evolve. There will be other visions, initiatives and declarations beyond Cape Town. This is exactly the point. The Cape Town signatories have committed to developing further strategies, especially around open technology and teaching practices. (http://www.capetowndeclaration.org/)

Accordingly the notion of openness should also be considered in the context of technology and how it is used. Both the technology tools which are employed in open learning and the ways those tools are created and developed can be 'open' processes. Since the free software movement of the mid 1990s, the genesis of the open source software movement in 1998, and the creation of the creative commons in 2001, the concepts of 'free-for-use' (i.e., without licensing fees) and openness have been a feature of the design, development, and use of a range of technology tools which support open learning initiatives (Wiley & Gurrell, 2009). 'Open source software' refers to software in which the programming code is accessible to any programmers who may wish to make modifications, additions, or improvements to the existing versions of the software. Free open source software (FOSS) is a key ingredient not only in open learning in general, but also in the development of OERs in particular owing to the types of tools being developed and the ways they are used. The freedom from licensing fees and the development of more open licensing practices allow existing products to be copied, modified, and reused. These practices continue to change the way that technology tools are created and developed.

This point deserves particular attention: The ethos of openness not only affects the availability of products for use but also makes them available for adaptation, modification, and ongoing development. This potentially changes the way we think of a 'resource'. Open resources are not mere static items to be used and reused 'as is'; they are dynamic materials which can be modified and repurposed, thereby expanding notions of what the 'use' of such resources is. When combined with the effective and convenient communications afforded by the Internet, and 'connected' ways of working that have emerged amongst networked groups of users, openness provides a very powerful mechanism to share and apply knowledge for the benefit of greater numbers of users.

Open source developers are continually creating applications which are open source products themselves and which can also be used to promote open activity through the creation, modification, and sharing of learning objects, media elements, and information. These tools include open source media creation tools such as Audacity (http://audacity.sourceforge.net/), HTML/XHTML editors such as eXe (http://exelearning.org/), learning management systems such as Moodle (http://moodle.org/), content managers such as Joomla (http://www.joomla.org/), and open source browsers such as Firefox (http://www.mozilla.com/en-US/firefox/personal.html). Together, these tools form an open infrastructure which supports open learning.

Openness and OERs

The particular issue of OERs as a facet of open learning focuses on the creation, use, modification, and reuse of educational resources. The notion of open access which underpins open learning has a particular significance in the context of OERs. OERs are part of broad social strategies aimed at using technology "to help equalise the distribution of high quality knowledge and educational opportunities for individuals, faculty and institutions…throughout the world" (Atkins, Brown, & Hammond, 2007, p. 2). The development and reuse of OERs support a more open, sustainable approach to the use of learning technologies and work to address issues of equity and access to high quality learning resources.

The movement toward openness in educational resources includes three main types of open resources (see also Wiley & Gurrell, 2009). The first is the open source software mentioned above. The affordability and accessibility of such products make them valuable resources to support open learning activities at a range of levels from the development of institution wide systems down to the creation of particular individual learning resources. The second type of open resource is 'open content', which includes the content of educational programs such as whole courses, individual units of work, textbooks, individual learning objects, and tests or other forms of assessment which support learning (Atkins et al., 2007). The Massachusetts Institute of Technology was one of the pioneers in this area, starting from a pilot of 20 course in 2001 and eventually opening the content of nearly its entire undergraduate and graduate catalogues for free public use worldwide (http://ocw.mit.edu/OcwWeb/web/about/about/index.htm). The third type of open resource is tools which support the creation and ongoing development of open resources. These tools include open wikis such as WE and other flexible repositories such as Flickr (http://www.flickr.com). This evolution includes a shift in focus from tools and materials to a philosophy of openness which supports ongoing educational development (d'Antoni, 2009).

SETTING THE STAGE

Wikis as OERs

Of interest in this chapter are the tools which support the creation and development of OERs, particularly wikis. Wikis are dynamic web-based tools which allow for the collaborative authoring of web-based artifacts. Generally, wikis allow all users to edit the contents of wiki pages and thereby create a continuous authoring-refinement process in which the pages represent the shared knowledge of all contributors. Open wikis are wiki environments with a creative commons license attached which allows users to create wiki pages which are free for duplication, modification, adaptation, and reuse.

In this way, and as noted above, open wikis lie at the intersection of two significant applications of learning technology. The first application is OERs, including learning materials for learners, support materials for teachers, and other material which facilitates the provision of high quality education (Johnstone, 2005). Open wikis provide the venue for the creation of open resources which represent the shared knowledge of all who contribute to them. Open wikis such as WE (http://www.wikieducator.org/Main_Page) leverage the flexibility and ease of editing inherent in wiki tools to create OERs in wiki format which are freely accessible, open for use or modification, and easily editable.

The second application is collaborative authoring environments. The emergence of increasingly sophisticated collaborative authoring tools is intertwined with the evolution of the World Wide Web to Web 2.0, also known as the read/write web. In this generation of web technologies, users have shifted their roles from passive consumers of web-based information to active producer/consumers (or "prosumers" (Thompson, 2008)) who both produce knowledge in the form of electronic, web-based artifacts and consume web-based knowledge and information. A critical feature of Web 2.0 tools is the social connectivity that they provide and the associated potential for collaboration. In particular, wiki tools enable groups of individuals to work jointly on a single web-based artifact to create a collaborative product. The increasing sophistication of wiki tools has added features which support productive collaboration, such as archiving previous versions of an artifact, tracking user changes, providing a separate space for parallel discussions of the collaboration, and allowing reversion to previous forms of the artifact.

WikiEducator

WE is an open community working within a wiki environment to build capacity in the use of wikis for collaboration and open content creation, develop free educational content, facilitate community networks related to free content initiatives, and foster technologies which benefit education (see http://www.wikieducator.org/WikiEducator:About). It is supported by the Commonwealth of Learning, an intergovernmental organization supported by Commonwealth member nations. Since its establishment in 2006, WE has been pursuing the goal of developing a free, open curriculum for all levels of education.

WE provides a free, open environment for the creation of educational content (learning objects, resources, presentations, etc). Being a wiki environment it caters for online collaborative production, including collaborative authoring and peer review. All content within WE is licensed under the creative commons 'Attribution-Share alike' license which allows users to copy, remix, distribute, and transmit content with the stipulations that they attribute the work to the source and that any modified versions of the content be relicensed using the same (or equivalent) attribution share-alike arrangement.

WE functions as a large, online community. Like other net-based user communities, member-users of WE are driven by a common interest, namely open education, which includes the development of a repository of open educational content. As such, much of the activity within the WE online environment is oriented toward individual and collaborative development of OERs. Working within a wiki infrastructure, the community has developed a set of tools which support the activities of the community, including the development of OERs. These tools include information on the background of OERs, tutorials on the use of wikis, templates for wiki content creation, and a large collection of exemplar OERs.

CASE DESCRIPTION

Overview

The case study presented in this chapter is based on *Instructional Design for E-learning*, a postgraduate course offered by the College of Education at Massey University. The course is part of the College's specialized Master of Education programs in Distance and Online Learning, Educational Technologies, and E-Learning. The program caters to in-service educators in a variety of sectors of education from pre-schooling/early years education, through all levels of schooling, post compulsory education, and lifelong and life-wide learning. Most learners in the program are situated in New Zealand, but a growing number are located in other countries.

The intent of the course is to provide learners with a foundational understanding of (a) instructional and learning design processes, (b) key views of learning and related pedagogical approaches, (c) the role and potential uses of technology to support learning, (d) familiarity with a range of contemporary learning technologies, and (e) hands-on experience with practical design work for e-learning situations.

The design of the course involves a balance of theoretical and practical work. The course includes three theory modules on the basics of instructional design, exploration of learning technologies, and issues related to design for e-learning. A key component of the course is the design project which requires learners to work in a design team with a particular design brief to produce a complete set of materials for a unit of work within a learning program. Fully one-third of the course is devoted to a practical design project which involves the creation of an OER on WE.

Course Delivery and Use of Technology

The course is offered via print supported online delivery. A small package of print materials is sent to each student at the start of the course, but the bulk of the materials are provided electronically in a combination of online environments including a learning management system, an electronic portfolio system, and the open wiki at WE. The main offering of the course exists in MasseyStream, a customized local version of Moodle supported by Massey University. A parallel form of the course is maintained in WE.

Learners are asked to work with a combination of resources, including electronic text, print materials, rich-media resources, and other material which they locate and bring to the course environment to complete learning tasks which structure the learning process for course participants. While the course designers acknowledge that learning takes place in a wide variety of settings, the communication and production tools housed in the online learning environment provide a venue for a combination of individual and collaborative learning activity.

Use of WikiEducator

WE is used in the course in two ways, both of which are forms of an OER. First, the course content exists on WE. Used in this way, WE is primarily a presentation tool. Enrolled students can visit the course content there as part of their work on the design project in WE. However, the course is freely available to all users for copying, distribution, modification, and reuse, under the 'Attribution Share-alike' creative commons license outlined above. Second, students use WE to create OERs as part of their design project. In this way, the wiki environment is deployed as a tool to create new OERs. Following the perceived advantages of using an open wiki described above, this use of WE allows students to engage in the creation of OERs in a very authentic way as part of the WE community. Students' learning activity is purposeful not only insofar as it meets the requirements of the course, but also in making a contribution to the growing collection of OERs which reside within WE. That learning is supported by background information which outlines the basic elements of the OER movement and the operation of WE as well as explicit tutorials which help students learn to use the wiki interface. Support is also provided in the form of exemplars within the site from other developers who are adding OERs on a regular basis.

Rationale for the Use of Technology in This Way

The decision to offer the course in parallel, with one version in the 'closed' learning management system and one version in the open wiki environment, was based on several considerations. The course teaching team recognized the advantages of offering the course as an OER in an open wiki. Chief among these was the desire to 'open' the course content and make a visible contribution to the OER movement. The WE environment seemed to provide a 'good fit' in terms of accessibility, membership in an open learning community, and the opportunity to contribute to a wider program of development. The flow on benefits for course participants were seen to include (a) introducing them to the use of open wikis as OERs, (b) engaging students in the activities of the WE community as proponents of the OER movement, and (c) providing an exemplar of an OER which linked the theoretical aspects of the course to the practical design project. Moreover, the technical functionality of WE seemed sufficient to support the sort of collaborative activity that was built into the course design. Each WE page includes layers which allow users to see the page as it exists, track the history of the page, discuss page content, including ongoing development, and work with source code (as needed) to modify the page.

However, the course teaching team also recognized the advantages provided by the use of a learning management system. Primary amongst these is that the MasseyStream online learning environment which exists within the learning management system is supported by the university. This support includes technical assistance in the form of maintenance of the environment and troubleshooting advice for technical problems. It also includes administrative support in the form of a single sign-on for all of the university's online support platforms, including the e-portfolio system, and each student's personalized access portal for the university's online services. This convenience was seen as a great benefit to online learners as it increased the ease of access to a range of university support services, including the online learning environment, e-portfolio, the library portal, and other support mechanisms. The online environment was also preferred because of the diversity of tools it contains. The various types of discussion forums, student blogs, wikis, messaging facilities, and a virtual classroom were seen as supportive of learning activity and were therefore considered indispensable. Moreover, as the learning management system is used by all online courses in the program, it is familiar to students in that program. This 'one-stop-shop' of integrated e-learning services was seen as too valuable not to be used for the variety of learning tasks included in the course design.

CURRENT CHALLENGES FACING THE ORGANIZATION

The use of WE in this course has revealed tensions between 'doing the right thing' and 'doing the job right'. The ideals of open education provide a motive for the development and use of OERs which is linked to long standing traditions of knowledge sharing in academic communities. However, the practicalities of using open wikis in general and WE in particular create potential conflicts between 'open' activities and existing notions of quality assurance – for example, institutional materials development processes, the use of existing authoritative texts which are held under proprietary license, and maintenance of quality in open collaborative communities. It is important for practitioners considering the use of open wikis to apply a critical eye to the application of open wikis in order to (a) understand the tensions between the benefits of openness and the need for quality, and (b) make informed decisions about any potential trade-offs between those agendas. These tensions are exemplified in this section in the discussion of two current challenges related to the use of WE as an OER in this case and based on the twin points of view highlighted throughout this chapter: the tension between an ethos of openness and the need for the use of authoritative texts which are held under proprietary license; and present limitations on realizing the potential of WE's collaborative learning environments,.

Open Courses, Closed Content

The first challenge emerging from the design and development of the course in WE was the tension between the perceived advantages of openness and the need for quality in course material which is related to the use of authoritative texts. The willingness of the course teaching team to make a meaningful contribution to the WE community combined with the opportunity to engage cohorts of postgraduate students with that community as part of an authentic learning design experience and the ability to create educational resources which were available not only to their creators but also to a much wider international education community provided a strong motive for the development of an open version of the course in WE. However, the designers of the course were immediately confronted with the creative commons 'Attribution, Share-alike' licensing of WE which precluded the use of authoritative texts which were protected by copyright and accessible to the institution via its copyright agreements with publishers. While the content generated by the course developers could be licensed under the creative commons licenses at the discretion of the developers, the third-party content including book chapters, journal articles, commercially sourced learning objects, and other proprietary content was essentially 'closed'. It could be distributed to students enrolled with the institution, but it could not be included in an 'open' environment for distribution, modification, or reuse.

For the course developers, this was an issue of quality in which three alternatives emerged. The first alternative was to remove the course content from WE and use the space primarily for learner activity in the development of OERs as part of their design project. While this option was seen to address the licensing conflict, it also mitigated some of the key motivators for using WE in the configuration of a postgraduate course in instructional design. The second alternative was to include only the course content that could be licensed under the creative commons scheme. This would allow the course to be included in WE as a 'whole', but there were questions of quality related to the use of authoritative texts as a key component of higher education. The course developers recognized that they could include a relatively higher proportion of open content in the course; however, this was a potentially labor intensive process of redevelopment which did not address the questions of quality. It was determined that the inclusion of only open content would compromise the quality of the course and increase the labor cost of redeveloping the course. The third alternative was to create two versions of the course: an 'open' version which included all parts of the course which could be distributed under the creative commons license; and a 'closed' version of the course which included materials held under proprietary copyright. This option preserved the motives for using WE and met the quality concerns of the development team with the trade-off of having to run the course in two parallel versions. In the end, this option was preferred as a 'best fit' which preserved the motives of the project and met the needs of students enrolled in the course.

Wikis as Collaborative Learning Environments

The second challenge in the use of wikis addressed here is the learning associated with being able to use the wiki environment. Wikis use a particular syntax which defines the formatting of a wiki page. While most users are familiar with word processing interfaces and similar 'what you see is what you get' (WYSIWYG) interfaces, wiki syntax requires users to understand a textual 'code' which relates to a set of formatting instructions. In WE, there is a simple WSIWYG interface for basic formatting, but the creation of more complex pages with special formatting requires users to invest time and energy in learning to use the WE environment. This particular need is not unique to WE. To some extent, a number of tools used in e-learning require a similar investment in learning to learn online. However, such investment cannot be discounted and must be considered in the use of the WE environment.

There are other issues related to online collaboration in a wiki. The use of wikis is primarily asynchronous. One user at a time edits the wiki and saves changes, and over time the resulting document evolves as it is built up, edited, rebuilt, and refined. However, for any author at any given time working in a collaborative authoring situation, it is not apparent at a glance what changes have been made within a document and who has made those changes. While WE (like many other wikis) tracks the history of a particular page or document, it is not possible to see a combination of (a) what changes have been made (relative to a previous version) and (b) who made those changes in a single view.

This poses multiple problems for learners in collaborative learning situations. First, the openness of the wiki environment as a virtual 'blank slate' can be confronting to learners who are accustomed to working within defined activity spaces. The experiences with wikis in the case in question indicate a need to consider the role of supportive structure (relative to 'freedom') in wiki-based writing projects. Given the importance of structure in online learning (Coomey & Stephenson, 2001), wiki-based writing activities will need to be considered carefully for the potential lack of structure in a 'blank' wiki page.

Second, the lack of identifiable collaborative partners may undermine users' ability to collaborate meaningfully. This relates to users' experiences of one another in a technology mediated environment and their abilities to relate to one another in a meaningful, productive way. Owing to a lack of attributions in their respective wiki contributions, collaborative authors are more-or-less anonymous to one another unless they communicate via another channel. Such effective anonymity may have negative effects on collaborative production. For example, even within a small group of collaborative authors, the meanings attributed to the writing of a particular contributor may be linked to that contributor's authority. A lack of attribution of particular contributions to particular (known) authors may affect the ability of collaborative authors to develop shared understandings based on the context provided by attributed authorship.

Furthermore, using only the page editing features, wiki authors are able to convey a very limited sense of online social presence and are not immediately accessible to one another for interaction. One likely result is limited interpersonal relations among the authors, which affects the quality of their collaboration. Without an evident connection, collaborative authors may struggle to achieve the intersubjective understandings which are part of intense, productive collaboration. These points provide a rationale for the inclusion of linked 'discussion' pages which accompany each wiki page. Learning designers seeking to incorporate wikis into their designs for collaborative writing activities must consider the relationship between the wikis as authoring environments and the discussion pages as discussion environments in order to provide a well-supported collaborative learning situation.

SOLUTIONS AND RECOMMENDATIONS

The preceding section of the chapter illustrated the use of open wiki technology at WE within the course from two different points of view. The first point of view, focused on using wikis as a presentation tool by the course teaching staff, highlighted the perceived advantages of this approach and the anticipated challenges faced by faculty in the use of open wikis. Discussion of this point of view also emphasized crucial issues for faculty in terms of their respective roles in teaching and administration. The second point of view, centered on using wikis as a collaborative production tool by learners, identified opportunities for enriching learning experience provided by the use of open wikis as well as the challenges faced by teaching staff in supporting learning in this environment. Particular issues canvassed included the addition of authenticity to learning and explicit support for collaborative activity provided by features of the technology, counterbalanced by technical constraints on the attainment of interpersonal relations and intersubjective understandings.

Solutions to these current challenges facing the organization are neither obvious nor immediate. Indeed, ongoing evolution of the technical aspects of WE is likely to address existing concerns about its collaborative learning potential (the second point of view and challenge) more quickly and comprehensively than are the systemic barriers constraining the 'open courses, closed content' conundrum (the first point of view and challenge) liable to amelioration. To understand why this is so, we need to examine the wider terrain in which contemporary higher education is situated.

In particular, as with individual learners and faculty members, so too higher education institutions occupy an ambivalent position and an unstable space. On the one hand, inter-institutional collaboration is officially encouraged and rhetorically praised, on the grounds of conserving resources and maximizing sustainability. This approach is underpinned by a view of knowledge as being socially constructed and by an understanding of learners as autonomous agents. On the other hand, the reality is that universities compete for students, and that collaboration in this context seems to produce losers as well as winner (see also Cardini, 2006). This situation is unlikely to change any time soon, given the continuing marketization of higher education provision as part of a broader neoliberal agenda by governments, certainly in Western countries (Danaher, Gale, & Erben, 2000). Furthermore, and as a consequence of that agenda, the social construction of knowledge and the status of learners as autonomous agents sit uneasily beside the entrenched privileging of individualized assessment of students' learning and practices such as the increased use of plagiarism detection software. Many of these contradictions are encapsulated in the notion of the "enterprise university" (Marginson & Considine, 2000), which alerts us to the multiple expectations of, and the competing pressures on, contemporary higher education institutions.

Viewed from this perspective, the use of WE as an OER in the course under review here can be seen as part of a wider commitment to expanding educational access and disrupting taken for granted assumptions about the relative roles and responsibilities of learners, faculty, and course designers and developers. At the same time, the larger forces identified above have the capacity to shape and constrain that commitment in ways that are not necessarily comfortable or welcome. As noted above, solutions to this conundrum will not be easy to conceptualize and implement.

For us, any such solutions must be directed foursquare at the broader terrain in which these contradictory forces are located. Our specific recommendations for doing that are concentrated on faculty and course designers and developers, with the hope and expectation that their actions will enlist the support of learners, university administrators, and ultimately government policy-makers. Accordingly we recommend that faculty and course designers and developers should:

- Continue to support the philosophy and practice underpinning such developments as wikis and creative commons licensing.
- Explore and exploit greater opportunities for cross-departmental and cross-institutional collaborations using these technologies.
- Highlight the pedagogical and social advantages of open courses, and the limitations and disadvantages of closed content, to learners and university administrators.
- Conduct and publish research evaluating the learning outcomes of WE and other wikis.
- Lobby government and other policy-makers to increase public support for these developments.

While we do not underestimate the size of the task confronting us, and while we recognize that some if not all of these recommendations might appear idealistic and even naïve, nevertheless we are convinced that it is only through concerted actions of these kinds that welcome initiatives like OERs can be nurtured and sustained. Our great fear is that unless this kind of support for OERs gains maximum momentum they are at risk of being subsumed and rendered futile by the neo-liberal agenda identified above. Such an outcome would have highly deleterious consequences for learners, teachers, universities, and ultimately humanity. This is the larger context framing this chapter's discussion of wikis, OERs, and efforts to overcome the challenges and realize the potential in extending the reach of digital technologies in contemporary higher education.

REFERENCES

Atkins, D. E., Brown, J. S., & Hammond, A. L. (2007). *Review of the open educational resources (OER) movement: Achievements, challenges and new opportunities*. Menlo Park, CA: William and Flora Hewitt Foundation.

Cardini, A. (2006). An analysis of the rhetoric and practice of educational partnerships in the UK: An arena of complexities, tensions and power. *Journal of Education Policy, 21*(4), 393–415. doi:10.1080/02680930600731773

Challborn, C., & Reimann, T. (2005, July). Wiki products: A comparison. *International Review of Research in Open and Distance Learning, 6*(2). Retrieved April 19, 2009, from http://www.irrodl.org/index.php/irrodl/article/view/229/859

Choy, S. O., & Ng, K. C. (2007). Implementing wiki software for supplementing online learning. *Australasian Journal of Educational Technology, 23*(2), 209-226. Retrieved April 19, 2009, from http://www.ascilite.org.au/ajet/ajet23/choy.html

Coomey, M., & Stephenson, J. (2001). Online learning: It is all about dialogue, involvement, support and control – according to the research. In Stephenson, J. (Ed.), *Teaching and learning online: Pedagogies for new technologies* (pp. 37–52). London: Kogan Page.

d'Antoni, S. (2009). Open educational resources: Reviewing initiatives and issues. *Open Learning: The Journal of Open and Distance Learning, 24*(1), 3–10. doi:10.1080/02680510802625443

Danaher, P. A., Gale, T. C., & Erben, T. (2000, April). The teacher educator as (re)negotiated professional: Critical incidents in steering between state and market in Australia. *Journal of Education for Teaching, 26*(1), 55–71. doi:10.1080/02607470050007138

Ferris, S. P., & Wilder, H. (2006, June/July). Uses and potentials of wikis in the classroom. *Journal of Online Education, 2*(5). Retrieved April 19, 2009, from http://www.innovateonline.info/index.php?view=article&id=258

Foley, B., & Chang, T. (2006). *Wiki as a professional development tool.* Paper presented at the annual conference of the American Educational Research Association, San Francisco, CA. Retrieved April 19, 2009, from http://www.csun.edu/~bfoley/AERA_Wiki.pdf

Johnstone, S. M. (2005). Open educational resources serve the world. *EDUCAUSE Quarterly, 3*(28), 15–18.

Kamel Boulos, M. N., Maramba, I., & Wheeler, S. (2006). Wikis, blogs and podcasts: A new generation of Web-based tools for virtual collaborative clinical practice and education. *BMC Medical Education, 6*(41). Retrieved April 19, 2009, from http://www.biomedcentral.com/1472-6920/6/41/

Lund, A., & Smørdal, O. (2006). Is there a space for the teacher in a WIKI? In *Proceedings of the 2006 international symposium on wikis* (pp. 7-46). Odense, Denmark. Retrieved April 19, 2009, from http://portal.acm.org/citation.cfm?id=1149453.1149466

Marginson, S., & Considine, M. (2000). *The enterprise university: Power, governance and reinvention in Australia.* Melbourne, Australia: Cambridge University Press.

O'Neill, B., Schuchardt, J., Pankow, D., Porter, N., Seiling, S., Branch, J., & Miller, J. (2007). eXtension: A high tech resource for improving financial security. *Consumer Interests Annual, 53.* Retrieved April 19, 2009, from http://cnr.consumerinterests.org/files/public/ONeill_eXtensionAHighTechResourceforImprovingFinancialSecurity.pdf

Pan, G., & Bonk, C. J. (2007, November). The emergence of open-source software in North America. *International Review of Research in Open and Distance Learning, 8*(3). Retrieved April 19, 2009, from http://www.irrodl.org/index.php/irrodl/article/view/496/950

Robertson, I. (2008). Learners' attitudes to wiki technology in problem based, blended learning for vocational teacher education. *Australasian Journal of Educational Technology, 24*(4), 425-441. Retrieved April 19, 2009, from http://www.ascilite.org.au/ajet/ajet24/robertson.html

Schwartz, L., Clark, S., Cossarin, M., & Rudolph, J. (2004, April). Educational wikis: Features and selection criteria. *International Review of Research in Open and Distance Learning, 5*(1). Retrieved April 19, 2009, from http://www.irrodl.org/index.php/irrodl/article/view/163/692

Thompson, C. (2008). Dialogism and social computing: Academic authorship in cyberspace. In J. McConachie, M. J. G. Singh, P. A. Danaher, F. Nouwens, & G. R. Danaher (Eds.), Changing university learning and teaching: Engaging and mobilising leadership, quality and technology (pp. 359-374). Teneriffe, Qld, Australia: Post Pressed.

Wheeler, S., Yeomans, P., & Wheeler, D. (2008, November). The good, the bad and the wiki: Evaluating student-generated content for collaborative learning. *British Journal of Educational Technology, 39*(6), 987–995. doi:10.1111/j.1467-8535.2007.00799.x

Wiley, D., & Gurrell, S. (2009, February). A decade of development.... *Open Learning: The Journal of Open and Distance Learning, 24*(1), 11–21. doi:10.1080/02680510802627746

FURTHER READING

Anderson, T. (2008, June 2). *Open educational resources plus social software: Threat or opportunity for Canadian higher education?* Paper presented at the annual conference of the Canadian Society for the Study of Higher Education, University of British Columbia, Vancouver, BC. Retrieved May 4, 2009, from http://auspace.athabascau.ca:8080/dspace/handle/2149/1609

Bissell, A. N. (2009, February). Permission granted: Open licensing for educational resources. *Open Learning: The Journal of Open and Distance Learning, 24*(1), 97–106. doi:10.1080/02680510802627886

Blackall, L. (2008, March). Open educational resources and practices. *TESL-EJ, 11*(4). Retrieved May 4, 2009, from http://tesl-ej.org/ej44/a8.html

Brown, J. S., & Adler, R. P. (2008, January-February). Minds on fire: Open education, the long tail, and Learning 2.0. *Educause Review, 43*(1). Retrieved May 4, 2009, from http://foruminnova.files.wordpress.com/2007/12/minds_on_fire.pdf

Carey, T., & Hanley, G. L. (2008). Extending the impact of open educational resources through alignment with pedagogical content knowledge and institutional strategy: Lessons learned from the MERLOT community experience. In Iiyoshi, T., & Kumar, M. S. V. (Eds.), *Opening up education: The collective advancement of education through open technology, open content, and open knowledge* (pp. 181–195). Cambridge, MA: Massachusetts Institute of Technology.

Caswell, T., Henson, S., Jensen, M., & Wiley, D. (2008, February). Open Educational Resources: Enabling universal education. *International Review of Research in Open and Distance Learning, 9*(1). Retrieved May 4, 2009, from http://www.irrodl.org/index.php/irrodl/article/viewArticle/469/1001

Downes, S. (2007). Models for sustainable Open Educational Resources. *Interdisciplinary Journal of Knowledge and Learning Objects, 3.* Retrieved May 4, 2009, from http://ijello.org/Volume3/IJKLOv3p029-044Downes.pdf

Geith, C., & Vignare, K. (2008). Access to education with online learning and open educational resources: Can they close the gap? *Journal of Asynchronous Learning Networks, 12*(1). Retrieved May 4, 2009, from http://www.distanceetdroitaleducation.org/contents/JALN_v12n1_Geith.pdf

Geser, G. (Ed.). (2007). *Open educational practices and resources: OLCOS Roadmap 2012.* Salzburg, Austria: Open eLearning Content Observatory Services. Retrieved May 4, 2009, from http://www.olcos.org/cms/upload/docs/olcos_roadmap.pdf

Gourley, B., & Lane, A. (2009, February). Reinvigorating openness at The Open University: The role of Open Educational Resources. *Open Learning: The Journal of Open and Distance Learning, 24*(1), 57–65. doi:10.1080/02680510802627845

Hylén, J. (2006). *Open Educational Resources: Opportunities and challenges.* Retrieved May 4, 2009, from http://www.oecd.org/dataoecd/5/47/37351085.pdf

Keats, D. (2009, February). The road to Free and Open Educational Resources at the University of the Western Cape: A personal and institutional journey. *Open Learning: The Journal of Open and Distance Learning, 24*(1), 47–55. doi:10.1080/02680510802627829

Lane, A. (2008). Widening participation in education through open educational resources. In Iiyoshi, T., & Kumar, M. S. V. (Eds.), *Opening up education: The collective advancement of education through open technology, open content, and open knowledge* (pp. 149–163). Cambridge, MA: Massachusetts Institute of Technology.

Larson, R. C., & Murray, M. E. (2008). Open Educational Resources for blended learning in high schools: Overcoming impediments in developing countries. *Journal of Asynchronous Learning Networks, 12*(1). Retrieved May 4, 2009, from http://www.distanceandaccesstoeducation.org/contents/JALN_v12n1_Larson.pdf

Mora, M. J. (2008, August). *Open Educational Resources: Motivations, governance, and content protection.* Unpublished Master of Applied Science in Technology Innovation Management thesis, Department of Systems and Computer Engineering, Carleton University, Ottawa, ON. Retrieved May 4, 2009, from http://learn.creativecommons.org/wp-content/uploads/2008/10/open-educational-resources-motivations-governance-and-content-protection.pdf

Okada, A., & Connolly, T. (2008). Designing Open Educational Resources through knowledge maps to enhance meaningful learning. *The International Journal of Learning, 15*(7), 209–220.

Parker, K. R., & Chao, J. T. (2007). Wiki as a teaching tool. *Interdisciplinary Journal of Knowledge and Learning Objects, 3*, 57-72. Retrieved May 4, 2009, from http://ijklo.org/Volume3/IJKLOv3p057-072Parker284.pdf

Pereira, M. (2007, November-December). Open educational resources: A bridge to education in the developing world. *Educational Technology Magazine: The Magazine for Managers of Change in Education, 47*(6), 41–43.

Petrides, L., Godwin, A., & Jimes, C. (2007). Building engagement, collaboration and context into open teaching and learning resources. In C. Montgomerie & J. Seale (Eds.), *Proceedings of world conference on educational multimedia, hypermedia and telecommunications 2007* (pp. 4358-4359). Chesapeake, VA: AACE. Retrieved May 4, 2009, from http://www.editlib.org/?fuseaction=Reader.ViewFullText&paper_id=26007

Petrides, L., & Jimes, C. (2008, May). Building open educational resources from the ground up: South Africa's free high school science texts. *Journal of Interactive Media in Education.* Retrieved May 4, 2009, from http://jime.open.ac.uk/2008/07/jime-2008-07.html

Petrides, L., Nguyen, L., Jimes, C., & Karaglani, A. (2008). Open educational resources: Inquiring into author use and reuse. *International Journal of Technology Enhanced Learning, 1*(1-2), 98–117. doi:10.1504/IJTEL.2008.020233

Raman, M., Ryan, T., & Olfman, L. (2005). Designing knowledge management systems for teaching and learning with wiki technology. *Journal of Information Systems Education, 16*(3), 311–320.

Stacey, P. (2007, April 2). Open educational resources in a global context. *First Monday, 12*(4). Retrieved May 4, 2009, from http://firstmonday.org/htbin/cgiwrap/bin/ojs/index.php/fm/article/view/1769/1649

Wiley, D. (2006). On the sustainability of open educational resource initiatives in higher education. Paper commissioned by the OECD's Centre for Educational Research and Innovation (CERI) for the project on Open Educational Resources. Retrieved May 4, 2009, from http://www.oecd.org/dataoecd/33/9/38645447.pdf

Wilson, T. (2008, February). New ways of mediating learning: Investigating the implications of adopting open educational resources for tertiary education at an institution in the United Kingdom as compared to one in South Africa. *International Review of Research in Open and Distance Learning, 9*(1). Retrieved May 4, 2009, from http://www.irrodl.org/index.php/irrodl/article/viewArticle/485/998

KEY TERMS AND DEFINITIONS

Creative Commons Licensing: A set of legal tools which allows authors and developers of creative works to retain certain rights to their work while allowing others to share, remix and use the work for other purposes.

Open Education: A flexible approach to teaching and learning which emphasizes freedom from barriers to the creation and use of particular resources.

Open Educational Resources (OERs): Freely available materials that can be shared, modified, adapted, and reused in diverse learning contexts.

Open Source Software: Software in which the programming code is accessible to any programmers who may wish to make modifications, additions, or improvements to the existing versions of the software.

Proprietary Licensing: An exclusive legal arrangement which reserves all rights associated with a product and its use to those who hold the license. This usually denotes a 'fee-for-use' arrangement in which users pay to gain access to a particular product or service.

Wiki: A piece of software which allows users to create and edit web-based content (i.e. 'web pages'). Access to wikis is generally 'open' which allows for collaborative authoring to take place online.

APPENDIX: SUPPORTING MATERIAL

Abstract

Open wikis lie at the intersection of two significant applications of learning technology: open educational resources (OERs), which are freely available materials that can be shared, modified, adapted, and reused in diverse learning contexts; and collaborative authoring environments. The case discussion includes an illustration of the use of open wiki technology at WikiEducator within the course from two different points of view: the use of wikis as a presentation tool by the course teaching staff; and as a production tool by learners seeking to create OERs as part of an instructional design project.

Questions and Answers

1. What is the overall problem in this case?

The central problem in this case is the application of WikiEducator as an OER in the context of a postgraduate course. This problem involves consideration of a range of tensions between 'open' and 'closed' approaches to education and the potential role of digital technologies to help facilitate productive responses to those tensions.

2. What organizational issues affected the use of OERs in the case?

Three main types of organizational issues were described. One is the tension between 'open' learning and 'closed' resources. A second is the tension between established systems of providing learning support which are 'closed' and the desire for openness via participation in open educational communities. A third is the general tension between 'doing the right thing' and 'doing the job right' which is part of development in education which leads to innovations which provide improvements in one area whilst potentially sacrificing quality in another area.

3. What issues related to students' use of OERs emerged from the case?

Students were affected by the use of the open wiki as a presentation tool and as a collaborative environment. The use of wikis as a presentation tool was limited owing to the provision of a parallel 'closed' learning management system which housed a suite of online learning tools. The use of wikis as a collaborative environment highlighted the need for thoughtful use of the wiki environment to support not just the act of online authoring, but also the related interpersonal interaction and associated meaning making.

4. How does the case inform the ongoing use of open wikis in formal education?

Generally, the case highlights tensions between 'open' education and more established, formal, 'closed' processes which are in place in educational institutions such as the university in question. More particularly, the case highlights the issues of open licensing in educational materials development, the conflict between proprietary publication and open education, potential limits of wikis as 'online learning environments', and specific issues related to online collaboration in a wiki environment.

Epilogue and Lessons Learned

The case of WE as an OER illustrates both the potentials of more open approaches to education via OERs and open licensing and the tensions between status quo approaches to higher education and the development of more inclusive, wider reaching alternatives. More particularly:

WE is a potentially powerful open resource which may provide benefit to many, but must continue to be used in a carefully thought out way to maximize benefits for users and inform the ongoing development of understandings of its use. Clearly, the use of open wikis such as WE is not entirely straightforward. The best intentions of practitioners to promote open learning do not mitigate the reality that OERs are a new idea that are not well understood at either operational or institutional levels. Designers and developers must carefully consider the use of open wikis in a purposeful way which is supported by a range of other technologies and/or tools.

Institutions must interrogate their own practices to identify ways in which the tools of open education can be used to benefit both the institutions themselves and the wider communities they serve. The case in point begins to illustrate the tensions between the market-driven competition which motivates 'closed' institutional approaches and the more open approaches which provide benefit to a wider community via the sharing of knowledge. Either position can be supported but neither position can be supported at the exclusion of the other. The 'middle ground' is a broad terrain. Institutions much work hard to strike a balance between sustainability and indeed survival on the one hand and maximizing the benefits of their activity on the other.

Individual course designers, developers, and teachers must continue to innovate, to record their innovations, and to catalogue the results so that there is an evidence base for informing ongoing development in the use of open wikis, OERs, and other tools of open education. While the case in question may be considered a marginal success in introducing 'openness' to a previously closed postgraduate course, it is clearly not an overall success in creating a fully functional open postgraduate course. Further development, informed by a growing body of evidence to support good practice, is needed.

Chapter 6
Doctoral Faculty 2020:
Preparing for the Future in Organizational Leadership

Peter E. Williams
University of La Verne, USA

L. Hyatt
University of La Verne, USA

ABSTRACT

Leaders are in demand and leadership institutions are necessary to prepare students for important roles in our society (Green, Alexander, & Boryczka, 2001). Faculty are a central factor in graduate and post-graduate programs as they are responsible for guiding student learning (Bryant, 2003). This case reports on an exploratory case study of 21st century competencies for faculty in an organizational leadership doctoral program. Esteemed researchers have conducted studies regarding transitioning students to become new faculty (e.g. Austin, 2002; Austin, Connolly, & Colbeck, 2008; Gardner, 2005; Purcell 2007); however, little research exists specific to the new-century skills necessary for doctoral faculty in leadership programs. As the surge in technology continues to bring about global changes, preparing potential leaders is our best hope going forward. It follows then, that it is important to discover the competencies doctoral faculty will need in order to address the challenges of the future.

BACKGROUND

U.S. Doctoral Education

By the mid-1800s higher education institutions in America had begun to recognize a need for further intellectual preparation (Storr, 1969). Rather than representing the "completion of formal study," as was its original intent, undergraduate degrees became known as a "first degree of academic life" (p. 1). Even though these degrees provided students with sufficient general knowledge about certain fields e.g. philosophy, religion, mathematics, and social and physical sciences, Storr states that students "...did not necessarily love good literature, recognize their own special talents, or command any profound knowledge of things outside the limits of conventional learning" (p. 2).

Although undergraduate level institutions provided new materials for students, they rarely

DOI: 10.4018/978-1-61520-869-2.ch006

treated subjects thoroughly. Storr (1969) notes that the professors did not necessarily leave lasting impressions with students, and coverage of materials offered only occasional opportunities for student dialogue and debate. The need for universities to offer more than undergraduate studies and preparation for specific areas, such as medicine and law, inevitably gave rise to the graduate school.

In 1861, Yale University awarded the first U.S. doctorates. It took another decade for the University of Pennsylvania and Harvard University to begin conferring doctorates. In addition to acknowledging a need for graduate and post graduate education, there were additional events that drove an increase in doctoral education in America. The two Morrill Land Grant Acts, the first in 1862, provided land for states to establish colleges to meet the new industrial needs of society. The second Morrill Land Grant Act in 1890 led to the development of colleges in response to segregation resulting in historically black colleges and universities (HBCUs). While the Morrill Land Grant Acts were growing the number of public higher education institutions, there was also an increase in the number of private colleges and universities forming (e.g.: Johns Hopkins University, 1876; Stanford University, 1891; University of Chicago, 1892) and/or reorganizing (e.g.: Columbia and Harvard) to offer graduate education. Although the U.S. model of doctoral education was established by the late 1880s and early 1900s, large numbers of American students were still drawn to European institutions especially those in Germany. This was attributed to a lack of regulations and accountability, and a perceived inconsistency in the quality of U.S. colleges and universities (Speicher, 2000).

To stem the tide of the student exodus, 14 leading U.S. doctoral-granting institutions sent representatives to a conference in January, 1900 at the University of Chicago. This resulted in the formation of the Association of American Universities (AAU). The founding AAU member institutions are listed in Figure one.

During the 1930s, 1940s, and 1950s U.S. graduate and post graduate education grew steadily. The federal government increasingly looked to universities for research in technology and policy in the New Deal era of the 1930s. The emphasis on research continued producing alliances with such federal government agencies as the National Institutes of Health (NIH) in 1946, The Office of Naval Research (ONR) 1949, and the National Science Foundation (NSF) in 1950 (Geiger, 1993). A significant driver of U.S. graduate and post graduate education came from another European event. The Soviet Union's launching of the Sputnik satellite in 1957 resulted in another growth spurt in institutions granting doctorates. Research and development spending tripled between 1957 and 1970 and higher education more than doubled rising from three million to seven million (Thurgood, Golladay, & Hill, 2006).

Steady but slowed growth characterized the 1980s and most of the 1990s. However, at the beginning of the 21st century, in 2003, the successful plotting of the human genome fostered renewed interest in universities and research. Currently, university research attentions are fo-

Table 1. Colleges and universities at the 1900 AAU meeting (AAU, 2003)

Catholic University of America	Johns Hopkins University	University of Michigan
Clark University	Princeton University	University of Pennsylvania
Columbia University	Stanford University	University of Wisconsin-Madison
Cornell University	University of California-Berkeley	Yale University
Harvard University	University of Chicago	

cused on new technologies that increase mobility, stem-cell research, organ farming, cognitive and neuro-processes, understanding the complexities of human behaviors such as leadership, and robotics, etc. By 1900 fewer than 20 universities conferred about 250 doctorates (Thurgood, Golladay, & Hill, 2006). At the start of the 21st century 426 higher education institutions in the U.S. had awarded approximately 1.4 million doctorates.

The U.S. doctorate is conceptualized as education arranged around rigorous real-world research experiences that prepares students to "discover, integrate, and apply knowledge, as well as communicate and disseminate it" (CGS, 1990, p.1).

Graduate education began to fill the void in U.S. universities and was aimed at "bringing the student to an understanding of the conceptual structure of his field at the frontier, and research that is aimed to push the frontier a little further" (Rees, 1972, p. 144). The mastery of certain disciplines allowed the expansion of research within those areas in an organized manner. Explaining the necessity of graduate schools, Rees posits that:

The thrill of intellectual discovery, of insight into the mysteries of antiquity, of understanding of the motives and lives of those who made our civilization; the excitement that human beings can find from looking into the physical and biological universe and into the world of human creations are still a part of significant human experience. The graduate schools are needed to sustain and enhance their significance. But so also are the applications of our competencies to better social solutions, to the betterment of lives in our own country and abroad. To find a better way is the task that lies ahead. (p. 144)

The creation of specific graduate programs would then increase the competencies of the student and appropriately prepare them for a society waiting for leaders that will guide them towards a better world.

Doctoral Leadership Programs

The historical importance of graduate and post graduate education serves as a backdrop for this study. According to Green, Alexander, and Boryczka (2001), these leadership institutions are necessary, as charisma and interpersonal skills are insufficient to meet the needs of large organizations. Universities that specialize in doctoral leadership education allow students to "...increase their personal mastery and self-awareness, improve their interpersonal communication skills, and learn to influence people" (p. 69). The products of leadership study show a direct correlation to the original intention of the graduate institution: to take material presented in the classroom and appropriately present it to the outside world (Rees, 1972). Since doctoral degree programs in leadership are evolving rapidly (Crawford, Brungardt, Scott, & Gould, 2002), it is necessary to explore the issues that will drive the changing competencies necessary for doctoral leadership program faculty in the next decade.

Doctoral programs in leadership prepare students for a variety of venues including higher education, government, K-12 school administration, for profit and nonprofit organizations. Faculty play a significant role in the quality and value of doctoral education. The faculty in leadership programs will have to address the changes we are beginning to see today in society and those we envisage in the coming decades.

Recent studies have focused on preparing current students or new faculty in areas other than leadership (e.g. Austin, 2002; Gilis, Clement, Laga, & Pauwels, 2008). In addition, Purcell (2007) studied senior faculty perceptions about preparing new faculty in biological sciences, English, mathematics, and non-clinical psychology. Austin and McDaniels (2006) used Boyer's (1990) four types of scholarship to look at graduate programs in general as preparation for future faculty. Tigelaar, Dolmans, Wolfhagen, and Van (2004) developed a framework of teaching competencies for faculty in higher education for purposes of evaluation. There is a paucity of literature specifically focused on organization leadership doctoral faculty.

Doctoral faculty in leadership programs are expected to continuously increase their proficiencies for instruction, scholarship and praxis. Advances in technologies, increased cultural diversity, geographically distributed students, and abundant and immediate access to information are just some of the factors influencing the changing doctoral landscape. This changing landscape prompted the authors to investigate 21st century competencies for faculty in an organizational leadership doctoral program.

Doctoral Faculty Issues and Competencies

If faculty in leadership programs are expected to continuously enhance their skills, how do they determine which proficiencies, or competencies, are needed? The challenge of staying relevant in a rapidly changing society can be formidable, particularly when the societal changes are unclear. It is important for faculty to identify the issues. Well documented advances in technologies offering copious data with 24/7 access and communications regardless of location are just some of the issues influencing the changing doctoral landscape.

There have been a number of competency studies over the last eighty years: Lindeman (1938) focused on adult learning, and Knowles (1962) studied the competencies of doctoral candidates. In the field of human resource development, competency studies are a common approach to defining roles and necessary skills within organizations (Nadler, 1968; Pinto & Walker, 1978; McLagan & McCullough, 1983; Foshay, Silber, & Westgaard, 1986; Stein & Hutchison, 1988; McLagan & Suhadolnik, 1989; Hale, 1989; Rothwell & Cookson, 1997; Piskurich & Sanders, 1998). In colleges and universities, faculty development has taken on renewed importance at least since Boyer's "Scholarship Reconsidered" (1990), and as a result, competencies have received considerable attention (e.g. Andenoro, 2005; Austin, 2002; Austin, Connolly, & Colbeck, 2008). More specific to technology-mediated learning in higher education, and including roles beyond those of faculty, Thach (1994) and Williams (2003) identified competencies for distance education programs in higher education.

CASE DESCRIPTION

This exploratory case study was conducted using research methods that included a comprehensive literature review and interviews of organizational leadership doctoral faculty. Content analysis followed to identify emerging themes. Case studies allow for deeper discovery about a specific situation and emphasize contextual analyses of events or related conditions. Yin (1984) defines the case study research method as "an empirical inquiry that investigates a contemporary phenomenon within its real-life context; when the boundaries between phenomenon and context are not clearly evident; and in which multiple sources of evidence are used" (p. 23). There is little literature specific to competencies of doctoral faculty who teach in leadership programs. Therefore, an exploratory case study was an appropriate method for initial discovery.

The chapter authors employed five steps generally suggested by case study methods experts (e.g. Stake, 1995; Yin, 1984).

1. Define the central research question
2. Select the case and data collection and analysis techniques
3. Gather data
4. Analyze data
5. Report results

The central research question was: *What competencies will be necessary for doctoral faculty in leadership programs to meet the challenges of the next decade?*

Study Site and Sample Population

Following Institutional Review Board approval and site permission, the authors selected Very Good University (VGU) as the site for the case study (Hyatt & Goor, 2009). VGU was established in the 1890s and is a doctoral granting university. This private, non-profit, regionally accredited institution grants bachelors, masters, and doctoral degrees and serves a diverse student population of approximately 8000. It is located in a small community within 40 miles of an urban metropolis in California surrounded by a concentration of private and public universities. The doctoral leadership program was developed over 30 years ago, continues to innovate, and is recognized as a leading program in the state. The sample consisted of 10 participants (*N*= 10) who met the following criteria established for inclusion in the study:

1. Faculty who have an earned doctorate;
2. Persons who are designated as faculty in a leadership doctoral program at a regionally accredited university;
3. Persons who have been faculty in a leadership doctoral program for at least one year.

The doctoral faculty in the leadership program represented the sample population for this case study with 10 voluntarily agreeing to participate.

Data Collection and Analysis Techniques

Data collection began with a review of the literature, followed by the development of an interview instrument. The interview instrument consisted of demographic questions and semi-structured interview questions. The semi-structured questions queried participants first about issues, trends, and challenges that will impact doctoral faculty in leadership programs as they function in various expected roles in the next 10 years. The next set of questions asked participants to identify skills and competencies that doctoral faculty will need to function in the roles of teaching, advising, faculty scholarship (researcher), university service, and colleague. The interview instrument was reviewed by a panel of three experts all of whom had a doctorate degree and served as faculty in a leadership doctoral program in various institutions other than VGU. The panel of experts came to consensus that the interview questions would yield data to inform the central research question.

Interviews were conducted by the researchers, transcribed, and analyzed for prominent themes and patterns. Content analysis was employed using reduction (searching for all possible themes and meanings); horizontalization (individual statements lead to the creation of meaning units followed by clustering the meanings); textual description (what was experienced); and structural descriptions (how it was experienced) (Miles & Huberman, 1994). A second rater provided inter-rater reliability with resultant themes discussed and agreed upon for clarity and reliability (Patton, 2001). Results are displayed textually in the subsequent section.

RESULTS: ISSUES AND CURRENT CHALLENGES

Issues

Faculty members were asked two questions: (1) What issues, trends, and challenges will impact doctoral faculty in leadership programs as they function in various expected roles in the next 10 years; and (2) Given the issues you have mentioned, what competencies will doctoral faculty need to function in their differing roles? The following issues and related competencies were common themes arising from their responses to these two semi-structured questions.

Globalization: cultures coming into contact with each other, was identified as a trend that will increasingly impact organizations and consequently leadership programs. One participant stated it this way:

Students are diversifying in age, experience, cultures... A wonderful trend. Globalization is what/ who we are. This trend will grow. The idea that we'll run everyone through the same experience to get the same outcome is an archaic notion and simply wrong. (Participant 1, personal communication, 2009)

Along with identifying globalization as an issue, subjects also recognized that knowledge of global trends was an important competency.

Another issue identified by faculty that is closely related to globalization, and partially a result of the increased contact among cultures, is the greater diversity of students, or as one participant put it, "we have a richer stakeholder pool"(Participant 5, personal communication, 2009). Faculty identified the need to recognize that students are coming increasingly from other cultures, languages, and generations. Another aspect contributing to diversity is that students in the leadership program are coming from many types of organizations, from non-profits, corporations, higher education institutions, government agencies and K-12 schools. The diversity of settings is also recognized in the literature as an issue already effecting academic programs in general and likely to increase in the future (Austin 2002; Keller 2001; Syverson, 1996).

As a result of the increasing diversity among students in leadership doctorate programs, the faculty in this study recognized that they must have or develop competencies such as being able to communicate and engage different generations of learners, ability to accept and value others, and the ability to work with diverse groups of people.

New technologies: The rise of online learning and other technologies involved in planning, teaching, and accessing library and information resources was identified by the faculty in this study as an issue that would continue to impact the doctoral leadership program. One aspect of the rise of new technologies, particularly the internet and the increased bandwidth available throughout communities, is that faculty are increasingly expected to use technologies to teach (Austin 2002).

Closely related to the rise of new technologies is the issue of abundance of accessible information. Hyatt, Evans, and Haque (2009) coined the term "knowledge velocity" to describe the phenomenon, explaining, "The availability of global information on-demand has created the phenomenon of knowledge velocity. Abundance, speed, and complexity will create a paradigm shift from parsimonious information management to munificence through knowledge sharing" (p. 120). These issues are intertwined with more user friendly and robust communications technologies allowing people to have access to a wider range of information than ever before: text, images, video, audio, data, and scholarly publications to name a few types of information. Often this information is available the moment it is published, so it is timelier than traditional publication modes. The implications for a doctoral leadership program are at least partially captured by one participant who stated:

Today it is more important to teach processes than facts. Information is doubling every 18 months or so. Within a career, from the time the student enters school, information has increased over 100,000 times, so learning facts isn't as important as learning processes.... Our programs have to become developmental to prepare students to develop over time ... we have to develop them as much as we can within the program and prepare them to continue to develop after they leave the program; this means continually developing new skills and competencies rather than to just keep learning more facts. (Participant 10, personal communication, 2009)

The communications technologies and the access they provide to massive amounts of information fuel a sense of constant change, another issue identified by the faculty. The participants expressed concern over keeping programs updated in face of rapid change is significant. The perception is that societal and organizational change is happening fast, so the leadership program must have a dynamic process for staying current and being innovative even while maintaining quality and compliance with standards that may be more reflective of the past than the future.

In this context of new technologies, abundant and accessible information, and the perception of rapid societal change, the faculty participants suggested that the following competencies will be necessary:

- Use appropriate technologies to deliver instruction, to facilitate research and collaboration
- Teach using blended environments that have online and face-to-face events. This implies making good decisions about what instructional activities to do online, what to do face-to-face, what to do in an asynchronous environment such as a learning management system and what to do in a synchronous setting such as a web conference (using a tools such as Acrobat Connect, Elluminate, WebEx, etc.)
- Pedagogical understanding is required to make good decisions in blended environments; decisions that are learner centered.
- Ability to be innovative and adaptive in an academic program that could be constantly changing to meet the needs of a dynamic society with ever-changing organizations.

Changing nature of organizations and leadership: Organizations and leadership within organizations are changing, including hierarchies, communication patterns, and ways of sharing information, for example. A participant stated:

There are shifts in organizations -- structural shifts and the way they function. So we as faculty if we are to represent organizations broadly, we'll have to work diligently to stay current with what's going on in organizations. Dying out are the traditional hierarchical structures, replaced by different structures with different communication patterns. Not so much command and control now. (Participant 8, personal communication, 2009)

Not only are organizational structures becoming more diverse, recent events have led to more oversight and scrutiny of organizations in many sectors, resulting, in some cases, in reduced resources and increased accountability.

To deal with the changing nature of organizations and with what is perceived as diminishing resources coupled with increasing accountability, the faculty suggested several competencies:

- Faculty scholarship that results in peer reviewed publications. As VGU emphasizes faculty research, the faculty themselves feel the dynamics of a changing organization and gain firsthand experience with the challenges involved.
- Experience with variety of organizational types to gain knowledge of the rapidly changing dynamics in different industry sectors.
- Awareness of organizational trends and challenges.
- Ability to be innovative and adaptive in dealing constructively with rapid change.
- Within this changing environment, the ability to be supportive of the organizational mission (for faculty, the university mission) and the program goals and values.

Unprepared students: Increased number of students that lack basic skills and experience including limited English skills and limited ability to read critically, analyze, synthesize and write. As one participant explained, "Incoming students have less and less experience, because they are younger. The average age of doctoral students has dropped. This represents a huge difference in amount of experience they bring to the program" (Participant 6, personal communication, 2009).

While it isn't part of this study to determine whether or not this trend is increasing, the fact that it was mentioned by several participants is important. As the student body becomes more diverse, it is likely that there will be a wider range of skills beyond those traditionally valued academically. With high expectations for reading and writing required in a doctoral program, the sense of students being less prepared may be not only a challenge but also a source of frustration for students and faculty. In response to the question about faculty competencies, subjects gave the following suggestions which are directly related to assisting students who may not be prepared for doctoral level academic work:

- Be able to guide students to produce quality written work
- Be available to students
- Have effective coaching techniques

The competencies and issues identified here will assist faculty to create relevant professional development plans to meet future challenges.

Current Challenges

In this environment, the challenges of maintaining a quality doctoral leadership program are apparent, flowing directly from the issues mentioned in the interviews. The challenges for this particular program, and perhaps for many others, are as follows.

1. A one-size-fits-all set of curricular experiences may not be appropriate for developing leaders for organizations that will be operating in an increasingly global society. Properly deployed technologies could help address the individualization needed to deliver curricular experiences and track student progress.
2. The increasing diversity of the student body will require a rethinking of student support services to address their widely varying strengths and needs.
3. In a rapidly changing technology landscape, it is a challenge to achieve deployment of learning technologies that is driven by program goals, learner needs, and faculty usability. This challenge is being addressed in some faculty support services now offered that focus on how to improve teaching in a technology enriched learning environment as opposed to training that focuses on how to use the technology (Andenoro 2005).
4. Furthermore, the fragmentation of faculty responsibilities, as noted by various authors (Austin & McDaniels, 2006; Austin, 2002; Boyer, 1990), poses the question, of how to deploy technological systems that help faculty integrate and document the different aspects of their work: research (or discovery), teaching, application, and integration.
5. The changing nature of organizations and leadership requires that faculty in the doctoral leadership program keep a "finger in the pool" (Participant 2, personal communication, 2009) to maintain program viability. This requires multiple communication channels be available and that faculty have the tools and skills to collaborate with external organizations. These tools might include audio and web conferencing tools and other technologies used to communicate, collaborate, manage projects, share documents, and work on teams.
6. Closely related is the challenge of providing students in the doctoral leadership program with applied experiences, including technology use, which will help them be more effective leaders. Faculty members have to be able to model proper use of technology to support organizational change, decision making, and communications.

7. Supporting students that come to the program with disparate educational and professional backgrounds presents several challenges. Primarily, the challenges revolve around creating a supportive environment in which students can access help in various areas related to academic achievement: writing, research, study skills, technology use, communications, career services, advisement and counseling, and others. These services are typically available to campus based students, but the doctoral leadership program students at VGU, like many doctoral and other graduate programs, are mainly employed elsewhere, commute to campus for courses, and therefore may need to be able to access such services at different hours and from different locations.

SOLUTIONS AND RECOMMENDATIONS

Solutions

Findings from this study add to the current knowledge in the field of leadership programs. New technologies and sweeping global changes will impact universities with doctoral programs in organizational leadership consequently affecting hundreds of faculty who teach in these programs. In addition, doctoral program administrators and the institutions they serve will find this information useful as they plan for the future. Researchers can use this exploratory research to inform further efforts to identify competencies and issues for faculty of the future.

Recommendations

The following recommendations may be applicable for doctoral leadership programs:

1. Establish an environmental scanning work group that consists of faculty and administration who are innovators, who enjoy evaluating new technologies and practices to improve instruction and support for faculty and students. The work group (or a similar one) should also monitor changes in the nature of organizations, their use of information and communications technologies, and the impact of globalization.
2. Further study and exploration will be needed to understand how information and communication systems can support what Boyer calls the scholarship of integration – the making of connections across disciplines and organizations to inform and enhance research and practice.
3. Provide faculty and student development opportunities on how to use technology to improve instruction.
4. Exploit social networking in virtual environments to augment learning and encourage community.
5. Routinely evaluate needs and provide student support relative to a variety of services that are accessible to adult learners in doctoral leadership programs.

REFERENCES

Andenoro, A. C. (2005). *Competencies of leadership professionals: A national study of premier leadership degree programs*. Ph.D. dissertation, Texas A&M University, United States—Texas. Retrieved April 25, 2009, from Dissertations & Theses: Full Text database. (Publication No. AAT 3246442).

Association of American Universities (AAU). (2003). *The letter of invitation to the founding conference of AAU.* Retrieved on May, 10 2009 from: http://www.aau.edu/aau/Invit.html

Austin, A. E. (2002). Preparing the next generation of faculty. *The Journal of Higher Education, 73*(1), 94–122. doi:10.1353/jhe.2002.0001

Austin, A. E., Connolly, M. R., & Colbeck, C. L. (2008). Strategies for preparing integrated faculty: The center for the integration of research, teaching, and learning. *New Directions for Teaching and Learning*, (113): 69–81. doi:10.1002/tl.309

Austin, A. E., & McDaniels, M. (2006). Using doctoral education to prepare faculty to work within Boyer's four domains of scholarship. *New Directions for Institutional Research*, (129): 51–65. doi:10.1002/ir.171

Bernthal, J. E. (2001). Strategies to recruit and retain doctoral-level teacher-scholars. *ASHA Leader, 6*(12), 35. Boyer [*Scholarship reconsidered: Priorities of the professoriate*. Princeton, NJ: Carnegie Foundation for the Advancement of Teaching.]. *E (Norwalk, Conn.), L*, 1990.

BizEd. (2003). *Doctoral crisis looms, says commission, 3*(1), 8.

Boyer, E. L. (1990). *Scholarship reconsidered: Priorities of the professoriate*. Princeton, NJ: Carnegie Foundation for the Advancement of Teaching.

Bryant, M. T. (2003). *The portable dissertation advisor*. Thousand Oaks, CA: Corwin Press.

Council of Graduate Schools (CGS). (1990). The doctor of philosophy degree: A policy statement. Washington, DC.

Crawford, C. B., Brungardt, C. L., Scott, R. F., & Gould, L. V. (2002). Graduate programs in organizational leadership: A review of programs, costs and delivery methods. *The Journal of Leadership Studies, 8*(4), 64–74. doi:10.1177/107179190200800406

Fabian, C. A. (2006). A five-year analysis of university initiatives to increase faculty engagement. *Journal of Computing in Higher Education, 17*(2), 3–24. doi:10.1007/BF03032696

Foshay, W., Silber, K., & Westgaard, O. (1986). *Instructional design competencies: The standards*. Iowa City, IA: The International Board of Standards for Training, Performance and Instruction.

Gardner, S. K. (2005). Faculty preparation for teaching, research, and service roles: What do new faculty need? *Journal of Faculty Development, 20*(3), 161–166.

Geiger, R. L. (1986). *To advance knowledge: The growth of American research universities, 1900–1940*. New York: Oxford University Press.

Gilis, A., Clement, M., Laga, L., & Pauwels, P. (2008). Establishing a competence profile for the role of student-centered teachers in higher education in Belgium. *Research in Higher Education, 49*(6), 531–554. doi:10.1007/s11162-008-9086-7

Green, M. T., Alexander, J., & Boryczka, R. (2001). Developing an interdisciplinary doctoral program in leadership studies. In Outcalt, C. L., Faris, S. K., & Mc Mahon, K. N. (Eds.), *Developing non-hierarchical leadership on campus: Case studies and best practices in higher education* (pp. 225–237). Westport, CT: Greenwood Press.

Hale, J. (1989). *Training manager competencies: The standards*. Batavia, IL: The International Board of Standards for Training, Performance & Instruction.

Hyatt, L. Evans, L., & Haque, Md. (2009). Leading across cultures: Designing a learning agenda for global praxis. In M. A. Moodian (Ed.), Contemporary leadership and intercultural competence. Thousand Oaks, CA: Sage Publications.

Hyatt, L., & Goor, M. B. (2009, April). *Creating a faculty research culture: The times are a-changing*. American Educational Research Association (AERA) 2009 Annual Meeting: Disciplined Inquiry: Education Research in the Circle of Knowledge. San Diego, CA.

Irby, B., & Lunenburg, F. (2007, October 12). Doctoral Program Issues: Accreditation of Programs. Retrieved from the Connexions Web site: http://cnx.org/content/m14599/1.3/

Keller, G. (2001). The new demographics of higher education. *Review of Higher Education, 24*, 219–235. doi:10.1353/rhe.2001.0004

Knowles, J. (1962). A general theory of the doctorate in education. *Adult Education Quarterly, 12*(3). doi:10.1177/074171366201200302

Lindeman, E. (1938). Preparing leaders in adult education. In Dixon, N. & Henkelman, J. (Eds.), (1991). Models for HRD practice: The academic guide. Alexandria, VA: American Society for Training and Development.

McLagan, P., & McCullough, R. (1983). *Models for excellence: The conclusions and recommendations of the ASTD training and development competency study*. Alexandria, VA: The American Society for Training and Development.

McLagan, P., & Suhadolnik, D. (1989). *Models for HRD practice: The research report*. Alexandria, VA: American Society for Training & Development.

Miles, M., & Huberman, M. (1984). *Qualitative data analysis: A source book for new methods*. Thousand Oaks, CA: Sage Publications.

Nadler, L. (1968). A study of the needs of selected training directors in Pennsylvania which might be met by professional education institutions. (Doctoral dissertation, Columbia University, 1962). *Dissertation Abstracts International, 24*(2) 601.

Patton, M. Q. (2001). *Qualitative research and evaluation methods* (3rd ed.). Thousand Oaks, CA: Sage.

Perry, J. A., & Imig, D. G. (2008). A stewardship of practice in education. *Change, 40*(6), 42–49. doi:10.3200/CHNG.40.6.42-49

Pinto, P., & Walker, J. (1978). *A study of professional training and development roles and competencies*. Alexandria, VA: American Society for Training and Development.

Piskurich, G., & Sanders, E. (1998). *ASTD models for learning technologies: Roles, competencies, and outputs*. Alexandria, VA: American Society for Training & Development.

Purcell, J. M. (2007). *Perceptions of senior faculty concerning doctoral student preparation for faculty roles*. Ph.D. dissertation, University of South Florida, United States– Florida. Retrieved February 14, 2009, from Dissertations & Theses: Full Text database. (Publication No. AAT 3306885).

Rees, M. (1972). Graduate education – a long look. In Kent, L. J., & Springer, G. P. (Eds.), *Graduate education today and tomorrow* (pp. 139–151). Albuquerque, NM: University of New Mexico Press.

Rifkin, T. (1995). ERIC review: Faculty evaluation in community colleges. *Community College Review, 23*(1), 63. doi:10.1177/009155219502300107

Rothwell, W., & Cookson, P. (1997). *Beyond instruction: Comprehensive program planning for business and education*. San Francisco: Jossey-Bass.

Ryan, M., Carlton, K. H., & Ali, N. S. (2004). Reflections on the role of faculty in distance learning and changing pedagogies. *Nursing Education Perspectives, 25*(2), 73–80.

Santilli, S., & Beck, V. (2005). Graduate faculty perceptions of online teaching. *Quarterly Review of Distance Education*, *6*(2), 155–160.

Smith, K. S., & Simpson, R. D. (1995). Validating teaching competencies for faculty members in higher education: A national study using. *Innovative Higher Education*, *19*(3), 223. doi:10.1007/BF01191221

Speicher, A. L. (2000). The association of American universities: A century of service to higher education. Retrieved on May 1, 2009, from: http://www.aau.edu/

Stake, R. E. (1995). *The art of case study research*. Thousand Oaks, CA: Sage.

Stein, F., & Hutchison, C. (1988). Instructor competencies: The standards, Vols. 1 & 2. Batavia, IL: The International Board of Standards for Training, Performance & Instruction.

Storr, R. J. (1969). *The beginnings of graduate education in America*. New York: Arno Press.

Syverson, P. (1996). The new American graduate student: Challenge or opportunity? *CGS Communicator, 29*(8), 7-8. Retrieved from http://www.capnet.org/vcr/cctr610.htm

Thach, E. C. (1994). *Perceptions of distance education experts regarding the roles, outputs, and competencies needed in the field of distance education*. Ph.D. dissertation, Texas A&M University, Texas, U.S. Retrieved May 1, 2009, from Dissertations & Theses: Full Text database. (Publication No. AAT 9506728)

Thurgood, L., Golladay, M. J., & Hill, S. T. (2006). U.S. doctorates in the 20th Century. National Science Foundation, Division of Science Resources Statistics, NSF 06-319, Arlington, VA.

Tigelaar, D. E. H., Dolmans, D. H. J. M., Wolfhagen, I. H. A. P., & Van, V. (2004). The development and validation of a framework for teaching competencies in higher education. *Higher Education*, *48*(2), 253–268. doi:10.1023/B:HIGH.0000034318.74275.e4

Williams, P. E. (2003). Roles and competencies for distance education programs in higher education institutions. *American Journal of Distance Education*, *17*(1), 45. doi:10.1207/S15389286AJDE1701_4

Yin, R. K. (1984). *Case study research: Design and methods*. Thousand Oaks, CA: Sage.

KEY TERMS AND DEFINITIONS

Competency: A collection of skills, knowledge, attitudes and characteristics of an individual that contribute to performance.

Dissertation Advisor: A role usually played by a faculty member in which he/she guides a doctoral student in conducting a research project and writing a report on the research that meets the standards commonly accepted in the field of study.

Doctorate: A terminal degree, usually post-Masters, that provides a high level of skills commonly recognized in the discipline. There are several types of doctorates including Doctor of Philosophy (Ph.D.), Doctor of Education (Ed.D.), Doctor of Business Administration (D.B.A.), and Doctor of Psychology (Psy.D.) among others.

Faculty: Typically responsible for a combination of teaching research and service, depending upon institutional and program mission and goals.

Leadership: The formal and informal use of influence and power to bring about change in an organization.

APPENDIX: SUPPORTING MATERIAL

Abstract

This chapter reports on an exploratory case study of 21st century competencies for faculty in an organizational leadership doctoral program. As the surge in technology continues to bring about global changes, preparing potential leaders is our best hope going forward. It is important to discover competencies doctoral faculty will need to address the challenges of the future.

Questions and Answers

1. What is the significance of this case study?

Doctoral programs in leadership prepare students for a variety of leadership opportunities. Faculty play a significant role in the quality and value of doctoral education. Since doctoral programs in leadership are evolving rapidly the results of this study will assist faculty, administrators, and the students they serve.

2. Name at least three issues identified as expected to be prominent in 2010.

Globalization, Changes in organizations and leadership, New technologies, Volume of information, Funding and resources, accountability, and Students who are unprepared.

3. What 5 faculty roles are mentioned in this study?

Teaching, Advising, Researcher, Community Service, and Colleague

4. Name 3 skills that faculty identified as necessary for teaching in the next decade.

Teach and integrate theory and practice; Use of appropriate Technologies; Interpersonal skills; Model and teach ethics; Communication skills; Knowledge of organizational trends and challenges; Knowledge of global issues.

5. Discuss why you think the skills you named in question 4 are important for leaders.

For instance, new technologies and the access they provide to massive amounts of information fuel both a sense of constant change and anticipation. As a result, faculty in this study noted that keeping current in technology skills will be necessary for leaders to communicate with and engage others.

Epilogue and Lessons Learned

This case study attempted to give voice to faculty in a leadership doctoral program about what issues they would face in the future and what competencies they would need. One underlying theme that was pervasive was the sense of constant and rapid change. This notion of change is tangentially related to new technologies that are disruptive, either changing the way we do things, or requiring new skills, or both. Faculty expressed optimism about the future and the new opportunities that will undoubtedly come with changing technologies.

It is important to note that technologies should be deployed thoughtfully, in alignment with program goals and values, with faculty input, and with sufficient opportunity for faculty to learn to use them effectively. While we don't really know what the future holds and can only guess what challenges and changes organizations will face, leaders should make every attempt to gauge where organizations are and the global trends and issues they will be facing. Keeping academic programs current and continually improving learning are two of the challenges that will not change.

This chapter reports on an exploratory case study of 21st century competencies for faculty in an organizational leadership doctoral program. As the surge in technology continues to bring about global changes, preparing potential leaders is our best hope going forward. It is important to discover what issues doctoral faculty think they will face and what competencies they will need to address the challenges of the future.

Chapter 7
Technoethical Study of Electronic Technology Ab/Use at University

Rocci Luppicini
University of Ottawa, Canada

ABSTRACT

This case explores how university students view non-work related use of electronic technology within universities (I.e., electronic monitoring technology and personal use of electronic technologies). Of particular interest are student experiences and ethical stances concerning non-work related use of electronic technologies within universities as well as the variables that affect their decision to engage in or not engage in personal electronic technology use during class. To this end, a technoethical case study utilizes research literature and conversational data derived from online group work taken from a research course offered by the communication department of a large urban university. Findings indicate the presence of ethical tensions and contradictions in how students rationalize non-work related use of electronic technology within universities. This case study sheds light on student's attitudes, subjective norms, attributions of responsibility, and factors affecting students' ethical stances towards non-work related technology use at university. It also offers recommendations on how to leverage mutual understanding and consensual decision-making in similar contexts where ethical and social controversies arise, surrounding technology and its use in society.

BACKGROUND: ELECTRONIC TECHNOLOGY AB/USE AT UNIVERSITY

The widespread integration of electronic technologies in universities is transforming organizational operations as well as how students, faculty members, support staff, and administration interact with one another. This can partly be attributed to the many educational and organizational advantages perceived to accompany electronic technology use within university settings. New electronic technologies allow university members to exchange more information in less time and with greater

DOI: 10.4018/978-1-61520-869-2.ch007

flexibility than possible through face-to-face interactions. Electronic technologies include, but are not limited to, computer monitoring and filtering systems, surveillance cameras, IM and other chat tools, electronic mail, Internet, audio and video conferencing tools, mobile devices, and personal data assistants (Luppicini, 2008a). Non-work-related use of electronic technologies may include personal use of electronic technologies as well as institutional uses of counter measure electronic technologies to control personal use.

Non-work related use of electronic technologies within universities is a relatively understudied area of research. This is particularly salient in the lack of practical research focusing on insider perspectives and attitudes towards electronic technology use within universities. To date, only a few studies have specifically focused on individuals' personal views and attitudes towards non-work related electronic technology use in organizational contexts and none have focused specifically on insider views and attitudes towards non-work related electronic technology use within university contexts. One relevant study of non-work related Internet use at work by D'Abate (2005) found that individuals may rationalize non-work related use of the Internet during work hours in a variety of ways including, viewing themselves as capable of simultaneously conducting work and non-work related tasks, viewing non-related Internet use a justified reward for completed work, and viewing themselves as feeling tempted by the convenience of access. Although this study does not address personal views and attitudes towards non-work related electronic technology use within university contexts, it does provide compelling evidence to suggest that individuals' personal views and attitudes about non-work related electronic technology use within work contexts plays a powerful role in shaping professional conduct and organizational actions revolving around non-work related electronic technology. Moreover, it highlights the importance of understanding the role of ethical values and rationalization processes in shaping individuals' approach to non-work related electronic technology.

SETTING THE STAGE

What is Technoethics? In referring to the *recent Handbook of Research on Technoethics*, Luppicini (2008) provides the following definition:

Technoethics is defined as an interdisciplinary field concerned with all ethical aspects of technology within a society shaped by technology. It deals with human processes and practices connected to technology which are becoming embedded within social, political, and moral spheres of life. It also examines social policies and interventions occurring in response to issues generated by technology development and use. This includes critical debates on the responsible use of technology for advancing human interests in society. To this end, it attempts to provide conceptual grounding to clarify the role of technology in relation to those affected by it and to help guide ethical problem-solving and decision making in areas of activity that rely on technology (p. 5).

This technoethical case study explores how university students view non-work related use of electronic technologies within university, a technoethical case because it focuses on the ethical and social aspects of technology use in society. In view of the importance of electronic technologies within university contexts, there is a need to get an insider perspective from students to better understand how electronic technologies are used and abused within their university. This case is intended to shed light on students' attitudes and ethical stances concerning non-work related electronic technology use within their university. This case is also intended to identify areas of concern about non-work related use of electronic technology within universities and offer possible solutions to help guard against potentially destructive activities with electronic technologies within university settings.

In spite of their ubiquity and remarkable benefits of electronic technologies in organizational settings, research has uncovered substantial obstacles to effective and responsible electronic technology use which, in turn, has given rise to heated debates. In the area of organizational studies, personal use of electronic technologies during work hours is a serious concern because it represents a misuse of limited organizational resources that can take away valuable work time. Misuses of electronic technology within work organizations can range from counterproductive to non-productive to inappropriate activities as reflected in research on cyberloafing, network attacks, information theft, unauthorized transmission of confidential information, transmission of offensive jokes, deceptive communication, exchanging online pornography, online flaming, and online identity deception (Donath, 1999; Gurak, 2001; Lim, 2002; Redding, 1996; Wilson, 2005).

Controversial use of electronic monitoring of organizational members (countermeasure technology) is included in debates about the misuse of electronic technology within organizational settings. Many work organizations have introduced electronic monitoring to guard against electronic technology abuse among organizational members. Such countermeasures are considered by some to be a further misuse of non-work-related electronic technology within organizations. Counter measures aimed at controlling personal use of electronic technologies, include surveillance cameras, computer monitoring and filtering systems, and electronic technology use policies. Recent research has begun to examine various aspects of organizational countermeasure use including, social implications of surveillance cameras (Whittaker, 1995; Zweig & Webster, 2002), electronic technology use policies (Martin, 1999), and computer monitoring and filtering systems (Alge, 2001; Urbaczewski & Jessup, 2002). Taken together, the growing body of research on non-work related use of electronic technologies and counter measures within organizations has helped highlight how actual organizational benefits and limitations offered by electronic technology relies to a large extent on the individuals that use them.

CASE DESCRIPTION

Case Context

This technoethical case study explores non-work related use of electronic technologies within the university classroom. The grounded theory approach of Strauss and Corbin (1998) is used to guide the data collection and analysis. "Grounded theories, because they are drawn from data, are likely to offer insight, enhance understanding, and provide a meaningful guide to action"(Strauss & Corbin, 1998, p. 12). The following research question guides this case study: How do students view non-work related abuse of electronic technology at university?

Communication Concerns with Non-Work Related Use of Electronic Technologies

What is unknown is how the non-work related use of electronic technologies and counter measures are viewed within educational contexts like universities. Within universities, electronic technologies are used in teaching, research and administrative functions. Electronic technologies are also used extensively by the student body, which makes up the majority of university members at most, if not all universities. Because there is little research available on how students view non-work related use of electronic technologies and counter measures within their own university, this case study focuses on students personal views and attitudes towards non-work related use of electronic technologies and counter measures within their own university.

Data Collection and Analysis Tools for Exploring Electronic Technology Ab/Use

This case is organized as follows. First, a review of the research literature on non-work related use of electronic technology within educational and work settings is conducted to help ground the study in relevant research. Second, conversational data is collected from an online lab activity carried out in groups of two to gather student perspectives about non-work related use of electronic technology within university. Findings are based on preliminary data collected from the online lab activity completed within an undergraduate qualitative research methods course taught by the study author. In terms of study analysis, conversation data are coded using grounded theory approach. Key concepts uncovered are compared with one another and those that appeared to pertain to a similar phenomenon were grouped into categories (open coding). A second tier of coding (axial coding) was used to establish links between categories and sub-categories by analyzing individual categories in terms of their underlying conditions, context, interactions, and outcomes (Strauss & Corbin, 1998). The findings and interpretations are presented below.

FINDINGS: KEY THEMES, ISSUES, AND CHALLENGES

Emergent Themes

A number of moderately related themes emerged in an analysis of selected conversation data. These were grouped into the following categories illustrated in Figure 1.

E-Technology Abuse in Class

What is the nature of electronic technology abuse in university classes? This study involved undergraduate university students situated within a larger urban university in North America. When asked about non-work related use of electronic technology in class, there was widespread acknowledgement of its occurrence within their classroom environment. One student stated that "a lot of technologies are abused and serve as more of a distraction to students, rather than(sic)

Figure 1. E-technology abuse in class

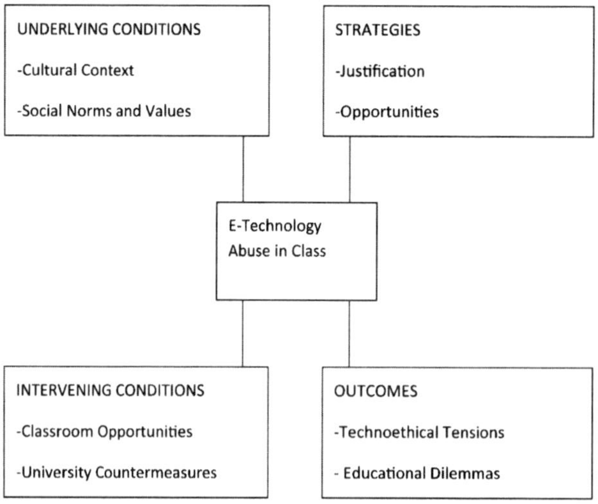

helping them with their education"(excerpt). Moreover, student has an acute awareness of different types of e-technology abuse. As stated by one student, " The most common abuse mention was "surfing the net or playing games to pass the class time" (excerpt). Despite the best intentions of students to use laptops for class work only, the temptation is often too hard to resist. As remarked by one student, "I always start out taking notes, but usually end up surfing the web" (excerpt) This temptation is present despite the presence of breaks between classes where students can use laptops freely. Another student indicated, "Sometimes it can wait until class is done, but it's right there and it's so easy and quick that sometimes I do it" (excerpt).

Non-work related cell phone use during class was the second most discussed e-technology abuse discussed. Many students use cell phones at university. As stated by one student, "I also use my cell phone to keep in contact with people while I'm on campus. It keeps me connected to my friends and family" (excerpt). However, personal cell phones are compact and portable, permitting convenient in-class use despite student awareness of its disruption to others. One student noted "I would have to admit that I've had my cell phone ring in class, which is not a good thing, ha ha it disturbs the flow of the class when something like that happens" (excerpt). Another student indicated a personal need to use cell phones in class despite problems it might create for others, "I couldn't figure out how to turn the key tone noise off on my new phone, but really wanted to text my friend anyways. I knew I was disrupting a few students but I just had to text lol".

A moderate level of student discussion focused on the entertainment value of e-technology as a distraction within large classroom learning environments with limited opportunity for active student engagement. In connecting with existing research, Bugeja (2007) linked classroom abuse of e-technology to student experiences of passive lecture based teaching where professors asked and answered their own questions (also referred to as Sesame Street Syndrome) and student expectations to be entertained while they learn. This suggests that students may be acting as 'cognitive misers' avoiding active class participation in favor of dividing attention between passive information note taking and e-technology entertainment (E.g., web surfing, visiting social networking sites, etc.). Another possible explanation comes from Thurlow's (2002) study based on gratification theory, which suggests that e-technology use is affected by the capacity of e-technology to satisfy individuals' needs by enabling them to feel connected and intimate with others across time and space. Overall, the appears to be a clear indication of electronic technology abuse within university classroom environments. There is also an apparent contraction in student behavior where students complain about e-technology abuse as a distraction in class but admit to doing it themselves. The question is, what underlying conditions give rise to this contradictory classroom behavior?

Underlying Conditions

What conditions allow for electronic technology abuse in university classes to occur? In examining conversational data, there appeared to be a moderate level of discussion about the underlying context that permitted electronic technology abuse at work to occur. Some students felt that technology was an important part of contemporary culture and society that they grew up with. One student indicated that "we live in a world controlled by technologies and we are always going to have to use them, so we should get used to the fact that they will be surrounding us for a long time" (excerpt)." Another student viewed the technological culture of communications as reflective of their generation, "our generation has been so immersed in this technological culture that it makes it seem natural for us to use these forms of communication" (excerpt). Within this technological culture and society, students expressed an awareness of the rapid pace of life and the value added by technology to help individuals stay connected with one another. One student indicated, "As busy professionals and students, we have a constant need to be in touch with colleagues and families" (excerpt). Student responses help explain tendencies to abuse e-technology in class because it seen as a normal cultural practice within a technological society. In this sense, e-technology may be seen as an acceptable and essential practice connected to their cultural and social identities.

There was also mention of an educational culture defined by active engagement and student collaboration within a classroom environment viewed as a learning community. Electronic technology abuse was viewed as a threat to the classroom educational culture. One student indicated, "using my electronic technologies prevents me from [learning]" (excerpt). Another student conveyed a sensitivity to the demands of the educational culture, the mere idea of failing and not graduating because I was un-engaged and didn't participate in class is enough for me not to use electronic devices for my personal use during class" (excerpt). The high level of distraction created by electronic technology abuse within current educational culture is recognized in the research literature. As indicated by Bird, Cain, and Jones (2008):

"In addition to the more traditional types of distraction such as crossword puzzles, mobile computing devices offer online shopping, instant messaging, Facebook, online fantasy sports games, and web browsing. Aside from the general annoyance this may create for instructors, computer-aided distraction has the potential to negatively impact learning" (p. 2).

In a study of laptop use in the classroom, Cole (2008) argues that laptops threaten the integrity of the educational culture by removing students from it, "[Laptops] take the student out of the classroom discussion, which itself has collective costs for the learning environment as a whole."

In further contextualizing this study, the researcher noted in the data collection how easy it was for students to abuse e-technologies in the classroom for extended periods without being detected. According to this researchers field notes, "The easy portability of laptop computers, Internet access from anywhere on campus, and large class size provides a context of convenience for e-electronic technology abuse" (researcher field notes).

There appears to be underlying influences arising from a tension between technological culture and educational culture at work. On the one hand, continual use of e-technologies is recognized by students as part of the technological culture of society. This permits e-technology abuse in class to appear acceptable. On the other hand, there is a recognition among some students of an educational culture defined by active engagement, class participation, and the avoidance of learning distractions such as the non-work related use of e-technologies in class.

E-Technology Strategies in the Classroom

What is the ethical stance of students concerning their personal use of electronic technologies during class time? When discussing ethical implications of e-technology abuse in the classroom, there were mixed responses. There was a moderate tendency among some students to justify their personal use of electronic in terms of their personal rights and freedoms. One student stated, "Students should have a choice to use what they are most comfortable with and if they want to use it for something that doesn't relate to class then it's really their problem and they alone will have to deal with the consequences" A second student indicated, "I feel like I should be the one making that decision" (excerpt). Another strategy by students was to divert attention away from the e-technology abuse by taking a laissez-faire approach, """ if it's not laptops or cell phones or mp3 players then it'll be something else to distract [students]" (excerpt).

There was also a moderate tendency among some students to judge e-technology use in a negative light. According to one student, "Any kind of device in the classroom is only going to hurt the learning process" (excerpt). Other students believed e-technology abuse violated acceptable social protocols. One student indicated, "I just think that it's rude because it doesn't have anything to do with class" (excerpt). A second student limited their disapproval of e-technologies to certain aspects of classroom activity, "I think it's rude during presentations, though. Which I would distinguish from a lecture" (excerpt). A third student reasoned that only some e-technologies are acceptable in the classroom while others are not. Other students had technology specific or context specific views. One student approved of laptops but viewed cell phones as "having no place in a classroom because it hinders the learning experience (excerpt)". Another student indicated that," if you sit in the back of the class that [distraction]can no longer be an issue" (excerpt). This tendency to rationalize e-technology abuse follows D'Abate's (2005) findings that individuals rationalize non-work related use of the Internet during work hours.

There is a division in student responses that appears to reflect a technoethical tension between student ethical stances on technology as duty and technology as a right. On one hand, students made the case that electronic technology abuse (albeit regretful) is the right of the student. As indicated by one student, "if it's their education and money, why not let them do what they want in class?" (excerpt). This follows an ethics of rights rooted in the writings of Thomas Hobbes, John Locke, and John Rawls and is based on assumptions of rights owed to all individuals by the collective they are part of. Social contracts are often used to ensure that individual rights are upheld in society. Under this account, students have the right to abuse electronic technologies within university classes to the extent that it does not infringe on the rights of others. On the other hand, students who opposed e-technology abuse in the classroom tended to view it as an ethical violation of duty to faculty and the university. As indicated by one student, *"I don't think students should use any other sort of electronic device during class time like cell phones or i-Pods because they should show some respect to the professor " (excerpt). This follows a d*uty ethics focused on obligations one has to others in society (E.g., duty to respect professors). This ethical perspective is rooted in the work of Kant and what individuals ought to do in order to live an ethical life. The question is, which ethical stance is right and which one should people follow?

Intervening Conditions

What is the ethical stance of students concerning university countermeasures to control the personal use of electronic technologies during class time? When asked about the use of counter measures (E.g., surveillance cameras, restriction policies, computer monitoring and filtering software, etc) ethical stances of students were predominantly against countermeasures to control e-technologies in the classroom. One student reasoned, "If the university takes them (technologies) away, it will upset students because it will seem like the university is taking away our right to use laptops or whatever device we prefer" (excerpt). Another student indicated "We're all adults and if we choose not to pay attention to class for whatever reason, then the university shouldn't try to control that by using counter measures." A third student discussed countermeasures in terms of respect and public accountability, "Such a ban would stifle-decrease student body respect for the institution as a respectable academic entity. It would adversely affect the University's image and identity" (excerpt). A modest number of students did not judge countermeasures to be unethical. As indicated by one student, "Banning all electronics would make the classroom ambiance more intimate. The students would be more connected with what's happening in the classroom rather than on their screen."

As was the case with ethical stances concerning personal use of e-technologies, there is a division in student responses between student ethical stances on technology as duty and technology as a right. On one hand, students made the case that countermeasure violated students' rights to decide for themselves whether to abuse e-technologies in the classroom or not. On the other hand, there were students who tended to favor countermeasures to protect the integrity of the learning environment and perceived duty to professors. As stated by one student commenting on countermeasures, "I actually think it would be a better learning environment (excerpt)". "

Consequences

What would affect individuals' decision to use or not use electronic technologies for personal use during class time? One of the main factors mentioned by students that would alter their approach to e-technology abuse in the classroom was to take away the opportunities to use e-technologies in the classroom. As stated by one student, "Site is built so that students don't get internet of cell phone reception in the classes" (excerpt). Other factors mentioned to reduce opportunities included, removing laptop plug-ins from classrooms, or disallowing students from bringing e-technologies on campus. A second, factor mentioned by students involved reducing student choices by implementing university classroom policies to ban personal use of e-technologies along with mechanisms for punishment in the event that policies are violated. A third, consequence, and one followed by some student was to avoid e-technology use through the recognition of its potential negative impact on academic success and how it detracts from "the quality of learning (excerpt)". Another student admitted that reflecting on the negative learning impact of using personal technologies in class convinced her to stop this behavior due to fear of "failing and not graduating because I was unengaged and didn't participate in class" (excerpt). This fear is supported by existing research linking personal use of e-technology in class to distraction, lower academic performance and learning depth. Fried (2008) which found that "laptop use by fellow students was the single most reported distracter, accounting for 64% of all responses" (Fried 2008, 907). As stated by Freid (2008) "[Too] many sources of information can create cognitive overload, and new information coming in can cause attention shifts and distraction… Computers and other high-tech equipment are likely sources of overload and distraction…" (p. 908). In a study of e-technology influences on academic performance, Grace-Martin and Gay (2001) found that the more time students spent surfing the internet during class the lower grades they tended to receive (Grace-Martin & Gay 2001). In a follow-up study on the effects of multitasking, Hembrooke and Gay (2003) found that students who used their laptops to multitask in class had memory recall of course compared to students not multitasking. material that had been presented (Hembrooke & Gay 2003). This is mirrored in expert opinions from faculty as indicated by Poldrack (2006),"Even if you learn while multitasking, that learning is less flexible and more specialized, so you cannot retrieve the information as easily... The best way to improve memory and learning is to pay full attention" (p.14).

DISCUSSION

Issues and Challenges

General findings provided evidence of a relation between perceptions of the classroom learning context and factors affecting personal choice and opportunity to abuse e-technologies during class time. At the same time, a number of specific issues and challenges emerged worth noting. One major issue revolves around the role of faculty members in dealing with the new distraction of electronic technologies in their classroom. The high level of distraction created by electronic technology use in the classroom has provoked a variety of responses from faculty members in an effort to improve the situation. This, however, has proven challenging with mixed reception as is illustrated in the following excerpt:

"My professor used to ask all the people with laptops to sit at the front so that he could keep an eye on what they're using it. The thing is the front rows used to fill up very quickly, and when people with laptops used to come in late they weren't able to use their laptops since they couldn't find empty seats at the front. The professor would never let them use it at the back so they used to have a lot of arguments about that".

Apart from the limited space issue, it is not clear that placing laptop users in the front will eliminate classroom distractions. As indicated by one student, I personally don't like the lap tops in class, its distracting when someone is in front of me, I tend to look at the screens" (excerpt). In other words, there appears to be no easy way to displace electronic technology users in the classroom that satisfies the needs of all students.

One option for faculty is to completely eliminate student use of electronic technologies in the classroom in an effort to protect learning opportunities for all students. This, however, could create other learning issues. As indicated by one student, "It would be disadvantageous for the people who love to take laptop notes" (excerpt). A second student added, "I think it would be very tough for me to cope with that ban; I am used to typing all my notes since I am very untidy when it comes to writing them down on a paper. I would probably panic when it is time to study for my exams/tests since all my notes will be messy and unreadable" (excerpt). There appears to be no mutually acceptable strategy yet to deal with distraction of electronic technologies in their classroom that does not create problems in other areas.

A second major issue concerns how the economic reality of university teaching and learning creates opportunities for electronic technology abuse in university classroom? The anonymity of large class sizes provides ample opportunity for students to disengage from classroom learning without faculty awareness. This is largely due to the large class size and low student to faculty ratio at many universities. It is not uncommon at many North American universities to have up to 500 students per course section taught by a single faculty member. In connecting with the current study, this researcher noted the challenge of controlling electronic technology abuse in the classroom, "With almost 100 students sandwiched into this advanced undergraduate research class, it is impossible to police electronic technology abuse. There is no room to circulate to see student laptop screens and cells can be easily hidden from the podium" (researcher log excerpt). Unfortunately, the financial burden of hiring more faculty or reducing student enrollments to increase student to faculty ratios are not options for many universities with limited funding.

A third major issue is the long-term risk to students created by an overreliance on electronic technologies leading to technology addiction, inappropriate social behavior, and psychological damage. This is one area that future research should address. When using ICT's to communicate with someone else during a face-to face social situation, individuals commit themselves to two different social contexts simultaneously—the face-to-face social context and an online social context. Garcia-Montes et al. (2006) likened this division in these two worlds as a splitting of the self into a "schizophrenic individual–institutional structure" (p. 72). If this indeed the case, then electronic technology can be seen as a driver of this split in self at the intersection of face-to-face and online worlds. This phenomenon could be influencing electronic technology abuse (online interactions) during university lectures (face-to-face interactions) because many student are accustomed to using ICT's continuously. This can lead to a dividing of limited cognitive capacities between the face-to-face lecture and online environment. In the short-term, this could can lead to low level learning and poorer performance. This is supported by a small but growing body of research showing that multitasking negatively influences learning. In the long-term, this could reinforce electronic technology abuse in inappropriate face-to-face situations and a blurring of reality, increased risk of delusional mental states, and psychological breakdowns.

Solutions and Recommendations

In connecting key chapter findings, issues and challenges, it is apparent that electronic technology abuse is a complex and controversial phenomena within university classrooms.. Findings revealed mixed perspectives on electronic technology abuse and how to deal with it. For instance, if countermeasures are used by the university to curtail e-technology abuse (I.e., restricting internet connections in classrooms) then the opportunities for abuse are eliminated at the expense of individual student rights. On the other hand, offering students the choice to abuse e-technologies may remove the respect and sense of duty concerning ethical values and conduct in educational settings. The latter ethical perspective, although seemingly controversial, does follow the pioneering writings of Ivan Illich's (1970)*Deschooling Society* and its rejection of the privileged role of educational institutions exert within society as a controlling mechanism. Instead, Illich viewed ideal educational systems as more open and flexible. According to Illich (1970):

A good educational system should have three purposes: it should provide all who want to learn with access to available resources at any time in their lives; empower all who want to share what they know to find those who want to learn it from them; and, finally, furnish all who want to present an issue to the public with the opportunity to make their challenge known.

Based on this line of reasoning, one recommendation would be to re-design universities to be more flexible and sensitive changing's contexts and public interests. E-technology is well suited to allow more flexible types of educational engagement reflecting the technological landscape of current society. In this sense, electronics offers a powerful tool for re-calibrating education around the interests of its users rather than recalibrating student values and conduct around university rules and regulations.

A second option, and the one recommended in this chapter, would seek to identity key areas of technoethical tension and differences in perspective to be used in modeling learning conversations between stakeholders (students, instructors, university administration, technical support staff). Based on this study, key technoethical tensions by which to model a topic focused learning conversation (I.e., learning conversation about electronic technology solutions for university classrooms) can be illustrated, (see Figure 2).

Based on conversation theory derived from Gordan Pask (see Luppicini, 2008b), a learning conversation about about electronic technology solutions for university classrooms would emerges in two steps: (1) a student (receiver) shares a concept with an instructor (sender) when the student is able to make sense of the sender's explanation (demonstrate) and (2) the student and the instructor understand one another when the student is able to make sense of the instructor's explanations of the receiver's explanations (explain). In the most basic learning conversation model there is a minimum of two levels of interaction to leverage mutual understanding/knowledge of the how and why of a topic (learning conversation).

Within this conversation, instructors would

Figure 2. Model of technoethical tensions in electronic technology A/buse

Values: Self interest for entertainment, social affiliation, and distraction		Values: Collective interest for distraction free learning
Underlying Context: Assumption of technological culture and society	⟺	Underlying Context: Assumption of educational culture and community of learners
Intervening Conditions: Personal rights and freedom to decide e-technology uses.		Intervening Conditions: Institutional responsibility and duty to protect students from e-tech abuses
Consequences: Electronic technology overreliance, mental stress and information overload, risk of lower grades		Consequences: Electronic technology withdrawal risk, higher grades and learning potential

be responsible for conveying all information about electronic technology tensions and possible solutions for university classrooms. Students would have the opportunity to actively engage in learning conversations in an effort to reach mutual understanding and agreement. This simple learning conversation model would be applied to all stakeholder groups until mutual understanding is achieved and a set of acceptable solutions are identified which all stakeholders can agree to. This type of approach is well suited for complex areas of shared human interest where competing values and multiple perspectives need to be understood in order to guide democratic decision-making which takes all perspectives and views into consideration. This type of approach is particularly important in this study where controversies are deeply rooted in ethical tensions arising from competing assumptions underlying ethical theories and actions. This approach is validated by existing work focusing on ethics and technology (technoethics). As highlighted by Luppicini (2008a):

The problem with relying on ethical theories as a stand alone approach for dealing with social and ethical issues is that ethical theories are based on different assumptions about the nature of reality and the obligations of individuals within it. Ethical tensions arise when the fundamental assumptions underlying different ethical theories leads to different conclusions concerning what constitutes ethical conduct (12).

Although conversation modeling strategies are recognized as a useful tool for navigating complex and controversial areas of shared human interest (E.g., e-technology abuse in universities), there are limitations to note. The major limitation of this approach is that it is time consuming and requires invested interest of all stakeholders to continue learning conversations to completion (the point at which mutual understanding and consensual agreements are reached).

CONCLUSION

The core conclusion can be summarized as follows. First, most students were critical of the negative distraction created by e-technology abuse within the classroom, but admitted that they continued the behavior anyway. This follows organizational communication theories distinguishing between contractions in individuals espoused theories and theories in action. Second, there appears to be cultural and social tensions underlying students' ethical stance and values about electronic technology abuse in the classroom. On the one hand, some students complained about electronic technology detracting from a healthy community of learning (learning culture) involving active engagement, collaboration, and class participation. On the other hand, some students defended electronic technology abuse as a normal part of a technological society where 'being connected' all the time and everywhere is valued. Third, there was a moderate level of tension between individuals ethical stances regarding ethical duties and rights concerning individual electronic technology abuse within classrooms and university countermeasures to block such abuse. Students who highlighted individual's right to control their own decisions tended to be against university countermeasures and typically justified their ethical position in terms of basic human rights to make one's own personal choices concerning electronic technology use. Students who tended to be more critical of individual electronic technology abuse and supportive of university countermeasures typically highlighted ethical duties of students and universities to uphold certain standards to protect the classroom learning environment. Finally, a number interesting options are available for dealing with pervasive issues and challenges in overcoming e-technology abuse in university classes, including strategies to frame technoethical tensions and strategies to model learning conversations aimed at resolving technoethical tension by leveraging mutual understanding and consensual decision-making among all stakeholders affected (or potentially affected) by e-technology abuse in the classroom.

REFERENCES

Alge, B. J. (2001). Effects of computer surveillance on perceptions of privacy and procedural justice. *The Journal of Applied Psychology*, *86*(4), 797–804. doi:10.1037/0021-9010.86.4.797

Bird, E. R., Cain, J., & Jones, M. (2008). Mobile Computing Initiatives Within Pharmacy Education. *American Journal of Pharmaceutical Education*, *72*, 1–7.

Bugeja, M. (2007). *Distractions in a wireless classroom.* The chronicle of higher education. Retrieved November 15th from http://fp.arizona.edu/geog695c/PDFs/wireless.classroom.pdf.

Cole, D. (2008, October 23). Why I ban Laptops in my Classroom. *Encyclopedia Britannica Blog.* Retrieved November 20, 2008, from http://www.britannica.com/blogs/2008/10/why-i-ban-laptops-in-my-classroom/

D'Abate, C. P. (2005). Working hard or hardly working: A case study of individuals engaging in personal business on the job. *Human Relations*, *58*, 1009–1032. doi:10.1177/0018726705058501

Donath, J. A. (1999). Identity and deception in the virtual community. In Smith, M. A., & Kollock, P. (Eds.), *Communities in cyberspace* (pp. 29–59). London: Routledge.

Fried, B. (2008). In-class laptop use and its eVects on student learning. *Computers & Education*, *50*, 906–914. doi:10.1016/j.compedu.2006.09.006

Garcia-Montes., et al. (2006). Changes in the self as a resulting from the use of mobile phones. *Media Culture & Society*, *28*, 67–81. doi:10.1177/0163443706059287

Grace-Martin, M., & Gay, G. (2001). Web browsing, mobile computing, and academic performance. *Journal of Education Technology*, *4*, 95–107.

Gurak, L. J. (2001). *Cyberliteracy: Navigating the Internet with awareness*. New Haven, CT: Yale University Press.

Hembrooke, H., & Gay, G. (2003). The laptop and the lecture: The effects of multitasking in learning environments. *Journal of Computing in Higher Education, 15*, 46–64. doi:10.1007/BF02940852

Illich, I. (1970). *Deschooling Society, ournature.org*. Retrieved February 1, 2009, from http://ournature.org/~novembre/illich/1970_deschooling.html

Lim, V. K. G. (2002). The IT way of loafing on the job: Cyberloafing, neutralizing and Distraction versus destruction. *Cyberpsychology & Behavior, 9*(6), 730–741.

Luppicini, R. (2008a). Introducting the field of Technoethics. In Luppicini, R., & Adell, R. (Eds.), *Handbook of Research on Technoethics* (pp. 1–18). Hershey: Idea Group Publishing.

Luppicini, R. (2008b). Introducing conversation design for instructional applications. In Luppicini, R. (Ed.), *Handbook of Conversation Design for Instruction* (pp. 1–18). Hershey: Idea Group Publishing.

Martin, J. (1999, March). Internet policy: Employee rights and wrongs. *HRFocus, 75*, 11.

Mastrangelo, P. M., Everton, W., & Jolton, J. A. (2006). Personal use of work computers: organizational justice. *Journal of Organizational Behavior, 23*, 675–694.

May, S. (2006). *Case Studies in Organizational Communication: Ethical Perspectives and Practices*. Thousand Oaks, CA: Sage.

Urbaczewski, A., & Jessup, L. M. (2002). Does electronic monitoring of employee Internet usage work? *Communications of the ACM, 45*(1), 80–83. doi:10.1145/502269.502303

Whittaker, S. (1995). Rethinking video as a technology for interpersonal communications: Theory and design implications. *International Journal of Human-Computer Studies, 42*(5), 501–529. doi:10.1006/ijhc.1995.1022

Wilson, C. (2005). *Computer attack and cyberterrorism: Vulnerabilities and policy issues for Congress*. Washington, DC: CRS Reports.

Zweig, D., & Webster, J. (2002). Where is the line between benign and invasive? An examination of psychological barriers to the acceptance of awareness monitoring systems. *Journal of Organizational Behavior, 23*(5), 605–633. doi:10.1002/job.157

FURTHER READING

Adams, D. (2006). Wireless laptops in the classroom (and the sesame street syndrome). *Association for Computing Machinery. Communications of the ACM, 49*(9), 25. doi:10.1145/1151030.1151049

Barak, M., Lipson, A., & Lerman, S. (2006). Wireless laptops as means for promoting active learning in large lecture halls. *Journal of Research on Technology in Education, 38*(3), 245–264.

Campbell, A. B., & Pargas, R. P. (2003). Laptops in the classroom. *Technical Symposium on Computer Science Education archive*. New York: ACM.

Campbell, S. (2006). Perceptions of mobile phones in college classrooms: Ringing, cheating, and classroom policies. *Communication Education, 55*(3), 280–294. doi:10.1080/03634520600748573

Campbell, S. W. (2007). A cross-cultural comparison of perceptions and uses of mobile telephony. *New Media & Society, 9*(2), 343–363. doi:10.1177/1461444807075016

Carnevale, D., & Young, J. R. (2006). The challenges and benefits of requiring students to buy laptops. *The Chronicle of Higher Education, 52*(38), 39–40.

Gattiker, U., & Kelley, H. (1999). Morality and computers: Attitudes and differences in moral judgments. *Information Systems Research, 10*(3), 233–254. doi:10.1287/isre.10.3.233

Gilroy, M. (2004). Invasion of the classroom cell phones. *Education Digest: Essential Readings Condensed for Quick Review, 69*(6), 56–60.

Harrington, S. (1996). The effect of codes of ethics and personal denial of responsibility on computer abuse judgments and intentions. *Management Information Systems Quarterly, 20*(3), 257–278. doi:10.2307/249656

Koskela, H. (2000). The gaze without eyes: video-surveillance and the changing nature of urban space. *Progress in Human Geography, 24*(2), 243–265. doi:10.1191/030913200668791096

Lavoie, J. A. A., & Pychyl, T. A. (2001). Cyberslacking and the procrastination superhighway: A web-based survey of online procrastination, attitudes, and emotion. *Social Science Computer Review, 19*(4), 431–444. doi:10.1177/089443930101900403

Lever, K. M., & Katz, J. E. (2007). Cell phones in campus libraries: An analysis of policy responses to an invasive mobile technology. *Information Processing & Management, 43*(4), 1133. doi:10.1016/j.ipm.2006.07.002

Luppicini, R. (2008). Introducing technoethics. In Luppicini, R., & Adell, R. (Eds.), *Handbook of research on technoethics* (pp. 1–18). Hershey: Idea Group Publishing.

Marshall, K. (1999). Has technology introduced new ethical problems? *Journal of Business Ethics, 19*(1), 81–90. doi:10.1023/A:1006154023743

Nilson, L. B., & Weaver, W. E. (2005). Laptops in Class: What Are They Good For? What Can You Do with Them? *New Directions for Teaching and Learning, 101*, 3–13.

Poldrack, R. (2006). iPods and Learning: Not Always a Good Mix. *American society for training and development, 60*, 14.

APPENDIX: SUPPORTING MATERIAL

Abstract

This chapter explores how university students view non-work related use of electronic technology within universities (I.e., electronic monitoring technology and personal use of electronic technologies). To this end, a technoethical case study utilizes research literature and conversational data derived from online group work taken from a research course offered by the communication department of a large urban university.

Questions and Answers

1. What is Technoethics and how is it defined?

Technoethics is an interdisciplinary field concerned with all ethical aspects of technology within a society shaped by technology. It deals with human processes and practices connected to technology which are becoming embedded within social, political, and moral spheres of life. It also examines social policies and interventions occurring in response to issues generated by technology development and use. This includes critical debates on the responsible use of technology for advancing human interests in society. To this end, it attempts to provide conceptual grounding to clarify the role of technology in relation to those affected by it and to help guide ethical problem-solving and decision making in areas of activity that rely on technology

2. What is the overall aim of the case and what does it offer to the reader?

The aim of the case is to explore how university students view non-work related use of electronic technologies within university, a technoethical case because it focuses on the ethical and social aspects of technology use in society. This case is intended to shed light on students' attitudes and ethical stances concerning non-work related electronic technology use within their university. This case is also intended to identify areas of concern about non-work related use of electronic technology within universities and offer possible solutions to help guard against potentially destructive activities with electronic technologies within university settings.

3. What were the main study findings regarding electronic technology abuse in the classroom?

There was a clear indication of electronic technology abuse within university classroom environments and an apparent contraction in student behavior where students complained about e-technology abuse as a distraction in class but admitted to doing it themselves.

4. What were the three purposes of an educational system according to Illich (1970)?

A good educational system should have three purposes: it should provide all who want to learn with access to available resources at any time in their lives; empower all who want to share what they know to find those who want to learn it from them; and, finally, furnish all who want to present an issue to the public with the opportunity to make their challenge known.

5. What strategies were mentioned in the chapter for dealing with pervasive issues and challenges in overcoming e-technology abuse in university classes?

First, strategies were provided for framing technoethical tensions. Second, strategies were provided to model learning conversations aimed at resolving technoethical tension.

6. According to the chapter discussion, why are ethical theories inadequate for dealing with social and ethical dilemmas in real life?

The problem with relying on ethical theories as a stand alone approach for dealing with social and ethical issues is that ethical theories are based on different assumptions about the nature of reality and the obligations of individuals within it. Ethical tensions arise when the fundamental assumptions underlying different ethical theories leads to different conclusions concerning what constitutes ethical conduct.

Epilogue and Lessons Learned

One of the most interesting findings in this chapter was that most students were critical of the negative distraction created by e-technology abuse within the classroom, but admitted that they continued the behavior anyway. It would be interesting to examine in a follow-up case involving all key stakeholders (students, administration, faculty, staff) whether the phenomenon of e-technology abuse is common in all stakeholder ground. This could provide a useful indicator of the problem across the university to inform the creation of a comprehensive policy to deal with e-technology abuse for all university members (students, administration, faculty, staff).

Lessons Learned

1. Each university is a complex system which requires context specific analyses. The study of e-technology abuse in the classroom cannot be generalized across universities and must be tailored to each context.
2. E-technology use policies, while helpful, will not completely solve the problem since individuals acknowledge that they would not change their behaviour. There is a deeper problem related to personal and professional ethics that needs to be resolved through ethical and moral educational interventions.
3. The proposed conversational approach to study perspective sharing and participatory decision-making within the university has its limits. One major limit in this study was the time required to analyze data. It provides a rich level of detail but at the expense of efficiency. The second problem is related to interest. It is a challenge to get busy university stakeholders to agree to give up valuable time. This would have to be a mandatory intervention which may create problems of interest and a sense of forced participation.

Chapter 8
Faculty Training and Mentoring at a Distance: Learning Together in the Virtual Community

Rena M. Palloff
Fielding Graduate University, USA

Keith Pratt
Fielding Graduate University, USA

ABSTRACT

Evidence suggests that a good instructor is the key to student persistence in an online course. Because of this, the hiring, training, and evaluation of good online instructors has become high priority for most online institutions. Providing good training and also providing incentives for keeping good online faculty have become critical concerns for most colleges and universities. However, not all universities are able to provide good training even under the best of circumstances. Many factors can wreak havoc with well-intended plans to provide training for online faculty. This case looks at the characteristics of a good online instructor as well as the faculty training needed to ensure high quality course design and delivery. Models of effective faculty training and evaluation are reviewed. Two cases, Delgado Community College in New Orleans and Excelsior Community College in Kingston, Jamaica are also reviewed to illustrate how critical needs for the delivery of high quality faculty training were met at a distance under less than ideal conditions. The cases illustrate the importance and impact that good training can make.

INTRODUCTION

Colleges and universities are faced with an increasingly diverse student body, competition for enrollment, changing policies and societal demands, as well as technological changes that are impacting the way instructors teach and students learn. A response to this has been increased development and adoption of online courses, with mixed results. Many administrators view online learning as a way to increase flagging enrollments and extend the reach of the institution or, in simple terms, as an easy way to maximize profits and attract new students. Many students view online courses as a more convenient way to go to school and even

DOI: 10.4018/978-1-61520-869-2.ch008

sometimes, mistakenly, as an easier way to earn credit. Faculty who are given the responsibility to develop and teach online courses, however, might not see online education in such a positive light. The absence of good training to support new and seasoned online instructors alike is part of the problem – good faculty development for online teaching is the solution.

Evidence suggests that a good instructor is the key to student persistence in an online course. Because of this, the hiring, training, and evaluation of good online instructors has become high priority for most online institutions. Providing good training and also providing incentives for keeping good online faculty have become critical concerns for most colleges and universities. However, not all universities are able to provide good training even under the best of circumstances. Many factors can wreak havoc with well-intended plans to provide training for online faculty. This chapter begins by looking at the characteristics of a good online instructor as well as the faculty training needed to ensure high quality course design and delivery. Models of effective faculty training and evaluation will be reviewed.

Following that discussion, two cases, Delgado Community College in New Orleans and Excelsior Community College in Kingston, Jamaica will be reviewed to illustrate how critical needs for the delivery of high quality faculty training were met at a distance under less than ideal conditions. The cases illustrate the importance and impact that good training can make. Additionally, the cases provide evidence for the organizational change that occurs when faculty development for online teaching goes beyond the simple use of technology in teaching.

THE IMPORTANCE OF FACULTY TRAINING FOR ONLINE TEACHING

Faculty are rarely provided with training in the pedagogical skills they need to teach online. A 2002 survey of faculty who teach in various disciplines and are located throughout the United States, yielded results that appear to be the norm of faculty experience, as 75% indicated that they had received approximately 30 hours of technical training in the course management system they would be using; however, only one-third reported receiving any pedagogical training. A subset of surveyed faculty were interviewed; they described the difficulties they were having engaging students in online discussion and their perceived need for pedagogical training (Pankowski, 2004). Given that White and Weight (2000) note that teaching techniques that work in the face-to-face classroom may not work online and that faculty are asking for additional support for effective teaching, it is clear that pedagogical training is lacking. Milam, Voorhees, and Bedard-Voorhees (2004) note, "…the online paradigm holds that learning itself may be different in the online environment" (p.74). Given that learning itself is different online, shouldn't faculty training be addressed differently as well?

Faculty Online

Teaching online requires faculty to move beyond traditional models of teaching and to adopt what may be new practices for them that facilitate student learning. Gone is the traditional lecture and in its place is the need to create a strong learning community (Palloff and Pratt, 2007), facilitate good discussion, and engage students in collaborative learning. Thus, the ability to present oneself well in text, known as the creation of social presence, has been receiving significant research attention and is now considered a critical factor in community building and in teaching online classes. Both instructors and students need to be able to present themselves as "real people" in the online classroom. This ability is positively linked to student satisfaction with online learning as well as successful achievement of learning outcomes (Garrison, Anderson, & Archer, 2003; Gunawardena and Zittle, 1997; Picciano, 2002; Rovai & Barnum, 2003).

In addition to the ability to develop social presence, successful online instructors are willing to give up a fair degree of control in the teaching and learning process. They are able to empower their learners and build a learning community. In other words, they are learner-focused instructors. Huba and Freed (2000) note that in a learner-centered paradigm, students construct knowledge by gathering and synthesizing information together by using inquiry, communication, critical thinking, and problem solving. The instructor's role is to facilitate the process and instructors and students together assess learning. Engaging in these practices may be new and even a bit threatening to an instructor who has been seen as "in charge" of the learning process in the face-to-face classroom and who is more comfortable with lecturing.

The ability for an online instructor to move to new means by which to deliver instruction impacts not only student learning but student persistence in the course as well. Ackridge, DeMay, Braunlich, Collura, and Sheahan (2002) suggest that student retention online is dependent on three factors: Selecting the right students for the right program; using a highly learner-focused delivery model; and engaging learners at a personal level. Hebert (2006) discovered that the responsiveness of faculty to perceived student needs helps to increase persistence in online courses and creates a greater degree of satisfaction with the learning process. This is an essential component of what it takes to teach online and yet, if faculty are only receiving technical training before they embark on teaching their first online course, how would they know how to do this?

An instructor who is willing to use collaborative, active learning techniques and ideas, and who allows for personal interaction, brings in real-life examples, and builds reflective practice into teaching, is a good candidate for teaching online (Palloff and Pratt, 2007). The open and flexible instructor needs support, however, to make the transition to the online classroom successful. This support rests in training and mentoring.

TRAINING TO SUPPORT THE TRANSITION

Faculty cannot be expected to know intuitively how to design and deliver an effective online course. Although courses and programs about the use of technology in education are emerging, and attendance at conferences on the topic continues to grow markedly, faculty have not been fully exposed to the techniques and methods needed to make online work successful. In fact, the study reported by Pankowski (2004) notes that only 56% of faculty who teach online have taken an online course themselves. She notes, "It is very difficult to teach in a medium in which one has never experienced learning" (Faculty as students, ¶ 1).

However, training faculty to help them get started and to support their ongoing teaching online does help. When that training is delivered online, using the course management system in which they will be teaching, faculty have the opportunity to experience the online environment as both a student and an instructor, serving to increase their effectiveness. In an online training course, the best practices involved in online teaching can be demonstrated. The best practices relate to the activities of teaching and learning and not to the technology itself. The online training course should be long enough so that faculty can be encouraged to develop the skeleton of their own course or at least one unit or lesson that other participants can critique. The facilitator of the training should model good techniques for building a learning community within the course and for empowering the participating faculty to explore both the medium and the material.

We have found that it is best to include faculty who will imminently teach their first online courses in the online training. Faculty who are about to teach online are highly motivated to learn good techniques for doing so. When the group is made up of those who will be teaching online immediately and those who are simply interested in teaching online at some point in the future, those who will not be teaching online immediately do not feel as compelled to comply with participation expectations for the course. They may drop out and create frustration for those who stay with the training and who depend on the group to learn how the online learning process works.

Elements and Models of Good Training

Bates (2000) notes that in institutions where best practices in the implementation of technology are followed, faculty development focuses on teaching and learning and not on the technology itself. There is little doubt that faculty are in need of developing skills in computer literacy before they can move into teaching online. However, as has been emphasized, the focus in faculty development should be on pedagogical methods and not on the software in use.

Pankowski (2004) notes that the faculty interviewed in her study cited the need for mentoring to support the transition to online teaching. Creating a mentoring relationship through the pairing of faculty who are more experienced online with those who are just starting helps to break down barriers and provides real concrete examples of what works and what does not. Those in Pankowski's study felt that without the support of a more experienced colleague to guide them, they would most likely have discontinued their involvement with online teaching beyond their first course. Using a mentoring approach to the training of online instructors can help to determine who will succeed and who might not be well suited to teaching online.

Mandernach, Donnelli, Daily, and Schulte (2005) describe the very extensive mentoring model used by Park University in Missouri. In this model, all instructors who teach online first go through faculty training for online teaching and then are assigned a peer faculty mentor who monitors their performance in an online course. In the Park University model, the mentor not only observes the online teaching of the new online instructor, but conducts five formative reviews of teaching performance during the first term. This very intensive model may not be appropriate to all universities, but a mentoring approach can be quite useful in faculty development by allowing the new instructor a peer to consult with and who can make suggestions to improve practice while the course is in progress. When mentoring programs are established, however, it should be with the clear understanding of how the resulting data will be used. Generally, the results of mentoring should be used for development purposes and not for faculty evaluation.

The University of Central Florida has established a comprehensive faculty development program that addresses four key areas of readiness for online work: the institution, faculty, courses, and learners. The areas can be used to generate a checklist to help institutions and faculty evaluate which aspects of their program or courses need attention. Institutional readiness includes such aspects as a clear mission for the online program, a robust campus infrastructure to support courses, programs, faculty, and students, and a strong commitment to assessment and evaluation. Faculty readiness includes the following elements that also determine components to be included in faculty training:

- A willingness to learn
- A willingness to surrender some control over class design and teaching style
- An ability to collaborate with peers
- A willingness to change the traditional faculty role
- An ability to build a support system
- Patience with technology
- An ability to learn from others
- Demonstrated understanding of the technology in use
- Demonstrated understanding of the pedagogy required for online teaching

- Demonstrated understanding of the logistics of the course production process

(Truman-Davis, Futch, Thompson, & Yonekura, 2000)

Fielding Graduate University developed a robust and rigorous online faculty development program, the Teaching in the Virtual Classroom academic certificate program, that is open to faculty from any institution. This comprehensive program spans two academic semesters and focuses on both the effective facilitation of online courses as well as effective course development. Developed by the authors of this chapter, the program focuses on the critical element of community building in the effective development and delivery of online classes. The program itself is conducted completely online and reviews the theoretical underpinnings of adult learning and online teaching while providing activities and examples that encourage faculty to experiment with multiple modes of course delivery, such as the use of wikis, blogs, and virtual classroom technology, as well as working in collaborative groups to explore concepts. Faculty participants are expected to create both lessons and full courses by the time they complete the program and to apply what they are learning to their online classrooms along the way. Fielding has negotiated partnerships with several community colleges as a means by which to provide economical faculty development to cohorts of faculty who are either new to online teaching or who are interested in improving their online course delivery. Two such partnerships with Delgado Community College in New Orleans, Louisiana and with Excelsior Community College in Kingston, Jamaica were initiated because of critical needs the institutions were facing.

What happens when critical needs arise that force institutions to abandon a well-planned approach to faculty development and move more quickly toward the implementation of online courses? The case of Delgado Community College is one such example.

THE DEVELOPMENT OF A VIRTUAL COMMUNITY COLLEGE

Delagado Community College lost 70 percent of its physical plant and significant enrollment due to Hurricane Katrina. Prior to the storm, the college was the largest community college in the state of Louisiana, enrolling upwards of 17,000 students. The college was already moving toward the development and delivery of online classes prior to Katrina. A push to begin offering online courses had begun with a three-year plan to increase online offerings and train faculty for online delivery. Before the storm, Delgado was proud to offer 67 fully online courses taught by 20 members of its faculty.

The devastation brought by Hurricane Katrina is widely known and undeniable. The staff, faculty, and students of Delgado were significantly impacted – many evacuated the New Orleans area to different parts of the country and it was not known where people were or who might have perished in the storm. Delgado's Chancellor worked with their e-Learning Coordinator to establish an area on the college's website where people could check in, tell their storm stories, and reconnect with the Delgado community. In addition, the college quickly realized that the only way to remain vital was to move its course offerings online, particularly since most of the physical plant was unusable, would be so for at least five years, and students and faculty were no longer in the local area. Luckily, the college's Blackboard server was safe and functioning. Consequently, a special fall semester was held in 2005 using Blackboard. Approximately 150 faculty stepped forward to teach online courses – most had never taught a course online before and had no training in doing so. One-day "crash courses" were offered by the more seasoned online faculty either in faculty's homes, if they were in New Orleans, or in the cities to which they had evacuated, and approximately 7,000 students were able to continue their education as a result. Faculty taught themselves and each other to work within this new framework for delivering education, but realized that there was much more that they needed to learn to move forward.

OK, Now What Do We Do?

As the reality of the situation in New Orleans set in and the long-term impact for Delgado was realized, it became clear to the college that a new strategy was in order – one that involved significant numbers of course offerings through online means. In addition, although faculty had stepped up to teach online when needed, they were asking for help and training in order to do a better job of online course development and teaching. The college had lost most of its technology as well as physical space for faculty development, so a new approach was in order. Additionally, there was a need to apply for a substantive change with the accrediting agency, Southern Association of Colleges and Schools.

A staff member at Delgado, who was also a doctoral student at Fielding Graduate University reached out to a student colleague of hers, someone she knew to be involved professionally with strategic planning work and who was also well-connected and networked and could potentially bring help to a college in need. He, in turn, reached out to one of the authors, a faculty member at Fielding and as a result, others from Fielding were brought into the discussions. A series of phone meetings between Fielding and Delgado personnel ensued. A resulting partnership was created with Fielding Graduate University to assist with strategic planning for substantive change as well as training and coaching for faculty in online course design and delivery, led by the authors.

Timeline for Change

The following is the timeline that outlines the work that occurred once the partnership was created:

January 2006

Planning meeting held between Fielding, DLIT (Distance Learning and Instructional Technology) office, and Professional Development office

- Needs explored
- Resources identified
- Initial plan for services developed

February and March 2006

A plan for faculty coaching and training was developed, culminating in a face-to-face meeting in April 2006

- Professional Development and DLIT promote online coaching for all of Delgado's online faculty
- Faculty sign up for the coaching
- Palloff/Pratt given access to all online instructors' classes who volunteered to be reviewed

April 2006

Palloff/Pratt, along with the Dean of the School of Educational Leadership and Change from Fielding travel to New Orleans to assess additional needs and train/coach faculty

- Decision is made to offer the annual Delgado Summer Institute virtually
- Date set for July 10 - 14
- LearningTimes is solicited for help and donates their Elluminate classroom as well as technical support and planning assistance for the virtual event
- Fielding Graduate University offers the services of Palloff and Pratt to facilitate the event
- PR website is developed

May 2006

- E-mail sent to all DCC faculty with link to PR website
- Faculty complete the online form to register
- Room that is available for opening session is located and booked
- Faculty are notified of their registration and room location

June 2006

- Reminder e-mails sent
- Donation solicited by Rick Daniels – Funds used to hire local tech support person for faculty to rely on for help with Blackboard technical issues

July 2006

- Final e-mail reminder sent
- Summer Institute held July 10 – 14 with 30 faculty participating
- Evaluation of Summer Institute by participants July 14
- Evaluation of Summer Institute by leaders July 17

When Life Gives You Lemons...

The Virtual Summer Institute, hosted by LearningTimes and facilitated by the authors, was attended by approximately 60 faculty and was considered a tremendous success. As a result, a decision was made to continue to offer the Institute in virtual fashion in subsequent years. The partnership between Fielding and Delgado did not end with the Summer Institute and is ongoing. In the fall of 2006, 12 Delgado faculty members enrolled in Fielding's Teaching in the Virtual Classroom program to further develop their skills as online instructors and course developers. A five-year plan was developed for ongoing training of faculty and the Teaching in the Virtual Classroom program became an integral part of the plan. Each fall, eight Delgado faculty enter and complete the program as part of Delgado's ongoing faculty development and continuous quality improvement effort. Fielding continues to offer consulting and training services as Delgado assesses and addresses ongoing needs.

In the spring of 2007, Delgado's enrollment approached its pre-Katrina levels. One additional classroom building is now available on campus. The college is now offering 314 fully online classes and 51 hybrid classes.

The challenge moving forward is in sustaining the faculty development effort as well as evaluating the quality improvement of online courses. Additionally, creating administrative structures to support and continue the work has been a challenge. Ongoing faculty training needs are being assessed as is the organizational structure that will sustain the efforts made to date. The participating faculty, to this point, have done this work because they are committed to rebuilding the college. Will that commitment be sustainable over the long haul, however? This is the major question still to be tackled at Delgado. But, in the meantime, efforts continue to rebuild enrollment through the offering of high quality, well facilitated online courses – and it appears to be working.

What appears to have supported and sustained this effort was the empowerment of faculty by the institution to take on the responsibility for making it happen. Certainly, there was a sense of urgency involved and the need to transform the college in order to survive. But, faculty took on the tasks not because there were extrinsic rewards involved; rather the challenge of moving forward into new territory, learning something new, and collaboratively creating a new learning model both initiated and sustained the work. Delgado now views itself as primarily a virtual community college, something the institution would not have considered prior to the storm. As noted by one staff member who wrote about this effort,

"Perhaps of the various theoretical conclusions that can be drawn…one that stands out…is that if positive transformation is to occur, it is necessary to allow it to occur, to provide an environment for it to occur, to support it as it is occurring, and to create equitable circumstances in which it may continue to be a source of inspiration and purpose for those individuals who choose to act on it" (Breckenridge, 2008).

BECOMING A LEADER IN A DISTANCE LEARNING CONSORTIUM

Unlike the situation at Delgado Community College, Excelsior Community College has been faced with transformation of a different sort. As noted by Excelsior's Principal, Dahlia Repole, "The profile of the student in the world today continues to change, and as such, the demands on educational institutions to respond to these needs continue to be intense. One such demand is the need to have access to programme offerings which are available anytime, anywhere" (Repole, 2007, p.1).

Background

Excelsior Community College was established in 1974 and was the first Community College established in Jamaica. The College has served Jamaica for 33 years in Kingston community and 13 years in Morant Bay. Excelsior Community College is part of the Excelsior Education Centre (EXED) of schools, which together have served the nation for over seventy five years.

Excelsior offers a wide range of programs including Bachelor Degrees, Associate Degrees, Certificates and Modular Courses and boasts ten departments with approximately 2000 students enrolled each year. The College has received accreditation for its Bachelor and Associate Degree Programs in Computing and Hospitality. Over the years, the institution has established vital linkages with its community through its association with neighborhood groups as well as the private sector, and has been responsive to their developmental needs while also creating opportunities to address the challenges faced by its members. The College also has firm linkages with the University of the West Indies, the University of Technology Jamaica, and with universities and colleges in the United States of America, Canada and the United Kingdom.

In this very dynamic, global and competitive educational environment, the college is re-positioning itself to meet the opportunities that have been created with the advent of the information age (Repole, 2007).

In 2006, the Ministry of Education and Youth of Jamaica, drafted and presented for consideration of its stakeholders, an integrated National Strategic Planning Framework 2006-11. This Framework presents great and new opportunities for all institutions at the tertiary level, and especially for the community colleges. The Framework speaks to the importance of developing opportunities in the Information Technology sector, such as the use of distance education to expand access. The Framework also demands that each individual institution respond by developing its own Strategic Plan that is congruent with, and expands upon, individual directions within the Framework. Education providers are therefore creating new courses, using new technologies, including online distance learning courses, to meet this demand. This coincides perfectly with the College's vision and mission "to be a dynamic learning institution, providing tertiary level educational and training opportunities in an environment that is responsive, adaptable, nurturing and inclusive, and enhances lifelong learning in support of the changing educational and employment needs of individuals and society" (Repole, 2007, p.3).

Meeting the Demand

Community Colleges through the Council of Community Colleges of Jamaica have developed a plan focusing on Open and Distance Education. The emerging employment opportunities in Jamaica demanding education and training to which the Community Colleges can respond are predominately in four major sectors: IT, Manufacturing, Hospitality and Tourism and Business. Within these sectors, there are many sub-sectors, to many of which the Community Colleges can also respond. However, to expand their program offerings, the Colleges will need to evaluate their existing infrastructure, availability of human resources at a variety of levels, systems and policies and financial resources, plan carefully and determine their strategic direction for the next five to ten years.

In response, the Council of Community Colleges put forth the following strategic vision and plan:

The Council of Community Colleges of Jamaica/Open and Distance Education Vision Statement

"Going the Distance"

Mission Statement

Providing expanded, sustainable opportunities for access to high quality relevant education and training through distance education without boundaries.

Objectives

In determining the objectives for Open and Distance Education in the Community Colleges, it was decided that four primary areas that must guide the change and development processes: *people, processes, infrastructure* and *finance.*

Developing a focus for ODE objectives in the Community Colleges

- Affordability
- Quality Assurance
- Support Services
- Program Development and Sustainability
- Human Resource Management
- Access
- Technology

Objectives for Distance Education in the Community Colleges:

Following are the related sub-objectives for Open and Distance Education in the Community Colleges:

- Develop and offer affordable Distance Education
- Provide student support systems to ensure successful completion of programmes
- To develop sustainable programs that satisfy client needs
- To provide access through a variety of technologies
- Develop partnerships that will expand resources and relationships with other institutions
- Ensure the availability of a trained, highly motivated cadre of DE facilitators and support staff
- Development of a system to assure the quality of Community Colleges' methods, educational products and outcomes (Repole, 2007, pp. 6-7)

Implementing the Strategy

Excelsior Community College realized that in order to make this strategy a reality, there was a need to focus on personnel, specifically the development of their Information Technology department to provide support and training faculty to develop and deliver effective online courses. Additionally, the college recognized that other interrelated systems also needed to be in place – provision of high quality course materials, student support, and responsive administrative structures. The expertise to make this happen did not exist in Jamaica. Consequently, Excelsior Community

College entered into an agreement with Fielding Graduate University to train a cohort of 10 faculty members through the Teaching in the Virtual Classroom program.

To begin this venture, the authors traveled to Kingston and delivered a face-to-face training about the transition to online learning to over 200 participants from various community colleges in Jamaica and other Caribbean islands. From that group, 10 volunteered to be part of the initial cohort. Many unforeseen issues inhibited the initial progress of the group of 10, however. They were:

- Distance – The facilitators were in the United States and all of the participants were in close geographical proximity to one another in Jamaica. It was clear that there were conversations, including conflicts and differences of opinion that were being aired on the ground in Jamaica, but not shared with the facilitators. At one point, the conflict did emerge on the asynchronous discussion board and the facilitators had to call on administrators in Jamaica to intervene. This inability to intervene directly became an issue that resurfaced later in the program, as it had caused misunderstanding and misinterpretation of intent.
- Cultural differences – The cultural differences experienced were many. A major difference focused on the British-based educational system to which the group was accustomed. In this system, faculty are referred to by Professor or Doctor rather than by first names, which is part of the culture at Fielding. The cohort was initially quite uncomfortable with this and also had difficulty expressing this discomfort. Because of the warmth and friendliness of the members of the group, the discomfort came as a surprise to the facilitators. Additionally, it was difficult for the group to explore course design that might go beyond the use of lectures and exams, since this has been so much a part of the delivery of education in Jamaica.
- Further issues with formality – The group were used to being rather formal with one another and in working independently from one another and even competitively with one another. Because the program relies to a great degree on community building and collaboration for the completion of assignments, this posed another hurdle for the participants. The concept of community was quite familiar to them and helped them to overcome this barrier for the most part. But the element of competition between members was present throughout.
- Infrastructure issues – The technological infrastructure in Jamaica is somewhat fragile. Access issues were common. During the time that the cohort was engaged in the program, two hurricanes hit the island which knocked out power and internet capability for two weeks at a time. Regrouping after the storms was an issue.

Program Outcomes and Lessons Learned

Of the 10 faculty members who made up the Excelsior cohort, eight successfully completed the program and went on to become trainers and support people for the faculty who are now developing online courses for the college. A follow-up session with representatives of the group six months after completion indicated positive results including greater comfort with instructional techniques beyond lecturing, implementation of hybrid learning approaches in existing college classes, and a desire to engage others in the online learning process. One member of the group was asked by college administration to develop a training program for other faculty who will be teaching online and developed a training program that is based on the principles that underlie the Teaching in the Virtual Classroom Program. Despite the challenges, movement toward the goals of the college's strategic plan has begun as the result of participation in online faculty training and development at a distance.

CONCLUSION AND IMPLICATIONS

There is a movement occurring in the academic world; academic institutions need to be increasingly responsive to those they serve, resulting in a shift from the traditional faculty-centered institution to a learner-focused one. The student is seen as a customer whose needs for technologically-based education must be met. In this context, the need for good training to support online delivery of courses is increasing. The ability to deliver that training in the same mode through which instruction will be delivered allows faculty to see both sides of the picture – what it is like to be an online student and what it is like to design and deliver courses online. This ability to work from two perspectives only serves to strengthen online course design and delivery.

The challenges encountered in both of the cases presented were educational for all – participants as well as facilitators – and helped prospective online instructors see in a very real way what can and does go wrong as well as what makes things go well. These were very important lessons learned. What was key to both of these cases is that instructors were empowered to take on their own learning – something that will translate into their own online teaching.

When instructors and students are able to reap the benefits of a well designed online course, the end result is excitement about what is possible in the online realm and about the new relationships that are developed between instructor and student; among students; and among instructor, students, and knowledge creation. The resultant excitement about learning helps to stimulate new creative approaches to online teaching.

REFERENCES

Akridge, J., DeMay, L., Braunlich, L., Collura, M., & Sheahan, M. (2002). Retaining adult learners in a high-stress distance education learning environment: The purdue university executive MBA in agribusiness. Motivating & Educating Adult Learners Online. Essex Junction, VT. Retrieved from GetEducated.com

Bates, A. W. (2000). *Managing technological change*. San Francisco: Jossey-Bass.

Breckenridge, A. (2008). *The sharpening stone: Crisis as impetus for individual and organizational transformation,* Fielding Graduate University: Unpublished paper.

Garrison, D., Anderson, T., & Archer, W. (2003). A theory of Critical Inquiry in Online Distance Education. In Moore, M. G., & Anderson, W. G. (Eds.), *Handbook of Distance Education* (pp. 113–127). Mahwah, NJ: Lawrence Erlbaum Associates.

Gunawardena, C. N., & Zittle, F. (1997). Social presence as a predictor of satisfaction within a computer mediated conferencing environment. *American Journal of Distance Education, 11*(3), 8–25. doi:10.1080/08923649709526970

Hebert, M. (2006). Staying the course: A study in online student satisfaction and retention. *Online Journal of Distance Learning Administration, 9*(4).

Huba, M. E., & Freed, J. (2000). *Learner-Centered Assessment on College Campuses: Shifting the Focus from Teaching to Learning*. Needham Heights, MA: Allyn & Bacon.

Mandernach, B. J., Donnelli, E., Dailey, A., & Schulte, M. (2005). A faculty evaluation model for online instructors: Mentoring and evaluation in the online classroom. *Online Journal of Distance Education Administration,* 8(3).

Milam, J., Voorhees, R., & Bedard-Voorhees, A. (2004). Assessment of online education: Policies, practices, and recommendations. In Serban, A. M., & Friedlander, J. (Eds.), *Developing and implementing assessment of student learning outcomes. New Directions for Community Colleges*. San Francisco: Jossey-Bass.

Palloff, R. M., & Pratt, K. (2007). *Building online learning: Effective strategies for the online classroom*. San Francisco: Jossey-Bass.

Pankowski, P. (2004, September). Faculty training for online teaching. *T.H.E. Journal*. Retrieved from http://thejournal.com/articles/16956

Picciano, A. (2002, July). Beyond student perceptions: Issues of interaction, presence, and performance in an online course. *JALN*, *6*(1), 21–40.

Repole, D. (2007). *Open and distance education proposal,* Excelsior Community College: Unpublished paper.

Rovai, A. P., & Barnum, K. T. (2003). On-Line Course Effectiveness: An Analysis of Student Interactions and Perceptions of Learning. *Journal of Distance Learning*, *18*(1), 57–73.

Truman-Davis, B., Futch, L., Thompson, K., & Yonekura, F. (2000). Support for online teaching and learning. *EDUCAUSE Quarterly*, *2*, 44–51.

White, K., & Weight, B. (2000). *The Online Teaching Guide*. Needham Heights, MA: Allyn & Bacon.

APPENDIX A: ADDITIONAL RESOURCES

Teaching in the Virtual Classroom Certificate Program Fielding Graduate University 2112 Santa Barbara St Santa Barbara, CA 93105 www.fielding.edu/elc/tvcC Contact: Nathan Lewin, Program Coordinator E-mail: nlewin@fielding.edu
Quality Matters (www.qualitymatters.org)
Moodle (www.moodle.org)
Elluminate (www.elluminate.com)
LearningTimes (www.learningtimes.org)

APPENDIX B: SUPPORTING MATERIAL

Abstract

Providing good training and also providing incentives for keeping good online faculty have become critical concerns for most colleges and universities. However, not all universities are able to provide good training even under the best of circumstances. Many factors can wreak havoc with well-intended plans to provide training for online faculty. This chapter looks at the characteristics of a good online instructor as well as the faculty training needed to ensure high quality course design and delivery. Models of effective faculty training and evaluation are reviewed. Two cases, Delgado Community College in New Orleans and Excelsior Community College in Kingston, Jamaica are also reviewed to illustrate how critical needs for the delivery of high quality faculty training were met at a distance under less than ideal conditions. The cases illustrate the importance and impact that good training can make.

Questions and Answers

1. What is the overall problem(s) in this case?

In both cases, the institutions had a need to move quickly to develop online courses and to train faculty effectively to do so. Due to constraints posed by natural disaster, technological infrastructure issues, and lack of availability of resources, it was determined that online faculty training would best meet these needs.

2. What are the factors affecting the problem(s) related to this case?

At Delgado Community College, the significant loss of physical resources along with the disbursement of personnel following Hurricane Katrina posed huge obstacles to providing effective faculty training for online teaching. In the case of Excelsior Community College, resources to provide training were not available locally. An unstable technology infrastructure created additional concerns for training and delivery of online courses.

3. Discuss managerial, organizational, and technological issues and resources related to this case.

In both cases, faculty had to be empowered to take charge of the training and development process and project. Without that level of empowerment, it is unlikely that faculty would have volunteered to be trained or would have taken on the responsibility for developing the ongoing training program for other faculty.

4. What role do different players (decision-makers) play in the overall planning, implementation and management of the information technology applications?

In both cases, senior managers gave their approval for online faculty training and helped to recruit those who would participate and then got out of the way, allowing faculty to take charge of the process and move it forward. The support of the decision-makers was critical in setting the wheels in motion.

5. What are the possible alternatives and pros and cons of each alternative facing the organization in dealing with the problem(s) related to the case?

In the case of Delgado, had movement to online course delivery not occurred, the institution would likely have floundered following Hurricane Katrina. With only 30% of its physical plant available, enrollment would have seriously suffered and the survival of the institution is questionable. In the case of Excelsior, the administration and faculty would have been at the mercy, so to speak, of other decision-makers, namely the Ministry of Education and the other universities who were moving forward. They chose to take leadership in this initiative rather than being followers. In so doing, they were able to proactively meet the needs of their own students and institution rather than hoping that those needs might be met by the efforts of others.

6. What are some of the emerging technologies that should be considered in solving the problem(s) related to the case?

Moodle, Skype, and Elluminate were the technologies used to deliver training in both cases, along with the use of wikis and blogs. Not only did participants gain facility with these technologies, they were instrumental in creating a community of practice in both cases.

7. What is the final solution that can be recommended to the management of the organization described in the case? Provide your arguments in support of the recommended solution.

The final solution recommended to both institutions was the one adopted – the delivery of online training to groups of faculty who are going to be teaching online. Training outcomes were successful and both institutions now have cadres of instructors who can instruct others on best practices in online teaching and course design. The effort is sustainable, even if instructors do not continue to participate in the Teaching in the Virtual Classroom program. They have gained valuable skill in the use of technology in teaching and effective facilitation of online courses. In addition, they are now adept at evaluating courses for quality and are engaging with their institutions to continue this effort.

Epilogue and Lessons Learned

Epilogue: Delgado Community College

Delgado Community College continues to successfully offer an increasing number of online courses as well as blended or hybrid courses as their enrollment increases to pre-Katrina levels. As more buildings come back online, the number of face-to-face courses offered is also increasing. Delgado recently received a faculty development grant from the State of Louisiana to continue their faculty training. The intent now is to create a cadre of "master instructors" for both face-to-face and, in particular, for online delivery. The instructors who have completed the Teaching in the Virtual Classroom Program are prime candidates to be trained as master instructors and will likely become mentors to those who are just embarking on online teaching. Additionally, several Delgado faculty have completed the Quality Matters training and are evaluating the design of online courses both at Delgado and for other institutions. Although the college may never emerge as a completely online institution, its work in the online arena as the result of a natural disaster has significantly transformed the college and the role of its faculty in effective course design and delivery.

Epilogue: Excelsior Community College

Of the 10 faculty members who made up the Excelsior cohort, eight successfully completed the program and went on to become trainers and support people for the faculty who are now developing online courses for the college. A follow-up session with representatives of the group six months after completion indicated positive results including greater comfort with instructional techniques beyond lecturing, implementation of hybrid learning approaches in existing college classes, and a desire to engage others in the online learning process. One member of the group was asked by college administration to develop a training program for other faculty who will be teaching online and developed a training program that is based on the principles that underlie the Teaching in the Virtual Classroom Program. Despite the challenges, movement toward the goals of the college's strategic plan has begun as the result of participation in online faculty training and development at a distance.

Lessons Learned

The need for good training to support online delivery of courses is increasing. The ability to deliver that training in the same mode through which instruction will be delivered allows faculty to see both sides of the picture – what it is like to be an online student and what it is like to design and deliver courses online. This ability to work from two perspectives only serves to strengthen online course design and delivery. Online faculty development for online faculty is the method of choice in training excellent instructors.

The challenges encountered in both of the cases presented helped prospective online instructors see in a very real way what can and does go wrong in an online class in addition to what makes things go well. These were very important lessons learned. What was key to both of these cases is that instructors were empowered to take on their own learning – something that will translate into their own online teaching. Faculty need to be an integral part of the effective design and delivery of online courses to assure successful outcomes.

Chapter 9
The Potential for Student Engagement Using Clickers in a Large Introductory Class

Jenepher Lennox Terrion
University of Ottawa, Canada

Victoria Aceti
University of Ottawa, Canada

ABSTRACT

This pilot project employed personal response systems, or clicker technology, in an effort to address student inattention and the distractions created by electronics in a large, first-year introductory communication class. The objectives of the project were to increase student engagement through a more hands-on, active and collaborative learning environment and to better gauge student understanding of important concepts throughout the lecture. This case discusses the challenges of student engagement, in particular with today's millennial students, examines the role of technology generally in engaging students and the personal response systems specifically, describes the pilot project and presents a series of exercises that may be used to most effectively take advantage of this technology in the classroom.

INTRODUCTION

Engaging students has become more of a challenge than ever. Students (and faculty members) perceive themselves as part of an increasingly fast-paced world where multi-tasking and information overload are the norm. Today's students, called millennials by Strauss and Howe (2000, 2003), noted authorities on generational identities and behaviors, were born in 1982 or later and are the first university cohort to have grown up with the internet, the cell phone, and a host of instant-communication and social networking technologies. As a generation, millennials are constantly wired and connected to their friends, their media and the internet through their cell phones, MP3 players, and laptops. Jones (2002), in his study of the impact of internet use of college students' daily lives and academic and social routines, found that 72% of all students check their email daily, and 26% of college students use instant messaging on an average day. A 2008 survey reported that 87% of American adults in the 18-29 age range participated in online activities (Pew Internet Project, 2008). These data show that university

DOI: 10.4018/978-1-61520-869-2.ch009

and college classrooms are made up of participants who are likely in a constant state of distraction -- playing on laptops, watching videos on Youtube, communicating with friends on various hand-held technologies and checking their Facebook pages (Rice & Bunz, 2006). These distracting behaviors interfere with both the student's own ability to attend to and understand the course material as well as that of his or her peers sitting nearby, and is likely to have a negative impact on student engagement.

What is Student Engagement?

Student engagement is understood to mean "the time and energy students devote to educationally sound activities inside and outside of the classroom, and the policies and practices that institutions use to induce students to take part in these activities" (*Kuh, 2003, p. 25).* It is clear from this definition that if they want their students to invest time in their classes, instructors must find ways to maintain the interest and attention of students, and that students need to be involved in meaningful, participatory classroom practices in what Coates (2005) calls the "joint proposition" of learning. Research shows that student engagement is among the better predictors of learning and personal development (*Carini, Kuh, & Klein, 2006*) and thus is critical to the academic achievement and retention of post-secondary students (Kuh, 2003).

The Role of Technology in Student Engagement

While technology may be blamed for much of the distraction in university and college classrooms, it can also offer solutions to this problem by enhancing student engagement. Millenials are adept at learning, are used to handheld devices and are eager early adopters of new technologies, As Prensky (2001) describes them, millenials are "digital natives in a land of digital immigrants" so it may well be that the most effective approach to engaging these students is to meet them where they are.

As Chickering and Ehrmann (1996) suggest, technology can be used as a lever to advance the seven principles of effective undergraduate education developed by Chickering and Gamson (1987). In sum, Chickering and Gamson argue that good practice encourages contact between students and faculty, develops reciprocity and cooperation among students, encourages active learning, gives prompt feedback, emphasizes time on task, communicates high expectations, and respects diverse talents and ways of learning.

One technology that offers hope is the personal or classroom response system (PRS/CRS) commonly referred to as the *clicker*. This technology is being used in schools internationally in an attempt to bring students' focus back to the lecture. In classrooms equipped with a receiver and the appropriate software, students each have a hand-held remote control, purchased along with their textbook for about $20. Students "click" in their responses to multiple choice questions posed by the lecturer that are projected on the screen from within a slide presentation. When all responses are received, the results are projected onto the screen for the entire class to see (either anonymously or with respondents identified). Individual student and collective class data are saved for each session, allowing for responses to be recorded, analyzed and graphed. As Rice and Bunz (2006) argue, clickers create the opportunity for collaborative learning, which they define as a group- or team-based approach to and which allows for "the fundamental roles of direct interaction with information, and of social interaction in learning" (p. 2). These authors point out that the clicker technology at once fosters participation by requiring every student to provide a response and, depending on how it is used, can encourage collaboration if students discuss questions before posting their answers. Participation and collaboration, according to Kuh (2003), are both critical aspects of student engagement and, ultimately, learning.

LITERATURE REVIEW: THE IMPACT OF CLICKERS ON STUDENT ENGAGEMENT

Research suggests that, when used thoughtfully and appropriately, clickers are very effective in engaging students and facilitating active learning. Duncan (2006) explains that, "the success of even an exemplary lecture is limited by the passive role that students take in an ordinary lecture" (p. 72). Thus learning technologies, such as clickers, may be the key to creating an active learning environment, which in turn enhances student engagement. Previous studies, conducted at a number of different universities in a variety of disciplines, conclude that clickers are beneficial in improving student engagement and overall student success in the course in which they are used (Rice & Bunz, 2006; Kaleta & Joosten, 2007; Hoekstra, 2008; Twetten, Smith, Julius, & Murphy-Boyer, 2007). The popularity of the clickers in many universities has led to a vast literature on the benefits, challenges, and best practices of implementation. The "common consensus among the many studies and experiences of students and faculty is that class interaction and engagement is enhanced" (Ellozy, 2007, p.2). Reviewing the research on clickers is critical in creating realistic expectations of the extent to which the clickers will affect student engagement.

Empirical studies have illustrated the pedagogical benefits of clickers in the classroom, including a recent study conducted by Rice and Bunz (2006) who found that clickers have led to "greater student engagement in the classroom, high satisfaction, and gains in student learning across the disciplines" (p. 3). The authors further break down the benefits for students, stating that clickers facilitate more participation and interaction (Markey & Spiering, 2005; Scott Barrett, Bornsen, Erickson), collaboration, cognitive involvement, self-assessment (Draper, Cargill, & Cutts, 2002) shared knowledge, material review (Judson & Sawada, 2002; Scott Barrett et al.), and lecture discussion (Draper et al.; Fies & Marshall, 2006).

Kaleta and Joosten (2007) studied 3,500 students in 28 courses and 19 disciplines at the University of Wisconsin who employed clicker technology in the classroom and found that 94% of faculty strongly agreed/agreed that students were more engaged and 72% strongly agreed/agreed that clickers benefited learning. Further, 69% of students agreed or strongly agreed that the use of clickers made them feel more engaged (Kaleta & Joosten). The researchers conclude that clickers are ameliorating the problems of medium to large classes. This study illustrates that clickers are not successful in only one specific discipline or field of study, but across disciplines and post-secondary levels.

A recent ethnographic evaluation of clickers confirms the conclusions of previous quantitative analyses. Hoekstra (2008) evaluated student responses to clickers in an introductory Chemistry course over three years with different students. Through observational notes, interviews, and survey questions, Hoekstra found that, "clickers create a more engaging learning environment than would be the case with lecture alone" (p. 334). The author goes further to claim that clickers allow for a more accountable student who is then able to engage with course material during lectures. Researchers conclude that clickers are ameliorating the problems of disengagement associated with medium and large classes. This study illustrates that clickers are successful across many disciplines and post-secondary levels.

While clicker technology holds promise, not all research has touted the positive impacts of clickers in post-secondary education. In their study of the impact of clicker technology in a microeconomics course, Johnson and Robson (2008) found that nearly 90% of students reported that they were 'engaged' or 'somewhat engaged'. However, the data showed no significant difference in student engagement between students in a course which employed clickers and those in the control group who did not use the technology. In explaining the results, the researchers state that the implementation of the clickers through a simple transfer to the classroom without changing the pedagogy of the course affected the statistical significance of the results (Draper & Brown, 2004; Johnson and Robson; Judson & Sawada, 2002; Trees & Jackson, 2007). These findings illustrate the importance of adapting pedagogical techniques to incorporate with clicker exercises.

Simply put, empirical studies support the use of clickers in the classroom and claim that the technology is a moderately inexpensive way to engage learners in the educational process and to enrich their experience" (Twetten et al., 2007, p. 5). The positive impact of clickers on engagement has led to another question: what it is it about the clicker that works to engage students so effectively? Bruff (2009) tried to determine how clickers engage students and stated that, "students are usually more engaged with a task when they are asked to produce a deliverable" (p. 199). In other words, it is the act of coming up with something that engages students, according to Bruff.

Other scholars have discussed the unique attributes of clicker technology and argued that it is these which contribute to enhanced student engagement. There are four main attributes of clickers which enhance student engagement: response anonymity, immediate feedback, tangible act of answering question, and accountability for class preparation. When students are posed with a verbal question in traditional lectures, they have to respond through visual signs (e.g. raising a hand or nodding). This form of answering is not anonymous and usually not entirely truthful as students may answer according to what is deemed socially acceptable. Clickers give students the opportunity to answer anonymously, thus facilitating more fruitful class discussions which enhance student engagement. Students feel less anxious in answering honestly, are able to see the distribution of diverse responses and are able to engage in more fruitful classroom discussions. (Bruff, 2009). Students find that the anonymity of the clickers allows for answering questions in lectures more palatable – in particular those that seek opinions or ideas – as these are more revealing of personal, and possibly embarrassing, views.

Clickers allow for students to not only respond anonymously but also to think independently. Bruff (2009) explains that this independent thinking can increase student engagement as students respond before knowing how their peers have answered. Furthermore, the immediate feedback provided allows the student to better assess their knowledge of major concepts, as well as their level of understanding in comparison to their peers (Kaleta & Joosten, 2007). This immediate feedback allows the instructor to better understand students' understanding of lecture materials. Further, if students are grasping a concept easily (as seen in their clicker responses), the instructor is able to move the lecture along more quickly, thus keeping the attention of the students. In contrast, if students are not grasping a concept – as evidenced by their incorrect clicker responses – the lecturer can reinforce those concepts. Immediate feedback thus allows for better student engagement as the lecture is able to move along at the learning pace of the students.

Learning styles vary among students and yet the traditional lecture usually only accommodates auditory or, with the use of slides or overheads, visual learning. The tangible act of answering a question using a clicker increases engagement, especially in students who are kinesthetic learners (Bruff, 2009). This action expands the student's role from a passive participant to an active contributor. Incorporating the needs of all styles of learners increases student engagement as each student is able to learn effectively through one of the delivery approaches – auditory, visual or kinesthetic – of the lecture.

In Kaleta and Joosten's (2007) study at the University of Wisconson, students reported their "need to come to class ready to participate and pay attention" (p. 9) when the lecture incorporated clickers. Students are aware that if clickers are used in lecture, they must be prepared to answer the questions. In addition, "It also creates a learning environment with higher expectations for student preparation prior to class" (Trees & Jackson, 2007, p. 25). As a result, students have another motivation to read all materials required for lecture, resulting in more engagement in lecture discussions. Kaleta and Joosten further claim that clickers allow for a more accountable student who is then able to engage with course material during lectures.

CASE DESCRIPTION: CLICKER USE AT THE UNIVERSITY OF OTTAWA

Based on the literature, we have developed a pilot project that draws on insights from research findings as well as the unique pedagogical approaches used in the discipline of communication.

In an effort to address student inattention and the distractions created by electronics in a large, first-year introductory communication class, the researchers will add a number of clicker innovations to our existing pedagogical approaches. CMN 1148, Introduction to Organizational Communication, is a relay-taught course in which three professors each teach a 4 week section of the course. The course is lecture- based and uses Microsoft Powerpoint slides with infusions of multimedia and online tools. Each lecture will incorporate many different clicker activities, which have the potential to help in holding the student's attention longer. Gaining the students' attention is the first step in engaging students with the course material and increasing participation in class discussions. Through different exercises, quizzes, case studies, and team-based activities, we hope not only to increase student engagement, but also to create a climate of active learning. Further, the use of quizzes with the lectures will allow the instructors to gauge student understanding. This testing mechanism has benefits for students who may not admit they did not understand a particular concept in the lecture. In the case of questions eliciting attitudes, the anonymity afforded by use of the clickers may encourage students to be more truthful with their answers, without feeling embarrassed. Information gained from specific responses to content-based questions, on the other hand, allows the professor to target where more instruction is required, based on the needs of the students. This allows the lecture to move along quickly on easier subjects and to repeat sections that are more difficult, thus creating a more student-focused lecture.

In the past, new technological advances, proven to be helpful in addressing student inattention, did not always gain a foothold because of the implementation challenges associated with large class sizes. However, clickers are designed specifically to be used in large classes, and they have been shown in numerous studies to be helpful in overcoming the challenges faced with student inattention and distractions (Boyle & Nicol, 2003).

This pilot project has three main objectives:

1. To increase student engagement with course material and in-class discussions.
2. To increase active learning through hands-on activities that encourage dialogue among students and professors.
3. To better gauge student understanding of important concepts throughout the lecture.

The Kinds of Activities That Work Really Well

The following section presents five activities that were developed for this pilot project to enhance student engagement through active and collaborative learning and to enable prompt feedback through the use of the clickers.

1. Quizzes

Quizzes can be used at the beginning of the lecture to assess understanding of readings or at the end of challenging sections in lectures to check understanding. As Chickering and Ehrmann (1987)

Figure 1.

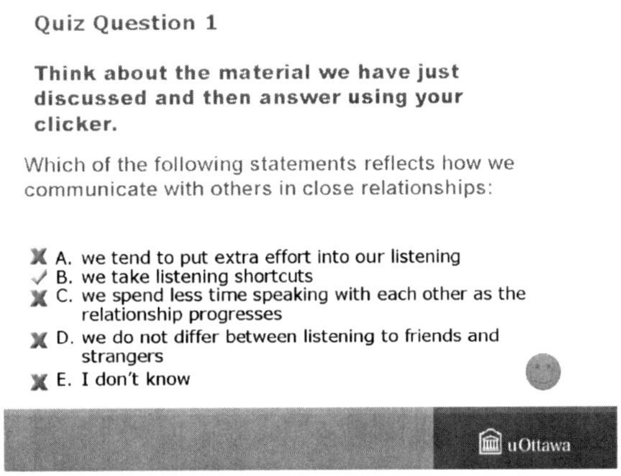

argue, knowing what you know and don't know focuses your learning and quizzes can help students (and the instructor) to assess existing knowledge and identify gaps, which can then be clarified or emphasized in the lecture.

As the following slide shows, the lecture has focused on theories of listening and shown that, surprisingly, people put less effort into listening to those with whom they have a close relationship. The quiz will ask a series of questions about this material, including this question, which aims to emphasize the unexpected "shortcuts" that we take. This type of question could also be used at the beginning of the lecture to measure students' understanding of material that students were required to have read before arriving at class. Note that the option "I don't know" is included to keep students from guessing.

2. Discussion Questions about Attitudes or Opinions

As Chickering and Gamson (1987) suggest in their principles of good practice in undergraduate education, when students share their own ideas and respond to the reactions of other students and the instructor, this activity sharpens their thinking and deepens their understanding. Further, as Bonwell and Eison (1991) argue, effective lectures incorporate active learning strategies where students are encouraged to explore their own meaning, attitudes, and values. As the following slide shows, students are asked first to share their opinion with a neighbour and then, after this processing exercise, are asked to post their own viewpoint. As shown on the slide, there is no "right" answer to this question but rather the slide would show the frequency of responses to each choice. Note that the option "Other" is included on this slide so that students with an opinion other than those identified by the instructor can choose this option, allowing for discussion about what some other points of view might be.

3. Questions about Student Opinions on Awkward or Embarrassing Topics Example

Because answers can be posted anonymously, the clicker gives the instructor the chance to gauge student viewpoints and behaviors much more effectively than by asking for a show of hands, particularly when the subject matter is awkward, embarrassing or very personal. As shown on the slide below, there is no "correct" answer posted, and the instructor has left two options for students who don't see that any of the first three answers is a good fit. Option 5 allows for the instructor to

Figure 2.

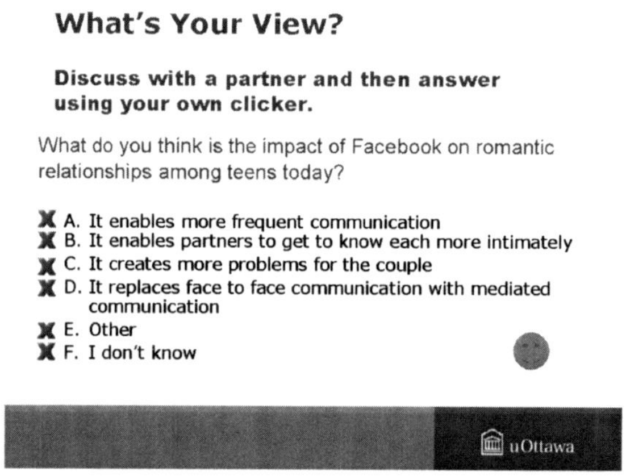

open a discussion about why none of the answers might be appropriate (for example if a student is already married!), but this must be done with care in order to avoid putting students on the spot about sensitive issues. This example also shows how the use of clickers can help to create the kind of secure and supportive classroom that is essential for learning to occur.

4. Exercises to Promote Interest and Discussion and To Illustrate Concepts

As Chickering and Gamson (1987) state, learning is not a spectator sport, and thus it requires the full participation of the student. Bonwell & Eison (1991) describe active learning strategies as those that involve "students in doing things and (have the students) think about the things they are doing" (p. iii). Exercises, where students are actively involved in challenging, interesting and stimulating activities, are easily accomplished using the clickers, as demonstrated in the slide below. Research shows that if the clickers are used to ask students to answer mundane questions or perform menial tasks, then students lose interest in the technology and in the lecture.

Figure 3.

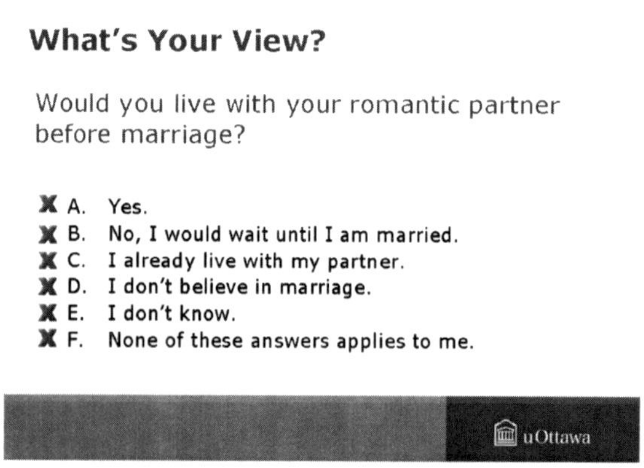

5. Peer Instruction to Promote Active Learning and Collaborative Learning

As Chickering and Gamson (1987) argue, good learning is collaborative and social, not competitive and isolated. To achieve collaborative learning, an effective approach, and one that works particularly well with clickers, is peer instruction, a technique developed by Eric Mazur (1997) to help make lectures more interactive and to get students intellectually engaged with the material by having them think critically about the material and discuss their ideas and insights with their neighbors. This technique works as follows: After a short lecture that exposes students to a concept, theory, model or process, present a slide with a question. Have students answer individually first using their clickers but do not display the correct answer. Ideally there will be a range of answers (which demonstrates that the topic is challenging, that there is not universal understanding and, thus, that peer instruction is *necessary*). Then have students discuss with those sitting next to them and answer again using their own clickers. Only reveal the correct answer after the peer instruction is completed.

Evaluation of this Pilot Project

As with the implementation of any program, it is important to determine the degree to which the intervention is accomplishing the objectives it was designed to achieve and this may be done through a summative evaluation, which assesses the impact of a program on its completion. As well, formative evaluation, which gathers information about the success of a program and makes recommendations toward improving it, is especially useful in order to make changes while the program is underway.

For this pilot project, informal formative evaluation is conducted throughout the semester by the instructor and the teaching assistant. Specifically, the teaching assistant is present at every lecture taking notes on the students' immediate reactions to each clicker activity. From this feedback, future activities within the course can be adjusted in order to complement students' preferences for different clicker exercises. As the ultimate aim in adopting the clicker technology is to engage students more effectively in order to increase their understanding of course content and improve their chances of academic success, it is important to evaluate and adapt the use of the clickers on an ongoing basis.

As for summative evaluation, this will be accomplished during regular University of Ottawa course evaluations, where students will be asked additional questions revolving around clicker use

Figure 4.

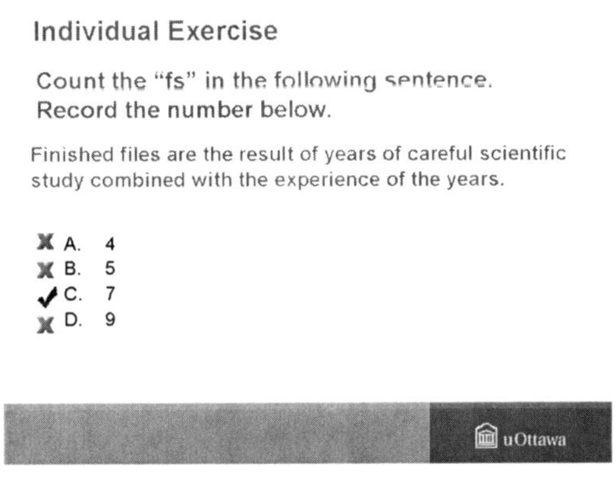

Figure 5.

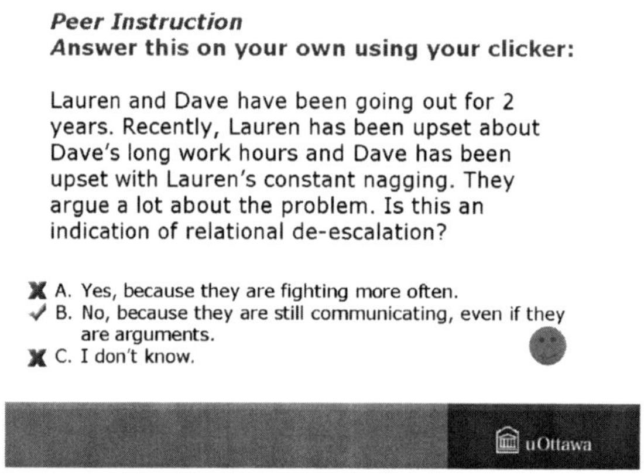

within the lectures. This evaluation will provide quantitative evidence as to the success of the project and determine whether the three main objectives were achieved. In addition, it will provide the opportunity to improve upon the clicker activities for future courses.

Some sample questions which will be included in the end-of-semester course evaluation to which students will be asked to respond are the following:

One a scale of 1 (Disagree) to 5 (Agree), please rate the use of clickers in this class with regard to the items listed below:

- The professor made good use of the Clickers
- Clickers contributed significantly to my learning.
- Clickers were well integrated into the course.
- The clickers used in this course were easy to use.
- The technology used in this course worked well.
- As a result of using Clickers in this course I interacted more with other students on the course material.
- The use of the Clickers in this course was appropriate for achieving the course objectives.

CONCLUSION

Employing clickers is a relatively simple, low cost, and effective means to engage students and facilitate active learning. However, the implementation of this technology requires various forms of support or commitment at three levels: institution, professor, and student. The lack of support from one of these levels will negatively impact the effectiveness of clicker use in the classroom.

At the institutional level, there must be recognition that clicker technology is an innovative way to improve learning. From this, the educational institution must be able to afford the accompanying clicker technology. Although some institutions pass the cost of the clicker on to students, clicker receivers and software must be purchased by the institution. Along with the purchasing of technology, training and technical support, either internal or external, must be made available to professors and teaching assistants. Clickers are a financial investment it helps if more than one class adopts the clickers, and if only one brand of clicker technology is adopted across the institution. This is beneficial in three ways. First, it cuts costs as only one receiver and software system has to be purchased and learned. Second, as more faculty members incorporate clickers, their expertise and experiences can be passed on, easing the burden on technical support services. Finally, students are able to reuse the clickers in other courses. Studies have shown that when students are required to buy more than one clicker for different courses, their perceptions of the technology grow sour.

A main hindrance of clicker adoption is the fear that the technology will malfunction during class. Professors realize that students' attention span is short and technical issues can interrupt attention and also frustrate the students. Thus, technical support must be available to quickly help professors during lectures, as well as to provide adequate training and troubleshooting prior to the course beginning. In addition to this support, educational materials must be created and made available to professors to assist in integrating clickers successfully. As the literature has shown, pedagogical techniques must be altered to incorporate the clickers rather than the clickers simply being an add-on to the original lecture.

Further, inconsequential use of the clickers in lecture will cause the students to respond negatively. As the students are purchasing the clickers, it is crucial that the clickers be used to their utmost potential. If clickers are used for only attendance purposes, students will feel that the clicker was a waste of money, may become more disengaged, and may not be open to using clickers in the future when other professors employ the technology. Thus, student support of clickers is imperative as the use of clickers creates a shift in the classroom environment where more active participation is required from students (Trees & Jackson, 2007). For first-year students, this change may not even be noticed; however, in upper year courses where students are used to taking a more passive role in the lecture, lecturers who employ clickers may face more resistance.

Here are a few tips which can assist in employing the use of clickers effectively. Before the course begins, instructors must make certain that they are familiar with the software and know how to solve minor technical problems. Also, they need to assure that they have enough time to create clicker activities and alter their lecture to incorporate the extra time needed to conduct the exercises. Gaining support from the students is the most important aspect of assuring the successful use of clickers. Avoid using the clickers for attendance purposes only, and try to use the clickers regularly, but without overusing them as this can be perceived as too repetitive and thus tedious. Finally, explain to students how the clickers will be used, and emphasize that the clickers are not a tracking system, but a learning tool for the student's direct benefit.

In this chapter we have explored the theoretical foundations and practical applications of clickers in the classroom. As can be seen from this discussion, clickers are an effective learning tool which can be used to enhance student engagement. However, they must be used appropriately and with support from many different levels. With this support and appropriate preparation for their employment, clickers offer potential to enhance student engagement.

REFERENCES

Bonwell, C., & Eison, J. (1991). *Active Learning: Creating Excitement in the Classroom AEHE-ERIC Higher Education Report No.1*. San Francisco: Jossey-Bass

Boyle, J. T., & Nicol, D. J. (2003). Using classroom communication systems to support interaction anddiscussion in large class settings. *Association for Learning Technology Journal*, *11*(3), 43–57.

Bruff, D. (2009). *Teaching with Classroom Response Systems: Creating Active Learning Environments*. San Francisco: Jossey-Bass.

Carini, R. M., Kuh, G. D., & Klein, S. P. (2006). Student engagement and student learning: Testing the linkages. *Research in Higher Education*, *47*(1), 1–32. doi:10.1007/s11162-005-8150-9

Chickering, A. W., & Ehrmann, S. C. (1996). Implementing the Seven Principles: Technology as Lever. *American Association of Higher Education Bulletin, October*, 3-6.

Chickering, A. W., & Gamson, Z. F. (1987). Seven principles for good practice in undergraduate education. *American Association of Higher Education Bulletin, March,* 3-7

Coates, H. C. (2005). The value of student engagement for higher education quality assurance. *Quality in Higher Education*, *11*(1), 25–36. doi:10.1080/13538320500074915

Draper, S. W., & Brown, M. I. (2004). Increasing interactivity in lectures using an electronic voting system. *Journal of Computer Assisted Learning*, *20*, 81–94. doi:10.1111/j.1365-2729.2004.00074.x

Draper, S. W., Cargill, J., & Cutts, Q. (2002). Electronically enhanced classroom interaction. *Australian Journal of Educational Technology*, *18*, 13–23.

Duncan, D. (2006). Clickers: A new teaching aid with exceptional promise. *Astronomy Education Review*, *5*, 70–88. doi:10.3847/AER2006005

Ellozy, A. (2007). New initiative: "Clickers" in our classrooms. *New Chalk Talk, 6*(8). Retrieved June 11, 2009, from http://www.aucegypt.edu/academics/llt/clt/ChalkTalk/Documents/V6Issue8.pdf

Fies, C., & Marshall, J. (2006). Classroom response systems: A review of the literature. *Journal of Science Education and Technology*, *15*(1), 101–109. doi:10.1007/s10956-006-0360-1

Hoekstra, A. (2008). Vibrant student voices: Exploring effects of the use of clickers in large college courses. *Learning, Media and Technology*, *33*(4), 329–341. doi:10.1080/17439880802497081

Howe, N., & Strauss, W. (2000). *Millennials Rising: The Next Great Generation*. New York: Vintage Books.

Howe, N., & Strauss, W. (2003). *Millennials Go to College: Strategies for a New Generation on Campus*. Washington, DC: American Association of Collegiate Registrars and Admissions Officers.

Johnson, M., & Robson, D. (2008). Clickers, student engagement and performance in an introductory economics course: A cautionary tale. *Computers in Higher Education Economics Review*, *20*, 4–12.

Jones, S. (2002). The internet goes to college: How students are living in the future with today's technology. *Pew Internet & American Life Project*. Retrieved online June 11, 2009, from http://www.eric.ed.gov/ERICDocs/data/ericdocs2sql/content_storage_01/0000019b/80/1a/bb/a7.pdf

Judson, E., & Sawada, D. (2002). Learning from the past and present: Electronic response systems in college lecture halls. *Journal of Computers in Mathematics and Science Teaching*, *21*, 167–181.

Kaleta, R., & Joosten, T. (2007). Student response systems: A University of Wisconsin system study of clickers. *EDUCAUSE Center for Applied Research: Research Bulletin*, *10*, 1–12.

Kuh, G. D. (2003). What we're learning about student engagement from NSSE. *Change*, *35*(2), 24–32. doi:10.1080/00091380309604090

Mazur, E. (1997). *Peer Instruction: A User's Manual*. Upper Saddle River, NJ: Prentice Hall.

Pew Internet & American Life Project. (2008). Retrieved June 11, 2009, from http://www.pewinternet.org/Static-Pages/Data-Tools/Download Data/~/media/Infographics/Trend%20Data/January%202009%20updates/Demographics%20of%20Internet%20Users%201%206%2009.jpg

Prensky, M. (2001). *Digital Natives, Digital Immigrants. On the Horizon, 9*(5). Retrieved June 12, 2009. from http://www.twitchspeed.com/site/Prensky%20-%20Digital%20Natives,%20Digital%20Immigrants%20-%20Part1.htm

Rice, R., & Bunz, U. (2006). Evaluating a wireless course feedback system: The role of demographics, expertise, fluency, competency, and usage. *Studies in Media and Information Literacy Education*, (3), 1-23.

Scott Barrett, M., Bornsen, S. E., Erickson, S. L., Markey, V., & Spiering, K. (2005). The personal response systems as a teaching aid. *Communication Teacher, 19*(3), 89–92. doi:10.1080/14704620500201806

Trees, A. R., & Jackson, M. H. (2007). The learning environment in clicker classrooms: Student processes of learning and involvement in large university-level courses using student response systems. *Learning, Media and Technology, 32*(1), 21–40. doi:10.1080/17439880601141179

Tweeten, J., Smith, M. K., Julius, J., & Murphy-Boyer, L. (2007). Successful clicker standardization. *EDUCAUSE Quarterly, 4*, 63–67.

KEY TERMS AND DEFINITIONS

Active Learning Strategies: A mode of instruction where students are required to actively participate in the classroom experience.

Clicker: A handheld device used in a classroom to communicate a student's response to a question posed by the instructor.

Clicker Attributes: There are four main attributes of clickers which enhance student engagement: response anonymity, immediate feedback, tangible act of answering question, and accountability for class preparation.

Collaborative Learning: A group or team-based approach to learning where students work together to interact with information.

Formative Evaluation: An approach to program evaluation which gathers information about the success of a program and makes recommendations toward improving it,

Millenial: A term used to describe the demographic cohort following Generation X (after about 1982).

Peer Instruction: An in-class activity where, at given points during a lecture, students turn to their neighbors and explain the concept being discussed to each other.

Student Engagement: The effort that students contribute to their learning experience both inside and outside of the classroom and the ways that colleges and universities try to encourage this investment.

Summative Evaluation: An approach to program evaluation which assesses the impact of a program on its completion.

APPENDIX: SUPPORTING MATERIAL

Abstract

This pilot project employed personal response systems, or clicker technology, in an effort to address student inattention and the distractions created by electronics in a large, first-year introductory communication class. The objectives of the project were to increase student engagement through a more hands-on, active and collaborative learning environment and to better gauge student understanding of important concepts throughout the lecture. This chapter discusses the challenges of student engagement, in particular with today's millennial students, examines the role of technology generally in engaging students and the personal response systems specifically, describes the pilot project and presents a series of exercises that may be used to most effectively take advantage of this technology in the classroom.

Questions and Answers

1. Why is student engagement important?

Research shows that student engagement is among the better predictors of learning and personal development (*Carini, Kuh, & Klein, 2006*) and thus is critical to the academic achievement and retention of post-secondary students (Kuh, 2003).

2. What is it about clickers that seems to engage students?

There are four main attributes of clickers which enhance student engagement: response anonymity, immediate feedback, tangible act of answering question, and accountability for class preparation.

3. What is the problem that the pilot study in this case tries to address?

This pilot project employed personal response systems, or clicker technology, in an effort to address student inattention and the distractions created by electronics in a large, first-year introductory communication class.

4. What were the objectives of this pilot study?

This pilot project had three main objectives:

1. To increase student engagement with course material and in-class discussions
2. To increase active learning through hands-on activities that encourage dialogue among students and professors
3. To better gauge student understanding of important concepts throughout the lecture

5. What are three benefits of clicker technology in the classroom?

Clicker technology encourages collaborative learning, enhances active learning, and allows for anonymity.

Chapter 10
The Knee Bone Connected To the Thigh Bone:
A Case Study of Teaching Anatomy to Engineering Students Using State-of-the-Art Anatomical Software

T. J. Joyce
Newcastle University, UK

P. McCormack
Newcastle University, UK

ABSTRACT

Bioengineering is a multidisciplinary subject which necessitates that engineering students, who typically have no knowledge of medicine, must quickly and effectively gain a thorough understanding of the complexities of human anatomy. Teaching on a Bioengineering module at Newcastle University's School of Mechanical and Systems Engineering employed a combination of Primal Pictures anatomical software, bespoke teaching materials and peer to peer learning. This allowed Bioengineering students to quickly construct an understanding of anatomical principles which they used in individual, assessed projects on total joint replacement. Anonymised, written feedback gathered from the students revealed overwhelmingly positive learning experiences and assessed projects indicated deep knowledge of the anatomical descriptions necessary to understand and work with the science of joint replacement.

ORGANIZATION BACKGROUND

Newcastle University is a member of the Russell Group, comprising 20 leading research institutions in the UK. The 2008 Research Assessment Exercise (RAE) found that in over two thirds of subjects assessed, at least half of all research was placed in the top two categories of 4* (world leading) and 3* (internationally excellent). Based on these results, Newcastle University is among the top 20 higher education institutions in the UK in terms of research power, according to the publication, Research Fortnight.

The School of Mechanical and Systems Engineering at Newcastle University has a history dating back to 1871 and has strong links to local

DOI: 10.4018/978-1-61520-869-2.ch010

and international engineering industry. The 2008 RAE placed the School in the top 10 mechanical engineering departments in the UK for research. The University's mission statement is to be a world-class research- intensive university, to deliver teaching of the highest quality and to play a leading role in the economic, social and cultural development of the North East of England. The University has three faculties, one of which is Science, Agriculture and Engineering (SAgE). Mechanical and Systems Engineering (MSE) is one of ten Schools within SAgE. The School of Mechanical and Systems Engineering has 19 full-time lecturing staff and a student cohort of approximately 400 undergraduate and postgraduates undertaking a range of BEng, MEng and MSc degrees.

SETTING THE STAGE

In the School of Mechanical and Systems Engineering the subject of Bioengineering is taught as a 15 credit module over two semesters to fourth year MEng undergraduate students as well as postgraduate MSc students. Two members of academic staff teach the course, taking 1/3 and 2/3 shares of the teaching load. On alternate years they swap the teaching load so that one year they teach 1/3 and the next 2/3. Course delivery and assessment previously followed a conventional pattern of lectures and tutorials with assessment based on a written examination at the end of the module. In the 2008-09 academic year the lead author became module leader. Based on his pedagogical views and experiences a number of changes were introduced to the Bioengineering module. For his 'third' of the module, assessment was swapped from final exam to an individual, 3000 word project based on a critique of a commercially available total joint replacement. As such a critique needs to be founded on a full appreciation of the anatomy of the human joint that is being replaced, so the challenge was how to facilitate student learning of the complex subject of anatomy. In addition, for the majority of the bioengineering students, this would be the first time they had been formally introduced to anatomy and the associated medical terminology.

CASE DESCRIPTION

Introduction

Bioengineering - the application of engineering principles and techniques to the medical field - contributes towards the improvement of medical interventions in many ways. One of the discipline's most important contributions has been the design of artificial joints, a development which is recognised as the twentieth century's major advancement in orthopaedics. Millions of joint replacements have been implanted leading to improved quality of life for many thousands of people suffering from crippling musculo-skeletal diseases. These artificial joints are designed by engineers who need to be fully conversant with human anatomy and the associated medical language. The challenge then, is how to immerse undergraduate engineering students quickly and efficiently in an alien subject and give them sufficient knowledge for them to apply engineering principles to this exciting topic?

Pedagogical Background

Functional anatomy is a strongly three-dimensional subject where spatial visualisation is key (Van Sint Jan et al., 2003). Commentators have noted that medical students frequently encounter problems in understanding certain dynamic aspects of functional anatomy (Van Sint Jan et al., 2003) and this is likely to be the case with engineering students too. It has also been shown that the application of multimedia has helped students to increase their 3D anatomical understanding by giving them spatial direction about the underlying anatomy and its dynamic behaviour (Van Sint Jan et al., 2003). Additionally it has been noted that if students can interact with lecture content, then their assimilation of that material should be increased compared to situations where there is no opportunity to interrelate (Benbunan-Fich, 2002).

By gaining a full understanding of the anatomy of human joints, the intention was that Bioengineering students would appreciate the inherent challenges of joint replacement and the problems facing clinicians who have to implant such devices. The anatomical software chosen was Primal Pictures Systemic edition. Details of the software can be found on the company's website (http://www.primalpictures.com/). To date no formal independent evaluation appears to have been published and this chapter may therefore offer the first such pedagogical assessment of the software.

The Bioengineering Module

The Primal Pictures software was introduced to students undertaking the Bioengineering module offered by the School of Mechanical and Systems Engineering at Newcastle University and this is usually the first exposure that students have to the subject.

In the academic year which the Primal Pictures software was introduced, the lead author taught one third of the Bioengineering module, with a focus on total joint replacement. After a series of lectures on total hip replacement and biotribology which introduced background knowledge through a case study of the most common and successful type of joint replacement, students were allocated an individual project. In their projects each student was asked to critique a specific design of replacement joint and describe the anatomy of the relevant natural joint. Deliberately each of these projects was intended for one of the less commonly replaced human joints, specifically the shoulder, elbow, wrist, ankle and the various finger and toe joints.

This methodology allowed case-based, problem-based, and project-based learning, where students' learning was organised around attempts to solve authentic problems that occur in bioengineering. Such methods can help students develop the conditionalised knowledge and understanding that lets them think productively about problems in the discipline (Harris, Bransford, & Brophy, 2002).

Methodology

Dedicated teaching materials were provided to the students in the form of bespoke training notes, written by the lead author, for the Primal Pictures software. Students worked through these notes with the software, in pairs, at their own pace, during dedicated sessions. The lead author led these sessions and was available to answer any questions which arose around anatomical principles or medical terminology.

It has been noted that valuable features of web-based learning include its potential for empowering the learner, for enabling individualised instruction and collaborative peer-to-peer learning, and for transferring greater control to learners to decide when, how much, and to what extent study and instruction takes place (Curran, Hoekman, Gulliver, Landells, & Hatcher, 2000). By presenting information and instructional materials in various formats, individual learning styles and preferences can be addressed (Curran et al., 2000).

By signifying that a fundamental understanding of anatomy is required to tackle subsequent assessed course material related to artificial joint replacement, and by pointing out how many people have their lives improved through joint replacement, it was considered that the 'need to learn' and the 'want to learn' aspects of Race's model of learning would be facilitated (Race, 1994). Supervision was deliberately small group or one-to-one and non-hierarchical so that students felt they were gaining personal attention in a constructive learning environment, as suggested by Tinto's model of integration (Tinto, 1975). Additionally the value of providing time for student-instructor and student-student interactions in the classroom has been shown (Roselli & Brophy, 2003). Students were paired up to tackle questions related to the software, thus encouraging immediate learning by doing and augmenting this through peer-to-peer learning. Both of these tactics supported Kolb's ideas of experiential learning, thus facilitating deeper learning (Kolb, 1984). Moreover, it has been recognised that opportunities to work collaboratively can enhance students' abilities to learn and can help students receive feedback about their thinking.

At the end of his third of the module, anonymised questionnaires were passed to the students by the lead author. The questionnaires contained a number of sections and were intended to gather feedback on this part of the Bioengineering course. The first section of the questionnaire consisted of ten questions which requested answers on a five-point scale. The second section asked the student to offer two good features of the course and two suggestions for improvement, before offering the opportunity for further comments to be made. The third section focussed on the 'innovative' features of the course, including the Primal Pictures software. Here the dedicated questions were 'to what extent did Primal Pictures software help you to understand human anatomy?' and 'if you accessed Primal Pictures software outside of taught sessions, to what extent was this useful?'.

Results and Discussion

Students interacted well with the software and asked very few technical questions, while the pairing mechanism encouraged pertinent discussion and sharing of opinion. It was also interesting to note the majority of students mimicking the actions of human joints shown on computer screens, for example by lifting their shoulders to imitate elevation or 'wagging' fingers to copy the flexion-extension motion.

Student feedback on use of the Primal Pictures software was overwhelmingly positive. Students said that using the software was 'fun' and 'easy' and one commented specifically about the learning experience, 'the Primal Pictures software made me appreciate what a sophisticated and still not fully understood bearing the natural elbow joint is'. One student described the software as 'an excellent graphical aid and introduction to the anatomical language'. Another said the Primal Pictures software was 'very useful for the project, in naming bones and muscles and all related terms to do with the joint'. A third student offered this review of the software. 'It was very good for learning about the muscles, ligaments and bones considering you had to click on each part'.

Another student offered the following opinions, 'I found the software easy to use with its simple search and contents options'. 'It was easy to navigate through the program'. 'What I found most useful about the software were the interactive 3D models of the area of interest which could be rotated and altered. When looking at a specific joint it allowed me to appreciate the complexity of it in 3D but also made it very accessible to explore as each component within the joint could be highlighted by clicking on it, then the name and a brief description was given at the side of the model. The 3D models could also be built up layer by layer from the bone showing the different tendons, ligaments, muscles etc which allowed you to simplify your view of an otherwise complex "organ" within the body'.

Perhaps the most positive comment about the Primal Pictures software was the following: 'With the program being so simple to use it urged me to look at other sections of the body out of interest purely as a learning experience. The program overall does not give a great deal of in-depth information about specifics within the body but its greatest ability is to show otherwise complex organs, joints and systems within the body in an interactive 3D way which is very user friendly'.

Two formal questions were asked of the students, and an answer requested to each on a five-point scale. These questions were: 'to what extent did Primal Pictures software help you to understand human anatomy?'; and 'if you accessed Primal Pictures software outside of taught sessions, was this useful?'. Twenty completed questionnaires were received from students, although one student did not respond to the second question. Results are shown in figures 1 and 2.

As can be seen from figure 1 the majority of students (90%) thought that the software helped them to understand human anatomy a 'great deal' or a 'very great deal'. In addition, as indicated in figure 2, the majority of students thought that it was 'very useful' to be able to access the Primal Pictures software outside of the taught sessions.

As has been stated, each student was assigned an individual project which concerned a critique of a currently available artificial joint. As part of this evaluation, students were asked to describe the anatomy of the relevant natural joint, describing the main bones, muscles and ligaments. The average mark awarded on this section of the projects was 62% and almost all the students had used Primal Pictures software to describe the appropriate natural joint thereby indicating the important role that the software had in their understanding of anatomy.

Throughout his third of the module, the lead author employed small group and interactive teaching wherever possible. General feedback from students should therefore be seen in this light but students' comments as to positive aspects of the module included the following: 'entirely new and interesting topic, self directed learning (project)'; 'the project is good and I learned a lot'; 'very interactive learning, encouraged thinking/problem solving'; 'the software was useful, the teaching was very clear to us'; 'course work assessment, no biology knowledge assumed'.

CURRENT CHALLENGES FACING THE ORGANIZATION

At the completion of the project the only main challenge to the lead author was the marking of all the individual student projects. The aim of these projects was to encourage deeper learning, and it was felt that this aim was achieved. However, the time commitment for marking from the lecturer is significant. A challenge for the future will be to maintain funding for the Primal Pictures software.

Figure 1. Students' answers to first specific question on use of Primal Pictures software

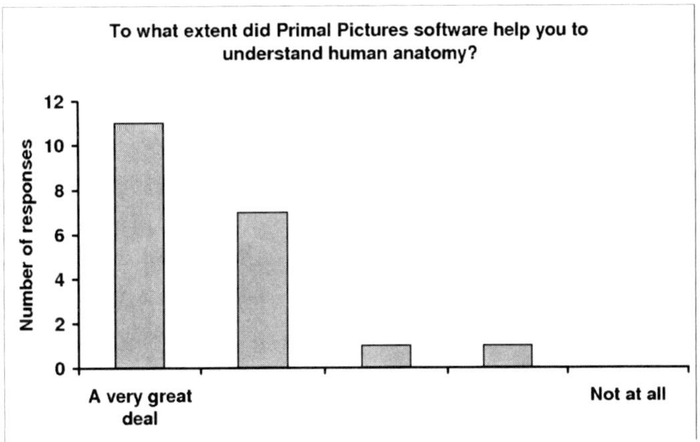

Figure 2. Students' answers to second specific question on use of Primal Pictures software

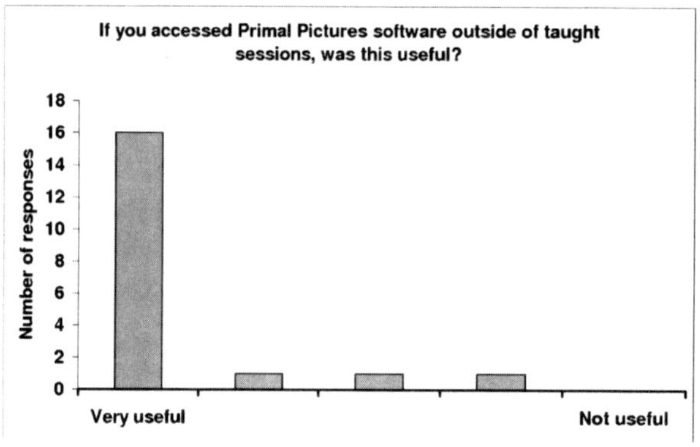

This has been achieved for the next academic year. The first year of funding was obtained from a one-off teaching award while the second year will be provided by the School, but longer-term it would be preferred if financial support could be received at a University level.

SOLUTIONS AND RECOMMENDATIONS

Given the challenges just listed, one potential solution to the issue of marking would be to ask for project reports from pairs of students. Students would be allowed to select who they pair up with and, on submission of the project, students would be asked to allocate the proportion of marks between them. Hopefully this peer-moderated assessment should help to account for a potential situation where one student puts in more effort than the other. Regarding the funding issue, it is felt that the longer the software is embedded into the Bioengineering module, the more difficult it will be to justify removal. In addition, contacts exist between the School of Mechanical and Systems Engineering and the Medical School at Newcastle University and staff at the latter are interested in the opportunity of introducing the Primal Pictures software into their teaching. If the Medical School introduce the software then it is most likely that access to the software will then be financed at a University level.

FUTURE TRENDS

The promotion of active, non-hierarchical, peer-supported learning is not new. From Socrates onwards teachers have engaged in critical pedagogy (Kincheloe, 2008) and nurtured students as "candles to be lit" rather than "vessels to be filled". The hope is that such techniques encourage critical thinking (Bloom, Engelhard, Furst, Hill, & Krathwohl, 1956; Dillon, 1990; Gokhale, 1995; Mills, 1995) and in the work described in this chapter, encourage students to work, and to work together, in a manner which goes some way to emulating situations they will meet as professional engineers in the workplace.

The increased use of ICT in teaching and the continued professionalisation of higher education teaching is helping to drive the promotion of distributed, self-directed and experiential learning, moving further from the traditional knowledge transmission and recall systems and nearer to Wenger's communities of practice (Wenger, nd). Technology provides diverse tools which can 'create an environment that supports and encourages inquiry, broaden the learner's experience of the subject matter, and elicit active and critical reflection by learners on their growing experience base' (Kim & Bonk, 2006). The aims of active, problem-based, experiential learning and distributed, self-directed, technology-based learning serve each other well.

When using software such as Primal Pictures, students move away from the long theoretical narrative found in lectures and books and explore their own paths, examine areas of knowledge deficiency and construct their own understanding according to personal preferences. This is all made easier by software which is 3D, illustration-heavy and presented in small sections via multiple interconnected paths.

When looking at how future trends may allow improvements in the course described this will probably be along two strands. Firstly, in the near future 3D graphical software like Primal Pictures is likely to continue to improve as hardware advancements allow increased programming power. So detail, speed, ease of movement around the software and the amount of content presented should all get better. Specific content is continually being added to the Primal Pictures' suite and in the case of this course, the provision of a package which simulates joint replacement surgery in regions other than the hip and the knee would be a great addition. Looking further into the future we could one day expect this course to be using 3D, touch sensitive, projected images which the students could physically grab and move around with their hands. The commercial technology for this is already available (IO2_Technology, nd).

Secondly, the use of peer to peer and distributed learning within the course could be increased. One of the most interesting current technological developments in this area is the use of multi user virtual environments (MUVEs). The most widely used of these in the UK is Second Life. MUVEs can encourage learning to be even more self-directed, experiential and problem-based – all crucial skills required for the professional engineer. Second Life environments are already well established within UK higher education and proponents point to its capacity for collaboration between users and the ability to create structures in the virtual world that would not be possible in the real world (Toro-Troconis et al., 2008; Zhang, 2007). Perhaps more interestingly Dawley (Dawley, nd) claims that learning in Second Life promotes andragogy and if we are interested in students as apprentice professional engineers and as interdependent, self-motivated, inquisitive learners, this development is an exciting one.

REFERENCES

Benbunan-Fich, R. (2002). Improving education and training with IT. *Communications of the ACM, 45*(6), 94–99. doi:10.1145/508448.508454

Bloom, B. S., Engelhard, M. D., Furst, E. J., Hill, W. H., & Krathwohl, D. R. (1956). *Taxonomy of educational objectives, handbook 1: cognitive domain*. New York: Longmans.

Curran, V. R., Hoekman, T., Gulliver, W., Landells, I., & Hatcher, L. (2000). Web-based continuing medical education (I): Field test of a hybrid computer-mediated instructional delivery system. *The Journal of Continuing Education in the Health Professions, 20*(2), 97–105. doi:10.1002/chp.1340200206

Dawley, L. (nd). Emerging territories in second life for socially networked teaching & learning.

Dillon, J. T. (1990). *The practice of questioning*. London: Routledge.

Gokhale, A. A. (1995). Collaborative learning enhances critical thinking. *Journal of Technology Education, 7*(1).

Harris, T. R., Bransford, J. D., & Brophy, S. P. (2002). Roles for learning sciences and learning technologies in biomedical engineering education: a review of recent advances. *Annual Review of Biomedical Education, 4*(1), 29–48. doi:10.1146/annurev.bioeng.4.091701.125502

IO2_Technology. (nd). *IO2 Technology homepage*. Retrieved August 7, 2009, from http://www.io2technology.com/index.htm

Kim, K.-J., & Bonk, C. J. (2006). The future of online teaching and learning in higher education: "the survey says.... *EDUCAUSE Quarterly*, 4.

Kincheloe, J. L. (2008). *Knowledge and critical pedagogy: an introduction*. London: Springer. doi:10.1007/978-1-4020-8224-5

Kolb, D. A. (1984). *Experiential Learning: Experience as the source of learning and development*. Upper Saddle River, NJ: Prentice-Hall.

Mills, J. (1995). Better teaching through provocation. *College Teaching*, *46*, 21–25. doi:10.1080/87567559809596228

Race, P. (1994). *The Open Learning Handbook*. London: Kogan Page.

Roselli, R. J., & Brophy, S. P. (2003). Redesigning a biomechanics course using challenge-based instruction. *IEEE Engineering in Medicine and Biology Magazine*, *22*(4), 66–70. doi:10.1109/MEMB.2003.1237504

Tinto, V. (1975). Dropout from Higher Education: A Theoretical Synthesis of Recent Research. *Review of Educational Research*, *45*, 89–125.

Toro-Troconis, M., Mellstrom, U., Partidge, M., Meeran, K., Barrett, M., & Higham, J. (2008). Designing game-based learning activities for virtual patients in Second Life. *Journal of CyberTherapy & Rehabilitation*, *1*(3), 227–239.

Van Sint Jan, S., Crudele, M., Gashegu, J., Feipel, V., Poulet, P., & Salvia, P. (2003). Development of multimedia learning modules for teaching human anatomy: Application to osteology and functional anatomy. *Anatomical Record. Part B, New Anatomist*, *272B*(1), 98–106. doi:10.1002/ar.b.10020

Wenger, E. (nd). *Communities of practice*. Retrieved August 7, 2009, from http://www.ewenger.com/theory/

Zhang, J. (2007). *Second Life: hype or reality? Higher education in the virtual world*. DE Oracle.

FURTHER READING

Ashwin, P. (Ed.). (2006). *Changing higher education: the development of learning and teaching*. London: Routledge.

Baillie, C., & Moore, I. (2004). *Effective learning and teaching in engineering*. New York: Routledge Falmer. doi:10.4324/9780203415986

Bell, B., & Cowie, B. (2001). *Formative assessment in science education*. The Netherlands: Kluwer Academic Press.

Comeaux, P. (Ed.). (2005). *Assessing online learning*. Bolton, MA: Anker.

Galloway, P. D. (2008). *The 21st century engineer: A proposal for engineering education reform*. Reston, UK: ASCE Press.

Hall, S. R., Waitz, I., Brodeur, D. R., Soderholm, D. H., & Nasr, R. (2002). *Adoption of active learning in a lecture-based engineering class*. Paper presented at the 32nd ASEE/IEEE Frontiers in Education Conference, Boston. HEA. (nd). *Higher education academy engineering subject centre*. Retrieved August 7, 2009, from http://www.engsc.ac.uk/

Jacques, D. (2000). *Learning in groups: A handbook for improving group working* (3rd ed.). London: Kogan Page.

Joly, K. (2007). A second life for higher education? Retrieved August 7, 2009, from http://www.universitybusiness.com/viewarticle.aspx?articleid=797

Laurillard, D. (2002). *Rethinking university teaching: A conversational framework for the effective use of learning technologies* (2nd ed.). London: Routledge. doi:10.4324/9780203304846

NEEDS. (nd). *A digital library for engineering education*. Retrieved August 7, 2009, from http://www.needs.org/needs/

Vest, C. M. (2005). *Disturbing the educational universe: Universities in the digital age - dinosaurs or prometheans?* Cambridge, MA: MIT.

APPENDIX: SUPPORTING MATERIAL

Abstract

Anatomical software, supported by bespoke teaching materials and peer to peer learning, was introduced to a Bioengineering module at a UK university. This combination allowed students to quickly construct an understanding of anatomical principles which they used in individual, assessed projects on total joint replacement. Anonymised, written feedback gathered from the students revealed overwhelmingly positive learning experiences.

Questions and Answers

1. What is the overall problem in this case?

Bioengineering often necessitates that engineering students achieve a competence in medical terminology and a good understanding of basic human anatomy. However, these are complex subjects and achievements of competencies should not be an end in itself, but a springboard to the application of engineering principles within a medical context. The question then is how to teach these concepts quickly and effectively.

2. What were the main challenges in introducing the software?

One issue is the cost of the software, at approximately £4,400 for ten seats for one year. For a single module with a cohort of approximately 30 students this may be unsustainable, although the software was also used by undergraduate students undertaking individual bioengineering projects. The second challenge was the issue of writing bespoke teaching materials.

3. How else could anatomy be learnt by the bioengineering students

The conventional method would be from text books. However, it is noted that anatomy is a three-dimensional subject where spatial visualisation is key therefore learning from 2D texts can be challenging, especially for engineering students who have likely not studied the subject previously. Another option would be to use models of human joints.

4. What are the disadvantages of using the software and then asking students to undertake an individual project, as opposed to 'conventional' lectures and a written exam?

The main issue has been that of the time taken to assess 30 individual, 3000 word projects where each concerns a different type of artificial joint. This demands not only a significant time commitment from the lecturer but also a deep knowledge of the subject of joint replacement.

5. What then are the advantages?

Students interact well with the software and the interactive, small-group teaching. They seem to enjoy the 'lectures' more, and so too does the lecturer. The projects encourage deeper learning rather than simply testing memory, which exams might do.

Epilogue and List of Lessons Learned

The long-range effects of this case include: increased use of software in teaching in the School of Mechanical and Systems Engineering; the first use of the Primal Pictures software at Newcastle University; the introduction of more interactive teaching in a module where there was little previously; and the successful introduction of project based assessment in a module which was previously 100% examined by final exams.

Lessons Learned

- Undergraduate mechanical engineering students can quickly learn anatomy and related medical terminology, given access to appropriate software, well-written bespoke teaching materials and small group teaching.
- The introduction of such software and teaching methods was noted to be novel in the context of that currently offered in the School of Mechanical and Systems Engineering.
- Students said that they enjoyed using the software and this opinion was supported by the view of the lead author when he was 'teaching' the software.

Chapter 11
Improvement of Engineering Students Education by E-Learning

George. A. Sorial
University of Cincinnati, USA

Babak Noroozi
University of Guilan, Iran

ABSTRACT

Traditional education for engineers has shifted towards new methods of teaching and learning through the proliferation of Information and Communication Technologies. The continuous advances in technology enable the realization of a more distributed structure of knowledge transfer. Virtual Learning Environment has become an increasingly ambiguous term in recent years because of essential elements facilitating a consistent environment for learners. It has the potential to position the learner within a meaningful context to a much greater extent than traditional interactive multimedia environments. The 3D environment acquaints students with features of different shapes and objects, and can be particularly useful in teaching younger students different procedures and mechanisms for carrying out specific tasks. This case explains the key issues and success factors regarding the e-Learning for engineering education especially in developing countries.

BACKGROUND: ENGINEERING EDUCATION AND CHANGES

Recent years have seen dramatic changes in engineering education in terms of increased access to lifelong learning, increased choice in areas of study and the personalization of learning. To advance across all domains seems to necessitate incompatible changes to the learning process, as practitioners offer individualized learning to a larger, more diverse engineering student base. To achieve this cost effectively and without overwhelming practitioners requires new approaches to teaching and learning coupled with access to a wide range of resources: practitioners need to be able to source and share engineering materials, adapt and contextualize them to suit individual needs, and use them across a variety of engineering educational models (Littlejohn, et al., 2008). Hence a great deal of effort has focused on the integration of new technologies

DOI: 10.4018/978-1-61520-869-2.ch011

such as multimedia video, audio, animation, and computers, with associated software, to achieve the improvement of traditional engineering education. The internet technologies have also been popularly applied to web-based learning (Hung, et al., 2007). The growth of the information society provides a way for fast data access and information exchange all over the world. Computer technologies have been significantly changing the content and practice of engineering education (Gladun, et al., 2008). Information and communication technologies (ICT) are rightly recognized as tools that are radically transforming the process of learning. Universities, institutions and industries are investing increasing resources to advance researches for providing better and more effective learning solutions (Campanella, et al., 2007).

Nowadays, the use of ICT has improved learning, especially when coupled with more learner-centered instruction, or convenience, where learning and exchange with the instructor can take place asynchronously at the learners own pace or on as-needed basis (Motiwalla, 2007). The consequent applications of all multimedia and simulation technologies, computer-mediated communication and communities, and Internet-based support for individual and distance learning have the potential for revolutionary improvements in education (Gladun, et al., 2008).

Hence, electronic collaboration (e-collaboration) technologies for engineers are technologies that support e-collaboration. An operational definition of e-collaboration is collaboration among different individuals using electronic technologies to accomplish a common task. These e-collaboration technologies include several Internet-based technologies, such as e-mail, forums, chats, and document repositories (Padilla, et al., 2008).

The first computer-supported collaboration system emerged in 1984 from the need of sharing interests among product developers and researchers in diverse fields. This revolutionary approach was called computer-supported collaborative work and it was used to support learning by means of desktop and video conferencing systems. Consequently, a new paradigm arose around educational institutions which were defined as computer-supported collaborative learning (CSCL). This emerging system was based on the contributions of constructivist learning theories about the term collaborative learning, which focus on social interdependence and maintain that engineering students consolidate their learning by teaching one another. CSCL environments were created for using technology as a mediation tool within collaborative learning methods of instruction. Since then, and thanks to the great evolution of network technologies, engineering education is moving out of traditional classrooms. These collaborative e-Learning environments have caused a revolution in the academic community, providing a great amount of advantages for using both the Internet and technologies for 'any-time, any-place' collaborative learning (Jara, et al., 2008). Figure 1 shows a brief history of distance learning (Hamza-Lup, 2007; Harper, 2004).

SETTING THE STAGE: E-LEARNING AND ENGINEERING STUDENTS

The final objective of a learning object is to realize three fundamental learning goals:

- To inform the engineering students to be responsible of their learning, capable to manage processes to reach aims and to understand their learning needs;
- To promote real and meaningful learning environments and contexts, enabling the engineering students to retrieve information and build knowledge by using different learning ways;
- To create stimulating situations and learning dynamics that prelude to wider learning tasks

Figure 1. The history of distance learning

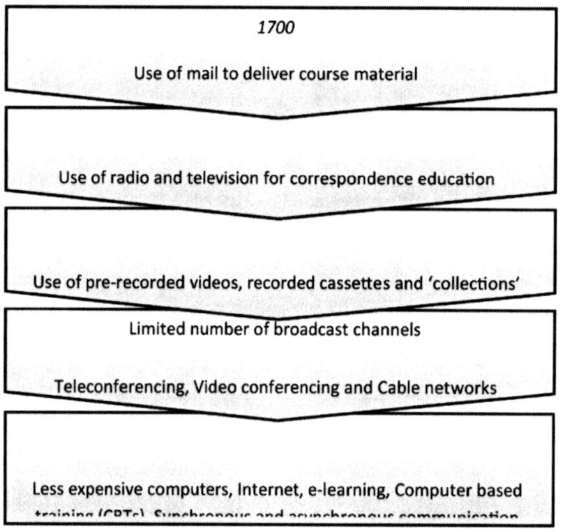

The most important aspects of a focused learning for engineering students are shown in Figure 2.

It should be noted that e-Learning is becoming one of the most popular solutions to meet new needs especially in technical courses. In e-learning course development and management for engineers the emphasis is often on technical aspects, whereas the relevance of learning products for the actual process of learning is not considered in depth. Indeed the most important aspect of a learning product is its aptitude to provide knowledge and skill by stimulating in dept study, further

Figure 2. The most important and meaningful characteristics for engineering instruction

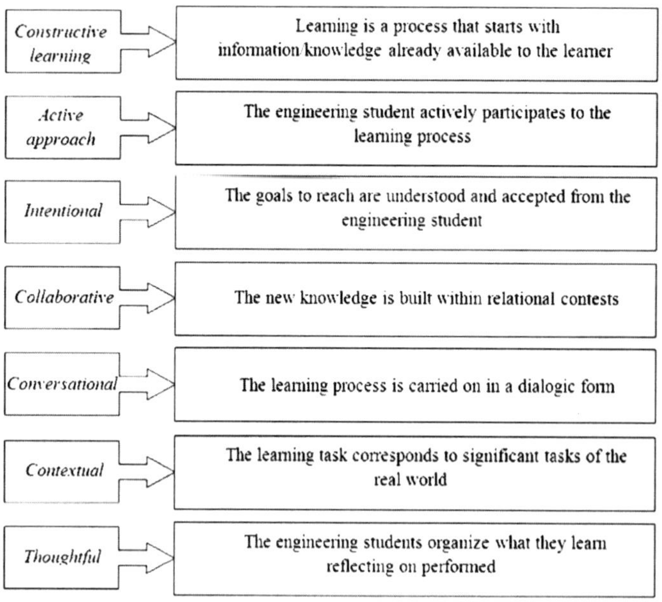

researches and close investigations (Campanella, et al., 2007).

The present chapter is a study on the growth of e-Learning in engineering education as the most important objective area of science apart from the medical science. Using the definitions and aptitudes of e-Learning we tried to find a more specialized way to develop e-Learning in engineering education. To this aim, we have investigated the progresses being made on engineering e-Learning, and the benefits and difficulties of implementing e-Learning in engineering education. The study has focused on the importance of e-Learning design for engineering education; therefore, the concept of instructional design has been reviewed and oriented for engineering e-Learning. This study also presents an overview on International potential for designing e-Learning, with selected case studies of developing countries.

CASE DESCRIPTION

Case Context

The definition of e-Learning for engineers may vary significantly, but perhaps "... learning the engineering concept is aided by information and communication technologies..." is one of the definitions, which is very close to reality. However, some authors and users define e-learning only as "... the delivery of content via all electronic media, including the internet, intranets, extranets, satellite, broadcast, video, interactive TV, and CD ROM...". In this case the emphasis is only at the delivery and many unworthy engineering courses have been "developed" by this way –just delivery to students of existing files with handouts. This has the only advantage of reduced cost, but the educational results do not have significant value. Many authors support the first view that e-Learning should develop materials, which will increase the pedagogical effectiveness, and then deliver these to engineering students. Only in this case the full power of e-Learning can be utilized (Tabakov, 2008).

E-Learning for engineering students, at its best, is the kind of learning that complements traditional methods and gives a more effective experience to the learner. Simply, e-Learning for engineers is the use of technology to support the learning process. Fundamentally, it is about putting the learner first by placing resources at the learner's fingertips. The engineering e-learner is able to dictate the pace and balance of learning activities in a way that suits him/her. E-Learners can absorb and develop knowledge and skills in an environment that has been tailored to suit them – and at their own pace. As opposed to online courses in their strictest sense, e-Learning does not necessarily lead to an engineering certification or an engineering degree programmer but may be tailored, for example, to suit the needs of a specific company (Magoha&Andrew, 2004).

Engineering Education Improvement Concerns

Despite the dramatic expansion in e-Learning and distance education, e-Learning in engineering education still faces a number of setbacks that prevent an equivalent expansion rate. For effective and complete learning in engineering, science and technology, engineering education requires a mixture of theoretical and practical sessions. In order to understand how theoretical knowledge can apply to real world problems, practical exercises are essential. While it is relatively easy to simulate experiments, performing practical experiments online has continued to be a challenge. Coupled with this, engineering software is often very expensive and may not be easily affordable by the ordinary e-Learner. Although low cost alternatives that utilize freeware have been successfully developed and tested, practical laboratories that support engineering education are still difficult to implement online (Magoha&Andrew, 2004). E-learning system for engineering education is able to be interpreted in various ways such as "computer based, education delivery system which is provided through the Internet", or "an educational method that is able to provide opportunities for the needed people, at the right place, with the right contents, and the right time" (Lee&Lee, 2008).

Engineering education relies heavily on capital-intensive laboratory equipment. Collaboration with developed countries would, therefore, be one path to enhance learning in engineering concepts for developing countries. A collaborative laboratory component can bridge the gap between regular e-learning and e-learning in engineering. This can be achieved through an Internet laboratory, examples of which are several Internet-based laboratories have already been developed and have been described elaborately. Most of these laboratories are based on standard hardware systems, such as those provided by National Instruments (NI), and are commercially available. However they are costly and often require specialized training. The solution is to develop low cost systems that rely partially on expensive hardware at the server and open software at the client (Magoha&Andrew, 2004).

Examples of Engineering Education Developments

Numerous digital applications have been developed to demonstrate laboratory experiments, real-world landscape processes or microscopic objects. Engineering students learned faster and liked their classes more than students in traditional on-campus classes. Cognitive scientists believe that to learn, the material must have meaning to the learner.

Medical Physics and Engineering (MEP) is an example among the first professions to develop and apply e-Learning. An indicator for this is the first international prize in the field (EU Leonardo da Vinci Award) presented to European Medical Imaging Technology (EMIT) Consortium in 2004. During the last 15 years, a number of activities and publications addressed the questions of MEP Education and Training. These led to rapid development of the profession worldwide and now the next stage of e-learning is to be addressed. A special issue on the subject was published by the Journal of Medical Engineering and Physics in 2005.

Using three dimensional graphics for more realistic and detailed representations of topics, offering more viewpoints and more inspection possibilities compared to 2D education. For example the WebTOP system helps in learning about waves and optics by visually presenting various kinds of physical phenomena, may are not available in the real world, but have invaluable potential for education (Chittaro&Ranon, 2007).

In improvement of engineer education, some authors use CFD (Computational Fluid Dynamics) program to run the case and observe the physical phenomena on single-plane software rather than via internet. Frederick et al. (Hung, et al., 2007) used the commercial software, FlowLab, to create a CFD education interface for engineering course and laboratories, had been proven that is an effective and efficient tool to help students learning.

The concept of thermal-hydraulics e-learning system was initiated by Hung et al. (Hung, et al., 2007). They merged existing computational fluid dynamics capability into the e-learning concept to improve traditional engineer education in fluid flow and heat transfer. In the paper, they referred to HTML (Hyper text markup language) and ASP (Active server pages) where an interactive user interface as the core of the system and system structure has been preliminarily planned. The prototype of a postprocessor program was also established. But the ability of post-processor in drawing for flow field, stream lines, and isothermal contours has to be further enhanced. Liu et al. (Liu, et al., 2006) quoted the concept of Hung et al (Hung, et al., 2007) to implement and strengthen the architecture of this thermal hydraulics e-learning system. In order to establish a cross platform for e-learning, they used an HTML embedded scripting language, PHP (Hypertext Preprocessor), and integrated with MySQL database management system to manage all teaching materials (Hung, et al., 2007).

Comparing Traditional and E-Learning Education

E-Learning for engineering education offers unique pedagogical opportunities to enhance student learning: In the realm of e-education, there are clear benefits that can be derived from e-Learning as follows:

- It promotes exploratory and interactive modes of inquiry.
- It supports and facilitates team-orientated collaborations and expands the ease of access to engineering education across institutional, geographical and cultural boundaries, among others.
- Class notes and materials are posted on the Internet and students can access the sites from anywhere in the world.
- This is quite unlike distance learning, where an engineering student is given course materials and reads solely on his/her own until examination time.
- E-Learning is interactive; the software permits the engineering student to communicate, not only with the lecturer, but also with fellow classmates. It enriches and supplements the classroom experience by engaging the Web.
- E-Learning has the ability to communicate consistently to learners by providing the same concepts and engineering information – unlike classroom learning, where different instructors may not follow the same curriculum or teach different things within the curriculum.
- E-Learning is cost effective in terms of learners per instructor. In addition, it saves classroom time and this is very significant for learners who are employed on a full-time basis.
- Engineering students, instructors and evaluators can track learning outcomes more easily (Magoha&Andrew, 2004).

It has been found that all of the respondents considered the online course materials beneficial to their overall learning experience. Obtained results have shown a positive effect on engineering student learning, problem-solving skills, and critical thinking skills, with females responding more positively than males. Comparing undergraduates who completed quizzes online with engineering students who took traditional paper-based quizzes leads to reveal that students who took the quizzes online significantly outperformed engineering students who took the pencil-and-paper quizzes. It has been asserted that web-enhanced learning improves instruction and course management and offers numerous pedagogical benefits for learners. Engineering students in Web-enabled learning environments become more active and self directed learners, who are exposed to enhanced learning materials. Course Websites have proved to be an effective means of delivering learning materials, with students responding positively to the quality resources they make available (Buzzetto-More, 2008).

For all its potential in dealing with learners individually, online learning does have its own invisibility problems. The other side of online learning can seem far away and isolated. For the learner, the price of empowerment is the responsibility of wielding that power. As with all distance learning, e-Learning relies on self-motivation. With no enforced discipline or deadlines, it is easy for the learner to be distracted and put off work for a distant tomorrow. With no human presence, it is also impossible for a learner with a problem to obtain help easily. Thus, personal interaction between the instructor and engineering students is either absent or else very different from traditional face-to face learning. Other subtle disadvantages of e-Learning include the ability to read text from the computer screen. Research has shown that linear text is often difficult for people to read from the computer. Hence, learners often have to reformat the text and print it out for reading, necessitating the need for a printer. The problems of invisibility, anonymity and isolation can be dealt with in several ways. Once more, the key solution is communication and there are several channels available to learners. The first is a national help line where learners can talk to someone trained to give them advice on their course. Many e-Learners are also assigned an online tutor who checks on their progress and can be contacted by e-mail with any queries or worries. Online message boards and chat rooms provide learners with the means to contact and talk to other people doing the same course, exchanging advice, ideas and encouragement. For those without access to computer at home or who require additional support there is a network of centers across countries. Surely, no engineering educator would argue against a legitimate teaching method that highly motivates students to learn their subject matter and promotes student interaction in the process. To witness students achieve an increased mastery of ideas, while also setting greater expectations for themselves, would be fulfilling educators' dreams.

A Brief Review of Case Studies in Developing Countries

Thailand

E-Learning in Thailand like many other developing countries, deals with barriers such as culture, organization, limited technology and availability low household penetration of the ICT such as telephones, Satellites, PC's, Internet connections, broadband and etc. here again technologies available during the last decade did not appear to support the engineering education sector perfectly. They have been rare, limited and relatively expensive for engineering educational purposes. Multimedia presentation is a well-presented (and well tested) form of learning that requires a large bandwidth for the transmission of the contents to all destination users, certainly pushing the broadband diffusion too. It is important not to forget the localization as Thai students do not love studying non-Thai contents and this is why almost well known foreign (English) contents did not succeed in Thailand market. The majority of existing e-Learning Contents available are in English. Thus, e-Learning Contents in non-English are highly in demand (Sirinaruemitr, 2004; Vate-U-Lan, 2007; Witsawakiti, et al., 2006).

The first traces of e-Learning for engineers in Thailand returns to 1993. When after several years of usage of internet in 1-2 academic centers in Thailand, i.e. Asian Institute of Technology and Chulalongkorn University, they felt that Internet should be made available to the whole Assumption University (AU). The outcome was implementing a project, called AuNet. Purposing (Chorpothong&Charmonman, 2004):

1. To educate the engineering students, faculty and staff members on the concepts of local and international networking.
2. To prepare the engineering students to enter into information society where networking will be the norm rather than the exception.
3. To provide full Internet access to all engineering students, faculty and staff members for their personal and educational usage.

Concerning to the rapid expansion of knowledge and widespread demand of engineering education, in 2002 this program proposed a project on e-Learning with the aim of (Chorpothong&Charmonman, 2004):

1. To serve the country by allowing those interested in engineering education the opportunity to continue their studies conveniently, no matter from where or when.

2. To promote Life-Long Learning by using the Internet.
3. To expand Assumption University from traditional classroom-based engineering education to Internet-based distance education.
4. To increase the number of students at Assumption University from about 18,000 persons in 2002 to 100,000 persons later.

Establishment of the College of Internet Distance Education on April 25, 2002, with over 2000 Internet terminal and 1000 phone lines, and mirror sites for degree programs from other countries has been the first step of this project which looks for degree-level e-Learning in Thailand. The College of Internet Distance Education of Assumption University has entered into cooperation with many universities such as UKeU and UNITAR, hoping that by the year 2010, the target of 100,000 students, will be reached. Now the attempts on developing e-Learning seem to be more on e-Learning designing and overcoming infrastructure problems. Local case studies are more emphasizing on the role of design of hypertext or hyperlink and the flexibility of presentation (Morse&Suktrisul, 2006; Siritongthaworn&Krairit, 2004; Vate-U-Lan, 2007; Witsawakiti, et al., 2006).

Furthermore, Thailand is quite slow in deploying the services including the necessary (broadband) infrastructure and transforming the ways of learning and the (digital) contents are very rare too. In some open universities such as Rhamkhamhaeng University, and Sukhothai Thammatirat University, it's true that they are working on e-Learning projects but they are still familiar with one way broadcasting or two-way video conferencing through the satellite and Fiber Optics. This is because the digital contents available may not deliver to the learners or students by means of using effective broadband ADSL for lack of availability. As a step ahead, ICT ministry of Thailand has launched a program to address provincial home market and enabled people in the rural areas to have home computers. In addition, low-cost software has been introduced to support the hardware program and in turn Thailand can now see quite a low cost of Microsoft licenses and freeware such as Linux and Pladao being deployed. Ministry sponsored low cost software's and cheap computers as a result of high competitions and reduced production cost have for the first time allowed Thai people to be able to afford reasonable computers at home in larger and growing quantities. However, people still perceive that Internet access cost is still too high. This is the barrier to the use of Internet for education. Broadband access fees are also still relatively high and are considered as a premium. Affordability is still an important consideration as far as broadband was concerned (Sirinaruemitr, 2004).

India

E-Learning or electronic learning in India is gaining prominence slowly, but indeed steadily. This is due to the fact that more than half the population of India today is below 25 years of age and the number of Internet users is growing continuously. According to UNESCO reports at 2006, 65.2% of adults and 81.3% of youth are literate (UNESCO, 2006). The tremendous growth of the economy in the recent past has also helped in the growth of online education in India. E-Learning in India is especially popular with the young professionals who have joined the work force quite early but still would like to continue their education that may help them move up their career ladder quickly and safely. They find online education in India very convenient, as the nature of the course work does not require them to attend regular classes. Moreover reputed institutes like Indian Institute of Management, Indian Institute of Technology, Indian Institute of Foreign Trade are today offering e-Learning courses. The scope of online education in India is actually much wider. Apart from proper course works, some E-Learning portals in India are also conducting mock tests for various competitive examinations like engineering, medical, management etc.

In India, the engineering education has got both government and private players in the market. It consists of arts, science, and management, technical and professional education. Since the Indian knowledge industry is entering into the take off stage, the strategy of survival is high. The foreign players are also trying to join the competition. And hence the less effective educational institutions for engineers are forced to merge themselves with others or they are forced to go out of market. However there is a paradox in e-Learning among various institutes in India. Few institutions join the race, while the rest suffer from lack of knowledge or from lack of realization of the importance of e-Learning. Institutes like IITs are adopting all latest technologies and are keeping their engineering students enlightened from various parts of the world. E-Learning has vast potential in India.

The IT service sector export of India has grown up from US $ 754 million in 1995-95 to US $ 12,000 million in 2004-05. The annual growth based on the trend analysis is US $ 573 in India and US $ 1038 in Tamil Nadu. The Indian IT sector especially Tamilnadu IT sector is growing at a faster rate. This same speed of growth is not replicated in e-Learning application. If all these efforts, are directed properly the ups and downs in knowledge growth can be removed.

In engineering education, virtual classroom or a teacher free classroom has got bright future in India. A virtual classroom is one where the virtual reality is enhanced. It is a totally technology enabled class room environment. Virtual Reality (V.R.) is a 3D learning environment where the learner can explore the learning concept. Learning is experienced through games or simulated situation. It brings a real environment while wearing a headset and data glove in an immersive virtual reality environment. In the areas of Medicine, Engineering, Astronomy and other skill trainings, virtual e-Learning will become indispensable (Nelasco, et al., 2007).

China

Cyber-education has been growing rapidly in China since the late 1990s, especially in the fields of higher education and basic education. Technical and engineering institutions in China are currently encountering a high pressure onto their schooling capacity due to an increasing population of education pursuers. Cyber-education is considered as a fast and economic approach to ease the pressure. In September 1998, the MOE started to grant special licenses to Tsinghua University, Beijing Post and Telecommunication University, Zhejiang University, and Hunan University as the first set of higher educational institutions pioneering cyber-education. In 1999, Beijing University and the Central Broadcast and Television University were added to the pioneer list. Simulated by favorable policies, a considerable number of Chinese universities started to invest in Cyber-education since then. At the end of 2002, up to 67 universities in China have received cyber-education licenses. It is estimated that over 1.6 millions of students are enrolled in these cyber-education institutions, involved in 140 specialties from 10 academic disciplines. Besides, the Central TV University which has over 2 million of students, enrollment is moving to cyber-education (Zhiting, 2004).

Iran

The first traces of e-Learning returns to 25 years ago with distance learning. Iran is a country with a high interest in education. This country has an expanded network of private, public and state affiliated universities offering degrees in higher education. Reports of UNESCO show that up to 2006, 84.0% of adults and 97.6% of youth are literate and this is well balanced between male and female population. Furthermore a significant majority of the youth population is at or approaching collegiate levels (UNESCO, 2006). However the tendency of getting higher levels graduates is obviously growing between the youth population and particularly in graduated students.

Therefore the development of e-Learning in Iran glances in a brief view. Several universities in Iran has started e-Learning programs for distance education, specially Sharif University of Technology which is the most prestigious technical university in Iran and middle east, with different on-line courses on mechanic, electronic, and advanced modeling methods. However, many other authentic universities such as University of Tehran, Amirkabir University of Technology, University of Science and Industry and University of Shiraz have developed several on-line courses with the main concentration on engineering education.

Despite of all the efforts being made to expand e-Learning methods in educational structure of Iran, the process of transferring the traditional education in the Iranian society involves many pressing difficulties which according to the recent studies can be abridged as (Dilmaghani, 2003; Giveki, 2003; Hejazi, 2007; Noori, 2003):

- Lack of realistic comprehension concerning the process of learning
- Ambiguous understanding about students' educational needs in different levels
- Defective implementation of computer hardware and software
- Limited experienced IT professionals
- Incompatible educational resources for e-Leaning

SOLUTIONS AND RECOMMENDATIONS

Implementation of e-Learning for engineering students in developing countries could be tailored to satisfy the needs of a limited educational infrastructure. Moreover, for e-Learning design to succeed in the developing world, it needs to build one important pillar: the existence of infrastructure, along with some degree of connectivity. Nevertheless a key challenge could be technological requirements which must be kept to a minimum in order to increase the participation of developing countries in e-Learning design for engineering students. Virtual 3D models can be used in engineering education to stimulate processes to enhance the understanding of the concepts used in a particular process. Students could experience the 3D structure of a specific process and the means of controlling direction and movement within a system. 3D Virtual Reality, software tools and associated Web technologies are mature enough to be used in conjunction with advanced e-learning systems. 3D based content can enhance communication of ideas and concepts and stimulate the interest of students.

REFERENCES

Buzzetto-More, N. A. (2008). Student Perceptions of Various E-Learning Components. *Interdisciplinary Journal of E-Learning and Learning Objects*, *4*, 113–135.

Campanella, S., Dimauro, G., Ferrante, A., Impedovo, D., Impedovo, S., & Lucchese, M. G. (2007). Engineering e-learning surveys: a new approach. *International Journal of Education and Information Technologies*, *1*(2), 105–113.

Chittaro, L., & Ranon, R. (2007). Web3D technologies in learning, education and training: Motivations, issues, opportunities. *Computers & Education*, *49*, 3–18. doi:10.1016/j.compedu.2005.06.002

Chorpothong, N., & Charmonman, S. (2004). An eLearning project for 100,000 students per year in Thailand. *International Journal of The Computer, the Internet and Management, 12,* 111-118.

Coimbra, Portugal.Hung, T. C., Wang, S. K., Tai, S. W., & Hung, C. T. (2007). An innovative improvement of engineering learning system using computational fluid dynamics concept. *Computers & Education, 48*, 44-58.

Dilmaghani, M. (2003). *National providence and virtual education development capabilities in higher education.* Paper presented at the Virtual University Conference. Kashan, Iran.

Giveki, F. (2003). *Learning New Methods in Distance Higher Education*. Paper presented at the Virtual University Conference, Kashan, Iran.

Gladun, A., Rogushina, J., Garcıa-Sanchez, F., Martınez-Bejar, R., & Fernandez-Breis, J. T. (2009). An application of intelligent techniques and semantic web technologies in e-learning environments. *Expert Systems with Applications, 36*(2), 1922–1931. doi:10.1016/j.eswa.2007.12.019

Hamza-Lup, F. G., & Stefan, V. (2007). *Web 3D & Virtual Reality - Based Applications for Simulation and e-Learning*. Paper presented at the 2nd International Conference on Virtual Learning, ICVL. Constanta, Romania.

Harper, K. C., Chen, K., & Yen, D. C. (2004). Distance learning,virtual classrooms,and teaching pedagogy in the Internet environment. *Technology in Society, 26*, 585–598. doi:10.1016/S0160-791X(04)00054-5

Hejazi, A. (2007). *New wine-old bottles*. Retrieved from http://ictarticles.blogspot.com/2007/05/new-wine-old-bottles.html

Hung, T., Liu, C., Hung, C., Ku, H., & Lin, Y. (2007, September 3 – 7). *The Establishment of an Interactive E-learning System for Engineering Fluid Flow and Heat Transfer*. Paper presented at the International Conference on Engineering Education – ICEE 2007

Jara, C. A., Candelas, F. A., Torres, F., Dormido, S., Esquembre, F., & Reinoso, O. (2009). Real-time collaboration of virtual laboratories through the Internet. *Computers & Education, 52*(1), 126–140. doi:10.1016/j.compedu.2008.07.007

Lee, J., & Lee, W. (2008). The relationship of e-Learner's self-regulatory efficacy and perception of e-Learning environmental quality. *Computers in Human Behavior, 24*, 32–47. doi:10.1016/j.chb.2006.12.001

Littlejohn, A., Falconer, I., & Mcgill, L. (2008). Characterising effective eLearning resources. *Computers & Education, 50*, 757–771. doi:10.1016/j.compedu.2006.08.004

Liu, C. C., Hung, C. T., Hung, T. C., Pei, B. S., & Zhang, L. (2006). *The development of an innovative interactive e-learning system in computational thermal-hydraulics for engineers.* Paper presented at the EDMEDIA.Magoha

Morse, A., & Suktrisul, S. (2006). Introducing eL-earning into Secondary Schools in Thailand. *Special Issue of the International Journal of the Computer, the Internet and Management, 14*, 8.1-8.5.

Motiwalla, L. F. (2007). Mobile learning: A framework and evaluation. *Computers & Education, 49*, 581–596. doi:10.1016/j.compedu.2005.10.011

Nelasco, S., Arputtharaj, A. N., & Alwinson, E. G. (2007). ELearning for Higher Studies of India. *Special Issue of the International Journal of the Computer. The Internet and Management, 15*, 161–167.

Noori, M. (2003). *Traditional education or learning with computer*. Paper presented at the Virtual University Conference at Kashan Payam-e Noor College, Kashan, Iran

P. W., & Andrew, W. O. (2004). The global perspectives of transitioning to e-learning in engineering education. *World Transactions on Engineering and Technology Education, 3*(2), 205–210.

Padilla-Melendez, A., Garrido-Moreno, A., & Aguila-Obra, A. R. (2008). Factors affecting e-collaboration technology use among management students. *Computers & Education*, *51*, 609–623. doi:10.1016/j.compedu.2007.06.013

Sirinaruemitr, P. (2004). Trends and forces for eLearning in Thailand. *International Journal of The Computer, the Internet and Management*, *12*, 132-137.

Siritongthaworn, S., & Krairit, D. (2004). Use of Interactions in E-learning: A Study of Undergraduate Courses in Thailand. *International Journal of The Computer, the Internet and Management*, *12*, 162-170.

Sun, P., Cheng, H. K., Lin, T., & Wang, F. (2008). A design to promote group learning in e-learning: Experiences from the field. *Computers & Education*, *50*, 661–677. doi:10.1016/j.compedu.2006.07.008

Tabakov, S. (2008). e-Learning development in medical physics and engineering. *Biomedical Imaging and Intervention Journal*, *4*(1), e27. doi:10.2349/biij.4.1.e27

UNESCO. (2006). *UIS statics in brief-Iran*. Retrieved from http://stats.uis.unesco.org/unesco / TableViewer/document.aspx?ReportId=121&IF_Language=eng&BR_Country=3640.

Vate-U-Lan, P. (2007). Readiness of eLearning connectivity in Thailand. *Special Issue of the International Journal of the Computer, the Internet and Management*, *15*, 21.21-21.27.

Witsawakiti, N., Suchato, A., & Punyabukkana, P. (2006). Thai language E-training for the hard of hearing. *Special Issue of the International Journal of the Computer. The Internet and Management*, *14*, 41–46.

Zhiting, Z. (2004). The development and applications of elearning technology standards in China. *International Journal of The Computer, the Internet and Management 12*, 100-104.

APPENDIX: SUPPORTING MATERIAL

Abstract

This chapter is a study on the growth of e-Learning in engineering education as the most important objective area of science. Using the definitions and aptitudes of e-Learning we tried to find a more specialized way to develop e-Learning in engineering education. The study has focused on the importance of e-Learning design for engineering education. This study also presents an overview on International potential for designing e-Learning, with selected case studies of developing countries.

Questions and Answers

1. What is the overall problem(s) in this case?

E-Learning for engineering students, is the kind of learning that complements traditional methods and gives a more effective experience to the learner. Simply, e-learning for engineers is the use of technology to support the learning process which its wide range of application allows increasing education quality and delivery of information.

2. What are the fundamental learning goals?
   a. To inform the engineering students to be responsible of their learning
   b. To promote real and meaningful learning environments and contexts,
   c. To create stimulating situations and learning dynamics

3. Discuss managerial, organizational, and technological issues and resources related to this case.

Integration of new technologies such as multimedia video, audio, animation, and computers, with associated software help to achieve the improvement of traditional engineering education. Information and communication technologies (ICT) are rightly recognized as tools that are radically transforming the process of learning.

4. What are some of the tools and techniques that should be considered in solving the problem(s) related to the case?

During recent years University Education has to experience an important progress with respect to the resources used for lecturing. New methodological approaches have to introduce in order to value an active learning as opposed to a traditional passive learning.

5. What is the final solution that can be recommended to the management of the organization described in the case? Provide your arguments in support of the recommended solution.

Implementation of e-Learning for engineering students in developing countries could be tailored to satisfy the needs of a limited educational infrastructure. Nevertheless a key challenge could be technological requirements which must be kept to a minimum in order to increase the participation of developing countries in e-Learning design for engineering students.

Epilogue and Lessons Learned

Virtual Learning Environment has become increasingly ambiguous term in recent years because of essential elements facilitating a consistent environment for learners. It has the potential to position the learner within a meaningful context to a much greater extent than traditional interactive multimedia environments. The 3D environment makes acquainted students with features of different shapes and objects, and can be particularly useful in teaching younger students different procedures and mechanisms for carrying out specific tasks.

Lessons Learned

1. The continuous advances in technology enable the realization of a more distributed structure of knowledge transfer. This becomes critically important for developing countries that lack the resources and infrastructure for implementing engineering education practices.
2. *The two main themes of technology in designing e-Learning for engineering education in developing countries focus either on aspects of technological support for traditional methods and localized processes, or on the investigation of how such technologies may assist distance learning.*
3. *Virtual Reality is mature enough to be used for enhancing communication of ideas and concepts and stimulate the interest of students*

Chapter 12
Purpose-Oriented Small Software:
A Case Study for Some Engineering Subjects

Giancarlo Anzelotti
University of Parma, Italy

Masoumeh Valizadeh
University of Guilan, Iran

ABSTRACT

This case emphasizes on the power of virtual tools for engineering subjects. As a more accessible approach, the authors suggest the development and application of Purpose-Oriented small software. The aim of developing these e-tools is enhancing the understanding of concepts taught in the undergraduate and graduated Mechanical, Material, Civil and many other engineering branches. The main idea behind this case is to show that even light software which is focused on a particular subject can be used as a key for engineering education.

INTRODUCTION

The critical tenet of engineering education reform is the integral role of virtual environment capabilities which is provided by fabulous advances in information technology. Current technological progresses combined with changes in engineering content and instructional method require engineering instructors to be able to design intensive and concentrated lessons for exploration and discovery of the engineering concepts through appropriate computer applications. In actual practice, however, most computer applications provided for engineering education consist of software designed for a specific educational purpose. Furthermore, economical constraints often stand in the way of incorporating such special purpose software into an instructional setting.

Owing to all the revolutions made and is being made in information transfer and computer capabilities and speed, recent decades have been witnessed many changes in the methods of engineering education and there are many new researches and methods for this task (Willis 1993; Koksal 1998; Kaufman 2000; Cloete 2001; Wankat 2002; Baker 2005; Hutten 2005; Yu 2006; Burnely 2007; Moreno

DOI: 10.4018/978-1-61520-869-2.ch012

2007; Haghi 2008; Monahan 2008; Shih 2008; Toth 2008; Vadillo 2009). This paper discusses an alternative to the traditional approach which shifts the instructional focus from specific computer applications to more sophisticated uses of general purpose software. In particular, educational uses of purpose-oriented small software which can be implemented in multi purpose software are exampled as an introduction to this approach. In another vision, purpose-oriented small software can be designed as a cost-effective approach to provide practical experience to undergraduate students. The concept which is called '*Virtual Laboratory*' and is being widely developed in engineering schools and educational programs (Gervasi 2004; Ramasundaram 2005; Kukreti 2008; Tan 2008; Vadillo 2009).

The software and approaches described here have been presented to graduate and undergraduate engineering education majors in a continuing education course in universities or factories.

NEW APPROACHES IN ENGINEERING EDUCATION

Since the first years of its emergence in mid 20th century (1940-1945), the computers have been welcomed and started to be employed by governments, companies, factories and moreover in education. By this new invention of human being the computations needed the handling of big amount of data and calculations have been "translated" in computer language and little by little have been automatized and implemented by this powerful contrivance. It changed the approach to design radically and convinced the engineers, mathematicians, economists, industrialists all over the world to employ it as a potent tool in their activities. Since that time we have been witnessing significant jumps in the science of computing and design. Nowadays, thanks to the enormous power of today's computers respect to what was available just few years ago, we are able to solve complex, multifarious tasks involving different science fields and may need weeks or months of work if they would have been done by hands.

Along with the significant changes in designing and calculating methods, occurred through the application of electronic devices like calculating machines as a simple example, but mostly the computers, the methods of teaching the design and modeling techniques have changed remarkably. However comparing to all the present branches of science and technology, the engineering and engineering education have evolved more and have progressed fabulously. Nowadays the use of computer-aided design software (CAD) or finite element systems (FEA) have become *de facto* a standard and the essential topics in engineering courses, both at school and university levels. In the next step, further improvements in the field of computer languages has made the use of custom-made software more widely possible, and has empowered the engineers to solve different requirements of the industries.

Professional programming languages like Python™ or Visual Basic® have been developed with a reasonably user friendly, easy learning curve and practical performances, providing lower investment costs for users. On the other hand to confront with more complicated calculations middle-level languages like C++ or High-level languages like FORTRAN represent a fairly better performance in a more admissible time. Furthermore, concerning to the fact that the software may be used in different operating systems and to aid the students to use them in laboratory or at home then a cross-platform programming approach consisting of languages, tools, libraries, etc. that let the programmer to port easily the code from one operating system to another one can be more favorable.

However, the field of education is usually concerned about the understanding of concepts as well as how to speed-up the learning process, where the ease of knowledge transfer from the teacher to the students is the key issue. In this area, one of the problems is the lack of suitable thinking approach. The students are used to solve design problem still based on analytical approach, not based on synthetic approach. They have difficulty in applying the acquired specific knowledge to their design task, although they have already learned that from related nature science or engineering science courses. However, the engineers of 21st century need not only innovative talents but also interdisciplinary abilities to develop new technologies and products. Appropriate teaching aids are therefore necessary for the challenge of engineering design education. In addition to teaching the knowledge of engineering science, today the design and simulation methodology play more and more an important roll in engineering. Therefore it seems that new requirements on the curriculum of engineering design courses are necessary to enforce the students to use the present facilities to actuate and accelerate their learning progressions (Tsai 2008).

Concerning to this task, a wide range of professional software have been made that can be used to increase the effectiveness of learning as well as teaching such as SolidWorks®, AutoCAD®, ArchiCAD®, Abaqus®, LabView®, Matlab® *etc.* Although the professional software provide noteworthy facilities in both industrial and educational fields, but for many of the educational centers it is not affordable to pay for their licenses and to employ them for educational affairs. However the fact that there are always possibilities to enhance students' cognition through some proper ploys such as developing e-tools and freeware or small software sounds encouraging.

Relevant visual tools ensure quick and comprehensive transfer of information and convey data, coding of which in written or spoken form takes longer time and more facilities, or in many situations even it is impossible. The main forms of visualization can be counted as images, animations and simulations (Upitis 2008).

DEVELOPING PURPOSE-ORIENTED SMALL SOFTWARE IN ENGINEERING EDUCATION

The authors believe that even with purposeful small software especially with a plain, but intelligible graphic interface, the students will be able to reach a better understanding of the design and simulation courses, admitting that there is no other branch of science as objective, tangible and virtualizable as engineering. Thus, in this field the application of script languages, embedded inside general purpose (Endnote 1) software is preferable like Python™ that has embedded inside Abaqus®. According to the authors' experience, the use of Visual Basic® for Application (VBA) for the beginner level of programming inside an engineering course, aimed to solve simple design problems and not directly to programming is usually a good choice.

Programming itself may sometimes help the students to clarify the complex mathematical environment needed to solve engineering problems. Regarding to this fact that math is just a powerful tool in the hands of the engineers it is the essential term of every designing or simulation, but should not be considered as the main task of the engineering.

Focusing on mechanic, civil and material engineering as the branches of the engineering which are sorely involved in design and simulation, the next sections will present some examples of software aimed to help the students to understand better the design and material properties and behavior concepts.

CAMCREATOR

The design of a camshaft or simply of a single cam is usually a difficult task to solve. Because it deals not only with the design of the shape and to make the lever in a way that follows a certain displacement law, but also it needs to take into account the speed and more important the acceleration law for the lever (and sometimes also the jerk, first derivative of the acceleration). When the general geometry of the cam and the lever are simple and the applied displacements and loading system are not complex, the design and its calculations can be solved manually. But to design more complicated systems, the use of a computer aided approach is unavoidable. A problem-oriented software is able to define different geometries using a trial-and-error algorithm in few minutes. While the number of input and output variables is high, a congruous computer software gives the possibility to the user to focus on just few of them a time and to draw graphs of the variation of the output respect to the change of input. Through an automatic algorithm based on trial-and-error or more complex optimization schemes like genetic algorithm (GA),the software may be even able to determine the best design itself.

However the programmer has to consider that for the educational purposes, graphical user interface (GUI), its ease of use, comprehensiveness and visual aspects, plays a very important role, because it is the main object attracts the learners and incite them to focus on the lesson. Here the virtual environments may offer better facilities. Through applying this approach, more clear and exact illustrations of the objects and the problems will be available. Therefore every sketch, drawing or schemes, but moreover the simulated animations and movies may accelerate the learning process. As an example Figure 1 shows a graphical user interface designed for the definition of the input needed to design a desmodromic cam. In Figure 1a the software asks for the general properties of the cam so it provides the opportunity to import the geometrical information. Figure 1b introduces a simple 7-steps acceleration law, so it asks for loading system.

Programming for such specialized software needs the deep and comprehensive understanding of the programmer about the designing of the desmodromic cam, to consider every kind of mistake the user may make and prevents them by providing appropriate warnings or error messages.

Figure 1. Graphical user interface (GUI) of CamCreator

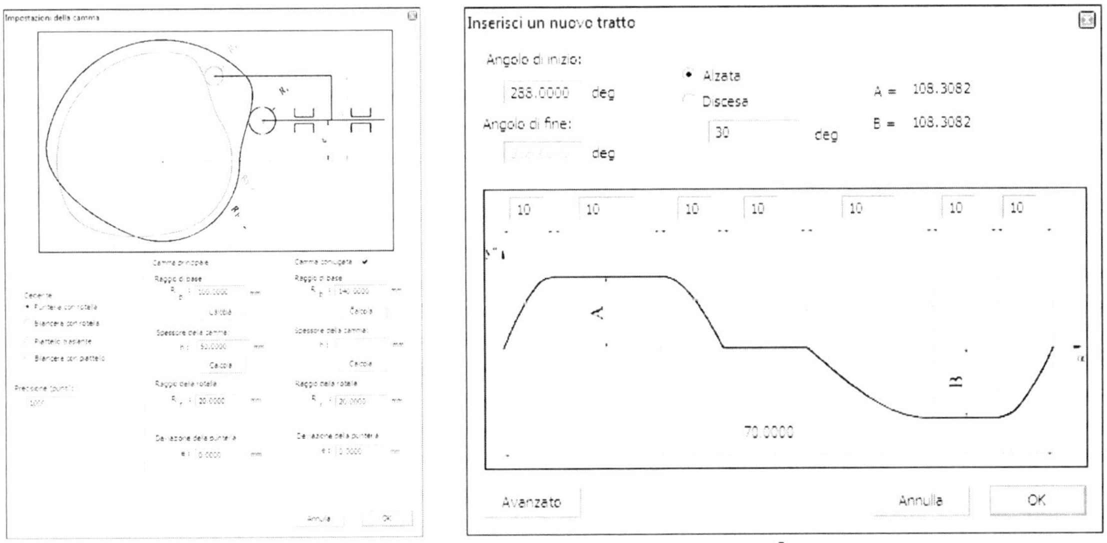

a b

Figure 2. A small software like CamCreator can lead to precious statements

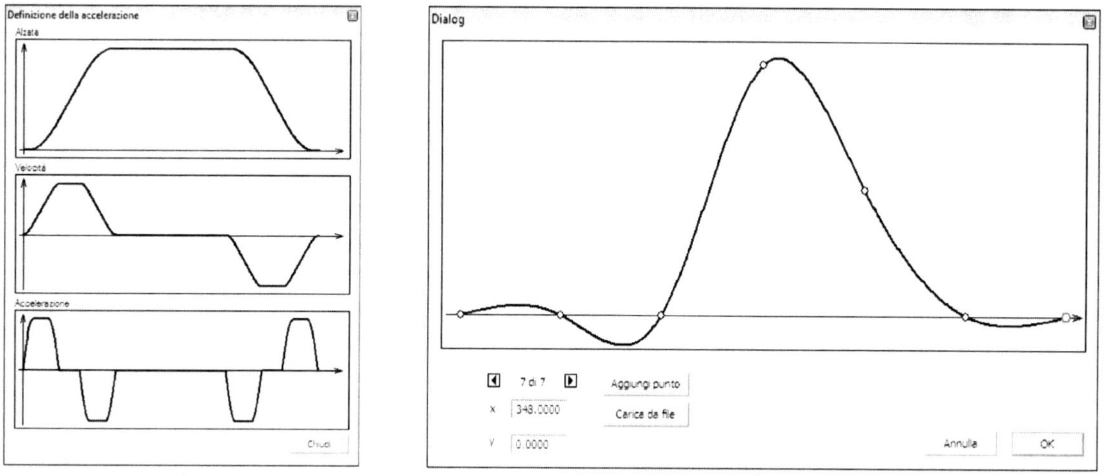

a b

Figure 2 shows how the software can easily present different representing graphs, such as the displacement (on the top of figure 2a) to the acceleration (on the bottom of figure 2a). Such software can be equipped by virtual 3D configuration which is the forte of computer aided engineering education. This appliance supplies a live performance of the machine and its kinematical mechanisms or its dynamics in a 3D world, without building the real part or prototyping it. To make this scenario cost-effective there are freeware utilities such as OpenGL, to animate the final results. This application has been shown in figure 3.

GEAR-CUT

Another example is Gear-Cut software to teach the gears and the interaction between the gears to the students. This subject usually it is not deeply clear to the students. The influence of corrections on the change of the geometry or the undercut phenomenon is most of the times a complicated subject. For this purpose laboratory sessions may help them to figure out the mechanism, but this needs the laboratory being equipped with a milling machine or some kind of milling system able to cut the gear profile out of a cylindrical piece of metal. Then, according to the course time and the disbarments to the course, just few specimens may be cut to show the students, or the same specimens should be showed at each year.

Figure 3. 3D visualization: a key to deep understanding

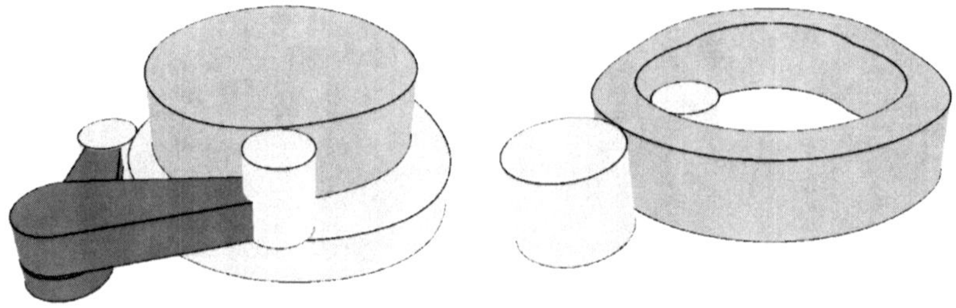

Figure 4. Gear simulation by Gears-Cut software

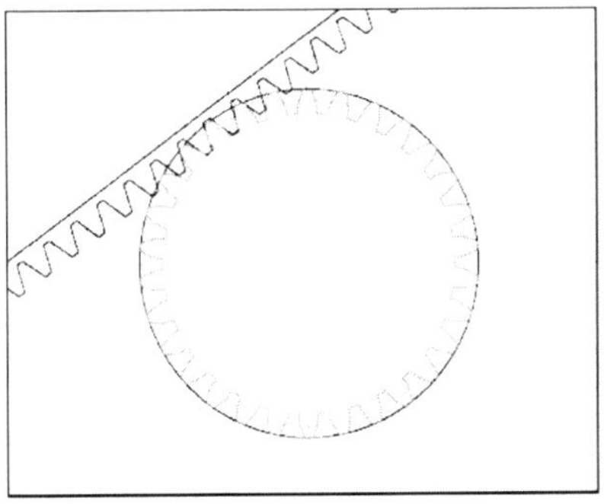

a

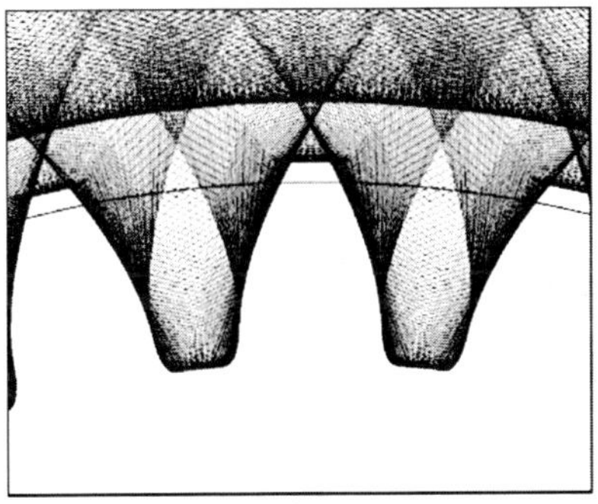

b

To solve these limits, purpose-oriented software has been developed by the authors in order to represent different gears geometry to the students.

In figure 4a a simple approach to gears-cut is presented. The virtual rotation without slipping of a rack on a smooth circle is creating the shape of the gears. As shown in figure 4b, several possible position of the rack can be visualized.

Testing of strange combinations of the input variables makes the lessons more interesting to the students and more over it also introduces concepts like the minimum number of teeth. Usually this is introduced as the result of an equation aimed to obtain geometry of the gear in order to avoid the teeth interference.

Through the visual approach of such software the student can also easily realize how the shape of teeth is changing from a high number of teeth to the low number of teeth, as shown in figure 5; where we have just 5 teeth (meanwhile the classical minimum number of teeth is around 17 for a pressure angle of 20 degrees).

The use of a well-designed user interface and a real-time changing of the visual results may help students to "play" with the inputs and to see the result of their combinations directly.For example

Figure 5. An example of 5 teeth gear designed by Gear-Cut

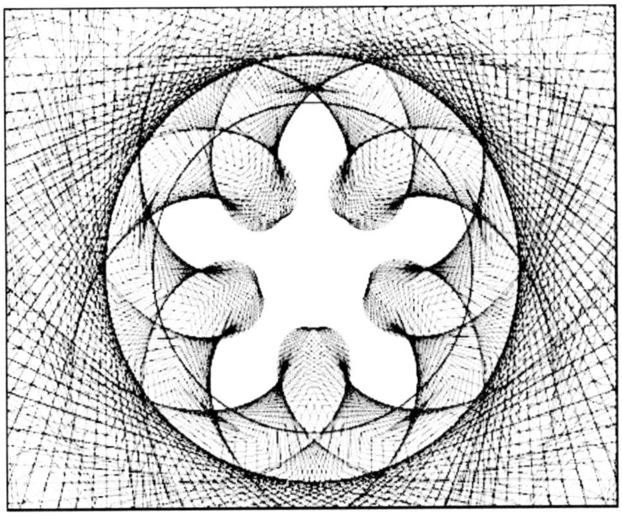

the use of a slide may easily teach the influence of a parameter to a student watching directly the changing of the geometry from a very low value to a very high value of that parameter.

EMPLOYING DIFFERENT GENERAL PURPOSE SOFTWARE

The authors believe that an effective educational approach is not just the use of one particular tool or software even if it is very powerful, but make the students used to system of tools as the best choice. This may be sometimes time consuming and they may require a level of knowledge which is not easily accessible in every school or factory. However the use of different general purpose software, smartly connected to each other, is a fast and flexible technique which can be adapted to several problems with small changes.

The example which is presenting here is the parametric design of a loft. This problem involves the design skills of the students. It is also a good example of how to combine the masteries of CAD and programming to design an educational appliance.

The design of pillars, beams, stairs and the parapet requires particular knowledge of different courses and push the students on the use of local or international norms, as a structure addresses many people and high safety standards have to be concerned. To design such structure weight and properties of different materials (steel, wood, plastic, etc.) used to build it have to be considered. On the other hand taking in to account different input variables needs a parametric design.

Excel®, Calc, Numbers, Matlab®, Octave and much other software can be used. Even some freeware software may provide enough professional capabilities. Considering the necessity of application of a spreadsheet Microsoft® Excel® can be a good choice as it is a standardized utility in many factories and universities. The use of a spreadsheet let the students to design easily a user interface where inputs and outputs are well presented and also where all the materials are written in tables, equipped by all their properties needed for the design.

Once introduced the inputs, a series of well-linked cells may lead to a series of outputs giving us the opportunity to draw the complete structure. However this is possible only if simple approaches are to be used. The task shows itself more strongly concerning to the fact that the iterative design is not always accessible (especially if the design presents several branches). In this case the connection between the cells may become incredibly complex or even impossible. Moreover the debug of the algorithm will be a very complex task as well. Thus the use of Visual Basic® for Application may solve these limits and let the student to embed the design algorithm inside the spreadsheet, but using a simple programming language.

The students have to study all kinds of simple structures that constitute the loft such as beams and pillars and draw the designs by hands. The algorithms have to be solved leaving parametric input variables. They have to be able to distinguish all the limits in the calculations and designing in order to encounter the warning and error messages that they will face with during using the e-tool approaches caused by applying improper combinations of values of the parameters.

The present spreadsheet is able to design even each small bolt. To avoid the time consuming step of updating all the dimensions by the designer after making each kind of changes and moreover, to prevent the errors due to the accidental forgetfulness the worksheet has been connected directly to a CAD system. Thus it allows the drawings to be updated automatically at each change of the input parameters. Finally thanks to realistic rendering software like Blender or 3DStudio it is possible to convert the engineering drawing of the structure to a more desirable "realistic" representation (Figure 6).

In this example all calculations are considered and solved by VBA (some of them in closed form,

Figure 6. Employing a system of software to present a virtual reality

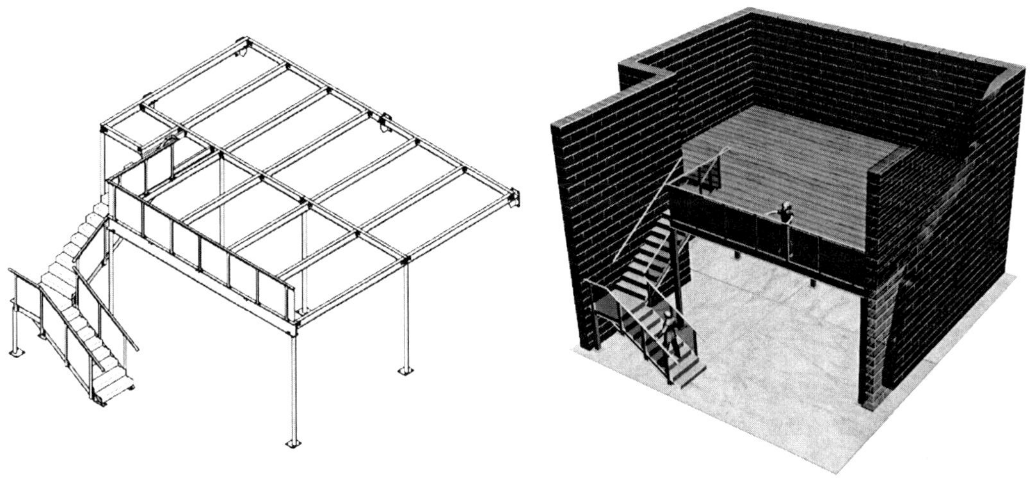

others by iterative calculations). The cells of the spreadsheet are organized in a way that the user finds easily the series of necessary input and the series of important output. Using a 3D parametric CAD software like SolidEdge®, the user can connect the output cells of the spreadsheet (representing all the dimensions of all the part of the loft) to the CAD system using OLE (Object Linking and Embedding) approach. To do this the CAD model of the loft has to be drawn and each dimension has to be linked to the spreadsheet.

3D-PORE

In different fields of engineering, the study of the influence of pores on the fatigue life of mechanical parts is a very important task. In fact the pores are defects of empty volumes presenting in material due to the production process and are very expensive to reduce or control.

Recent studies on this area are more focused on a better understanding of the influence of the pores in order to predict the fatigue life or to induce special morphology distribution of pores during the producing process and to control the mechanical properties. To get closer to the natural morphology of the pores, now the researchers are more interested in three dimensional characterizations of pores which present the actual shape and volume of the pores.

Computed tomography (CT) is a technique to identify the volumetric distribution of the "density" of the material, describing the pores three dimensionally. CT is a precise digital geometry process able to generate three dimensional volumes of the inside of an object using a large series of two dimensional images and joining them together. The information held in the volumetric pixel, the voxel, is the absorption coefficient of the material, which is somehow related to the density of the material itself.

The student may be interested in the three-dimensional description of a pore, starting from the volumetric information of a specimen portion. This is useful to understand the real shape of a complex phenomenon that can be for example the casting of metal materials, and it may be also useful for a subsequent finite element analysis based on real morphology and not an approximation.

In Figure 7a it is possible to see the distribution of pores inside a small cylindrical specimen of 4mm diameter this model has been made in 3D-Pores using the measured data of 3D X-ray.

Figure 7. Pore 3D approach VS. 2D

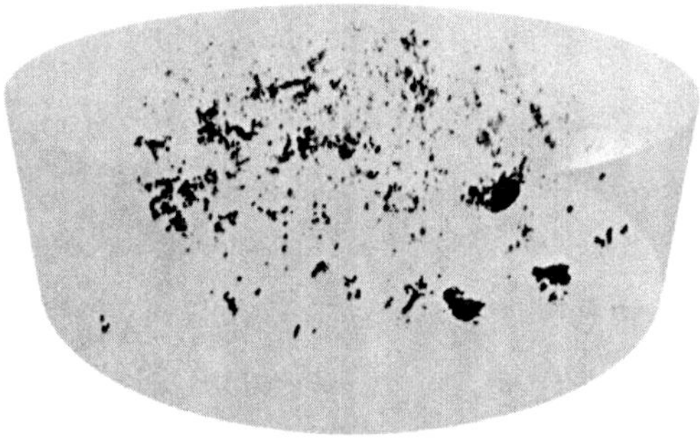

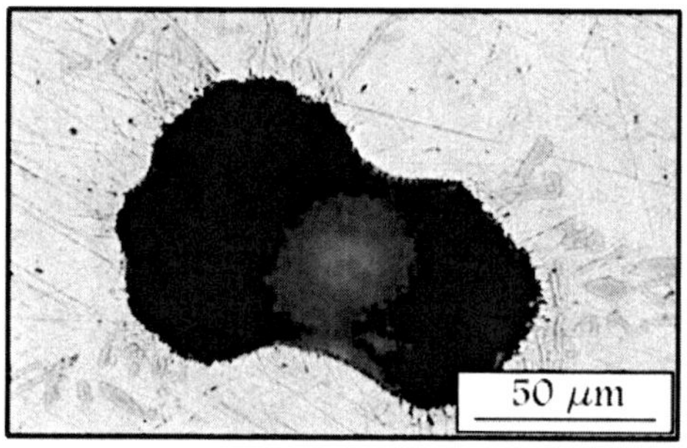

Figure 7b is a typical portion of cross-section of such a specimen. However the 2D pore cross-section would not help the student to understand the correct shape as the real three-dimensional reconstruction. The three-dimensional pore shown in Figure 8 is an example of a real pore reconstructed by 3D-Pores.

DIC APPROACH FOR STRAIN MEASUREMENT

The other example which is related to several deviations of engineering is measuring the material properties and mechanical behaviors. These are usually the main subject of many engineering courses. In addition to many theoretical lessons, the students have to make the experiments in laboratory and gain a deep understanding of different properties and different behaviors.

Experiment design, making the measurements, collecting the data, statistical investigation and interpretation of data are different part of real experiments that is more productive if are done by the students themselves rather than being based on just the theoretical sessions.

Many mechanical processes are strain-driven, thus it is very important to understand its behavior due to loading. In order to experience different approaches to strain measurements, there are different devices used to help the students to understand the meaning of deformation and heterogeneity. The classical and older method to teach strain measurements to the students is measuring the strain by clamping the specimen and applying the load. This method is usually the less precise and it needs some specific cares such as finding the adopted gage-length. Extensometer is a more accurate method which needs a higher attention during the installation and implementation processes Extensimetry is a desired method to measure the local strains and for most of engineering materials with a small level of heterogeneity or homogeneous materials. In this case the theory behind the strain-gage working principle and the attention to the implementing procedure is taught to the students.

Figure 8. Pore reconstruction

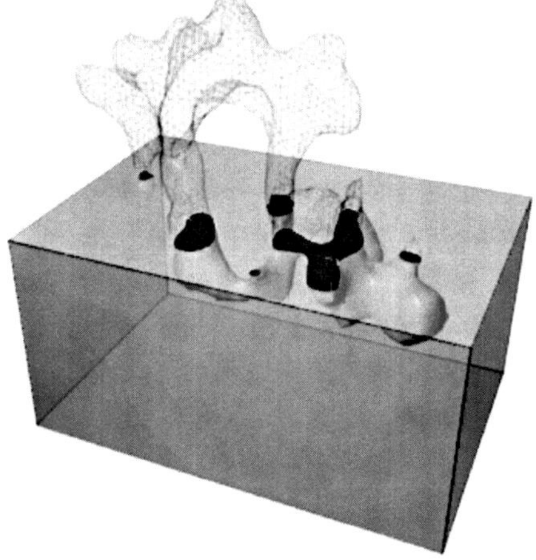

A relatively new and progressing technique to have full-field strain information of the specimen surface is the digital image correlation (DIC). This is an optical non-contact method able to identify the displacement field of a specimen, employing the observation of the specimen surface by a digital camera. The algorithm is based mainly on the analysis of the images taken from the surface of a specimen and describing their changes using the constitutive law of the solid continuous mechanics. The image taken at the undeformed state is called *master picture* and each of the following images, describing a special deformed state, are called *slave images*. As it is shown in Figure 9 the algorithm starts with identifying a number of sub-windows on the master picture. Each of them is representing an area of the specimen using a characteristic matrix of grey-level pixels. The aim is to follow the displacement and deformation of these sub-windows in each of the slave picture. At the end of the analysis the algorithm leads to a series of time-changing displacements for each sub-window (Endnote 2). According to the magnification of the acquisition device the user may have general information about the specimen or quite detailed information at the meso- or micro-level (Anzelotti 2008; Nicoletto 2008; Nicoletto 2009; Nicoletto in Press).

DIC is practically based on visual concepts. It introduces the image processing algorithm to the students, make them familiar with the explanation of the displacements calculations and moreover it is a good approach to activate the students interests in the topic of strain measurement. DIC is a measuring method mostly used by the researchers and as an upcoming and growing method has been less used for educational purposes. However it is potentially capable of being used in engineering education as it easily provides the visual requirements to motivate the students effectively. The fact that DIC approach can be implemented for different kinds of materials such as metals, ceram-

Figure 9. Applying DIC approach for strain measurement

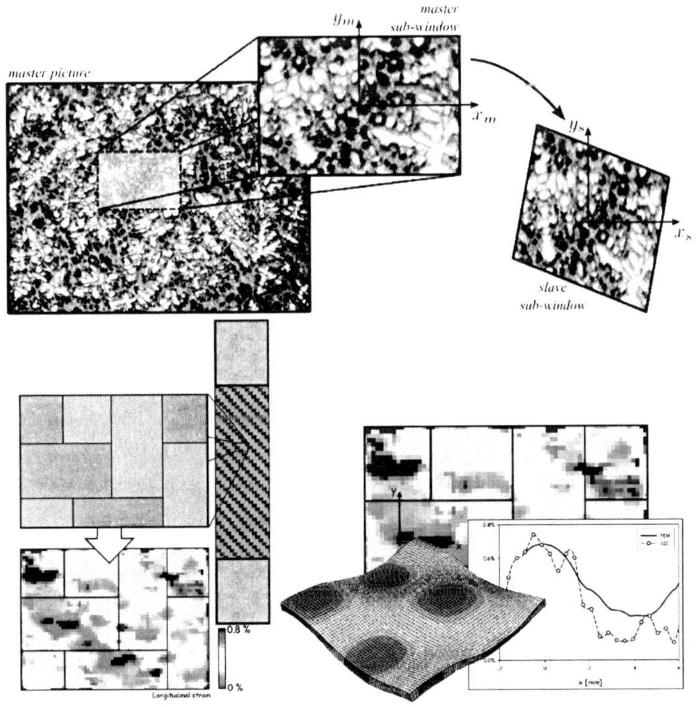

ics, composites and even more heterogeneous structures such as textiles empowers it to be employed in several engineering fields.

CONCLUSION REMARKS

Recent experience in different engineering education programs have shown that only systematic, research based, approach could be used for engineer training and education. The engineering education designers have to consider the engineering market demands. The industries would like to employ well educated skilled engineers and a skilled engineer is the engineer who has experience. Time and costs as two essential parameters do not let the engineering educational centers to train enough skilled engineers. To cope with this task and in order to reach an effective engineering education approach, a comprehensive educational design is required; starting from the schools and continuing to universities or research centers. An effective educational design is based on adequate and appropriate tools connected to each other through definite standards.

This chapter emphasizes on the power of virtual tools for engineering subjects. The aim of developing these *e-tools* is enhancing the understanding of concepts taught in the undergraduate and graduated Mechanical, Material, Civil and many other engineering branches. To exert such a virtual environment, the authors' suggestion is to develop and/or employ purpose-oriented small software along the professional software. The idea of this chapter is to show that even light software which is focused on a particular subject can be used as a key for engineering education. The specifications of this approach can be counted as:

- Purpose-oriented small software has a clear thought behind of it, it is concentrated on the subject and is directly pointing to the problem;
- It is easy to develop and implement;
- The students can effortlessly communicate with it, therefore it is practically appropriate to be utilized in the subjects and courses that have to be taught in one semester and according to the curriculum;
- Visuals and motions can be combined in a single format so that complex or abstract concepts can be illustrated through visual simulation (the old apothegm: "a picture is worth a thousand words");
- It is easy to make it adapted with different operating systems, so that the students can use it with no trouble even at home or at school;
- It can be joined and employed by novel education systems such as e-learning or generally distance education;
- It is cost effective;
- It is effectively a motivative, inspiring tool.

The virtual environment is expected to enhance the understanding of how and why one phenomenon happens, why a material behavior differs from the other, what is the optimum design for a device or a structure and help the students to realize the material properties and behavior. Students can use the purpose-oriented small software to verify the assumptions of the theories they have learned. It can also be employed to illustrate the influence of the change in assumptions and to realize the limitations and boundaries. Hence the students will be able to simulate mechanical behavior connecting their theoretical knowledge to the virtual experiments.

With the same idea of the virtual laboratories, the purpose-oriented software discussed above is being developed with the goal of making them a useful tool to enhance the understanding of theoretical concepts taught in the engineering courses. The virtual environment of these e-tools would positively impress the learning experience of the engineering students and make learning an enjoyable experience.

REFERENCES

Anzelotti, G., Nicoletto, G., & Riva, E. (2008). *Heterogeneous microscopic strains in a cast Al-Si alloy by digital image correlation.* Paper presented at the Symposium on Advances in Experimental Mechanics, České, Budějovice.

Baker, A., Navarro, E. O., & van der Hoek, A. (2005). An experimental card game for teaching software engineering processes. *Journal of Systems and Software*, *75*, 3–16. doi:10.1016/j.jss.2004.02.033

Burnely, S. (2007). The use of virtual reality technology in teaching environmental engineering. *Engineering Education. Journal of the Higher Education Academy Engineering Subject Center*, *2*(2).

Cloete, E. (2001). Electronic education system model. *Computers & Education*, *36*, 171–182. doi:10.1016/S0360-1315(00)00058-0

Gervasi, O., Rignelli, A., Pacifici, L., & Lagana, A. (2004). VMSLab-G: a virtual laboratory prototype for molecular science on the Grid. *Future Generation Computer Systems*, *20*, 717–726. doi:10.1016/j.future.2003.11.015

Haghi, A. K., Mottaghitalab, V., & Akbari, M. (2008). *The Scholarship of Teaching Engineering: Some fundamental issues*. Hershey: IGI Global.

Hutten, H., Stiegmaier, W., & Rauchegger, G. (2005). KISS—A new approach to self-controlled e-learning of selected chapters in Medical Engineering and other fields at bachelor and master course level. *Medical Engineering & Physics*, *27*, 611–616. doi:10.1016/j.medengphy.2005.05.003

Kaufman, D. B., Felder, R. M., & Fuller, H. (2000). Accounting for individual effort in cooperative learning teams. *Journal of Engineering Education*, *89*(2), 133–140.

Koksal, G., & Egitman, A. (1998). Planning and design of industrial engineering education quality. *Computers & Industrial Engineering*, *35*, 639–642. doi:10.1016/S0360-8352(98)00178-8

Kukreti, A., & Zaman, M. (2008). *Virtual laboratory modules for undergraduate STReNGTH of materials course.* Paper presented at the Engineering Education, Loughbrough, London.

Monahan, T., McArdle, G., & Bertolotto, M. (2008). Virtual reality for collaborative e-learning. *Computers & Education*, *50*, 1339–1353. doi:10.1016/j.compedu.2006.12.008

Moreno, L., Gonzalez, C., Castilla, I., Gonzalea, E., & Sigut, J. (2007). Applying a constructivist and collaborative methodological approach in engineering education. *Computers & Education*, *49*, 891–915. doi:10.1016/j.compedu.2005.12.004

Nicoletto, G., Anzelotti, G., & Riva, E. (2008). Mesomechanic strain analysis of twill-weave composite lamina under unidirectional in-plane tension. *Composites. Part A, Applied Science and Manufacturing*, *39*(8), 1294–1301. doi:10.1016/j.compositesa.2008.01.006

Nicoletto, G., Anzelotti, G., & Riva, E. (2009). Mesoscopic strain fields in woven composites: Experiments vs. finite element modeling. *Optics and Lasers in Engineering*, *47*(3-4), 352–359. doi:10.1016/j.optlaseng.2008.07.009

Nicoletto, G., Marin, T., Anzelotti, G., & Roncella, R. (in press). Application of high magnification digital image correlation technique to micromechanical strain analysis. *Strain*.

Ramasundaram, V., Grunwald, S., Mangeot, A., Comerford, N. B., & Bliss, C. M. (2005). Development of an environmental virtual field laboratory. *Computers & Education*, *45*, 21–34. doi:10.1016/j.compedu.2004.03.002

Shih, W. C., Tseng, S. S., & Yang, C. T. (2008). Wiki-based rapid prototyping for teaching-material design in e-Learning grids. *Computers & Education, 51*, 1037–1057. doi:10.1016/j.compedu.2007.10.007

Tan, A. C. C., Tang, T., & Paterson, G. (2008). *Web-based Remote Vibration Experimental Laboratory.* Paper presented at the Engineering Education, Loughbrough, London.

Toth, P. (2008). *New Method in Quality Assurance of Electronic-based Teaching Materials.* Paper presented at the Engineering Education, Loughbrough, London.

Tsai, S., Yeh, T. L., Lee, C. K., & Wang, N. C. (2008). *Teaching Strategies for Design Realization in Engineering Design Education.* Paper presented at the Engineering Education, Loughbrough, England.

Upitis, G., Maziais, J., & Rudnevs, J. (2008). *Problen-Oriented E-tools for Studies in Mechanical Engineering.* Paper presented at the Engineering Education, Loughborough, England.

Vadillo, M. A., & Matute, H. (2009). Learning in virtual environments: Some discrepancies between laboratory- and Internet-based research on associative learning. *Computers in Human Behavior, 25*, 402–406. doi:10.1016/j.chb.2008.08.009

Wankat, P. C., Felder, R. m., Smith, K. S., & Oreovicz, F. S. (2002). *The scholarship of teaching and learning in engineering.* Washangton, DC: AAHE/Carnegie Foundation for the Advancement of Teaching.

Willis, B. D. (1993). *Distance Education-A Practical Guide.* Englewood Cliffs, CA: Educational Technology Publications.

Yu, C. Y., & Shaw, D. T. (2006). *Fostering Creativity and Innovation in Engineering Students.* Paper presented at the 2006 International Mechanical Engineering Education Conference, joined Conference by ASME and CMES, Beijing, China.

ADDITIONAL READING

Monahan, T., McArdle, G., & Bertolotto, M. (2008). Virtual reality for collaborative e-learning. *Computers & Education, 50*, 1339–1353. doi:10.1016/j.compedu.2006.12.008

Montero, E., Aguilar, F., Alonso, C., & Gonzalez, M. J. (2008). *Interactive learning objects in the delivery of e-learning engineering courses.*

Toth, P. (2008). *New Method in Quality Assurance of Electronic-based Teaching Materials.* Paper presented at the Engineering Education, Loughbrough, London.

ENDNOTES

1 Here the concept of "general purpose" is referred to the possibility to use the software to solve different problems in different courses.

2 This is not the only existing algorithm but it is quite used by researchers and the authors do not want to present an exhaustive treatise about DIC, but just introduce it as teaching experience in engineering courses.

APPENDIX: SUPPORTING MATERIAL

Abstract

This chapter emphasizes on the power of virtual tools for engineering subjects. As a more accessible approach, the authors suggest the development and application of Purpose-Oriented small software. The aim of developing these *e-tools* is enhancing the understanding of concepts taught in the undergraduate and graduated Mechanical, Material, Civil and many other engineering branches. The main idea behind of this chapter is to show that even light software which is focused on a particular subject can be used as a key for engineering education.

Questions and Answers

1. What is the overall problem(s) in this case?

Owing to all the advantages made and is being made in modern Engineering, the recent decades have been witnessed that the engineering education methods needs extreme changes to be more compatible with the requirements of both the industries and researches. It seems that the classic methods of engineering education which are mainly based on teacher-classroom-printed textbook have to be changed to something which is more adapted with the current engineering approaches.

2. What is the advantage of this case study?

The revolution in information transfer and computer capabilities and their speed has powered the educational specialist to plan powerful e-tools to facilitate engineering education, the main example that this case study is referring to it is the purpose oriented small software for engineering education.

3. What are the factors affecting the problem(s) related to this case?

Developing purpose-oriented small software is aimed to be an aid for engineering education. Some of the affecting factor in developing and applying of such approach can be counted as: preparing the student to make relation and use these educational tools, the design of the software, speed, performance, user interface, the ease of making relation, cost and effectiveness.

4. What are some of the emerging technologies that should be considered in solving the problem(s) related to the case?

In order to make purpose-oriented small software, we do not need a very high or complicated technology, but a skilled programmer who is familiar with the field that the software is being designed for it and mainly is a specialist in the same filed. On the other hand this specialist programmer has to have the experience of teaching to be able to design the software according to the needs of learners.

5. What are the roles of different players in the overall planning?

There are two main players in engineering education performance: the teacher and the learner. However in this case study we have introduced the third player which is the purpose-oriented small software. The role of purpose-oriented small software is to make a connection between the teacher and the learner. However it plays as an aid for the learner to understand the topics which are planned to be transferred to him.

Epilogue and Lessons Learned

In this chapter the aspect of the purpose-oriented software has been introduced. The main goal of this educational tool is to enhance the understanding of theoretical concepts taught in the engineering courses. The virtual environment of these e-tools would positively impress the learning experience of the engineering students and make learning an enjoyable experience.

Chapter 13
Managing Learning Activities in E-Learning Systems

Mehregan Mahdavi
University of Guilan, Iran

Ali Sajedi Badashian
Islamic Azad University of Lahijan, Iran

ABSTRACT

The advent of computers and later the Internet has led to trends in Computer Aided Learning (CAL). The learning process is rapidly transforming from traditional learning to electronic learning. Computer-based systems enable effective delivery and access to learning materials, at a time and place chosen by the student. This case explores Learning Activity Management (LAM) systems, which are new tools for designing, managing and delivering online collaborative learning activities. LAM systems provide instructors with a flexible environment in which to design, organize and monitor the learning activities of the learners. We describe components and key features of LAM systems and also explore the challenges that exist in this field.

INTRODUCTION

In recent years, computer-based systems have become widely used for learning purposes. They enable the use of a range of delivery modes (Web/GUI, text/multimedia) for effective delivery. Via the Internet, they enable learners to use the learning material at a time and place of their choosing. Electronic Learning (E-Learning) refers to the use of computers for delivering learning materials. Learning Management Systems (LMS) are Web-based software applications used to plan, implement, and assess a specific learning process. LMSs allow learners to connect to and interact with the educational material through the Internet. Typically, a learning management system provides an instructor with a way to create and deliver content, monitor learners' participation, and assess their performance. A learning management system may also provide learners with the ability to use interactive features such as threaded discussions, video conferencing, and discussion forums.

Learning Activity Management (LAM) systems are flexible learning design tools that enable instruc-

DOI: 10.4018/978-1-61520-869-2.ch013

tors to organize and monitor learning activities of the learners. These activities include assignments, quizzes, and also collaboration. Collaborative learning is a process during which learners collaborate with each other for solving problems. Collaborative learning is particularly useful in promoting team work in the learning process. Assessment is also an integral part of LAM systems; enabling instructors effectively evaluate learners' activities in the learning process. In this chapter we study learning activity management systems and the main components that such systems should provide in order for instructors and learners to effectively participate in the learning process.

BACKGROUND: LEARNING ACTIVITY MANAGEMENT (LAM) SYSTEMS

Constructive learning is a process in which learners build new thoughts, ideas and concepts making use of their knowledge and experience (Beatty, 2003). An important aspect of constructive learning is that it gives responsibility and control over the learnt material to the learner. Constructive learning is enhanced by interaction with instructors and classmates, rather than simply interacting with content (Alexander, 2008). Traditional e-learning systems have focused on content delivery and individual interaction with this content. Learning activity management systems extend this by combining content delivery with collaboration. They aim to combine the benefits of e-learning with the collaborative aspects of traditional (classroom-based) education, thus resulting in a more effective on-line learning environment. Some LAM systems have already been built to realize the above ideals. We describe some of the more prominent examples and then discuss the remaining challenges in developing such systems.

Nor Azan (2007) has developed a LAM system named SPAP, based on ideas from the IMS Learning Design framework. In particular, it used the Conceptual Model to provide a containment framework that can describe the design of teaching and learning processes in a formal way. SPAP allows teachers to plan, manage and monitor learning activities, and enables learners to carry out these learning activities. SPAP provides a set of seven activity tools based on teaching methods such as discussion, problem solving and simulation. SPAP includes five modules, the most important of which are the authoring and learner modules. The authoring module provides a graphical interface that allows teachers to describe a sequence of learning activities (a learning design) and save the design. The learner module guides students through the learning designs specified by the teacher, using a graphical interface to clearly indicate progress. It also gives them access to a course overview developed by the teacher in a synopsis module. A monitoring module allows the teacher to track the progress of all students through the learning activities.

Dalziel (2003) has developed a system called LAMS, which is perhaps the most complete LAM system currently available. Like SPAP, LAMS provides authoring, learning, and monitoring modules (which we describe in more detail below). Unlike SPAP, it has achieved widespread acceptance, due in part to its release as open-source software (Alexander (2008) notes that LAMS users number roughly 3200 in 80 countries). An additional factor in its adoption is that LAMS has been designed based on Learning Design standards so that designs may be shared, re-used, and re-purposed. Also, it has been designed so that it can work either as a stand-alone system or in conjunction with other Virtual Learning Environments (VLEs) and Learning Management Systems (LMSs).

The following example (from Dalziel (2003)) gives some idea of the capabilities of LAMS. It was initially designed for a class of 20-30 high-school history students, potentially located in more than one physical location, around the topic "What is Greatness?", and implemented using the LAMS system. The activity lasts for

Figure 1. Authoring environment[1]

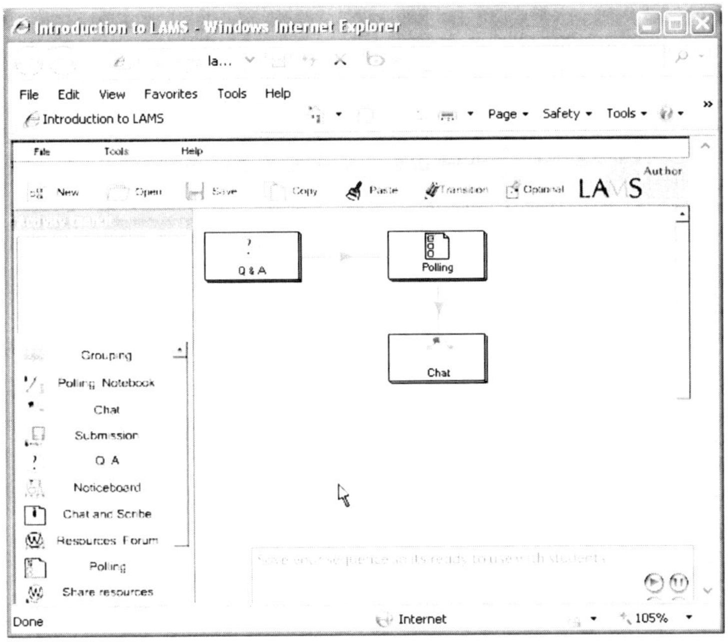

four weeks. In the first week, all students discuss their views on the topic in an online forum. In the second week, students are given access to a range of material on the topic, and asked to find an example web-site on the topic, which they then share and comment on to the whole class. In week 3, students are put into small discussion groups, where they chat interactively on-line to deal with questions provided by the teacher; one student acts as a "scribe" to record the discussion. The conclusions reached by each group are then posted for the whole class. Finally, in the fourth week, students individually write a report on the initial question ("What is Greatness?") which they submit via the system for marking. The activity concludes when the students receive marks and feedback from the teacher.

One of the powerful features of the learning activity approach is that the content of a sequence can be easily changed to suit a different discipline, while leaving the activity structure unchanged (the above example has been re-used to deal with the question "What is Jazz?"). The learning activity sequence can provide a "pedagogical template" which may be useful in many contexts by changing the "content" to suit different discipline areas. The focus on easy re-use with LAMS means that these changes can be implemented and ready to run with a new student group. Moreover, the pedagogical template itself should be modifiable, so that if a teacher wishes to change the order of the tasks, or add/remove activities from the template, this can be easily achieved. In LAMS, this is possible within the authoring environment using a simple drag-and-drop system which makes explicit the teaching and learning processes as a series of discrete activities. Figure 1 shows the authoring interface of LAMS (Dalziel, 2003). For customization, activities are dragged from the left pane into the middle pane and the links between activities are created using the given tools. The learner module enables learners perform learning activities that are designed by the teachers. Learners are given a clear visual path of their progress via the progress bar which is visible at all times. The monitoring module enables monitoring the students' progress in performing learning activities at any time. Figure 2 shows the monitoring module where each row in the middle pane indicates a learner.

Mann (2008) considers the impact of online collaboration on the learning process. He notes advantages of online collaboration as the free sharing of ideas and freedom from physical and time constraints. Despite the advantages, he also identifies a disadvantage: learners involved in unstructured online collaboration may find themselves in a situation similar to chatting on "MSN", which is more in line with socializing instead of learning. In other words, learners may misuse the online environment so that its effectiveness as a learning environment is significantly reduced. In other words, monitoring tools may be useful in order to lead learners to learn when they perform a learning activity. LAM environments may also provide a live monitoring tool for educators in order to monitor the progress of students so that inappropriate behaviors of misusing the collaboration tool in a destructive way can be minimized.

Fan and Jiaheng (2008) describe sequencing of activities based on ontologies and activity graphs in personalized learning environments. As a result, the creation and sequencing of content-based, single learner, and self-paced learning objects would be enabled.

Course Maker[3] is a Web-based package for creating course content. It provides a visual environment for creating and changing the course design. It also provides a number of pre-designed course templates that can be used for creating interactive multimedia learning materials such as image maps and quizzes. Other examples of such systems include Sakai[4], LRN[5], Moodle[6], BlackBoard[7], and WebCT[8].

As mentioned before, assessment is an integral part of learning systems. Web work[9] is an Internet-based system for generating and delivering homework problems to students. Its goal is to make homework more effective and efficient. Each Web Work problem set is personalized. That is, each student has a different version of each problem; for example the numerical values in

Figure 2. Monitoring environment for different learners[2]

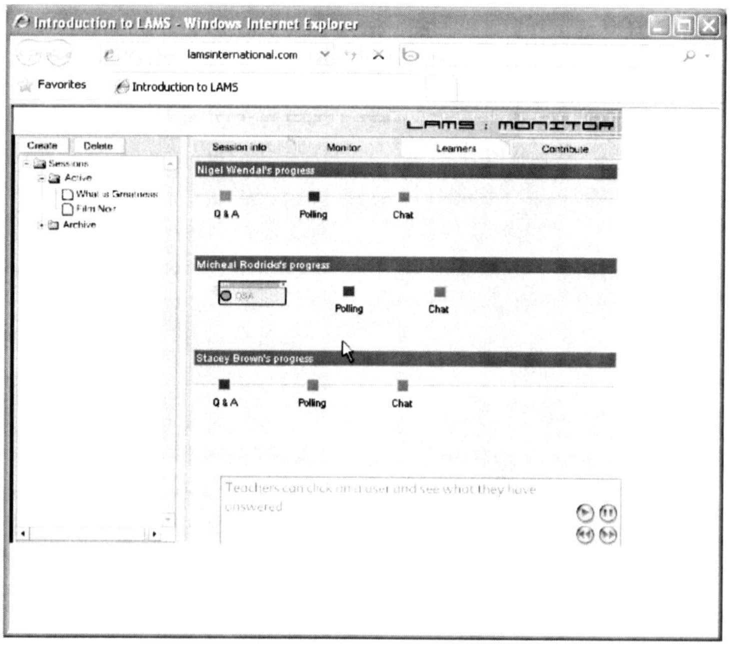

the formulas may be slightly different. Students complete the assignments, log onto the Internet and enter their answers using a Web browser. Web Work system responds students by telling them whether an answer (or a set of answers) is correct or not and also records whether the student answered the question correctly or not. The students are free to try a problem as many times as they wish until the due date. A key educational benefit of this system is that if a student gets a wrong answer, he gets immediate feedback while the problem is still fresh in his mind. The student can then correct a careless mistake, review the relevant material before approaching the problem again, or seek help (frequently via e-mail) from his friends, the TA or the instructor. It increases the effectiveness of traditional homework as a learning tool by:

- Providing students with immediate feedback on the validity of their answers and giving students the opportunity to correct mistakes while they are still thinking about the problem
- Providing students with personalized versions of problems, meaning that instructors can encourage students to work together, while still requiring that each student develop an answer to his own version of the problem

It also increases the efficiency of traditional homework by:

- Providing automatic grading of assignments
- Providing information on the performance of individual students and the course (or section or recitation) as a whole

LEARNING ACTIVITIES AND IN LAM SYSTEMS

In this part, we discuss the properties of a LAM system and its components. One of the benefits of LAM systems is that they can reduce staff uptake. Also, higher levels of pupil motivation are expected using the coherent, integrated and structured LAM systems, compared to traditional courses. Moreover, the self-paced LAM environment encourages students with anonymous favors develop their confidence, autonomous learning, and meta-cognitive skills. As a result, the users of such systems become more inclusive from the traditional ones.

The possible activities in a LAM system are not limited, but we can name a number of standard and common tasks and activities in current systems. Some of the most important activities are:

Informative Activities

These activities include those that play an informative role for users. More important activities include:

- **Notice board:** It is a straightforward way of providing content to the learners (as a bulletin of the professors). It can be implemented in two methods. Firstly, a brief link-based legend index of items can be presented. This index points to different targets. Secondly, a larger area can provide as much content as possible. It might also use links. The content can be rich text, html, links, word documents, audio, video, etc.
- **Share resources:** The learners can share their resources using this activity.
- **Task list:** This activity allows learners to inform the monitors and the authors the completed tasks. It may be an individual's activity to manage the activities too.

- **Meeting with the instructor:** This activity enables the learners to participate in meeting sessions with their instructor(s) and resolve their possible problems.

Evaluative Activities

These activities include those that are used in the evaluation process. Some of the important activities in this category include:

- **Multiple choices:** This activity is a quiz consisting of several questions each of which containing several items to choose from. The learners should select the correct answer of each question in the specified time. The multiple choices are designed for each part of the course according to the needs of that part.
- **True/False questions:** True/False questions are used to assess conceptual knowledge of students in a quick way. The students' answers to these questions can show if they have understood the essence of the learning material.
- **Drag and drop:** Drag and drop activities are those in which students require to place text or images by dragging in the correct positions on the page.
- **Hotspot:** This is an activity in which students should select the correct area within an image.
- **Drop down list:** It is a selection list in which a set of answers is revealed so that students can select the answer to a question from the list.
- **Freeform text entry:** In this activity, students should answer a question by writing a text.
- **Sequence:** In this activity, students should arrange a series of options by dragging them in a certain order.
- **Submit files:** The learner's work or answers to exercises can be received by the system in different ways. One of these ways is submitting files. Learners can create files from their work and submit them in the specified area for assessment.
- **Research activity report:** The learners should inform the instructors the research activities/results of their current tasks.
- **Screen capture:** For some disciplines such as computer science, the result of students' activities should be evaluated carefully. The details should be considered by both the students and the professors. As a result, capturing a video from the steps of the students' activities could be an effective and powerful evaluation tool.

Collaborative Activities

There are a number of activities that enable collaboration between learners. Some of these activities include:

- **Chat:** It is a popular activity for the learners. They can chat together, to the monitor/instructor based on their needs.
- **Scribe:** It is the reports that the learners write.
- **Forum:** It is an asynchronous discussion environment for the learners. The discussion threads usually are created by the authors.
- **Group communications:** the learners can join together as a group and communicate with each other. For example, file and resource sharing between them can be done.
- **Group survey:** The learners can complete a survey about a specified topic together. This makes both learning course materials and problem solving easier. This activity can also be considered as a reflective activity.

Reflective Activities

These activities reflect the learners' ideas or thoughts during the learning process. Examples of these activities include:

- **Question and Answer (Q & A):** The learners can ask questions and the instructors answer them. The important aspect is that all questions and answers are presented in a single page visible to all.
- **Notebook:** It is an activity for recording learners' thoughts during a sequence.
- **Survey:** It collects the learners' surveys and opinions about a topic.
- **Voting:** It allows the learners to vote on a specific idea in the sequence, topic, or learning object.
- **Learner bulletin:** It is a place for the learners to inform the others about anything in the learning space.

KEY FUNCTIONALITIES OF DIFFERENT ROLES IN LAM SYSTEMS

In LAM systems, there are different roles participating simultaneously such as educational roles, controlling roles, advertising roles and so on. But in all of them, there are three common roles constituting the main LAM foundation: Learner (Student), Monitor (Assistant) and Author (Instructor). In the followings we describe these roles.

Learner (Student)

The students can study and learn what an instructor wants in a controlled manner. In fact, a LAM system works just like the instructor is asking questions, assigning tasks, teaching and briefly monitoring the answers to the tasks/assignments to be done. These tasks include reading the provided lessons (in the form of plain text, html, and multimedia), chat, scribe, voting, exam and other previously mentioned activities. However, these tasks are not limited and can be extended to any other digital contributions.

The overall tasks/assignments can be shown and classified as progress bar or sequence of tasks. Each task in the sequence is represented by a specified name, shape and color. For example, as in Alexander (2008), the completed tasks are shown with blue circles. The in-progress tasks are indicated with red squares and the tasks that haven't been reached are shown with green triangles. However, this is only an assumption and can include more comprehensive states and situations. The task progress bar (or task sequence) navigation can be facilitated with interactive user-friendly navigation tools including exposure to text, tables, images, video, and audio.

In the lower level, after selecting each task, the learner can contribute to the learning process specified by the instructor. For example, if the activity is an html scribe task, the learner should write something specific. If the activity is a multiple choice, then the learner should choose between the multiple choice(s). A notebook tool is also available for the students to write statements to be viewed entirety or collated into a set of entries available to be viewed by the instructor. An example of different possible areas for the learners is shown in Figure 3. Moreover, Figure 4 shows a sample activity arrangement.

Monitor (Assistant)

A key feature in LAM systems is monitoring. By this feature, the instructors (or their assistants) can control the students' learning. There are three major parts for this feature: Lesson, Sequence, and Learner.

Lesson-related monitoring activities: The instructor (or his assistants) can control the overall properties of each lesson and the students that use

Figure 3. An example of different possible learner areas

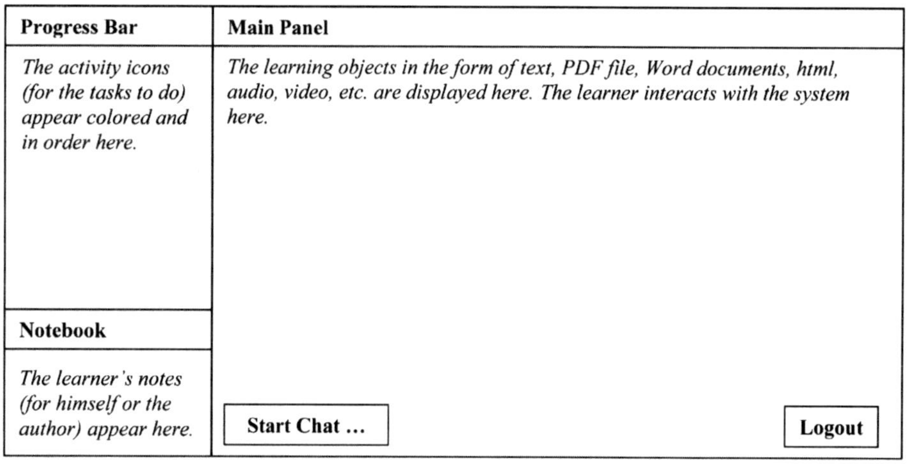

Figure 4. Part of a sample activity arrangement for a learner

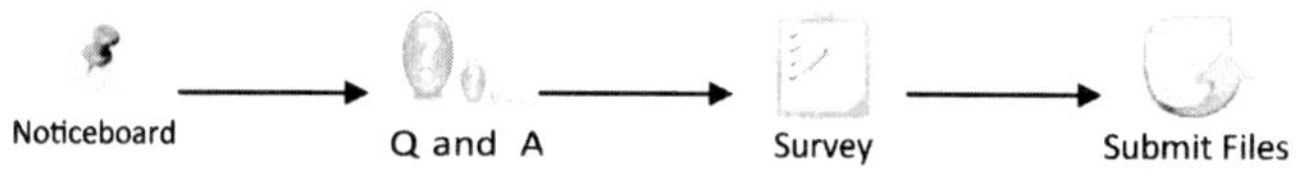

them. He can also disable lessons, archive them, etc. The important properties of this activity may include:

- Viewing the lessons' status
- Viewing the statistics of each class, its learners and their selected lessons
- Viewing the number of online learners for the lesson at each time
- Viewing the total number of learner logins for a lesson in a period of time
- Viewing the sequence status of the learners for the lesson

Sequence-related monitoring activities: A sequence is a chain of tasks or activities for the learners as defined by the instructors (see Figure 5). The monitoring tasks for a particular sequence are:

- Grouping the learners (performed by the monitors)
- Assigning activities to the groups
- Choosing scribes
- Viewing the overall status of the learners in each sequence
- Viewing the total number of learners doing each task (online or offline)
- Refreshing the system to be synchronized with the sequence status of the current learner
- Controlling the learners such as opening or closing gates[10], forcing the learners to move to a specific activity (by moving their icon to the desired activity) or moving out the learners from an activity or a sequence
- Making minor sequence content changes by adding or removing particular activities

Learners-related monitoring activities: Monitoring the learners' progress is an important aspect of LAM systems. In the traditional systems

Figure 5. A sample of a sequence

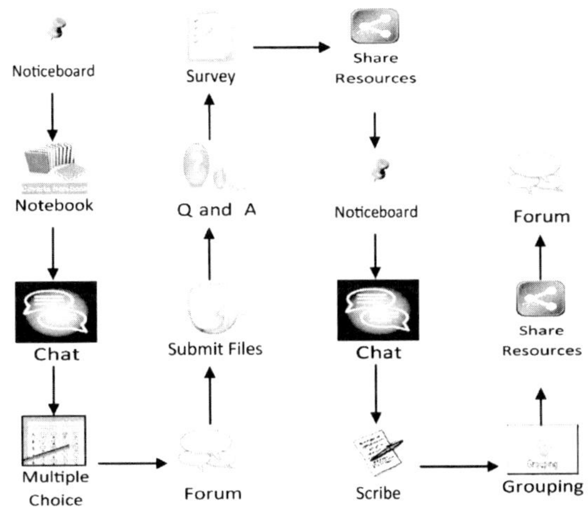

it is constituted from several face-to-face contacts during the learning period. The learners-related monitoring tasks include:

- Viewing the overall progress of learners
- Viewing the sequence progress of learners (completed, current and new activities that haven't been undertaken)
- Viewing the detailed status of the learners in each sequence (according to the selected learner)
- Editing permissions of the learners to sequences (or parts of them) created by the authors (instructors)
- Exporting portfolios for a learner or a group of learners in groupware activities

Author (Instructor)

Each activity in a LAM system should be started by or under supervision of the author. In fact, creating multiple fascinating pathways for the learners is not a troublesome task today, but having a meaningful consistent set of controlled structures with unified educational goals in such systems makes it hard to be implemented, considering the collaboration between different parts of the system. In such a system, an author can control the system in these ways:

- Creating, storing, modifying and reusing the learner activity sequences
- Viewing a preview of their authored sequences
- File operations (new, open, save, and save as)
- Editing operations (copy–paste and cut–paste)
- Sequencing tools (transition, optional activity, flow, gate, grouping, branching, and preview)
- Importing and exporting sequences to be shared with colleagues

CONCLUSION

In this chapter, we studied learning activity management systems as a tool for designing, managing and delivering online collaborative learning activities. We also described components and key features of e-learning systems. These systems enable more effective delivery of digital learning materials to the learners. They also enable more efficient assessment of learners' activities as a result of using software tools. In LAM systems, the learning materials are normally shared via the Internet. They provide a flexible framework that can be customized by the instructor. They can be used in universities, high schools, academies, etc. Their flexible framework enables the instructors to update the contents of the system periodically.

Another advantage of LAM systems is sharing resources between learners. Whilst some social networks permit users to share resources, integrating these sharing activities along with other common learning activities makes them useful. Moreover, these systems can be used independent from time and location.

An overall comparison between LAM and traditional systems shows that LAM systems lead to lower cost, more motivation for learners, more effective education, and adaptability with different educational environments. These systems help instructors preserve the integrity of their course contents.

On the other hand, some people believe that these new learning systems encourage learners to individual activities and discourage social and group activities. Some controlling aspects also remain disputable due to the vast provision of resources and availability of the Internet for younger learners. These are challenging issues in such systems compared to traditional learning systems where face to face conversations, sessions, meetings, scientific tours, etc. are common. As a result, such face to face activities might be necessary in parallel to these systems or have to be somehow integrated with them.

REFERENCES

Alexander, C. (2008). An overview of LAMS (Learning Activity Management System), Teaching English with Technology Journal, 8(3).

Alexander, C., (2009), LAMS Revisited. *Teaching English with Technology Journal, 9*(1).

Beatty, K. (2003). *Teaching and Researching Computer-Assisted Language Learning. Harlow*. London: Longman.

Cameron, L., & Dalziel, J. (2008). Perspectives on Learning Design. In *Proceedings of the 3rd International LAMS & Learning Design Conference* (p.p. 81-86), Sydney: LAMS Foundation.

Dalziel, J. (2003). Implementing Learning Design: The Learning Activity Management System (LAMS). In *Proceedings of the 20th Annual Conference of the Australian Society for Computers in Learning in Tertiary Education* (ASCILITE).

Fan, Z., & Jiaheng, C. (2008). Learning Activity Sequencing in Personalized Education System. *Journal of Natural Science, 13*(4), 461–465.

Mann, S. (2008). The problems of online collaboration for junior high school students: Can the Learning Activity Management System (LAMS) benefit students to learn via online learning? In L. Cameron & J. Dalziel (Eds.), *Proceedings of 3rd International LAMS & Learning Design Conference 2008: Perspectives on Learning Design* (pp. 81-86). Sydney: LAMS Foundation.

Nor Azan, M. Z. (2007). Learning Activities Management System (SPAP), In *Proceedings of International Conference on Electrical Engineering and Informatics*. Institut Teknologi Bandung, Indonesia.

FURTHER READING

Alexander, C. (2007a), Using the Internet in TESOL. In S.Walker, M. Ryan & R, Teed. (Eds.), Proceedings of Design for Learning (pp. 28-34). Australia: Greenwich University.

Alexander, C. (2007b). A case study of English language teaching using the Internet in Intercollege's language laboratory. *The International Journal of Technology. Knowledge and Society, 3*(1), 1–15.

Britain, S. (2004). *A Review of Learning Design: Concept, Specifications and Tools: A Report for the JISC E-Learning Pedagogy Programme*. Retrieved May 20, 2008, from http://www.jisc.ac.uk/uploaded_documents/ACF1ABB.doc

Cohen, R. F., Meacham, A., & Skaff, J. (2006). Teaching Graphs to Visually Impaired Students Using an Active Auditory Interface. In *Proceedings of the 37th SIGCSE technical symposium on Computer science education* (pp. 279-282), Houston, TX.

Crescenzi, P., & Nocentini, C. (2007). Fully integrating algorithm visualization into a CS2 course: a two-year experience. In *Proceedings of the 12th Annual Conference on Innovation and Technology in Computer Science Education* (pp. 296-300), Dundee, Scotland.

Curzon, P., & McOwan, P. W. (2008). Engaging with Computer Science through Magic Shows, *ACM. SIGCSE Bulletin*, *40*(3), 179–183. doi:10.1145/1597849.1384320

Dalziel, J. (2003a). *Discussion Paper for Learning Activities and Meta-data. Macquarie E-learning Centre of Excellence (MELCOE).* Retrieved May 10, 2008, from http://www.lamsinternational.com/documents/LearningActivities.Metadata.Dalziel.pdf

Erkan, A., VanSlyke, T. J., & Scaffidi, T. (2007). Data Structure Visualization with LaTeX and Prefuse. In Proceedings of the 12th Annual Conference on Innovation and Technology in Computer Science Education, Dundee, Scotland.

Lauer, T. (2006). Learner interaction with algorithm visualizations: viewing vs. changing vs. constructing, *ACM SIGCSE Bulletin, 38*(3).

Levy, P., Aiyegbayo, O., Little, S., Loasby, I., & Powell, A. (2008). *Designing and Sharing Inquiry-Based Learning Activities: LAMS Evaluation Case Study*. (Centre for Inquiry-based Learning in the Arts and Social Sciences, University of Sheffield). Retrieved June 20, 2008, from http://www.jisc.ac.uk/media/documents/programmes/elearning-pedagogy/desilafinalreport.pdf

Myller, N., Laakso, M., & Korhonen, A. (2007). Analyzing engagement taxonomy in collaborative algorithm visualization. In *Proceedings of the 12th Annual Conference on Innovation and Technology in Computer Science Education* (pp. 251-255). Dundee, Scotland.

Russell, T., Varga-Atkins, T., & Roberts, D. (2005). Learning Activity Management System Specialist Schools Trust pilot. *A Review for Becta and the Specialist Schools and Academies Trust by CRIPSAT.* Centre for Lifelong Learning, University of Liverpool. Retrieved March 10, 2008, from http://www.cripsat.org.uk/current/elearn/bectalam.htm

Schweitzer, D., & Brown, W. (2007). Interactive visualization for the active learning classroom, *ACM SIGCSE Bulletin, 39*(1).

Subramanian, K. R., & Cassen, T. (2008). A cross-domain visual learning engine for interactive generation of instructional materials, *ACM SIGCSE Bulletin, 40*(1).

ENDNOTES

1 http://www.lamsinternational.com/CD/html/support/intro_to_lams.html
2 http://www.lamsinternational.com/CD/html/support/intro_to_lams.html
3 http://www.coursemaker.co.uk
4 http://sakaiproject.org/index.php?option=com_content&task=view&id=103&Itemid=208
5 http://dotlrn.org
6 http://en.wikipedia.org/wiki/Moodle
7 http://en.wikipedia.org/wiki/Blackboard_Inc
8 http://en.wikipedia.org/wiki/WebCT
9 http://webwork.csis.pace.edu/webwork
10 Professors can generate stop points somewhere in a sequence by gates. Gates halt the process of learners through a sequence until a specified condition is met.

APPENDIX: SUPPORTING MATERIAL

Abstract

In this chapter, an overview of e-learning systems that are new tools for designing and managing online material is described. We show how such systems provide instructors with a flexible environment in which to design, organize and monitor the learning activities of the learners. We also describe components and key features of such systems.

Questions to Ponder

1. Which informative, evaluative, collaborative and reflective activities are managed in e-learning systems?
2. Discuss the basics of three different roles in a learning activity management system.
3. What is a sequence and how does it appear for different roles as an author and a learner?
4. Discuss the main advantages and disadvantages of e-learning systems.
5. What do you think of the future of e-learning systems?

Epilogue and Lessons Learned

The learning activities in the e-learning systems are managed automatically under the supervision of an author (professor) and one or more monitors. Each activity is normally started by or under the supervision of an author and can be monitored by him or his assistants.

E-learning systems also promote collaborative learning during which learners collaborate with each other for solving problems.

Lessons Learned

1. Each Learning Activity Management (LAM) system has different components. Usually three major components exist in all of them; authoring, monitoring and learning components. Each component is normally managed in a separate environment. Such systems connect all the members of the learning community online in the provided environment.
2. A sequence is an arrangement of activities that a learner should do. An author arranges theses activities based on the topic. Different roles see different views of sequences. The authors see a detailed view of the sequence. The monitors see the current position of each learner and the completed/current activities. Finally, the learner sees a progress bar of the activities. The important aspect of the system is providing an online control. When a learner moves on to the next activity, the monitor can control his progress.
3. Learning activity management systems can be used in any educational community. Examples of these communities are universities, high schools, academies, etc. However, customization may be needed in each case.

Chapter 14
Architectural Web Portal and Interactive CAD Learning in Hungary

Attila Somfai
"Széchenyi István" University, Hungary

ABSTRACT

It is the aim of this case to show the teaching web portal of the Faculty of Architecture at "Széchenyi István" University (www.arc.sze.hu/indexen.html) and its many uses. Nowadays, the Internet helps us to look into Hungarian and foreign study aids, and architectural websites. The Internet has created potential new and effective ways of cooperation between lecturers and students of the university and other institutions of higher education. The teaching web portal mentioned above realizes diversity and complexity of architecture, with efficient grouping of information, while being attentive to high professional standards. Computer Aided Architectural Modeling (www.arc.sze.hu/cad) is one of the new types of online lecture notes, where many narrated screen captured videos show the proper usage of cad software instead of texts and figures. This interactive type of learning assists students to become more independent learners. This type of teaching modality provides the opportunity for students who need more time to acquire subject matter through viewing video examples. The success of our departments' common web initiations can be measured through Internet statistics and feedback of the students and external professionals.

MAIN GOALS AND PHILIOSOPHY

It is high time to speak of the importance of the electronic knowledge-bases in the teaching of Hungarian architects and students, as well its multidirectional possibilities for use. The professional web portal of the "Széchenyi István" University in Győr is introduced, together with some of its subject matter of instruction. In today's wolld, the Internet provides access to teaching packages from domestic and foreign sources, professional portals and novel topics. Moreover, it makes possible to effectively cooperate among lecturers, professors and students, as well as among institutions of higher

DOI: 10.4018/978-1-61520-869-2.ch014

education. The Internet initiative discussed in this chapter receives 2300 visitors in a month. The URL-address of the portal, and links to actual works are incorporated onto the homepages of numerous institutions dealing with the profession or the education in general.

Our "Database for Architecture" (www.arc.sze.hu/indexen.html) started in 2001 with the target to provide up-to-date and easily useable, editable knowledge materials that can be easily accessed at any time and from any place, to the education of architects at any level in Győr. A more effective education at a higher level can be achieved with the help of electronic subject matter following the changes in the profession in a flexible way. Knowledge of the fields of related branches, the most recent aims of science and technique, and examples realized in practical life are dynamically coupled with basic knowledge. Through the step-by-step building up of the complexity-aimed database-concept of several special branches, versatility and richness of our profession has also been outlined.

Realization of the above targets in the area of building construction entails that lecture notes, practical guides and study aids with references, electronic stores of drawings, and planning and construction sheets and brochures of leading companies manufacturing building materials – all that can be done at the same place. In addition to that, further homepages of professional and scientific character, journals, reviews and periodicals from Hungary and abroad, as well as a selection of independent articles can be found here. Successful operation of a database for architecture is provides numerous special services (search possibilities, integrated dictionaries, forum, students' administration, news bar).

Today, county borders are getting more and more permeable within Europe of the regions – thereby making wide-ranging collaborate and cooperation very easy. An important precursor and catalyst of this process is the world wide web (WWW) where results of international research and practical achievements can be published. The Internet is, however, much more then simply a media because cooperation can be established and practised on a daily basis among different institutions of higher education owing to its interactivity. There is a possibility for reasonable sharing of the activities, or publishing the results in a common knowledge base. As educational tools, electronic knowledge bases are interactive. At the same time, it must always be taken into consideration that education of future architects has the characteristic feature of often being highly individual regarding the duties given and solutions obtained. Therefore, a personal teacher-student contact is and shall be of the uppermost importance. The knowledge base provides a very useful background for these works, too, for example in informing a variety of tasks.

ELECTRONIC TEACHING KNOWLEDGE BASES AS ARCHETYPES

Based on existing professional databases and idea exchange, electronic teaching databases were believed to be suitable for the above detailed wide-ranging demands at our university. We were familiarized with one initiative in 1999 presented at the Conference on Building Construction where the educational computer program package on building construction (called "FAL", meaning "Wall") developed at the Budapest Technical University was introduced us by Nándor Bártol (see: Figure 1). The author wished to integrate the electronic lecture aids from the university department and links from outside of the university – representing the professional life – into a common knowledge base. The ideas on the structure of the database, the professional requirements and the way of actualizing were formulated as follows:.

Another ingenious contribution to professional knowledge transfer is the work of Dr. József Orbán from Pécs and a catalogue on building materials published by the company Orisoft in Pécs (see:

Figure 1. "FAL": Conceptual scheme of an educational program package on building construction developed at the Budapest Technical University (© 1999, Nándor Bártol. used with permission)

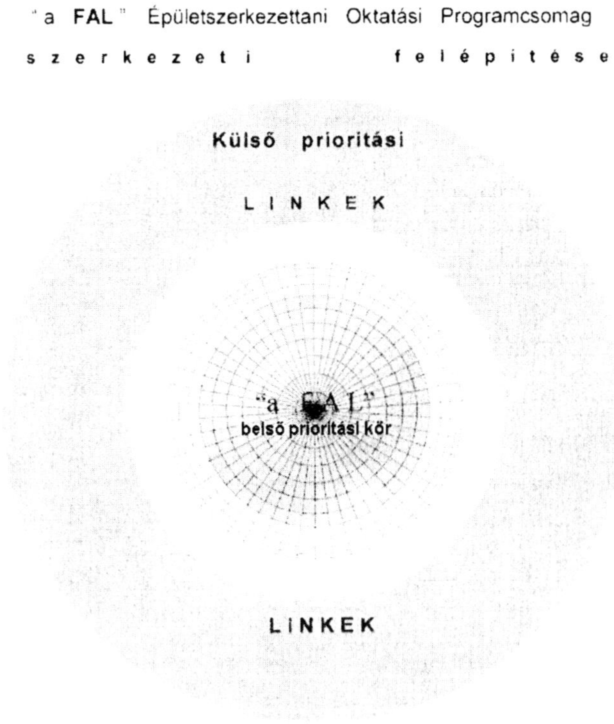

Figure 2). Professional knowledge and skill can be accessed in a clearly and distinctly detailed hierarchy. This compilation is utilized both in the practical life and education, owing to its encyclopaedia-like structure.

After having selected the main theme desired, the subgroups in the Orisoft Catalogue provided in a matrix-array made it possible to choose from the secondary and tertiary points of view of information collecting. So it was possible to choose from different company information within one single product group or to choose a product group within an actual company. Another advantage of the matrix principle is its compactness, i.e. being unexpanded. Activities of a great number of companies become easily visible and comparable. However, in the small grid field there is only place enough for one link. Therefore information attached is seen when the mouse cursor on top of the link moves and displays an information windows with variable content besides the matrix. In case more information should be needed, users can click onto the link in the grid field and navigate away onto a new page.

STRUCTURE AND USE OF THE KNOWLEDGE BASE FROM GYŐR

At the time of establishing the Architectural Database in Győr (Figures 3 and 4) our target was not only to utilize already available knowledge and tools but to find new areas for advancement. Visitors are greeted on the main page showing a mosaic in details from the most beautiful sceneries of the town. Then comes a picture directing users to a webpage with professional information. Catching the eye of our visually susceptible students,

Figure 2. Scheme of a catalogue on building materials (company: Orisoft in Pécs) organized by main themes, and one selected of the subgroup matrices

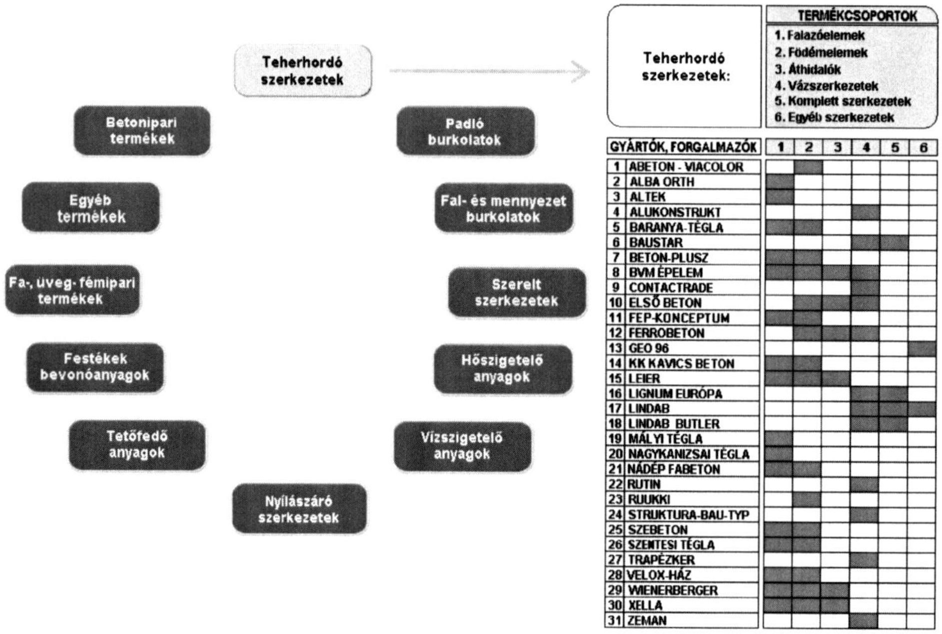

their interest is going to be increased by a header toolbar in individual design showing animation over the main themes.

In the database, university lecture notes, additional supporting materials, and selected outside homepages, documents and videos (of

Figure 3. Architectural database for students (designed in Győr)

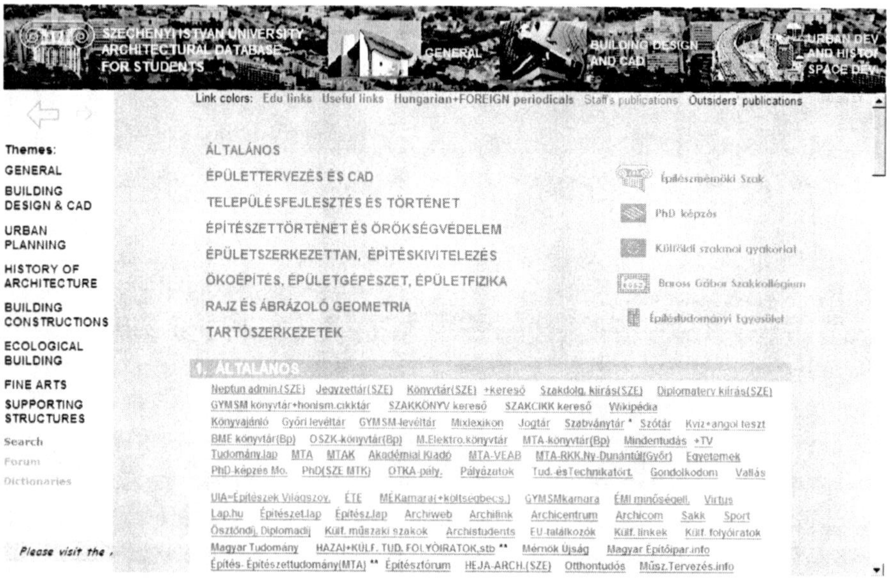

informative, research, company information, etc. character) are available. It has a distinctly theme-oriented structure, and even more, it is quite unique among domestic (Hungarian) web portals since its main structure orientation is subject to that of the university lectures of the teaching students of architecture. This organizational construction is one of our targets in achieving complexity-oriented education because all of the main segments and parts of our profession compose true unity beside each other as elements.

At the starting location of the professional surface, one of the following main themes can be selected:

- GENERAL
- BUILDING DESIGN & CONSTRUCTION, AND CAD
- URBAN & SETTLEMENT DEVELOPMENT, AND HISTORY
- HISTORY OF ARCHITECTURE, AND PROTECTION OF HERITAGE
- BUILDING CONSTRUCTION SCIENCE, AND BUILDING EXECUTION
- ECOLOGICAL (GREEN) BUILDINGS, BUILDING INSTALLATION, AND BUILDING PHYSICS
- DESIGN DRAWING AND DESCRIPTIVE GEOMETRY
- SUPPORTING STRUCTURES

If one changes the main theme selected before, it is not necessary to go back to the top of the homepage because there are direct links for the main themes on the side bar, too. At the very beginning of the professional surface, but distinctly separated in graphical way from the main themes, certain emphasis is given to the access to some of the most important homepages (e.g. Department of Architect Engineering, PhD Education, Professional Practice Abroad, College "Baross Gábor" for Advanced Technical Studies, or a link to the homepage of the Association of Building Construction Science Branch in Győr). The structure of the database is

Figure 4. On-line lecture notes and practical aids for each semester on building construction and building effectuation

similar to a site-map (a kind of link-maps) with links organized into five subgroups kept apart by spectacular colour markings. The following subgroups can be found within all of the main themes:

- Education material (lilac);
- Useful professional links (blue);
- Domestic and foreign periodicals, journals, etc. (red);
- Articles written by university lecturers (green);
- Certain articles of higher importance written by authors "from the outside" (brown).

Owing to this multi-level grouping, it is easier to search for something. This site-map principle makes several information gaining strategies possible. It is also possible to decide whether to choose from the five subgroups within each main theme, or the subgroups with the same colour (i.e. periodicals, journals, etc.) representing the primary point of view for the search and the selection of a certain main theme (i.e. a given field of profession), which remains at the second level (secondary point of view).

Since there are several links in the cluster selected on the basis of both the primary and the secondary selection point of view (i.e. several journals on building construction), a third level of differentiation can be derived. Through modification of the link names, a quaternary differentiation may partly also be realized:

- Separation of lecture notes from education supports and aids with the help of determining additional words;
- Discrimination of the most important document owners with supplemental words (authors, universities, countries, etc.);
- Emphasized display of the names of periodicals and journals from foreign countries by capital letter;
- Separation of periodicals and journals with on-line full-text from those with only content information (these latter-mentioned are distinguished with the supplementary word "info").

These spectacularly coloured site-map markings can be easily overviewed through a simple mouse scrolling, therefore allowing the last mentioned particular points of view to be chosen as primary selection features (and thereby it is possible to browse only e.g. the cluster of foreign periodicals, or that of the university lecture notes, etc.).

This multi-differentiated site-map as shown can flexibly be developed; however, it is our important target to support our students only with pre-selected information that can be reviewed at a glance. Sometimes when an expansion of the material occurs, certain other elements are removed, or links that are close to or in strong relationship with each other (e.g. practical guides and helping supplements for building construction) are compiled onto a single independent page to be opened by a single click.

SPECIAL SERVICES OBTAINABLE FROM THE KNOWLEDGE BASE

Through these special services, efficiency of use and up-to-date information transfer are significantly increased. The links already visited are displayed in and distinguished with a slightly changed background shade thereby allowing systemic (or on the contrary, "on the random basis") browsing of the database items, and the return onto a former item are greatly facilitated. Not only "search what you see" but some kinds of "computer-aided search" options can also be chosen. A simple quick search (CTRL+F) is used for searching among link names, and an individually modified purpose-oriented Google-service (under "Search" of the side bar) helps in finding something within the full content of the university's web-documents. This menu point is also suitable for use with the Google Scholar search machine developed for educational and scientific purposes.

From the side menu it is possible to enter the "Forum" page. This is a kind of interactive discussion surface where students and teachers, lecturers and "outside" participants working in the line of business can communicate with each other. Themes of this "virtual round-table" are determined by the user, and anybody can add a comment to them. At the very beginning, some themes were designated as start-up topics by the lecturer in order to facilitate deeper discussions and formation of professional directions (e.g. Designers' Forum, Forum for Urbanists and Heritage Protection, Forum for Building Constructors). This is also the very forum that can create a community, a kind of society among our students who stay in different foreign countries under the work with "Leonardo" or "Erasmus" programs. Help can be obtained during browsing homepages in foreign languages when the on-line dictionaries (developed by SZTAKI) in five languages and in both translation directions are turned on through clicking on the bottom part of the side bar menu. On the lowest part of the side bar menu, actual and latest news are temporarily running (e.g. about certain lectures, exhibitions, conferences, "Day of Open Gates", admission information).

From the homepage, "Neptun" (an administrative service for students) can be accessed where information regarding different subjects and time schedules are published. This is one of the ways for students to register themselves for learning a subject and later for exams, and here they can also check their graduation notes. This kind of information on documents and graduation is subject to change only with a password of the university department.

Scrolling down onto the bottom of the database, the Database for Architecture can be set with a single click as a start page in the internet browser; and there is the possibility to jump to a download page of free software to accommodate commonly used file types (extensions .pdf, .doc, .ppt, .xls).

HAVE A TASTE FROM THE CURRICULAR SCHOOL-WORKS OF THE KNOWLEDGE BASE

In case of certain subjects – for example, building construction, building execution, history of architecture – curricular school works were published on a CD ten years ago. Because of their HTML format they could easily be inserted into the internet knowledge base. Through the recently used side bar menu and read-windows the notes became easier to overview, and their use is also more convenient. Other school-works can be accessed not in HTML but the also most popular PDF format (e.g. Organization of Building Activities, Planning of Buildings).

Our newest (and also on CD accessible) school work is the "Computer-Based Architectural Modelling" which is intended to support ArchiCAD teaching. Important roles are given – besides the texts and pictorial information – to educational videos and interactive practicing examples. This material was prepared in 2006 within the framework of HEFOP-program, and its realization was also supported by the company Hyperionics with its "HyperSnap" screen capture software and "HyperCam" screen recorder software.

In the videos, example solutions can be documented, the oral explanation of the lecturer can be heard, and the places of mouse clicks are also marked with colours. This educational film can be run by the students with the CAD-software; it can be stopped and re-started, etc. These films are never-stopping educational supports to learn step-by-step the examples. The students can thereby more efficiently learn the special knowledge. When using ArchiCAD, preparation of technical drawings is similar to the classical and traditional drawing on tracing-paper with china-ink but spatial modelling requires a specific way of ArchiCAD-Thinking. Therefore greater emphasis has been laid upon this (see: Figure 5).

Today, numerous architect offices prepare own homepages and even accept orders, not only for architectural planning, but web design-type works, thereby turning visual art abilities into business. In accordance with the challenges of our time, in the above mentioned lecture note on CAD there is a short summary given about publishing of vision schemes on an internet webpage with interactive web design-examples (when modifying the software lines written in HTML in the practical examples, different results as reactions can be displayed).

Figure 5. Computer aided architectural modelling (online lecture notes)

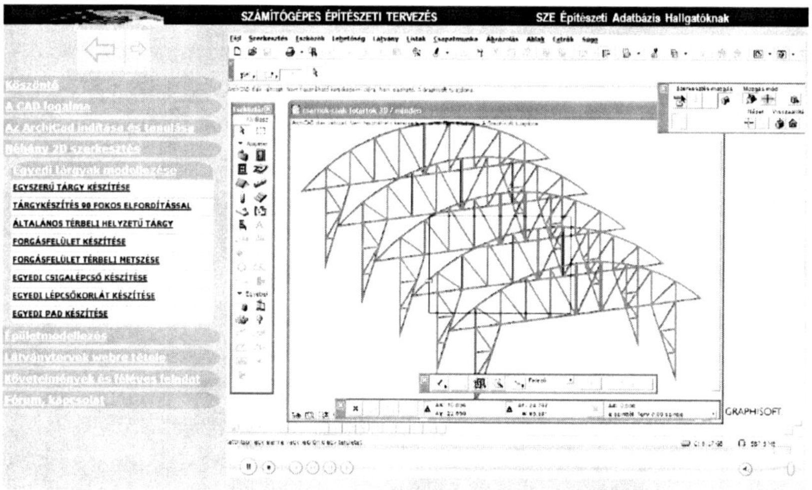

Figure 6. Visitor-statistics of arc.sze.hu

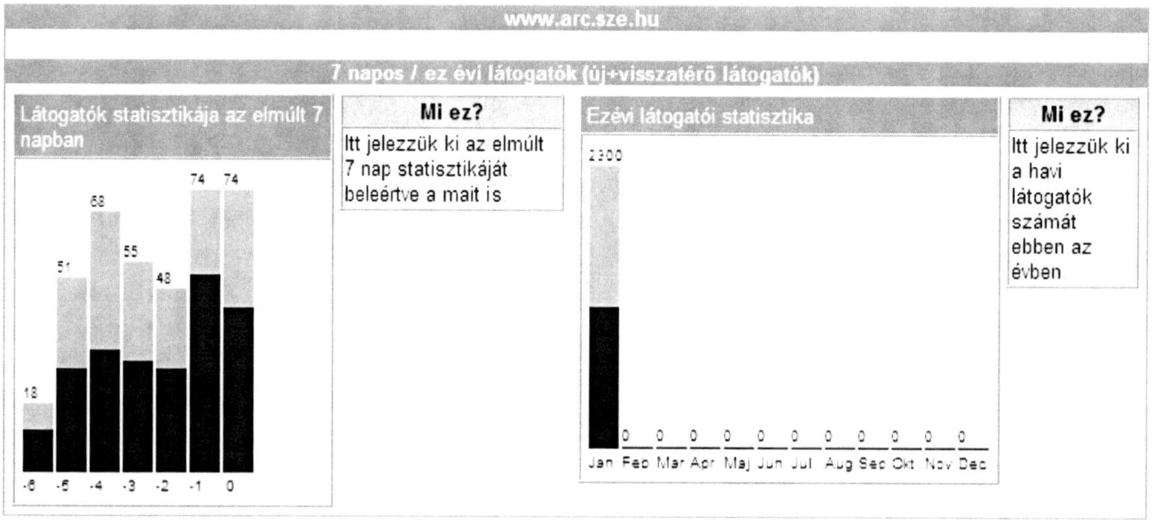

MAINTENANCE OF THE KNOWLEDGE BASE: FURTHER DEVELOPMENTS

Construction and editing of the internet knowledge base is based in general on html-knowledge, but is accompanied with numerous Java Script applications (animations, interactive VR-panorama, on-line dictionary request, etc.). Both editing and automated looking for link-failure are realized with free software. During steady maintenance and actualization, ideas, proposals and opinions of the users are taken into account. Our students give reports on the great help this knowledge base provides them in learning and being informed, while the visitor-statistics give also high access figures as feedback (see: Figure 6).

The Database for Architecture is continuously in development. It is our plan to prepare further school projects as we try to utilize the new innovations developed in computer science. Our professional web portal is integrated both into the homepage of "Széchenyi István" University, Department of Architecture and into those of the related special departments. So this Knowledge Base provides new opportunities for both the students and their lecturers for thinking together.

ADDITIONAL READING

Bártol, N. (1999). Új segédanyag az épületszerkezettan hatékonyabb oktatásáért. (New Education Aids for a More Effective Teaching of Building Construction Theory.) In Proceedings of *XXIVConference on Building Construction* (pp. 54-62) "Széchenyi István" University, Győr, Fátrai, György (1998). *Építéskivitelezés online-jegyzet (On-Line Lecture Notes on Building Effectuation)*. www.arc.sze.hu/kivitelea

Koppány, A. (1998 and 2006). *Épületszerkezettan online-jegyzet (On-Line Lecture Notes for Building Construction)*. www.arc.sze.hu/epszerkea

Molnárka, G. (2006). *Hallgatói mobilitási portál (Mobility Portal for Students)*. http://www.sze.hu/leonardo

Orbán, J. (2000-2007). *Orisoft Építőanyagipari Katalógus (Orisoft Catalogue of Building Materials)*. www.orisoft.pmmf.hu

Somfai, A. (2006). *Számítógépes Építészeti Modellezés online-jegyzet (On-Line Lecture Notes on Computer Aided Architectural Modelling)*. www.arc.sze.hu/cad

APPENDIX: SUPPORTING MATERIAL

Abstract

It is the aim of this chapter to show the teaching web portal of the Faculty of Architecture at "Széchenyi István" University (www.arc.sze.hu/indexen.html) and its many uses. Nowadays, the Internet helps us to look into Hungarian and foreign study aids, and architectural websites. The Internet has created potential new and effective ways of cooperation between lecturers and students of the university and other institutions of higher education. The teaching web portal mentioned above realizes diversity and complexity of architecture, with efficient grouping of information, while being attentive to high professional standards. Computer Aided Architectural Modeling (www.arc.sze.hu/cad) is one of the new types of online lecture notes, where many narrated screen captured videos show the proper usage of cad software instead of texts and figures. This interactive type of learning assists students to become more independent learners. This type of teaching modality provides the opportunity for students who need more time to acquire subject matter through viewing video examples. The success of our departments' common web initiations can be measured through Internet statistics and feedback of the students and external professionals.

Questions and Answers

1. What are the overall problems in this case?

How to construct a small, simple and well articulated database for university students, fully managed by architect lecturers, without informatics engineering skills.

2. What are the factors affecting the problems related to this case?

The main factors are suitable computer systems and internet facilities, inventing advantageous database structure and website appearance, along with choosing easy usable and widely known software.

3. Discuss managerial, organizational, issues related to this case.

This project involved the teamwork of some departments at the School of Architecture in Győr, Hungary. Many lecturers took part in its development by licensing their electronic documents or giving useful suggestions. This project needed a founder manager and some enthusiastic co-workers.

4. What are the possible alternatives and pros and cons of each alternative facing the organization in dealing with the problems related to the case?

Databases designed with up-to-date PHP/MySQL are better solutions than plain HTML, but needs employing informatics engineers. This professional PHP/MySQL based solutions may have user-friendly data input forms, still often resulting big databases but very small searching fields (instead of smaller but well articulated colorful tree-view solution described in the case study above).

Epilogue and Lessons Learned

In inventing and developing this small database, our teamwork aimed to provide "smaller, simpler, and cheaper" solutions for architect lecturers who are non-informatics engineers. Colored sitemap principles proved to be successful according to student feedback. We tried to utilize our training and experiences while cooperating with informatics experts. More specifically, we found that:

- In the case of smaller projects it is often advantageous to work in a smaller developing teamwork to achieve higher efficiency and avoid exorbitant sharing of tasks.
- If we have good ideas, it is worth dealing with self training in solving several informatics problems.
- In the case of bigger projects we have to recognize the necessity of cooperating with informatics experts.

Chapter 15
Blended Learning in Engineering Curricula Through the Meaningful Use of ICT Tools

Yih-Ruey Juang
Jinwen University of Science and Technology, Taiwan

ABSTRACT

Blended learning, which combines various ICT tools into conventional face-to-face classroom activities, has proved to be more effective in enhancing the learners' motivation, communication skills and learning achievement than teaching by employing a single approach. The meaningful use of ICT tools is critical to the successful promotion and implementation of blended learning. This case introduces a study of blended learning using the WIRE model that links pre-class warm-up, interaction in class, and review as well as post-class exercises into a continuous learning experience with basic to advanced mental skills. The WIRE model has been experimented in the Department of Information Management of a university of science and technology in Taiwan. The findings from the learning achievement, questionnaire, and focus group interview revealed some significant differences between the experimental and control groups in the degree of motivation, interaction between teacher and students, and collaboration among students. The WIRE model can thus help enhance learning motivation, interaction between teacher and students and among students, and learning achievement.

BACKGROUND

With reference to recent literature, Graham (2006) has defined blended learning into three perspectives: (1) combining instructional modalities or delivery media (such as Bersin & Associates, 2003), (2) combining instructional methods to gain an optimal learning outcome with or without instructional technology (such as Driscoll, 2002), and (3) combining online and face-to-face instruction (such as Rooney, 2003; Osguthorpe & Graham, 2003). In this study, the third perspective is more appropriate for considering the implementation of blended learning research. The emphasis on blended learning as described in this chapter refers particularly

DOI: 10.4018/978-1-61520-869-2.ch015

to the meaningful use of technology as a way of effectively achieving educational objectives.

Can blended learning serve as an important strategy for technology enhanced learning both at present and in the future? Interestingly, in Kim and Bonk's (2006) survey on the future growth (continuing up to 2013) of online teaching and learning in higher education, the respondents expected future emphasis to be placed more on blended learning than on full online courses. Up until the present, this trend has continued in the same direction and seems to be increasingly common. These investigators also suggested that follow-up studies might focus on the types of blended learning, design of activities, and instructor training with respect to the blended-learning situation (Kim & Bonk, 2006). Yet, even in the context of corporate training, many organizations remain confused about what blended learning involves and how it is implemented (Kim, Bonk, & Oh, 2008). More empirical studies should therefore be undertaken for the blended learning models that will be needed in the future.

According to the literature regarding the implementation of blended learning on campus, the use of Information Technology and Communication (ICT) tools within teaching and learning has generally been encouraged. Moreover, most campuses (more than 90%) have deployed commercial or homegrown course management systems (CMSs) or learning management systems (LMSs) for teaching and learning (Hawkins & Rudy, 2008); however, most tools provided in these systems are merely used for message broadcasting, the sharing of learning resources, homework management, and online quizzes rather than being closely integrated into an instructional model (Hartman, 2008).

This chapter presents a study of blended learning model—the WIRE model, which was proposed by Juang in the book "*Web-based engineering education: Critical design and effective tools*" (Juang, 2009). The WIRE model comprises four learning activities within three stages—a pre-class warm-up, interaction during class, and post-class review and exercises. The first letter of each activity forms the basis for the WIRE acronym. Under this simple concept, instructional plans can be designed using various combinations of the four learning activities in order to obtain the best learning outcome. The WIRE model has experimented with in the Department of Information Management of one university in Taiwan. The preliminary findings from the learning achievement, questionnaire, and focus group interview show some significant differences between the experimental group and control group, including the degree of the motivation, interaction between teacher and students, and collaboration among students. The following sections introduce the basic concept of WIRE model, describe the research design, research results and discussion, with final comments being made in the conclusion.

INTRODUCTION TO THE WIRE MODEL

The WIRE model is an instructional model for implementing blended learning and suggests that the instructional design should include the following three essential elements throughout the process of instruction:

a. The development of students' mental skills: The whole process should be designed with appropriate serial learning activities suitable for the current level of mental skills of students that spans the simple to the complex according to Bloom's Taxonomy (Bloom, 1956).
b. Meaningful adoption of educational technology: A successful adopter of educational technologies for the design of blended learning should meaningfully integrate the ICT tools into each various learning stages by answering the following essential questions: (1) What technologies are easy to use? (2) What

technologies are teachers currently relatively familiar with? (3) What technologies can be closely integrated into the instructional strategy? (4) What technologies can enhance the learning effect (Juang, 2009)? Although many modern educational software or learning devices have been proposed and promoted over the years, the technologies teachers are willing to use are invariably restricted and are usually straightforward, rapid, effective, and relatively easy.

c. Continuous learning experience: A teacher is responsible for arranging appropriate activities, according to the objectives, into a continuous learning experience for learners who will acquire knowledge and skills in a step by step manner. The WIRE model proposes an adaptable instruction process that can provide a continuous learning experience in a blended learning modality. The instruction process involves four activities, including the pre-lesson warm-up, interaction with teachers and classmates, review of the lesson, and the exercise or assignment (Juang, 2009).

In addition, the WIRE model can be applied as a way of creating instructional plans for any scale of learning content and can be adapted for any course having different objectives. A learning unit or a whole course can be designed to match the different objectives as a way of systematically developing the mental skills of learners. The time spent on learning the major content will be more than that spent on other information. The time allocation and difficulty for each stage of the learning process should therefore be adaptable according to the teacher's intentions of what content the students should learn.

Based on the concepts described above, the WIRE model was designed to have three stages: the pre-class warm-up, interaction in class, and the post-class review and exercises. The learning activities of the three stages were arranged to function as a cyclic process that incorporates various ICT tools into face-to-face and online contexts. The ICT tools used in the WIRE model are not new, but are meaningfully integrated for use with each learning activity, and accord with the requirements mentioned above. The processes in each stage are described briefly as follows.

1. *Warm-up* stage: Before the class meets, where all students are asked to read the learning materials, in printed or digital form, and then to individually answer the warm-up questions supplied by the teacher on the web or by email. The teacher can browse through the answers before entering the classroom to clarify the background knowledge of the students and possible misunderstandings. The information obtained can thus help the teacher to adapt the difficulty and emphasize the learning content as required in order to effectively exploit the time for interaction in classroom.
2. *Interaction* stage: Since the students are expected to have read the learning materials and have replied to questions during the warm-up stage, they will have therefore already memorized some information about the materials and will be more ready to learn. Whereas students bring questions and motivation to the classroom, the teacher should take advantage of the highly participatory attitude arising to conduct interactive activities that are able to sustain interest in the field of learning concerned. First, the teacher should provide students with a concept test to check they are sufficiently prepared. Depending on the test results, the teacher can then provide a mini-lecture to clarify the answer required that will include an introduction to background knowledge with regard to the test items, and a follow up in the form of a complex question to be discussed by the students amongst themselves. All the test and discussion results need to

be recorded in digital form on the teacher's computer or the web-based learning system for the purpose of future reference.

3. *Review and exercise* stage: The follow-up learning subsequent to the classroom interaction should concentrate on deepening the comprehension and application of the knowledge and skills acquired, and then advance to a high-order thinking activity that involves synthesis and evaluation. Instead of traditional homework, students, therefore, simply revise their previous answers to the warm-up questions and to some of the more advanced questions if applicable. The mini problem-based learning (PBL) modality provides a good option to then inspire students towards implementing more advanced thinking skills with regard to the further exercises.

The three stages that include the four learning activities can be arranged in various combinations (called a scenario) into a cyclic process that could be implemented in a lesson, chapter, unit, or even in the case of an entire semester involving a complete course. A scenario could be a combination of the three stages, but should preserve the sequence warm-up, interaction, review, and exercises stages. In other words, a scenario may consist of multiple warm-ups, interactions, reviews, or exercises based on the attributes of the learning content. For example, the study presented in this chapter formulated a scenario based on WIRE that lasted up to three weeks and involved five cycles in a semester. The details of this scenario are described in the following section.

RESEARCH DESIGN

Participants

The experiment consisted of 88 participants who came from a university of science and technology in Taiwan who had registered at the Department of Information Management of the Further Education School. Most of participants worked during the daytime and studied courses during the evening from Monday to Friday. The excessive demands therefore meant that the participants did not possess enough time to digest the newly acquired knowledge and skills. Blended learning, however, is suitable for the needs to such students because it provides flexible time allocation for learning. During the first week, the teacher explained how blended learning works and how to be an active course learner, as well as the requirements involved in the present experiment. It should also be added, that most of the participants in the experimental group expressed a great interest in the experiment.

The participants were divided into two groups (classes). The experimental group consisted of 45 students while the control group comprised 43 students. The experimental group adopted the WIRE model while the control group adopted lecture-based instruction but was verbally encouraged to warm-up and review lessons. Since the students had already been divided into two classes when they joined the department, the researchers could not reorganize and randomly assign them into two new classes just for the experiment. All the participants were asked to take a test of prior ability, which covered basic Java programming and algebra. The test results revealed no significance according to Levene's test of homogeneity of variance ($F = .824$, $p = .429 > .05$). This shows that the discrete distribution of the two classes reveals no significant difference, with the participants confirming an almost equal background knowledge and ability to learn the subject "Data Structure." In addition, the students from each class were divided into several heterogeneous groups of three to five students for the purpose of group work.

In order to control for variables arising from employing a different instructor, the two groups of students were taught by the same teacher using the different instructional models.

Figure 1. The WIRE scenario spread over 21 days (3 weeks)

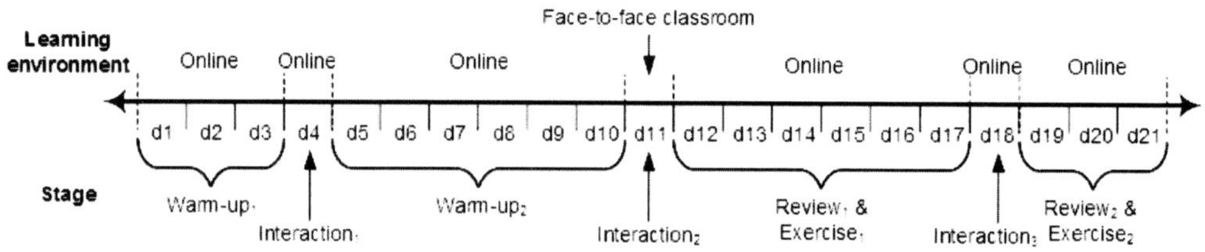

Instructional Design

The WIRE model was experimented with in the subject of Data Structure for 18 weeks of a semester. The course was originally offered in the form of distance learning, but the researchers changed this in order to implement the blended mode, which was interwoven with some of the face-to-face classes. Data Structure is the subject of this study and is fundamental to any course on data processing. Therefore, the WIRE scenario designed for each chapter of the learning material consists of two warm-ups and interactions followed by two stages for review and exercise (see Figure 1). The complete process regarding this scenario was conducted over a three-week period that covered one chapter of the course textbook; accordingly, there are five chapters provided in the experiment (see Figure 2).

By following the general class scheduling rules of universities, this study supposed that each week is comprised of one day for synchronous interaction either online or in face-to-face classroom interactions, such as days 4, 11, and 18, as shown in Figure 1. Each WIRE cycle therefore had only one face-to-face classroom interaction (*Interaction$_2$* on day 11), and the other two interactive activities (*Interaction$_1$* and *Interaction$_3$*) were conducted by synchronous text chat on an e-learning platform. For all warm-ups, the learning content for the stage *Warm-up$_1$* concentrated on the comprehension of new knowledge, so the intention of the stage *Interaction$_1$* was to clarify any confusion arising regarding new knowledge; and then the stage *Warm-up$_2$* consisted of six days for preparing the learning content to be taught in stage *Interaction$_2$* by way of face-to-face contact. The remaining days after the stage *Interaction$_2$* were allocated to the Review and Exercise phase, which included stage *Interaction$_3$* for consulting about the exercise(s) or mini-PBL.

Since each three-week WIRE scenario consisted of one week for face-to-face classroom interaction (denoted as 'C' in Figure 2) and two

Figure 2. Time allocation for the whole semester (w# denotes the week number)

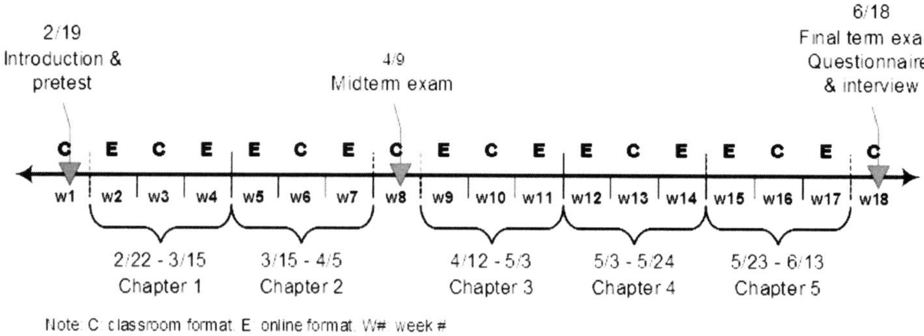

weeks for online learning (denoted as 'E' in Figure 2), five scenarios for five chapters of the learning content for the entire 18 weeks of the semester were organized. In addition, there were three weeks arranged for activities in relation to preparing for the WIRE model during the first week, midterm exam in week 8, and the final term exam during the last week, respectively. The time allocation for the whole semester is summarized in Figure 2 where it can be seen that this consists of eight weeks for face-to-face classroom meetings and ten weeks for online learning activities.

The Use of ICT Tools

The main educational technology utilized for the experimental group consisted of forum, homework, chat, and group tools, acquired through the e-learning platform. "Blackboard" which is a course management system, was a further tool also employed in this study. The way these ICT tools were used at each stage and step during the experimental procedure is listed below.

- Warm-up stage
  - Step 1: The teacher provides 1 to 3 warm-up questions to students using the forum tool on the Blackboard e-learning platform.
  - Step 2: After reading both the printed text and learning materials developed and uploaded by the instructor, the students answer the warm-up questions with respect to the forum.
  - Step 3: The teacher briefly browses through the warm-up answers before entering the classroom forum.
- Interaction stage
  - Step 1: For each learning chapter, the teacher applies a simple test to check the warm-up stage by way of the Classroom Response System (CMS), which is a remote control procedure that allows each student to reply to questions.
  - Step 2: The teacher gives a mini-lecture based on the test results and provides further advanced questions for peer discussion by using MS PowerPoint.
- Review and exercise stage
  - Step 1: The teacher assigns 1-3 exercise or a small project, if needed, for individuals or groups via the homework tool and group tool on the Blackboard.
  - Step 2: The students revise the warm-up answers and finish the assigned exercise(s) or projects individually or collaboratively through the homework tool and discussion forum on the Blackboard.

Research Questions

The researchers attempted to answer the following questions in this study through the learning achievement test, questionnaire, and focus-group interview.

1. Can the WIRE model effectively motivate students to learn?
2. Can the WIRE model effectively facilitate interaction either between teacher and students or among students?
3. Can the WIRE model effectively increase the learning achievement of students?

Research Tools

The examination paper for evaluating the difference in learning achievement between the two groups was made by the instructor according to the learning content, and was taken in the last week. In addition, the researchers created a questionnaire to assess the views of the experimental group using the WIRE model. Finally, 10 students from the experimental group were invited to a focus-group interview. The selection principle was hetero-

Table 1. Group statistics for the learning achievement test

	Group	N	Mean	Std. Deviation	Std. Error Mean
Score of learning achievement test	Experimental group	45	63.870	19.500	2.907
	Control group	43	52.691	13.467	2.054

geneous, that is, the interviewees had different attributes with regard to learning achievement, participatory degree of learning activities, and different level of recognition to the WIRE model.

The questionnaire was consisted of a five-point Likert scale. The pretest samples consisted of 32 students who came from another class of the same department and grade, and had adopted the WIRE model for one semester. After the pretest, the researchers retained 16 items for the purpose of the formal questionnaire by using item and factor analysis. The factors included the strategy with respect to warm-up lessons, interactive activities in class, and the strategy employed with regard to review and exercises after class. The reliability estimates for these items using Cronbach's Alphas were 0.627, 0.870, and 0.911, respectively. Taken as a whole, the Cronbach's Alpha reliability coefficient thus came to 0.892.

Research Procedure

The research procedure is listed as follows.

- Step 1: Give both experimental and control groups a test for prior ability in basic Java programming and algebra so as to evaluate the sample representativeness and then to adjust the lesson plan and difficulty of concept questions for each instructional stage.
- Step 2: Apply the WIRE procedure to the experimental group as shown in Figure 1 and 2 with the control group being treated with lecture-based instruction and collective discussions.
- Step 3: Apply a test to both groups in learning achievement. The experimental group also took part in the questionnaire and a few selected participants were invited to a focus-group interview.

RESULTS AND DISCUSSIONS

By analyzing the data from the learning achievement test, the average score of the experimental group was found to be higher than the control group by about 11.2 points (100 points represent maximum marks). In this respect, the t-test, which examined the difference between the means of the two groups, reached a significant level ($t(88) = 3.116$, $p < .05$). This result reveals that the WIRE model can effectively enhance the learning achievement of students. The detailed results of the group statistics for the learning achievement test and the corresponding independent samples test are shown in Table 1 and 2.

With respect to the questionnaire survey, the research group conducted a questionnaire (using a five-point Likert scale, in which 1 = strongly disagree or poor and 5 = strongly agree or excellent) so that the participants could evaluate the motivation, interaction, and learning achievement experienced from being involved in the WIRE model. Of the 45 responses received, those possessing fixed responses, having too many unanswered questions, and with unreasonable replies were eliminated, which finally gave 41 valid responses (validation rate = 91.1%) that were used for statistical purposes.

In order to answer the research issues, the questions in the questionnaire were divided into three categories, motivation, interaction, and learning achievement. From the statistics, the three weighted averages for the three categories

Table 2. Independent samples test and the results of the learning achievement test

	Levene's Test for Equality of Variances		t-test for Equality of Means						
	F	Sig.	t	df	Sig. (2-tailed)	Mean Difference	Std. Error Difference	95% Confidence Interval of the Difference	
								Lower	Upper
Equal variances assumed	5.962	0.017	3.116	86	0.0025	11.179	3.588	4.046	18.313
Equal variances not assumed			3.141	78.419	0.0024	11.179	3.559	4.094	18.264

were 3.78, 3.72, and 3.73, respectively (see Table 3). This reveals that most participants agreed that the course employing the WIRE model effectively increased learning motivation, interaction between teacher and students, and learning achievement more than the courses that did not adopt the WIRE model. Since all the students were asked to answer the warm-up questions, they had to have read the text and digital content provided by the teacher in order to be prepared before class. In contrast with traditional instructional methods, the students became more responsible and paid more attention to classroom activities (avg. = 3.90); they answered the teacher's questions, because the lectures stimulated their minds. In addition, the students can easily connect the knowledge acquired before and after classroom learning, because they were provided with the opportunities to rethink and review the warm-up questions during the review stage. By taking advantage of having the fresh memories of learning content after the review activity, the participants appreciated that the additional exercises can enhance the proficiency in applying the knowledge and skills acquired and then increased their learning achievement (avg. = 4.02).

From the results of the focus-group interview, most interviewees generally accepted that the

Table 3. The questionnaire results

Categories	Questions (N = 41)	Average
Motivation	The warm-ups increased my learning motivation for the course.	3.66
	I was engaged in the classroom activities because of the warm-up before class.	3.73
	Unlike other courses, I paid much attention during classroom learning.	3.90
	Unlike other courses, I was very motivated during classroom learning.	3.83
Interaction	The warm-ups increased my interaction with my teacher.	3.61
	The warm-ups increased my interaction with my classmates.	3.80
	Unlike other courses, I interacted more with my teacher during classroom activities.	3.44
	Unlike other courses, I interacted more with my classmates during classroom activities.	3.73
Learning achievement	The warm-ups increased my learning achievement on this course.	3.66
	Revising the warm-up questions as part of the lesson review after class helped me connect the knowledge acquired before and after classroom learning.	3.63
	The exercises assigned after class enhanced my learning achievement.	4.02

WIRE model led to an enhancement of attention, interaction, and motivation with regard to classroom activities, and therefore learning achievement was promoted. Participants also expressed an interest in trying out the novel delivery model. Several of the positive replies from interviewees are quoted below.

Interviewee 1: I like the new learning style. When I encountered the questions that I had no idea how to solve, I took this seriously and discussed it further with my classmates instead of just giving up. And then, I felt a sense of accomplishment when I came to solve the questions. I also understood the lessons relatively better than was the case with the other courses.

Interviewee 2: I found I had much more time to interact with classmates. The group discussion forced me to learn about the materials from others. When I was hesitant or felt embarrassed to ask questions in classroom, I was able to use the forum on the Blackboard to post questions. This is very convenient and saves a lot of time.

Interviewee 5: The WIRE model allowed me to control my learning time and become more active and enthusiastic in discussions with my classmates.

Interviewee 7: It felt good. At least, I learned much more from this way of working than the others. The flexible time allocation let me really concentrate on the learning content at my own pace as and when I wanted to learn.

As most participants first took the e-learning course with blended learning, the sense of freshness and novelty may have led to a greater motivation to participate more fully in the learning activities. However, since the WIRE procedure was repeated five times during the whole semester, the participants should have gradually become habituated to the novel learning style. The positive feedback revealed two important items of information: (1) The WIRE model could facilitate the interaction between teacher and students and among students, and (2) the WIRE model can provide more opportunities for students to think and reflect about the knowledge and skills the teacher wishes to deliver.

During the interview phase, some negative feedback and suggestions also arose. First, two interviewees hoped that they might have had more time for face-to-face classroom learning (see the following excerpt from interviewee 4), although they nevertheless seemed to appreciate the advantages to be gained from using distance learning according to the WIRE model.

Interviewee 4:...some questions found in the warm-up or exercise stage were difficult to solve. I hoped that I could find someone to help me or discuss the answers rather than post questions on the forum. It this comes too late, I might have had to go to work and was also very busy during the daytime and, even when off work, I have no time to sit in front of the computer for accessing the Internet. I would very much appreciate interactive learning in a face-to-face classroom context.

Interviewee 8: My computer doesn't work so I needed to go to the school at times when I was obliged to post answers for the warm-up, review, and exercises. So it was quite inconvenient for me to use the WIRE model.

These students preferred to learn from the teacher through face-to-face discussion for solving the questions from the warm-up or exercise stages. As had been found in some of the research results regarding online learning, those learning strategies that employ communication online focus on the affordance provided by tools to support learning motivation, interaction, and cooperation. However, some people will always prefer to discuss lessons with others in a face-to-face setting. The two interviewees, however, may be a special case due to the fact they have very busy jobs during the daytime, and so prefer to learn through real interaction. Perhaps future study will be able to take more account of this issue, i.e., the difference between the fulltime student and student at work.

Second, some warm-up questions were difficult to solve. Since the WIRE procedure in relation to this experiment only provided an opportunity for face-to-face interaction for each learning chapter, the teacher could not precisely predict the actual capabilities of students in order to be able to sufficiently prepare and assign the appropriate warm-up questions and exercises. An essential factor to the success of the WIRE model was to ask the appropriate questions at all three stages. These questions must reflect the concepts typified by the learning materials up to a moderate level of difficulty so that the self-confidence of learners could be encouraged. In future research of the WIRE model, the teacher might therefore prepare questions with various levels of difficulty for flexible use in face-to-face learning activities. The thoughts of the students in response to such questions can then provide some clues as to the level of difficulty required for subsequent questions.

Finally, two interviewees expressed the view that they might have expected to experience more practice exercises in order to gain more confidence for the midterm and final exams (see the following excerpts from Interviewees 3 and 9). The researchers also found that most of the students making such comments possessed relatively strong learning achievement and were highly active in all the learning activities. On the other hand, three interviewees expressed the view that they preferred not to receive too many exercises because they were only part-time students. It is therefore also a challenge for the teacher to control the amount of exercises either in the case of classroom teaching or during the online activities, as well as to continue to remain sensitive to the demands of students as much as possible.

Interviewees 3: I didn't have enough confidence to pass the exams because I was afraid I would be unable to answer the various exercises I did during the warm-up and exercise stage. So, the exercises did not provide enough practice. I suggest more exercises should be uploaded to the Blackboard, if possible, so that we can practice more often.

In summary, it seems that the WIRE model can indeed help to increase learning motivation, learning achievement, and interaction between teacher and students and among students. However, the problems and challenges also found in the experiment could represent obstacles for teachers in adopting WIRE model. The workload of teachers will increase to tackle those problems. However, the bulk of the work will be done when teachers repeatedly take the same subjects.

CONCLUSION

Blended learning has been proposed and promoted in higher education for many years, but most teachers have not taken full advantage of ICT tools and incorporated them into teaching and learning activities. The WIRE model emphasizes the meaningful use of ICT tools for teaching and learning by blending these into a series of learning activities. The pre-class *Warm-up* that uses the forum tool enables students to mentally obtain some information about the learning content, which arouses their curiosity and elicits questions. Along with a more motivated sensibility, the *Interaction* in class, using the Classroom Response System, facilitates discussions and debates that help clarify concepts and solve the individual problems identified during the warm-up. Subsequently, the post-class Review and Exercise, using the homework and forum tools, provide more profound learning and application to help gain insight into the acquired knowledge. The results of the current study show that most students provided positive feedback to the model, although some personal reservations were also expressed. The WIRE model, however, still requires more research in various areas with respect to a more diverse range of ICT tools.

REFERENCES

Bersin, (2003). *Blended learning: What works?: An industry study of the strategy, implementation, and impact of blended learning*. New York: Bersin & Associates.

Bloom, B. S. (1956). *Taxonomy of educational objectives, Handbook I: The cognitive domain*. New York: David McKay Co Inc.

Driscoll, M. (2002). *Blended learning: Let's get beyond the hype, IMB Global Services*. Retrieved August 22, 2009, from http://www-8.ibm.com/services/pdf/blended_learning.pdf

Graham, C. R. (2006). Blended learning systems: Definition, current trends, and future directions. In C. J. Bonk & C. R. Graham (Eds.), The handbook of blended learning: Global perspectives, local designs (pp. 3-21). SanFrancisco: Pfeiffer Publishing.

Hartman, J. L. (2008). Moving teaching and learning with technology from adoption to transformation. *EDUCAUSE Review*, Nov.-Dec., 24-25.

Hawkins, B. L., & Rudy, J. A. (2008). *EDUCAUSE Core Data Service - Fiscal Year 2007 Summary Report*. Retrieved Jun. 13, 2009, from http://net.educause.edu/ir/library/pdf/PUB8005.pdf

Juang, Y.-R. (2009). WIRE: A Blended Model for Teaching and Learning in Engineering Curricula. In Russell, D. L., & Haghi, A. K. (Eds.), *Web-based engineering education: Critical design and effective tools*. Hershey, PA: IGI Global.

Kim, K.-J., & Bonk, C. J. (2006). The future of online teaching and learning in higher education: A survey substantiates some ideas about online learning and refutes others. *EDUCAUSE Quarterly*, *4*, 22–30.

Kim, K.-J., Bonk, C. J., & Oh, E. J. (2008). The present and future state of blended learning in workplace learning settings in the United States. *Performance Improvement*, *47*(8), 5–16. doi:10.1002/pfi.20018

Osguthorpe, R. T., & Graham, C. R. (2003). Blended learning environments: Definitions and directions. *The Quarterly Review of Distance Education*, *4*(3), 227–233.

Rooney, J. E. (2003). Blending learning opportunities to enhance educational programming and meetings. *Association Management*, *55*(5), 26–32.

FURTHER READING

Barbian, J. (2002). Blended Works: Here's Proof! *Online Learning*, *6*(6), 26–31.

Bersin, J. (2004). *The blended learning book: Best practices, proven methodologies, and lessons learned*. San Francisco: Pfeiffer.

Cavus, N., & Ibrahim, D. (2007, May 3-5). Is blended learning the solution to web-based distant engineering education? Paper presented at the *7th International Educational Technology Conference (IETC)*, Nicosia, Turkish Republic of Northern Cyprus. eLearning Guide Research (2008). *Snapshot Report on Learning Modalities*. Retrieved Jun. 13, 2009, from http://www.elearningguild.com/research/archives/index.cfm?action=viewonly2&id=129&referer=http%3A%2F%2Fwww%2Eelearningguild%2Ecom%2F

Center for Educational Research and Evaluation. (2005). *Report on the survey of higher education teachers in 2004*. Retrieved Jun. 13, 2009, from http://www.cher.ntnu.edu.tw/analyze/data/edu92_teacher/pdf/2/2-2.pdf

Gudimetla, P., & Iyers, R. M. (2006). The role for e-learning in engineering education: Creating quality support structures to complement traditional learning. In *Proceedings of 17th Annual Conference of the Australasian Association for Engineering Education*, Auckland, New Zealand.

Kerres, M., & De Witt, C. (2003). A didactical framework for the design of blended learning arrangements. *Journal of Educational Media*, *28*(2-3), 101–103. doi:10.1080/1358165032000165653

Lane, L. M. (2008). Toolbox or trap? Course management systems and pedagogy. *EDUCAUSE Quarterly*, *2*, 4–6.

Laurillard, D. (1993). *Rethinking university teaching: a framework for the effective use of educational technology*. London: Routledge.

Law, N., Pelgrum, W. J., & Plomp, T. (Eds.). (2008). *Pedagogy and ICT use in schools around the world: Findings from the IEA SITES 2006 study*. Hong Kong: CERC-Springer.

Mortera-Gutiérrez, F. (2006). Faculty best practices using blended learning in e-learning and face-to-face instruction. *International Journal on E-Learning*, *5*(3), 313–337.

Pulichino, (2006). *The trends in blended learning research report*. Santa Rosa, CA: The eLearning Guild.

Rossett, A., Douglis, F., & Frazee, R. V. (2003). *Strategies for building blended learning, Learning Circuits*. Retrieved Jun. 13, 2009, from http://www.astd.org/LC/2003/0703_rossett.htm

Siau, K., Sheng, H., & Fiona Fui-Hoon Nah, F. F.-H. (2006). Use of a classroom response system to enhance classroom interactivity. *IEEE Transactions on Education*, *49*(3), 398–403. doi:10.1109/TE.2006.879802

Singh, H. (2003). Building effective blended learning programs. *Educational Technology*, *43*(6), 51–54.

Smith, J. M. (2001). *Blended learning: An old friend gets a new name*. Retrieved Jun. 13, 2009, from http://www.gwsae.org/Executiveupdate/2001/March/blended.htm

Troha, F. J. (2002). Bulletproof instructional design: A model for blended learning. *USDLA Journal*, *16*(5).

Valiathan, P. (2003). Blended learning models. *Learning Circuits*, Retrieved June13, 2009, from http://www.astd.org/LC/2002/0802_valiathan.htm

Zenger, J., & Uehlein, C. (2001) Why blended will win. *T+D*, *55*(8), 54-62.

APPENDIX: SUPPORTING MATERIAL

Abstract

This chapter explores a case of blended learning by adopting the proposed WIRE model in a university. The WIRE model stresses a continuous learning process with meaningful use of ICT tools to build a highly interactive learning experience. By the simple concept, that are the warm-up before class, interaction in class, and review and exercise after class, the students can keep focus and enthusiasm in learning activities so as to increase learning motivation, interaction, and learning achievement.

Questions and Answers

1. What is the overall problem(s) in this case?

The overall problem in this case is how to closely integrate technologies into teaching by meaningful use of ICT tools in order to increase students' learning motivation, learning achievement, and interaction between teachers and students and among students.

2. What are the factors affecting the problem(s) related to this case?

The key factor affecting the problems related to this case is the usage and attitude of integrating ICT tools into teaching to adequately help gain the best learning effect of students. Other factors such as the difficulty of learning materials, time allocation, quantity of exercises, and interesting interaction with teacher and classmates are also important to control the quality of learning.

3. Discuss managerial, organizational, and technological issues and resources related to this case.

- *Managerial*: As a teacher who is carrying out the blended learning, it is difficult to observe, memorize, and reflect all students' learning statuses. If every teacher has assigned a teaching assistant, the heavy work could be reduced to be affordable for more consideration on adopting appropriate teaching strategy.
- *Organizational:* Many researchers have agreed that blended learning can more effectively enhance motivation, communication skills, and learning achievement compared to single-form teaching methods; however, an important factor for the success of blended learning is the attitude toward and method of adopting ICT tools for teaching and learning. Most organizations (campuses or schools) cannot only provide information hardware and software for teachers but also organize the teachers' community of teaching practice to share and advance the professional development on pedagogy in blended learning. Holding the regular conference for sharing experiences also can form a promoting force to generate more cases of best practice.
- *Technological:* The technological issue occurred in this case is not difficult to tackle, because the products for digital teaching or learning are easier to use than the past ten years. Most campuses have purchased or homegrown one or more e-learning platforms and even the other assisted systems or tools. The possible issue could be how teachers can take the full

advantage of them in their teaching. More training and assistance for teachers in using those technologies are the important issues in the near future.

4. What role do decision-makers play in the overall planning, implementation and management of the information technology applications?

The decision-makers in this case, such as the administration team of e-learning and the dean of Academic Affairs Office, were not only bring computer hardware and software in front of them, but also more active and constructive on supporting teachers in meaningful use of ICT tools in teaching. For example, they broke the rule of general academic affairs to temporarily allowed that the students who took the experimental subject just came to school only 6 times in the whole semester, and the teacher can flexibly arrange the learning content, time allocation, and learning environment. These support brought teaching autonomy for teachers and let teacher freely implement their various teaching innovations.

5. What are the possible alternatives and pros and cons of each alternative facing the organization in dealing with the problem(s) related to the case?

The possible alternatives of the blended learning model have many variations which depend on the subject, issue, learning objectives, and teacher's preferred teaching method. However, according the literature review about the usage of CMS (course management system, which is a representative of e-learning tools), most tools are just used for message broadcasting, sharing of learning resources, homework management, and online quizzes rather than being closely integrated into an instructional model. From the organizational view, the possible pros are the high percentage of teachers who have adopted e-learning and the high number of digital learning materials, but the numbers can not represent the teaching quality and students' learning achievement are approaching to high. Therefore, the schools or campuses should take into account how to facilitate the meaningful use of the ICT tools into teaching, otherwise the using of ICT tools are just another burden for teachers.

6. What are some of the emerging technologies that should be considered in solving the problem(s) related to the case?

The personal learning environment (PLE) is the trend of learner-centered instructional concept that can be used to integrate contemporary information technologies into blended learning, such as Web 2.0, mobile computing, massive multiplayer online games (MMOGs), and classroom learning technologies (e.g. Classroom Response Systems, Interactive Whiteboard, etc.). In addition, by using these technologies to provide authentic learning environment either online or face-t0-face is also a potential in tackling the meaningful use of ICT tools in blended learning. For example, the blogs can be designed as a personal learning environment by blogging the notes of warm-up before class, interaction with teachers and peers in class, and review and exercise after class. At the end of each semester, the blog has recorded not only the personal learning processes and portfolios but also the interaction logs of discussions with the teachers and peers.

7. What is the final solution that can be recommended to the management of the organization described in the case? Provide your arguments in support of the recommended solution.

The study case adopted a simple strategy to closely integrate appropriate ICT tools into a serial of learning activities which comprise the ***W***arm-up learning before class, highly ***I***nteractive learning in class, and ***R***eview and ***E***xercise after class. That is the ***WIRE*** model.

The forum tool or blog can be used by students to reply the warm-up questions asked by the teacher for recalling the old knowledge and inspiring the learning of new knowledge. The classroom response system can be used for classroom interactive learning activity and allows teachers to know the students' learning effects just-in-time. The group discussion tool can be used to record the conclusions or unsolved problems discussed in face-to-face class if applicable. Finally, the stage of review and exercise can use the forum tool or blog to revise the answers posted in warm-up stage and to do exercises assigned by the teacher after class. Sometimes, the group discussion tool can be used for group exercise after class, such as the mini project of problem-based learning (PBL).

On the overview of whole learning process of the WIRE model, the ICT tools have been meaningfully integrated into the learning activities to form a highly interaction learning experience that can effectively achieve the corresponding objectives of each stage.

Epilogue and Lessons Learned

Right ICT tools should be adopted in right instructional strategy at right time to obtain the best learning outcome with technology. Blended learning stresses on the combination of online and face-to-face modalities to enrich and extend learning resources and gateways, but without meaningful use of ICT tools the additional way to learning is just an additional burden to teacher and an additional load to students. The learning outcome will be limited when the ICT tools are used independently. An instructional designer of blended learning should consider what ICT tool can play what role in the whole instructional plan to effectively achieve the learning objectives.

Lessons Learned

1. When the ICT tools were used as a medium to link all learning activities either online or face-to-face settings into a complete learning experience or model, the learning effect is better than the independent use of the ICT tools.
2. Most teachers definitely know that the warm-up before class is helpful for class interaction, but less strategy used can work effectively. By answering the warm-up questions asked by teachers before class on the web-based forum or personal blog, the teacher can initially know what misconceptions and background knowledge the students have by the browse of students' answers before class. In addition, those answers can be recorded in digital form and be used for the review of lessons after class. All the content of personal learning process is also a complete record for personal learning portfolio which can be an important reference for the further learning in the future.
3. The workload of teachers will increase in adopting WIRE model. However, the bulk of the work will be done in once when teachers repeatedly take the same subjects.

Chapter 16
Designing Effective Web-Based Courses in Engineering

Stelian Brad
Technical University of Cluj-Napoca, Romania

ABSTRACT

Developing engineering study programs of high quality, able to satisfy customized needs, with flexible paths of study, with easy and rapid access to the most appropriate educational facilities and lecturers is a critical and challenging issue for the future of engineering education. The latest developments in communication and information technologies facilitate the creation of reliable solutions in this respect. Provision of web-based courses in engineering represents one of these solutions. However, the absence of physical interactions with the training facilities and the specificity of remote collaboration with lecturers rise up additional challenges in designing a high-quality web-based engineering course. In order to define superior solutions to the complex set of requirements, quality planning and an innovative problem solving are parts of web-based engineering courses design process. In this context, the present chapter introduces a generic roadmap for competitive design of web-based engineering courses. Methodology application is illustrated in a case study. An important conclusion arising from the case study is that no unique, best-of-the-world solution exists in developing a web-based engineering course; therefore customized approaches should be considered for each course category to maximize the impact of the web-based educational process.

INTRODUCTION

Today's evolutions in science and technology lead to a rapid depreciation rate of knowledge in engineering. There are areas where this rate is less than one year; however, countless opinions consider an average depreciation rate of knowledge in engineering around three years. Producing companies operate in environments influenced by globalization, emphasising horizontal integration, innovation and customer satisfaction, while focusing on small number of business areas. In this very demanding economic

DOI: 10.4018/978-1-61520-869-2.ch016

environment, continuous training of engineers is vital for ensuring business competitiveness from technological perspectives. The very wide areas in engineering study rise up many challenges on how to approach properly the educational process. Experience clearly shows there is no general pattern for success. Depending on the subject area, personalized models and means are required to maximize the impact of the educational process (Barros, Read & Verdejo, 2008; Brad, 2005; Ogot & Okudan, 2007; Popescu, Brad & Popescu, 2006). Dynamics of changes in the economic environment determines both undergraduate and postgraduate students in engineering to look for flexible, high quality and financially affordable paths of study, for easy and rapid access to the most appropriate educational facilities and to the most appropriate lecturers and trainers to satisfy specific needs. A good opportunity in front of such expectations stands in web-based education, which exploits the facilities provided by the latest developments in communication and information technologies to remotely access, either off-line and/or on-line, real and virtual labs, libraries, documentation, tutorials, seminars, courses, etc. (e.g. Bhatt, Tang, Lee & Knovi, 2009; Callaghan, Harkin, McGinnity & Maguire, 2008; Du, Li & Li, 2008, Ebner & Walder, 2008; Helander & Emami, 2008).

Provision of web-based courses is not a simple task (Finger, Gelman, Fay & Szczerban, 2005; Lau, Mak & Ma, 2006; Li & Wang, 2007). Beyond the immanent technological challenges, there are other issues that require meticulous treatment. Life-cycles of most engineering courses are very short, therefore a major concern on designing and developing high-quality courses from the very first time occurs; that is, a concern for effective and efficient engineering course design. Web-based engineering courses rise up supplementary requirements and must overpass additional constrains than classical, face-to-face courses, like: virtual collaborative experimentation, interactive remote approach, collaborative remote learning, off-line active learning, cross-institutional collaboration, remote test and assessment (e.g. Helander & Emami, 2008; Hutchings, Hadfield, Horvath & Lewarne, 2007; Jou, Chuang, Wu & Yang, 2008; Mackey & Ho, 2008; Rizzotti & Burkhart, 2006; Wang, Dannenhoffer, Davidson & Spector, 2005). Therefore, a comprehensive planning is required to design a high-impact web-based engineering course (Bier & Cornesky, 2001; Brad, 2005; Brad, 2009; Koksal & Egitman, 1998; Ogot & Okudan, 2008).

For web-based engineering courses, special attention should be given to course structure, course subject, communication technology, teaching process management, costs, effort and time to prepare the course, dynamics of information, dynamics of the educational models, technology to provide the information, etc. (Barros, Read, & Verdejo, 2008; Du, Li & Li, 2008; Ebner & Walder, 2008; Helander & Emami, 2008; Li & Wang, 2007; Saygin & Kahraman, 2004; Sessink, van der Schaaf, Beeftink, Hartog & Tramper, 2007; Toral, Barrero & Martinez-Torres, 2007; Vargas, Sanchez, Duro, Dormido, Farias, Dormido, Esquembre, Salzmann & Gillet, 2008; Xuelian, 2008). All these areas of intervention are important for setting up a competitive web-based course in engineering. From this perspective, a web-based engineering course is revealed as a complex adaptable system (Brad, 2008). A web-based engineering course, seen as a "living" complex adaptable system, should be able to internalize information, to modify its parameters and behavior over its life-cycle, to compress information gathered from the interaction with the external environment and to "learn" from this interaction. Thus, a web-based engineering course should be evolutionary; and from this point of view the search is not for the "best of the world" solution (because it does not exist) but for mature solutions able to balance various dimensions characterizing a web-based engineering course. Elementary aspects about these dimensions are further brought into discussion.

The first dimension is referring to the course structure. The web-based course structure usually has some additional elements than a classical course. On one hand, this is because a web-based course is provided remotely, via electronic means. On the other hand, the limitations in terms of interaction between student and teacher require additional sections in the course structure, which could contain in some cases explanations on how to use the course material, as well as additional materials in electronic format that support the core unit of the course.

Content is another dimension of analysis for a web-based course. In principle, the content should be similar as in the case of a face-to-face course. However, a web-based course should contain supplementary questions and answers and/or supplementary case studies and exercises. Also, the information itself should be user-centric organized such as the information to be delivered in a more intuitive way – because of the remote, limited and less natural interaction of student with teacher and with other students. Sometimes, a web-based course could include supplementary explanations to compensate the lack of student interaction with the teacher. The volume of information should be carefully dimensioned, too, in order to avoid overloading the student's study time.

For storing the information of a web-based course, electronic formats are mainly used. Nowadays, a quite large variety of electronic formats for storing information is met. This ranges from usual "static" electronic files where information is stored in text, graphics and picture formats to more animated formats like web pages, electronic books, movies, simulations, interactive games, remote test benches, virtual instrumentation, etc. Focal points in this area are also about easy access of students to information using web technologies and about handling with minimum effort the course files on computers.

Communication technology is another key issue in the case of web-based engineering courses. It varies from already well-known, usual communication means like e-mails, web conferences and chats with web cameras as part of the system (e.g. Yahoo Messenger, Skype), to complex web-based video conference systems, web-based smart boards and remote desktop control server applications for interacting in the teaching/learning environment.

Management of the teaching process rises up specific challenges in the framework of web-based courses in engineering, too. A lot of web-based software platforms are available onto the market for handling various aspects of the teaching process like course scheduling, course content administration, student profiles, student attendance and results administration, forums, role management, access rights and so on. More and more popular are the open-source learning management systems (LMS) or virtual learning environments (VLE) like, for example, Moodle.

Besides the above mentioned characteristics, any initiative of setting up and running web-based courses requires a careful planning from financial, as well as economic points of view. This involves calculation of financial indicators for the investment in a web-based course like return on investment and internal rate of return, to which economic indicators like economic net present value can be added. The cost-benefit analysis should represent a major element for deciding the form in which a web-based course in engineering has to be designed and delivered.

Moreover, the dynamics and evolution of the educational environment should not be excluded from the list of relevant dimensions to which a web-based course is planned, designed and implemented. Dynamics of the educational environment is reflected in the interaction between the life-cycles of four sub-systems that describe the educational product – market needs and requirements, teaching-learning process, study program and educational provider. The four life-cycles must be well-balanced in order to create favourable premises for the provision of successful web-based courses in engineering (Popescu, Brad & Popescu, 2006). Evolution of the educational environment is reflected in the evolutions of the four sub-systems mentioned before as a consequence of various attractors. Attractors have to be seen as aggregated effects of some external influence factors acting with a relevant intensity upon these sub-systems, thus generating bifurcation points in their evolutions. For example, technological progress in the area of remote communication tools will influence the evolution of the teaching-learning process; as well, various transformations in the social and economic environments will influence the evolution of the educational provider models, etc.

Even if several new tools and paradigms have been developed and tested in the attempt of adapting the training in engineering to nowadays' needs, there are still many unknowns on how to develop a web-based course as a whole, not only limited to the teaching and learning methods. Almost any topic in engineering has particular characteristics, which implicitly requires a deep customization of a web-based course. Thus, a collection of complex problems must be crossed over to set up mature web-based courses in engineering. In conclusion, a web-based course in engineering must be "designed for customization" as any other kind of tailor-made product or service in order to achieve high quality levels (Brad, 2008; Brad, 2009). But such approaches require radical innovation and use of adequate planning tools during the conceptualization process of the web-based course. The next section of this chapter is going to propose such planning and synthesis methodology.

These circumstances ask for competitive design of web-based courses, where competitive design should be viewed as the implementation of an optimal framework and the use of adequate concepts, methods and tools in all aspects that define the engineering study in order to define, design and develop, from the very beginning and in a timeframe required by the educational market dynamics, of a high-impact engineering course. In other words, quality must be "designed" within the course before delivering the course to the students (Brad, 2005).

This chapter is going to introduce a roadmap for quality planning and innovation of web-based engineering courses. The methodology is exemplified in a case study dealing with the design of a web-based environment to support delivery of courses in robotic engineering. Quality planning is performed by combining QFD-type planning matrices (Bier & Cornesky, 2001; Brad, 2005; Kaminski, Ferreira & Theuer, 2004; Kumar & Labib, 2004; Ogot & Okudan, 2007; Popescu, Brad & Popescu, 2006; Raharjo, Xie, Goh & Brombacher, 2007; Suliman, 2006) with AHP/Saaty-type matrices (Raharjo, Xie, Goh & Brombacher, 2007; Saaty & Vargas, 2001). Innovation is supported by means of the TRIZ method (Altshuller, 2000; Brad, 2008).

METHODOLOGY

The methodology for systematic planning and innovation of a competitive web-based course in engineering integrates in a novel way QFD-based planning matrices with TRIZ inventive vectors in order to display and rank priorities of intervention and to formulate innovative solutions to various challenges. The methodology consists of several steps that are further revealed.

Step 1: The methodology starts with definition of business objectives in relation to the web-based course. Here, they are denoted with $BO_1, BO_2, \ldots, BO_m$, where m is the number of business objectives. In order to lead the planning process under various constrains (e.g. time, budget, technology, etc.), business objectives have to be ranked. The AHP method is proposed for performing this task. At the end of this process the following set of ranked business objectives is obtained: $BO(R(t)) = \{BO_1(\underline{R}_1(t)), BO_2(\underline{R}_2(t)), \ldots, BO_m(\underline{R}_m(t))\}$, where $\underline{R}_i(t)$, $i = 1, \ldots, m$, is the estimated degree of importance of the business objective BO_i, $i = 1, \ldots, m$, at the moment in time t when the course is delivered. Working with estimates instead of static values underlines the inconsistency of information between the moment of web-based course planning, conceptualization and development and the moment when the course is commercialized; thus showing the dynamic and evolutionary nature of the educational program. In other words, the importance given now to the business objectives might be different after *N* months (time t) when the course is delivered. Thus, because of the evolving educational environment, ranks at moment t can be only estimated, the accuracy of the estimates depending on the level of understanding the evolution and interaction of the influential factors of the educational environment. This philosophy is also transferred to the next steps of the methodology.

Step 2: In order to meet the business objectives, a set of target-functions is further formulated $TF = \{TF_1, TF_2, \ldots, TF_n\}$, where n is the number of target-functions. To see the consistency of the target-functions with the business objectives, a relationship matrix is worked out. It relates the business objectives (located on the rows of the matrix) with the target-functions (located on the columns of the matrix) by means of the so-called relationship coefficients (located at the intersections between the rows and the columns of the matrix).

The following categories of relationships between the business objectives and the target-function are taken into account: 0 – no relationship; 1 – weak/possible relationship; 3 – medium relationship; 9 – strong relationship; 27 – very strong/critical relationship (Brad, 2008). Along each column, at least a strong relationship must exist such as the corresponding target-function to be relevant. The estimated value weight $\underline{W}_j(t), j = 1, \ldots, n$, at the moment t, of each target-function is calculated with the formula:

$$\underline{W}_j(t) = \sum_{k=1}^{m} \underline{R}_k(t) \cdot a_{kj}, \quad j = \overline{1, n}, \qquad (1)$$

where a_{kj}, $k = 1, \ldots, m; j = 1, \ldots, n$ are the relationship coefficients between the business objectives and the target-functions. It is simple to deduce that designing for life-cycle of a web-based course requires consideration of various value weights of the target-functions at various life-time moments.

Step 3: For each target-function, requirements are formulated and ranked. For ranking, tools like AHP could be also used. Further, measurable performance characteristics are defined and related to requirements. There are denoted with $RE_h[TF_j], h = 1, \ldots, g[TF_j]$ the requirements related to the target-function TF_j, $j = 1, \ldots, n$, and with $\underline{U}_h(t)[TF_j], h = 1, \ldots, g[TF_j]$ the estimated degrees of importance of requirements $RE_h[TF_j]$, $h = 1, \ldots, g[TF_j]$ at the moment t. There are denoted with $PC_f[TF_j], f = 1, \ldots, d[TF_j]$ the performance characteristics related to the target-function TF_j, $j = 1, \ldots, n$. The estimated value weights of these performance characteristics, at the moment t, are denoted with $\underline{V}_f(t)[TF_j], f = 1, \ldots, d[TF_j]$ and calculated with the formula:

$$\underline{V}_f(t)[TF_j] = \sum_{l=1}^{g[TF_j]} \underline{U}_l(t)[TF_j] \cdot b_{lf}[TF_j], \quad f = \overline{1, d[TF_j]}, \quad j = \overline{1, n} \qquad (2)$$

where $b_{lf}[TF_j], f = 1, \ldots, d[TF_j]$ are the relationship coefficients of the planning matrix corresponding to the target-function TF_j, $j = 1, \ldots, n$. The value weights $\underline{V}_f(t)[TF_j]$, $f = 1, \ldots, d[TF_j]$ give a perspective of the most relevant performance characteristics in relation to the web-based course with respect to the target-function TF_j, $j = 1, \ldots, n$, at the moment t.

Step 4: The correlations between performance characteristics to the level of each target-function are identified. The negative correlations are extracted. A negative correlation between two performance characteristics occurs when attempting to improve one of the performance characteristics a harmful effect is generated upon the other one. Where negative correlations occur, innovation is required to define mature solutions of the web-based course. This kind of innovation is called in this paper "performance characteristic-oriented innovation". TRIZ method is applied at this step for each negative correlation in order to define vectors of innovation of the web-based course.

Step 5: For each performance characteristic a target is established. Achieving in a very short time high levels of quality of the web-based course represents a big challenge for any educational provider. This automatically requires innovation, which is here called "target-oriented innovation". For setting up appropriate lines of innovation of the web-based course, TRIZ method is applied at this step of the methodology. This step is related to each performance characteristic of each target-function.

Step 6: Development of a web-based course could meet some supplementary barriers coming up from financial, organizational and human resources constrains. This category of barriers necessitates further innovative solutions in setting up a competitive web-based course. Innovation in this area is called here "system-oriented innovation". TRIZ method could be also used at this point for tackling properly the innovative problem solving process. This step is related to each target-function.

Step 7: The set of vectors of innovation identified at steps 4, 5 and 6 are exploited for formulating local solutions of the web-based course. Each local solution should move towards satisfying as much as possible the requirements of the corresponding target-function, towards a so-called "local qualitative optimality". Local variants of the web-based course effectively show the "multiple" facets of the same system. They reveal the differences in relevance of the modules of the same system when it is placed in different contexts. This step actually brings to live one of the most important properties of complex systems: in a complex world there is no single best solution – otherwise the problem would not be considered complex. Thus, a set of n local solutions of the web-based course are elaborated at the end of this step. The set of local solutions is denoted $S = \{S_1, S_2, \ldots, S_n\}$.

Step 8: Local solutions have to be aggregated into a final solution, which, in principle, should comprise to the maximum possible extend the strengths of all local solutions. In order to generate the final solution of the web-based course as an aggregated result of the local solutions, a specific algorithm is required. An aggregation algorithm in five stages is further proposed.

The aggregation algorithm starts with the identification of the correlation types and correlation levels between the target-functions TF_1, $TF_2, \ldots, TF_n$. The correlation coefficients between the target-functions are denoted here with C_{jk}, $j = 1, \ldots, n, j \neq k$. The correlation coefficients could have negative values, positive values or null values, depending on the characteristics of the target-functions when they are compared each other (i.e. support, conflict or no relative influence). For defining the levels of correlation between the target-functions, the following values are very often used in practice: 0 – no correlation; 1 – weak positive correlation; 2 – medium positive correlation; 3 – strong positive correlation; -1 – weak negative correlation; -2 – medium negative correlation; -3 – strong negative correlation.

Further, the aggregation algorithm considers information from step 2 of the methodology. The target-function with the highest value weight in the set will be taken as the starting point in the aggregation algorithm. It is symbolized with *PTF* the target-function having the highest value weight from the n target-functions $TF_1, TF_2, \ldots, TF_n$. If $\underline{W}_{\max}(t)$ denotes the maximum value weight at the moment t, the following relationship comes up:

$$\underline{W}_{\max}(t) = \max\{\underline{W}_1(t), \underline{W}_2(t), \ldots, \underline{W}_n(t)\}\,. \quad (3)$$

In the next stage, the other target-functions are grouped relative to *PTF*. *PTF* is correlated with the other n–1 target-functions in various ways:

positive, negative or not correlated, as well as at various strengths. The type of correlation between two target-functions is determined by the correlations between their constitutive requirements. In this respect, the rest of the n–1 target-functions can be sorted on three categories: the group of those target-functions that are positive correlated with *PTF*, the group of those target-functions that are not correlated with *PTF* and the group of those target-functions that are negative correlated with *PTF*.

Further, the algorithm asks to order the target-functions inside each of the three groups. Considering that the *PTF* is the k-th target-function in the set *TF* from step 2, for the target-functions that are positive or negative correlated with *PTF* an index will be calculated; index denoted with $\underline{H}_j(t)$, $j = 1, \ldots, n, j \neq k$, as the product between the value weight $\underline{W}_j(t)$, $j = 1, \ldots, n, j \neq k$ and the correlation coefficient C_{jk}, $j = 1, \ldots, n, j \neq k$. This formula is shown below:

$$\underline{H}_j(t) = \underline{W}_j(t) \cdot C_{jk},\ j = \overline{1,n},\ j \neq k,\ C_{jk} \neq 0\,. \tag{4}$$

In the group of target-functions that are positive correlated with *PTF*, the target-functions will be ordered starting with the one having the highest H and ending with the one having the lowest H. The same rule is kept for the group of target-functions that are negative correlated with *PTF*. It is highlighted the fact that $C_{jk} < 0$ in the group of negative correlated target-functions, so the one with the highest H will have the lowest magnitude in absolute value, too. The target-functions that are not correlated with *PTF* will be ordered starting with the one having the highest value weight W and ending with the one having the lowest value weight W.

In the last stage, the aggregated solution is generated following an iterative approach. The aggregated solution will result as a "compromise & combination" of the set of n local solutions. In this respect, the following rule is applied:

a. The solution corresponding to the *PTF* will be taken and analyzed together with the solution corresponding to the first target-function in the group of the target-functions that are positive correlated with *PTF*. Because the two target-functions are positive correlated, the best ideas from the local solutions will be combined, resulting an improved hybrid solution.
b. The hybrid solution from (a) will be then analyzed against the local solution corresponding to the second target-function in the group of the target-functions that are positive correlated with *PTF*. The new variant will result as a combination of the best ideas from the hybrid solution generated at phase (a) and from the current local variant.
c. The process will go on in the manner above described until all target-functions from the group of target-functions that are positive correlated with *PTF* are consumed. After that, the group of no correlated target-functions is taken into account and the process is continued until all of these target-functions are consumed. At the end, the group of target-functions that are negative correlated with *PTF* will be taken into account. Because at this phase potential conflicts could occur, they have to be solved without compromises, if possible. In this respect, it is firstly required to identify pairs of conflicting problems between the compared variants. Afterwards, innovative solutions have to be formulated. Methods like TRIZ could offer a real support in this respect. At the end of this process, the complete overall solution will be defined.

Step 9: The result is reviewed with respect to the most relevant performance characteristics of each target-functions and with respect to a cost-objective. Relevance of the performance characteristics for each target-function TF_j, $j = 1, \ldots, n$, is given by their value weights $\underline{V}_f(t)[TF_j]$, $f = 1, \ldots, d[TF_j]$. If failures are identified both in terms of cost and technical performances, improvements are further formulated. To perform this task properly, various innovative problem solving tools could be also considered (e.g. TRIZ, ARIZ, Su-Field, USIT, ASIT).

CASE STUDY

In order to exemplify the methodology, a case study is elaborated. The application example is referring to a web-based course about engineering design of industrial robots, which has to be delivered to a branch *X* of the university *Y*, placed in other locality. The course includes lectures and project work (e.g. engineering design of a robotic module). To keep the case study relative simple, as well as in a reasonable paper volume, only a limited set of target-functions and requirements describing the target-functions will be further considered.

Thus, in this application example, the following business objectives have been considered to frame the analysis and design space of the web-based course: BO_1 – to minimize possible frustrations of the students located in the facility *X* because of less face-to-face contact with the lecturers [37%]; BO_2 – to be relative easy accepted and adopted by the lecturers with less experience in using information and communication technologies and tools [12%]; BO_3 – the quality of the teaching process not being affected because of the remote performance [33%]; BO_4 – the operation and maintenance costs to be acceptable [9%]; BO_5 – the return on investment to be attractive [9%]. Values between brackets reveal the relative ranks of the business objectives, as they have been determined with the AHP method.

In relation to the business objectives, the following target-functions will be taken into account: design for easy and fast scalability [TF_1], design for cost affordability [TF_2], design for fast development and implementation [TF_3], and design for reliability [TF_4]. Table 1 reveals the deployment process of the business objectives into target-functions. The relationship matrix, the correlation matrix and the calculated value weights of the target-functions are put into evidence.

According to the results in Table 1, for this case study a special attention should be given to design for reliability and design for cost affordability. For each target-function the set of requirements and related performance characteristics are defined. The deployment process of requirements into performance characteristics is revealed for

Table 1. Deployment of business objectives into target-functions

TF_4					
TF_3					+1
TF_2					-2
TF_1			-1	+2	
Target-functions		TF_1	TF_2	TF_3	TF_4
Business objectives	Degree of importance	Relationship matrix (bottom) and Correlation matrix (up)			
BO_1	3.7	3		1	27
BO_2	1.2	3		27	9
BO_3	3.3	9		9	27
BO_4	0.9	9	27	1	9
BO_5	0.9	9	27	27	
Value weight [%]		14.9	11.9	22.3	50.9

Table 2. House of scalability

$PC_8[TF_1]$									
$PC_7[TF_1]$									+1
$PC_6[TF_1]$									
$PC_5[TF_1]$									+1
$PC_4[TF_1]$						+1		+1	+1
$PC_3[TF_1]$									
$PC_2[TF_1]$				+1	+1	+1			
$PC_1[TF_1]$									
Metric		$PC_1[TF_1]$		$PC_3[TF_1]$	$PC_4[TF_1]$	$PC_5[TF_1]$			$PC_8[TF_1]$
Optimization trend		min	max	min	min	min	max	min	min
Requirement	$U \backslash D$	1	2	3	4	2	2	2	2
$RE_1[TF_1]$	3.2	9	27	1	27	27		1	1
$RE_2[TF_1]$	3.2	27	3	27	3	9		3	1
$RE_3[TF_1]$	1.8		1		9	9	9	3	9
$RE_4[TF_1]$	1.8		3		3	9	27	9	27
Value weight		115.2	103.2	89.6	117.6	147.6	64.8	34.4	71.2
Value weight [%]		15.5	13.9	12.1	15.8	19.8	8.7	4.6	9.6
Global weight [%]		2.3	2.1	1.8	2.4	2.9	1.3	0.7	1.4
Most relevant		x	x		x	x			
Target		< 60 s	All	< 600 s	< 1 h	→ 0	> 50	< 600 s	→ 0

each target-function in Tables 2, 3, 4 and 5. In the case of target-function TF_1 (design for easy and fast scalability), the following requirements are considered: $RE_1[TF_1]$ – Good functional scalability (system enhancement by adding new functionalities at minimal effort: fast and easy adding new files in any format, fast and easy adding or removing communication tools, fast and easy adding or removing new multi-media applications, etc.); $RE_2[TF_1]$ – Good load scalability (fast and easy expanding or contracting its resource pool, fast and easy adding new files to the course, fast modification of files' content and structure, etc.); $RE_3[TF_1]$ – Good geographic scalability (maintenance of performance, usefulness and usability regardless of expansion and concentration to a more distributed geographic area); $RE_4[TF_1]$ – Good administrative scalability (capacity to increase easy and fast the number of terminals for sharing a single distributed system). The degrees of importance for these requirements are determined with the AHP method and have the following values: $U[TF_1] = \{32\%, 32\%, 18\%, 18\%\}$. The related performance characteristics are: $PC_1[TF_1]$ – Time required adding new files; $PC_2[TF_1]$ – Number of file formats allowed; $PC_3[TF_1]$ – Time required modifying information; $PC_4[TF_1]$ – Time required integrating new tools; $PC_5[TF_1]$ – Cost required integrating new tools; $PC_6[TF_1]$ – Number of remote terminals; $PC_7[TF_1]$ – Time required integrating/removing new terminals; $PC_8[TF_1]$ – Cost required integrating/removing new terminals.

For the target-function TF_2 (design for cost affordability), the related requirements are as follow: $RE_1[TF_2]$ – Affordable life-cycle costs (operating costs, maintenance costs, replacement costs, scalability costs, disposal costs, support

Table 3. House of affordability

$PC_5[TF_2]$						
$PC_4[TF_2]$						+2
$PC_3[TF_2]$						
$PC_2[TF_2]$				+2	+1	+2
$PC_1[TF_2]$			+1	+1	+2	+1
Metric		$PC_1[TF_2]$	$PC_2[TF_2]$	$PC_3[TF_2]$	$PC_4[TF_2]$	$PC_5[TF_2]$
Optimization trend		max	max	max	min	min
Requirement	$U \setminus D$	5	4	3	3	2
$RE_1[TF_2]$	4.0	9	27	27	27	27
$RE_2[TF_2]$	3.0	27	27	9	27	
$RE_3[TF_2]$	3.0	27	27	3	9	1
Value weight		198	270	144	216	111
Value weight [%]		21.1	28.8	15.3	23.0	11.8
Global weight [%]		2.5	3.4	1.9	2.7	1.4
Most relevant		x	x		x	
Target		> 250%	> 0	> 1	< 1.5 years	< 5%

Table 4. House of development

$PC_5[TF_3]$						
$PC_4[TF_3]$						
$PC_3[TF_3]$					+1	+1
$PC_2[TF_3]$						
$PC_1[TF_3]$			+1			
Metric		$PC_1[TF_3]$	$PC_2[TF_3]$	$PC_3[TF_3]$	$PC_4[TF_3]$	$PC_5[TF_3]$
Optimization trend		min	min	min	min	min
Requirement	$U \setminus D$	3	5	2	3	2
$RE_1[TF_3]$	2.0	27	27	9	9	9
$RE_2[TF_3]$	3.5	9	1	27	1	1
$RE_3[TF_3]$	1.5		9	9	27	1
$RE_4[TF_3]$	3.0	3	9	9	3	27
Value weight		94.5	98.0	153.0	71.0	104.0
Value weight [%]		18.2	18.8	29.4	13.6	20.0
Global weight [%]		4.1	4.2	6.5	3.0	4.5
Most relevant		x	x	x		x
Target		< 20% of the time required to elaborate a classical course	< 20% of the costs required to elaborate a classical course	< 1 h	< 2 h	< 300 s

Table 5. House of reliability

$PC_8[TF_4]$									
$PC_7[TF_4]$									+1
$PC_6[TF_4]$								+1	+1
$PC_5[TF_4]$									+2
$PC_4[TF_4]$						+2			
$PC_3[TF_4]$					-2	+1			
$PC_2[TF_4]$				-1	-2				
$PC_1[TF_4]$			-2	+1	+1				
Metric		$PC_1[TF_4]$	$PC_2[TF_4]$	$PC_3[TF_4]$	$PC_4[TF_4]$				$PC_8[TF_4]$
Optimization trend		max	min	min	max	max	min	min	max
Requirement	$U \backslash D$	5	5	4	3	5	4	3	4
$RE_1[TF_4]$	2.5	27	27	27	27				3
$RE_2[TF_4]$	2.5	3	27	27	27	27			9
$RE_3[TF_4]$	1.0		1				3	9	
$RE_4[TF_4]$	1.5						27	27	
$RE_5[TF_4]$	1.5	27	27	9	9				3
$RE_6[TF_4]$	1.0		3			9			27
Value weight		115.5	179.5	148.5	148.5	76.5	43.5	49.5	61.5
Value weight [%]		14.0	21.8	18.0	18.0	9.3	5.3	6.1	7.5
Global weight [%]		7.1	11.1	9.2	9.2	4.7	2.7	3.1	3.8
Most relevant		x	x	x	x				
Target		> 12 h continuous work	< 6 Mb/s	< 40 ms	> 1024 × 768	> 90%	< 150 s	< 600 s	> 90%

costs, administrative costs, etc.); $RE_2[TF_2]$ –Affordable level of the initial investment (system's price, installation and testing costs, training costs, etc.); $RE_3[TF_2]$ – Attractive financial indicators. The degrees of importance for these requirements are determined with the AHP method and have the following values: $U[TF_2]$ = {40%, 30%, 30%}. The main performance characteristics related to the target-function TF_2 are the followings: $PC_1[TF_2]$ – Return on investment; $PC_2[TF_2]$ – Net present value; $PC_3[TF_2]$ – Benefit/cost ratio; $PC_4[TF_2]$ – Payback period; $PC_5[TF_2]$ – Percentage of the annual operational costs from the initial investment.

In this case study, in relation with the target-function TF_3 (design for fast development and implementation) the key requirements for web-based course planning are the followings: $RE_1[TF_3]$ – Easy and fast adaptation of a classical course to a web-based course; $RE_2[TF_3]$ – Short time required to train students and lecturers in using the system; $RE_3[TF_3]$ – Short time for setting up the system; $RE_4[TF_3]$ – Short time for initiating working sessions (lectures, project work, consultancy, etc.). The AHP method is also applied to calculate the degrees of importance for TF_3-related requirements. They have the following values: $U[TF_3]$ = {20%, 35%, 15%, 30%}. The performance characteristics associated to the target-function TF_3 are the followings: $PC_1[TF_3]$ – Time required to adapt a classical course to a web-based course;

$PC_2[TF_3]$ – Costs required to adapt a classical course to a web-based course; $PC_3[TF_3]$ – Time required to train students/lecturers to use the system; $PC_4[TF_3]$ – Time required to set up the system (hardware and software); $PC_5[TF_3]$ – Time required to initiate the working session.

For the target-function TF_4 (design for reliability) the selected requirements for system's planning are: $RE_1[TF_4]$ – High quality of signal transmission (signal continuity, sound quality, image quality, etc.); $RE_2[TF_4]$ – High capacity of interaction student-teacher (speaking, seeing, writing, drawing, cooperation); $RE_3[TF_4]$ – Easy testing of the system; $RE_4[TF_4]$ – Easy error tracking and fast problem fixing; $RE_5[TF_4]$ – Low internet resources required; $RE_6[TF_4]$ – Good course management (session record, file management, student work management, etc.). In the case of the target-function TF_4 the degrees of importance of the related requirements are: $U[TF_4]$ = {25%, 25%, 10%, 15%, 15%, 10%}.

The main performance characteristics taken into account for the target-function TF_4 are the followings: $PC_1[TF_4]$ – Mean time between failures; $PC_2[TF_4]$ – Average bandwidth required; $PC_3[TF_4]$ – Delay; $PC_4[TF_4]$ – Resolution; $PC_5[TF_4]$ – Level of interaction relative to a face-to-face meeting; $PC_6[TF_4]$ – Time required to identify the problem; $PC_7[TF_4]$ – Time required to fix the most complex problem and restart the system; $PC_8[TF_4]$ – Monitoring level of students with respect to a face-to-face meeting.

Table 2 illustrates the deployment of TF_1-related requirements into TF_1-related performance characteristics. The set of matrices from Table 2 is called "house of scalability". According to the results in Table 2, the most relevant performance characteristics for web-course optimization in relation to TF_1 are: time required integrating new tools, cost required integrating new tools, time required adding new files and number of file formats allowed. With D, in Table 2, as well as in Tables 3, 4 and 5 is denoted the degree of difficulty to solve performance characteristics. The rank of D is given on a five-point Likart scale (from 1 "less difficulty" to 5 "very high difficulty"). Difficulty is seen from organizational and financial points of view.

With respect to D, for the target-function TF_1, innovation should be mainly directed towards the performance characteristic $PC_4[TF_1]$ (time required integrating new tools). According to the results in Table 2, no "performance characteristic-oriented innovation" is specially required because only positive correlations exist between performance characteristics (see step 4 of the methodology). With respect to the current state of technological progress, "target-oriented innovation" (see step 5 of the methodology) should be mainly directed towards $PC_5[TF_1]$ (cost required to integrate new tools).

Thus, with respect to $PC_4[TF_1]$, the mini-problem which necessitates innovation could be formulated as: (a) to reduce the time for integrating new tools by involving low costs; and (b) to reduce the time for integrating new tools by involving low efforts. In TRIZ-language, this problem shows like: time [9] versus amount of substance [26]; and time [9] versus energy spent by moving objects [19] (Altshuller, 2000). Numbers in brackets show the position of the generic parameters in the "TRIZ table of generic parameters causing conflicts" (Altshuller, 2000). For the first set of generic conflicts, the following generic directions of intervention are recommended by TRIZ: use the resonance frequency [18], replace a continuous action with an impulse (and if it necessary use pauses between impulses to introduce additional actions) [19], replace "solid" parts with "fluidic" parts [29], enrich the "atmosphere" with supplementary components [38]. Numbers in brackets show the position of the directions of intervention in the "TRIZ table of inventive vectors" (Altshuller, 2000). For the second set of generic conflicts, the following generic directions of intervention are recommended by TRIZ: compensate a certain "weight" with forces coming from the external environment [8], make the system more dynamic (with components able to change their position, with higher mobility and interchangeability, with capacities of automatic adjustments) [15], change the degree of flexibility or density or volume [35], enrich the "atmosphere" with supplementary components [38].

In accordance with the above recommended directions of innovation, a possible solution of the web-based course to meet the major scalability requirements is the following: materials can be prepared in any format (e.g. .ppt, .pdf, .doc, .xls, .jpg, .cdr, .avi, etc.) – principle 18; students can download files from a repository system (e.g. Moodle) – principle 19; students can open any file on their computers (alternatively, the file can be displayed on a screen by means of a multimedia projector) – principle 35; multiple modes of communication are ensured (e.g. off-line via e-mails; on-line via Skype, Yahoo messenger, etc.) – principle 29; web-cameras are used for visual contact – principle 38; alternatively, for a better interaction with the classroom, a videoconference system replaces the communication on web messenger systems and web-cameras – in this respect, two video cameras are used: one camera broadcasts person(s) A (e.g. the teacher) and displays the image that the other camera broadcasts; the other camera broadcasts person(s) B (e.g. the students) while displaying image received from the place where person(s) A is(are) located – principle 38; teacher can handle remotely each camera – principle 8; both teacher and student have to have direct internet connections and real IP addresses (a broadband internet connection is recommended) – principle 15; teacher works on his/her tablet PC, which has to have a direct internet access – principle 38; teacher uses a remote desktop control server application (e.g. a free license, like VNC) in order to display remotely any application that runs on his/her computer – principle 35; if the PC is a tablet PC, teacher can use a virtual whiteboard to interact even more with students (e.g. CorelGrafigo, Windows Journal, etc.) – principle 38; moreover, teacher can run a system application for remote monitoring of computers in the network – principle 35. These solutions allow a comprehensive and multimodal provision of the course content (drawings, films, text, simulations, dynamic annotations, on-line hand written and sketches, on-line running of any application on computers, etc.).

In order to meet the target with respect to the performance characteristic $PC_5[TF_1]$, the following TRIZ mini-problems are revealed: (a) amount of substance [26] versus harmful side effects [31]; (b) amount of substance [26] versus loss of information [24]; and (c) amount of substance [26] versus convenience of use [33]. The generic directions of interventions recommended by TRIZ are: group (a): transition from a homogeneous structure to a heterogeneous structure of the system or of the external environment [3], change the degree of flexibility or density or volume [35], define a composite structure of the system [40], introduce a neutral "substance" or "additive" [39]; group (b): use a mediator to do the action [24], replace "mechanical" components with "simple or complex fields" [28], change the degree of flexibility or density or volume [35]; group (c): change the degree of flexibility or density or volume [35], replace "solid" parts with "fluidic" parts [29], make use of "waste material" or make the system to serve itself [25], carry out in advance some actions or put the components of the system such as to come fast into action when necessary [10].

In addition to the technical elements defined a paragraph before, the following ones should be considered to meet the major scalability requirements: build the web-course system having both web-cameras and videoconference units – principle 3; provide also materials with detailed information and explanations on how to use the course, considering supplementary case studies and exercises, thus facilitating off-line learning – principle 28; provide records of the course, and simulations, etc. – principle 28; use local assistants to support teacher for any small inconvenient caused by the remote interaction – principle 24;

record the session for later use – principle 25; combine remote sessions with one or two face-to-face sessions – principle 40; train the users in advance on how to use the system (e.g. demos, intuitive guiding manuals, face-to-face practical sessions) – principle 10.

An analysis of these technical elements against the most relevant scalability performance characteristics highlighted in Table 2 shows the web-based course system meets the intended targets (e.g. any file format is supported, any software application running on the teacher's desktop is seen on students' screens, time required to use any new software application is almost instantaneous, etc.).

Table 3 illustrates deployment of TF_2-related requirements into TF_2-related performance characteristics. The set of matrices from Table 3 is called "house of affordability". According to the results in Table 3, the most relevant performance characteristics for web-course optimization in relation to TF_2 are: return on investment, net present value and payback period. In terms of "system-oriented innovation" (factor *D* in Table 3), innovations from organizational and financial points of view should be mainly directed towards high return on investment and net present value. In other words, this requires relative low initial investments, as well as continuous and significant savings, relevant incomes even from early phases of course launching, supplemented by low operating and administrative costs. As in the case of design for scalability, no innovations generated by conflicts between performance characteristics are necessary. In terms of targets, innovations are mainly on achieving a high rate of the return on investment.

In this case, the following conflicting problems are formulated: (a) durability of the moving object [15] versus amount of substance [26]; and (b) brightness [18] versus amount of substance [26]. With respect to these conflicting problems, the following generic directions of innovation are suggested by TRIZ: group (a): transition from a homogeneous structure to a heterogeneous structure of the system or of the external environment [3], change the degree of flexibility or density or volume [35], carry out in advance some actions or put the components of the system such as to come fast into action when necessary [10], define a composite structure of the system [40]; group (b): increase the segmentation of the system [1], replace a continuous action with an impulse (and if it necessary use pauses between impulses to introduce additional actions) [19].

In order to meet cost-affordability requirements (see results in Table 3), the web-based course could comprise the following main technical elements: use open source repository systems (e.g. Moodle), where any file format can be uploaded/downloaded – principle 35; multiple free communication modes are ensured (e.g. off-line via e-mails; on-line via Skype, Yahoo messenger) combined with usual web-cameras for visual contact – principle 40; teacher uses a free license remote desktop control server application (e.g. VNC) in order to display remotely any application that runs on his/her computer – principle 35; file formats are limited to those which are immediate accessible to the teacher, with no supplementary costs for realization – principle 1; train the users in advance on how to use the system by means of face-to-face practical sessions and/or a simple guiding procedure – principle 10; use local assistants from the audience – principle 3; let students know in advance how to set up the system for the next session – principle 10; use asynchronous means to learn (e.g. links to specialized web-sites, electronic books, etc.) – principle 19; compensate the lack of good interactivity with more detailed written materials and run the course for larger groups of students at a time – principle 1. This solution involves low investment. Combined with qualified teachers and high quality written materials, this solution could lead to attractive values of the return on investment.

Table 4 illustrates deployment of TF_3-related requirements into TF_3-related performance characteristics. The set of matrices from Table 4 is called "house of development". According to the results in Table 4, the most relevant performance characteristics for web-course optimization in relation to TF_3 are: time required to adapt a classical course to a web-based course, costs required to adapt a classical course to a web-based course, time required to train students/lecturers to use the system and time required to initiate the working session. There are no conflicts between the performance characteristics, thus no innovations are required in this dimension. However, organizational innovations should be considered in relation to factor *D*, mainly for reducing costs necessary to adapt a classical course to a web-based course (see Table 4), as well as to meet the target (less than 20% from the development costs of a classical course).

In the case of target-function TF_3, the following generic conflicting problems are formulated with respect to organizational challenges: (a) amount of substance [26] versus convenience of use [33]; (b) amount of substance [26] versus capacity [39]. With respect to meeting key targets, the following TRIZ-type challenges are defined: (c) "tension (pressure)" [11] versus volume of non-moving object [8]; (d) "tension (pressure)" [11] versus harmful side effects [31]. TRIZ recommends the following paths of intervention for these problems: group (a): change the degree of flexibility or density or volume [35], replace "solid" parts with "fluidic" parts [29], make use of "waste material" or make the system to serve itself [25], carry out in advance some actions or put the components of the system such as to come fast into action when necessary [10]; group (b): inversion (do the things vice versa than usual) [13], replace "solid" parts with "fluidic" parts [29], transition from a homogeneous structure to a heterogeneous structure of the system or of the external environment [3], replace an expensive system with several inexpensive systems, comprising some properties [27]; group (c): change the degree of flexibility or density or volume [35], use a mediator to do the action [24]; group (d): extract or separate some disturbing parts from the system [2], apply homogeneity principles [33], replace an expensive system with several inexpensive systems, comprising some properties [27], use the resonance frequency [18].

The solution related to the target-function "design for fast development and implementation" shall follow several directions of intervention that are common with the target-function "design for scalability". In this respect, materials can be prepared in any format (e.g. .ppt, .pdf, .doc, .xls, .jpg, .cdr, .avi, etc.) and a repository system is used for file management (e.g. Moodle) to upload and download files on computers, too – see principle 35. Multiple communication modes are implemented (e.g. e-mail; Skype, Yahoo messenger, web-cameras) – see principle 18. For a better interaction with the classroom, a videoconference system can be taken into account. Teacher uses a remote desktop control server application (e.g. VNC) for handling remotely any application that runs on his/her computer. If a tablet PC is part of the system, teacher can use a virtual whiteboard to interact even more with students (e.g. CorelGrafigo, Windows Journal, etc.). Moreover, teacher can run specialized applications for monitoring computers in the network. In addition, students can work in close connection with the teacher for structuring the classical course to a web-based course. In this respect, each student can receive a small homework with the purpose of adapting a sub-chapter of the classical course into a web-based one. This means they will reformulate the content according to their understanding, will add questions and will indicate where more explanations and exercises are required. Thus, teacher can easier and faster intervene to develop the web-based course. This action is in accordance with principle 13. Principle 27 encourages the use of virtual modules to train students (e.g. for the course of industrial robot design that is treated in this case study, students can use robot off-line programming and modelling systems like RobotStudio, which have the capability to be installed on a server and accessed via internet from any location). The use of local assistants for supporting teacher in classes is also indicated in this case (principle 24). According to principle 2, it is encouraged to replace the classical pedagogical methods with problem-based and project-based learning methods. Cooperative learning strategies are highlighted by principle 33. The solution meets the targets established for fast development and implementation of the web-based course (review the targets in Table 4).

In Table 5, deployment of TF_4-related requirements into TF_4-related performance characteristics is revealed. The set of matrices from Table 5 is called "house of reliability". Major considerations in web-course design should be given to improve the following metrics: mean time between failures, average bandwidth required, signal delay and resolution. With respect to this target-function, several innovations are required to overpass the conflicts existing between various metrics (see Table 5). Thus, innovative solutions are necessary to avoid signal loss at low bandwidth, to avoid signal delays at low bandwidth, to ensure high resolution at low bandwidth and to avoid delays if the resolution has to be kept high. From organizational point of view, innovation is required for keeping a high level of interaction between students and teachers. From targets point of view, the main focus is on student-teacher interaction and quality of signal transmission (see Table 5).

In the case of TF_4, the vectors of innovation are directed towards three major areas: (a) to approach the conflicts between performance characteristics, (b) to approach targets, and (c) to approach organizational challenges. For the first category of problems, TRIZ reflects the following generic conflicts: (a_1) loss of information [24] versus speed (time) [9]; (a_2) stability of object [13] versus speed (time) [9]; (a_3) brightness [18] versus speed (time) [9]; (a_4) brightness [18] versus harmful side effects [31]. For the second category of problems, the following challenges have to be tackled: (b_1) accuracy of process [29] versus power [21]; (b_2) accuracy of process [29] versus volume of moving object [7]; (b_3) accuracy of process [29] versus amount of substance [26]; (b_4) capacity [39] versus power [21]; (b_5) reliability [27] versus speed (time) [9]. For the third category of problems, the following TRIZ-related generic conflicting parameters have to be approached: (c_1) convenience of use [33] versus complexity of system [36]; (c_2) convenience of use [33] versus "shape" (type of course) [12].

In relation to this, the following generic inventive vectors are revealed by TRIZ matrix of contradictions: group (a_1): use simple and inexpensive "copies" of the system [26], use "additives" to see processes that are difficult to see or change the "colour" or the level of transparency of the system [32]; group (a_2): apply homogeneity principles [33], make the system more dynamic (with components able to change their position, with higher mobility and interchangeability, with capacities of automatic adjustments) [15], replace "mechanical" components with "simple or complex fields" [28], use the resonance frequency [18]; group (a_3): carry out in advance some actions or put the components of the system such as to come fast into action when necessary [10], inversion (do the things vice versa than usual) [13], replace a continuous action with an impulse (and if it necessary use pauses between impulses to introduce additional actions) [19]; group (a_4): change the degree of flexibility or density or volume [35], replace a continuous action with an impulse (and if it necessary use pauses between impulses to introduce additional actions) [19], use "additives" to see processes that are difficult to see or change the "colour" or the level of transparency of the system [32], introduce a neutral "substance" or "additive" [39]; group (b_1): use "additives" to see processes that are difficult to see or change the "colour" or the level of transparency of the system [32], extract or separate some disturbing parts from the system [2]; group (b_2): use "additives" to see processes that are difficult to see or change the "colour" or the level of transparency of the system [32], replace "mechanical" components with "simple or complex fields" [28], extract or separate some disturbing parts from the system [2]; group (b_3): use "additives" to see processes that are difficult to see or change the "colour" or the level of transparency of the system [32], use "flexible membranes" [30]; group (b_4): change the degree of flexibility or density or volume [35], make objects of the system to operate continuously, without pauses [20], carry out in advance some actions or put the components of the system such as to come fast into action when necessary [10]; group (b_5): perform harmful operations at very high speeds [21], change the degree of flexibility or density or volume [35], compensate for the relatively low reliability of the system by taking countermeasures in advance [11], replace "mechanical" components with "simple or complex fields" [28]; group (c_1): use "additives" to see processes that are difficult to see or change the "colour" or the level of transparency of the system [32], use simple and inexpensive "copies" of the system [26], apply the equipotentiality principle [12], use multi-level assembly of the system / move the problem into several "dimensions" [17]; group (c_2): make the system more dynamic (with components able to change their position, with higher mobility and interchangeability, with capacities of automatic adjustments) [15], reject and regenerate parts of the system [34], replace "solid" parts with "fluidic" parts [29], replace "mechanical" components with "simple or complex fields" [28].

In the case of the last target-function, a large set of vectors of innovation are proposed to support the conceptualization process of the web-based course system. Many of them are already met in relation to the previous target-functions (e.g. principles 33, 35, 29, 15, 28, 18, 10, 19, 39, 2, 11). Solutions proposed in those cases are naturally included here, too. Thus, materials can be prepared in any format and students can download files from a repository system (e.g. Moodle). Students can open any file on their computers (alternatively, the file can be displayed on a screen by means of a multi-media projector) and multiple modes of communication are provided (e.g. e-mails, Skype, Yahoo messenger, etc.). Web-cameras and/or videoconference systems are integrated. Teacher uses a tablet PC and a remote desktop control server application (e.g. VNC) in order to handle remotely any application that runs on his/her tablet PC. The tablet PC, together with specific software applications (e.g. CorelGrafigo, Windows Journal, etc.), acts as a virtual interactive whiteboard. A specific application for remote computer monitoring is integrated to "see" and "record" any action of each student on his/her terminal. Thus, a comprehensive and multimodal provision of the course content is ensured. Materials with detailed information and explanations on how to use the course material, with supplementary case studies and exercises are also provided, thus facilitating off-line learning. Local assistants are included in the scheme. Sessions are recorded for further use. Remote sessions are combined with one or two face-to-face meetings. All users are trained in advance for handling the system (e.g. demos, intuitive guiding manuals and face-to-face practical meetings). A group of students could also cooperate with the teacher before course delivery to "translate" the classical course to a web-based course (students are granted for this effort). Problem-based and project-based learning methods should be the core pedagogical approaches for course delivery. Cooperative learning strategies are also included. To these components of the web-based course system, some additional elements should be considered. They are suggested by the inventive principles 26, 32, 30, 20, 21, 26, 12, 17 and 34. Thus, films and simulations that are free on internet could be included in various places of the course to improve information content – principle 26. In the same spirit, courses can be recorded in advance and uploaded on the repository system. Complex designs (as it is the case of industrial robots) and complex hardware technical systems can be replaced with virtual systems (today, there are simulators for robots, PLCs, controllers, etc.). Development of partnerships with local companies for facilitating access of the students to various hardware solutions should be taken into account – principle 32. According to the same principle, students can be pre-grouped to work together in activity centres (when this thing is possible). According to principle 30, it is encouraged that some students to mentor other students. Principle 20 suggests a continuous evaluation of students, not only at the end phase of the course and encourages project-based and exercise-based course delivery. Principle 21 focuses on quality of transmission. In this respect, videoconference systems with facilities of fast resetting should be the option. In addition, the consideration of redundant solutions for communication is required (web-cameras, internet messaging systems), thus acting as a "plan B". Moreover, courses have to be recorded in advance, as a "plan C" for the cases of longer period internet connection breakdown – principle 26. Principle 12 clearly asks to consider multiple technologies of course delivery that can be easy and fast adapted to meet varying student needs. Principle 17 recommends the use of experiential learning rather than theoretical learning; therefore simulation tools which replicate accurately the real systems are necessary (e.g. in the case of industrial robot design, students can use web-based modelling and simulation tools like RobotStudio, which replicate real systems with very high accuracy). Projects can be remotely analyzed by the teacher, too, using the virtual whiteboard and the tablet PC, as well as a remote desktop control server application and a videoconference system. Principle 34 suggests the use of practical activities in companies. This is possible even for web-based courses. Also, this principle encourages for periodical change of the instructional activities in order to keep student interest for the course. This can be done by means of exercises.

The solutions proposed above converge to the main targets expressed by the function "design for reliability". Specifically, they are able to ensure a good interaction between student and teacher, and from technical point of view (e.g. signal quality) are feasible, too.

The next step of the methodology requires aggregation of the local solutions. According to the proposed algorithm, *PTF* is in this case study associated to TF_4. The aggregation flow for this case study starts by combining the local solution related to TF_4 with the local solution related to TF_3. The hybrid result, here named HF_1, is further combined with the local solution of TF_1. The new hybrid, named HF_2, is further combined with the local solution of TF_2.

From aggregation point of view, the first two steps raise up no problems, because solutions are either positive (TF_4 with TF_3) or not correlated (HF_1 with TF_1). The challenge occurs when aggregation is required between HF_2 and the local solution related to TF_2. Thus, HF_1 will incorporate all common components of the local solutions related to TF_4 and TF_3, to which all individual components of the local solutions related to TF_4 and TF_3 are added (please review the local solutions for TF_4 and TF_3). Moreover, HF_2 will include all components of HF_1, to which the individual components of the local solution related to TF_1 are added (please review the local solution for TF_1).

Analyzing the main characteristics of the local solution related to TF_2 against the hybrid solution HF_2, the following major conflicting problems occur: (a) need of videoconference system (HF_2) versus avoidance of expensive equipment (TF_2); (b) need of simulation tools which accurately replicate real systems (HF_2) versus avoidance of expensive software (TF_2). Both cases are subjected to the same TRIZ generic problem: capacity (TRIZ parameter 39) versus harmful side effects (TRIZ parameter 31); and convenience of use (TRIZ parameter 33) versus amount of substance (TRIZ parameter 26). The inventive principles proposed by TRIZ in connection to these problems are: apply the equipotentiality principle [12], use the "resonance frequency" [18], convert harm into benefit [22], change the concentration and flexibility [35], and introduce a "neutral substance" or an "additive" [39].

Principle 12 highlights the importance of analyzing conflicts in the context of each course. In this respect, for the course of industrial robot design, principle 18 suggests selecting software solutions for robot simulation from providers that have educational licenses (e.g. ABB is the producer of RobotStudio; the company provides free educational licenses for 50 users; similar educational programs have other companies like Fanuc, Siemens, etc.). Principle 39 suggests renting videoconference systems, if attractive offers exist. However, an alternative is to buy the videoconference system using a long term payment scheme (e.g. quarterly rates, over several years time horizon) – principle 35. Principle 22 suggests exploiting various opportunities for attracting funds to buy a high quality technology for web-based courses. In this respect, this principle asks applying for grants, sponsorships from several available programs (e.g. in Europe: European Social Fund, Leonardo da Vinci Program, Erasmus Program, etc.).

Comprising all recommendations, the final solution of the web-based course in industrial robot design comprises five units. They are further detailed.

1. Course structure unit: the course contains lectures, seminars, project work, practical activities and individual work – all these components are delivered remotely; however, at least two face-to-face meetings between lecturer and students should be considered (this action is feasible because the remote class is located in a single place); problem-based and project-based learning methods are included – students must individually work to design a robot module (e.g. an intelligent gripping system) and in cooperation to solve one or two real mini-problems taken from industry (they have to spend this time in companies).
2. Course support unit: consideration of .ppt and .avi files for on-line lectures; consideration of .doc, .pdf, .jpg and .avi files for off-line information delivery; guiding manual to support the project work is provided in .pdf format; during seminar and lecture classes, supplementary files could be generated (see the use of whiteboards and simulation tools) – these files can be saved in .jpg, .htm, .avi and other formats for later review; materials with detailed information on how to use files are necessary; supplementary case studies and exercises should be included for the complex parts of the course – thus, off-line learning is facilitated; two local assistants are taken into account (students that support teacher in initializing and turning off the system); each session is recorded by the videoconference system for later use, both by students and teacher; a specific software tool for remote computer monitoring can be activated to "record" any action performed by each student on his/her terminal.
3. Simulation unit: use educational licenses for specialized web-based robot simulation and programming software – in this case RobotStudio and Robot HandlingPro are included in the training program because their producers provide free licenses for educational purposes; other CAD/CAR/CAE/CAP software tools and PLC simulation tools can be accessed by students via the remote desktop control application (e.g. VNC).
4. Course management unit: an open source repository system is implemented (e.g. Moodle); Moodle offers sufficient features for a good management of the web-based course (e.g. upload/download of files, forums, course scheduling, role assignment, and many other facilities which practically cover all usual actions for managing a course remotely); both teachers and students are trained in advance on how to use the

technology for communication and interactive/cooperative work (training manuals and training sessions have to be taken into account); students can contribute to the adaptation of the course for the web-based delivery.

5. Communication and interactive/cooperative work unit: a videoconference system is installed – a standard videoconference system between point A and point B uses two video cameras: one, at point A, broadcasts person(s) A (e.g. the teacher) and displays the image that camera B broadcasts; camera B broadcasts person(s) B (e.g. the students) while displaying image received from point A; two multi-media projectors are installed in the classroom, one connected with the computer where the remote desktop control application is installed (e.g. VNC) and another one connected to a videoconference camera (e.g. Polycom); in order to increase system's robustness, additional communication means are integrated – they comprise e-mail, Skype and Yahoo messenger, with web camera included on both sites; interaction between students and teacher is increased using the tablet PC and an interactive whiteboard (e.g. CorelGrafigo); in order to make different annotations on the work performed by students, specific software applications, like Windows Journal, are integrated; projects and homework can be remotely analyzed by the teacher using the virtual whiteboard and the tablet PC, as well as the remote desktop control server application and the videoconference system.

The scenario for communication and interactive/cooperative work between teacher and students looks like this: (a) teacher and students can see each other by using the standard videoconference system based on two video cameras; each camera needs to have a direct internet connection and a real IP address; a broadband internet connection is recommended; (b) the broadcast quality is usually a standard TV broadcast quality (for example a PAL video system has a 720 x 576 pixel resolution); (c) teacher watches students on a computer monitor that is directly connected to his/her videoconference camera; (d) teacher works on his tablet PC which needs to have a direct internet access; it needs to run a remote desktop control server application (e.g. VNC); teacher runs the course presentation or any support applications on his/her tablet PC; (e) students watch teacher on a projection screen; their videoconference camera is connected to the multimedia projector; (f) students are connected to the teacher's tablet PC by using a remote desktop control client application like VNC and are able to see teacher's desktop, i.e. the presentation or any other application (students need to have internet access); they may even remotely work on teacher's computer (even an on-line exam may be performed in this way); (g) teacher controls who or if anyone can remotely control his/her desktop; teacher may accept connections in read-only mode when presenting his/her course and then allows connections with control rights for any interactive tasks. Figure 1 suggestively illustrates this scenario.

The architecture of the web-based course revealed in this case study has a high degree of versatility, meaning that with low effort and in a very short time it can be adapted to many other web-based courses in engineering. The system described in this case study has been effectively tested in practice, providing a very good satisfaction both to students and teachers. After one year of implementation, it was adopted by other ten engineering courses (i.e. Computer Aided Design, Creativity and Innovation in Engineering, Quality Engineering and Management, Machine Elements Design, Mechanisms Design, Hydraulic and Pneumatic Systems, Objected Oriented Programming, Integrative Project, Process Monitoring and Control, Machine Tool Design).

Figure 1. Communication between teacher and students by means of a videoconference system

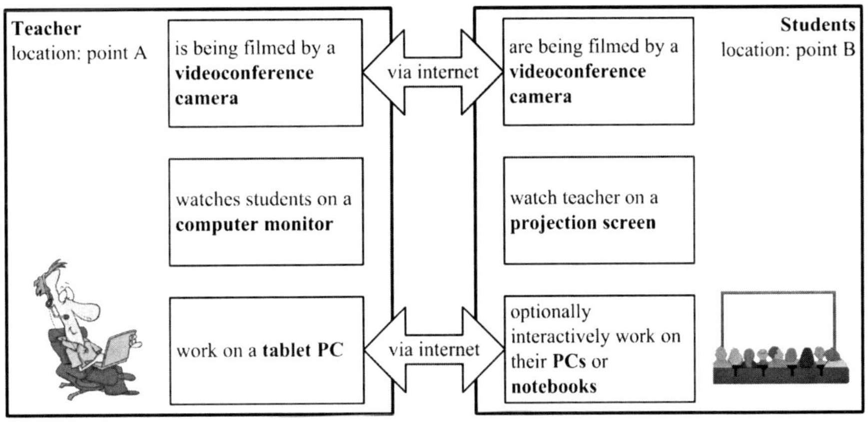

FURTHER RESEARCH DIRECTIONS

Researches presented in this material could be continued by including in the planning scheme additional target-functions. Two of the most challenging ones are "design for web-based course content quality" and "design for fast web-based course customization". Both design for course content quality and course customization lead to a significant number of conflicting problems. As a consequence, adequate planning and innovation is required to overpass crisis points in web-based course system conceptualization, development and implementation.

Performance planning could be further deployed to the level of teaching and learning processes, as well as to the pedagogical methods. Here, there is a huge space of action, where competitive design methods and methodologies would be extremely useful to handle less tangible dimensions and incomplete data.

Development of more realistic and intuitive simulation tools for web-based courses should be another area where competitive design would play an important role. Actually, this is a generous area for future developments, because every producing organization will have to become conscious that provision to universities of simulation tools related to their products will represent a competitive weapon. These tools will have to operate effectively via internet. In this respect, future developments of web technologies will support this process. Moreover, new organizational models of the educational providers will have to be considered.

Universities will have to enhance their partnerships with producing organizations, acting as "extended open universities". In this area, competitive design will provide a reliable framework to ensure a superior balance between effort and effect in web-based course conceptualization, development and delivery.

Further challenges in web-based course development will occur. They will be related to the development of a new generation of web-based courses in engineering. Such courses will consider remote interactions with hardware systems, also including capabilities for "sensing" the remote environment. In this area, competitive design will play an important role for setting up ingenious and commercial sustainable solutions, too.

CONCLUSION

The consideration of competitive design philosophy for setting up successful web-based courses in engineering is introduced in this material. Web-based courses in engineering are complex systems, which have to face with various challenges from technical, technological, financial and organizational points of view. From this perspective, such courses have to be designed and developed in strong connection with the context where they are going to be implemented, thus no "best-of-the-world" solution exists, and only context-related optimal solutions could be proposed at the best. Therefore, application of performance planning and innovative problem solving tools is necessary during the conceptualization and design of such courses.

This chapter introduces a novel framework for concurrent planning of a web-based course considering its multiple facets. The planning process starts from the incipient phases of web-based course development. The goal is to formulate a competitive solution in an effective and efficient way, with lower development costs and in a reasonable period of time. Several concluding remarks derive from the application of methodology on the case study.

First, designing a successful web-based course in engineering requires simultaneous consideration of multiple sides characterizing the respective course. Second, the complex nature of the course necessitates an innovative approach of solution formulation in order to overpass inevitable conflicting problems of technical, technological, organizational and financial nature. Third, a web-based course in engineering should be seen as a dynamic system, whose evolution in time is strongly dependent by the correlations between the life-cycles of its major sub-systems (e.g. communication unit, management unit, simulation unit, support unit, etc.).

REFERENCES

Altshuller, G. (2000). *The innovation algorithm. TRIZ, systematic innovation and technical creativity*. Worcester, MA: Technical Innovation Center.

Barros, B., Read, T., & Verdejo, M. F. (2008). Virtual collaborative experimentation: An approach combining remote and local labs. *IEEE Transactions on Education*, *51*(2), 242–250. doi:10.1109/TE.2007.908071

Bhatt, R., Tang, C. P., Lee, L. F., & Knovi, V. (2009). A case for scaffolded virtual prototyping tutorial case-studies in engineering education. *International Journal of Engineering Education*, *25*(1), 84–92.

Bier, I. D., & Cornesky, R. (2001, April). Using QFD to construct a higher education curriculum. *Quality Progress*, 64-68.

Brad, S. (2005). Need for radical innovation to ensure high quality of continuous education in engineering. In C. Oprean, & C. Kifor (Ed.), *3rd Balkan Region Conference on Engineering Education* (pp. 77-80). Sibiu: Lucian Blaga University Press.

Brad, S. (2008). Complex system design technique. *International Journal of Production Research*, *46*(21), 5979–6008. doi:10.1080/00207540701361475

Brad, S. (2009). Concurrent multifunction deployment. *International Journal of Production Research*, *47*(19), 5343–5376. doi:10.1080/00207540701564599

Callaghan, M. J., Harkin, J., McGinnity, T. M., & Maguire, L. P. (2008). Intelligent user support in autonomous remote experimentation environments. *IEEE Transactions on Industrial Electronics*, *55*(6), 2355–2367. doi:10.1109/TIE.2008.922411

Du, J., Li, F., & Li, B. (2008). The case of interactive web-based course development. In E. Leung, F. Wang, L. Miao, J. Zao, & J. He (Ed.), *2nd Workshop on Blended Learning* (pp. 65-73). Berlin, Germany: Springer

Ebner, M., & Walder, U. (2008). E-education in civil engineering – a promise for the future? In P. Vainiunas & L. Juknevicius (Ed.), *6th AECEF Symposium on Civil Engineering Education in Changing Europe* (pp. 16-26). Vilnius, Lithuania: Vilnius Gediminas Technical Univ. Press.

Finger, S., Gelman, D., Fay, A., & Szczerban, M. (2005). Supporting collaborative learning in engineering design. In W. Shen, A. James, K. Chao, M. Younas, & J. Barthes (Ed.), *9th International Conference on Computer Supported Cooperative Work in Design* (pp. 990-995). Coventry, UK: Coventry Univ. Press.

Helander, M. G., & Emami, M. R. (2008). Engineering e-laboratories: Integration of remote access and e-collaboration. *International Journal of Engineering Education*, *24*(3), 466–479.

Hutchings, M., Hadfield, M., Horvath, G., & Lewarne, S. (2007). Meeting the challenges of active learning in web-based case studies for sustainable development. *Innovations in Education and Teaching International*, *44*(3), 331–343. doi:10.1080/14703290701486779

Jou, M., Chuang, C. P., Wu, D. W., & Yang, S. C. (2008). Learning robotics in interactive web-based environments by PBL. In IEEE (Ed.), *IEEE Workshop on Advanced Robotics and Its Social Impacts* (pp. 206-211). Taipei, Taiwan: Nat. Taiwan Normal Univ. Press.

Kaminski, P. C., Ferreira, E. P. F., & Theuer, S. L. (2004). Evaluating and improving the quality of an engineering specialization program through the QFD methodology. *International Journal of Engineering Education*, *20*(6), 1034–1041.

Koksal, G., & Egitman, A. (1998). Planning and design of industrial engineering education quality. *Computers & Industrial Engineering*, *35*(3-4), 639–642. doi:10.1016/S0360-8352(98)00178-8

Kumar, A., & Labib, A. W. (2004). Applying quality function deployment for the design of a next-generation manufacturing simulation game. *International Journal of Engineering Education*, *20*(5), 787–800.

Lau, H., Mak, K., & Ma, H. (2006). IMELS: An e-learning platform for industrial engineering. *Computer Applications in Engineering Education*, *14*(1), 53–63. doi:10.1002/cae.20067

Li, L. Y., & Wang, H. J. (2007). A new method for building web-based virtual laboratory. In H. Liu, B. Hu, X.W. Zheng, & H. Zhang (Ed.). *1st International Symposium on Information Technologies and Applications in Education* (pp. 555-558). Kunming: Shandong Normal Univ. Press.

Mackey, T., & Ho, J. (2008). Exploring the relationship between web usability and students' perceived learning in web-based multimedia (WBMM) tutorials. *Computers & Education*, *50*(1), 386–409. doi:10.1016/j.compedu.2006.08.006

Ogot, M., & Okudan, G. (2007). A student-centered approach to improving course quality using quality function deployment. *International Journal of Engineering Education*, *23*(5), 916–928.

Popescu, S., Brad, S., & Popescu, D. (2006). The engineering study program as a customized product: barriers and directions for intervention, In E. Westkaemper (Ed.), 1st CIRP International Seminar on Assembly Systems, (pp. 289-294). Stuttgart, Germany: IFF Univ. Stuttgart.

Raharjo, H., Xie, M., Goh, T. N., & Brombacher, A. C. (2007). A methodology to improve higher education quality using the quality function deployment and analytic hierarchy process. *Total Quality Management & Business Excellence*, *18*(10), 1097–1115. doi:10.1080/14783360701595078

Rizzotti, S., & Burkhart, H. (2006). Web-based test and assessment system: Design principles and case study. In V. Uskov (Ed.), *5th IASTED International Conference on Web-based Education* (pp. 37-42). Puerto Vallarta, Mexico: Acta Press.

Saaty, T. L., & Vargas, L. G. (2001). *Models, methods, concepts & applications of the analytic hierarchy process*. New York: Springer.

Saygin, C., & Kahraman, F. (2004). A Web-based programmable logic controller laboratory for manufacturing engineering education. *International Journal of Advanced Manufacturing Technology*, *24*(7-8), 590–598. doi:10.1007/s00170-003-1787-7

Sessink, O., van der Schaaf, H., Beeftink, H., Hartog, R., & Tramper, J. (2007). Web-based education in bioprocess engineering. *Trends in Biotechnology*, *25*(1), 16–23. doi:10.1016/j.tibtech.2006.11.001

Suliman, S. M. A. (2006). Application of QFD in engineering education curriculum development and review. *International Journal of Continuing Engineering Education and Life-long Learning*, *16*(6), 482–492. doi:10.1504/IJCEELL.2006.011892

Toral, S., Barrero, F., & Martinez-Torres, M. (2007). Analysis of utility and use of a web-based tool for digital signal processing teaching by means of a technological acceptance model. *Computers & Education*, *49*(4), 957–975. doi:10.1016/j.compedu.2005.12.003

Vargas, H., Sanchez, J., Duro, N., Dormido, R., Farias, G., & Dormido, S. (2008). A systematic two-layer approach to develop web-based experimentation environments for control engineering education. *Intelligent Automation and Soft Computing*, *14*(4), 505–524.

Wang, X., Dannenhoffer, J., Davidson, B., & Spector, M. (2005). Design issues in a cross-institutional collaboration on a distance education course. *Distance Education*, *26*(3), 405–423. doi:10.1080/01587910500291546

Xuelian, H. (2008). Research and practice on web-based distance education of master of engineering. In L. Maoqing (Ed.), *3rd International Conference on Computer Science & Education* (pp. 1511-1514). Kaifeng, China: Xiamen Univ. Press.

Yeo, R. (2008). Brewing service quality in higher education: Characteristics of ingredients that make up the receipe. *Quality Assurance in Education*, *16*(3), 266–286. doi:10.1108/09684880810886277

Chapter 17
Web-Based Approaches in Engineering Education

Masoumeh Valizadeh
University of Guilan, Iran

Giancarlo Anzelotti
University of Parma, Italy

Arezou S. Salehi
NV Bekaert SA, Belgium

ABSTRACT

Among different branches of human knowledge and sciences, engineering, like medicine, is more involved in practical and daily-life aspects where the virtual utilities and educational software can be utilized to consummate the practical features of engineering education. Furthermore the virtual environment of e-learning courses can provide cheaper, safer, more comprehensive and more inclusive approaches to engineering educational material. The aim of this case is to count the requirements of engineering education and to accord the facilities and inadequacies of e-learning as training technique in engineering instruction.

INTRODUCTION

Distance learning is a progressive method of pedagogy employing the electronic technology to transfer the education to the students who are not on site and allows them to participate in educational activities on their own time. Since 1728 which the first ideas of distance learning has flickered through application of postal services, this technique has passed through several transition states like radio, television, telephone, computer and internet. Emersion of internet made a revolution in distance learning leading to a new generation called web-based learning. Web-based learning is practically the milestone of electronic learning or e-learning, profiting the popularity of the internet as a fast information source.

Connolly and Stansfield have categorized the historical progress of web-based training through three distinct generations. The first generation took place from 1994-1999 and was marked by a passive use of the Internet where traditional materials were simply repurposed to an online format. The second generation appeared through 2000-2003.

DOI: 10.4018/978-1-61520-869-2.ch017

This spectrum is marked by the transition to higher bandwidths, rich streaming media, increased resources, and the move to create virtual learning environments that integrated access to course materials, communications, and student services. Internet, Intranets, local area networks (LAN) and wide area networks (WAN) have offered the learners the opportunity to use distance learning beyond pre-recorded classes, educational software and virtual laboratories. The third generation is currently in progress and it is marked by the incorporation of greater collaboration, socialization, project based learning, and reflective practices, through e-portfolios, wikis, blogs, social bookmarking and networking and online simulations. Online forums, blogs and discussion boards have become a precious resource in Learning Management Systems (LMSs). They allow learners to communicate with their compeers and tutors, empowering them to socialize and learn together online. Furthermore, the third generation is progressively being influenced by advances in mobile communicating (Harper 2004; Connolly 2007; Monahan 2008).

Due to its singular capabilities, web-based learning has entered and is widely used in every field of science and technology. It is not only warmly welcome at schools and universities, but also in factories and houses. However utilization of web-based learning technique requires tender and comprehensive attentions in designing, applying and assessing configurations, directed by when, where and for which purpose it is being employed.

Among different branches of human knowledge and sciences, engineering as well as medicine is more involved in practical and daily-life aspects, where the virtual utilities and educational software can be utilized to consummate the practical features of engineering education. Furthermore the virtual environment of e-learning courses can provide cheaper, safer, more comprehensive and more inclusive approaches to engineering educational material. What usually the students need to learn in laboratories and workshops and it is costive and demanding for the universities and the schools. The aim of this chapter is to count the requirements of engineering education and to accord the facilities and inadequacies of e-learning as training technique in engineering instruction.

ENGINEERING

Engineering is the discipline of implementing of science and mathematics to develop explanation for the problems and to find practical solutions that have an applicable outcome. Engineering is the knowledge of creating a new world based on the rules which science has already discovered. Engineers suppose to be inventors. They design and manufacture machines, processes, systems and even economical constitutions. Utilizing science and mathematics, they observe the world, find the troubles, dream up new ideas and realize the dreams to improve the quality of life and make our world a more comfortable place to live.

Based on scientific principles, every engineering discipline has two main tasks (Wintermantel 1999):

1. To model subsystems using the theoretical and methodological scientific knowledge. In this respect, engineering is not different from the natural sciences.
2. To develop methods and procedures, which allow real systems in all their complexity to be designed and constructed even if not all subsystems have been precisely modeled due to a lack of a thorough knowledge of the underlying physics and chemistry.

The Engineers Council for Professional Development (ECPD), in USA has defined the term of engineering as: "the creative application of scientific principles to design or develop structures, machines, apparatus, or manufacturing processes, or works utilizing them singly or in combination; or to construct or operate the same with full cognizance of their design; or to forecast their behavior under specific operating conditions; all as respects an intended function, economics of operation and safety to life and property" (Science 1941).

REQUIREMENTS TO MAKE THE BEST ENGINEER

An engineer supposes to solve complex problems by the simplest solutions. They are often responsible for directly creating a new product or service. The main functions of an engineer have been defined through 7 terms by Encyclopedia Britannica (Smith 2009):

1. *Research*, Using mathematical and scientific concepts, experimental techniques, and inductive reasoning, the research engineer seeks new principles and processes.
2. *Development*, Development engineers apply the results of research to useful purposes. Creative application of new knowledge may result in a working model of a new electrical circuit, a chemical process, or an industrial machine.
3. *Design*, in designing a structure or a product, the engineer selects methods, specifies materials, and determines shapes to satisfy technical requirements and to meet performance specifications.
4. *Construction*, The construction engineer is responsible for preparing the site, determining procedures that will economically and safely yield the desired quality, directing the placement of materials, and organizing the personnel and equipment.
5. *Production*, Plant layout and equipment selection are the responsibility of the production engineer, who chooses processes and tools, integrates the flow of materials and components, and provides for testing and inspection.
6. *Operation*, The operating engineer controls machines, plants, and organizations providing power, transportation, and communication; determines procedures; and supervises personnel to obtain reliable and economic operation of complex equipment.
7. *Management and other functions*, in some countries and industries, engineers analyze customers' requirements, recommend units to satisfy needs economically, and resolve related problems.

By integrating all above mentioned functions, the required skills for all engineering disciplines can be sorted in 3 categories: mathematics and science, team working and curiosity, creativity and innovation (Figure 1). Every educational curriculum for engineering education has to fulfill these themes comprehensively.

Mathematics and science: math and science are the basis of engineering. Physics, chemistry,

Figure 1. The essential requirements of being an engineer

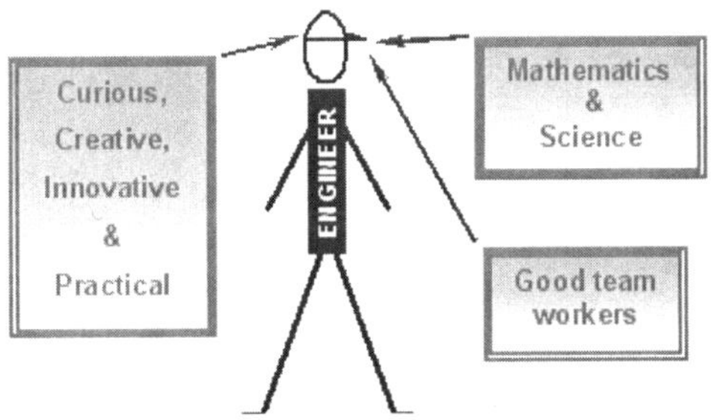

biology, economics, psychology as the laws, forces and resources of nature are the primal necessities of different engineering disciplines. The physical sciences are concerned with the laws that govern the world and the realities of nature. Mathematic however is a comprehensive concept that, in spite of being inspired by the rules of nature, does not bound up with it. It can exist and grow within itself. Mathematics and basic sciences are pure. Engineering, in contrast, is not pure. The process of training an engineer to apply the basic rules of science and to design a machine or a process requires a study of engineering models and deep understanding of basic science and the mathematical techniques. Those models require correspondence with reality in their conception, and precision in their description. And those mathematical techniques, like all mathematical techniques, require practice, sophistication and rigor. Consequently, the technological world of an engineer has been constructed on the pure disciplines of mathematics and basic sciences, but it is not contained in them (Chatterjee 2005).

Teamwork: Most engineers work as a team. Therefore they should be good team players and acquire reasonable skills in communicating with others. This is highly important when planning and creating new projects. Teamwork and group work are increasingly common elements of engineering learning. When group activities and projects are assigned, two types of learning outcomes will emerge:

- *Product outcomes*: outcomes related to the content of the course;
- *Process outcomes*: outcomes related to team skills and contribution in group work activities.

The aims of teamwork development are that the members work interdependently and work towards both personal and team goals. They understand these goals are accomplished best by communal support. They feel a sense of ownership towards their role in the group because they committed themselves to goals. Members work in partnership together and use their talent and experience to supply the success of the team's purposes. As a part of every mutual work, members try to be honest, respectful, and listen to others point of view. They see conflict as a part of human nature and they react to it by treating it as an occasion to hear about new ideas and opinions. Members participate equally in decision-making, but each member understands that the leader might need to make the final decision if the team cannot come to a common consent (Kaufman 2000).

Practical, Innovative personality: Conceptual advances have always been the driving force behind scientific progresses. This in turn relies on creativity and the ability to continue the production of new insights and innovative ideas. The history has given us many discoveries (especially in engineering and the sciences) linked to a sudden recognition, which are the outcomes of creative, dreamer mind of human beings. An engineer is who dreams, then assesses the realization possibilities of the dream and finally makes the dream a reality. Therefore an engineering student on one hand should have the talent and on the other hand has to be trained up appropriately to be able to follow the steps of an engineering decision according to Figure 2 and to create and find the answers for questions like:

1. What is the problem?
2. What do I want to do?
3. What are the benefits of this solution? And are they significant?
4. How can I implement the solution?
5. How can I know that if I have reached the benefits?
6. How can I represent a better solution with my new experiences?

Figure 2. Decision making in engineering processes

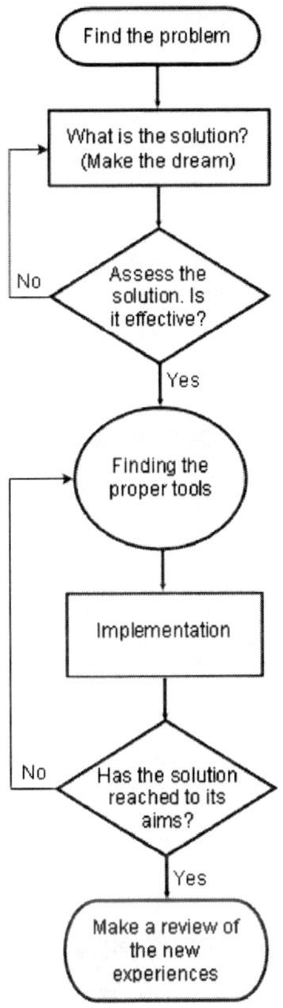

ENGINEERING EDUCATION REQUIREMENTS

In a continuously changing world, many challenges and opportunities face the engineering profession and engineering education. Based on various technological and economic developments, fundamental changes have taken place over the last few years that affect the methods in engineering education. In consequence, the actual training trends like the trend to virtual and classical Instructional methods, the global availability of information on one hand and of information resources and accessibility on the other hand, the rise of learning demands and the particularities of engineering education require a strategic streamlining of each of these options. The basis for this strategic planning should be the instructional principal abilities and the use of the general available enabling technologies.

Engineering professionals working in industry are in general unsatisfied with the level of real-world preparedness acquired by recent university graduates entering the work market. Their dissatisfaction is understandable. In order for these graduates to be productive in an industrial setting, one idea is that the organizations which hire them must supplement their university education with extensive on-the-job training and preparation that provides them with the skills and knowledge they lack (Conn 2002; Baker 2005).

On the other hand, following the tremendous progress in science and technology, engineering teaching materials are currently under development by the multidisciplinary (production engineers, computer scientists, economists) project teams. The philosophy behind this approach is to give access to all information that is relevant to understand and to work on the topic of interest. The background of the didactic approach of these projects is teaching and learning by distance instructions. The central focus is the specification of event-oriented lessons and seminars such as computer supported role-plays for distributed problem-solving, gaming in an open environment and multinational web-based teaching, where students will learn to work on open problems in different fields of engineering, having an active connection with other universities and also the manufacturers. They will be guided from theoretical learning in lessons via interdisciplinary distributed games to international teamwork in cooperation with partner universities. Step by step, their capabilities and entrepreneurial spirit to apply theoretical knowledge will increase, as well as their social and managerial skills. This approach takes up the idea of e-learning to enhance traditional more or less passive reception of knowledge by students what we know as learning by listening, towards an active, self-directed learning and cooperative knowledge creation learning by trying (Hirsch 1998; Pyrz 2003; Baker 2005; Grunbacher 2007).

Concerning to the necessities of modern life, engineering education requires essential transitions in methods and tools to accord with modern societies. So that, engineering education designers endeavor to design and to employ the most consistent methods which fulfill this purpose.

As a potent approach web-based training technique is one of the modern methods of distance learning which plays an advancing role in every field of education. It can be applied solely or joined with the traditional education systems.

WEB-BASED TRAINING

In order to overcome the problems of incompatibility and employ a new way of linking made possible by computers, called hypertext, a group of scientists at the European Laboratory for Particle Physics (CERN) in Geneva, Switzerland, began developing an Internet tool in 1989 to link the information achieved by all of the CERN researchers. Rather than presenting information in a linear or hierarchical fashion, hypertext permits information to be linked in a web-like structure. The tool provided a way to link textual information on different computers and created by different scientists. Nodes of information could be linked to other nodes of information in multiple ways. As a result, users can dynamically interlace the information in order to make them most convenient. The CERN project resulted in an innovative front-end to the Internet, now called the World-Wide Web (WWW) (Gottschalk 2009).

For educators, the internet and HTML have provided a new occasion for distance training. The ability of putting together graphics, text, sound, animations and movies into a single tool has empowered the educators to build virtual classroom on their WebPages. By this mean the organizations or individuals can create their own home pages and link them to other home pages or share them with other computers. The educational home pages can be supported by virtual laboratories, virtual libraries, text lessons, virtual classrooms using video conferencing, exercises and exams. These are all the body builders of web-based training.

As a simple definition, web-based training is a form of training that can be developed by utilizing a network. 'Web-Based Training (WBT) is the Delivery of educational content via a Web browser over the public Internet, a private intranet, or an extranet. Web-based training often provides links to other learning resources such as references, e-mail, bulletin boards, and discussion groups. WBT also may include a facilitator who can provide course guidelines, manage discussion boards, deliver lectures, and so forth. When used with a facilitator, WBT offers some advantages of instructor-led training while also retaining the advantages of computer-based training' (Imperial-College-London 2009).

WBT is the innovative approach to distance learning in which training material is transformed by the technologies and attitudes of the internet and intranets. The specification of Web-based training is the presenting of live contents, in a structure allowing self-directed, self-paced instruction in any topic (Kilby 2009).

The same as all other distance learning techniques, WBT needs some indispensable components which can be categorized in 3 groups:

- Instructional design
- Knowledge delivery techniques
- Standards,

specifications and examples of these components are tabled in table 1 (Bergstrom 2001; Digitalthink 2003; Friesen 2004; IEEE 2005; Le@rningFederation 2008; Ryder 2008; DCMI 2009; IMS 2009). These are general concepts, details of which need to be revised and upgraded according to the demands in different educational fields.

Web-Based Training for Engineering Students

The engineering education is in fact the engineering training, explained as the way of improving a person's performance related to job environments by providing instructions. *Intention, designing, tools and media and assessment* are usually the components of training programs which can increase the effectiveness of the Engineering training. Though, intention is the motivation and willing to participate in parts of the training, the design is the systematic structure of the training. It determines each step while the learners go ahead with the new skills. It also includes instructional strategies and related measurement issues about these strategies. Tools and media are the means of instruction transfer. It could be a classroom, a web-based training system or combinations of different tools. To finalize the learning process, a formalized assessments and certification provide accountability of the training (YilDirim 2009).

Two basic components of web-based training technology are Ideal Learners and Ideal Instructions. These are the delicate concepts of WBT needing to be taken care for engineering education. As Horton states an Ideal Learner is who (Horton 2001):

- Has definite goals
- Opens to learn independently and view learning prohibitively
- Is self-disciplined and have good time management
- Is moderately capable of field and know basic concepts and facts
- Has enough good writing skills
- Has enough domination in computing skills
- Has positive attitude toward technology in business and learning
- Is so relaxed while there is any technical problem and can cope with these problems

An Ideal Engineering Learner in web-based training system, in addition to above mentioned items has to have notable skills in mathematics be able to adapt himself with the group working and the projects which are usually defined as part of the learners assessment plan and schedule of the course.

The most important and crucial aspect to reach to an advantageous Ideal Course is determining learners needs. In an ideal course, teaching is efficient. Precise objects are well defined and the learner acquires new knowledge by spending less time. Development process of WBT is the other crucial concern. Using web-based utilities, the designers can use several models and modulus for instructional objects.

The nature of WBT provides a remarkable array of opportunities and technologies such as XML (eXtensible Markup Language), Web Services, Peer-to-Peer and many other approaches. On the other hand there are many items in WBT environment influencing the outcome. Therefore one can find the most and the least useful information simultaneously. Hence the designers of WBT courses are responsible of performing the course in the most comprehensive and specific system.

Michael Allen counts three priorities for successful Ideal Course designing (Allen 2003):

Motivation: motivation is essential to learning because it induces attention, persistence and participation in learning activities. This concept is very familiar to literature of learning and instructional designers, but unfortunately, explicit managing of motivation seems to be creeping into educational plans very slowly. The fact is that highly motivated learners will find the means and the tools to access the learning material. Motivation is definitely a very effective task in engineering education, because it is directly connected to creativity and curiosity. A designed approach of motivation in engineering courses assists team working approaches and can encourage the students to exchange their knowledge more readily.

Table 1.

Concept	Aspects	examples
Standards	**Resource detection**	• ADL SCORM Content Aggregation Model • IEEE P1484.11 Computer Managed Instruction • IMS Content Packaging Specification • IMS Content Packaging Specification • IMS Simple Sequencing Specification
	Content management	• Dublin Core Metadata Element Set • UK LOM Core • IEEE 1484.12.1-2002 Learning Object Metadata standard • IMS Learning Resource Meta-data Specification • EdNA Metadata Standard • Gateway to Educational Materials Element Set • Canadian Core Learning Resource Metadata Application Profile • SingCore
	Accessibility	• Le@rning Federation Accessibility Specification • Web Content Accessibility Guidelines • IMS AccessForAll Meta-data Specification
	Interoperability	• ADL SCORM • IMS Resource List Interoperability Specification • IMS Enterprise Information Model • IMS Enterprise Services Specification • IMS Question & Test Interoperability Specification • IMS Shareable State Persistence Specification • IMS Digital Repositories • IMS Learner Information Package Specification • ISO/IEC JTC1 SC36/WG3 Learner Information
	Pedagogy Quality	• Le@rning Federation Educational Soundness Specification
	digital rights management	• ISO/IEC JTC1 SC36/WG4 Digital Rights Expression Language • Le@rning Federation Rights Management Specification
Instructional design	**Analysis** **Design** **Development** **Implementation** **Evaluation**	• ADDIE • ASSURE • ARCS • CSCL • CSILE
Knowledge delivery techniques	**Synchronous technologies:**	• Telephone and Mobile • Web-based conference • Video conference
	Asynchronous technologies:	• Postal materials • Audio and video cassettes • Radio and Television • Fax and E-mail • Voice mail, MMS and SMS • Message boards and Forums • E-portfolios and blogs

Directing: highly motivated learners are ready to use any tool helping them to reach the learning material. Therefore it is essentially important to design and provide appropriate educational materials upon a precise schedule. By this way the effectiveness of motivation credit will not be spoiled. Priming appropriate learning content includes providing excellent indexing helping the students to identify an appropriate learning material, or applying an assessment that specifies what the students (in more progressed educational courses, what every individual student) may need. For engineering aspects the relevant directions are even more important. The engineering aspects are widespread in different fields of science and technologies. Meanwhile being founded on basic sciences concepts; it has more connection with applied science. Engineering is in fact the most notable representative of applied science, and due to the broadness and variety of its subjects it requires thoroughly disciplined plan for courses.

Purposeful and impressive: an ideal course has to be designed for the wide spectrum of students with different capabilities. It has to be enough understandable for less skilled learners meanwhile it is privileging talent students to grasp deeper concepts with satisfactory and appealing supplements. However from another point of view providing appealing and purposeful material for the courses impresses the students and helps them to memorize and remember the instructional contents more easily. For engineering courses designing this approach is even more desirable and helpful, since as objective concepts, the engineering perceptions can be significantly described using the virtual aids of WBT. The main advantage of this approach is the ease of remembering the taught objects in real job status. To facilitate the instructional course with such configuration, the WBT designer may use the following utilities:

- Attractive context and new examples
- Providing a charming environment using several means represented by virtual world advantages, such as computer simulated environments
- Problem-solving scenarios
- Engaging themes, media and user interface elements
- Practices, that in WBT cases Virtual Laboratories may empower the instructional contents with virtual practical sessions.

To express the advantages of the above mentioned issues, some simple but very applicable examples are presented in the following paragraphs, revealing the application of WBT in some engineering subjects.

CASES

1. Thermodynamic is the fundamental knowledge of many branches of engineering such as chemical engineering, mechanical engineering, textile engineering, polymer engineering and many others. One of the fundamental lessons taught in this course is Carnot cycle to make an example of reversible heat engine. This cycle is defined by several adiabatic and isothermal steps including several changes in volume, pressure, enthalpy and entropy of the system. It is a fairly complicated introduction on second law of thermodynamic inaugurating the headwords for more elaborate concepts. As a pivotal subject, teachers usually have to put a lot of time on it and even in this case the students look still confused.

Professor Michael Flower from Department of physics, university of Virginia, has an online course on modern physics, entitled ‘Galileo and Einstein’ at http://galileoandeinstein.physics.virginia.edu, contenting different fundamental laws of physics such as Galileo’s Compound Motion, Kepler’s law, Doppler Effect, Carnot Cycle and many others. The advantage of his on-line course is simplification of subjects providing animations, graphs, definitions and states, and all these are connected to each other. Through the visual and virtual interface of this course, the student would be able to follow easily the instructions. They would have the opportunity to make the calculations on each point of cycle, and view the correspondent effects on states, graphs and the heat engine status which they have to learn. Moreover it is easier for the teachers to teach (Hwang 2004; Ion 2007; Flowers 2008).

2. Polymer chemistry is the fairly new subdivision of chemistry being taught in chemical engineering, polymer engineering, fiber production engineering, textile engineering, composite and material scientists. Polymer science which is in fact the chemistry, rheology and processing of macromolecules has intricate subjects for both students (to learn) and professors (to make sure that the taught subjects have been understood by the students). American chemical society has several short courses on chemistry and chemical engineering, including polymer courses. The ACS Short Courses in Polymer Chemistry targets industry professionals, chemists, materials scientists, and engineers with a B.S. or higher degree seeking greater understanding of principles governing polymer science and a comprehensive, up-to-date overview of polymer subjects. Since no assumptions are made regarding the background of the participants, the courses attempt to address a variety of learning styles and knowledge bases through lecture, demonstrations, laboratory exercises, and computer-based independent study (ACS 2009).

The department of polymer science of the University of Southern Mississippi has established an on-line center, called Polymer Science Learning Center (PSLC). This center contents polymer courses for different levels from beginners, even kids to polymer explorers. As a multi-level, multimedia polymer education resource, PCLS is an interactive web site in polymer education by pioneering an innovative hands-on, inquiry-based, multi-faceted learning environment for pre-kindergarten through researchers that will result in all polymer education ventures originating by choice with the PSLC. The mission is to teach polymer science to students of all levels in the most memorable manner possible to better prepare them for both chemical careers and life (Mathias 2009).

CONCLUSION

World-Wide Web and Internet technologies are the main support of modern communication. They have established foundations of modern educational systems which are offering an extraordinary volume of information to a wide spectrum of learners, even at schools, universities and factories, or house users which are looking for specific objects. Internet contains some of the vantage components of distance education naturally supplying time and place independency as the server computers are working 24 hours a day, all over the year.

With all the advantages happening in distance communication, the teaching and training technology is gravitating more and more toward web-based aspects. The main users of web-based training technologies are still the students of the universities and schools. However, due to its virtual supplements, web-based training can star more effectively in some particular branches of science such as engineering.

- Web-based training is a novel instructional technique offering many superior advantages over traditional methods. Potential capabilities of web-based training nominate it as a suitable method for engineering education, some of which can be counted as:
- WBT offers time-effective and cost-effective training services.
- WBT overcomes the disadvantages of traditional instructional methods based on printed course material. In WBT the educational content can be changed or added fast and easily.
- WBT provides standardized courses ensuring congruous training.

- The educational content can be easily designed to be consistent with different budgets and cultures.
- Course material can be easily adapted and updated for different learners and according to their needs.
- Virtual environment of WBT provides very powerful configurations that can replace the costive practical sessions required in engineering education.

In addition to all the advantages of WBT, it includes some disadvantages as well:

Initial implementation of a WBT system can be more costive than the cost of publishing course material as textbooks.

- Bandwidth limitations and other limitations on required electronic devices such as the capabilities of computers are considered as the constrains of WBT development.
- WBT is more adapted with self-directed students. But the students who are more used to traditional techniques of teacher-classroom - printed textbooks or the students who do not have enough skills in using computer or internet may find it difficult to get adapted.
- WBT provides time and place independency for the students; however the students are more possible to get interrupted because of the freedom they gain because of the natural self- dependency of WBT method.
- Even with the existence of Virtual laboratories, the students will not get the idea of the real training, as well as they are needed to be trained for their coming careers.

Collecting all the presented information, WBT can be counted as a powerful method when it is designed and applied in its right position. It is certainly the most perfect method to enter in the course content and actually start it, especially for engineering courses where the provided virtual environment of WBT can help the students to figure out the subject. WBT would be very effective when the technical capabilities of the students and their skills have been depicted realistically. The main advantage of WBT is that it can be easily customized regarding to the needs. The needs can be the level of education, the required skills, job aids, the culture of users and many other issues.

REFERENCES

ACS. (2009). *ACS Complete Short Course Listings*. Retrieved from http://portal.acs.org/portal/acs/corg/content?_nfpb=true&_pageLabel=PP_ARTICLEMAIN&node_id=273&content_id=CTP_006408&use_sec=true&sec_url_var=region1&__uuid=f3138678-d8ec-4b90-83a7-781b4b80b9bf

Allen, M. W. (2003). *Michael Allen's guide to e-learning: Building Interactive, Fun, and Effective Learning Programs for Any Company*. Hoboken, NJ: John Wiley & Sons, Inc.

Baker, A., Navarro, E. O., & van der Hoek, A. (2005). An experimental card game for teaching software engineering processes. *Journal of Systems and Software*, *75*, 3–16. doi:10.1016/j.jss.2004.02.033

Bergstrom. (2001). *CMI Guidelines for Interoperability AICC*. Retrieved from http://www.aicc.org/docs/tech/cmi001v3-5.pdf

Chatterjee, A. (2005). Mathematics in engineering. *Current Science*, *88*(3), 405–414.

Conn, R. (2002). Developing software engineers at the C-130J software factory. *IEEE Software*, *19*(5), 25–29. doi:10.1109/MS.2002.1032849

Connolly, T., & Stansfield, M. (2007). *Principles of effective online teaching*. Santa Rosa, CA: Informing Science Press.

DCMI. (2009). *Dublin Core Metadata Element Set, Version 1.1*. Retrieved from http://dublincore.org/documents/dces/

Digitalthink. (2003). *SCORM™:The E-Learning Standard*. Retrieved from http://www.adlnet.org/index.cfm?fuseaction=scormabt

Flowers, M., & Ching, H. W. (2008). *Lecture on Carnot Cycle*. Retrieved from http://galileoandeinstein.physics.virginia.edu/more_stuff/flashlets/carnot.htm

Friesen, N. (2004). *The E-learning Standardization Landscape*. Retrieved from http://www.cancore.ca/docs/intro_e-learning_standardization.html

Gottschalk, T. H. (2009). *Distance education at a glance*. Retrieved from http://www.uiweb.uidaho.edu/eo/distglan

Grunbacher, P., Seyff, N., Briggs, R. O., In Kitapci, H., & Port, D. (Eds.). Making every student a winner: The WinWin approach in software engineering education. The Journal of System and Software, 80, 1191-1200.

Harper, K. C., Chen, K., & Yen, D. C. (2004). Distance learning,virtual classrooms,and teaching pedagogy in the Internet environment. *Technology in Society*, *26*, 585–598. doi:10.1016/S0160-791X(04)00054-5

Hirsch, B. E., Thoben, K. D., & Hoheisel, J. (1998). Requirements upon human competencies in globally distributed manufacturing. *Computers in Industry*, *36*, 49–54. doi:10.1016/S0166-3615(97)00097-3

Horton, W. (2001). *Designing Web-Based Training: How to Teach Anyone Anything Anywhere Anytime*. New York: John Wiley & Sons.

Hwang, F. (2004). *NTNUJAVA Virtual Physics Laboratory Java Simulations in Physics: Enjoy the fun!* Retrieved from http://www.phy.ntnu.edu.tw/ntnujava/index.php?PHPSESSID=61e16b595f51a79534ea86dd507e6fce&topic=23.msg156#msg156

IEEE. (2005). *1484.12.1: IEEE Standard for Learning Object Metadata*. Retrieved from http://ltsc.ieee.org/wg12/

Imperial-College-London. (2009). *Information & Communication Technologies ICT; An E-Learning Glossary*. Retrieved from http://www3.imperial.ac.uk/ict/services/teachingandresearchservices/elearning/aboutelearning/elearningglossary

IMS. (2009). *Innovation Adoption Learning*. Retrieved from http://www.imsglobal.org/specifications.html

Ion, D. (2007). *Physics and Engineering*. Retrieved from http://www.cs.sbcc.cc.ca.us/~physics/

Kaufman, D. B., Felder, R. M., & Fuller, H. (2000). Accounting for individual effort in cooperative learning teams. *Journal of Engineering Education*, *89*(2), 133–140.

Kilby, T. (2009). *What is Web-Based Training?* Retrieved from http://www.webbasedtraining.com/primer_whatiswbt.aspx

Le@rningFederation. (2008). *Metadata Elements Comparison: Vetadata and ANZ-LOM*. Australia: Flexible Learning Network.

Mathias, L., Frantz, P., Brust, G., Montogery, J., Smith, V., Simmons, M., et al. (2009). *Polymer Science learning Center*. Retrieved from http://pslc.ws/macrog.htm

Monahan, T., McArdle, G., & Bertolotto, M. (2008). Virtual reality for collaborative e-learning. *Computers & Education*, *50*, 1339–1353. doi:10.1016/j.compedu.2006.12.008

Pyrz, R., Olhoff, N., Lund, E., & Thomsen, O. T. (2003). *Mechanic for.* Retrieved from http://me.aau.dk/GetAsset.action?contentId=1987778&assetId=3356989

Ryder, M. (2008). *Instructional design models*. Retrieved from http://carbon.cudenver.edu/~mryder/itc_data/idmodels.html#modern

Science. (1941). The engineers' council for professional development. *Science, 94*(2446), 456.

Smith, R. J. (2009). *Engineering*. Retrieved from http://www.britannica.com/EBchecked/topic/187549/engineering

Willis, B. D. (1993). *Distance Education-A Practical Guide*. Englewood Cliffs, NJ: Educational Technology Publications.

Wintermantel, K. (1999). Process and product engineering Ð achievements, present and future challenges. *Chemical Engineering Science, 54*, 1601–1620. doi:10.1016/S0009-2509(98)00412-6

YilDirim. S. (2009). *Web-Based Training: Design and Implementation Issues*, Retrieved from http://ocw.metu.edu.tr/informatics-institute/web-based-training-design-and-implementation

FURTHER READING

ACS. (2009). *ACS Complete Short Course Listings*. Retrieved from http://portal.acs.org/portal/acs/corg/content?_nfpb=true&_pageLabel=PP_ARTICLEMAIN&node_id=273&content_id=CTP_006408&use_sec=true&sec_url_var=region1&__uuid=f3138678-d8ec-4b90-83a7-781b4b80b9bf

Buzzetto-More, N. A. (2008). Student Perceptions of Various E-Learning Components. *Interdisciplinary Journal of E-Learning and Learning Objects, 4*, 113–135.

Cloete, E. (2001). Electronic education system model. *Computers & Education, 36*, 171–182. doi:10.1016/S0360-1315(00)00058-0

Connolly, T., & Stansfield, M. (2007). *Principles of effective online teaching*. Santa Rosa, CA: Informing Science Press.

Flowers, M., & Ching, H. W. (2008). *Lecture on Carnot Cycle*. Retrieved from http://galileoandeinstein.physics.virginia.edu/more_stuff/flashlets/carnot.htm

Harper, K. C., Chen, K., & Yen, D. C. (2004). Distance learning, virtual classrooms, and teaching pedagogy in the Internet environment. *Technology in Society, 26*, 585–598. doi:10.1016/S0160-791X(04)00054-5

Mathias, L., Frantz, P., Brust, G., Montogery, J., Smith, V., Simmons, M., et al. (2009). *Polymer Science learning Center*. Retrieved from http://pslc.ws/macrog.htm

APPENDIX: SUPPORTING MATERIAL

Abstract

Among different branches of human knowledge and sciences, engineering, like medicine, is more involved in practical and daily-life aspects where the virtual utilities and educational software can be utilized to consummate the practical features of engineering education. Furthermore the virtual environment of e-learning courses can provide cheaper, safer, more comprehensive and more inclusive approaches to engineering educational material. The aim of this chapter is to count the requirements of engineering education and to accord the facilities and inadequacies of e-learning as training technique in engineering instruction.

Questions and Answers

1. What is the overall problem(s) in this case?

An engineer supposes to solve complex problems by the simplest solutions. They are often responsible for directly creating a new product or service. They have to know how to research, how to design, how to construct and over all these they have to manage and direct the production or construction. The engineers of our progressing technological world have to be taught using some more effective tools to get prepared to manage all these requests.

2. What is the advantage of this case study?

This study has presented some introductions of engineering, engineering requirement and engineers characters. Counting all the requirement for the engineering education, this chapter is introducing web-based training as a powerful tool to engineering education using some studied examples in different fields of engineering.

3. What are the factors affecting the problem(s) related to this case?

Developing web-based training method is aimed to be a powerful aid for engineering education. Some of the affecting factor in developing and applying of web-based training can be counted as: preparing the student to make relation and use these educational tools, the design of the web-based software, performance, user interface, the ease of making relation, cost and effectiveness.

4. What are some of the emerging technologies that should be considered in solving the problem(s) related to the case?

The requirements of web-based training are:

1. A fast connection to Internet
2. Websites, Wikis, blogs and forums which are designed for educational purposes.
3. A fulfilled course to train how to use web-based e-tools to the students or learners.

5. What are the roles of different players in the overall planning?

There are two main players in engineering education performance: the teacher and the learner. However in this case study we have introduced the third player which is the purpose-oriented small software. The role of purpose-oriented small software is to make a connection between the teacher and the learner. However it plays as an aid for the learner to understand the topics which are planned to be transferred to him.

Epilogue and Lessons Learned

Internet and HTML have provided a new occasion for distance training. The ability of putting together graphics, text, sound, animations and movies all into a single tool has empowered the educators to build virtual classroom on their WebPages and making a low cost school.

Selected Readings

Chapter 18
A Needs Analysis Framework for the Design of Digital Repositories in Higher Education

Sue Bennett
University of Wollongong, Australia

Dominique Parrish
University of Wollongong, Australia

Geraldine Lefoe
University of Wollongong, Australia

Meg O'Reilly
Southern Cross University, Australia

Mike Keppell
Charles Sturt University, Australia

Robyn Philip
University of Sydney, Australia

ABSTRACT

As the notion of learning objects has grown in popularity, so too has interest in how they should be stored to promote access and reusability. A key challenge to all repository projects is to understand the various motivations and needs to those wishing to contribute to and access the collection. To date there has been considerable attention given to technical issues of repositories, with much less consideration of how to attend to the needs of those who will use them. This chapter presents a needs analysis framework that was developed to guide the design of a new repository currently being created for the Australian higher education sector, The Carrick Exchange. The project to develop the framework is described, outlining the findings from analysis of literature and existing repositories, with input from a survey of potential users. The purpose of the framework was to distil key issues that should be considered in the design of the repository and we offer it here as an analytical tool that could be applied by others.

INTRODUCTION

With the advent and adoption of the Internet it has become easy to share and distribute information. This has generated considerable interest in how digital resources can be stored and organised. In the early years of the Internet, many had visions of "virtual libraries," a digital analogy to the familiar physical library. More recently as the idea of reusable and sharable "learning objects" has emerged, attention has become focused on digital repositories.

In higher education, the vision is for learning objects developed for specific teaching purposes to be housed in digital repositories in which they are catalogued and described in ways that make the resources accessible across institutions (Littlejohn, 2003b; Littlejohn & Buckingham Shum, 2003). The activities involved in populating and using these repositories would create an economy in which individual academics design and prepare resources appropriate for reuse by others in exchange for access to a much wider range of similarly reusable resources contributed by other individual academics (Malcolm, 2005). In addition, institutions, government bodies, and commercial educational developers could also contribute to such an economy. There is also considerable interest within institutions to make the most of digital resources, a trend that can be observed in the current move to content management systems, though this issue is somewhat separate from the broader notions of the learning object economy.

It is difficult to define a "learning object" with any precision or authority as there is still significant debate in the literature as to what should be regarded as a learning object (see Agostinho, Bennett, Lockyer, & Harper, 2004). For the purposes of this chapter, the term will be used to encompass teaching and learning materials and guides that range in granularity from single files to full courses. As such, learning objects can be considered items relevant to the teaching and learning process that are made available for others to use and adapt to their own contexts.

Thus, learning objects made available in digital repositories promise a new way of creating learning environments within and outside the traditional boundaries between courses, disciplines, and institutions. Digital repositories that accommodate high quality learning objects could be of assistance to university teaching by increasing the reusability of content thereby:

- Saving time and money in course development,
- Enhancing students' learning experiences, and
- Engaging teaching staff in a dynamic community of practice.

The basis of digital repositories is the sharing of digital resources. The fundamental premise is that digital resources are submitted according to specified criteria and accessed according to another set of conditions. The submission of digital resources may occur in a variety of ways, for example:

- Contributors freely provide digital resources that may be assessed, enhanced, or peer reviewed before being accessed from the repository (e.g., Apple Learning Interchange, Connexions, and iLumina).
- Only registered members are able to contribute digital resources that may be peer reviewed prior to being made available to repository users; for example, Campus Alberta Repository of Educational Objects (CAREO), Cooperative Learning Object Exchange (CLOE), EducaNext, Education Network Australia (EdNA), Jorum, and Multimedia Educational Resource for Learning and Online Teaching (MERLOT).

- An education advocate selects, develops or designs digital resources that are made available from the repository (e.g., Blue Web'n and INTUTE).
- Educators design and produce digital resources for a specific higher education course or purpose and use the repository as a means for dissemination (e.g., LEARNet, Massachusetts Institute of Technology (MIT) Open CourseWare (OCW) and Scottish electronic Staff Development Library (SeSDL)).
- Contributors provide details and/or information about the digital resource and a link to the Web address where the resource is housed, external to the repository (e.g., Educause and Learning Resources Community (LRC) Project).
- Registered members use tools that are made available through the repository to create digital resources that once developed are described by metadata and added to the repository for other registered members to reuse; for example, European Knowledge Pool System (ARIADNE) and The Carnegie Foundation for the Advancement of Teaching (KEEP).

The diversity of digital repository implementation strategies indicates some of the complexity faced by those embarking on the design of a new initiative. Although, there is a range of options for repository management, all require effective search mechanisms to assist users in their assessment and selection of a resource. To do this well the designers of any repository must develop a sound understanding of the potential users of their system and of the culture into which the repository will need to be integrated. In this chapter we focus on how the notions of learning objects and digital repositories informed the conceptualisation and planning for *The Carrick Exchange*, a repository under development for the Australian higher education community, and in particular on the framework developed to capture users' needs.

BACKGROUND

The Carrick Institute for Learning and Teaching in Higher Education was established by the Australian Commonwealth government in 2004 with the aim of promoting and advancing learning and teaching in Australian higher education. In addition to administering competitive grant funding for teaching and learning initiatives and overseeing a system of national teaching awards, part of the Institute's brief is to establish *The Carrick Exchange*, "a new online service that will provide learning and teaching resources and functions to support communication and collaboration across the (Australian) and international higher education sector" (Carrick Institute, 2007, p. 3). This project is part of the wider *Resource Identification and Networking Portfolio* charged with identifying, disseminating, and embedding good practices in higher education and with promoting the development of networks and communities (see http://www.carrickinstitute.edu.au/carrick/go/home/rin). The development of networks and communities of practice is seen as a key component to enable the sector to engage with *The Carrick Exchange,* moving beyond the idea of just exchanging resources.

The Carrick Institute's initial collection will comprise teaching and learning resources and research outcomes funded under current projects and grant schemes, and an archive of material funded by earlier government initiatives. It will include a directory of contributors, a description of their expertise, and will provide space for the developing network of educators to dialogue through *The Carrick Exchange*. There will also be a federated search mechanism linking it with other national and international repositories. The purpose of *The Carrick Exchange* is to provide:

- Access to quality resources that support teaching and learning by searching and browsing;
- Access to learning materials available for sharing and repurposing;
- Information about new technologies that impact on teaching practice and student learning experiences;
- Ideas about learning and practice;
- Opportunities to network with other academics with similar interests in group spaces and/or through creating networks of colleagues;
- The ability to save resources and search results;
- The ability to comment on and exchange ideas on the relevance and usefulness of particular teaching resources and to view the comments of others;
- The ability to participate in discussions, debates and dialogue about teaching in higher education (Carrick Institute, 2007, p. 3).

To inform the development of the repository, a project was established to investigate the "state of play" with respect to digital resources for enhancing teaching and learning in the higher education sector, the key success factors and issues in the utilisation of such digital repositories, and requirements for a successful reusable resource repository. Undertaken in late 2006, the purpose of this project was to develop a sound understanding of existing repository initiatives in Australia and around the world, and relate those to the particular context of the project.

One of the major difficulties in the uptake of digital repositories is their adoption by individual academics and institutions, and the application of resources in contexts other than the development environment. The aim of the project was to examine strategies for incorporating the use of these repositories into normal academic work practices. Much of the research and development in this area has focussed on technical and supply-side issues, with insufficient attention paid to the needs of the people using repositories. Understanding the needs of users, and contexts of use, for such digital repositories is a neglected area, and a better evidence base is urgently needed to avoid unwise investment and development strategies.

The approach adopted by the research team was to concurrently undertake an analysis of the relevant research literature and an analysis of existing repositories in Australia and around the world. The team also developed an online survey of potential users, seeking volunteers from the membership of three professional associations in Australia—*ascilite* (http://www.ascilite.org), the Open and Distance Learning Association of Australia (http://www.odlaa.org) and the Higher Education Research and Development Society of Australia (http://herdsa.org.au). The survey asked respondents a series of multiple-choice questions to determine: (1) their disciplinary/topical area of interest; (2) the likelihood they would access a learning object repository to support a range of content selection, activity design or professional learning tasks; (3) the importance they placed on various characteristics of a repository, such as local content, easy access, detailed metadata; (4) the importance of various types of recognition for contributions they might make to a repository; (5) their awareness of major repositories. Options were also provided for respondents to add additional information as free text where they wished. A total of 86 respondents completed all questions in the survey, which, though too small to be considered representative of the sector, was useful in gathering some background information from those who might use the system. The outcome of the project was the development of a needs analysis framework which was presented at a "think tank" meeting that included key stakeholder representatives from across the sector to inform the further development of the repository.

KEY THEMES DERIVED TO INFORM THE NEEDS ANALYSIS FRAMEWORK

Use of Digital Repositories

There is very little information or research to conclusively determine the extent to which university educators are using existing digital repositories. This is particularly so of very large repositories that seek to appeal to a mass audience, rather than within-institution or more targeted initiatives with a smaller number of potential users. One empirical study to support the notion that educators are using digital repositories is that of Najjar, Ternier, and Duval (2004). This study investigated the ways in which users interacted with learning object repositories by logging the queries of the ARIADNE digital repository over periods of 4 to 10 months. These queries when analysed equated to 4,723 queries from about 390 different users, and were found to have come predominantly from educational institutions. However, the authors concluded that it was difficult to draw conclusions about the motivations of users from their search activities.

It appears that educators are using digital repositories in different ways and with varying purposes. A review of literature (Bradley & Boyle, 2004; Campbell, Littlejohn & Duncan, 2001; Koppi & Lavitt, 2003; Koppi, Bogle, & Lavitt, 2004; Lambropoulos & Christopoulou, 2004; Littlejohn, 2003a; Malcolm, 2005; Oliver, 2001; Poupa & Forte, 2003; Wilson & Mundell, 2004), the online survey conducted to inform this project, and case studies reported in digital repositories indicate that some of the reasons educators are using digital repositories are to:

- Acquire resources to develop or enhance learning and teaching experiences or course materials;
- Manage information and knowledge for sharing among communities of practice; the repurposing and subsequent development of digital resources, by educators from various departments, faculties and universities, can be stored and shared from a common repository;
- Promote the collegial and collaborative development of learning and teaching resources and practices across communities of practice;
- Save time that might otherwise be spent developing new learning and teaching resources or course materials;
- Gain recognition, educators who have put time and effort into developing learning resources are able to share the products and communicate the educational developments with peers;
- Archive course resources for students to access (e.g., the background reading for a lecture or the actual lecture taped for students to access and review prior to the face-to-face session so that other forms of instruction/topics can be covered in class);
- Provide students with additional resources to supplement or consolidate their learning (e.g., WebQuests with real-world implications that allow learners to revise, analyse and synthesize data);
- Document evidence of excellence in teaching, for promotion and tenure.

As part of this project an online survey was conducted to ascertain why respondents might access digital repositories. A summary of responses, shown in Table 1, suggests that obtaining resources to use in teaching would be a significant motivation to access a repository.

GENERAL ISSUES FOR THE IMPLEMENTATION OF DIGITAL REPOSITORIES

Rogers (1995) proposed a list of features that largely determine or impact on the acceptance of technology. Some of these features are relevant for the acceptance of digital repositories and can be adapted as questions that should underpin consideration of the key success factors and issues in the use of digital repositories:

Is the operation of the repository easy to understand, maintain, and use?

- Are the benefits of the repository as an educational tool obvious?
- Is the use of the repository more convenient, more worthwhile?
- Does the repository address the needs of the potential users?
- Is there enough support for the use of the repository?
- Is there enough time, energy, money, and resources to ensure the repository's success?

A register of contributing conditions can also be generated to anticipate potential reasons for the failure of an innovative initiative, such as the introduction of a digital repository. Latham (1988) identified a number of features common to failed innovations that could be relevant to the introduction of a digital repository. Understanding these features could ensure that barriers do not thwart key success factors or exacerbate challenges to the use of digital repositories. In terms of the current project, these include the following possibilities:

- Practitioners become disenchanted and disillusioned because the use of the digital repository is more difficult than expected, causing unnecessary disruptions and lengthy delays to their progress.
- Champions for the digital repository leave or are not available.
- People lack training in the use of the digital repository and subsequently lose enthusiasm.
- Funding to support the implementation and promotion of the digital repository runs out.
- There is inadequate supervision and support for users accessing the digital repository.
- The transitional stage of the digital repository's introduction lacks accountability, monitoring, review, assessment, and or evaluation.
- There is a "take-it-or-leave-it" attitude on behalf of the repository's promoters.

Table 1. Reasons for accessing a digital repository (n=86)

I would access a repository to obtain:	never	rarely	some-times	often	always
a. A learning object to complement an aspect of a lecture or other learning experience I was developing (e.g., text, images, video, sound)	0%	12%	34%	**48%**	7%
b. An activity for a lesson I was teaching (e.g., quiz, discussion starter, workbook, exercise, assessment task)	2%	16%	**38%**	35%	8%
c. A plan for a session in a course I was teaching (e.g., tutorial, workshop, lecture).	6%	28%	**37%**	24%	5%
d. A course program for a subject I was teaching (including lecture notes, tutorial sessions, workshops, recorded lecture presentations, assessment tasks, etc.)	8%	**40%**	28%	20%	5%
e. Information about learning and teaching pedagogy	5%	17%	**38%**	31%	8%

KEY FACTORS CONTRIBUTING TO THE SUCCESS OF DIGITAL REPOSITORIES

There have been a number of studies and literature reviews conducted evaluating digital repositories and proposing motivating factors for their use (Bradley & Boyle, 2004; Gosper, Woo, Gibbs, Hand, Kerr, & Rich, 2004; Littlejohn, 2003a; Littlejohn, Jung, & Broumley, 2003). A summary of the factors proposed in these studies and literature identifies the following as incentives for using digital repositories:

- Saves time in preparation,
- Quality assurance,
- Communities of practice,
- Acknowledgment,
- Provides flexibility, and
- Access and control of educational information.

Saves Time in Preparation

Educators can save time and money in the development of teaching activities, sessions, or courses by reusing and adapting existing educational resources for a new context. Instead of creating every learning resource from scratch, which is an activity that consumes many educators' time; digital repositories provide a mechanism that enables educators to access quality resources aligned to teaching aims. The time required to search for, access, and adapt resources available from digital repositories is far less than that required to create a learning resource from scratch, which is an enormous incentive for educators to use digital repositories.

The studies of Gosper et al. (2004) and Koppi and Lavitt (2003) both found that time and workload pressures were incentives in the utilisation of digital repositories. However, it is important to note that participants in both these studies indicated they were prepared to spend time searching for learning objects if they were confident that the available resources were:

- Relevant to teaching aims,
- Quality resources,
- Atypical or uncommon and
- Potential assets to enhance students' learning.

Campbell (2003), in support of the notion that time saving is a powerful incentive for educators to utilise digital repositories added that this was conditional on the digital resources being contained in a pedagogical framework. The incentive for using digital repositories to save time is dependent on the perceived quality and value of the learning objects stored in the repository. As such, the management of most digital repositories includes some form of quality assurance to warrant and promote the merit of the learning objects it contains.

Quality Assurance

Quality assurance is critical for widespread adoption of a digital repository (Poupa & Forte, 2003). Enthusiasm for reusing learning objects housed in digital repositories is influenced by the quality control mechanisms engaged by the repository. There are three different aspects of quality assurance related to resources contained in digital repositories:

- The technical quality of a learning object, and
- The quality of a learning object's content, and
- Ease of use.

It would be assumed and expected that digital repository learning objects should be technically sound in relation to standards and usability, and that they function as expected. However, quality assurance of content does not necessarily hold the same guarantee. Most digital repositories engage a peer review process of some sort to exercise control over the quality of the objects collected and to encourage the participation of community members. There are varying protocols for the review process undertaken by digital repositories but the intentions of these are largely concerned with an assessment of the:

- Validity and quality of the content,
- Pedagogical value of the learning object, and
- Overall contribution of the learning object to student learning.

Methods are also emerging to assist educators to judge the quality of the learning resources for themselves. The generation of dynamic histories, to provide users with the ability to search for the most widely used learning objects on a given topic, is one strategy being investigated as a mechanism for learning object validation (Campbell, 2003).

Educators accept that resources published in peer-reviewed books and journals are of adequate quality. However, aligning this judgment of quality to the learning objects housed in digital repositories appears to be a little more difficult. Peer review that is facilitated within communities of practice is assisting this transition and serving as an incentive for using digital repositories.

Communities of Practice

Many digital repositories are created with a specific community in mind, for example a university repository will primarily serve its community of university students, educators, and academics. These repositories can be either public or restricted to serve only the community, or can provide mixed access with a blend of privileges depending upon user identity and role.

There are incentives for using repositories that target a community of practice, particularly in regard to the resources they house. The resources in these repositories will predominantly be developed by members of the particular community of practice to address the needs and focus areas of that community. Consequently, the learning resources will inevitably be content appropriate with only contextual modification by the user necessary. The availability of this calibre of resource will make the development of learning and teaching resources a far more efficient process.

Accessing resources in these repositories is time efficient, as the metadata attached to the resources is relevant and familiar to the members of the community of practice. As such, searches within the repository can be explicit and refinement of the available resources more exact.

Gosper et al. (2004) reported that educators would be willing to share resources on a professional basis in an effort to develop a community of practice. These educators were also keen to engage in a learning object economy within this community because it exposed them to new ideas and high-quality practice. By sharing learning resources educators could see that they were contributing to building communities of practice in which academics assisted each other to provide students with high quality learning resources.

A further incentive for using digital repositories is the opportunity and mechanism they provide for educators to promote their contributions and efforts within their particular community of practice to other members of the community. This is a means of gaining acknowledgement and recognition in much the same way as an educator's contributions to peer reviewed books and journals will achieve. Identification of a network of expertise, including individuals with similar interests and specific strengths, results in a valuable community of practice to be supported by a repository such as *The Carrick Exchange*.

Acknowledgment

Acknowledgement of an individual's contributions in the development of a learning object is highly regarded as an incentive for contributing resources to digital repositories. Gosper et al. (2004) found acknowledgement was a far greater incentive for sharing learning objects than was payment.

The online survey further endorsed this finding with respondents confirming that financial remuneration was not as great an incentive for contributing to a digital repository as was formal recognition and acknowledgement of the contribution by the repository's management or the contributor's university, faculty, or department (see Table 2).

Educators, according to Koppi and Lavitt (2003), require professional recognition of the contributions they make to digital repositories especially if that recognition could possibly lead to promotion. This notion is supported in other literature affirming the importance of recognising digital repository contributions in tenure or promotion processes (Campbell, 2003; Taylor & Richardson, 2001). Engagement in the learning object economy needs to align to the opportunities and rewards provided through traditional forms of sharing in academic circles.

Acknowledgement of repository contributions is a significant innovation in the CLOE repository. Members who submit learning objects receive yearly updates on CLOE letter-head, signed by the director and providing details of how many different courses benefited from the learning object throughout the year, at what level those courses were offered and how many students were involved. Additionally, submitters receive written notification advising when their learning objects are accepted by CLOE for reuse. These activities are specifically intended to assist submitters in promotion and tenure processes, and to include in their curriculum vitae.

Provides Flexibility

Flexibility is applicable to two aspects of digital repository use. First, flexibility is the capacity for educators to repurpose or customise learning objects to suit their specific learning requirements; for example, changing the wording of a learning object to give a local voice or changing content examples to suit a particular student group. According to Gosper et al. (2004) an educator's ability and rights to customise learning objects is an essential criterion in their use of learning objects and a subsequent incentive for using digital repositories.

Table 2. Incentives for contributing to a digital repository (n=86)

Rate the following in terms of how strongly you agree or disagree	strongly disagree	disagree	neutral	agree	strongly agree
a. I would be willing to contribute a learning object to a learning repository.	1%	2%	15%	**60%**	21%
b. I would be willing to contribute a learning object to a learning repository if I received formal recognition from the repository's management of my contribution.	0%	2%	12%	**60%**	26%
c. I would be willing to contribute a learning object to a learning repository if I received formal recognition of my contribution from my University/ Faculty/ Department.	0%	2%	16%	**53%**	28%
d. I would be willing to contribute a learning object to a learning repository if I received remuneration for my contribution.	8%	17%	**40%**	27%	8%

This incentive is the essence of why digital repositories are created; consequently, measures to reinforce this aspect of flexibility are often promoted in the operation and management of a repository. Some repositories encourage the repurposing of learning objects by providing tools to assist users to customise the digital resource (e.g., the tools for modifying learning objects that are available from the ARIADNE repository and the KEEP toolkit offered for users in the Carnegie Foundation for the Advancement of Teaching repository).

The second aspect of flexibility that is an incentive for using digital repositories is the flexibility that educators have through federated searches to access resources from a range of digital repositories and not just the one source. The digital resource economy provides educators with the flexibility and resources to adapt, adopt, and add to their course materials as desired.

Access and Control of Educational Information

The most common reason for educators to choose a learning object was the object's relevance to curriculum according to Gosper et al. (2004). The educators in this study specifically reported that when choosing between resources, they were more likely to look for relevant materials that were easy to locate, access, and acquire. Apart from educational efficacy, the reported appeal of learning objects for teachers in the Gosper et al. (2004) study was the potential to improve the efficiency of their work through the provision of a large repository of relevant objects that could be accessed via search mechanisms that used educational criteria relevant to their own context.

Participants indicated that they were generally unsatisfied with the outcomes of Internet searches, and required systems that categorised learning objects in a way that more closely matched their local syllabus and curriculum outcomes, as was the case with some digital repositories. These educators also indicated that they preferred learning objects that had clear instructions for use, to ensure they selected resources that all students could access and had the technical skills to use. Overall, the teachers in this study placed educational efficacy and efficiency as the main concerns for using and choosing between learning objects.

Unlike the Web, digital repositories can provide certain control functionalities. Some repositories provide educators with the ability to:

- Determine who can access the published resources (e.g., access could be limited to those enrolled in a course/class, anyone registered with a particular university/universities, anyone possessing a valid user ID certificate, or to anyone in the world),
- Place restrictions on the reuse and repurposing of digital resources,
- Record details.

Other strategies offered in digital repositories to encourage reuse and repurposing of learning objects centre around the issue of rights security. Repositories often use licences, memorandums of understanding and terms and conditions to ensure the integrity of learning objects. In many instances learning objects cannot be submitted or accessed without attending to these agreements. These measures are intended to assure users of their rights and thereby encourage the reuse and repurposing of learning objects accessible from the digital repository.

Respondents to our online survey indicated that the most significant factors for selecting digital repositories are that the:

- Learning objects are easily accessed, downloaded, and manipulated;
- Search mechanism is consistent with Internet searching protocols;
- Repository provides detailed information (metadata) about the learning object; and

- Repository engages sound quality control practices that are applied to all learning objects prior to being accepted (see Table 3).

KEY BARRIERS TO THE SUCCESS OF DIGITAL REPOSITORIES

Digital repositories are capable of delivering significant benefits for communities of teachers and learners but the human barriers to encouraging sharing can be difficult to overcome. Wetterling and Collis (2003) found that the major problems in the utilisation of digital repositories were often culturally based in relation to collaboration among partners and a lack of overall willingness of users to participate in a learning object culture where educators share and use learning objects created by each other. Littlejohn, Jung, and Broumley (2003) identified barriers in the use of digital repositories as:

- Insufficient hardware to support the use of multimedia Web resources within classrooms;
- Too few reusable resources that would directly map with lesson objectives;
- Outdated resources that often require updating;
- Not enough time to search for good quality materials and evaluate existing materials;
- Lack of robustness of external materials;
- Poor accessibility of resources;
- Copyright issues;
- Insufficient time to use Web resources in class; and
- Lack of evidence of the effectiveness of using Web resources.

A summation of these and other factors identified in literature and research studies as disincentives for using digital repositories include issues related to:

- Intellectual property rights, copyright, and learning object management,
- Time, workload, and effort,
- Communities of practice,
- Quality control,
- Context appropriateness, and
- Interoperability.

Table 3. Reasons for accessing a digital repository (n=86)

Rate the following in terms of importance to you when selecting a learning repository	of no import-ance	not import-ant	not sure if it is import-ant	import-ant	vitally import-ant
a. The repository is suitable for the Australian context.	3%	8%	17%	**48%**	23%
b. The repository stores the actual learning object rather than directing the user to a secondary Web site where the object is held.	5%	22%	13%	**36%**	24%
c. The repository learning objects are easily accessed, downloaded and manipulated.	0%	0%	1%	31%	**67%**
d. The repository search mechanism is consistent with Internet searching protocols.	0%	2%	12%	**44%**	42%
e. The repository provides detailed information (metadata) about the learning object.	0%	7%	13%	**43%**	37%
f. The repository engages sound quality control practices that are applied to all learning objects prior to being accepted.	1%	5%	9%	**45%**	40%
g. The repository provides an evaluation (e.g., peer review, user review) of the learning objects.	1%	6%	17%	**57%**	19%

Intellectual Property Rights, Copyright, and Learning Object Management

The sharing of intellectual property is often conditional on certain copyright conditions. The management of these conditions can be daunting for some educators and the proposition of dealing with them a greater burden than many are willing to accept for the sake of sharing resources with others. The Gosper et al. (2004) study affirmed this premise that educators were not prepared to deal with unresolved copyright issues and that these copyright issues can be a disincentive to them for using digital repositories. They also found that a lack of knowledge about copyright was a deterrent to educators reusing learning objects. Educators in this case see the responsibility of copyright clearance a burden that they are not willing to bear to utilise the learning objects held in digital repositories.

A study conducted to investigate the use of ICT for teaching and learning found that educators were not as comfortable providing students with electronic resources as they were with supplying them with hardcopy materials. Their issues related to the copyright of materials, with educators feeling under scrutiny and insecure with regards to copyright of materials distributed to students online, compared with the distribution of paper-based resources (Littlejohn, Campbell, Tizard, & Smith, 2003). This is a disincentive to using digital repositories that is addressed in some repositories with a copyright statement. This statement or in some cases agreement is intended to elucidate the importance of exchange, requiring contributors to agree to users freely using, developing and adapting their materials either to improve their own practice or to help develop others' skills.

Some educators are wary of sharing their resources within and beyond their communities of practice if there is a perception that intellectual property rights are at risk of being violated. Concerns exist in relation to the repurposing of learning objects. If an original learning object is adapted, repurposed and republished by another user, then who is the recorded "author"? This inability to control intellectual property rights is often a disincentive for educators to share their resources.

Participants in the Gosper et al. (2004) study were conversely apprehensive about customising learning objects. They were concerned with limitations that could be imposed on them by the creators of learning objects. Inadequate resolution of these intellectual property issues, particularly in relation to customisation requirements, can have a negative effect on the use of digital repositories.

In addition there is often no formal means of recording learning object management information such as: acquisition details, the extent to which a resource can be distributed, whether or not it can be adapted, the boundaries of the community for which it is intended and the number of versions a single repository may hold. With the reuse of learning objects across communities of practice and international boundaries, many educators are reluctant to contribute to repositories when these management issues are not formally addressed in the submission or utilisation of digital resources (Campbell, 2003).

Time, Workload, and Effort

Although repositories can offer substantial time savings through the utilisation of resources that others have produced, there is a time commitment required to learn about and use this tool. Often the perception is that the commitment of time to learn about and use a repository is great. This is a barrier that technology cannot solve but is one that requires changing work practices and culture.

The studies both found that time and workload pressures were issues in the utilisation of digital repositories according to two recent studies (Gosper et al., 2004; Koppi & Lavitt, 2003). Participants in these studies indicated that institutions encouraging the reuse of learning objects needed to allocate sufficient time to allow educators to:

- Search for and acquire learning objects,
- Make the necessary changes to their curricula and teaching practices, and
- Attend professional development programs developing the underpinning technical and pedagogical skills required.

To ensure others can source materials from a digital repository, each resource submitted must be tagged with metadata during upload. A major shortcoming of using metadata, and a disincentive for submitting resources to digital repositories, is the time spent on completing metadata fields (Goodacre & Rowlands, 2005; Neven, Duval, Ternier, Cardinaels, & Vandepitte, 2003). This time pressure was highlighted amongst the issues identified in a study of the uptake of learning objects conducted by Koppi and Lavitt (2003). Staff found uploading and tagging their learning objects time-consuming and intrusive to their daily work.

Standards for recording Learning Object Metadata (LOM) have been instigated to warrant some consistency in the classification of learning objects. It has been noted, however, that the full set of 86 elements in LOM are not worthy of the investment of time required to compile the complete classification record (Goodacre & Rowlands, 2005; Mohan & Greer, 2004; Richards, McGreal, & Friesen, 2002). Even if it were possible to capture the metadata elements specified in LOM, the usefulness of the metadata in reusing learning objects is questionable (Farance, 2003; Mohan & Brooks, 2003; Wiley, 2002). For example, the LOM standard contains elements such as Semantic Density and Interactivity Level, which mean different things to different people therefore the benefits of standardisation are lost.

The time taken to enter metadata can be considerably reduced by using "application profiles" such as CanCore, which contains only 36 elements from the LOM, and are considered essential for promoting the discovery and reuse of learning objects. According to Neven et al. (2003), it is also possible to automatically generate several metadata fields before data entry by a human user.

Another solution is to make available tools that automatically create as much metadata as possible. Given access to these tools, tutors need not be concerned with metadata standards, though they are still required to describe a few, specific elements by selecting from a controlled vocabulary or by entering free text (Littlejohn, 2003a).

Culture Change

Research has shown that although educators are willing to reuse resources produced by others, many are much less willing to share their own materials (Campbell, Littlejohn, & Duncan, 2001). There are a number of reasons why this may be the case, and Duncan and Ekmekcioglu (2003) maintain that for some educators it may be more than an unwillingness to share, there may be a fear or insecurity of exposing how they teach.

Whilst collaboration is viewed as desirable, rivalry, particularly among universities where competition for students is high, does exist. Academics are generally happy to share resources with their colleagues in other universities if there is no competition for student enrolments, as is the case with subjects in high demand. However, in disciplines where there is greater competition for student enrolments and less demand for certain subjects, academics may be less likely to share with each other in order to protect their own interests (Gosper et al., 2004). Another significant disincentive for using digital repositories was that some faculties considered the learning objects held in digital repositories to be inappropriate to their learning and teaching programs (Gosper et al., 2004; Koppi & Lavitt, 2003).

A situation that has been encountered by some repositories is that in the early stages of operation people in some large institutions do not want to share with those in smaller institutions on an equal basis because they perceive that the smaller institutions gain more than they contribute, at the expense of the larger institutions. This issue has been managed in some instances with an agreement that states that all affiliated and participating institutions are bound to share equally.

These issues require a shift in the culture and perception of the learning object economy and adequate promotion of the benefits of a viable economy. Duncan and Ekmekcioglu (2003) advise that to realise the benefits of digital repositories, it is best to start with communities of noncompetitive, natural collaborators and quickly establish a critical mass of shared resources.

Quality Control

The perceived quality of available resources can influence educators' use of the digital repository. Educators are quite reluctant to spend time searching a repository for a resource if they believe that the quality of the resource they might acquire could be questionable. The content shared in a repository is key to its success. One primary motivation for using digital repositories is to get access to a wide variety of high-quality knowledge resources. If this need cannot be satisfied for any reason, users will not persist in using the repository. According to Koppi, Bogle, and Lavitt (2004), some users believe that their materials are not good enough to be considered "quality resources"; but this is a perception only based on the undefined subjective criteria of these individual users. In the case of the Universitas 21 Consortium (U21), regarding this notion of quality resources, a decision was made to let the owner of the resource make the decision (without formal criteria) as to whether or not the learning object would be submitted. Eventually it became a matter of trust with the recommendation made that teachers were trusted to provide their students with quality learning materials, so why should it be any different for the submission of resources to the digital repository.

Context Appropriateness

In general, when designing resources educators take into consideration the constraints of the educational setting within which they operate and consequently design learning objects to suit the context of their particular educational setting, resulting in resources that are context-dependent and less reusable in other settings.

Learning objects are predominantly designed and produced to meet specific educational needs, this motivation or stimulus for the creation of a learning object does not necessarily align to the requirements for a learning object to be transferable across educational settings, contexts and needs. Therefore educators utilising learning objects are often required to spend large amounts of time modifying the learning object which can equate to the time it would take to entirely develop the resource themselves.

To maximise their durability, it is generally agreed that resources must, as far as possible, be context-free. While contextual considerations may pervade the initial design process, specific context limitations should not, any more than necessary, constrain the durability of the object. Maximum durability requires the removal of as much contextual information as possible relating to approach, learner-target and even objective, from anywhere other than metadata (Oliver, 2001).

Interoperability

In order to participate in a learning object economy, educators must have access to the appropriate tools and resources such as content authoring and management systems, digital repositories and virtual and managed learning environments. Furthermore, if learning objects are to be shared then it is crucial that the tools, systems and components are "interoperable"; and the user and the contributor should be able to exchange information and use the information that has been exchanged (Campbell, 2003). An inability to provide or utilise this interoperability is a disincentive to using digital repositories.

The key principle of digital repositories is the interoperability between systems. Interoperability enables learning objects to be deployed in many systems, and it also enhances content sharability among individuals and between institutions (Mohan & Daniel, 2004). Currently there are many regional and international organisations working on the development of common standards for learning objects (e.g., ARIADNE, PROMETEUS, CEN/ISS; SCORM, CanCore, and CANARIE) to enhance the likelihood of this interoperability.

Users need to be able to search easily for and locate the learning object resources they require using a method that is consistent with Internet searching protocols. There should be a benchmark of standards set to ensure that learning objects are interoperable. Interoperability means that a resource would be delivered in a form that can be used by all, or at least most, other systems (Duncan & Ekmekcioglu, 2003).

A lack of interoperable standards among the different learning systems is a significant hindrance to system interaction. Though there are standards like IMS Global Learning Consortium, 2003 and SCORM (2004) to define and describe learning materials to be exchanged and reused across the different e-larning platforms the communication and interaction of learning objects can still be lacking.

A learning resource catalogue (LRC) that comprised records of learning objects was developed and used by members of the Universitas 21 Consortium for three years (Koppi, Bogle & Lavitt, 2004). The LRC provided a standardised means of identifying and describing learning and teaching materials in order to facilitate reuse and minimise replication. The interoperability qualities that the LRC set were aimed at academic staff and may be a model useful in negating the disincentive that a lack of interoperability can evoke.

The Web-based interface also needs to be fairly intuitive to accommodate the large numbers of people for whom training in the use of the digital repository is not feasible. If a user cannot operate the mechanics of the repository quickly they will inevitably disregard the resource as a viable educational tool.

NEEDS ANALYSIS FRAMEWORK

Using the emerging themes from the literature, existing repository projects and the online survey, the project team developed a needs analysis framework, reproduced in full in Appendix A. The framework was used to structure a one-day "think tank," which brought together 50 representatives of stakeholder groups from around Australia, including teaching staff, researchers, administrators, and technical experts. The outcomes of this meeting were used to further guide the development of specifications for the repository.

The framework is founded on the assumption that the following factors need to be considered in the design of a digital repository if the eventual repository is to be effective and successful:

- Adequate and appropriate encouragement for contributors;
- Willing and extensive sharing of learning objects;
- Viable rewards for both contributors and users of the repositor;
- Broad promotion of the digital repository.

The framework comprises a list of considerations that have been developed based on the success factors and key issues for using digital repositories identified within the context of *The Carrick Exchange* project. However, it is possible to apply these more generally and developers of other repositories may find them helpful in informing their process in identifying requirements for a project. The items could be used as a basis for discussions amongst stakeholders, or as the basis for survey or interview questions in the collection of data from potential users or a repository. Further, this structure could be used in reporting options or decisions made back to stakeholders. Importantly, it would support a methodical approach to address key issues in repository design and development. It is important to note that this is not an exhaustive list and can be adapted or appended according to the context. Decisions made on the basis of such a framework could then be used to inform technical specifications.

A JISC-funded project in the UK, Community Dimensions of Learning Object Repositories (CDLOR), recently released their study on the barriers and enablers to engagement in such repositories (http://www.academy.gcal.ac.uk/cdlor/). Their research, coupled with the ongoing research by *The Carrick Exchange* research team, will aim to address some of the major issues identified through the design and development phase of *The Carrick Exchange* (Lefoe, O'Reilly, Parrish, Bennett, Keppell, & Gunn, 2007; Littlejohn, 2005; Margaryan & Littlejohn, 2007). This collaboration will inform future development of this and similar projects.

FUTURE TRENDS

Although the project had initially been focused on a repository as a means of storing, cataloguing and sharing teaching and learning resources, the key stakeholders participating in the "think tank" identified a need to go beyond the conventional notion of a repository to one where tools for networking and communicating were integrated. The potential for adopting Web 2.0 technologies for communication and collaboration to foster the development of a learning community in higher education, whilst also providing a central access point to an extensive database of resources was agreed to be the way forward. This has led to an emphasis on *The Carrick Exchange* as a "hub for Australian higher education, and integrating communities, users, networks, and resources."

Thus, one of the future trends for repository developers is to understand how emerging technologies, such as social bookmarking and community ratings, can enhance the usability and value of a resource repository in order to attract and engage users. The strategies that will be successful are the ones that take into account the needs of their target users, and in higher education this means understanding the needs and work practices of time-pressured teaching academics and support staff attempting to cater for a diverse student population. Furthermore, we need to learn much more about what can attract university educators to reusing learning resources created by others and to sharing resources they have created themselves in an academic culture that is slow to change.

CONCLUSION

Since the emergence of the learning object concept there has been considerable interest from educators, researchers, and technical experts. Key to the success of any learning object initiative is the provision of repositories that enable effective storage and retrieval. To be successful the design of such repositories must be based on a sound understanding of the needs and motivations of potential users. Without such an understanding the initiative is likely to fail.

This chapter has presented a needs analysis framework for developing repository functionality to meet the needs of potential users of the system. Although developed to inform *The Carrick Exchange* project, it offers a more generic framework that could be adapted or appended for other repository development projects. Frameworks of this kind are necessary to inform the technical decision making of any repository initiative.

ACKNOWLEDGMENT

Support for this research has been provided by the Carrick Institute for Learning and Teaching in Higher education, an initiative of the Australian Government Department of Education, Science, and Training. The views expressed in this chapter do not necessarily reflect the views of The Carrick Institute for Learning and Teaching in Higher education. We also wish to acknowledge the additional support provided by the *ascilite* executive team, especially Cath Gunn, and *The Carrick Exchange* Project Team including Project Leader Prof Jan Orrell, Project Coordinator, Elizabeth Greener, and Senior Fellow, Rob Phillips.

REFERENCES

Agostinho, S., Bennett, S., Lockyer, L., & Harper, B. (2004). Developing a learning object metadata application profile based on LOM suitable for the Australian higher education context. *Australasian Journal of Educational Technology, 20*(2), 191-208.

Bradley, C., & Boyle, T. (2004). The design, development, and use of multimedia learning objects *Journal of Educational Multimedia and Hypermedia, 13*(4), 371-389.

Campbell, L.M. (2003). Engaging with the learning object economy. In A. Littlejohn (Ed.), *Reusing online resources: A sustainable approach to e-learning* (pp. 35-45). London: Kogan Page.

Campbell, L.M., Littlejohn, A.H., & Duncan, C. (2001). Share and share alike: Encouraging the reuse of academic resources through the Scottish electronic staff development library. *Association of Learning Technologies Journal (ALT-J), 9*(2), 28-38.

The Carrick Institute. (2007). The Carrick exchange overview 2007. Retrieved March 28, 2008, from http://www.carrickinstitute.edu.au/carrick/webdav/site/carricksite/users/siteadmin/public/rin_carrickexchange_overview_2007.pdf

Dalziel, J. (2006). Building communities of designers. In H. Beetham & R. Sharpe (Eds.), *Design for learning: Rethinking pedagogy for a digital age*. RoutledgeFalmer: London.

Duncan, C., & Ekmekcioglu, C. (2003). In A. Littlejohn (Ed.), *Reusing online resources: A sustainable approach to e-learning* (pp. 135-145). London: Kogan Page.

Farance, F. (2003). IEEE LOM standard not yet ready for "prime time." *Learning Technology, 5*(1).

Goodacre, C., & Rowlands, D. (2005). Real world metadata management for resource discovery: Proof of concept across education and library sectors in Tasmania. In J. Dalziel, R. Philip, & J. Clare (Eds.), *The COLIS project: Collaborative online learning and information services* (pp. 163-185). Sydney, NSW: Macquarie University E-Learning Centre of Excellence.

Gosper, M., Woo, K., Gibbs, D., Hand, T., Kerr, S., & Rich, D. (2004). Learning objects: User perspectives on the conditions surrounding their use. In L. Cantoni & C. McLoughlin, (Eds), *Proceedings of World Conference on Educational Multimedia, Hypermedia and Telecommunications 2004* (pp. 66-72). Chesapeake, VA: AACE.

IMS Global Learning Consortium. (2003). *IMS learning design best practice and implementation guide version 1.0 final specification*. IMS Global Learning Consortium Inc. Retrieved October 11, 2006, from http://www.imsglobal.org

Koppi, T., Bogle L., & Lavitt, N. (2004). Institutional use of learning objects: Lessons learned and future directions. *Journal of Educational Multimedia and Hypermedia, 13*(4), 449-463.

Koppi, T., & Lavitt, N. (2003). Institutional use of learning objects three years on: Lessons learned and future directions. In D. Lassner & C. McNaught (Eds.), *Proceedings of World Conference on Educational Multimedia, Hypermedia and Telecommunications 2003* (pp. 644-648). Chesapeake, VA: AACE.

Lambropoulos, N., & Christopoulou, M. (2004). Cultural-based learning objects in a blended environment for Greek and Greek-Cypriot students in U.K. In L. Cantoni & C. McLoughlin (Eds.), *Proceedings of World Conference on Educational Multimedia, Hypermedia and Telecommunications 2004* (pp. 1851-1856). Chesapeake, VA: AACE.

Latham, G. (1988). The birth and death cycles of educational innovations. *Principal, 68*(1), 41-43.

Learning Technology Standards Committee. (2002). IEEE Standard for Learning Object Metadata. IEEE Standard 1484.12.1, Institute of Electrical and Electronics Engineers, New York. Retrieved March 28, 2008, from http://ltsc.ieee.org/wg12/files/LOM_1484_12_1_v1_Final_Draft.pdf

Lefoe, G., O'Reilly, M., Parrish, D., Bennett, S., Keppell, M., & Gunn, C. (2007). The Carrick exchange: Not just another repository. In C. Montgomerie & J. Seale (Eds.), *Proceedings of World Conference on Educational Multimedia, Hypermedia and Telecommunications 2007* (pp. 108-113). Chesapeake, VA: AACE.

Littlejohn, A. (Ed.) (2003a). *Reusing online resources: A sustainable approach to e-learning.* London: Kogan Page.

Littlejohn, A. (2003b). An incremental approach to staff development in the reuse of learning resources. In A. Littlejohn (Ed.), *Reusing online resources: A sustainable approach to e-learning* (pp. 221-233). London: Kogan Page.

Littlejohn, A. (2005). Keynote presentation: Community dimensions of learning object repositories. In H. Goss (Ed.), *Balance, fidelity, mobility: Maintaining the momentum? Proceedings of the 22nd Annual Conference of ascilite* (p. 3). Brisbane: Teaching & Learning Support Services, QUT.

Littlejohn, A., & Buckingham Shum, S. (2003). JIME special issue on reusing online resources. *Journal of Interactive Media in Education.* Retrieved March 28, 2008, from http://www-jime.open.ac.uk/2003/1/

Littlejohn, A.H., Campbell, L.M., Tizard, J., & Smith, A. (2003). From pilot project to strategic development: Scaling up staff support in the use of ICT for teaching and learning, *Journal of Further and Higher education, 7*(1), 47-52.

Littlejohn, A., Jung, I., & Broumley, L. (2003). A comparison of issues in the reuse of resources in schools and colleges. In A. Littlejohn (Ed.), *Reusing online resources: A sustainable approach to e-learning* (pp. 212-220). London: Kogan Page.

Malcolm, M. (2005). The exercise of the object: Issues in resource reusability and reuse, *British Journal of Educational Technology, 36*(1), 33-41.

Margaryan, A., & Littlejohn, A. (2007). Community dimensions of learning object repositories. In C. Montgomerie & J. Seale (Eds.), *Proceedings of World Conference on Educational Multimedia, Hypermedia and Telecommunications 2007* (pp. 4335-4343). Chesapeake, VA: AACE.

Mohan, P., & Brooks, C. (2003, July). Engineering a future for learning objects. *Proceedings of the International Conference on Web Engineering* (pp. 120-123). Oviedo, Spain.

Mohan, P., & Daniel, B. (2004). The learning objects approach: Challenges and opportunities. In G. Richards (Ed.), *Proceedings of World Conference on E-Learning in Corporate, Government, Healthcare, and Higher education 2004* (pp. 2512-2520). Chesapeake, VA: AACE.

Mohan, P., & Greer, J. (2003). Reusable learning objects: Current status and future directions. In D. Lassner & C. McNaught (Eds.), *Proceedings of World Conference on Educational Multimedia, Hypermedia and Telecommunications 2003* (pp. 257-264). Chesapeake, VA: AACE.

Najjar, J. Ternier, S., & Duval, E. (2004). User behaviour in learning objects repositories: An empirical analysis. In L. Catoni & C. McLoughlin (Eds.), *Proceedings of World Conference on E-Learning in Corporate, Government, Healthcare, and Higher education 2004* (pp. 4373-4378). Chesapeake, VA: AACE.

Neven, F., Duval, E., Ternier, S., Cardinaels, K., & Vandepitte, P. (2003). An open and flexible indexation and query tool for ARIADNE. In D. Lassner & C. McNaught (Eds.), *Proceedings of World Conference on Educational Multimedia, Hypermedia and Telecommunications 2003* (pp. 107-114). Chesapeake, VA: AACE.

Oliver, R. (2001). Learning objects: Supporting flexible delivery of online learning paradigms. In G. Kennedy & T. Petrovic (Eds.), *Proceedings of Annual Conference of the Australian Society for Computers in Learning in Tertiary Education* (pp. pp 453-460). Melbourne: Melbourne City Press.

Poupa, C., & Forte, E. (2003). Collaborative teaching with learning objects in an international, non-profit context. The example of the ARIADNE community. *Educational Media International, 40*(3/4), 239-248.

Richards, G.R., McGreal, R., & Freisen, N. (2002, June). Learning object repository technologies for telelearning: The evolution of POOL and CanCore. In *Proceedings of the IS2002, Informing Science + IT Education Conference*. Cork, Ireland: IS2002. Retrieved March 28, 2008, from http://proceedings.informingscience.org/IS2002Proceedings/papers/Richa242Learn.pdf

Rogers, E.M. (1995). *Diffusion of innovations* (4th ed). New York: Free Press.

SCORM. (2004). Advanced distributed learning - SCORM. Retrieved March 28, 2008, from http://www.adlnet.gov/scorm/

Taylor, P.G., & Richardson, A.S. (2001). *Validating scholarship in university teaching*. Canberra, Australia: Higher education Division, Department of Employment, Education, Training and Youth Affairs.

Wenger, E., McDermott, R., & Snyder, W. (2002). *Cultivating communities of practice*. Boston, MA: Harvard Business School Press.

Wetterling, J., & Collis, B. (2003). Sharing and reuse of learning resources across a transnational network. In A. Littlejohn (Ed.), *Reusing online resources: A sustainable approach to e-learning* (pp. 182-194). London: Kogan Page.

Wiley, D.A. (2000). Connecting learning objects to instructional design theory: A definition, a metaphor, and a taxonomy. In D.A. Wiley (Ed.), *The instructional use of learning objects*. Retrieved March, 28, 2008, from http://reusability.org/read/chapters/wiley.doc.

Wiley, D.A. (2002). The instructional use of learning objects. Retrieved March, 28, 2008, from http://www.reusability.org/read/

Wilson, S., & Mundell, R. (2004). E-learning development using re-usable learning objects. In L. Catoni & C. McLoughlin (Eds.), *Proceedings of World Conference on E-Learning in Corporate, Government, Healthcare, and Higher Education 2004* (pp. 4373-4378). Chesapeake, VA: AACE.

KEY TERMS AND DEFINITIONS

Community of Practice: Communities of practice are characterised by a shared domain of knowledge, a shared community, and shared practices built up over time. Wenger, McDermott, and Snyder (2002, p. 4) define a community of practice as "A group of people who share a concern, a set of problems, or a passion about a topic, and who deepen their knowledge and expertise. .. by interacting on an ongoing basis."

Digital Repository: A collection of items in digital format that can be accessed via an online catalogue. The collection might be colocated on a single server or distributed across numerous locations. The collection may be made available to users within a particular computer network, to registered users or to the public.

Granularity: Granularity refers to the "size" or "extent" of a learning object. A fine grained learning object may be a single file, but also be tightly focused on a single concept or idea. A learning object of larger granularity would contain more extensive content, perhaps linking together multimedia concepts or with multiple activities for learners.

Learning Object: The term is often used quite broadly, and for the purposes of this chapter the term refers to teaching and learning materials and guides that range in granularity from single files to full courses. The term also has a very specific meaning in certain research fields. Wiley (Wiley, 2000, p.7) defines a learning object as "Any digital resource that can be reused to support learning." The IEEE Learning Technology Standards Committee includes nondigital objects in the definition: "Any entity, digital or nondigital, which can be used, re-used or referenced during technology supported learning (The Learning Technology Standards Committee, 2002). A more specific definition is that offered by Dalziel (2002): "An aggregation of one or more digital assets, incorporating metadata, which represents an educationally meaningful, stand-alone unit."

Learning Object Economy: The learning object economy refers to the process whereby learning objects are shared and exchanged through mechanisms such as licensing or royalties.

Needs Analysis: A needs analysis is carried out upon the initiation of a project to determine the characteristics and the needs of users of a system or intervention.

Reusability: Reusability is essential to the notion of the learning object in that a learning object can be more effectively shared and used if it can be adapted to multiple contexts.

APPENDIX A

Needs Analysis Framework for Developing Repository Functionality for Users

1. What personnel, skills, and roles are required to create and manage the digital repository?
    - Will there be specialised contributors, reviewers of repository resources?
    - Will the repository require day-to-day management and therefore need an administrator or management team?
2. How will resources be submitted?
    - Will there be restrictions on who can contribute resources to the repository?
    - How will learning resources be uploaded to the repository?
        - How can the submission tool or process be user friendly and intuitive?
    - Will there be standards for the learning resources set?
        - What is the baseline level of accessibility and quality?
        - Will metadata standards be used to provide an effective means for describing and cataloguing individual learning objects?
    - How will learning resources be classified and labeled?
        - How will issues of intellectual property rights be addressed?
        - What framework will be used for efficient and effective searching?
        - Could templates be used, underpinned by consistent standards?
        - How can this assist the evaluation of the resources to ascertain whether they meet specific needs?
    - What is the best way to store information?
        - Will the learning resources be housed in the repository or will it provide descriptions of the resources and then a link to the resource housed elsewhere on the Internet?
    - What guidelines are required to assist contributors to develop effective learning objects that can be reused, re-purposed and referenced?
3. How will resources be utilised?
    - Will there be a cost for accessing the repository's resources?
        - Will the collection be perceived of as having more value if it comes at a cost?
        - Should the cost be charged to the university and only members access the repository?
        - Is there a question mark over the quality of material where no charge is made?
    - Will there be restrictions on who can access the resources?
    - How will users search for their desired learning resources?
        - Is the search function easy and simple to use? Can users select just one or two metadata elements to form their learning resource queries so time investment is small?
    - Will there be an authoring capability provided?
    - What are the technical considerations in regard to reliability, usability and accessibility of the learning object?
    - Will participating universities consider providing academic and teaching staff, time and assistance to facilitate digital repository contributions?

4. How will quality assurance be addressed?
    - How will quality control be managed?
        - What personnel, skills, and roles are required?
        - What will be the focus of quality control measures (e.g., quality of content, potential effectiveness as a teaching-learning tools, and ease of use)?
        - Will formal peer review be used as a means of quality control? Will informal peer review by the users such as commentary or star ratings be used?
        - How will quality assurance be integrated into the whole content creation process? What guidelines and standards should underpin the development of content?
    - What quality assurance will there be for the functionality and usability of the actual repository?
5. What incentives will there be for educators to contribute to the digital repository? How will this relate to promotion practices within universities?
6. How will the repository be promoted?
    - How will educators and students be made aware of the strategies and advantages of using digital repositories?
    - What support and training will be provided? Will it be face to face or online or both?
    - Is there opportunity for repository promotion through Carrick networks and activities?
    - What opportunities are there for repository review publications to be used for promotion?
7. What are the strategies for monitoring, assessment and evaluation?
    - What monitoring strategies are there for regularly checking the progress of the repository? And who is responsible for this monitoring?
    - What are the targets and timeframes for these targets that can be measured and formally assessed to make an informed decision about the progress of the repository? And who will be responsible for conducting these planned assessments?
    - What are the specific aims, goals or objectives that will inform an evaluation of the project? And who will perform this evaluation?
    - Could these monitoring assessment and evaluation activities be managed in a similar manner to journals with an editorial board and reviewers?

This work was previously published in Handbook of Research on Learning Design and Learning Objects: Issues, Applications, and Technologies, edited by L. Lockyer; S. Bennett; S. Agostinho; B. Harper, pp. 607-628, copyright 2008 by Information Science Reference (an imprint of IGI Global).

Chapter 19
ICT Integration Efforts in Higher Education in Developing Economies:
The Case of Addis Ababa University, Ethiopia

Dawit Tibebu
Bahir Dar University, Ethiopia

Tridib Bandyopadhyay
Kennesaw State University, USA

Solomon Negash
Kennesaw State University, USA

ABSTRACT

A situational modified version of Tearle's model (2004) is utilized in this study to understand the integration of ICTs in the educational process. The study evaluated self efficacy beliefs, institutional support and policy in the context of developing economies where challenges of inadequate resources and insufficient skills persist. We assess the state of affairs, and the challenges faced by teachers and management at Addis Ababa University, Ethiopia. The results show that educators are generally appreciative of ICTs role in the teaching/learning process.

INTRODUCTION AND MOTIVATION

Today's networked economy is information and knowledge intensive. It is characterized by evolving global marketplaces coupled with business processes and sophisticated work environments. Competitive economic capabilities and success factors are now more centered on knowledge than ever. In order to remain effectively integrated in the global economy, a country's priorities should include education and training to increase the skill sets of their workforce.

Higher education (post secondary education) has been attempting to provide training to an ever increasing audience, to ensure that their graduates have the necessary knowledge and skills for the networked economy and generally prepare them for lifelong learning. To meet these challenges, educational institutions have concurrently aimed on expanding access, improving internal efficiency, and promoting the quality of teaching and learning (Haddad & Jurich, 2002). Information and Communication Technology (ICT) is used by many educational institutions to increase the quality of teaching and learning in a cost effective manner (Means and Olson, 1995). In this networked economy higher education graduates are expected to be versatile in a world of communications that includes email, Intranet, Internet, and the world-wide web, and be able to apply higher cognitive skills (analyzing, summarizing and synthesizing information) in order to engage in creative and critical thinking (Vogel and Klassen, 2001). It has also been argued that higher education should incorporate proven pedagogical strategies such as group work, cooperative learning, peer teaching, idea sharing and reflection (Ramsden, 1992 in Lockyer, et al., 2001). ICTs have been found useful in facilitating these strategies (Lockyer, et al., 2001) and their implementation has become an indispensable part of educational reform (Law, 2004 in Sabaliauskas and Pukelis, 2004).

Table 1. Opportunities from ICT integration in education: Research findings

ICT Impact Attributes in Education	Finds full/partial support in
Brings positive changes in the social organization of the classroom; achieves higher student-centric focus and delivery	Capper, 2003; Cradler and Bridgforth, 2005.
Enhances teaching and learning through dynamic, interactive, and engaging content	Davis and Tearle, 1999; Capper, 2003; Yusuf, 2005.
Develops, enriches, accelerates, and deepens student skills	Davis and Tearle, 1999; Capper, 2003.
Relates school experience to work place, provide opportunity for connection between school and world	Davis and Tearle, 1999.
Enhances learning opportunities and resources to the students and teachers	Byron and Gagliardi, 2001; OTA, 1997 in Cradler and Bridgforth, 2002; Department of Education and Skills, 2002 in Tearle 2003; Becta 2003a.
Enhances student motivation in the learning process which then • Accentuates enjoyment and interest in the learning process, • Achieves higher commitment, increases independence, self esteem and confidence in students.	Cox, 1997 in Cox et al. 1999; OTA, 1995 in Cradler and Bridgforth, 2002; Capper 2003.
Stimulates, motivates and sparks students' appetite for learning and helps to create a culture of success	Becta, 2003c.

The potential benefits of ICTs in education have been extensively researched. The benefits of integrating ICT in the teaching/learning process has been found to be layered, multifaceted, and comprehensive as shown in Table 1.

ICT integrated benefits of wider access, quality processes, facilitated delivery, and enriched learning and teaching experiences come with challenges. Such challenges are more accentuated for a low income country (LIC). There are major obstacles to ICT integration in schools and the wider community in LICs (IDRC, 1995) and there are economic, technological, and educational (contextual) factors that constrain the potential impact of ICT integrated education programs in LICs (Kozma & Wagner, 2005).

Cross sectional studies point out common challenges faced by LICs, however, there are specific factors that are different between countries. Thus there is a general need to identify and understand the specific contextual factors higher education faces in LICs. There is a dearth of academic research on the challenges faced by higher education when integrating ICT. In this study we attempt to recognize these challenges. In particular, we study the challenges faced by Addis Ababa University (AAU), a large public institution in Ethiopia, and bring the insights of context specific manifest difficulty as experienced there. The goals of this study as well as the questions that we asked to delve these inquisitions are presented in Exhibit A.

We have selected African continent as the backdrop of this study primarily because of the large concentrations of LICs. The selection of Ethiopia is congruent with our best ability to conduct detailed on-site research. We select AAU in Ethiopia because of the following reasons:

- AAU is the Flagship University of Ethiopia (ranked 32 in African Continent[1]), located at the capital city of Addis Ababa, and likely mirrors the concerns and intents of the LIC with minimum time delay.

Exhibit A

Goals of this study	A. Assess the extent to which ICT has been integrated into the teaching and learning process at AAU B. Understand the challenges encountered by teachers in the process of integrating ICT into the teaching and learning process.
Questions we asked facing the above goals	1. How is ICT utilized in the teaching and learning processes at AAU? 2. Does AAU management encourage and provide apex support to the integration of ICT into the teaching and learning process? 3. What are the challenges encountered by teachers in terms of integrating ICT into the teaching and learning processes? 4. Do teachers have a positive attitude towards utilizing ICT in the teaching and learning process? 5. Do teachers at AAU possess adequate skills to enable them use ICT in teaching and learning? 6. Are teachers confident in their ability to use computer technologies in the teaching and learning process? 7. Do teachers receive training on how to use ICT in teaching and learning? If there are existing training programs for the teachers, to what extent are they adequate? 8. Do teachers receive support (technical and pedagogical) to help them integrate ICT into teaching and learning? 9. Are there adequate resources that could help teachers to integrate ICT in their teaching? Are these resources easily accessible?

- AAU is the most comprehensive university in Ethiopia, and likely offers the greatest heterogeneity in terms of opportunities of ICT integration and multiplicity of challenges.
- AAU is one of the forerunners among Ethiopian universities attempting ICT integration in their teaching-learning processes.
- AAU has 8 campuses and has the single largest enrolment among all the universities in Ethiopia. It thus represents the single largest group of providers in higher education, embracing the changes, and facing the myriad challenges of ICT integration in Ethiopia.

The rest of the paper is organized in the following manner: Section 2 lists and explains our basic assumptions of the study, and Section 3 provides a background of ICT integration efforts at AAU. Section-4 explains our effort in understanding and identifying the underlying factors of ICT integration from extant research, especially from the Tearle's model of ICT integration. Section-5 explains situational modification of Tearle's model and our design of experiment. Section-6 presents detailed data analysis of this study. Section-7 summarizes our observations and remarks, and section-8 provides the set of references that we have used in this work. In appendix-1, we have included the survey instrument that we have operationalized to collect data for this study.

ASSUMPTION OF THE STUDY

Positive Impact of ICT on AAU Student Learning

Inline with the initiatives that we have observed at AAU (e.g. ICTDO[2]), our discussion with numerous university officials, and from our readings of the body of research in high and low income countries that report positive impact of ICT on student achievement (Table-1), this study presumes that AAU actively believes that ICT would impact the teaching-learning processes.

ICT as Enabler and Integrator at AAU

The roles of ICT in education have been identified by researchers. For instance, Pelgrum & Law (2003: 23) identify three distinctive roles[3] for ICT in education: from being a subject of learning to integral part of higher education. Anderson (1996, in Miller, 1997) note that computer assisted education means using the computer where it is the best medium to support the learning goal. Evidence suggests that ICT can contribute significantly to changes in teaching practices (Wagner, 2005). Kozma & Wagner (2005) emphasize that the way ICT is used in the classroom can make a big difference in the impact of an ICT-augmented program or project. In discussing integration of ICT into teaching and learning at AAU, we make the assumption that ICT is used **not** to support 'learning about ICT' but to support 'learning with ICT' and 'learning through ICT'. Integration of ICT into teaching and learning in this study is, therefore, defined as utilizing the power and ability of the computer and communication technologies to support teaching and learning.

THE BACKGROUND OF ICT INITIATIVES AT AAU

Higher education in Ethiopia has experienced slow penetration of ICT. Schools, colleges and universities in the country do not adequately utilize ICT in teaching and learning. Dzidonu (2006) notes that the Ethiopia's higher education currently faces a number of challenges in facilitating the process of development, deployment and exploitation of ICT in assisting teaching and learning processes. However, the promise of ICT in education is recognized by policy makers including the Ethiopian ICT for Development Agency (Dzidonu, 2006). The role of ICT in the national development and poverty reduction process of the country is widely accepted, and has gained high considerations from the government of Ethiopia. Similarly, AAU endeavors to integrate ICT into its education system.

AAU is the oldest multi-campus comprehensive university offering undergraduate and graduate programs in Ethiopia. It has over 40,000 students. AAU has installed a university-wide network infrastructure, AAUNet, in 2001 to enable ICT resource sharing, cooperation, and information. Three of the eight campuses (Sidist Kilo, Amist Kilo and Arat Kilo campuses) have implemented the first phase of the project. ICT Development Office (ICTDO) at AAU was established in 2003 to benefit from AAUNet by integrating it to future projects. The ICTDO mandate is to facilitate the integration of ICT into the curricula and administrative functions; supporting distance learning through platforms, efficient maintenance and support on ICT infrastructure; building staff capacity; providing ICT research and consultancy; promoting good governance; and nurturing democracy within AAU (ICT Development Office of AAU, 2004).

ICTDO has strategic objectives and priority areas implemented and managed by three units: i) Network and Communication Services has the responsibility of carrying out the central system administration and helpdesk, including expansion plans to provide a better internet and e-mail services, ii) The Computing Services is responsible for providing all computing services including procurement, and management of software and applications, iii) Training, Research and Consultancy has the responsibility on overall coordination of training, consultancy and research, and supports the planning, budgeting and revenue management of the office.

Under this general backdrop we study the challenges that AAU stakeholders face while integrating ICT in their teaching and learning process. In our effort, we recognize and emphasize the significant role faculty members' play in integration of ICT education to support teaching/learning in and outside the classroom. Although we make a conscious choice to focus our study on teachers, neither do we suggest that teachers are the only key stakeholders in the university, nor do we opine that ICT integration in registration and other university administrative activities are any less important or desirable outcomes.

UNDERSTANDING CONTRIBUTING FACTORS TO ICT INTEGRATION AT AAU

We adopt a simplified version of Tearle's model (2004) to operationalize the factors that contribute to ICT integration at AAU.

Tearle extensively review literature and propose a set of coherent issues that are important to implement ICT in education. While developing the framework, she categorized the literatures on two fields: Literatures which directly address ICT implementation in education systems and those which focus on change management, both from within and outside education in recognition of the view that the introduction of ICT into a school setting is a specific example of a change. Across these two fields of literature, she studied 424 relevant documents and proposes a comprehensive framework for ICT implementation (Tearle, 2004). Tearle then conducts a hold-out case study in a school where ICT is adopted and is in regular use by most teachers. Finally, she maps the case study outcomes back to the theoretical framework to identify areas of agreement, additional features, and inconclusive elements in the framework. Tearle's final model (Figure-1) shows validated factors for successful ICT implementation (Tearle, 2004).

In Tearle's model the outer ellipse has five factors that represent the whole school characteristics; these are organizational environment factors that affect the ICT implementation. The inner ellipse has five factors that represent the nurturing environment of the ICT implementation process. Actual ICT usage is characterized by the five individual factors at the center of the model, highlighting their central importance.

In the following section, we first review the whole school characteristics (outer ellipse), ICT implementation process (inner ellipse) and individual factors (constructs at the center) from Tearle's model (2004) vis-à-vis our case study at AAU, and propose our simplified research model.

Whole School Characteristics: The Outer Ellipse

Tearle (2004) reviews literature (Kennewell *et al*, 2000; Ridgeway & Passey, 1995; McCormick, 1992) on whole school culture and ethos which are influential in effective ICT implementation. Factors thus considered important in whole school characteristics for effective ICT implementation in the model include i) strong whole school leadership, ii) the culture of the school as one which promotes and encourages learning and could be described as both adaptive and collaborative, iii) the change orientated culture of the whole school, iv) the positive and proactive attitude to external influences, and v) well-established whole school internal processes. Tearle categorizes these as organizational factors which are related to the characteristics, culture and ethos of educational institutions.

In our simplified research model we have concentrated only inside the outermost ellipse and did not include organizational environment. Our conscious decision in this stems from the facts that AAU does not have a history of technology integration: culture and ethos of technology integration at AAU do not appear to have congealed, and that we do not intend to compare and contrast the challenges faced at AAU with educational institutions. Thus we assume that organizational environment factors are implicitly manifest on the 'Implementation Characteristics' (the inner ellipse) which we do include in our model framework.

ICT Implementation Process: The Inner Ellipse

Tearle's model depicts resources, time, support and training, planning and management, and quality of key people as the practical/material factors in ICT implementation process. These factors find support in numerous research findings.

Figure 1. Tearle's model (2004) for ICT integration factors

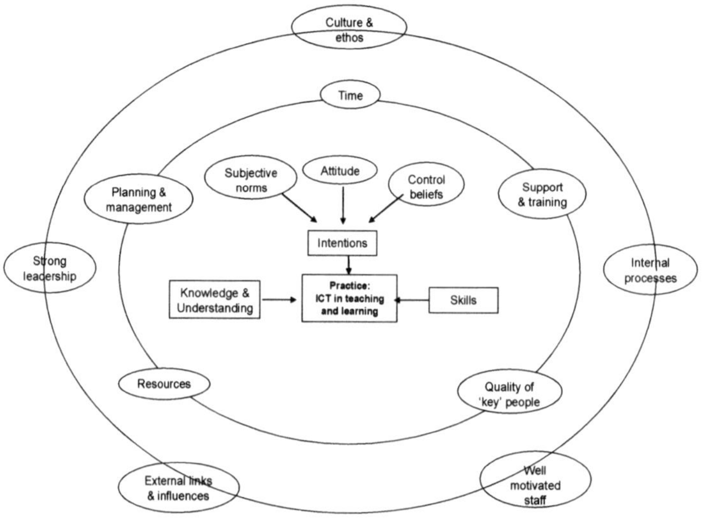

Williams, et al (2000) emphasize that appropriate training in terms of skills, knowledge, delivery; ready access to ICT resources; and ongoing support and advice are essential for effective ICT integration in teaching and learning. Pelgrum and Law (2003) point out access to computers, network and Internet; appropriate training of teachers; resources for ICT-based curriculum; and technical support for the academic staff as essential conditions to successfully integrate ICT into the teaching and learning process. The Office of Technology Assessment (1995) in Cradler and Bridgforth (2002) emphasizes that i) suiting technology to education goals and standards, ii) having a vision for the use of technology to support curriculum, iii) providing both in-service and pre-service training for teachers, ensuring access to appropriate technology, providing administrative support for technology use, allowing time for teachers to plan and learn how to integrate technology and iv) ensuring ongoing technical support are some of the requirements for effective use of technology in education.

Granger, et al., (2002) conduct qualitative case studies of four schools and their findings suggest that appropriate training, supportive and collaborative relationships among teachers, a commitment to pedagogically sound implementation of new technologies, and principals' encouragement of teachers to engage in their own learning as highly useful factors for successful implementation of ICT into teaching and learning. A nationwide survey of teachers in the USA finds teachers' motivation and commitment to their students' learning, support from schools, and sufficient access to technology as the three major factors in teachers' successful integration of computers into teaching practices (Sheingold and Hadley (1990) in Mumtaz (2000).

That quality of key[4] people is important in the integration of ICT into teaching and learning has been identified in several studies. Sandholtz et al., (1997) in Wilmore & Betz, (2000) report that one of the key factors of teachers' successful integration of technology in classroom was the level of support they received from school administrators. The International Society for Technology in Education (ISTE) point out that vision with support and proactive leadership from the education system, and policies and standards supporting new learning environments are among the most essential conditions for successful use of technology in teaching and learning (ISTE, 2000 in Capper, 2003).

In our simplified model we consider that all the factors of the implementation process (Tearle, 2004) are important and pertinent for AAU, and we adopt the inner ellipse of Figure-1 in its entirety. Additionally, we elaborate the unified construct 'Support and training' into three independent factors 'technical support', 'pedagogical support' and 'training' in our simplified research model. We make this choice because although technical support, pedagogical support and training are considered as equally important in successful ICT integration in the literature, our document analysis at AAU could not clarify whether ICTDO has the mandate to provide differentiated pedagogical support to teachers at AAU, or who is responsible for planning and implementation of specific training programs to different faculty bodies. That such support and training could come from more than one source, makes it essential for us to identify the component factors of the construct of 'Support and training' separately, and in an explicit manner.

Individual Characteristics: The Central Factors

In line with Tearle's model (2004) we include the triad of knowledge and understanding, skills and intentions leading to the actual practice of ICT integrated teaching practices at AAU. However, in our proposed model intention is a function of attitudes, and control beliefs. We do not include subjective norms. Tearle (2004) defines subjective norms as perceptions of the teachers in the way other peers have used ICT in their teaching, and their reflections of esteem. However, the impact of this construct on integration of ICT in teaching and learning is not adequately supported by other research findings and (as we have argued before) AAU does not have a history of technology integration, and our initial discussions with the stakeholders at AAU also suggested that teachers had barely started ICT integration in their teaching-learning process. Thus we argue that it is premature to consider that AAU faculties share subjective norms in the sense that Tearle defines it. Note that this exclusion of subjective norms is also consistent with the exclusion of the outer ellipse of environmental influence in our proposed model.

Moreover, we have renamed control beliefs, as self-efficacy beliefs in our proposed model. Although control belief and self efficacy share similar connotation, self-efficacy belief is a more familiar and well documented construct in the literature of the use of ICT in teaching and learning (Bandura, 1977, in Kinzie, et al., 1994; Albino, 1999; Wang, Ertmer, & Newby, 2004, in Pierson and McLachlan, 2004; Collins, 1982; and Lent et al., 1984, in Johnson & Wardlow, 2004).

OUR RESEARCH MODEL

Our research model as explained above is depicted in Figure 2.

Research Design

In this section we describe the descriptive survey research methods employed including the sampling and mechanistic aspects of the study.

Participants of the Study

The primary target group in this study was the teachers of AAU, while ICTDO personnel and the management staff of AAU were sampled as a secondary (support) group.

Sampling Technique and Instruments

AAU is composed of 17 entities[5]. The ICTDO report suggests that only 4 out of these 17 entities have reasonable ICT network facility. The four campuses with ICT facilities were i) the Main Campus, ii) faculty of Business and Economics (FBE), iii) faculty of Technology, and iv) faculty

Figure 2. Our simplified research model for factors in ICT integration at AAU

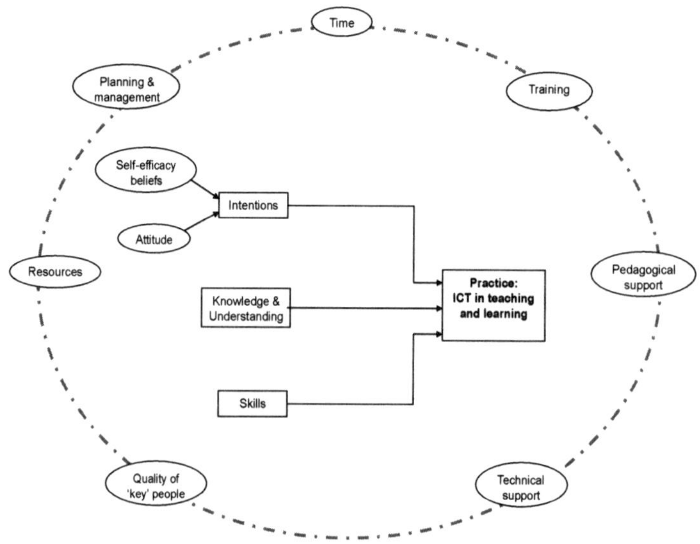

of Science. Accordingly, we used only these four campuses in our study. The number of departments and instructors in the selected four campuses, as obtained from AAU's 2004/05 Academic Staff List bulletin, are shown in Table 2.

Because teachers belonged to different programs with unequal total populations, we employed a proportional stratified sampling technique in this study. First, the participants were categorized into 4 strata with each campus as a stratum, see Table 1. All colleges within the sample campuses had more than one department except the Faculty of Law. Thus, to ensure that each instructor in the departments within the sample gets equal chance of being chosen as a participant, proportional number of instructors from each department was selected using simple random sampling technique. Accordingly, a total of 234 instructors, 35% from each stratum, were taken as representative sample of the population of interest. We utilized survey questions to assess the input of this primary group of participants.

For the secondary target (support) group, one key official each from ICTDO and AAU management were selected as participants to this study. However, because this secondary group was fundamentally different in terms of their role in ICT implementation at AAU, and also because of the dissimilarity in the sizes of the primary and secondary groups, these individuals' inputs were received through semi-structured interviews.

In addition, supplementary input was accessed through document analysis of ICTDO and AAU management bulletins and communiqués in the public domain.

The Questionnaire

Barring a few open-ended ones, the questionnaire predominantly consisted of closed type questions. Based on the types of information required, the final questionnaire comprised three sections:

1. The first part was intended to collect background and demographic information about the participants, and consisted of 6 items.
2. The second part was designed to assess information regarding respondents' perception of ICT resource availability at AAU, their levels of ICT skills/knowledge, their practices with different ICT components, and their perception of the challenges to ICT integration in their teaching and delivery. This part contained 22 items.
3. The third part of the questionnaire has 2 parts (A, and B), elicited information on respondents' attitude and perceived con-

Table 2. Distribution of full time teaching faculties in the selected campuses

No.	Campus	Faculty/College/Institute	No. of Instructors
1.	Main	College of Education	122
		College of Social Sciences	50
		Faculty of Law	20
		Faculty of Informatics	46
		Institute of Language Studies	67
2.	FBE	Faculty of Business and Economics	80
3.	Technology	Faculty of Technology	151
4.	Science	Faculty of Science	133
Total number of Instructors			671

fidence/self-efficacy beliefs towards using ICT in teaching and learning. These were adopted from Kinzie, Delcourt & Powers (1994). Section-A (9 items) and Section-B (29 items) each utilized a 4 point rating scale, and measured teachers' attitude towards computer technologies and teachers' perceived self efficacy towards the use of computer technologies in teaching and learning processes respectively.

The above questionnaire was pre-processed through the following steps before finalization:

1. A separate pilot testing was conducted on items located in part three of the questionnaire. This was felt necessary in view of our selective adoption of items from Kinzie, Delcourt & Powers (1994):
   - Section-A, Part-3 of the original questionnaire had 19 items. To ensure suitability for AAU teachers, and in line with our pruning strategy, we calculated the Cronbach Alpha coefficient of reliability of each of the 19 items separately, and then successively compared each alpha value with that of the rest of the items. Finally we included 9 items, each with alpha greater than 0.77, to measure the teachers' attitude towards computer technology.
   - Similarly, section B, Part-3 of the questionnaire originally had 46 items distributed in 6 sections. For the purpose of this study, only four sections[6] were chosen for inclusion in our questionnaire. Acceptable values of internal consistency (alpha) estimates of all the items in each section were available from the instrument developers. Accordingly, 5 items from 'word processing', 10 items from 'electronic mail', 6 items from 'spreadsheet' and 8 items from 'presentation tools' sections with Cronbach Alpha coefficient of reliability of 0.81, 0.79, 0.76, and 0.77 were selected for inclusion in the final questionnaire.
2. Before administering to the research participants, the questionnaire was given to 5 individuals to examine the extent to which the items were appropriate in eliciting relevant information to serve the purpose of the study[7]. Our final questionnaire, which was administered to the primary target group, incorporated suggestions from the pilot study.

The administered questionnaire had 60 items, excluding demographic questions from Part I. The survey was accompanied by a letter of solicitation to the participants[8].

The Interview

Items for the interviews were constructed based on the proposed research model. Before administering the interviews Feedback on appropriateness and clarity of questions was solicited from three AAU graduate students.. The interviews were conducted with one official each from ICTDO and the management of AAU.

The goal of the interview with the official at ICTDO was to gather information on ICTDO initiatives towards utilization of ICT in the University's education system and to uncover the challenges encountered by the office during such initiatives.

The purpose of the interview with the official at the AAU management group was to assess the University's awareness of the role of ICT in education, the elements and modes of support that AAU extended to ICTDO and to investigate the management's view of the challenges faced by the University in their way of integrating ICT.

The semi-structured format was chosen to enable a free flow of perceptions and ideas from the interviewee.

The Document Analysis

The document analysis confirmed much of the responses we received from the questionnaire and interviews. It also provided additional insights complementing the questionnaire and interviews.

Data Collection Procedure

The survey questions were sent to the department office. The department office administered the survey to the instructors and collected the responses.

The interview was conducted in two halves. In the first half, the primary investigator explained the purpose and mode of the study to the interviewee. A semi-structured interview was conducted in the second half. The interview session (second half) with the ICTDO official was recorded with permission.

DATA ANALYSIS AND RESULTS

In what follows, we analyze the collected data from the survey questionnaire, interviews, and document analyses.

Survey Demographics

Out of a total of 234 surveys, 169 were received complete (response rate 72.2%). Demographic data of the respondents are presented in Table 3.

Table 3. Background information of the respondents

Characteristics	Category	No.	%
Gender	Male	157	92.9
	Female	12	7.1
	Total	169	100
Qualification	Bachelor's	4	2.4
	Master's	103	60.9
	Doctoral	62	36.7
	Total	169	100
Teaching Experience	1-5 years	54	32.0
	6-10 years	34	20.1
	11-15 years	34	20.1
	16 years & above	47	27.8
	Total	169	100
College/Faculty/Institute	Education	34	20.1
	Social Science	15	8.9
	Informatics	10	5.9
	Language Studies	18	10.7
	Law	6	3.6
	Business & Economics	18	10.7
	Science	35	20.7
	Technology	33	19.5
	Total	169	100

The number of male respondents, 92.9%, reflects the low number of female Ethiopian teachers in higher education. This is in line with the low number of female teachers in Ethiopia's higher education[9].

Female instructors teaching on a regular basis at AAU stand at 11.1 % (Education Management Information Systems, 2005). A slightly higher proportion of the males in our respondents (compared to average gender proportions at AAU) can be attributed to the selection of the departments/faculties for the survey: technology and business areas are traditionally lopsided in male population.

The demographics suggest that a great majority (97.6 %) of the teachers at AAU had Master's or Doctoral degrees; 32 % of the teachers had 1-5 years of teaching experience, 20.1 % each had 6-10 and 11-15 years of teaching experience, and 18.3 % had teaching experience of 16 years and above. Majority of the participants, 68 %, had more than 6 years teaching experience.

Current Level of ICT Use at AAU

In order to evaluate the extent to which ICT is utilized in teaching and learning, teachers were given a list of activities (in four point rating scale[10]) and asked to provide feedback on their frequency of application of ICT tools to accomplish those activities. Assuming that a general level of ICT integration could involve utilization of ICT tools often (i.e. 2.0 as the test value) we have conducted one sample *t* test. T-test results are presented in Table 4.

The respondents showed higher ICT utilization in two activities: finding information and educational material (item #3 in Table 4) and furthering professional development (item #8 in Table 4). In contrast ICT utilization is significantly lower for activities like creating presentations/lectures, preparing lessons, communicating with students and colleagues, teaching specific subjects, publishing lecture notes and reference materials, and monitoring and evaluating students' progresses. Table 4 indicates that with the exception of ICT enabled information gathering, teachers at AAU inadequately employ ICT in the teaching-learning process.

More specifically, we asked teachers about their frequency of general Internet usage in teaching responsibilities (Table 5). The mean value of 2.47, which falls in between once a week and several days a week, suggests significantly lower level[11] of Internet utilization by AAU teachers (referencing several days a week, i.e. 3.0 as the test value).

Table 4. Teachers' utilization of ICT in teaching activities

No.	Activity/Purpose	Mean	SD	t test (One sample)	df
1.	Teaching specific subjects	0.52	0.861	-21.477*	155
2.	Teaching computer skills	0.28	0.735	-29.686*	159
3.	Finding information and educational materials	2.23	0.603	4.716**	159
4.	Making presentations/lectures	1.18	0.619	-16.834*	159
5.	Preparing lessons	1.62	0.708	-6.810*	159
6.	Publish lecture notes and reference materials	0.14	0.384	-60.41*	155
6.	Communicating with students and colleagues	1.28	0.626	-14.519*	159
7.	Monitoring and evaluating students' progress	0.62	0.512	-33.59*	155
8.	Further professional development	2.22	0.597	4.604**	161
Owing to omitted responses, number of respondents for each of the activities does not add up to 169.					

Table 5. Teachers' utilization of the internet in teaching activities

Item	Every day (4)		Several days a week (3)		Once a week (2)		Once a month (1)		Never (0)		Mean
	No.	%	No.	%	No.	%	No.	%	No.	%	
If you have access to the Internet, how often do you use?	23	13.6	44	26.0	97	57.4	-	-	5	3	2.47

Table 6. Teachers' expertise on selected technology applications

No.	Basic ICT skills	Mean	SD	t-test (One sample)
1.	Word Processing (e.g. MS Word)	2.33	0.86	4.903*
2.	Spreadsheet (e.g. MS Excel)	1.53	1.11	-5.556*
3.	Presentation Tools (e.g. MS PowerPoint)	1.50	1.31	-5.009*
4.	Database Management (e.g. MS Access)	1.22	1.15	-8.777*
5.	E mail (e.g. Yahoo mail)	2.29	0.96	4.002*
6.	Internet browsing (e.g. Internet Explorer)	2.25	0.97	3.410*
7.	Statistical Tools (e.g. SPSS)	0.64	0.95	-18.589*
8.	Web page designing (e.g. Page Maker)	0.48	0.84	-23.571*

$p < 0.05$. Criterion value of 2.0, good level of skill, for one sample t-test

Teachers' Attitude, Skill and Self Efficacy Beliefs in ICT

One of the major purposes of this study was to assess the extant level of the teachers' ICT skills. Towards that end, we asked teachers on their levels of proficiency in selected ICT skills, and the specific activities that they perform utilizing these ICT tools. Analysis of the survey data suggests that teachers' expertise on spreadsheets, presentation tools, database management, statistical tools and web page designing are significantly below the expected[12] (average) value. Three ICT skills: word processing, e-mail, and Internet browsing were found significantly above[13] the expected value (Table 6). Skill deficiency in presentation tools is noteworthy because this is the primary ICT enabled vehicle to disseminate knowledge in class.

Because successful application of skills requires professional confidence i.e. self efficacy beliefs (Compeau and Higgins. 1995), we also inquired about teachers' perceived self efficacy. We grouped self efficacy questions in four ICT aspects. Table 7 depicts the results, including our criterion value and *t*-test results. Consistent with the results from Table 6, teachers' self efficacy in word processing and e-mail were higher than the criterion values while their self efficacy towards use of spreadsheets and presentation tools in teaching and learning were significantly below the criterion values. In order to test whether teachers' self efficacy beliefs were realistically pegged on to their actual levels of ICT skills, as opposed to other incidental/environmental factors, we have checked ICT (symmetric) correlations between skills and self efficacies of the teachers at AAU (Table 8).

Positive correlation was found between teachers' skills and self-efficacy beliefs in word processing, presentation tools and e-mail. This suggests intrinsic relationships, significant at $\propto=0.001$. We were, however, surprised by the low, albeit positive

Table 7. Teachers' perceived self efficacy towards computer technologies

Variable	N	Test Value	Mean	SD	t
Word processing	169	12.5	16.4	1.42	35.7*
E-mail communication	169	25	26.72	6.54	6.54**
Spreadsheets	169	15	10.69	3.18	17.56*
Presentation Tools	169	20	14.32	4.28	17.23*
* => ($p < 0.001$), ** => ($p < 0.01$)					

Table 8. Relationship between skill in technology applications and self efficacy

Skill Variables	Word processing	Spreadsheet	Presentation tools	E mail
Self efficacy in word processing	0.74*	---	---	---
Self efficacy in spreadsheets	---	0.31**	---	---
Self efficacy in presentation tools	---	---	0.71*	---
Self efficacy in e-mail	---	---	---	0.77*
*$p < 0.001$ **$p < 0.01$				

correlation, between teachers' spreadsheet capabilities and efficacy beliefs, $r = 0.3$. An inspection of the raw data suggests that one reason for this surprising outcome in spreadsheet technologies could be a relatively high number of teachers who expressed lower self efficacy belief yet pointed out adequate skills in spreadsheet.

Although skills and self efficacy beliefs are critically important for integrating ICT in the teaching learning processes, propensity of actual utilization of ICT skills requires a positive attitude and hopeful expectation of outcome from ICT integration (Chau 2001). Delving this aspect, items in the questionnaire assessed attitudinal preferences of the teachers towards ICT integrated teaching/learning processes (Table 9). The mean score of teachers' composite attitude towards computer technologies, mean = 25.66, was found significantly above the test/ criterion value of 22.5[14]. This suggests that teachers' at AAU generally share a positive attitude towards using computer technologies in teaching/learning.

Challenges of Integrating ICT into Teaching and Learning

The main purpose of this study centers on identifying the challenges encountered by teachers in their attempt to integrating ICT into teaching and learning processes at AAU. In order to uncover those challenges faced by teachers, we obtained responses from teachers, ICTDO director, and management representative from the academic program office. In this section we present the challenges of ICT integration as reported by the respondents.

Availability and Adequacy of Pre-service and In-Service Trainings given to Teachers on ICT Related Issues

Inadequacy of critical skill sets (e.g. presentation technologies) can be a definite inhibitor of actual integration of ICT in teaching/learning processes at AAU. In order to analyze such absence of essential skill sets, we further investigated whether

Table 9. Teachers' attitude towards computer technologies (ATC)

Variable	No.	Mean	Test value	SD	t
ATC	169	25.66	22.5	1.94	21.17*
*p < 0.001					

Table 10. Teachers' pre-service training on basic ICT Skills

No.	Item	Response	Frequency	%
1	Did you receive any training on ICT before you joined the teaching profession (pre-service training)?	Yes	48	28.4
		No	121	71.6
2.	If your answer is 'Yes', was the training sufficient to help you use ICT in your teaching?	Yes	5	10.4
		No	42	87.5

teachers received adequate pre-service and in-service training on utilization of ICT.

Responses on pre-service ICT training indicate that only a small section, 28.4%, of the teachers had some pre-service ICT training before joining the profession (Table 10). Detailed (segmented) analysis suggests that among those who had responded receiving pre-service training, a very high percentage, 85.4%, were concentrated in the faculties of Business and Economics, Informatics, Science and Technology. A rather small section, 14.6%, of the teachers in other disciplines had received pre-service training at all. This suggests a lopsided distribution of ICT skill sets among AAU teachers. We also inquired about the perceived adequacy of pre-service training among teachers who responded positively to receiving pre-service training. Among those who reported receiving some pre-service training, 87.5 % felt that their pre-service trainings were not adequate for any effective utilization of ICT in the teaching processes. In essence, a very insignificant section (only 3%, i.e. 5 out of 169) of the teachers at AAU had actually begun their profession with some effective ICT training to help them integrate ICT in the teaching/learning process.

Because such initial deficiencies of ICT skills could be mitigated on-the-job at an institutional level, we then asked teachers on the availability and adequacy of in-service ICT trainings at AAU. In every ICT application we listed, less than half of the respondents noted that they had received any training; and barring word processing, close to ¾ of the respondents never received any training at all (Table 11).

Beyond the penetration of in-service training initiatives at AAU, we also inquired about the adequacy of ICT training conducted at AAU. An overwhelming majority, 95.5%, of the respondents felt that the in-service trainings were inadequate to enable them utilize ICT in teaching/learning processes. We also asked teachers whether they had received any in-service training on pedagogical integration of ICT in teaching, and an even larger section, 97%, reported that they had never received any pedagogical training on how to integrate ICT in teaching.

Our follow-up interviews with the ICTDO officials and the University management provided little insight. However, our documents analysis in the public domain did bring out such additional facts:

- Right after the completion of the first phase of AAUNet project (2002), training on selected contents were given to both academic and administrative staff in the Main Campus

Table 11. Availability and adequacy of ICT related technical and pedagogical in-service training

No.	Items	Response	Freq.	%
1.	Have you taken In-service training in which you learned to utilize the following technologies in teaching and learning?			
	Word Processing	Yes	75	44.4
		No	85	50.3
		Missing	9	5.3
	Spreadsheet/MS Excel	Yes	39	23.1
		No	120	71.0
		Missing	10	5.9
	MS PowerPoint	Yes	20	11.9
		No	130	76.9
		Missing	19	11.2
	Database/MS Access	Yes	25	14.8
		No	131	77.5
		Missing	13	7.7
	Internet browsing	Yes	21	12.4
		No	132	78.1
		Missing	16	9.5
	E mail	Yes	28	16.6
		No	132	78.1
		Missing	9	5.3
2.	Do you think that the in-service trainings that you have taken are adequate to help you utilize ICT in your teaching?	Yes	7	4.1
		No	145	85.8
		Missing	17	10.1
4.	Have you taken in-service pedagogical training on the use of ICT for teaching-learning?	Yes	5	3.0
		No	164	97.0
5.	Do you have sufficient time to attend ICT related in-service training, experiment with the technology, and prepare lessons using different technologies?	Yes	89	52.7
		No	80	47.3

Principal beneficiaries of these trainings were the faculties of Business and Economics, Science and Technology .The trainings were largely technical and aimed at introducing the academic staff on what they could do with using the AAUNet (Table 12)

- The ICTDO office had not organized any ICT training for the academic staff since its establishment in 2003.
- Training related to pedagogical use of ICT was non-existent. ICTDO did not have designated staff to provide, coordinate, and support ICT pedagogical training initiatives.

As a whole, it was revealed that the vast majority of teachers did not receive any training on the technical or pedagogical aspect of ICT integration in teaching/learning processes. Even if training

Table 12. AAUNet training of academic staff

No.	Training Content	No. of Trainees	Duration
1.	Network Concept	252	2 hrs
2.	Internet browsing	252	4 hrs
3.	E mailing	252	4 hrs
4.	Web publishing	252	6 hrs
(Source: ICTDO of AAU)			

Table 13. Availability of technical and pedagogical supports

No.	Items	Responses								Mean
		Very often (3)		Often (2)		Sometimes (1)		Never (0)		
		No.	%	No.	%	No.	%	No.	%	
1.	How frequently do you get technical support from staff at the University in your attempt to use ICT in teaching and learning?	-		24	14.2	112	66.3	19	11.2	1.03
2.	How frequently do you get pedagogical support from staff at the University in your attempt to use ICT in teaching and learning?	-		-		10	5.9	145	85.5	0.06
3.	How often do you fail to use computers or other ICT tools due to lack of technical & pedagogical support?	51	30.2	65	38.5	44	26.0	-	-	2.04

could be organized by the University, given existing workload, almost half of the teachers, 47.3%, believed that they could not have attended them. Teachers complained about paucity of time to attend ICT related in-service training, experiment with the technology and prepare lessons using different ICT applications. The teachers also had the opportunity to explain why they thought that they did not have sufficient time; a significant number, 62.5%, of them reported that they had too much teaching load and almost one-third, 31.3%, of them reported being burdened with additional administrative tasks. During our informal discussions, many wanted to be relieved from extra teaching loads and administrative tasks if they were to attend in-service trainings on ICT related issues.

Availability of Technical and Pedagogical Support to Teachers

We asked teachers whether they were getting technical and pedagogical supports upon request to help them use ICT in the teaching/learning process. Table 13 summarizes their response.

Teachers' response on the frequency of getting technical support had a mean value of 1.03 which is close to 'sometimes' in our relative scale. The frequency of getting pedagogical support, on the other hand, had a mean value of 0.06, meaning almost never. This suggests that ICT support at AAU is almost non-existent. In order to identify whether teachers actively sought technical and pedagogical support in their effort to utilize ICT, they were asked the extent to which they failed to use computers or other ICT tools due to lack of support, item 3 in Table 12. The mean value of

Table 14. Teachers' access to ICT resources at university and home

No.	Access to...	Location	Response	Frequency	%
1.	Computer	University	Yes	165	97.6
			No	4	2.4
		Home	Yes	66	39.1
			No	102	60.4
2.	Printer	University	Yes	36	21.3
			No	124	73.4
		Home	Yes	4	2.4
			No	160	94.7
3.	Scanner	University	Yes	12	7.1
			No	148	87.6
		Home	Yes	4	2.4
			No	160	94.7
4.	Internet	University	Yes	144	85.2
			No	22	13.0
		Home	Yes	21	12.4
			No	147	87.0
5.	Appropriate Softwares	University	Yes	15	8.9
			No	148	87.6
		Home	Yes	4	2.4
			No	160	94.7
5.	LCD Projector	University	Yes	14	8.3
			No	150	88.8

2.04 ($\overline{X}$=2.04) suggests that teachers often failed to utilize computers and other ICT tools due to lack of technical and pedagogical support.

Availability of ICT Resources on Campus and at Home

Survey items aimed at assessing the different ICT resources available on campus and at home were included. Table 14 depicts the summary statistics of the responses received.

Apparently, teachers at AAU have relatively high access to computers, 97.6%, and Internet, 85.2%, on campus. However, access to other resources like printers, scanners, appropriate software and LCD projectors was minimal. Access to different ICT resources at home was extremely limited, as low as 2.4%. This indicates the general inability of teachers to use any off-campus time to learn, design, or integrate ICT in their teaching efforts.

Although teachers at AAU pointed that they had high access to computers, our observation suggests that sometimes computer access on campus is available on a shared basis. In order, we asked teachers to denote the exact nature of their computer access at AAU to gain realistic idea of the teachers' access to computers, assess instances of shared computer usage (Figure 3). Interestingly, more than a quarter of the teachers at AAU gain basic computer access outside their

Figure 3. Teachers' access to computers in their office

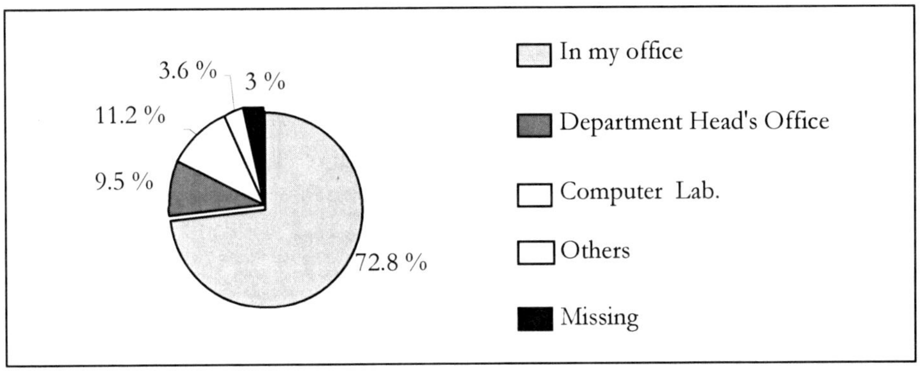

own offices. Of those who actually had access to a computer in their own offices, only a little over half, 55% or 68 out of 123, had Internet connection. Compared with the overall positive response on Internet availability, given the large number of respondents, 85.2%, having Internet access, a large number of teachers actually go elsewhere to access Internet services. It appears that between the barriers of inconvenience in shared resources and space, personal computer and Internet penetration at AAU is far from complete.

Teachers Perceived Challenges in ICT Integration

In an earlier section, we have explained the challenges AAU faces to integrate ICT in the teaching/learning processes. In this section, we report the stakeholders' perceived challenges, as reported in open ended interview questions regarding employing ICT in teaching/learning. We present teacher responses followed by stakeholder responses and compare the results. Towards this goal, we asked teachers to report their perceived challenge when integrating ICT. Summary statistic ranked by frequency is presented in Table 15.

While teachers' overall perceptions are in agreement with our survey findings, we report three noteworthy observations:

- Lack of ICT resources. Lack of accessible ICT resources ranks top among the perceived challenges faced by the teachers. Specifically, teachers reported lack of access to hardware (e.g. computers, LCD projectors, and printers) and inadequate access to the Internet in this category. It appears that in the absence of resources, the need for pedagogical and other training support facilities are less felt by the teachers.
- Lack of response in ICT integration. Seventy four respondents, 43.7%, did not mention anything as a challenge when integrating ICT into the teaching/learning process. Our

Table 15. Teachers' perception of challenges to ICT integration

No.	Challenges	Frequency	Rank
1.	Lack of accessible ICT resources	118	1
2.	Lack of adequate ICT skill	89	2
3.	Poor ICT background of students	68	3
4.	Lack of support	42	4

Table 16. Summary of ICT integration challenges

	ICT Integration Challenges at AAU
1	Lack of adequate teacher skills in ICT
2	Low self efficacy beliefs among teachers in using computer applications
3	Lack of adequate pre-service and in-service teacher training
4	Lack of technical and pedagogical support available for teachers
5	Lack of time for teachers to experiment, learn and employ different ICT tools
6	Lack of accessible ICT resources for teachers and students
7	Absence of institutional ICT policy for education
8	Lack of skilled ICT support staff
9	Absence of skilled staff in the ICT support office that can provide technical and pedagogical training to teachers

conjuncture is that rather than absence of challenges for these teachers, it might simply mean that either they have not yet started utilizing ICT in their teaching, or they are just reluctant to give response to this open ended item.

- Lack of student ICT skills. A large number of teachers indicated poor ICT background of students as a challenge in bringing ICT enabled changes in their teaching/learning process. This indicates that teachers perceive that students are not familiar/comfortable with using ICT or do not have access to such facilities. This may limit teachers' enthusiasm about integration of ICT in their teaching/learning processes. However, this aspect is beyond the scope of our study.

During the interview, we posed questions to the ICTDO officer and the management representative on their perception about the challenges of integrating ICT into the teaching/learning process at AAU. The responses were:

- The ICTDO officer listed lack of teachers' ICT skill and awareness, lack of adequate ICT resources (teachers and students), and absence of adequately trained support staff (technical and pedagogical), and as the main challenges to ICT integration at AAU. Our discussion also revealed that there is no clear ICT policy for education at the University. It was also apparent that the university is dependent on the Ministry of Education of Ethiopia for ICT usage directives[15]. However, we were also apprised of AAU's attempts to learn experiences from other comparable universities. However, no definitive discussions in related policy formulation/implementation followed.
- The management representative, from the office of academic programs, indicated that the University management was aware of the role of ICT in education[16]. He also indicated that all necessary support have been extended to ICTDO for ensuring adequate utilization of ICT in teaching/learning. We received reasonable agreement on this claim from the ICTDO officer as well. We also inquired on the observable under-utilization of ICT in the teaching/learning process. The management representative deferred this question to the ICTDO officer.

Overall, our interviews with the ICTDO officer and management representative reveal that there is an absence of comprehensive ICT policy at AAU. We also felt that the skill set of

Exhibit B

Study Recommendations for ICT Integration at AAU
1. Institute a clear ICT policy. ICTDO may find it useful to identify peer/comparable higher education institutions that have already integrated ICT, and bring experiential insights from them.
2. Avail resources to teachers. Network infrastructure and computational facilities need be augmented, and equitably allocated to teachers. Basic access to personal computer and Internet must be available to every teacher. This needs be complemented by extensive training on different ICT applications, followed by pedagogical training.
3. To effectively integrate ICT into the teaching and learning process:
1. Acquire ICTDO staff capable of providing/coordinating technical and pedagogical trainings to teachers.
2. Elevate teacher awareness, skill, and confidence towards ICT through differentiated training.
3. Motivate teachers to participate in training sessions and encourage them to integrate ICT enabled teaching. Some incentives to motivate teachers include: reduction in workload, peer-recognition, and certification.
4. Define responsibility/accountability structure for ICT implementation linking ICTDO and the University Management Board. Efficiency and efficacy of all interventions need be monitored, measured, reported and acted upon.
5. Access student ICT abilities. Consider offering introductory ICT courses as part of the general requirement for all students.
6. Encourage independent longitudinal studies to assess the state of affairs of ICT integration on a continued basis.

the ICTDO staff should be enhanced to ensure effective ICT implementation, especially in the areas of designing training programs for teachers and augmenting technical, pedagogical, and sundry support to faculty members.

CONCLUDING REMARK

Integrating ICT into the teaching/learning process is complex and time consuming. Unlike their counterparts in high-income countries, higher education institutions in low-income countries are just beginning ICT integration in education. The integration process, as we learned from the AAU case, is mired with challenges. We have attempted to understand the extent of ICT integration, and identified the challenges encountered by low-income countries. To operationalize our work we modified Tearle's original Model with situational factors and collected data from AAU stakeholders. We used survey questionnaire, semi-structured interviews, and public domain documents to conduct our analysis.

The modified model includes factors within the ICT implementation process, such as resource, time, training, technical and pedagogical support, coordination and management, and quality of key people. In addition, individual characteristics, such as knowledge and skills, attitude, and self-efficacy were found important for integrating ICT in the teaching/learning process.

We have not identified cultural changes that result from technology introduction because we believe the current ICT environment at AAU is too fluid and may obfuscate proper identification.

Instead, the identified factors in our model are interpreted as situation-pertinent.

The challenges we found at AAU, when integrating ICT in the teaching/learning process, are summarized in Table 16.

Our study did not find negative attitude and lack of management support among the challenges. However, lack of institutional ICT policy, although was not originally included in our model, stands out as another challenge to ICT integration at AAU. The study indicates that the majority of AAU teachers do not employ ICT in the teaching/learning process. As a result, students are largely unexposed to ICT mediated learning process. This may limit the competitive ability of graduates in the 21st century economy, a dynamic and information intensive world. We learned that teachers positively appreciate and realize the importance of ICT, share a positive attitude towards ICT utilization in teaching and learning, and are confident in at least some of the technology application in education. This, we believe, is a good foundation for a successful future integration of ICT in the teaching/learning process at AAU. We have summarized the above findings in a set of recommendations that may work as a planning template for ICT intervention/implementation at AAU.

We have investigated the expositional case of ICT integration in the teaching/learning processes at Addis Ababa University. Many Situational factors notwithstanding, this study provides certain generalizability of challenges that plague similar efforts in higher education among other low-income countries. This study is undertaken in an environment where ICT initiatives are nascent, and the implications for ICT integrated education processes are not well understood. We encourage other researchers to expand on this work by analyzing similar higher education institutions in low-income countries to better understand their ICT integrated education processes.

REFERENCES

Albino, P. R. (1999). *Self-Efficacy Beliefs as an Indicator of Teachers' Preparedness for Teaching with Technology*. Association for the Advancement of Computing in Education (AACE). Retrieved October 14, 2005 from http://www.usq.edu.au/users/albion/papers/site99/1345.html

Becta, (2003a). *What the research says about barriers to the use of ICT in teaching*. Retrieved October 14, 2005 from http://becta.org.uk/page_documents/research/wtrs_barriersinteach.pdf

Becta, (2003c). What the research says about ICT and Motivation. Retrieved October 14, 2005 from http://becta.org.uk/page_documents/research/wtrs_motivation.pdf

Byron, I., & Gagliardi, R. (2001). *State and Potential of Information and Communication Technologies in education*. Retrieved October 12, 2005 from http://www.idrc.ca/acacia/studies/ir-unes1.htm.

Compeau, D. R., & Higgins, C. A. (1995). Computer Self-Efficacy: Development of a measure and initial test. *MIS Quarterly*, *19*(2), 189-211.

Capper, J. (2003).Complexities and Challenges of Integrating Technology Into the curriculum. *TechKnowLogia*. Retrieved October 12, 2005 from http://www.techknowlogia.org/TKL_active_pages2/CurrentArticles/main.asp?IssueNumber=19&FileType=PDF&ArticleID=471

Chau, P. Y. K. (2001). Influence of Computer Attitude and Self-Efficacy on IT Usage Behavior. *Journal of End User Computing*, *13*(1), 26-33.

Cox, M., Preston, C., & Cox, K. (1999). *What Motivates Teachers to Use ICT?* Paper presented at the British Educational Research Association Annual Conference, University of Sussex at Brighton, September 2-5, 1999. Retrieved October 15, 2005 from http://www.leeds.ac.uk/educol/documents/00001329.htm

Cradler, J., & Bridgforth, E. (2002). *Recent Research on the Effects of Technology on Teaching and Learning*. Retrieved October 10, 2005, from http://www.wested.org/techpolicy/research.html

Cox, M., et al. (1999). *What factors support or prevent teachers from using ICT in their Classrooms*. Paper presented at the British Educational Research Association Annual Conference, University of Sussex, Brighton. Retrieved September 15, 2005 from http://www.leeds.ac.uk/educol/documents/00001304.htm

Davis, N. E., & Tearle, P. (1999). *A core curriculum for telematics in teacher training*. Teleteaching 98 Conference, Vienna. Retrieved December 7, 2005 from http://www.ex.ac.uk/telematics/T3/corecurr/tteach98.htm

Dzidonu, C. (2006). *The ICT-in-Education Implementation Strategy and Action Plan*. Ethiopian ICT Development Agency (EICTDA). Unpublished. Draft [Version 4.02].

Granger, C., Morbey, M., Lotherington, H., Owston, R., & Wideman, H. (2002). Factors contributing to teachers' successful implementation of IT [Electronic version]. *Journal of Computer Assisted Learning, 18*, 480-488.

Haddad, W. D., & Jurich, S. (2002). ICT for Education: Potential and Potency: In W. D. Haddad & Draxler, S. (Eds.), *Technologies for Education: Potential, Parameters, and Prospects*. For UNESCO by Knowledge Enterprise.

ICT Development Office of AAU, (2004). Five Year Strategic Plan (2004/05 to 2008/9). Addis Ababa University. Unpublished document.

IDRC, (1995). Information and Communication Technologies. Retrieved October 4, 2005 from http://web.idrc.ca/ev.php?id=11118_201&ID2=DO_TOPIC

Johnson, D., & Wardlow, G. (2004). Computer Experiences, Self-Efficacy, and Knowledge of Undergraduate Students Entering a Land-Grant College of Agriculture by Year and Gender [Electronic version]. *Journal of Agricultural Education, 45*(3).

Kinzie, M. B., Delcourt, M. A., & Powers, S. M. (1994). Computer Technologies: Attitudes and Self-Efficacy Across Undergraduate Disciplines [Electronic version]. *Research in Higher Education*, 35(6), 745-768.

Kozma, R. & Wagner, D. (2005). Core Indicators for Monitoring and Evaluation Studies for ICT in Education. In D. Wagener et al. (Eds.) *Monitoring and Evaluation of ICT in Educational Projects: A Handbook for Developing Countries. infoDev* Pre-Publication draft, Washington DC, USA. Retrieved December 15, 2005 from http://www.infodev.org/files/2942_file_M_E_ICT_Education_draft_WSIS_optimized.pdf

Lockyer, L., Patterson, J., & Harper, B. (2001). ICT in higher education: evaluating outcomes for health education [Electronic version]. *Journal of Computer Assisted Learning, 17*, 275-283.

Means, B., & Olson, K. (1995). Technology's Role in Education Reform. Findings from a National Study of Innovating Schools. Prepared for Office of Educational Research and Improvement. U.S. Department of Education: Washington, DC.

Miller, P.A. (1997). The Integration of Computers at Pinelands High School: A case study. Unpublished M. Ed Thesis, University of Pretoria. Retrieved January 23, 2006 from http://www.wcape.school.za/subject/CS/PHS/index.htm

Mumtaz, S. (2000). Factors Affecting Teachers' Use of Information and Communications Technology: a review of the literature [Electronic version]. *Journal of Information Technology for Teacher Education, 9*(3), 2000.

Pelgrum, W. J., & Law, N. (2003). ICT in education around the world. Trends, Problems and Prospects. Paris: UNESCO. Retrieved September 10, 2005 from http://unesdoc.unesco.org/images/0013/001362/136281e.pdf

Pierson, M., & McLachlan, A. (2004). Case Studies of Future Teachers: Learning to Teach with Technology. *Winner of the 2004 National Educational Computing Conference (NECC).* Retrieved from http://center.uoregon.edu/ISTE/NECC2004/handout_files_live/KEY_673094/pierson_case_studies.pdf

Sabaliauskas, T. and Pukelis K., (2004). Barriers to Integration of Information and Communication Technologies into the Teaching and Learning Process. Retrieved September 20, 2005 from http://www.leeds.ac.uk/educol/documents/00003861.htm

Tearle, P. (2004). A theoretical and instrumental framework for implementing change in ICT in education [Electronic version]. *Cambridge Journal of Education, 34*(3), 331-351.

Tearle, P. (2003). ICT implementation. What makes the difference? [Electronic version]. *British Journal of Educational Technology, 34* (5), 567-583.

Vogel, D., & Klassen, J. (2001). Technology-supported learning: status, issues and trends [Electronic version]. *Journal of Computer Assisted Learning, 17,* 104-114.

Wagner, D. (2005). Monitoring and Evaluation of ICT for Education. An Introduction. In Wagener, D., et al. (Eds.) Monitoring and Evaluation of ICT in Educational Projects: A Handbook for Developing Countries. *infoDev Pre-Publication draft,* Washington DC, USA. Retrieved December 15, 2005 from http://www.infodev.org/files/2942_file_M_E_ICT_Education_draft_WSIS_optimized.pdf

Williams, D., Coles, L., Wilson, K., Richardson, A., & Tuson, J., (2000). Teachers and ICT: current use and future needs [Electronic version]. *British Journal of Educational Technology, 31*(4), 307-320.

Wilmore, D., & Betz, M. (2000). Information Technology and Schools: the principal's role [Electronic version]. *Educational Technology & Society, 3*(4).

Yusuf, M. (2005). Information and communication technology and education: Analysing the Nigerian national policy for information technology [Electronic version]. *International Education Journal. 6*(3), 316-321.

ENDNOTES

1 http://www.webometrics.info/top100_continent.asp?cont=africa

2 "The University is attempting to expand, utilize and integrate ICT in its academic and administrative area" - ICT Development Office, AAU, 2004.

3 i) 'Learning about ICT' which refers to ICT as a subject of learning in the school curriculum, e.g. Computer (ICT) Literacy and Computer Science, ii) 'Learning with ICT', which refers to the use of ICT, including multimedia, the Internet or the web as a medium to enhance instruction or as a replacement for other media without changing the beliefs about the approaches to and the methods of teaching and learning and iii) 'Learning through ICT' which refers to the integration of ICT as an essential tool into a course/curriculum, such that the teaching and learning of that course/curriculum is no longer possible without it.

4 The 'key people' includes various members of the ICT team, in particular the ICT coordinator and network manager, in terms of their interpersonal skills, planning, management, and commitment to task (Tearle, 2004).

5 Total number of Faculties, Colleges, Institutes, and Schools located at different campuses.

6 Word processing, Electronic mail, Spreadsheet, and MS PowerPoint.

7 Three of the pilot participants were graduate students from the Masters of Education in ICT program (M. Ed. in ICT) and the remaining two were external experts in survey Measurement and Evaluation.

8 A link to the survey instrument is available at http://science.kennesaw.edu/~snegash/research/AAUsurvey2005

9 During the 2004/05 academic year, for example, the total number of female instructors in all 23 state owned higher education institutions was only 9.1% (Education Management Information Systems, 2005).

10 The scales were "very often (3)', 'often (2)', 'sometimes (1)' and 'never (0).

11 -> We stated lower level compared to the mean score of 3. Once again more than 60% of the teachers (102/167 = 60.36%) use Internet once a week (97) or never (5) times hence we say it is lower than the mean value of 3 in a scale of 1 to 5. Our results in Table 5 shows that 102 teachers were using Internet once a week (97) or never (5), compared to 23 that use every day and 44 that use several times a week. As a result, we inferred Internet use 'inadequate'.

12 We have used a Likert scale of 1 through 5; in a strongly disagree (1) to strongly disagree (5) scale. The average in this scale is 3. The mean (i.e. the average, as calculated and presented in Table 6) indicates results of below 3. That is what we refer to as 'expected (average) value'.

13 The caveat in the way these observations should be interpreted includes the fact that the database management and statistical tools are skills significantly higher than say, Word Processing.

14 In the ATC section of the questionnaire, there are 9 questions (4 point scale). So, at the hypothetical (overall midpoint), we expected a score of 2.5x9=22.5. This is the criterion value. The responses, as received, yielded a mean of 25.66. A sample with mean value of 22.5 would suggest that in an overall sense, the responders are at the invariance about their ATC, exactly in the middle point between 'slightly agree and slightly disagree. In essence thus, we argue that they exhibit positive ATC in an overall sense. The variance is statistically significant.

15 Although the interviewee from ICTDO explained that there was no ICT policy for higher education in Ethiopia, we have since discovered that there is a draft document of ICT-in-Education Implementation Strategy and Action Plan (developed by Ethiopian ICT Development Agency in May, 2006). This can be important for improving future utilization of ICT in Ethiopia's higher education.

16 He pointed to the establishment of ICTDO as a strong indication of the University's awareness, belief, and commitment in integrating ICT.

This work was previously published in International Journal of Information and Communication Technology Education, Vol. 5, Issue 3, edited by L. A. Tomei, pp. 34-58, copyright 2009 by IGI Publishing (an imprint of IGI Global).

Chapter 20
Game Informed Virtual Patients:
Catalysts for Online Learning Communities and Professional Development of Medical Teachers

Michael Begg
University of Edinburgh, UK

David Dewhurst
University of Edinburgh, UK

Michael Ross
University of Edinburgh, UK

ABSTRACT

Modern medical education necessitates a complex interleaving of issues relating to practice, professional and personal development, teaching and learning. This complexity has led, in part, to medical education being persistently located in the vanguard of eLearning development. Here, the authors describe our approach to the development of virtual patient resources and in particular how this iterative dialogue arising from the allied processes of practice, reflection and pedagogy required to create new learning tools and resources has contributed to professional development of those engaged in teaching medical students and in building online learning communities at the University of Edinburgh.

INTRODUCTION

Communication and network technologies have played an increasingly visible role in global culture since the early 1990s when the Microsoft Windows operating system and the expansion of the Internet into what we now recognise as the World Wide Web brought affordable hardware and similarly cost effective innovations in data searching, content creation and communication. The education sector has, over time, increasingly turned to information and communication technology (ICT), largely with a view to increasing capacity and reducing costs across administrative and business operations, as well as to increasing the quantity of educational resources available to teachers and students.

ICT continues to impact upon the processes of teaching and learning, and is now broadly regarded to be an integral component of the learning landscape (Laurillard, 1993) typified by the increasingly widespread use of Virtual Learning and Teaching Environments (VLEs), digital learning and library resources, e-assessment tools and software packages and Web 2.0 applications. The range of tools and applications available to teachers continues to grow, while eLearning literature commonly reports an increased degree of learner satisfaction, potential for rich engagement, a high degree of interactivity, and increased student adoption of self-directed learning habits. Equally compelling factors influencing the integration of digital technology into teaching and learning are contemporary cultural drivers towards mass Higher Education, widening access and lifelong learning. Numerous countries have declared ambitions to significantly increase the number of students entering into Higher Education and it is advances in ICT in general and eLearning in particular which make such ambitions possible (Littlejohn, 2003).

However, eLearning is still a relatively young area of development and can perhaps still be considered to be in a period of transition (Laurillard, 2007). It also has very broad application across different disciplines and different levels of education. In an attempt to narrow the focus, in this chapter, we have focussed on a particular community of practice – medical education – and how its various processes related to teaching, learning, reflection, professional development and activity recording are attempting to engage with the affordances the new digital technologies in the most meaningful and appropriate way.

Although the term "eLearning" is often used in very general terms about ICT in educational contexts, it is perhaps more appropriately used when considering the range of pedagogic and related activities associated with personal learning and professional development. We believe that successful eLearning offers user-centred, flexible opportunities for self-directed, reflective learning practices. It offers the potential for contextualised learning opportunities and acts as an effective agent for developing learning communities through a broad range of direct user communication options such as email, Voice-Over Internet Protocol (e.g. Skype), discussion boards and online conferencing.

More recently, the eLearning landscape has seen the introduction of a plethora of so-called Web2.0 applications, typified by social networking sites such as MySpace, Facebook and Bebo, and benefitted from the associated opportunities for content creation, syndication and management, cross platform delivery and overall user control. Blogs, wikis, podcasts and vodcasts, social bookmarking and content-tagging are all becoming increasingly commonplace within our educational institutions. Whatever threats these advancements may pose to the traditional organisational and political structures of our institutions they are unquestionably having a direct impact upon our learning communities. Learners, at every level, can now easily locate, author, share, discuss and aggregate information, establish collaborative networking relationships and project partnerships with peers and, effectively, steer their own personal and professional development.

E-LEARNING

eLearning is not merely a phenomenon that impacts upon learners. The implementation of eLearning tools and applications impacts upon all other stakeholders within the learning environment – particularly teachers (Ellaway, Begg, Dewhurst, & Macleod, 2005). It would seem clear that in developing the skills required to create new learning materials in unfamiliar media, and adopting new, equally unfamiliar approaches to creating learning content and educational activities presents considerable challenges for teaching staff.

Virtual Learning Environments (VLEs) are becoming ubiquitous in European and North American Higher Education institutions and an increasing number of these institutions have integrated these "virtual" versions of their course identities so deeply as to now offer online distance learning degree programmes, often at a Masters level, whereby students undertake a full course of study without ever physically entering the fabric of the institution. The University of Edinburgh has developed a number of such online courses (http://postgraduateprogrammesonline.ed.ac.uk/) and prominent amongst those is the MSc in Clinical Education aimed at healthcare professional educators.

The needs of medical education are both singular and particular. While HE institutions may commonly acquire a license for one of a number of generic off-the-shelf VLE solutions, it is often the case in the UK and elsewhere, that medical programmes – due both to the singular structure and activity patterns of medical education and the fact that such courses are in the vanguard of new developments – will, where resources allow, opt for bespoke VLE solutions, even if this solution is viewed to sit at odds with the dominant institutional system (Cook, 2001). This inclination again towards adopting tailored solutions for the singular challenges posed by the constraints of medical education is another factor contributing towards a position of commitment towards developing, implementing and evaluating the highest possible quality of eLearning tools and activities.

Whilst, like VLEs, these highly flexible tools may sit somewhat awkwardly within the socio-political makeup of other institutional technologies (McGee & Begg, 2008), they also offer responsive opportunities for collaboration, collection, recording and community building activities within peer groups. This has seen educators effectively work "under the wire" beyond the reach of institutional systems in order to progress their teaching or professional development (Begg, Ellaway, Dewhurst, & Macleod, 2007a)

To understand why eLearning has developed such a particularly close relationship of innovation and integration with healthcare education it may be of some value to look at the evolving nature of medical education itself and how the adoption of new technologies into practice has prompted a symbiotic development of both educative and developmental domains, as clearly evinced by the emergence of virtual patients

MEDICAL EDUCATION

We use the term 'medical education' here to mean undergraduate and postgraduate training and continuing professional development of medical doctors. Evidence of medical education can be traced back at least 5,000 years (Calman, 2007), although historically very little attention has been paid to the appropriate training and support of medical teachers themselves. As with many other disciplines, there was an assumption that a good doctor would also be a good teacher - exemplified by the traditional medical adage "See one, do one, teach one". Over the past few decades, interest and research in medical education has progressed dramatically. Teaching techniques have become more complex and specialised with increasing focus on simulation, learning technologies and informatics. There has been a shift away from teaching traditional discipline-based subjects such as anatomy and physiology separately, towards more integrated systems-based approaches, where for example the anatomy, physiology, pathology, clinical presentations and treatments for diseases such as angina are learned together. Clinical case-based learning, early contact with patients and increasing emphasis on the importance of learning communication skills, ethics and practical procedures have also been given greater emphasis (Schmidt & Rickers 2007).

In almost all countries training and accreditation for those engaging in medical practice has long been carefully regulated (Parliament 1858; EU 1981; DOH 2007) - principally for reasons of patient safety. There has been no similar regulation and training for those involved in medical teaching. The relatively recent demand for more public accountability, quality assurance and transparency from the medical profession, together with the more pedagogical issues highlighted above, has had a very positive impact on medical education as a discipline. There has been a move towards all doctors being required to teach (GMC 2006a) and to include continuing professional development as a teacher in their annual appraisal (GMC, 2004). Some medical students are learning to teach as undergraduates (GMC, 2003), there is an expectation that those taking on more responsibilities in education will undertake further training or a higher degree (GMC 1999, 2006a; NES 2007; NMC 2007), and national and international organisations are working to define standards and appropriate training for medical teacher professional development (Association of American Medical Colleges 1998; GMC 2003; WFME 2003; Frank 2005; PMETB 2005; GMC 2007; Cumming & Ross 2008). Medical teaching as a discipline could therefore be said to be currently undergoing a process of 'professionalisation' (Academy of Medical Educators 2007; Calman, 2007)

Aspects of medical education that particularly stand-out from other disciplines in higher education include the teaching and learning and assessment of communication skills, clinical diagnostic skills, 'professionalism' and practical clinical procedures. Miller (1990) presents a helpful model of the stages of skill acquisition in which the learner first knows about the skill, then knows how to do it, then can show how to do it in a simulated environment, and then does it in practice. Whilst adequate exposure to real patients is essential to medical training at all levels, simulation enables core learning objectives to be contextualised without any risk to patients and is an important part of the preparation of medical students to treat real patients. Simulations include clinical problems, virtual patients, low-fidelity part-task mannequins (e.g. synthetic airways for intubation and skin for minor surgery), high-fidelity whole body simulators (used to simulate complex illnesses and emergency situations such as cardiac arrest) and standardised ('simulated') patients or actors briefed on how to give a realistic performance of a patient.

THE NATURE OF MEDICAL PRACTICE

It is not appropriate to consider teaching, teacher development and technologies in isolation when attempting to establish a model for supporting these multiple objectives within a single integrated development environment. It may be appropriate – and more digestible – to focus on one key area of modern healthcare education that has instigated significant changes to formal curricula, approaches to teaching and learning and has explicit ramifications for professional development - namely the emergence, growth and use of virtual patients.

Members of the public generally go to a medical doctor for an opinion. They expect, amongst other things, that the doctor will diagnose what the problem is and formulate an appropriate plan to address it. Virtual patients enable students to practise these and other skills and can, therefore, help students develop some of the core skills required for effective practice as a doctor. Diagnosis and patient management are some of the most complex and challenging skills that students have to master however, consequently there must be considerable flexibility and potential for complexity in virtual patients created for this task.

Figure 1 shows a simplified medical consultation in which the doctor will first seek to establish a relationship and gather information about the patient and the reason for their attendance by listening, questioning, clinical examination and from other sources. From this information, which is often imprecise and incomplete, together with their scientific knowledge and clinical experience, they will exercise 'clinical judgement' in formulating a provisional or definitive 'diagnosis'. The doctor will then explain the problem(s) to the patient, discuss and advise on any relevant treatment / management options, and provide support as required (Byrne & Long 1976).

This orderly approach in which the doctor gathers as much relevant information as possible and then formulates a diagnosis is generally

Figure 1. A simplified medical consultation

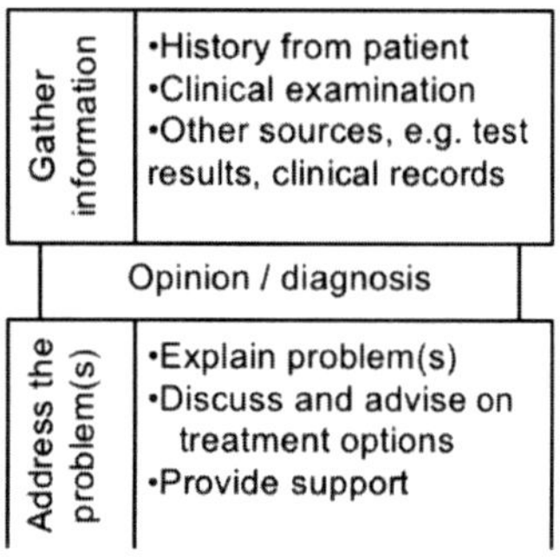

referred-to as the '**Inductive**' method of diagnosis. In a study of over 2000 audio-taped consultations, it was found that most medical consultations seem to follow such a sequence (Byrne & Long, 1976). What they did not detect from the recordings, however, were the doctors' thought processes – which subsequent research has shown do not generally follow such a logical analytical sequence (Elstein, Shulman, & Sprafka, 1978; Norman, Young, & Brooks, 2007). As doctors gain experience in clinical practice and interact with many individual patients, there is evidence that they collect in memory an increasingly large number of typical patterns of illness presentation and progression, sometimes called 'illness scripts' (Schmidt & Rickers, 2007). It seems that when an expert doctor is confronted with a familiar presentation of an ill patient they will formulate a provisional diagnosis very early in the consultation, sometimes within seconds, and will then strategically seek information to prove or disprove their hypothesis. If their hypothesis is disproved, or further information is gathered which suggests an alternative illness, a new provisional diagnosis will be made and tested. This has been referred-to as the '**Hypothetico-deductive**' method of diagnosis (Elstein, A. S., Shulman, L. S., & Sprafka, S. A., 1978; Norman, G., Young, M., & Brooks, L., 2007). It is likely that both novice and expert doctors actually use the hypothetico-deductive method in practice, although will revert to a more inductive method when confronted with an unfamiliar presentation of illness. Teaching students to use both approaches has been shown to result in improved diagnostic accuracy compared to using either alone (Kulatanga-Moruzi, Brooks, & Norman, 2001), and so this is the approach we have tried to adopt when developing virtual patients.

As an illustration of both diagnostic methods, imagine a previously healthy lady in her mid-thirties presenting to her general practitioner (GP) feeling 'tired all the time'. This is a common presentation in the UK, and statistically the most common cause by far is stress. There are numerous other potential causes of tiredness however, including depression, anaemia, thyroid problems, diabetes, chronic infections such as TB, heart or kidney failure, substance misuse, early rheumatoid arthritis, MS and various types of cancer and leukaemia (Hopcroft & Forte, 2003). An inductive approach to diagnosis in this case would involve taking a full history with questions relating to all possible causes, performing a full examination of all systems, and organising a battery of blood tests, x-rays and other investigations. The inductive doctor would then wait until they had all the information before making a diagnosis. Clearly this would take significantly longer than a typical 10-minute GP appointment. In practice, assuming the patient looks well and reports no worrying features (sometimes called 'red flags') the GP will often hypothesise early in the consultation that the cause of the tiredness might be stress, and will thus focus their questioning, examination and further management on proving or disproving this hypothesis. The hypothetico-deductive doctor will therefore focus on possible stressors, work and home situation, mood, sleep and the physical manifestations of stress. Critically, however, the doctor will also 'screen' for more serious potential causes of tiredness, with questions about weight loss, breathlessness and depression; inspection of the patient's records for previous serious illnesses; physical examination of the chest, abdomen, eyes and lymph glands; and possibly taking a blood test to check for anaemia, diabetes, thyroid problems, kidney failure and inflammation. The hypothetico-deductive doctor does not expect to find anything during this screen although remains vigilant, and does not check for all possible causes of tiredness, but seeks evidence which might refute their original hypothesis. If, for example, the patient reveals that they have lost weight without changing their calorie intake or exercise levels, or have enlarged lymph glands on examination, then more serious disease may be present and stress is less likely, so the doctor will make a new hypothesis to test.

Medical teachers are tasked with helping undergraduate students and postgraduate trainees develop and refine their expertise in clinical judgement and diagnosis. There are a number of problems inherent in trying to achieve this however, such as then high turnover and variability of patients presenting, and the lack of sufficiently detailed and immediate feedback typically available in clinical practice. These problems are being compounded by increasing student numbers, reduced numbers of hospital beds and enforced reductions on working hours for junior doctors. Becoming an expert in any field, whether sport, music or the medical diagnosis, requires a significant amount of deliberate practice. Some have even tried to quantify this in terms of the number of hours of practice required, with findings typically in the region of ten years or 10,000 hours (Ericsson, 2004; Ericsson, Krampe, & Tesch-Romer, 1993). The evidence suggests that deliberate practice is also required to maintain that expertise, and that when even highly experienced professionals are appropriately motivated they are able to gradually improve their objective performance in representative tasks from their domain of expertise (Ericsson, Krampe, & Tesch-Romer, 1993). To do this, they need to identify an area of their performance that they want to improve, and find a way to perform the same or similar tasks repeatedly with detailed and immediate feedback on their performance (Ericsson, 2004). Unlike in music or sport however, doctors are typically introduced to their field in their late teens or early twenties rather than in early childhood, and there are often no 'gold standard' expert performances to emulate (Ericsson, 2004). Many expert doctors find it difficult to reflect-upon and articulate to a novice the thought processes that they went through to arrive at a particular clinical judgement or diagnosis. Because their diagnoses are often heavily influenced by pattern-recognition with a previous patient or 'illness script' and hypothetico-deductive diagnostic methods, they may find it difficult to tease-apart and reason the different elements of their clinical judgement to help learners understand the processes involved (Schmidt & Rickers 2007). Experts also typically find it difficult to identify where students went wrong when they make errors in their diagnoses, and how best to help them improve their skills. In considering what factors contribute to good teaching in such circumstances, the concept of scholarship in teaching (Fincher R-ME, Simpson DE, Mennin SP, Rosenfeld GC, & Rothman A., 2000; Glassic, 2000) can be a helpful guide. Integral to the concept of scholarship is the notion that the teacher is also a learner – continually trying to improve their own understanding and practice whilst teaching others to improve theirs. Part of the success of eLearning in medical education may be due to the way in which it forces expert clinicians to learn new skills and to critically reflect on their prior approaches to clinical and teaching practice.

E-LEARNING IN MEDICAL EDUCATION

In the UK in the 1990s there were a number of national initiatives and a significant funding available to stimulate the use of ICT in higher education across a broad range of disciplines. Medical and biomedical education was prominent in many of these initiatives and the result was a plethora of interactive computer programs - commonly known as Computer-Assisted Learning (CAL) - and videos designed to support student learning of factual knowledge, principles and skills. Multimedia CDROMs, which incorporated a range of features to support learning (high-quality graphics; animation sequences to demonstrate dynamic principles; video (essential, for example, in illustrating abnormal gait patterns in some neurological conditions); audio; interactive self-assessments/quizzes; patient cases; simulated laboratory environments (virtual labs) in which students could collect data from simulated experiments) were the mainstay of e-learning during this period. Although this approach perhaps never achieved the cost-savings and efficiency gains predicted by those who funded such initiatives at that time, a number of studies in the biomedical sciences attempted to evaluate the educational effectiveness of these CAL programs. In general they demonstrated that students could manage their own learning very effectively, and that many of the learning objectives of the traditional teaching methods (lectures, practical classes) could be achieved (Coleman, Dewhurst, Meehan, & Williams, 1994; Dewhurst, Macleod, & Norris, 2000; Hughes, 2001; Rest, 1997; Tait, 1997)

The emergence of the Internet as a tool for supporting teaching and learning was the next major development and Virtual Learning Environments were becoming increasingly common by the end of the 20th Century.

'Virtual Learning Environments (VLEs) are a compelling and powerful way to support and manage modern medical education processes. A purposively aligned and built VLE, despite time and resource implications for development, can help to integrate and normalise procedures and provide a central access point and reference mechanism for all of a course's geographically and culturally diverse communities' (Ellaway, Dewhurst, & Cumming, 2003)

Medical education, especially the training of doctors, has always tended to be at the forefront of adoption of and innovation in eLearning. There are many possible reasons for this, including political factors and relatively good funding and support from the profession and Government, but one of the most significant factors is that of patient safety. Patient welfare is a defining principal of medical practice and training novices to make diagnoses, carry-out practical procedures and prescribe medication and other treatments is inherently fraught with potential dangers. Any method that presents a suitable opportunity to acquire the broad range of skills associated with professional practice without compromising patient safety is therefore of great interest. Case-based discussion and simulation training, using part-task mannequins, high-fidelity simulators, standardised patients and actors are examples of activities in which the core learning objectives can be contextualised and achieved without risk to patients. Another reason for early adoption of innovations in eLearning in medical education is to ensure learners are exposed to an adequate breadth of clinical experience. With increasing numbers of medical students passing through medical schools, drivers to reduce the number of patients in hospital their duration of stay, increasingly stringent directives governing doctors' working hours, and directives from governing bodies such as the UK General Medical Council declaring that "opportunistic learning" is no longer sufficient in healthcare education, it is difficult to ensure students have sufficient clinical exposure. All of these factors have stimulated the development of learning environments and resources where the virtual is increasingly expected to emulate, wherever it can, the real.

Another possible reason directly leading from this necessity for *reality*, and one which we will expand upon further, is the "practicum" nature of healthcare education. Schön (1987) defined the practicum as "a setting designed for the task of learning a practice. In a context that approximates a practice world, students learn... by undertaking projects that simulate and simplify practice; or they take on real-world projects under close supervision". Essentially, the suggestion is that the process of teaching should reflect as closely as possible the nature and context of the skills being taught and so the context of the teaching should, as closely as possible, reflect the reality of the practice. This sets the ground for the notion that the teacher and the pupil should, ideally, be sharing the same environment, the same resources, and, generally, accept that they are involved in a cyclical professional process of acquiring understanding, reflecting on that understanding, delivering insight, reflecting further upon feedback received, thereby returning to the point of acquiring understanding. Computer mediated activities, whether gaming, participating in an online social network such as Facebook or MySpace, or file-sharing, to name a few of the multiform activities undertaken online, are highly adaptable at connecting communities of individuals each of whom are empowered within the relevant environment. eLearning should be seen as no different in this. There can and should be appropriate representation and affordance for the full range of users in a single environment. It could, therefore, be suggested that a suitably constructed eLearning platform is a suitably aligned extension of the principles of the practicum.

CASE-BASED LEARNING AND VIRTUAL PATIENTS

Descriptions of individual patients and their medical problems, typically referred-to as 'Case Studies', have been used in medical education for centuries (Calman, 2007; Charlton & Walston, 1998). Typically they have been used to either exemplify a particular condition or clinical presentation and encourage students to generalise from the example, or alternatively to challenge generalisations and assumptions by offering exceptions to the rule and unusual or unexpected outcomes. In medicine there is also an increasing trend towards 'Narrative-based medicine' (Greenhalgh & Hurwitz, 1998), with increased awareness of the importance of patient's stories and the shortcomings of traditional positivist 'Evidence-Based Medicine' (Greenhalgh, 2006; Sackett, Straus, Richardson, Rosenberg, & Haynes, 2000). The development and use of virtual patients is an area of particularly rapid growth with several initiatives throughout Europe and the United States providing content, authoring tools and delivery platforms (Begg, 2008; Begg, Ellaway, Dewhurst, & Macleod, 2006). Meta frameworks, such as the Medbiquitous virtual patient standard have also emerged in order to maximise the potential for sharing of these virtual cases. Virtual patients are scenario-based learning activities, and are used in medical and veterinary education in numerous institutions worldwide. At the University of Edinburgh they are used in a variety of ways including: developing clinical diagnostic and decision-making skills; teaching and formatively assessing knowledge of basic and clinical sciences such as physiology and pharmacology; and enabling experiential learning ('learning through doing'). In some courses students particularly in the later years of their courses are engaged in developing their own virtual patients and this has proved to be a very effective and popular activity. The nature of the virtual patient also varies: some present a strongly didactic, linear and strictly codified exploration of key clinical data in information-gathering, diagnosis and treatment; others attempt to contextualise the learning experience by presenting believable narratives in realistic settings that invite the learner to *perform* in the role of a practitioner.

At Edinburgh the scalable creation of online resources has been facilitated by the in-house development of a range of easy to use authoring and delivery tools, suitable for academic and clinical teachers with little technical know-how. EROS (the Edinburgh Re-usable Object Sequencer), a web-based authoring tool, supports the creation of interactive, tutorial-style resources. It comprises a series of templates based on a range of common question types (MCQ, short text, extended matching, etc) which are most-often used for the development of formative self-assessment quizzes. Exemplars include a comprehensive pathology course (120+ individual modules), a number of clinical skills support resources and a wide range of case-based learning modules. These provide students with opportunities to test their understanding of the curriculum knowledge base, often within a contextualised and recognisable case narrative framework. EROS has had considerable impact in enabling content creation by academic staff with little intervention from learning technologists and to date in excess of 700 learning resources have been created in this way.

Another tool, Labyrinth, provides for the authoring of more complex "branching path" case narratives that take a game informed approach to the development of virtual patients(Begg, Dewhurst, & Macleod, 2005; Begg et al., 2006; Begg, Ellaway, Dewhurst, & Macleod, 2007b). Typically authors encourage learner engagement through a highly contextualised requirement for learners to adopt a meaningful role in the clinical scenario (e.g. junior doctor, patient, nurse), make critical clinical decisions (define the physical examination process they will follow, decide which tests to request, interpret the test data, come up with a differential diagnosis, and decide on a suitable treatment). Decisions have consequence and allowing the learner to work through even 'inappropriate' choices promotes learning. Learners apply critical, reflective reasoning whilst performing "in character" within a plausible real-life clinical scenario.

Labyrinth, like EROS, is designed to be usable by teachers with little technical knowledge, and the signs are that uptake by staff will be high. Locally, Labyrinth cases have already been embedded into the undergraduate MBChB programme in modules relating to clinical emergency training, general practice and surgery. The contextualised and character-rich cases are also playing a significant role in postgraduate training via the online distance MSc programme in Surgical Sciences, and further afield Labyrinth is being used in the development of new healthcare curricula in Malawi (Dewhurst & Chimalizeni, 2008)

The concept of game informed learning (Begg, 2008) is similar to the more familiar idea of games based learning (Prensky, 2000). Game informed learning proposes that through the concepts of play and narrative commonly attributed to successful games – contextual character roles for users, a responsive environment, a reasonable degree of empowerment for users within the game world, frequent feedback, etc – a richly compelling and immersive learning experience may be produced. Game informed learning differs from game based learning principally in that it argues that the resulting application need not be, explicitly, a game. Rather, it may be a learning activity, such as an interactive virtual patient case scenario, that applies the principals of games and narrative to enhance the impact of that activity.

Considering, once again, the level of experience and the variance of approaches that clinical practice implies we can draw parallels between diagnostic approaches and the particular style of virtual patient development accommodated by the two tools, EROS and Labyrinth. The inductive approach with its emphasis on methodical gathering of ordered evidence may be appropriately delivered via the strong linear framework of EROS, while the hypothetico-deductive approach may be best served by Labyrinth's ability to host multiple highly individualised pathways taken through a single case – allowing learners to explore multiple 'what if?' questions at each stage of their progress through a virtual case.

VIRTUAL PATIENT CREATION AND PROFESSIONAL DEVELOPMENT

The task of creating virtual patients requires medical teachers to reflect on their practice in a very focussed way that seems to be quite differ-

Figure 2. a) Example of a computer assisted learning (CAL) sequence, featuring a pair matching question concerned with reproductive health; b) The editing interface within the Edinburgh Reusable Object Sequencer (EROS) for the CAL self assessment page shown in figure 2a

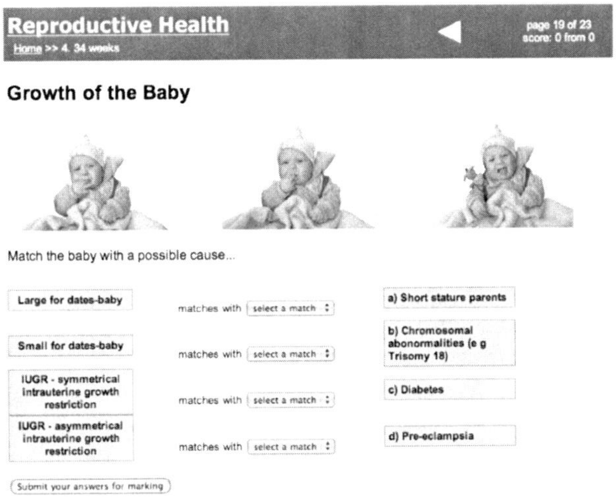

(a)

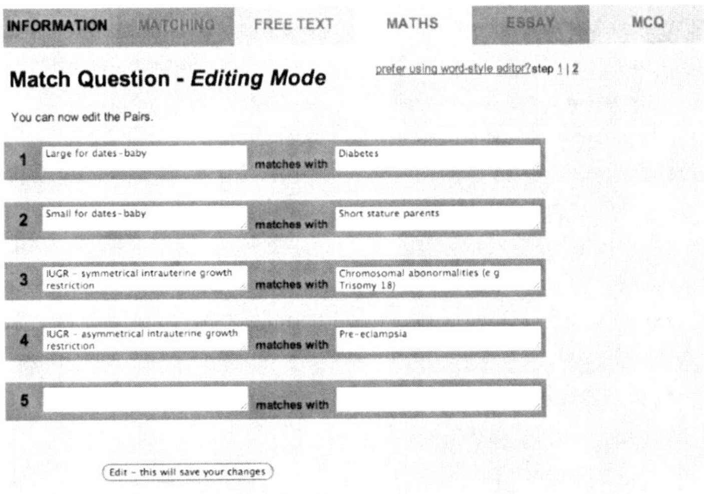

(b)

ent to their reflection in normal clinical practice. This would suggest that such enhanced reflection should improve their clinical practice and encourage them to be more reflective about other aspects of their practice (Schön, 1983; Schön, 1987). Active participation might also encourage them to take a more scholarly approach to their clinical teaching and practice, and make greater use-of, and contribute more to, the literature and to academic networks of like-minded practitioners (Boyer, 1990; Glassic, 2000). In our experience, active collaboration even on this small scale has also led to the establishment of small online communities of practice, which have been previously shown to be inherently beneficial to learning (Ellaway, 2005).

We have observed, through running virtual patient authoring workshops in Edinburgh, London and Malawi with a range of healthcare professional educators, how the process of applying the principles of game informed learning to the creation of virtual patients has led, somewhat inadvertently, to game informed teaching. As an illustration of this phenomenon consider how as healthcare professionals develop expertise much of their cognitive processing seems to take place at the subconscious level. This process, by which knowledge effectively becomes tacit (Baumard, 1999) or hidden, has also been called "thin-slicing" (Gladwell, 2005). This can lead to a problem with knowledge transfer between expert and apprentice due to the experts being unable to explain their own cognitive processes clearly, and unable to identify errors in learners' cognitive processes. The process of authoring realistic, context sensitive cases in Labyrinth requires clinical teachers – particularly when they are working collaboratively with peers – opportunities to *surface* their tacit knowledge through the need to describe and capture the processes to be accurately and appropriately set out in the case. A number of clinical, academic and basic science authors who have worked on such virtual cases have commented on the difficulty and complexity of such work, but also the considerable personal and academic gains and satisfaction associated with it. This has led an increasing number of clinical teachers to submit the work they do in authoring virtual patients as part of their professional CPD commitments. It is here that we can observe an illustration of the direct and explicit linking of practice, learning and professional development. Virtual patients reflecting real life and practice, are written by practitioners who, surface tacit knowledge through the process of authoring thereby increasing personal awareness and reflectivity, and at the same time they explicitly document these to develop and enhance the quality of a teaching resource. The issue then becomes how to frame the activities of multiple practitioners with a similar degree of flexibility and responsiveness.

PROFESSIONAL DEVELOPMENT OF MEDICAL TEACHERS

In seeking to offer undergraduate medical students a balanced education drawing on the strengths of evidence-based and narrative approaches, we have found virtual patients to offer many advantages to "traditional" learning and teaching methods.

Observation of the process of development of virtual patient case scenarios has shown that one of the positive consequences of using a game informed approach and making use of an online tool for collaborative authoring virtual patient cases is that medical teachers have, through engagement with the activity, been steered towards surfacing their own *tacit* professional knowledge. This has clear advantages if one assumes that one of the main drivers for students to undertake these virtual patient scenarios is to gain insight into the *reality* of clinical practice. Cleverly constructed online virtual patients that incorporate many of the principles of online games offer a real opportunity for medical teachers to support students in learning factual content as well as more complex skills such as the hypothetico-deductive method of diagnosis. The process of developing virtual patients also affords many direct opportunities for professional development of the teachers, including:

- Enhanced content knowledge and potentially enhanced clinical skills – whilst creating a virtual patient teachers will question, structure and identify gaps in their knowledge and are likely to go and read more about it.
- Development as educators – through reflection on current teaching practice, learning new skills and techniques and engagement with new, often unfamiliar, educational processes and methods in creating online learning resources for students.
- Community-building – in many instances VP development is a collaborative activity

Figure 3. a) A navigation chart of a game informed virtual patient scenario authored in the Labyrinth application. The figure illustrates the degree of branching complexity that can be introduced using this kind of technology; b) A screen grab from the complex branching case virtual patient scenario mapped out in figure 3a.

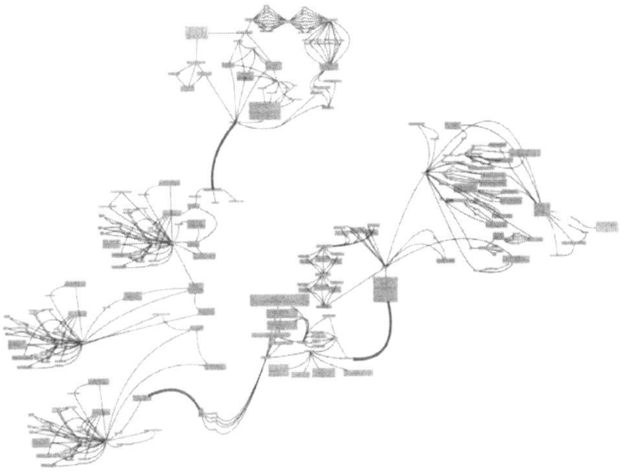

(a)

with development teams often comprising a small number of practicing clinicians and other professional (e.g. in one patient case there may be a psychiatrist, a GP, a learning technologist and physiologist developing a virtual patient together in an online environment). They will share and discuss knowledge and experience in an effort to develop a highly interactive and challenging learning resource. Often there is a challenge to develop a VP where the learner can adopt different roles – that of a junior/novice doctor, that of another healthcare professional (e.g. nurse) or that of the patient. Such peer learning is a particularly valuable staff development activity for all concerned.

- Reflective practice – by reflecting in and on action, as well as enhancing professional knowledge and skills, medical teachers may also develop their abilities and attitudes towards reflective practice itself (Schön, 1987).

- Enhanced integration of clinical and teaching roles – clinicians who have been involved in the development of virtual patients become more attuned to gathering material and examples from their everyday work which might be suitable for teaching. They are likely to think about and record this in a structure and format which is suitable for educational use.
- Increased awareness of the need for professional development – clinical teachers have a responsibility to support and assess student professional development (GMC, 2003, 2006b; NMC, 2007). Virtual patients can be used as a means to achieve this in a realistic yet safe environment. By creating realistic patient scenarios and ethical dilemmas to train and assess student professional development, educators are also forced to reflect and evaluate themselves.

Such processes of personal professional development, teaching skill and professional excellence cannot, in the present culture, be considered in isolation. There are complex interactions between all of these factors. There are also constraints on such interactions – not least of time, distance and funding. The requirements of practice, and the affordances of available technology, increasingly compel us towards a strategy that allows for integrated online environments in which such interactions and developments might take-place.

ONLINE COMMUNITIES OF MEDICAL TEACHERS

The potential benefits of interactive and supportive communities of practice are well described in the literature (Wenger, 1998). As we move into what some have described as the 'post-modern' era of education, there is increased recognition of the need to share knowledge, experience and insight between academic disciplines and professions – to break-down traditional barriers separating academic and professional groups and their exclusive 'silo' of knowledge, and to increase the value of such knowledge to society through a process of 'knowledge transfer' (Jacob, 2003; Ozga, 2007). Academics and practitioners can benefit immensely and immediately from increased interaction with similarly motivated groups, and have much to learn from each other. Traditionally there have been multiple cultural, social, financial, spatial and temporal constraints to such interaction. With the growth of transnational organisations, increasing economic integration and the rapid development of information technologies and telecommunications, sometimes collectively referred-to as 'globalisation', has come many new opportunities (Giddens, 1990). As Hudson and Lowe write:

"We may have to rethink our understanding of the nature of 'society' with its relatively fixed social structures and geographical boundaries... Globalisation is essentially about the networking of the planet – through the Internet, satellite telecommunications and rapid transport – by new forms of local, regional and transnational social connections, economic markets and political structures" (Hudson & Lowe, 2004).

Collaborative online virtual patient creation and development represents a fruitful exploration of such new opportunities, with potential benefits to those teachers and technologists involved in the creation process, students and trainees in medicine, veterinary medicine and allied health professions, and to the educational and healthcare institutions with which they are associated.

As experience of developing and using eLearning resources in medical education matures there are signs that a community lifecycle is emerging. An innovation (in this instance, virtual patients) leads to reflection on existing practice. Collaborative development of resources and adopting a novel approach (game-informed learning) to the development of resources leads to further innovation. The process of authoring itself engages further reflection and personal development (the "surfacing" of professional *tacit* knowledge) as well as indicating potential impact upon the evolution of the broader curriculum. Reflective commentary, observation, evaluation and other evidence gathering activities are gathered within the medical education community, as is data about how students engage with the innovative materials and whether they are fulfilling the learning objectives for which they were designed. The community dialogue leads (ideally) not only to further enhancement of authoring skills which might directly enhance and improve existing virtual patients, but also to the kind of informed, reflective community dialogue that leads both to the ongoing professional development of those involved and completes the "cycle" through the generation of new innovations.

FUTURE TRENDS

The University of Edinburgh is embarking on a process of deliberately expanding the role of the *traditional* VLE to accommodate the processes, practices and reflections of the growing community of healthcare educators. It is hoped that by increasing teachers' awareness and opportunities for interaction, by aggregating previously compartmentalised activities and related knowledge and skills such as case-authoring, CPD recording, portfolio development, reflection on student feedback and evaluation, by utilising the syndication and aggregation principals of Web 2.0, and by engaging in the emerging communities of practice that are growing around innovative applications such as Labyrinth; it should be possible to enhance healthcare education delivery and professional development in a number of ways:

- Improved alignment between activity creation and delivery
- Built in mechanisms for quality assurance (QA) through opportunities for peer review
- Increased levels of "buy-in" from healthcare educators due to broader base of activities relating to personal professional development, teaching and networking
- Improved quality of teaching and learning resources accorded by the *lifecycle* support in which students become competent educators within a single supported community framework

Exemplar models for nurturing online communities of practice through these kinds of approaches are emerging. In Malawi there is a great deal of activity addressing the identified need for curricular reform in the country's quest to generate greater numbers of healthcare professionals and self directed learners. An online collaborative working environment (CWE) proved to be a powerful way of enabling geographically disparate healthcare workers (doctors, clinical officers and nurses) across Malawi to collectively discuss case development, curricular prioritisation and resource collection, whilst authoring learning activities using Labyrinth and seeking peer feedback on case authoring activities. The Malawi Healthcare CWE is forming the heart of the emergent VLE for healthcare education and, critically, the teachers have not only bought-in to the online environment, they have, in a very real sense, created it.

Similarly, in a recent project with Chest, Heart and Stroke Scotland (CHSS) and National Health Service Education Scotland (NES) a CWE platform was developed which allowed groups of nurses, clinicians and teachers to gather and describe resources and requirements for a learning resource concerning the core competencies required by those working with those affected by strokes. Learning activities were collaboratively authored addressing each of the core competencies in turn and, as the project development reached completion the same environment formed the base for users to enter and undertake the activities. A self-assessment process underpinned with formal certification was also incorporated thereby presenting another complete model of a single environment supporting learning, reflection, content and activity development, delivery and recording of achievement.

In another initiative that more explicitly taps into the potential of virtual patient authoring to impact upon personal professional reflective practice The Royal College of Surgeons in Edinburgh, who are responsible for CPD of surgeons from all around the world, have recently put forward proposals to explore the usefulness of creating and engaging with interactive, scenario-based learning pathways or mazes (initially devised by small teams of 'expert' surgeons) as a means of acquiring and demonstrating their ability to apply specialist and up-to-date knowledge as part of the recertification process essential for continued practice.

It is arguably also the case that as long as eLearning activities attract funding streams largely out-with core institutional teaching and learning budgets, issues of related staff development – including teacher professional development – may also be forced out-with traditional institutional frameworks. Clinical teachers at the University of Edinburgh, as elsewhere, currently acquire information and knowledge from disparate sources such as subject specific special interest groups, practitioner mailing lists such as the UK's jiscmail service, as well as through the more traditional professional discourse afforded by institutional training, conferences, journals, networking, etc. Potentially such an outward search for support and information could isolate teachers from their own local context and community. In Edinburgh, we are actively seeking to capitalise on such external online resources, communities and activities by pooling them into 'ClinED' - an online collaborative learning environment for clinical educators, encouraging a shared collective engagement with external agencies (Ross, Blaney, Cameron, Begg, & Cumming, 2008). This online educator community environment is closely aligned to the Virtual Learning Environments for undergraduate medical teaching and the MSc in Clinical Education programme (www.clinicaleducation.mvm.ed.ac.uk). The anticipation is that, over time, the divide between different groups of clinical teachers undertaking professional development activities will become increasingly narrowed.

CONCLUSION

This chapter has focused on professional development of medical educators and in particular how their involvement in designing and creating innovative, scenario-based learning resources (virtual patients) has contributed to that activity. The formation of online communities of practice in medical education has also been explored and ways in which the technologies at their disposal in an online environment can support multi-specialty and multi-professional development have been described. It is clear that eLearning and ICT more generally can provide a vehicle for enhancing professional engagement with the education of students and for self-development in numerous ways.

Game informed virtual patients have proved to be extremely useful in helping students learn complex skills such as medical diagnosis. As a very welcome by-product of virtual patient construction, we have witnessed members of clinical and academic staff become more cohesive as a community, develop their understanding and skills in teaching and practice, and become more aware of themselves as learners and reflective practitioners. Whilst the training of medical teachers, the development of online learning communities and the creation of virtual patients themselves are all still at a relatively early stage, already there seems to be considerable potential gains for all involved.

Medical education is often in the vanguard of innovation and it is possible that what we are describing and observing in medical education practice now will extend into teacher professional development in other disciplines and at all levels in the future.

REFERENCES

Academy of Medical Educators. (2007). 14th December 2007, from http://www.medicaleducators.org/

Association of American Medical Colleges. (1998). *Learning objectives for medical student education.* Retrieved 15th April 2007, from www.aamc.org/meded/msop

Baumard, P. (1999). *Tacit knowledge in organizations.* London, UK: Sage.

Begg, M. (2008). Leveraging Game Informed Learning in Higher Education. *Medical Teacher, 30*(2), 155–158. doi:10.1080/01421590701874041

Begg, M., Dewhurst, D., & Macleod, H. (2005). Game Informed Learning: Applying computer game processes to Higher Education. *Innovate, 1*(6).

Begg, M., Ellaway, R., Dewhurst, D., & Macleod, H. (2006). Virtual Patients: considerations of narrative and gameplay. In M. Burmester, D. Gerhard, & F. Thissen (Eds.), *Digital Game Based Learning: 4th International Symposium for Information Design* (pp. 101 - 113). Stuttgart Media University: Universitatsverlag Karlsruhe.

Begg, M., Ellaway, R., Dewhurst, D., & Macleod, H. (2007a). *Logos and Mythos: the political dilemmas of Web 2.0 in an accreditation-driven educational environment.* Paper presented at the Ice 2007 - Ideas in Cyberspace Education, Loch Lomond, UK.

Begg, M., Ellaway, R., Dewhurst, D., & Macleod, H. (2007b). Transforming Professional Healthcare Narratives Into Structured Game Informed Learning Activities. *Innovate, 3*(6).

Boyer, E. L. (1990). *Scholarship reconsidered: priorities of the professoriate.* Princeton, New Jersey: Carnegie Foundation for the Advancement of Teaching.

Byrne, P., & Long, B. E. L. (1976). *Doctors talking to Patients.* London: HMSO.

Calman, K. C. (2007). *Medical education: past, present and future.* Edinburgh: Elsevier.

Charlton, B. G., & Walston, F. (1998). Individual case studies in clinical research. *Journal of Evaluation in Clinical Practice, 4*(2), 147–155. doi:10.1046/j.1365-2753.1998.00011.x

Coleman, I., Dewhurst, D., Meehan, A. S., & Williams, A. D. (1994). A computer simulation for learning about the physiological response to exercise. *The American Journal of Physiology, 11*, s2–s9.

Cook, J. (2001). *JTAP 623 - The Role of Virtual Learning Environments in UK Medical Education* (No. JTAP 623). UK: Institute for Learning and Research Technologyo. Document Number)

Cumming, A. D., & Ross, M. T. (2008). *The Tuning Project (medicine) – learning outcomes / competences for undergraduate medical education in Europe.* Edinburgh: The University of Edinburgh. Available online: www.tuning-medicine.com. Document Number)

Dewhurst, D., & Chimalizeni, Y. (2008). *Collaborative development of online virtual patients for medical and healthcare professional education in Malawi*. Paper presented at the eLearning Africa.

Dewhurst, D., Hardastle, J., Hardcastle, P. T., & Stuart, E. (1994). Comparison of a computer simulation program with a traditional laboratory practical class for teaching the principles of intestinal absorption. *The American Journal of Physiology, 12*(1), s95–s103.

Dewhurst, D., Macleod, H., & Norris, T. (2000). Independent Student Learning Aided by Computers: An Acceptable Alternative to Lectures? *Computers & Education, 35*, 223–241. doi:10.1016/S0360-1315(00)00033-6

DOH. (2007). *Trust, assurance and safety - the regulation of health professionals for the 21st Century*. London: Department of Health, HMSOo. Document Number)

Ellaway, R., Begg, M., Dewhurst, D., & Macleod, H. (2005). In A Glass Darkly: identity, agency and the role of the learning technologist in shaping the learning environment. *E-Learning, 3*(1), 75-87.

Ellaway, R., Dewhurst, D., & Cumming, A. (2003). Managing and supporting medical education with a virtual learning environment: the Edinburgh Electronic Medical Curriculum. *Medical Teacher, 25*(4), 372–380. doi:10.1080/0142159031000136789

Ellaway, R. H. (2005). *Evaluating a Virtual Learning Environment in Medical Education*. Unpublished PhD, University of Edinburgh, Edinburgh.

Elstein, A. S., Shulman, L. S., & Sprafka, S. A. (1978). *Medical problem solving: an analysis of clinical reasoning*. Cambridge, MA: Harvard University Press.

Ericsson, K. A. (2004). Deliberate practice and the acquisition and maintenance of expert performance in medicine and related domains. *Academic Medicine, 79*(10Supplement), S70–S81. doi:10.1097/00001888-200410001-00022

Ericsson, K. A., Krampe, R. T., & Tesch-Romer, C. (1993). The role of deliberate practice in the acquisition of expert performance. *Psychological Review, 100*(3), 363–406. doi:10.1037/0033-295X.100.3.363

EU. (1981). Council Directive 81/1057/EEC of 14 December 1981 concerning the mutual recognition of diplomas, certificates and other evidence of the formal qualifications of doctors, nurses responsible for general care, dental practitioners and veterinary surgeons respectively, with regard to acquired rights.

Fincher, R.-M. E., Simpson, D. E., Mennin, S. P., Rosenfeld, G. C., Rothman, A., & McGrew, M. C. (2000). Scholarship in teaching: an imperative for the 21st Century. *Academic Medicine, 75*(9), 887–894. doi:10.1097/00001888-200009000-00009

Frank, J. R. (2005). *The CanMEDS 2005 physician competency framework. Better standards. Better physicians. Better care.* Ottowa: The Royal College of Physicians and Surgeons of Canadao. Document Number)

Giddens, A. (1990). *The Consequences of Modernity*. Cambridge: Polity Press.

Gladwell, M. (2005). *Blink: the power of thinking without thinking*. New York: Little Brown & Co.

Glassic, C. E. (2000). Boyer's expanded definition of scholarship, the standards for assessing scholarship, and the elusiveness of the scholarship of teaching. *Academic Medicine, 75*(9), 877–880.

GMC. (1999). *The doctor as teacher*. London: General Medical Council.

GMC. (2003). *Tomorrow's doctors: recommendations on undergraduate medical education.* London: General Medical Council.

GMC. (2004). *Continuing professional development*. London: General Medical Council.

GMC. (2006a). *Good medical practice*. London: General Medical Council.

GMC. (2006b). *Strategic proposals for student fitness to practice: call for informal feedback*. London: General Medical Councilo. Document Number)

GMC. (2007). *The new doctor*. London: General Medical Council.

Greenhalgh, T. (2006). *How to read a paper: the basics of evidence-based medicine*. Oxford: Blackwell Publishing Ltd.

Greenhalgh, T., & Hurwitz, B. (1998). *Narrative based medicine*. London: BMJ Books.

Hopcroft, K., & Forte, V. (2003). *Symptom sorter* (2nd ed.). Abingdon: Radcliffe Medical Press Ltd.

Hudson, J., & Lowe, S. (2004). *Understanding the Policy Process: analysing welfare policy and practice*. Bristol: The Policy Press.

Hughes, I. E. (2001). Do computer simulations of laboratory practicals meet learning needs? *Trends in Pharmacological Sciences*, *22*, 71–74. doi:10.1016/S0165-6147(00)01605-9

Jacob, M. (2003). Rethinking Scicncc and Commodifying Knowledge. *Policy Futures in Education*, *1*(1), 125–142. doi:10.2304/pfie.2003.1.1.3

Kulatanga-Moruzi, C., Brooks, L. R., & Norman, G. R. (2001). Co-ordination of analytical and similarity-based processing strategies and expertise in dermatological diagnosis. *Learning and Teaching Medicine*, *13*, 110–116. doi:10.1207/S15328015TLM1302_6

Laurillard, D. (1993). *Rethinking University Teaching - A framework for the effective use of educational technology*. UK: Routledge

Laurillard, D. (2007). In H. Beetham & R. Sharpe (Eds.), *Rethinking Pedagogy for a Digital Age*. Oxford: Routledge.

Leathard, H. L., & Dewhurst, D. (1995). Comparison of the cost-effectiveness of a computer assisted learning program with a tutored demonstration to teach intestinal motility to medical students. *Assoc for Learning Technology Journal*, *3*(1), 118–125.

Littlejohn, A. (2003). Issues in reusing online resources. In A. Littlejohn (Ed.), *Reusing Online Resources: a sustainable approach to eLearning* (pp. 1-6). London: Kogan Page.

McGee, J. B., & Begg, M. (2008). What medical educators need to know about "Web 2.0". *Medical Teacher*, *30*(2), 164–169. doi:10.1080/01421590701881673

Miller, G. E. (1990). The Assessment of CLinical Skills / Competence / Performance. *Academic Medicine*, *65*(9), 63–67. doi:10.1097/00001888-199009000-00045

NES. (2007). *NES survey of Scottish consultant workforce*. Edinburgh: NHS Education for Scotlando. Document Number)

NMC. (2007). *Standards to support learning and assessment in practice: NMC standards for mentors, practice teachers and teachers*. Available online: http://www.nmc-uk.org/: Nursing and Midwifery Council.

Norman, G., Young, M., & Brooks, L. (2007). Non-analytical models of clinical reasoning: the role of experience. *Medical Education*, *41*, 1140–1145.

Ozga, J. (2007). Knowledge and Policy: Research and Knowledge Transfer. *Critical Studies in Education*, *48*(1), 63–78. doi:10.1080/17508480601120988

PMETB. G. a. (2005). *Principles of good medical education and training*. London: General Medical Council and Postgraduate Medical Education and Training Board.

Prensky, M. (2000). *Digital Game Based Learning*: McGraw-Hill.

Rest, T. (1997). Using video for teaching chemistry: A phoenix? *TLTP Newsletter*.

Ross, M. T., Blaney, D., Cameron, H. S., Begg, M., & Cumming, A. D. (2008). *ClinEd: developing a web-based collaborative learning environment for clinical educators at the University of Edinburgh.* Paper presented at the All Together Better Health IV.

Sackett, D. L., Straus, S. E., Richardson, W. S., Rosenberg, W., & Haynes, R. B. (2000). *Evidence-based medicine: how to practice and teach EBM.* London: Churchill Livinstone.

Schmidt, H. G., & Rickers, R. M. J. P. (2007). How expertise develops in medicine: knowledge encapsulation and illness script formation. *Medical Education, 41*, 1133–1139.

Schön, D. A. (1983). *The reflective practitioner: how professionals think in action*. London: Temple Smith.

Schön, D. A. (1987). *Educating the reflective practitioner: toward a new design for teaching and learning in the professions*. San Fransisco: Jossey-Bass.

Tait, B. (1997). Constructive Internet Learning. *Active Learning,* (7), 3-8.

The Medical Act (1858). UK Government.

Wenger, E. (1998). *Communities of Practice: Learning, Meaning and Identity*. New York: Cambridge University Press.

WFME. (2003). *Basic medical education: WFME global standards for quality improvement*. Copenhagen: World Federation for Medical Education.

This work was previously published in Online Learning Communities and Teacher Professional Development: Methods for Improved Education Delivery, edited by J. O. Lindberg, A. D. Olofsson, pp. 190-208, copyright 2010 by Information Science Reference (an imprint of IGI Global).

Compilation of References

Academy of Medical Educators. (2007). 14th December 2007, from http://www.medicaleducators.org/

ACS. (2009). *ACS Complete Short Course Listings*. Retrieved from http://portal.acs.org/portal/acs/corg/content?_nfpb=true&_pageLabel=PP_ARTICLEMAIN&node_id=273&content_id=CTP_006408&use_sec=true&sec_url_var=region1&__uuid=f3138678-d8ec-4b90-83a7-781b4b80b9bf

Agostinho, S., Bennett, S., Lockyer, L., & Harper, B. (2004). Developing a learning object metadata application profile based on LOM suitable for the Australian higher education context. *Australasian Journal of Educational Technology, 20*(2), 191-208.

Akridge, J., DeMay, L., Braunlich, L., Collura, M., & Sheahan, M. (2002). Retaining adult learners in a high-stress distance education learning environment: The purdue university executive MBA in agribusiness. Motivating & Educating Adult Learners Online. Essex Junction, VT. Retrieved from GetEducated.com

Albino, P. R. (1999). *Self-Efficacy Beliefs as an Indicator of Teachers' Preparedness for Teaching with Technology*. Association for the Advancement of Computing in Education (AACE). Retrieved October 14, 2005 from http://www.usq.edu.au/users/albion/papers/site99/1345.html

Alexander, C. (2008). An overview of LAMS (Learning Activity Management System), Teaching English with Technology Journal, 8(3).

Alexander, C., (2009), LAMS Revisited. *Teaching English with Technology Journal, 9*(1).

Al-Fahad, M. (2008). *Bridging the Global Digital Divide*. Saarbrucken, Germany: VDM Verlag.

Alge, B. J. (2001). Effects of computer surveillance on perceptions of privacy and procedural justice. *The Journal of Applied Psychology, 86*(4), 797–804. doi:10.1037/0021-9010.86.4.797

Allen, M. W. (2003). *Michael Allen's guide to e-learning: Building Interactive, Fun, and Effective Learning Programs for Any Company*. Hoboken, NJ: John Wiley & Sons, Inc.

Altshuller, G. (2000). *The innovation algorithm. TRIZ, systematic innovation and technical creativity*. Worcester, MA: Technical Innovation Center.

Andenoro, A. C. (2005). *Competencies of leadership professionals: A national study of premier leadership degree programs*. Ph.D. dissertation, Texas A&M University, United States—Texas. Retrieved April 25, 2009, from Dissertations & Theses: Full Text database. (Publication No. AAT 3246442).

Anzelotti, G., Nicoletto, G., & Riva, E. (2008). *Heterogeneous microscopic strains in a cast Al-Si alloy by digital image correlation*. Paper presented at the Symposium on Advances in Experimental Mechanics, České, Budějovice.

Association of American Medical Colleges. (1998). *Learning objectives for medical student education*. Retrieved 15th April 2007, from www.aamc.org/meded/msop

Association of American Universities (AAU). (2003). *The letter of invitation to the founding conference of*

AAU. Retrieved on May, 10 2009 from: http://www.aau.edu/aau/Invit.html

Atkins, D. E., Brown, J. S., & Hammond, A. L. (2007). *Review of the open educational resources (OER) movement: Achievements, challenges and new opportunities.* Menlo Park, CA: William and Flora Hewitt Foundation.

Austin, A. E. (2002). Preparing the next generation of faculty. *The Journal of Higher Education, 73*(1), 94–122. doi:10.1353/jhe.2002.0001

Austin, A. E., & McDaniels, M. (2006). Using doctoral education to prepare faculty to work within Boyer's four domains of scholarship. *New Directions for Institutional Research,* (129): 51–65. doi:10.1002/ir.171

Austin, A. E., Connolly, M. R., & Colbeck, C. L. (2008). Strategies for preparing integrated faculty: The center for the integration of research, teaching, and learning. *New Directions for Teaching and Learning,* (113): 69–81. doi:10.1002/tl.309

Baker, A., Navarro, E. O., & van der Hoek, A. (2005). An experimental card game for teaching software engineering processes. *Journal of Systems and Software, 75,* 3–16. doi:10.1016/j.jss.2004.02.033

Barros, B., Read, T., & Verdejo, M. F. (2008). Virtual collaborative experimentation: An approach combining remote and local labs. *IEEE Transactions on Education, 51*(2), 242–250. doi:10.1109/TE.2007.908071

Bates, A. W. (2000). *Managing technological change.* San Francisco: Jossey-Bass.

Baumard, P. (1999). *Tacit knowledge in organizations.* London, UK: Sage.

Beatty, K. (2003). *Teaching and Researching Computer-Assisted Language Learning. Harlow.* London: Longman.

Becta, (2003a). *What the research says about barriers to the use of ICT in teaching.* Retrieved October 14, 2005 from http://becta.org.uk/page_documents/research/wtrs_barriersinteach.pdf

Becta, (2003c). What the research says about ICT and Motivation. Retrieved October 14, 2005 from http://becta.org.uk/page_documents/research/wtrs_motivation.pdf

Begg, M. (2008). Leveraging Game Informed Learning in Higher Education. *Medical Teacher, 30*(2), 155–158. doi:10.1080/01421590701874041

Begg, M., Dewhurst, D., & Macleod, H. (2005). Game Informed Learning: Applying computer game processes to Higher Education. *Innovate, 1*(6).

Begg, M., Ellaway, R., Dewhurst, D., & Macleod, H. (2006). Virtual Patients: considerations of narrative and gameplay. In M. Burmester, D. Gerhard, & F. Thissen (Eds.), *Digital Game Based Learning: 4th International Symposium for Information Design* (pp. 101 - 113). Stuttgart Media University: Universitatsverlag Karlsruhe.

Begg, M., Ellaway, R., Dewhurst, D., & Macleod, H. (2007a). *Logos and Mythos: the political dilemmas of Web 2.0 in an accreditation-driven educational environment.* Paper presented at the Ice 2007 - Ideas in Cyberspace Education, Loch Lomond, UK.

Begg, M., Ellaway, R., Dewhurst, D., & Macleod, H. (2007b). Transforming Professional Healthcare Narratives Into Structured Game Informed Learning Activities. *Innovate, 3*(6).

Bell, R., Jung, J., & Zacharilla, L. (2009). *Broadband Economies: Creating the Community of the 21st Century.* New York: Intelligent Community Forum.

Benbunan-Fich, R. (2002). Improving education and training with IT. *Communications of the ACM, 45*(6), 94–99. doi:10.1145/508448.508454

Bergstrom. (2001). *CMI Guidelines for Interoperability AICC.* Retrieved from http://www.aicc.org/docs/tech/cmi001v3-5.pdf

Bernthal, J. E. (2001). Strategies to recruit and retain doctoral-level teacher-scholars. *ASHA Leader, 6*(12), 35. Boyer [*Scholarship reconsidered: Priorities of the professoriate.* Princeton, NJ: Carnegie Foundation for the Advancement of Teaching.]. *E (Norwalk, Conn.), L,* 1990.

Bersin, (2003). *Blended learning: What works?: An industry study of the strategy, implementation, and impact of blended learning.* New York: Bersin & Associates.

Bhatt, R., Tang, C. P., Lee, L. F., & Knovi, V. (2009). A case for scaffolded virtual prototyping tutorial case-studies in engineering education. *International Journal of Engineering Education, 25*(1), 84–92.

Bier, I. D., & Cornesky, R. (2001, April). Using QFD to construct a higher education curriculum. *Quality Progress*, 64-68.

Bird, E. R., Cain, J., & Jones, M. (2008). Mobile Computing Initiatives Within Pharmacy Education. *American Journal of Pharmaceutical Education, 72*, 1–7.

Birzea, C. (2000). *Education for democratic citizenship: a lifelong learning perspective*. Strasbourg, Germany: Council for Cultural Cooperation.

BizEd. (2003). *Doctoral crisis looms, says commission, 3*(1), 8.

Bloom, B. S. (1956). *Taxonomy of educational objectives, Handbook I: The cognitive domain*. New York: David McKay Co Inc.

Bloom, B. S., Engelhard, M. D., Furst, E. J., Hill, W. H., & Krathwohl, D. R. (1956). *Taxonomy of educational objectives, handbook 1: cognitive domain*. New York: Longmans.

Bonwell, C., & Eison, J. (1991). *Active Learning: Creating Excitement in the Classroom AEHE-ERIC Higher Education Report No. 1*. San Francisco: Jossey-Bass

Bower, M. (2007). Independent, synchronous and asynchronous—An analysis of approaches to online concept formation. Presented at ITiCSE '07. Dundee, Scotland

Boyd, G. (2004). Conversation theory. In Jonassen, D. (Ed.), *Handbook of educational communications and technology* (pp. 125–145). Mahwah, NJ: Laurence Erlbaum and Associates.

Boyer, E. L. (1990). *Scholarship reconsidered: Priorities of the professoriate*. Princeton, NJ: Carnegie Foundation for the Advancement of Teaching.

Boyle, J. T., & Nicol, D. J. (2003). Using classroom communication systems to support interaction anddiscussion in large class settings. *Association for Learning Technology Journal, 11*(3), 43–57.

Brad, S. (2005). Need for radical innovation to ensure high quality of continuous education in engineering. In C. Oprean, & C. Kifor (Ed.), *3rd Balkan Region Conference on Engineering Education* (pp. 77-80). Sibiu: Lucian Blaga University Press.

Brad, S. (2008). Complex system design technique. *International Journal of Production Research, 46*(21), 5979–6008. doi:10.1080/00207540701361475

Brad, S. (2009). Concurrent multifunction deployment. *International Journal of Production Research, 47*(19), 5343–5376. doi:10.1080/00207540701564599

Bradley, C., & Boyle, T. (2004). The design, development, and use of multimedia learning objects *Journal of Educational Multimedia and Hypermedia, 13*(4), 371-389.

Breckenridge, A. (2008). *The sharpening stone: Crisis as impetus for individual and organizational transformation,* Fielding Graduate University: Unpublished paper.

Brown, J. S., & Duguid, P. (2000). *The social life of information*. Boston: Harvard Business School Press.

Bruff, D. (2009). *Teaching with Classroom Response Systems: Creating Active Learning Environments*. San Francisco: Jossey-Bass.

Bruns, A., & Humphreys, S. (2007). Building collaborative capacities in learners: The M/cyclopedia project revisited. Presented at WikiSym '07. Montréal, Québec.

Bryant, M. T. (2003). *The portable dissertation advisor*. Thousand Oaks, CA: Corwin Press.

Bryant, S. L., Forte, A., & Bruckman, A. (2005). *Becoming Wikipedian: Transformation of participation in a collaborative online encyclopedia. Presented at GROUP '05*. FL: Sanibel Island.

Bugeja, M. (2007). *Distractions in a wireless classroom*. The chronicle of higher education. Retrieved November 15th from http://fp.arizona.edu/geog695c/PDFs/wireless.classroom.pdf.

Burnely, S. (2007). The use of virtual reality technology in teaching environmental engineering. *Engineering Education. Journal of the Higher Education Academy Engineering Subject Center, 2*(2).

Burrow, A. L. (2004). Negotiating access within Wiki: A system to construct and maintain a taxonomy of access rules. Presented at HT '04. Santa Cruz, CA.

Buzzetto-More, N. A. (2008). Student Perceptions of Various E-Learning Components. *Interdisciplinary Journal of E-Learning and Learning Objects, 4*, 113–135.

Byrne, P., & Long, B. E. L. (1976). *Doctors talking to Patients*. London: HMSO.

Byron, I., & Gagliardi, R. (2001). *State and Potential of Information and Communication Technologies in education.* Retrieved October 12, 2005 from http://www.idrc.ca/acacia/studies/ir-unes1.htm.

Callaghan, M. J., Harkin, J., McGinnity, T. M., & Maguire, L. P. (2008). Intelligent user support in autonomous remote experimentation environments. *IEEE Transactions on Industrial Electronics, 55*(6), 2355–2367. doi:10.1109/TIE.2008.922411

Calman, K. C. (2007). *Medical education: past, present and future*. Edinburgh: Elsevier.

Cameron, L., & Dalziel, J. (2008). Perspectives on Learning Design. In *Proceedings of the 3rd International LAMS & Learning Design Conference* (p.p. 81-86), Sydney: LAMS Foundation.

Campanella, S., Dimauro, G., Ferrante, A., Impedovo, D., Impedovo, S., & Lucchese, M. G. (2007). Engineering e-learning surveys: a new approach. *International Journal of Education and Information Technologies, 1*(2), 105–113.

Campbell, L.M. (2003). Engaging with the learning object economy. In A. Littlejohn (Ed.), *Reusing online resources: A sustainable approach to e-learning* (pp. 35-45). London: Kogan Page.

Campbell, L.M., Littlejohn, A.H., & Duncan, C. (2001). Share and share alike: Encouraging the reuse of academic resources through the Scottish electronic staff development library. *Association of Learning Technologies Journal (ALT-J), 9*(2), 28-38.

Capper, J. (2003).Complexities and Challenges of Integrating Technology Into the curriculum. *TechKnowLogia.* Retrieved October 12, 2005 from http://www.techknowlogia.org/TKL_active_pages2/CurrentArticles/main.asp?IssueNumber=19&FileType=PDF&ArticleID=471

Cardini, A. (2006). An analysis of the rhetoric and practice of educational partnerships in the UK: An arena of complexities, tensions and power. *Journal of Education Policy, 21*(4), 393–415. doi:10.1080/02680930600731773

Carini, R. M., Kuh, G. D., & Klein, S. P. (2006). Student engagement and student learning: Testing the linkages. *Research in Higher Education, 47*(1), 1–32. doi:10.1007/s11162-005-8150-9

Challborn, C., & Reimann, T. (2005, July). Wiki products: A comparison. *International Review of Research in Open and Distance Learning, 6*(2). Retrieved April 19, 2009, from http://www.irrodl.org/index.php/irrodl/article/view/229/859

Charlton, B. G., & Walston, F. (1998). Individual case studies in clinical research. *Journal of Evaluation in Clinical Practice, 4*(2), 147–155. doi:10.1046/j.1365-2753.1998.00011.x

Chatterjee, A. (2005). Mathematics in engineering. *Current Science, 88*(3), 405–414.

Chau, P. Y. K. (2001). Influence of Computer Attitude and Self-Efficacy on IT Usage Behavior. *Journal of End User Computing, 13*(1), 26-33.

Chickering, A. W., & Ehrmann, S. C. (1996). Implementing the Seven Principles: Technology as Lever. *American Association of Higher Education Bulletin, October*, 3-6.

Chickering, A. W., & Gamson, Z. F. (1987). Seven principles for good practice in undergraduate education. *American Association of Higher Education Bulletin, March,* 3-7

Chinn, M. D., & Fairlie, R. W. (2006). The Determinants of the Global Digital Divide: A Cross-Country Analysis of Computer and Internet Penetration. *Oxford Economic Papers, 59*(1), 16–44. doi:10.1093/oep/gpl024

Chittaro, L., & Ranon, R. (2007). Web3D technologies in learning, education and training: Motivations, issues, opportunities. *Computers & Education, 49*, 3–18. doi:10.1016/j.compedu.2005.06.002

Chorpothong, N., & Charmonman, S. (2004). An eLearning project for 100,000 students per year in Thailand. *International Journal of The Computer, the Internet and Management, 12,* 111-118.

Choy, S. O., & Ng, K. C. (2007). Implementing wiki software for supplementing online learning. *Australasian Journal of Educational Technology, 23*(2), 209-226. Retrieved April 19, 2009, from http://www.ascilite.org.au/ajet/ajet23/choy.html

Cloete, E. (2001). Electronic education system model. *Computers & Education, 36*, 171–182. doi:10.1016/S0360-1315(00)00058-0

Close the Gap International. (2009). *Close the Gap: Bridging the Digital Divide*. Retrieved February 3, 2009, from http://www.close-the-gap.org/pages/frontend/Home.aspx?menuitem=17

Coates, H. C. (2005). The value of student engagement for higher education quality assurance. *Quality in Higher Education, 11*(1), 25–36. doi:10.1080/13538320500074915

Coimbra, Portugal.Hung, T. C., Wang, S. K., Tai, S. W., & Hung, C. T. (2007). An innovative improvement of engineering learning system using computational fluid dynamics concept. *Computers & Education, 48*, 44-58.

Cole, D. (2008, October 23). Why I ban Laptops in my Classroom. *Encyclopedia Britannica Blog.* Retrieved November 20, 2008, from http://www.britannica.com/blogs/2008/10/why-i-ban-laptops-in-my-classroom/

Coleman, I., Dewhurst, D., Meehan, A. S., & Williams, A. D. (1994). A computer simulation for learning about the physiological response to exercise. *The American Journal of Physiology, 11*, s2–s9.

Colford, S. (2009, December/January). Explaining Free and Open Source Software. *Bulletin of the American Society for Information Science and Technology, 35*(2), 10–15. doi:10.1002/bult.2008.1720350205

Compeau, D. R., & Higgins, C. A. (1995). Computer Self-Efficacy: Development of a measure and initial test. *MIS Quarterly, 19*(2), 189-211.

Conn, R. (2002). Developing software engineers at the C-130J software factory. *IEEE Software, 19*(5), 25–29. doi:10.1109/MS.2002.1032849

Connaway, L. S. (2001). A web-based electronic book (e-book) library: The netLibrary model. *Library Hi Tech, 19*(4), 340–349. doi:10.1108/07378830110411961

Connolly, T., & Stansfield, M. (2007). *Principles of effective online teaching.* Santa Rosa, CA: Informing Science Press.

Cook, J. (2001). *JTAP 623 - The Role of Virtual Learning Environments in UK Medical Education* (No. JTAP 623). UK: Institute for Learning and Research Technologyo. Document Number)

Coomey, M., & Stephenson, J. (2001). Online learning: It is all about dialogue, involvement, support and control – according to the research. In Stephenson, J. (Ed.), *Teaching and learning online: Pedagogies for new technologies* (pp. 37–52). London: Kogan Page.

Costa, C. J., Nhampossa, J. L., & Aparicio, M. (2008) Wiki content evaluation framework. Presented at SIGDOC '08. Lisbon, Portugal.

Council of Graduate Schools (CGS). (1990). The doctor of philosophy degree: A policy statement. Washington, DC.

Cox, M., et al. (1999). *What factors support or prevent teachers from using ICT in their Classrooms.* Paper presented at the British Educational Research Association Annual Conference, University of Sussex, Brighton. Retrieved September 15, 2005 from http://www.leeds.ac.uk/educol/documents/00001304.htm

Cox, M., Preston, C., & Cox, K. (1999). *What Motivates Teachers to Use ICT?* Paper presented at the British Educational Research Association Annual Conference, University of Sussex at Brighton, September 2-5, 1999. Retrieved October 15, 2005 from http://www.leeds.ac.uk/educol/documents/00001329.htm

Cradler, J., & Bridgforth, E. (2002). *Recent Research on the Effects of Technology on Teaching and Learning.* Retrieved October 10, 2005, from http://www.wested.org/techpolicy/research.html

Crawford, C. B., Brungardt, C. L., Scott, R. F., & Gould, L. V. (2002). Graduate programs in organizational leadership: A review of programs, costs and delivery methods. *The Journal of Leadership Studies*, *8*(4), 64–74. doi:10.1177/107179190200800406

Creative Commons. (2009). Creative Commons. Retrieved February 3, 2009, from http://creativecommons.org

Cumming, A. D., & Ross, M. T. (2008). *The Tuning Project (medicine) – learning outcomes / competences for undergraduate medical education in Europe*. Edinburgh: The University of Edinburgh. Available online: www.tuning-medicine.com. Document Number)

Curran, V. R., Hoekman, T., Gulliver, W., Landells, I., & Hatcher, L. (2000). Web-based continuing medical education (I): Field test of a hybrid computer-mediated instructional delivery system. *The Journal of Continuing Education in the Health Professions*, *20*(2), 97–105. doi:10.1002/chp.1340200206

D'Abate, C. P. (2005). Working hard or hardly working: A case study of individuals engaging in personal business on the job. *Human Relations*, *58*, 1009–1032. doi:10.1177/0018726705058501

d'Antoni, S. (2009). Open educational resources: Reviewing initiatives and issues. *Open Learning: The Journal of Open and Distance Learning*, *24*(1), 3–10. doi:10.1080/02680510802625443

Dalziel, J. (2003). Implementing Learning Design: The Learning Activity Management System (LAMS). In *Proceedings of the 20th Annual Conference of the Australian Society for Computers in Learning in Tertiary Education* (ASCILITE).

Dalziel, J. (2006). Building communities of designers. In H. Beetham & R. Sharpe (Eds.), *Design for learning: Rethinking pedagogy for a digital age*. RoutledgeFalmer: London.

Danaher, P. A., Gale, T. C., & Erben, T. (2000, April). The teacher educator as (re)negotiated professional: Critical incidents in steering between state and market in Australia. *Journal of Education for Teaching*, *26*(1), 55–71. doi:10.1080/02607470050007138

Davis, N. E., & Tearle, P. (1999). *A core curriculum for telematics in teacher training*. Teleteaching 98 Conference, Vienna. Retrieved December 7, 2005 from http://www.ex.ac.uk/telematics/T3/corecurr/tteach98.htm

Dawley, L. (nd). Emerging territories in second life for socially networked teaching & learning.

DCMI. (2009). *Dublin Core Metadata Element Set, Version 1.1*. Retrieved from http://dublincore.org/documents/dces/

Dewhurst, D., & Chimalizeni, Y. (2008). *Collaborative development of online virtual patients for medical and healthcare professional education in Malawi*. Paper presented at the eLearning Africa.

Dewhurst, D., Hardastle, J., Hardcastle, P. T., & Stuart, E. (1994). Comparison of a computer simulation program with a traditional laboratory practical class for teaching the principles of intestinal absorption. *The American Journal of Physiology*, *12*(1), s95–s103.

Dewhurst, D., Macleod, H., & Norris, T. (2000). Independent Student Learning Aided by Computers: An Acceptable Alternative to Lectures? *Computers & Education*, *35*, 223–241. doi:10.1016/S0360-1315(00)00033-6

Di Iorio, A., & Vitali, F. (2005). From the writable Web to global editability. Presented at HT '05. Salzburg, Austria. ACM. 36.

Digital Divide Network. (2009). *Digital Divide Network*. Retrieved.

Digitalthink. (2003). *SCORM™:The E-Learning Standard*. Retrieved from http://www.adlnet.org/index.cfm?fuseaction=scormabt

Dillon, J. T. (1990). *The practice of questioning*. London: Routledge.

Dilmaghani, M. (2003). *National providence and virtual education development capabilities in higher education*. Paper presented at the Virtual University Conference. Kashan, Iran.

DOH. (2007). *Trust, assurance and safety - the regulation of health professionals for the 21st Century*. London: Department of Health, HMSOo. Document Number)

Donath, J. A. (1999). Identity and deception in the virtual community. In Smith, M. A., & Kollock, P. (Eds.), *Communities in cyberspace* (pp. 29–59). London: Routledge.

Dovey, J. (2009). *New Media: A Critical Introduction* (2nd ed.). New YorkRoutledge.

Draper, S. W., & Brown, M. I. (2004). Increasing interactivity in lectures using an electronic voting system. *Journal of Computer Assisted Learning, 20*, 81–94. doi:10.1111/j.1365-2729.2004.00074.x

Draper, S. W., Cargill, J., & Cutts, Q. (2002). Electronically enhanced classroom interaction. *Australian Journal of Educational Technology, 18*, 13–23.

Driscoll, M. (2002). *Blended learning: Let's get beyond the hype, IMB Global Services*. Retrieved August 22, 2009, from http://www-8.ibm.com/services/pdf/blended_learning.pdf

Du, J., Li, F., & Li, B. (2008). The case of interactive web-based course development. In E. Leung, F. Wang, L. Miao, J. Zao, & J. He (Ed.), *2nd Workshop on Blended Learning* (pp. 65-73). Berlin, Germany: Springer

Duncan, C., & Ekmekcioglu, C. (2003). In A. Littlejohn (Ed.), *Reusing online resources: A sustainable approach to e-learning* (pp. 135-145). London: Kogan Page.

Duncan, D. (2006). Clickers: A new teaching aid with exceptional promise. *Astronomy Education Review, 5*, 70–88. doi:10.3847/AER2006005

Dzidonu, C. (2006). *The ICT-in-Education Implementation Strategy and Action Plan*. Ethiopian ICT Development Agency (EICTDA). Unpublished. Draft [Version 4.02].

Ebner, M., & Walder, U. (2008). E-education in civil engineering – a promise for the future? In P. Vainiunas & L. Juknevicius (Ed.), *6th AECEF Symposium on Civil Engineering Education in Changing Europe* (pp. 16-26). Vilnius, Lithuania: Vilnius Gediminas Technical Univ. Press.

Ellaway, R. H. (2005). *Evaluating a Virtual Learning Environment in Medical Education*. Unpublished PhD, University of Edinburgh, Edinburgh.

Ellaway, R., Begg, M., Dewhurst, D., & Macleod, H. (2005). In A Glass Darkly: identity, agency and the role of the learning technologist in shaping the learning environment. *E-Learning, 3*(1), 75-87.

Ellaway, R., Dewhurst, D., & Cumming, A. (2003). Managing and supporting medical education with a virtual learning environment: the Edinburgh Electronic Medical Curriculum. *Medical Teacher, 25*(4), 372–380. doi:10.1080/0142159031000136789

Ellozy, A. (2007). New initiative: "Clickers" in our classrooms. *New Chalk Talk, 6*(8). Retrieved June 11, 2009, from http://www.aucegypt.edu/academics/llt/clt/ChalkTalk/Documents/V6Issue8.pdf

Elstein, A. S., Shulman, L. S., & Sprafka, S. A. (1978). *Medical problem solving: an analysis of clinical reasoning*. Cambridge, MA: Harvard University Press.

Ericsson, K. A. (2004). Deliberate practice and the acquisition and maintenance of expert performance in medicine and related domains. *Academic Medicine, 79*(10Supplement), S70–S81. doi:10.1097/00001888-200410001-00022

Ericsson, K. A., Krampe, R. T., & Tesch-Romer, C. (1993). The role of deliberate practice in the acquisition of expert performance. *Psychological Review, 100*(3), 363–406. doi:10.1037/0033-295X.100.3.363

EU. (1981). Council Directive 81/1057/EEC of 14 December 1981 concerning the mutual recognition of diplomas, certificates and other evidence of the formal qualifications of doctors, nurses responsible for general care, dental practitioners and veterinary surgeons respectively, with regard to acquired rights.

Even, R., & Tirosh, D. (2002). Teacher knowledge and understanding of students' mathematical learning. In English, L. D. (Ed.), *Handbook of international research in mathematics education* (pp. 219–240). Mahwah, NJ: Lawrence Erlbaum.

Fabian, C. A. (2006). A five-year analysis of university initiatives to increase faculty engagement. *Journal of Computing in Higher Education, 17*(2), 3–24. doi:10.1007/BF03032696

Fan, Z., & Jiaheng, C. (2008). Learning Activity Sequencing in Personalized Education System. *Journal of Natural Science*, *13*(4), 461–465.

Farance, F. (2003). IEEE LOM standard not yet ready for "prime time." *Learning Technology*, *5*(1).

Farkas, M. (2008). CMS the wiki way: Maintaining library web content with a wiki. In Practice: Technology. *American Libraries*, *39*(11), 35.

Ferris, S. P., & Wilder, H. (2006, June/July). Uses and potentials of wikis in the classroom. *Journal of Online Education*, *2*(5). Retrieved April 19, 2009, from http://www.innovateonline.info/index.php?view=article&id=258

Fies, C., & Marshall, J. (2006). Classroom response systems: A review of the literature. *Journal of Science Education and Technology*, *15*(1), 101–109. doi:10.1007/s10956-006-0360-1

Fincher, R.-M. E., Simpson, D. E., Mennin, S. P., Rosenfeld, G. C., Rothman, A., & McGrew, M. C. (2000). Scholarship in teaching: an imperative for the 21st Century. *Academic Medicine*, *75*(9), 887–894. doi:10.1097/00001888-200009000-00009

Finger, S., Gelman, D., Fay, A., & Szczerban, M. (2005). Supporting collaborative learning in engineering design. In W. Shen, A. James, K. Chao, M. Younas, & J. Barthes (Ed.), *9th International Conference on Computer Supported Cooperative Work in Design* (pp. 990-995). Coventry, UK: Coventry Univ. Press.

Flowers, M., & Ching, H. W. (2008). *Lecture on Carnot Cycle*. Retrieved from http://galileoandeinstein.physics.virginia.edu/more_stuff/flashlets/carnot.htm

Foley, B., & Chang, T. (2006). *Wiki as a professional development tool.* Paper presented at the annual conference of the American Educational Research Association, San Francisco, CA. Retrieved April 19, 2009, from http://www.csun.edu/~bfoley/AERA_Wiki.pdf

Forte, A., & Bruckman, A. (2007). Constructing text: Wiki as a toolkit for (collaborative?) learning. Presented at WikiSym'07. Montréal, Québec.

Foshay, W., Silber, K., & Westgaard, O. (1986). *Instructional design competencies: The standards.* Iowa City, IA: The International Board of Standards for Training, Performance and Instruction.

Frank, J. R. (2005). *The CanMEDS 2005 physician competency framework. Better standards. Better physicians. Better care.* Ottowa: The Royal College of Physicians and Surgeons of Canadao. Document Number)

Fried, B. (2008). In-class laptop use and its eVects on student learning. *Computers & Education*, *50*, 906–914. doi:10.1016/j.compedu.2006.09.006

Friesen, N. (2004). *The E-learning Standardization Landscape*. Retrieved from http://www.cancore.ca/docs/intro_e-learning_standardization.html

Garcia-Montes., et al. (2006). Changes in the self as a resulting from the use of mobile phones. *Media Culture & Society*, *28*, 67–81. doi:10.1177/0163443706059287

Gardner, S. K. (2005). Faculty preparation for teaching, research, and service roles: What do new faculty need? *Journal of Faculty Development*, *20*(3), 161–166.

Garrison, D., Anderson, T., & Archer, W. (2003). A theory of Critical Inquiry in Online Distance Education. In Moore, M. G., & Anderson, W. G. (Eds.), *Handbook of Distance Education* (pp. 113–127). Mahwah, NJ: Lawrence Erlbaum Associates.

Geiger, R. L. (1986). *To advance knowledge: The growth of American research universities, 1900– 1940.* New York: Oxford University Press.

Gervasi, O., Rignelli, A., Pacifici, L., & Lagana, A. (2004). VMSLab-G: a virtual laboratory prototype for molecular science on the Grid. *Future Generation Computer Systems*, *20*, 717–726. doi:10.1016/j.future.2003.11.015

Giannoukos, I., Lykourentzou, I., Mpardis, G., Nikolopoulos, V., Loumos, V., & Kayafas, E. (2008). *Collaborative e-learning environments enhanced by wiki technologies. Presented at PETRA '08* (pp. 1–5). Athens, Greece: ACM.

Giddens, A. (1990). *The Consequences of Modernity.* Cambridge: Polity Press.

Gilis, A., Clement, M., Laga, L., & Pauwels, P. (2008). Establishing a competence profile for the role of student-centered teachers in higher education in Belgium. *Research in Higher Education*, *49*(6), 531–554. doi:10.1007/s11162-008-9086-7

Giordano, R. (2007). An investigation of the use of a wiki to support knowledge exchange in public health. Presented atGROUP '07. Sanibel Island, FL, ACM. 269.

Giveki, F. (2003). *Learning New Methods in Distance Higher Education*. Paper presented at the Virtual University Conference, Kashan, Iran.

Gladun, A., Rogushina, J., Garcıa-Sanchez, F., Martınez-Bejar, R., & Fernandez-Breis, J. T. (2009). An application of intelligent techniques and semantic web technologies in e-learning environments. *Expert Systems with Applications*, *36*(2), 1922–1931. doi:10.1016/j.eswa.2007.12.019

Gladwell, M. (2005). *Blink: the power of thinking without thinking*. New York: Little Brown & Co.

Glassic, C. E. (2000). Boyer's expanded definition of scholarship, the standards for assessing scholarship, and the elusiveness of the scholarship of teaching. *Academic Medicine*, *75*(9), 877–880.

GMC. (1999). *The doctor as teacher*. London: General Medical Council.

GMC. (2003). *Tomorrow's doctors: recommendations on undergraduate medical education*. London: General Medical Council.

GMC. (2004). *Continuing professional development*. London: General Medical Council.

GMC. (2006a). *Good medical practice*. London: General Medical Council.

GMC. (2006b). *Strategic proposals for student fitness to practice: call for informal feedback*. London: General Medical Councilo. Document Number)

GMC. (2007). *The new doctor*. London: General Medical Council.

Gokhale, A. A. (1995). Collaborative learning enhances critical thinking. *Journal of Technology Education*, *7*(1).

Goodacre, C., & Rowlands, D. (2005). Real world metadata management for resource discovery: Proof of concept across education and library sectors in Tasmania. In J. Dalziel, R. Philip, & J. Clare (Eds.), *The COLIS project: Collaborative online learning and information services* (pp. 163-185). Sydney, NSW: Macquarie University E-Learning Centre of Excellence.

Gosper, M., Woo, K., Gibbs, D., Hand, T., Kerr, S., & Rich, D. (2004). Learning objects: User perspectives on the conditions surrounding their use. In L. Cantoni & C. McLoughlin, (Eds), *Proceedings of World Conference on Educational Multimedia, Hypermedia and Telecommunications 2004* (pp. 66-72). Chesapeake, VA: AACE.

Gottschalk, T. H. (2009). *Distance education at a glance*. Retrieved from http://www.uiweb.uidaho.edu/eo/distglan

Gouthro, P. A. (2002). Education for sale: at what cost? Lifelong Learning and the marketplace. *International Journal of Lifelong Education*, *21*(4), 334–346. doi:10.1080/02601370210140995

Grace-Martin, M., & Gay, G. (2001). Web browsing, mobile computing, and academic performance. *Journal of Education Technology*, *4*, 95–107.

Graham, C. R. (2006). Blended learning systems: Definition, current trends, and future directions. In C. J. Bonk & C. R. Graham (Eds.), The handbook of blended learning: Global perspectives, local designs (pp. 3-21). SanFrancisco: Pfeiffer Publishing.

Granger, C., Morbey, M., Lotherington, H., Owston, R., & Wideman, H. (2002). Factors contributing to teachers' successful implementation of IT [Electronic version]. *Journal of Computer Assisted Learning*, *18*, 480-488.

Green, M. T., Alexander, J., & Boryczka, R. (2001). Developing an interdisciplinary doctoral program in leadership studies. In Outcalt, C. L., Faris, S. K., & Mc Mahon, K. N. (Eds.), *Developing non-hierarchical leadership on campus: Case studies and best practices in higher education* (pp. 225–237). Westport, CT: Greenwood Press.

Greenhalgh, T. (2006). *How to read a paper: the basics of evidence-based medicine*. Oxford: Blackwell Publishing Ltd.

Greenhalgh, T., & Hurwitz, B. (1998). *Narrative based medicine*. London: BMJ Books.

Grunbacher, P., Seyff, N., Briggs, R. O., In Kitapci, H., & Port, D. (Eds.). Making every student a winner: The WinWin approach in software engineering education. The Journal of System and Software, 80, 1191-1200.

Gunawardena, C. N., & Zittle, F. (1997). Social presence as a predictor of satisfaction within a computer mediated conferencing environment. *American Journal of Distance Education*, *11*(3), 8–25. doi:10.1080/08923649709526970

Gunn, C. (2000). *Identity, Control and Changing Reality*. Paper presented at the ASCILITE 2000. Retrieved May 1, 2009, from http://www.ascilite.org.au/conferences/coffs00/papers/cathy_gunn_keynote.pdf

Gurak, L. J. (2001). *Cyberliteracy: Navigating the Internet with awareness*. New Haven, CT: Yale University Press.

Haddad, W. D., & Jurich, S. (2002). ICT for Education: Potential and Potency: In W. D. Haddad & Draxler, S. (Eds.), *Technologies for Education: Potential, Parameters, and Prospects*. For UNESCO by Knowledge Enterprise.

Haghi, A. K., Mottaghitalab, V., & Akbari, M. (2008). *The Scholarship of Teaching Engineering: Some fundamental issues*. Hershey: IGI Global.

Hale, J. (1989). *Training manager competencies: The standards*. Batavia, IL: The International Board of Standards for Training, Performance & Instruction.

Hamza-Lup, F. G., & Stefan, V. (2007). *Web 3D & Virtual Reality - Based Applications for Simulation and e-Learning*. Paper presented at the 2nd International Conference on Virtual Learning, ICVL. Constanta, Romania.

Hargittai, E. (April 2002). Second Level Digital Divide: Differences in People's Online Skills. *First Monday*, *7*(4-1). Retrieved February 3, 2009, from http://firstmonday.org/issues/issue7_4/hargittai/index.html

Harper, K. C., Chen, K., & Yen, D. C. (2004). Distance learning,virtual classrooms,and teaching pedagogy in the Internet environment. *Technology in Society*, *26*, 585–598. doi:10.1016/S0160-791X(04)00054-5

Harri-Augstein, S., & Thomas, L. (1991). *Learning conversations*. London: Routledge.

Harris, C. (2007). Can we make peace with Wikipedia? *School Library Journal*. Retrieved from www.alj.com

Harris, T. R., Bransford, J. D., & Brophy, S. P. (2002). Roles for learning sciences and learning technologies in biomedical engineering education: a review of recent advances. *Annual Review of Biomedical Education*, *4*(1), 29–48. doi:10.1146/annurev.bioeng.4.091701.125502

Hartman, J. L. (2008). Moving teaching and learning with technology from adoption to transformation. *EDUCAUSE Review*, Nov.-Dec., 24-25.

Hasan, H., Meloche, J. A., Pfaff, C. C., & Willis, D. (2007). *Beyond ubiquity: Co-creating corporate knowledge with a wiki*. Presented at the International Conference on Mobile Ubiquitous Computing, Systems, Services and Technologies. UBICOMM 2007, IEEE. 35.

Hawkins, B. L., & Rudy, J. A. (2008). *EDUCAUSE Core Data Service - Fiscal Year 2007 Summary Report*. Retrieved Jun. 13, 2009, from http://net.educause.edu/ir/library/pdf/PUB8005.pdf

Hebert, M. (2006). Staying the course: A study in online student satisfaction and retention. *Online Journal of Distance Learning Administration*, *9*(4).

Hejazi, A. (2007). *New wine-old bottles*. Retrieved from http://ictarticles.blogspot.com/2007/05/new-wine-old-bottles.html

Helander, M. G., & Emami, M. R. (2008). Engineering e-laboratories: Integration of remote access and e-collaboration. *International Journal of Engineering Education*, *24*(3), 466–479.

Hembrooke, H., & Gay, G. (2003). The laptop and the lecture: The effects of multitasking in learning environments. *Journal of Computing in Higher Education*, *15*, 46–64. doi:10.1007/BF02940852

Hepp, M., Siorpaes, K., & Bachlechner, D. (2007). *Harvesting wiki consensus: Using Wikipedia entries for knowledge management*. Semantic Knowledge Management.

Hernon, P., Hopper, R., Leach, M. R., Saunders, L. L., & Zhang, J. (2007). E-book use by students: Undergraduates in economics, literature, and nursing. *Journal of Academic Librarianship*, *33*(1), 3–13. doi:10.1016/j.acalib.2006.08.005

Hirsch, B. E., Thoben, K. D., & Hoheisel, J. (1998). Requirements upon human competencies in globally distributed manufacturing. *Computers in Industry*, *36*, 49–54. doi:10.1016/S0166-3615(97)00097-3

Hoekstra, A. (2008). Vibrant student voices: Exploring effects of the use of clickers in large college courses. *Learning, Media and Technology*, *33*(4), 329–341. doi:10.1080/17439880802497081

Hopcroft, K., & Forte, V. (2003). *Symptom sorter* (2nd ed.). Abingdon: Radcliffe Medical Press Ltd.

Horton, W. (2001). *Designing Web-Based Training: How to Teach Anyone Anything Anywhere Anytime*. New York: John Wiley & Sons.

Howe, N., & Strauss, W. (2000). *Millennials Rising: The Next Great Generation*. New York: Vintage Books.

Howe, N., & Strauss, W. (2003). *Millennials Go to College: Strategies for a New Generation on Campus*. Washington, DC: American Association of Collegiate Registrars and Admissions Officers.

Huba, M. E., & Freed, J. (2000). *Learner-Centered Assessment on College Campuses: Shifting the Focus from Teaching to Learning*. Needham Heights, MA: Allyn & Bacon.

Hudson, J., & Lowe, S. (2004). *Understanding the Policy Process: analysing welfare policy and practice*. Bristol: The Policy Press.

Hughes, I. E. (2001). Do computer simulations of laboratory practicals meet learning needs? *Trends in Pharmacological Sciences*, *22*, 71–74. doi:10.1016/S0165-6147(00)01605-9

Hung, T., Liu, C., Hung, C., Ku, H., & Lin, Y. (2007, September 3 – 7). *The Establishment of an Interactive E-learning System for Engineering Fluid Flow and Heat Transfer*. Paper presented at the International Conference on Engineering Education – ICEE 2007

Hutchings, M., Hadfield, M., Horvath, G., & Lewarne, S. (2007). Meeting the challenges of active learning in web-based case studies for sustainable development. *Innovations in Education and Teaching International*, *44*(3), 331–343. doi:10.1080/14703290701486779

Hutten, H., Stiegmaier, W., & Rauchegger, G. (2005). KISS—A new approach to self-controlled e-learning of selected chapters in Medical Engineering and other fields at bachelor and master course level. *Medical Engineering & Physics*, *27*, 611–616. doi:10.1016/j.medengphy.2005.05.003

Hwang, F. (2004). *NTNUJAVA Virtual Physics Laboratory Java Simulations in Physics: Enjoy the fun!* Retrieved from http://www.phy.ntnu.edu.tw/ntnujava/index.php?PHPSESSID=61e16b595f51a79534ea86dd507e6fce&topic=23.msg156#msg156

Hyatt, L. Evans, L., & Haque, Md. (2009). Leading across cultures: Designing a learning agenda for global praxis. In M. A. Moodian (Ed.), Contemporary leadership and intercultural competence. Thousand Oaks, CA: Sage Publications.

Hyatt, L., & Goor, M. B. (2009, April). *Creating a faculty research culture: The times are a-changing*. American Educational Research Association (AERA) 2009 Annual Meeting: Disciplined Inquiry: Education Research in the Circle of Knowledge. San Diego, CA.

ICT Development Office of AAU, (2004). Five Year Strategic Plan (2004/05 to 2008/9). Addis Ababa University. Unpublished document.

IDRC, (1995). Information and Communication Technologies. Retrieved October 4, 2005 from http://web.idrc.ca/ev.php?id=11118_201&ID2=DO_TOPIC

IEEE Internet Computing. 55. Hester, A. (2008). Innovating with organizational wikis: Factors facilitating adoption and diffusion of an effective collaborative knowledge management system. Presented at SIGMIS-CPR '08. Charlottesville, Virginia. ACM. 161-163. Hester, A. J. & Scott, J. E. (2008). A conceptual model of wiki technology diffusion.

IEEE. (2005). *1484.12.1: IEEE Standard for Learning Object Metadata*. Retrieved from http://ltsc.ieee.org/wg12/

Illich, I. (1970). *Deschooling Society, ournature.org*. Retrieved February 1, 2009, from http://ournature.org/~novembre/illich/1970_deschooling.html

Imperial-College-London. (2009). *Information & Communication Technologies ICT; An E-Learning Glossary*. Retrieved from http://www3.imperial.ac.uk/ict/services/teachingandresearchservices/elearning/aboutelearning/elearningglossary

IMS Global Learning Consortium. (2003). *IMS learning design best practice and implementation guide version 1.0 final specification*. IMS Global Learning Consortium Inc. Retrieved October 11, 2006, from http://www.imsglobal.org

IMS. (2009). *Innovation Adoption Learning*. Retrieved from http://www.imsglobal.org/specifications.html

In *Proceedings of the 41st Hawaii International Conference on System Sciences*. 1-8. Hill, M. D., Gaudiot, J.-L., Hall, M., Marks, J., Prinetto, P., & Baglio, D. (2006). A wiki for discussing and promoting best practices in research. *Communications of the ACM, 49*(9), 63-64.

IO2_Technology. (nd). *IO2 Technology homepage*. Retrieved August 7, 2009, from http://www.io2technology.com/index.htm

Ion, D. (2007). *Physics and Engineering*. Retrieved from http://www.cs.sbcc.cc.ca.us/~physics/

Irby, B., & Lunenburg, F. (2007, October 12). Doctoral Program Issues: Accreditation of Programs. Retrieved from the Connexions Web site: http://cnx.org/content/m14599/1.3/

Jacob, M. (2003). Rethinking Science and Commodifying Knowledge. *Policy Futures in Education, 1*(1), 125–142. doi:10.2304/pfie.2003.1.1.3

James, J. (2003). *Bridging the Global Digital Divide*. Northampton, MA: Edward Elgar Publishing.

Jantz, R. (2001). E-books and new library service models: An analysis of the impact of E-book technology on academic libraries. *Information Technology and Libraries, 20*(2), 104–115.

Jara, C. A., Candelas, F. A., Torres, F., Dormido, S., Esquembre, F., & Reinoso, O. (2009). Real-time collaboration of virtual laboratories through the Internet. *Computers & Education, 52*(1), 126–140. doi:10.1016/j.compedu.2008.07.007

Jing, H., & Fan, Y. (2008). Usability of wiki for knowledge management of knowledge-based enterprises. Presented at 2008 International Symposium on Knowledge Acquisition and Modeling. IEEE, 204.

Johnson, D., & Wardlow, G. (2004). Computer Experiences, Self-Efficacy, and Knowledge of Undergraduate Students Entering a Land-Grant College of Agriculture by Year and Gender [Electronic version]. *Journal of Agricultural Education, 45*(3).

Johnson, M., & Robson, D. (2008). Clickers, student engagement and performance in an introductory economics course: A cautionary tale. *Computers in Higher Education Economics Review, 20*, 4–12.

Johnstone, S. M. (2005). Open educational resources serve the world. *EDUCAUSE Quarterly, 3*(28), 15–18.

Jona, K. (2000). Rethinking the design of online courses. Paper presented at the ASCILITE. Retrieved from http://www.ascilite.org.au/conferences/coffs00/

Jones, S. (2002). The internet goes to college: How students are living in the future with today's technology. *Pew Internet & American Life Project*. Retrieved online June 11, 2009, from http://www.eric.ed.gov/ERICDocs/data/ericdocs2sql/content_storage_01/0000019b/80/1a/bb/a7.pdf

Jou, M., Chuang, C. P., Wu, D. W., & Yang, S. C. (2008). Learning robotics in interactive web-based environments by PBL. In IEEE (Ed.), *IEEE Workshop on Advanced Robotics and Its Social Impacts* (pp. 206-211). Taipei, Taiwan: Nat. Taiwan Normal Univ. Press.

Juang, Y.-R. (2009). WIRE: A Blended Model for Teaching and Learning in Engineering Curricula. In Russell, D. L., & Haghi, A. K. (Eds.), *Web-based engineering education: Critical design and effective tools*. Hershey, PA: IGI Global.

Judson, E., & Sawada, D. (2002). Learning from the past and present: Electronic response systems in college lecture halls. *Journal of Computers in Mathematics and Science Teaching*, *21*, 167–181.

Kagami, M., Masatsugu, T., & Giovannetti, E. (Eds.). (2004). *Information Technology Policy and the Digital Divide: Lessons for Developing Countries*. Northampton, MA: Edward Elgar Publishing.

Kaleta, R., & Joosten, T. (2007). Student response systems: A University of Wisconsin system study of clickers. *EDUCAUSE Center for Applied Research: Research Bulletin*, *10*, 1–12.

Kamel Boulos, M. N., Maramba, I., & Wheeler, S. (2006). Wikis, blogs and podcasts: A new generation of Web-based tools for virtual collaborative clinical practice and education. *BMC Medical Education*, *6*(41). Retrieved April 19, 2009, from http://www.biomedcentral.com/1472-6920/6/41/

Kaminski, P. C., Ferreira, E. P. F., & Theuer, S. L. (2004). Evaluating and improving the quality of an engineering specialization program through the QFD methodology. *International Journal of Engineering Education*, *20*(6), 1034–1041.

Kaufman, D. B., Felder, R. M., & Fuller, H. (2000). Accounting for individual effort in cooperative learning teams. *Journal of Engineering Education*, *89*(2), 133–140.

Keller, G. (2001). The new demographics of higher education. *Review of Higher Education*, *24*, 219–235. doi:10.1353/rhe.2001.0004

Kilby, T. (2009). *What is Web-Based Training?* Retrieved from http://www.webbasedtraining.com/primer_whatiswbt.aspx

Kim, K.-J., & Bonk, C. J. (2006). The future of online teaching and learning in higher education: A survey substantiates some ideas about online learning and refutes others. *EDUCAUSE Quarterly*, *4*, 22–30.

Kim, K.-J., Bonk, C. J., & Oh, E. J. (2008). The present and future state of blended learning in workplace learning settings in the United States. *Performance Improvement*, *47*(8), 5–16. doi:10.1002/pfi.20018

Kincheloe, J. L. (2008). *Knowledge and critical pedagogy: an introduction*. London: Springer. doi:10.1007/978-1-4020-8224-5

Kinzie, M. B., Delcourt, M. A., & Powers, S. M. (1994). Computer Technologies: Attitudes and Self-Efficacy Across Undergraduate Disciplines [Electronic version]. *Research in Higher Education*, 35(6), 745-768.

Kittur, A., Suh, B., & Chi, E. H. (2008). Can you ever trust a wiki? Impacting perceived trustworthiness in Wikipedia. Presented at CSCW '08. San Diego, CA.ACM, 477.

Kittur, A., Suh, B., Pendleton, B. A., & Chi, E. H. (2007). He says, she says: Conflict and coordination in Wikipedia. In Proceedings of the Online Representation of Self. San Jose, CA. ACM, 453.

Klein, R., & Smith, M. (2008). *Pursuing the peak of excellence: Wiki as a knowledge base. Presented at SIGUCCS '08* (pp. 167–171). Portland, OR: ACM.

Knowles, J. (1962). A general theory of the doctorate in education. *Adult Education Quarterly*, *12*(3). doi:10.1177/074171366201200302

Koksal, G., & Egitman, A. (1998). Planning and design of industrial engineering education quality. *Computers & Industrial Engineering*, *35*(3-4), 639–642. doi:10.1016/S0360-8352(98)00178-8

Kolb, D. A. (1984). *Experiential Learning: Experience as the source of learning and development*. Upper Saddle River, NJ: Prentice-Hall.

Koppi, T., & Lavitt, N. (2003). Institutional use of learning objects three years on: Lessons learned and future directions. In D. Lassner & C. McNaught (Eds.), *Proceedings of World Conference on Educational Multimedia, Hypermedia and Telecommunications 2003* (pp. 644-648). Chesapeake, VA: AACE.

Koppi, T., Bogle L., & Lavitt, N. (2004). Institutional use of learning objects: Lessons learned and future directions.

Journal of Educational Multimedia and Hypermedia, 13(4), 449-463.

Kozma, R. & Wagner, D. (2005). Core Indicators for Monitoring and Evaluation Studies for ICT in Education. In D. Wagener et al. (Eds.) *Monitoring and Evaluation of ICT in Educational Projects: A Handbook for Developing Countries. infoDev* Pre-Publication draft, Washington DC, USA. Retrieved December 15, 2005 from http://www.infodev.org/files/2942_file_M_E_ICT_Education_draft_WSIS_optimized.pdf

Kriplean, T., Beschastnikh, I., & McDonald, D. W. (2008). Articulations in WikiWork: Uncovering valued work in Wikipedia through Barnstars. Presented at CSCW '08. San Diego, CA. ACM, 50.

Kuh, G. D. (2003). What we're learning about student engagement from NSSE. *Change, 35*(2), 24–32. doi:10.1080/00091380309604090

Kukreti, A., & Zaman, M. (2008). *Virtual laboratory modules for undergraduate STReNGTH of materials course.* Paper presented at the Engineering Education, Loughbrough, London.

Kulatanga-Moruzi, C., Brooks, L. R., & Norman, G. R. (2001). Co-ordination of analytical and similarity-based processing strategies and expertise in dermatological diagnosis. *Learning and Teaching Medicine, 13*, 110–116. doi:10.1207/S15328015TLM1302_6

Kumar, A., & Labib, A. W. (2004). Applying quality function deployment for the design of a next-generation manufacturing simulation game. *International Journal of Engineering Education, 20*(5), 787–800.

Kuznetsov, S. (2006). Motivations of contributors to Wikipedia. *ACM SIGCAS Computers and Society, 36*(2).

Lakhani, K. R., & von Hippel, E. (2003, June). How Open Source Software Works: "Free" User to User Assistance. *Research Policy, 32*(6), 923–943. doi:10.1016/S0048-7333(02)00095-1

Lambropoulos, N., & Christopoulou, M. (2004). Cultural-based learning objects in a blended environment for Greek and Greek-Cypriot students in U.K. In L. Cantoni & C. McLoughlin (Eds.), *Proceedings of World Conference on Educational Multimedia, Hypermedia and Telecommunications 2004* (pp. 1851-1856). Chesapeake, VA: AACE.

Latham, G. (1988). The birth and death cycles of educational innovations. *Principal, 68*(1), 41-43.

Lau, H., Mak, K., & Ma, H. (2006). IMELS: An e-learning platform for industrial engineering. *Computer Applications in Engineering Education, 14*(1), 53–63. doi:10.1002/cae.20067

Laurillard, D. (1993). *Rethinking University Teaching - A framework for the effective use of educational technology.* UK: Routledge

Laurillard, D. (2007). In H. Beetham & R. Sharpe (Eds.), *Rethinking Pedagogy for a Digital Age.* Oxford: Routledge.

Lave, J., & Wenger, E. (1991). *Situated learning: Legitimate peripheral participation.* New York: Cambridge University Press.

Le@rningFederation. (2008). *Metadata Elements Comparison: Vetadata and ANZ-LOM.* Australia: Flexible Learning Network.

Learning Technology Standards Committee. (2002). IEEE Standard for Learning Object Metadata. IEEE Standard 1484.12.1, Institute of Electrical and Electronics Engineers, New York. Retrieved March 28, 2008, from http://ltsc.ieee.org/wg12/files/LOM_1484_12_1_v1_Final_Draft.pdf

Leathard, H. L., & Dewhurst, D. (1995). Comparison of the cost-effectiveness of a computer assisted learning program with a tutored demonstration to teach intestinal motility to medical students. *Assoc for Learning Technology Journal, 3*(1), 118–125.

Lee, J., & Lee, W. (2008). The relationship of e-Learner's self-regulatory efficacy and perception of e-Learning environmental quality. *Computers in Human Behavior, 24*, 32–47. doi:10.1016/j.chb.2006.12.001

Lee, S. T., Kim, H., & Gupta, S. (2009). Measuring Open Source Software Success. *Omega, 32*(2), 426. doi:10.1016/j.omega.2007.05.005

Lefoe, G., O'Reilly, M., Parrish, D., Bennett, S., Keppell, M., & Gunn, C. (2007). The Carrick exchange: Not just another repository. In C. Montgomerie & J. Seale (Eds.), *Proceedings of World Conference on Educational Multimedia, Hypermedia and Telecommunications 2007* (pp. 108-113). Chesapeake, VA: AACE.

Lerner, J., & Tirole, J. (2003). Some Simple Economics of Open Source. *The Journal of Industrial Economics, 51*(2), 197–234.

Li, L. Y., & Wang, H. J. (2007). A new method for building web-based virtual laboratory. In H. Liu, B. Hu, X.W. Zheng, & H. Zhang (Ed.). *1st International Symposium on Information Technologies and Applications in Education* (pp. 555-558). Kunming: Shandong Normal Univ. Press.

Lim, E.-P., Vuong, B.-Q., Lauw, H. W., & Sun, A. (2006). Measuring qualities of articles contributed by online communities. In *Proceedings of the 2006 IEEE / WIC / ACM International Conference on Web Intelligence*. IEEE.

Lim, V. K. G. (2002). The IT way of loafing on the job: Cyberloafing, neutralizing and Distraction versus destruction. *Cyberpsychology & Behavior, 9*(6), 730–741.

Lindeman, E. (1938). Preparing leaders in adult education. In Dixon, N. & Henkelman, J. (Eds.), (1991). Models for HRD practice: The academic guide. Alexandria, VA: American Society for Training and Development.

Littlejohn, A. (2003). Issues in reusing online resources. In A. Littlejohn (Ed.), *Reusing Online Resources: a sustainable approach to eLearning* (pp. 1-6). London: Kogan Page.

Littlejohn, A. (2003b). An incremental approach to staff development in the reuse of learning resources. In A. Littlejohn (Ed.), *Reusing online resources: A sustainable approach to e-learning* (pp. 221-233). London: Kogan Page.

Littlejohn, A. (2005). Keynote presentation: Community dimensions of learning object repositories. In H. Goss (Ed.), *Balance, fidelity, mobility: Maintaining the momentum? Proceedings of the 22nd Annual Conference of ascilite* (p. 3). Brisbane: Teaching & Learning Support Services, QUT.

Littlejohn, A. (Ed.) (2003a). *Reusing online resources: A sustainable approach to e-learning*. London: Kogan Page.

Littlejohn, A., & Buckingham Shum, S. (2003). JIME special issue on reusing online resources. *Journal of Interactive Media in Education.* Retrieved March 28, 2008, from http://www-jime.open.ac.uk/2003/1/

Littlejohn, A., Falconer, I., & Mcgill, L. (2008). Characterising effective eLearning resources. *Computers & Education, 50*, 757–771. doi:10.1016/j.compedu.2006.08.004

Littlejohn, A., Jung, I., & Broumley, L. (2003). A comparison of issues in the reuse of resources in schools and colleges. In A. Littlejohn (Ed.), *Reusing online resources: A sustainable approach to e-learning* (pp. 212-220). London: Kogan Page.

Littlejohn, A.H., Campbell, L.M., Tizard, J., & Smith, A. (2003). From pilot project to strategic development: Scaling up staff support in the use of ICT for teaching and learning, *Journal of Further and Higher education, 7*(1), 47-52.

Liu, C. C., Hung, C. T., Hung, T. C., Pei, B. S., & Zhang, L. (2006). *The development of an innovative interactive e-learning system in computational thermal-hydraulics for engineers.* Paper presented at the EDMEDIA.Magoha

Lockyer, L., Patterson, J., & Harper, B. (2001). ICT in higher education: evaluating outcomes for health education [Electronic version]. *Journal of Computer Assisted Learning, 17*, 275-283.

Lund, A., & Smørdal, O. (2006). Is there a space for the teacher in a WIKI? In *Proceedings of the 2006 international symposium on wikis* (pp. 7-46). Odense, Denmark. Retrieved April 19, 2009, from http://portal.acm.org/citation.cfm?id=1149453.1149466

Luppicini, R. (2008a). Introducting the field of Technoethics. In Luppicini, R., & Adell, R. (Eds.), *Handbook of Research on Technoethics* (pp. 1–18). Hershey: Idea Group Publishing.

Luppicini, R. (2008b). Introducing conversation design for instructional applications. In Luppicini, R. (Ed.), *Handbook of Conversation Design for Instruction* (pp. 1–18). Hershey: Idea Group Publishing.

Mackey, T., & Ho, J. (2008). Exploring the relationship between web usability and students' perceived learning in web-based multimedia (WBMM) tutorials. *Computers & Education*, *50*(1), 386–409. doi:10.1016/j.compedu.2006.08.006

Mader, S. (2008). *Wikipatterns*. Indianapolis, IN: Wiley Publishing.

Makice, K. (2006). *PoliticWiki: Exploring communal politics. WikiSym 2006* (pp. 105–118). Odense, Denmark: ACM.

Malcolm, M. (2005). The exercise of the object: Issues in resource reusability and reuse, *British Journal of Educational Technology*, *36*(1), 33-41.

Mandernach, B. J., Donnelli, E., Dailey, A., & Schulte, M. (2005). A faculty evaluation model for online instructors: Mentoring and evaluation in the online classroom. *Online Journal of Distance Education Administration,* 8(3).

Mann, S. (2008). The problems of online collaboration for junior high school students: Can the Learning Activity Management System (LAMS) benefit students to learn via online learning? In L. Cameron & J. Dalziel (Eds.), *Proceedings of 3rd International LAMS & Learning Design Conference 2008: Perspectives on Learning Design* (pp. 81-86). Sydney: LAMS Foundation.

Margaryan, A., & Littlejohn, A. (2007). Community dimensions of learning object repositories. In C. Montgomerie & J. Seale (Eds.), *Proceedings of World Conference on Educational Multimedia, Hypermedia and Telecommunications 2007* (pp. 4335-4343). Chesapeake, VA: AACE.

Marginson, S., & Considine, M. (2000). *The enterprise university: Power, governance and reinvention in Australia*. Melbourne, Australia: Cambridge University Press.

Martin, J. (1999, March). Internet policy: Employee rights and wrongs. *HRFocus*, *75*, 11.

Mastrangelo, P. M., Everton, W., & Jolton, J. A. (2006). Personal use of work computers: organizational justice. *Journal of Organizational Behavior*, *23*, 675–694.

Mathias, L., Frantz, P., Brust, G., Montogery, J., Smith, V., Simmons, M., et al. (2009). *Polymer Science learning Center*. Retrieved from http://pslc.ws/macrog.htm

May, S. (2006). *Case Studies in Organizational Communication: Ethical Perspectives and Practices*. Thousand Oaks, CA: Sage.

Mayes, J. T. (2004). *Learner centred pedagogy: Individual differences between learners*. JISC e-Learning Models Desk Study. Retrieved October 20, 2006, from http://www.jisc.ac.uk/uploaded_documents/Stage%202%20Learning%20Styles%20(Version%201).pdf

Mazur, E. (1997). *Peer Instruction: A User's Manual*. Upper Saddle River, NJ: Prentice Hall.

McFedries, P. (2006) It's a wiki, wiki world. Technically Speaking. IEEE Spectrum. Retrieved Jan. 22, 2009, from < www.spectrum.ieee.org >. 88.

McGee, J. B., & Begg, M. (2008). What medical educators need to know about "Web 2.0". *Medical Teacher*, *30*(2), 164–169. doi:10.1080/01421590701881673

McLagan, P., & McCullough, R. (1983). *Models for excellence: The conclusions and recommendations of the ASTD training and development competency study*. Alexandria, VA: The American Society for Training and Development.

McLagan, P., & Suhadolnik, D. (1989). *Models for HRD practice: The research report*. Alexandria, VA: American Society for Training & Development.

Means, B., & Olson, K. (1995). Technology's Role in Education Reform. Findings from a National Study of Innovating Schools. Prepared for Office of Educational Research and Improvement. U.S. Department of Education: Washington, DC.

Milam, J., Voorhees, R., & Bedard-Voorhees, A. (2004). Assessment of online education: Policies, practices, and recommendations. In Serban, A. M., & Friedlander, J. (Eds.), *Developing and implementing assessment of student learning outcomes. New Directions for Community Colleges*. San Francisco: Jossey-Bass.

Miles, M., & Huberman, M. (1984). *Qualitative data analysis: A source book for new methods*. Thousand Oaks, CA: Sage Publications.

Miller, G. E. (1990). The Assessment of CLinical Skills / Competence / Performance. *Academic Medicine*, *65*(9), 63–67. doi:10.1097/00001888-199009000-00045

Miller, P.A. (1997). The Integration of Computers at Pinelands High School: A case study. Unpublished M. Ed Thesis, University of Pretoria. Retrieved January 23, 2006 from http://www.wcape.school.za/subject/CS/PHS/index.htm

Mills, J. (1995). Better teaching through provocation. *College Teaching*, *46*, 21–25. doi:10.1080/87567559809596228

Mohan, P., & Brooks, C. (2003, July). Engineering a future for learning objects. *Proceedings of the International Conference on Web Engineering* (pp. 120-123). Oviedo, Spain.

Mohan, P., & Daniel, B. (2004). The learning objects approach: Challenges and opportunities. In G. Richards (Ed.), *Proceedings of World Conference on E-Learning in Corporate, Government, Healthcare, and Higher education 2004* (pp. 2512-2520). Chesapeake, VA: AACE.

Mohan, P., & Greer, J. (2003). Reusable learning objects: Current status and future directions. In D. Lassner & C. McNaught (Eds.), *Proceedings of World Conference on Educational Multimedia, Hypermedia and Telecommunications 2003* (pp. 257-264). Chesapeake, VA: AACE.

Monahan, T., McArdle, G., & Bertolotto, M. (2008). Virtual reality for collaborative e-learning. *Computers & Education*, *50*, 1339–1353. doi:10.1016/j.compedu.2006.12.008

Monahan, T., McArdle, G., & Bertolotto, M. (2008). Virtual reality for collaborative e-learning. *Computers & Education*, *50*, 1339–1353. doi:10.1016/j.compedu.2006.12.008

Moore, A., & Barber, L. R., Jr. (2008). Wiki-based extension fact sheets. Journal of Extension: 46(3). *Extension Journal, Inc. retrieved from:*http://www.joe.org/joe/2008june/tt1.php on March 4, *2009).*

Moore, T. D., & Serva, M. A. (2007). Understanding member motivation for contributing to different types of virtual communities: A proposed framework. Presented at SIGMIS-CPR '07. St. Louis, MS.

Moreno, L., Gonzalez, C., Castilla, I., Gonzalea, E., & Sigut, J. (2007). Applying a constructivist and collaborative methodological approach in engineering education. *Computers & Education*, *49*, 891–915. doi:10.1016/j.compedu.2005.12.004

Morse, A., & Suktrisul, S. (2006). Introducing eLearning into Secondary Schools in Thailand. *Special Issue of the International Journal of the Computer, the Internet and Management*, *14*, 8.1-8.5.

Motiwalla, L. F. (2007). Mobile learning: A framework and evaluation. *Computers & Education*, *49*, 581–596. doi:10.1016/j.compedu.2005.10.011

Mumtaz, S. (2000). Factors Affecting Teachers' Use of Information and Communications Technology: a review of the literature [Electronic version]. *Journal of Information Technology for Teacher Education*, *9*(3), 2000.

Mwai, N. (2006). Creation of a wiki-based code snippet repository. Student poster abstract. In *Proceedings of the Consortium for Computing Sciences in Colleges*. 293.

Nadler, L. (1968). A study of the needs of selected training directors in Pennsylvania which might be met by professional education institutions. (Doctoral dissertation, Columbia University, 1962). *Dissertation Abstracts International*, *24*(2) 601.

Najjar, J. Ternier, S., & Duval, E. (2004). User behaviour in learning objects repositories: An empirical analysis. In L. Catoni & C. McLoughlin (Eds.), *Proceedings of World Conference on E-Learning in Corporate, Government, Healthcare, and Higher education 2004* (pp. 4373-4378). Chesapeake, VA: AACE.

Nelasco, S., Arputtharaj, A. N., & Alwinson, E. G. (2007). ELearning for Higher Studies of India. *Special Issue of the International Journal of the Computer. The Internet and Management*, *15*, 161–167.

Nelson, M. R. (2008). E-books in higher education: Nearing the end of the era of hype? *EDUCAUSE Review*, *43*(2), 40–56.

NES. (2007). *NES survey of Scottish consultant workforce*. Edinburgh: NHS Education for Scotlando. Document Number)

Neven, F., Duval, E., Ternier, S., Cardinaels, K., & Vandepitte, P. (2003). An open and flexible indexation and query tool for ARIADNE. In D. Lassner & C. McNaught (Eds.), *Proceedings of World Conference on Educational Multimedia, Hypermedia and Telecommunications 2003* (pp. 107-114). Chesapeake, VA: AACE.

Nicoletto, G., Anzelotti, G., & Riva, E. (2008). Mesomechanic strain analysis of twill-weave composite lamina under unidirectional in-plane tension. *Composites. Part A, Applied Science and Manufacturing*, *39*(8), 1294–1301. doi:10.1016/j.compositesa.2008.01.006

Nicoletto, G., Anzelotti, G., & Riva, E. (2009). Mesoscopic strain fields in woven composites: Experiments vs. finite element modeling. *Optics and Lasers in Engineering*, *47*(3-4), 352–359. doi:10.1016/j.optlaseng.2008.07.009

Nicoletto, G., Marin, T., Anzelotti, G., & Roncella, R. (in press). Application of high magnification digital image correlation technique to micromechanical strain analysis. *Strain*.

NMC. (2007). *Standards to support learning and assessment in practice: NMC standards for mentors, practice teachers and teachers*. Available online: http://www.nmc-uk.org/: Nursing and Midwifery Council.

Noori, M. (2003). *Traditional education or learning with computer*. Paper presented at the Virtual University Conference at Kashan Payam-e Noor College, Kashan, Iran

Nor Azan, M. Z. (2007). Learning Activities Management System (SPAP), In *Proceedings of International Conference on Electrical Engineering and Informatics*. Institut Teknologi Bandung, Indonesia.

Norman, G., Young, M., & Brooks, L. (2007). Non-analytical models of clinical reasoning: the role of experience. *Medical Education*, *41*, 1140–1145.

O'Neill, B., Schuchardt, J., Pankow, D., Porter, N., Seiling, S., Branch, J., & Miller, J. (2007). eXtension: A high tech resource for improving financial security. *Consumer Interests Annual*, *53*. Retrieved April 19, 2009, from http://cnr.consumerinterests.org/files/public/ONeill_eXtensionAHighTechResourceforImprovingFinancialSecurity.pdf

O'Neill, M. E. (2005, Feb.). Automated use of a wiki for collaborative lecture notes. *SIGCSE '05*. St. Louis, MS.

Odamtten, T., & Millard, J. (2009, January). Learning from Others Within the Landscape of "Transitional Economies" and the Challenge in ICT Development for African Countries. *Society*, *23*(1), 51–61.

Ogot, M., & Okudan, G. (2007). A student-centered approach to improving course quality using quality function deployment. *International Journal of Engineering Education*, *23*(5), 916–928.

Oliver, R. (2001). Learning objects: Supporting flexible delivery of online learning paradigms. In G. Kennedy & T. Petrovic (Eds.), *Proceedings of Annual Conference of the Australian Society for Computers in Learning in Tertiary Education* (pp. pp 453-460). Melbourne: Melbourne City Press.

Open Content Alliance. (2009). *Open Content Alliance: Building a Digital Archive of Global Content for Universal Access*. Retrieved February 3, 2009, from http://www.opencontentalliance.org

Osguthorpe, R. T., & Graham, C. R. (2003). Blended learning environments: Definitions and directions. *The Quarterly Review of Distance Education*, *4*(3), 227–233.

Ozga, J. (2007). Knowledge and Policy: Research and Knowledge Transfer. *Critical Studies in Education*, *48*(1), 63–78. doi:10.1080/17508480601120988

P. W., & Andrew, W. O. (2004). The global perspectives of transitioning to e-learning in engineering education. *World Transactions on Engineering and Technology Education*, *3*(2), 205–210.

Padilla-Melendez, A., Garrido-Moreno, A., & Aguila-Obra, A. R. (2008). Factors affecting e-collaboration technology use among management students. *Computers & Education, 51*, 609–623. doi:10.1016/j.compedu.2007.06.013

Palloff, R. M., & Pratt, K. (2007). *Building online learning: Effective strategies for the online classroom*. San Francisco: Jossey-Bass.

Pan, G., & Bonk, C. J. (2007, November). The emergence of open-source software in North America. *International Review of Research in Open and Distance Learning, 8*(3). Retrieved April 19, 2009, from http://www.irrodl.org/index.php/irrodl/article/view/496/950

Pankowski, P. (2004, September). Faculty training for online teaching. *T.H.E. Journal*. Retrieved from http://thejournal.com/articles/16956

Pask, G. (1975). *The cybernetics of human learning and performance: A guide to theory and research*. London: Hutchinson.

Patterson, S. J., & Radtke, J. M. (2009). *Strategic Communications for Nonprofit Organization: Seven Steps to Creating a Successful Plan* (2nd ed.). Hoboken, NJ: John Wiley & Sons, Inc.

Patton, M. Q. (2001). *Qualitative research and evaluation methods* (3rd ed.). Thousand Oaks, CA: Sage.

Pelgrum, W. J., & Law, N. (2003). ICT in education around the world. Trends, Problems and Prospects. Paris: UNESCO. Retrieved September 10, 2005 from http://unesdoc.unesco.org/images/0013/001362/136281e.pdf

Perez, R. C., & Alaman, X. (2002). Creating E-books in a distributed and collaborative way. *The Electronic Library, 20*(4), 288–295. doi:10.1108/02640470210438883

Perry, J. A., & Imig, D. G. (2008). A stewardship of practice in education. *Change, 40*(6), 42–49. doi:10.3200/CHNG.40.6.42-49

Pew Internet & American Life Project. (2008). Retrieved June 11, 2009, from http://www.pewinternet.org/Static-Pages/Data-Tools/Download Data/~/media/Infographics/Trend%20Data/January%202009%20updates/Demographics%20of%20Internet%20Users%201%206%2009.jpgPrensky, M. (2001). *Digital Natives, Digital Immigrants. On the Horizon, 9*(5). Retrieved June 12, 2009. from http://www.twitchspeed.com/site/Prensky%20-%20Digital%20Natives,%20Digital%20Immigrants%20-%20Part1.htm

Picciano, A. (2002, July). Beyond student perceptions: Issues of interaction, presence, and performance in an online course. *JALN, 6*(1), 21–40.

Pierson, M., & McLachlan, A. (2004). Case Studies of Future Teachers: Learning to Teach with Technology. *Winner of the 2004 National Educational Computing Conference (NECC)*. Retrieved from http://center.uoregon.edu/ISTE/NECC2004/handout_files_live/KEY_673094/pierson_case_studies.pdf

Pinto, P., & Walker, J. (1978). *A study of professional training and development roles and competencies*. Alexandria, VA: American Society for Training and Development.

Piskurich, G., & Sanders, E. (1998). *ASTD models for learning technologies: Roles, competencies, and outputs*. Alexandria, VA: American Society for Training & Development.

PMETB. G. a. (2005). *Principles of good medical education and training*. London: General Medical Council and Postgraduate Medical Education and Training Board.

Poftak, A. (2001). Getting a read on E-books. *Technology & Learning, 21*(9), 22–36.

Popescu, S., Brad, S., & Popescu, D. (2006). The engineering study program as a customized product: barriers and directions for intervention, In E. Westkaemper (Ed.), 1st CIRP International Seminar on Assembly Systems, (pp. 289-294). Stuttgart, Germany: IFF Univ. Stuttgart.

Poupa, C., & Forte, E. (2003). Collaborative teaching with learning objects in an international, non-profit context. The example of the ARIADNE community. *Educational Media International, 40*(3/4), 239-248.

Prensky, M. (2000). *Digital Game Based Learning*: McGraw-Hill.

Priedhorsky, R., Chen, J., Lam, S. T. K., Panciera, K., Terveen, L., & Reidl, J. (2007). Creating, destroying, and restoring value in Wikipedia. GROUP '07. Sanibel Island, FL. ACM, 259 &266.

Priedhorsky, R., Jordan, B., & Terveen, L. (2007). *How a personalized geowiki can help Bicyclists share information more effectively.* Presented at WikiSym '07. Montréal, Québec.Raitman, R., Augar, N., & Zhou, W. (2005). Employing wikis for online collaboration in the e-learning environment: Case study. In *Proceedings of the Third International Conference on Information Technology and Applications* (ICITA '05). IEEE.

Purcell, J. M. (2007). *Perceptions of senior faculty concerning doctoral student preparation for faculty roles.* Ph.D. dissertation, University of South Florida, United States– Florida. Retrieved February 14, 2009, from Dissertations & Theses: Full Text database. (Publication No. AAT 3306885).

Pyrz, R., Olhoff, N., Lund, E., & Thomsen, O. T. (2003). *Mechanic for.* Retrieved from http://me.aau.dk/GetAsset.action?contentId=1987778&assetId=3356989

Race, P. (1994). *The Open Learning Handbook.* London: Kogan Page.

Raharjo, H., Xie, M., Goh, T. N., & Brombacher, A. C. (2007). A methodology to improve higher education quality using the quality function deployment and analytic hierarchy process. *Total Quality Management & Business Excellence, 18*(10), 1097–1115. doi:10.1080/14783360701595078

Ramasundaram, V., Grunwald, S., Mangeot, A., Comerford, N. B., & Bliss, C. M. (2005). Development of an environmental virtual field laboratory. *Computers & Education, 45,* 21–34. doi:10.1016/j.compedu.2004.03.002

Rao, S. S. (2003). Electronic books: A review and evaluation. *Library Hi Tech, 21*(1), 85–93. doi:10.1108/07378830310467427

Raymond, E. S. (1999). *The Cathedral & the Bazaar: Musings on Linux and Open Source by an Accidental Revolutionary.* Sabastopol, CA: O'Reilly & Associates, Inc.

Reagle, J. M., Jr. (2007). Do as I do: Authorial leadership in Wikipedia. Presented at WikiSym '07. Montréal, Québec.

Rees, M. (1972). Graduate education – a long look. In Kent, L. J., & Springer, G. P. (Eds.), *Graduate education today and tomorrow* (pp. 139–151). Albuquerque, NM: University of New Mexico Press.

Reinhold, S. (2006). WikiTrails: Augmenting wiki structure for collaborative, interdisciplinary learning. Presented at WikiSym '06. Odense, Denmark.

Repole, D. (2007). *Open and distance education proposal,* Excelsior Community College: Unpublished paper.

Rest, T. (1997). Using video for teaching chemistry: A phoenix? *TLTP Newsletter.*

Rice, R., & Bunz, U. (2006). Evaluating a wireless course feedback system: The role of demographics, expertise, fluency, competency, and usage. *Studies in Media and Information Literacy Education,* (3), 1-23.

Richards, G.R., McGreal, R., & Freisen, N. (2002, June). Learning object repository technologies for telelearning: The evolution of POOL and CanCore. In *Proceedings of the IS2002, Informing Science + IT Education Conference.* Cork, Ireland: IS2002. Retrieved March 28, 2008, from http://proceedings.informingscience.org/IS2002Proceedings/papers/Richa242Learn.pdf

Rifkin, T. (1995). ERIC review: Faculty evaluation in community colleges. *Community College Review, 23*(1), 63. doi:10.1177/009155219502300107

Rizzotti, S., & Burkhart, H. (2006). Web-based test and assessment system: Design principles and case study. In V. Uskov (Ed.), *5th IASTED International Conference on Web-based Education* (pp. 37-42). Puerto Vallarta, Mexico: Acta Press.

Robertson, I. (2008). Learners' attitudes to wiki technology in problem based, blended learning for vocational teacher education. *Australasian Journal of Educational Technology, 24*(4), 425-441. Retrieved April 19, 2009, from http://www.ascilite.org.au/ajet/ajet24/robertson.html

Rogers, E.M. (1995). *Diffusion of innovations* (4th ed). New York: Free Press.

Rooney, J. E. (2003). Blending learning opportunities to enhance educational programming and meetings. *Association Management, 55*(5), 26–32.

Roselli, R. J., & Brophy, S. P. (2003). Redesigning a biomechanics course using challenge-based instruction. *IEEE Engineering in Medicine and Biology Magazine, 22*(4), 66–70. doi:10.1109/MEMB.2003.1237504

Ross, M. T., Blaney, D., Cameron, H. S., Begg, M., & Cumming, A. D. (2008). *ClinEd: developing a web-based collaborative learning environment for clinical educators at the University of Edinburgh.* Paper presented at the All Together Better Health IV.

Roth, C. (2008). Viable wikis: Struggle for life in the Wikisphere. Presented at WikiSym '07. Montréal, Québec.

Rothwell, W., & Cookson, P. (1997). *Beyond instruction: Comprehensive program planning for business and education.* San Francisco: Jossey-Bass.

Rovai, A. P., & Barnum, K. T. (2003). On-Line Course Effectiveness: An Analysis of Student Interactions and Perceptions of Learning. *Journal of Distance Learning, 18*(1), 57–73.

Rowlands, I., & Nicholas, D. (2008). Understanding information behaviour: How do students and faculty find books? *Journal of Academic Librarianship, 34*(1), 3–15. doi:10.1016/j.acalib.2007.11.005

Ryan, M., Carlton, K. H., & Ali, N. S. (2004). Reflections on the role of faculty in distance learning and changing pedagogies. *Nursing Education Perspectives, 25*(2), 73–80.

Ryan, Y. (2001). The provision of learner support services online. In *The changing faces of virtual education* (pp. 71–94). Vancouver, BC: The Commonwealth of Learning.

Ryder, M. (2008). *Instructional design models.* Retrieved from http://carbon.cudenver.edu/~mryder/itc_data/idmodels.html#modern

Saaty, T. L., & Vargas, L. G. (2001). *Models, methods, concepts & applications of the analytic hierarchy process.* New York: Springer.

Sabaliauskas, T. and Pukelis K., (2004). Barriers to Integration of Information and Communication Technologies into the Teaching and Learning Process. Retrieved September 20, 2005 from http://www.leeds.ac.uk/educol/documents/00003861.htm

Sackett, D. L., Straus, S. E., Richardson, W. S., Rosenberg, W., & Haynes, R. B. (2000). *Evidence-based medicine: how to practice and teach EBM.* London: Churchill Livinstone.

Santilli, S., & Beck, V. (2005). Graduate faculty perceptions of online teaching. *Quarterly Review of Distance Education, 6*(2), 155–160.

Saygin, C., & Kahraman, F. (2004). A Web-based programmable logic controller laboratory for manufacturing engineering education. *International Journal of Advanced Manufacturing Technology, 24*(7-8), 590–598. doi:10.1007/s00170-003-1787-7

Schmidt, H. G., & Rickers, R. M. J. P. (2007). How expertise develops in medicine: knowledge encapsulation and illness script formation. *Medical Education, 41*, 1133–1139.

Schön, D. A. (1983). *The reflective practitioner: how professionals think in action.* London: Temple Smith.

Schön, D. A. (1987). *Educating the reflective practitioner: toward a new design for teaching and learning in the professions.* San Fransisco: Jossey-Bass.

Schuler, R. P., Grandhi, S. A., Laws, N., Jones, Q., & Bajaj, S. (2007). *Finding your way with CampusWiki: A location-aware wiki. CHI 2007: Work-in-Progress. San Jose, CA.Shirky, C. (2008). Here Comes Everybody: The Power of Organizing without Organizations.* New York: Penguin Group.

Schwartz, L., Clark, S., Cossarin, M., & Rudolph, J. (2004, April). Educational wikis: Features and selection criteria. *International Review of Research in Open and Distance Learning, 5*(1). Retrieved April 19, 2009, from http://www.irrodl.org/index.php/irrodl/article/view/163/692

Science. (1941). The engineers' council for professional development. *Science, 94*(2446), 456.

SCORM. (2004). Advanced distributed learning - SCORM. Retrieved March 28, 2008, from http://www.adlnet.gov/scorm/

Scott Barrett, M., Bornsen, S. E., Erickson, S. L., Markey, V., & Spiering, K. (2005). The personal response systems as a teaching aid. *Communication Teacher, 19*(3), 89–92. doi:10.1080/14704620500201806

Scott, B. (2001). Conversation theory. A constructivist dialogical approach to educational technology. *Cybernetics & Human Knowing, 8*(4), 25–46.

Sessink, O., van der Schaaf, H., Beeftink, H., Hartog, R., & Tramper, J. (2007). Web-based education in bioprocess engineering. *Trends in Biotechnology, 25*(1), 16–23. doi:10.1016/j.tibtech.2006.11.001

Sfard, A. (2003). Balancing the unbalanceable: The NCTM standards in light of theories of learning mathematics. In Kilpatrick, J., Martin, W. G., & Schifter, D. (Eds.), *A research companion to Principles and Standards for School Mathematics* (pp. 353–392). Reston, VA: National Council of Teachers of Mathematics.

Shih, W. C., Tseng, S. S., & Yang, C. T. (2008). Wiki-based rapid prototyping for teaching-material design in e-Learning grids. *Computers & Education, 51*, 1037–1057. doi:10.1016/j.compedu.2007.10.007

Sirinaruemitr, P. (2004). Trends and forces for eLearning in Thailand. *International Journal of The Computer, the Internet and Management, 12*, 132-137.

Siritongthaworn, S., & Krairit, D. (2004). Use of Interactions in E-learning: A Study of Undergraduate Courses in Thailand. *International Journal of The Computer, the Internet and Management, 12*, 162-170.

Smith, K. S., & Simpson, R. D. (1995). Validating teaching competencies for faculty members in higher education: A national study using. *Innovative Higher Education, 19*(3), 223. doi:10.1007/BF01191221

Smith, R. J. (2009). *Engineering.* Retrieved from http://www.britannica.com/EBchecked/topic/187549/engineering

Speicher, A. L. (2000). The association of American universities: A century of service to higher education. Retrieved on May 1, 2009, from: http://www.aau.edu/

Stake, R. E. (1995). *The art of case study research.* Thousand Oaks, CA: Sage.

Starkey, H. (2002). *Active citizenship and the lifelong learning agenda.* Paper presented at the Danish EU Presidency Conference: Lifelong learning - learning for adults in the 21st century, Snekkersten, Denmark.

Stein, F., & Hutchison, C. (1988). Instructor competencies: The standards, Vols. 1 & 2. Batavia, IL: The International Board of Standards for Training, Performance & Instruction.

Stickel, C., Holzinger, A., & Ebner, M. (2008). Useful oblivion versus information overload in e-learning examples in the context of wiki systems. In *Proceedings of the ITI 2008 30th International Conference on Information Technology Interfaces.* Cavtat, Croatia. 171 – 176.

Storr, R. J. (1969). *The beginnings of graduate education in America.* New York: Arno Press.

Suliman, S. M. A. (2006). Application of QFD in engineering education curriculum development and review. *International Journal of Continuing Engineering Education and Lifelong Learning, 16*(6), 482–492. doi:10.1504/IJCEELL.2006.011892

Sun, P., Cheng, H. K., Lin, T., & Wang, F. (2008). A design to promote group learning in e-learning: Experiences from the field. *Computers & Education, 50*, 661–677. doi:10.1016/j.compedu.2006.07.008

Syverson, P. (1996). The new American graduate student: Challenge or opportunity? *CGS Communicator, 29*(8), 7-8. Retrieved from http://www.capnet.org/vcr/cctr610.htm

Tabakov, S. (2008). e-Learning development in medical physics and engineering. *Biomedical Imaging and Intervention Journal, 4*(1), e27. doi:10.2349/biij.4.1.e27

Tait, B. (1997). Constructive Internet Learning. *Active Learning, (7)*, 3-8.

Tan, A. C. C., Tang, T., & Paterson, G. (2008). *Web-based Remote Vibration Experimental Laboratory.* Paper presented at the Engineering Education, Loughbrough, London.

Tapscott, D., & Williams, A. D. (2006). *Wikinomics: How Mass Collaboration Changes Everything.* New York: Penguin Group.

Taylor, P.G., & Richardson, A.S. (2001). *Validating scholarship in university teaching.* Canberra, Australia: Higher education Division, Department of Employment, Education, Training and Youth Affairs.

Tearle, P. (2003). ICT implementation. What makes the difference? [Electronic version]. *British Journal of Educational Technology, 34* (5), 567-583.

Tearle, P. (2004). A theoretical and instrumental framework for implementing change in ICT in education [Electronic version]. *Cambridge Journal of Education, 34*(3), 331-351.

Thach, E. C. (1994). *Perceptions of distance education experts regarding the roles, outputs, and competencies needed in the field of distance education.* Ph.D. dissertation, Texas A&M University, Texas, U.S. Retrieved May 1, 2009, from Dissertations & Theses: Full Text database. (Publication No. AAT 9506728)

The Carrick Institute. (2007). The Carrick exchange overview 2007. Retrieved March 28, 2008, from http://www.carrickinstitute.edu.au/carrick/webdav/site/carricksite/users/siteadmin/public/rin_carrickexchange_overview_2007.pdf

Thompson, C. (2008). Dialogism and social computing: Academic authorship in cyberspace. In J. McConachie, M. J. G. Singh, P. A. Danaher, F. Nouwens, & G. R. Danaher (Eds.), Changing university learning and teaching: Engaging and mobilising leadership, quality and technology (pp. 359-374). Teneriffe, Qld, Australia: Post Pressed.

Thurgood, L., Golladay, M. J., & Hill, S. T. (2006). U.S. doctorates in the 20th Century. National Science Foundation, Division of Science Resources Statistics, NSF 06-319, Arlington, VA.

Tiemann, M. (2009). *History of the OSI.* Retrieved February 3, 2009, from http://www.opensource.org/history

Tigelaar, D. E. H., Dolmans, D. H. J. M., Wolfhagen, I. H. A. P., & Van, V. (2004). The development and validation of a framework for teaching competencies in higher education. *Higher Education, 48*(2), 253–268. doi:10.1023/B:HIGH.0000034318.74275.e4

Tinto, V. (1975). Dropout from Higher Education: A Theoretical Synthesis of Recent Research. *Review of Educational Research, 45*, 89–125.

Toral, S., Barrero, F., & Martinez-Torres, M. (2007). Analysis of utility and use of a web-based tool for digital signal processing teaching by means of a technological acceptance model. *Computers & Education, 49*(4), 957–975. doi:10.1016/j.compedu.2005.12.003

Toro-Troconis, M., Mellstrom, U., Partidge, M., Meeran, K., Barrett, M., & Higham, J. (2008). Designing game-based learning activities for virtual patients in Second Life. *Journal of CyberTherapy & Rehabilitation, 1*(3), 227–239.

Toth, P. (2008). *New Method in Quality Assurance of Electronic-based Teaching Materials.* Paper presented at the Engineering Education, Loughbrough, London.

Trees, A. R., & Jackson, M. H. (2007). The learning environment in clicker classrooms: Student processes of learning and involvement in large university-level courses using student response systems. *Learning, Media and Technology, 32*(1), 21–40. doi:10.1080/17439880601141179

Truman-Davis, B., Futch, L., Thompson, K., & Yonekura, F. (2000). Support for online teaching and learning. *EDUCAUSE Quarterly, 2*, 44–51.

Tsai, S., Yeh, T. L., Lee, C. K., & Wang, N. C. (2008). *Teaching Strategies for Design Realization in Engineering Design Education.* Paper presented at the Engineering Education, Loughbrough, England.

Tweeten, J., Smith, M. K., Julius, J., & Murphy-Boyer, L. (2007). Successful clicker standardization. *EDUCAUSE Quarterly, 4*, 63–67.

UNESCO. (2006). *UIS statics in brief-Iran*. Retrieved from http://stats.uis.unesco.org/unesco /TableViewer/document.aspx?ReportId=121&IF_Language=eng&BR_Country=3640.

Upitis, G., Maziais, J., & Rudnevs, J. (2008). *Problen-Oriented E-tools for Studies in Mechanical Engineering.* Paper presented at the Engineering Education, Loughborough, England.

Urbaczewski, A., & Jessup, L. M. (2002). Does electronic monitoring of employee Internet usage work? *Communications of the ACM, 45*(1), 80–83. doi:10.1145/502269.502303

Vadillo, M. A., & Matute, H. (2009). Learning in virtual environments: Some discrepancies between laboratory- and Internet-based research on associative learning. *Computers in Human Behavior, 25*, 402–406. doi:10.1016/j.chb.2008.08.009

Van Sint Jan, S., Crudele, M., Gashegu, J., Feipel, V., Poulet, P., & Salvia, P. (2003). Development of multimedia learning modules for teaching human anatomy: Application to osteology and functional anatomy. *Anatomical Record. Part B, New Anatomist, 272B*(1), 98–106. doi:10.1002/ar.b.10020

Vargas, H., Sanchez, J., Duro, N., Dormido, R., Farias, G., & Dormido, S. (2008). A systematic two-layer approach to develop web-based experimentation environments for control engineering education. *Intelligent Automation and Soft Computing, 14*(4), 505–524.

Vate-U-Lan, P. (2007). Readiness of eLearning connectivity in Thailand. *Special Issue of the International Journal of the Computer, the Internet and Management, 15*, 21.21-21.27.

Viégas, F. B. (2007). The visual side of Wikipedia. In *Proceedings of the 40th Hawaii International Conference on System Sciences*. IEEE.

Vogel, D., & Klassen, J. (2001). Technology-supported learning: status, issues and trends [Electronic version]. *Journal of Computer Assisted Learning, 17*, 104-114.

Von Hippel, E., & von Krogh, G. (2003, March-April). Open Source Software and the "Private-Collective" Innovation Model: Issues for Organization Science. *Organization Science, 14*(2), 209–223. doi:10.1287/orsc.14.2.209.14992

Wagner, D. (2005). Monitoring and Evaluation of ICT for Education. An Introduction. In Wagener, D., et al. (Eds.) Monitoring and Evaluation of ICT in Educational Projects: A Handbook for Developing Countries. *infoDev Pre-Publication draft,* Washington DC, USA. Retrieved December 15, 2005 from http://www.infodev.org/files/2942_file_M_E_ICT_Education_draft_WSIS_optimized.pdf

Wang, L., Roe, P., Pham, B., & Tjondronegoro, D. (2008). An audio wiki supporting mobile collaboration. Presented at SAC '08. Fortaleza, Ceará, Brazil.

Wang, X., Dannenhoffer, J., Davidson, B., & Spector, M. (2005). Design issues in a cross-institutional collaboration on a distance education course. *Distance Education, 26*(3), 405–423. doi:10.1080/01587910500291546

Wankat, P. C., Felder, R. m., Smith, K. S., & Oreovicz, F. S. (2002). *The scholarship of teaching and learning in engineering.* Washangton, DC: AAHE/Carnegie Foundation for the Advancement of Teaching.

Warshauer, M. (2003). Demystifying the Digital Divide. *Scientific American, 289*(2), 6, &42.

Warshauer, M. (2004). *Technology and Social Inclusion: Rethinking the Digital Divide*. Cambridge, MA: The MIT Press.

Weber, S. (2005). *The Success of Open Source*. Cambridge, MA: Harvard University Press.

Wenger, E. (1998). *Communities of Practice: Learning, Meaning and Identity.* New York: Cambridge University Press.

Wenger, E. (nd). *Communities of practice*. Retrieved August 7, 2009, from http://www.ewenger.com/theory/

Wenger, E., McDermott, R., & Snyder, W. (2002). *Cultivating communities of practice.* Boston, MA: Harvard Business School Press.

Wetterling, J., & Collis, B. (2003). Sharing and reuse of learning resources across a transnational network.

In A. Littlejohn (Ed.), *Reusing online resources: A sustainable approach to e-learning* (pp. 182-194). London: Kogan Page.

WFME. (2003). *Basic medical education: WFME global standards for quality improvement*. Copenhagen: World Federation for Medical Education.

Wheeler, S., Yeomans, P., & Wheeler, D. (2008, November). The good, the bad and the wiki: Evaluating student-generated content for collaborative learning. *British Journal of Educational Technology, 39*(6), 987–995. doi:10.1111/j.1467-8535.2007.00799.x

White, K., & Weight, B. (2000). *The Online Teaching Guide*. Needham Heights, MA: Allyn & Bacon.

Whitehurst, J. (2009, January/February). Open Source: Narrowing the Divides Between Education, Business, and Community. *Educause, 44*(1), 70.

Whittaker, S. (1995). Rethinking video as a technology for interpersonal communications: Theory and design implications. *International Journal of Human-Computer Studies, 42*(5), 501–529. doi:10.1006/ijhc.1995.1022

Wiley, D., & Gurrell, S. (2009, February). A decade of development.... *Open Learning: The Journal of Open and Distance Learning, 24*(1), 11–21. doi:10.1080/02680510802627746

Wiley, D.A. (2000). Connecting learning objects to instructional design theory: A definition, a metaphor, and a taxonomy. In D.A. Wiley (Ed.), *The instructional use of learning objects.* Retrieved March, 28, 2008, from http://reusability.org/read/chapters/wiley.doc.

Wiley, D.A. (2002). The instructional use of learning objects. Retrieved March, 28, 2008, from http://www.reusability.org/read/

Williams, D., Coles, L., Wilson, K., Richardson, A., & Tuson, J., (2000). Teachers and ICT: current use and future needs [Electronic version]. *British Journal of Educational Technology, 31*(4), 307-320.

Williams, P. E. (2003). Roles and competencies for distance education programs in higher education institutions. *American Journal of Distance Education, 17*(1), 45. doi:10.1207/S15389286AJDE1701_4

Willis, B. D. (1993). *Distance Education- A Practical Guide*. Englewood Cliffs, CA: Educational Technology Publications.

Wilmore, D., & Betz, M. (2000). Information Technology and Schools: the principal's role [Electronic version]. *Educational Technology & Society, 3*(4).

Wilson, C. (2005). *Computer attack and cyberterrorism: Vulnerabilities and policy issues for Congress.* Washington, DC: CRS Reports.

Wilson, S., & Mundell, R. (2004). E-learning development using re-usable learning objects. In L. Catoni & C. McLoughlin (Eds.), *Proceedings of World Conference on E-Learning in Corporate, Government, Healthcare, and Higher Education 2004* (pp. 4373-4378). Chesapeake, VA: AACE.

Wintermantel, K. (1999). Process and product engineering Đ achievements, present and future challenges. *Chemical Engineering Science, 54*, 1601–1620. doi:10.1016/S0009-2509(98)00412-6

Witsawakiti, N., Suchato, A., & Punyabukkana, P. (2006). Thai language E-training for the hard of hearing. *Special Issue of the International Journal of the Computer. The Internet and Management, 14*, 41–46.

Wu, C.-S. A., Robinson, S. J., & Mazalek, A. (2008). Turning a page on the digital annotation of physical books. In *Proceedings of the Second International Conference on Tangible and Embedded Interaction* (TEI'08). Bonn, Germany.

YilDirim. S. (2009). *Web-Based Training: Design and Implementation Issues*, Retrieved from http://ocw.metu.edu.tr/informatics-institute/web-based-training-design-and-implementation

Yin, R. K. (1984). *Case study research: Design and methods.* Thousand Oaks, CA: Sage.

Yu, C. Y., & Shaw, D. T. (2006). *Fostering Creativity and Innovation in Engineering Students.* Paper presented at the 2006 International Mechanical Engineering Education Conference, joined Conference by ASME and CMES, Beijing, China.

Yusuf, M. (2005). Information and communication technology and education: Analysing the Nigerian national policy for information technology [Electronic version]. *International Education Journal. 6*(3), 316-321.

Zhang, J. (2007). *Second Life: hype or reality? Higher education in the virtual world.* DE Oracle.

Zhang, Y. (2006). Wiki means more: Hyperreading in Wikipedia. Presented at HT'06. Odense, Denmark.

Zhiting, Z. (2004). The development and applications of elearning technology standards in China. *International Journal of The Computer, the Internet and Management 12*, 100-104.

Zweig, D., & Webster, J. (2002). Where is the line between benign and invasive? An examination of psychological barriers to the acceptance of awareness monitoring systems. *Journal of Organizational Behavior, 23*(5), 605–633. doi:10.1002/job.157

About the Contributors

Rocci Luppicini is Assistant Professor, Department of Communication, University of Ottawa, Canada. He has published in a number of areas including virtual learning communities and practice (Quarterly Review Of Distance Education), research methodology on online instruction (Journal of Distance Education), issues in Higher Education, instructional design (Canadian Journal of Learning and Technology), and design research (International Journal of Technology and Design Education). His most recent edited books include, Online Learning Communities in Education (2007), Handbook of Conversation Design For Instructional Applications (2008), and the co edited (with Dr. Rebecca Adell), Handbook of Research on Technoethics: Volume I and II (2009). He is the founding Editor-in-Chief for the International Journal of Technoethics (forthcoming in 2010).

A. K. Haghi, is Professor and vice chancellor for research at University of Guilan (Iran). He also served as visiting Professor of Polymer science at Mahatma Gandhi University (India). He is author of more than 250 papers and contributed more than 30 chapters on books published in USA . He obtained his G.C.E in pure mathematics from England . He was then educated in USA where he was awarded his BSc and MSc in Engineering. He obtained his D.E.A. and Ph. D. from France.

* * *

Victoria Aceti received her Honours Bachelor of Arts in Communication from the University of Ottawa in June 2008, and is currently a Master of Arts student at the same institution. She has been a teaching assistant for an introductory communication course as well as a research assistant and is working with a teaching team to implement clicker technology in a large communication course. Her thesis is focused on the impacts of emerging wireless and mobile health technologies on physician-physician communication. Victoria hopes to continue her studies at the doctoral level in epidemiology and continue researching the communicative impacts of information and communication technology in health care and other contexts.

Giancarlo Anzelotti was born on February 1982 in Italy. He got graduated in Mechanical Engineering from University of Parma (Italy) in 2004 and he obtained his MSc from this university in 2006. He started his PhD studies at the Industrial Engineering Department of the University of Parma in 2007, working on the field of optical methods for strain measurements, especially in composite materials. Giancarlo has 5 years of experience in industrial design and composite material engineering training and research. He is interested in making software mainly in Mechanic and material engineering fields for both academic and industrial purposes. His research interests include: contact and non contact methods for strain measurements, finite element modeling and digital image correlation. Developing a software for digital image correlation is his recent activity. At the University of Parma Giancarlo teaches graduated courses in the field of computer aided design, mechanics of materials, finite element modeling.

Stelian Brad is Full Professor at the Technical University of Cluj-Napoca, Romania, leading the research group on Competitive Engineering in Design and Development. He is also the Director of the Department of Research, Development and Innovation Management of the same university. He has several years of experience in leading two offshore outsourcing software development companies, with customers in Europe, Northern America, Middle East and Far East. His main research fields of interest are: competitive engineering applied in robot design, software development, engineering education and industrial product design, science of complexity, engineering and management of innovation, as well as intelligent systems in industrial robotics.

Laura Bratanek is currently a Master's student studying communication at the University of Ottawa. She enjoys learning about the way that new technologies have the potential to transform traditional learning environments and how organizations face the challenges that technological advances pose. Previously, she attended Carleton University where she obtained a Bachelor of Public Affairs and Policy Management, focusing on Strategic Public Opinion and Policy Analysis.

P. A. Danaher, Ph.D., is Associate Professor (Education Research) in the Faculty of Education, and member of the Teaching, Learning, and Curriculum Research Cluster in the Centre for Research in Transformative Pedagogies, at the Toowoomba campus of the University of Southern Queensland in Australia, with research interests in the education of mobile communities.

Shalin Hai-Jew works as an instructional designer at Kansas State University. She teaches for WashingtonOnline (WAOL). She lived and worked at two universities in the People's Republic of China from 1988 – 1990 and 1992 – 1994. She has BAs in English and psychology, and an MA in English from the University of Washington; she has an Ed.D. from Seattle University, where she was a Morford Scholar. She is interested in socio-technical spaces, all forms of e-learning and related technologies, and complex instructional design projects. She was born in Huntsville, Alabama.

L. Hyatt is an Associate Professor in the Organizational Leadership Doctoral Program at the University of La Verne. She earned an MBA and a doctorate degree at Pepperdine University with research leading to the development of a model for the new paradigm of sustainable leaders. Other scholarly endeavors consist of writing numerous articles, presenting at conferences, serving as associate managing editor for a peer-reviewed journal and on several editorial boards, and authoring two books for McGraw-Hill. Research interests include leadership, learning and change, and the powerful climates created by our convergent stories as individuals, organizations and communities.

Tom Joyce is a senior lecturer in bioengineering in the School of Mechanical and Systems Engineering at Newcastle University in the UK. As well as teaching bioengineering he is also module leader for second year Design and foundation year Applied Mechanics. Other teaching workload includes third year, fourth year and postgraduate MSc projects as well as contributions to other modules. In late 2008 Dr Joyce was only one of five awardees from the UK and Ireland to win an ExxonMobil Excellence in Teaching award worth £40,000. In the School of Mechanical and Systems Engineering, Dr Joyce is Chairman of the School's Teaching and Learning Committee as well as the 'Teaching Champion', a role which aims to promote best practice in pedagogy in the School. Dr Joyce has also presented his pedagogical research at a number of international education conferences.

Yih-Ruey Juang, as known Jack Juang, is an assistant professor of the Department of Information Management in Jinwen University of Science and Technology in Taiwan. Previously, he received his master's degree from the Department of Computer Science and Information Engineering in National Chiao-Tung University, Taiwan, in 1995, and the Ph. D. degree from the Department of Computer Science and Information Engineering in National Central University, Taiwan, in 2007. Jack's research interests are focused on technology enhanced teaching and learning, information and computer education, and computer supported collaborative learning.

Benjamin Kehrwald is a senior lecturer in distance and online education in the College of Education at Massey University. He has been working with technology in learning situations for the last 15 years in the USA, Japan, Australia and New Zealand. His recent and ongoing work is in the development of blended learning systems which create productive combinations of face-to-face, online and distance education. His research interests include social learning theory, technology mediated social processes, online social presence and online teaching.

Jenepher Lennox Terrion is Associate Professor in the Department of Communication at the University of Ottawa in Ottawa, Ontario, Canada. She received her Ph.D. in Communication from Concordia University in Montreal, Quebec. Her research focuses on the impacts of a range of programs, including family support programs, mentoring programs, and addiction recovery programs. She is particularly interested in the impact of interpersonal relationships in the addiction recovery process and the development of social capital in vulnerable populations.

Mehregan Mahdavi is an Assistant Professor in the Department of Computer Engineering, University of Guilan, Iran. He received his PhD from the School of Computer Science and Engineering, University of New South Wales, Australia in 2005 in the area of caching dynamic data for Web applications. His research interests are in the area of Web and Database including Web Caching, Web Portals, Web Services, Web Data Integration, Electronic Learning and Data Versioning. He has published some conference and journal papers on these topics. His research area also includes Identity and Access Management, and Human Computer Interaction which he has also published some papers. He is a member of IEEE.

Pauline McCormack is a research associate in the Policy, Ethics and Life Sciences research centre based at Newcastle University in the UK. She examines emerging social and ethical issues associated with the treatment and care of rare neuromuscular disorders, as part of the TREAT-NMD European Network of Excellence. Prior to this Dr McCormack's career was in computer-based learning where she gained expertise in: the development of online, distance education; large scale digitisation; and the strategic implementation of learning technologies. Other research interests include: widening participation in UK higher education and UK post-16 education policy; and non-UK students' perceptions and expectations of work-based learning. She teaches research methods in education.

Roger McHaney is a University Distinguished Teaching Scholar and professor of management information systems in K-State's College of Business Administration. A K-State faculty member since 1995, McHaney teaches courses in enterprise systems, quality management and business computing. His areas of research include discrete event simulation, education technology, service simulations, and organizational computing. McHaney has a doctorate in computer information systems and quantitative analysis from the University of Arkansas. He has lectured in a variety of countries including New Zealand, Australia, China, the UK, and Italy. McHaney has published in numerous journals, written textbooks, and developed various instructional materials.

Babak Noroozi has 5 years of experience in bench scale research and chemical analysis with various analytical instruments in textile and environmental chemistry. His research interests include: processes for textile wastewater treatment such as ozone, electrochemical and adsorption by different adsorbents in single and multicomponent systems, modeling of adsorption systems (equilibrium and dynamics), use of biopolymers (chitin and chitosan) in production process of textiles and production of activated carbon, activated carbon fiber and nanofiber for controlling the quallity of water pollutants. At the University of Guilan, Dr Noroozi teaches graduate courses in the field of advanced topics in textile chemistry and principles of textile environmental problems. He also teaches undergraduate courses on textile wastewater treatment systems, textile fibre chemistry, and physical chemistry of dye adsorption. Now he is director of industry relation department at the university of Guilan.

Rena Palloff and Keith Pratt are the managing partners of Crossroads Consulting Group. Rena and Keith are program directors and faculty in the Teaching in the Virtual Classroom program at Fielding Graduate University, which trains instructors to teach online. They are the authors of the 1999 Frandson Award winning book Building Learning Communities in Cyberspace: Effective Strategies for the Online Classroom (Jossey-Bass, 1999), Lessons from the Cyberspace Classroom (Jossey-Bass, 2001), The Virtual Student (Jossey-Bass, 2003), Collaborating Online: Learning Together in Community (Jossey-Bass, 2005), and Assessing the Online Learner (2009). The second edition of Building Learning Communities in Cyberspace, now titled, Building Virtual Learning Communities was published in July 2007. The books are comprehensive guides to the development of an online environment that helps promote successful learning outcomes while fostering collaboration and building a sense of community among the learners. Drs. Palloff and Pratt have been presenting this work across the United States and internationally since 1994 as well as consulting to academic institutions regarding the development of effective distance learning programs.

Peter Rawlins is a senior lecturer at Massey University and the acting Programme Co-ordinator for the Graduate Diploma of Teaching (Secondary). His main area of teaching is in the field of mathematics education at both the graduate and postgraduate level. His main research interests include the use of formative assessment to enhance learning, and learners' perspectives of mathematics.

Ali Sajedi is a Lecturer in the Department of Computer Engineering, Islamic Azad University of Lahijan, Iran. He received his MS degree from the School of Computer Engineering, Amirkabir University of Technology, Iran in 2005 in the area of Kinetic Algorithms. His research interests are in the area of "Information Search and Retrieval", "Human Computer Interaction", "Electronic Learning", and "Information and Knowledge Management". He has published a number of papers on these topics. He has also been involved in industry as a database designer.

Arezou S. Salehi was born on March 21, 1977 in Tehran, Iran. In June 1994 she obtained a diploma in Mathematics and got graduated as Materials Science Engineer from the Tehran University (Iran) in January 1999. After 4 years working in industry, mainly in the fields of electro-plating and welding, in Iran (February 1999 till September 2003), Arezou started a Master in Materials Engineering (MME) at the Department of Metallurgy and Materials Engineering of K.U.Leuven in October 2003. She obtained her Master degree in Materials Engineering, METCER option, in July 2004 and completed a master thesis on the characterization of DLC (diamond like carbon) coatings. Form August 2004 till August 2007, she was a research scientist at the Department of Metallurgy and Materials Engineering of K.U.Leuven, conducting research on electro-erodable ceramic composites within the framework of the European Moncerat project. She obtained her PhD in Dec. 2008. Arezou S. Salehi currently is working for Bekaert company as R&D technology manager.

Heidi L. Schnackenberg is an Associate Professor of Educational Technology in Teacher Education at SUNY Plattsburgh in Plattsburgh, NY. She currently teaches both undergraduate and graduate classes on the use of technology to enhance teaching and learning in the P-12 classroom, social issues in education, and ethical issues in educational technology. Her various research interests include the integration of technology into pedagogical practices and the legal and ethical implications of western technologies in non-western and third world cultures.

Attila Somfai works as an associate professor at Szechenyi István University in Győr, Hungary. He graduated from Budapest University of Technology and Economics, Department of Public Building Design in 1996 and spent the next 13 years as a university lecturer and architect with an interval during that time as a PhD researcher. In his hometown Győr, he teaches courses and authors publications on computer aided architectural design, building constructions and regional and urban planning studies. Somfai is a member of the Public Body of the Hungarian Academy of Sciences and also a member of the International Council for Research and Innovation in Building and Construction.

George Sorial has 27 years of experience in bench scale and pilot scale research and chemical analysis with various analytical instruments. His research interests include: air biofiltration, electrochemical processes for destruction of organic contaminants, activated carbon adsorption (micropollutant removal from drinking water, adsorption of micropollutants by activated carbon and alternative adsorbents, characterization of adsorbent materials and natural organic matter, interactions between micropollutants and humic substances), modeling of adsorption systems (equilibrium and dynamics), remediation of contaminated soils, modeling of mercury speciation and chemical interactions in sediments and aquatic systems, development of analytical methods for analysis, and development of protocols for US EPA in effectiveness of surfactants on oil spills. At the University of Cincinnati, Professor Sorial teaches graduate courses in the field of Advanced Topics in Environmental Chemistry, Chemical Principles of

Environmental Systems, and a graduate laboratory course on Environmental Instrumentation. He also teaches an undergraduate course on Environmental Material Balances and coordinates in the undergraduate Capstone Course "Integrated Design Sequence".

Masoumeh Valizadeh was born on October 1978 in Iran. She has 7 years of experience in textile engineering training and research, in University of Guilan, Isfahan University of Technology and Islamic Azad University- branch of Rasht. She got graduated in Textile chemistry-Textile chemistry & Fibre Science from University of Guilan in 2001 and she obtained her MSc from Isfahan University of Technology in 2003. Masoumeh joined to the University of Guilan, Rasht in 2003 and spent 2 years working in Faculty of Engineering teaching undergraduate students. Starting her PhD studies in Isfahan University of Technology in 2005, she continued her cooperation with University of Guilan. After her PhD, she is the member of academy in the Faculty of Engineering, University of Guilan. Her research interests include: Mechanic of fabrics and yarns, Finite Element Modeling (FEM), Nanotechnology for fibers and multilayer, electrospinning of biopolymers and E-learning. At the University of Guilan, Masoumeh teaches graduate courses in the field of numerical Mathematic and Mechanic and Dynamic of Filament Yarns. She also teaches undergraduate courses on Physical chemistry, Polymer chemistry.

Eddie Vega has been in the field of Communications for over 20 years. During that time, he's been a cameraman, video editor, graphic designer, web developer, comic book and storyboard illustrator, and an instructor. In 2001, Eddie launched VISIONES, which in Spanish means "visions". The primary objective of the company is to meet the needs of individuals and create projects in the realm of digital media (or multimedia). He is currently an Adjunct Professor in Teacher Education at SUNY Plattsburgh in Plattsburgh, NY.

Peter E. Williams, Assistant Professor in the Organizational Leadership Doctoral program at University of La Verne, is certified in Texas to teach Spanish, English and English as a second language (ESL) and holds the professional school supervision certificate. He lived and taught for over five years in Honduras and has also worked in Costa Rica. Dr. Williams administered ESL programs in correctional instutions, directed distance learning programs at the Center for Distance Learning Research at Texas A&M University and at Rogers State University in Oklahoma. He has published in professional journals and made presentations at international conferences. In addition to faculty responsibilities, Dr. Williams manages Stewardship Learning, specializing in e-learning and organizational development.

Yih-Ruey Juang, known as Jack, was graduated from the Department of Elementary Teacher Education in Taipei Municipal Teacher's College (now has been changed to Taipei Municipal University of Education), Taipei City, Taiwan, in 1988. He received his Master's degree from the Department of Computer Science and Information Engineering in National Chiao-Tung University, Xin-Chu, Taiwan, in 1995, and the Ph. D. degree from the same department in National Central University, Jhoung-Li, Taiwan, in 2007. Jack's research interest is focused on learning technology, information and computer education, and computer supported collaborative learning.

Index

F

G

H

I

J

K

L

M

Q

R

S

T

U

V

W

X

Z